Viśākhadatta

MUDRĀRĀKSHASA

VIŚĀKHADATTA
MUDRĀRĀKSHASA

With the Commentary of
Ḍhuṇḍirāja

English Translation, Critical and Explanatory Notes, Introduction and Various Readings
by

M. R. Kale

MOTILAL BANARSIDASS
INTERNATIONAL
DELHI

Reprint Edition: Delhi, 2024
Sixth Edition: Delhi, 1976

ISBN : 978-93-95458-40-5 (Paper)
ISBN : 978-93-45848-42-9 (Cloth)

Also available at

MOTILAL BANARSIDASS INTERNATIONAL

H. O. : 41 U.A. Bungalow Road, (Back Lane)Jawahar Nagar, Delhi - 110 007
4261 (basement) Lane #3,Ansari Road, Darya Ganj, New Delhi - 110 002
203 Royapettah High Road, Mylapore, Chennai - 600 004
12/1A, 2nd Floor, Bankim Chatterjee Street, Kolkata - 700 073
Stockist : Motilal Books, Ashok Rajpath, Near Kali Mandir, Patna - 800 004

Printed in India
MOTILAL BANARSIDASS INTERNATIONAL

EXTRACT FROM THE PREFACE TO THE SECOND EDITION

This edition of the Mudrārākshasa is based on the printed texts of the play both at Bombay and Calcutta, and the various readings given therein. As the edition is meant for students, only the important readings are given in the foot-notes. The work of collating the available MSS and recording all the different readings found in them has been very carefully and ably done by Mr. Telang, and thereafter by Mr. Dhruva, edition 1900, and so it is not attempted here. An attempt is made, however, to make the book as useful to the students as possible. The translation attached herewith is so made as to explain the text, and the notes and the introduction have been written with a view to meet all the possible difficulties of students. The editions of Mr. Telang, and Mr. Dhruva were very useful to me, and I cannot adequately express my gratefulness to them. To Mr. Dhruva's scholarly work especially I am indebted for many useful suggestions and some good readings and quotations.... Any suggestions as to improvement etc. will be thankfully received. * * *

Bombay, 5th November, 1911. M. R. KALE

THE FOURTH EDITION

Several changes have been effected in this edition (such as the addition at the end of an index of the more important words occurring in the play, of some important readings from the ed. of A. Hillebrandt, Breslau, 1912, the summary of the plot in English etc.) so as to keep uniformity with other Sanskrit plays edited by me, and the translation and the notes have been carefully revised as far as was possible. It is hoped, therefore, that in its present form the book will be found increasingly useful by the students for whom it is chiefly intended.

Bombay, June 1927. M. R. KALE

PREFACE TO THE FIFTH EDITION

I HAVE great pleasure in bringing out the present edition of Mudrārākshasa, edited by my late father, Shri M. R. Kale, B. A. This and many others of his works are out of print for over twenty years; in spite of pressing demand of students from different parts of India. My thanks are due to M/s. Motilal Banarsidass, Delhi, who gladly undertook to publish this edition after getting it thoroughly revised from Prof. Satya Bhushan Yogi, Head of the Hindi and Sanskrit Dept. St. Stephens College, Delhi; and getting Hindi version from Prof. Lajpat Rai, New Delhi. My thanks are also due to these two learned professors for their efforts. For convenience of students, English and Hindi translations are printed opposite the text.

MAHIM, BOMBAY-16 (DD) V. M. Kale

PREFACE TO THE SIXTH EDITION

THE present edition is, in a way, the reprint of the Original Edition inasmuch as the Hindi Version of the text which is a new feature of the Fifth Edition has been totally eschewed.

This has been done in view of some important results. The student who has offered English as the medium of study would not bother about Hindi Version. He would rather appreciate the omission of Hindi Version, for he will have to spend less in buying the present edition than it would otherwise have been, had the Hindi Version been added.

Delhi, October 1976. —Publisher

CONTENTS

INTRODUCTION

I. THE SANSKRIT DRAMA.[1]

We shall begin with a brief outline of the general structure and arrangement of the Sanskrit Drama, without a knowledge of which the technical remarks on the construction of the present play here, as well as those made in the Notes, will not be intelligible to the general reader. Poetry in Sanskrit, from its inherent nature, as apart from its intrinsic merit, is divided into two kinds—दृश्य 'what is capable of being seen or exhibited and श्रव्य 'what can only be heard or chanted.' The drama falls under the first division. 'Rūpaka' is the general term in Sanskrit for all dramatic compositions, which also comprises a subordinate class called *Uparūpaka*. The 'Rūpaka[2] which has Rasa or Sentiment for its substratum, is divided into ten classes, *viz.*, नाटकं सप्रकरणं भाणः प्रहसनं डिमः । व्यायोगसमवकारौ वीथ्यङ्केहामृगा इति ॥. Of the Uparūpakas or Minor Dramas there are eighteen species, the most important of which are *Nāṭikas*, such as the Ratnāvalī, Viddhaśālabhañjikā, &c., *Troṭakas* such as the Vikramorvaśīya, and *Saṭṭakas* such as the Karpūramañjarī,—all differing very little from the general features of a *Nāṭaka*.

Having thus disposed of the divisions into which the whole of the scenic art is capable of falling, we turn to the principle of division among the *Rūpakas* themselves, which is threefold:[3]—(1) वस्तु or the Plot of the play; (2) नेता or the Hero; (3) and रस

---

1. The information given here has been mainly called from the Daśrūpaka. The minor particulars not noticed here will be found in my Sāhityasāraśaṃgraha. (Nir. Ed.).

2. अवस्थानुकृतिर्नाट्यं रूपं दृश्यतयोच्यते । रूपकं तत्समावेशाद्दशधैव रसाश्रयम् । D.-R.; रूप्यतेऽभिनयैर्यत्र वस्तु तद्रूपकं विदुः । नाटकाद्यैर्दशविधम् । *Nāṭya* is another and perhaps a wider term for the drama or the dramatic art, and is so called because it represents the different situations in (the scenes presented by) life. The sage Bharata is the founder of the science of music and dramaturgy and his work is styled the *Nāṭya-Śāstra*. *Nāṭya* is also *Rūpa*, inasmuch as it has *dṛśyatā* or the capability of being seen, and *Rūpaka* inasmuch as its subject-matter is represented by actors assuming particular characters.

3. वस्तु नेता रसस्तेषां भेदकः ।

or the Sentiment. These three are the essential constituents nay, the very life-blood, of every dramatic piece. Each of these we shall succinctly deal with in its order.

(A) Vastu or The Plot

Vastu is primarily of two kinds: आधिकारिक or 'principal' and प्रासङ्गिक or 'Accessary.' The Principal is that which relates to the chief characters or the persons concerned with the essential interest of the piece, and pervades the whole arrangement. The Accessary is that which appears in furtherance of the main topic, and is concerned with characters other than the Hero and the Heroine. This latter is of two kinds; *viz*. *Paṭākā* and *Prakarī*. The 'Paṭākā or 'Banner' is an episode by which the progress of the plot is illustrated, furthered, or hindered (so as to give additional interest to it). It is of considerable length, and sometimes extends to the very end of a play. The 'Prakarī' is also an episodical incident of limited duration and minor importance—one in which the principal characters take no part. Besides these two, there are three other elements requisite for the development of the plot. These are बीज or the seed, बिन्दु or the drop, and कार्यं or the final issue. *Bīja* is the circumstance leading to the ultimate end briefly stated, which, as the plot develops, bears multifarious results[1], and which is as it were the seed of the plot. *Bindu*[2] is what cements a break in the plot caused by the introduction of some other incident. *Kārya* is the final object of the plot, which being attained the whole is finished. These five are technically called Arthaprakṛitis (अर्थप्रकृतयः).

The *Vastu*, which is thus divided into five classes, may again be divided into three classes according to the source of its derivation. It may be borrowed from history or tradition, it may be fictitious, or mixed, *i. e.* partly drawn from history and partly the creation of the poet's fancy. A *Nāṭaka* belongs to the first class, a *Prakaraṇa* to the second.

As regards its development a dramatic plot has five stages or conditions called *Avasthās*. They are—(1) आरम्भ beginning or setting on foot of the enterprise, (2) यत्न effort (3) प्राप्त्याशा prospect

---

1. स्वल्पोद्दिष्टस्तु तद्धेतुबीजं विस्तार्यनेकधा ।
2. अवान्तरार्थविच्छेदे बिन्दुरच्छेदकारणम् ।

of success, (4) नियताप्ति certain attainment through the removal of obstacles, and (5) फलागम obtainment of the desired object. While these five stages are in progress there must be some links to connect them with the principal and subordinate parts of the main action (the episodes and incidents). These are called the *Saṃdhis*. They are five in number, answering to the five *Arthaprakṛitis*, each of which they join with its corresponding stage, *viz.* मुख, प्रतिमुख, गर्भ, अवमर्श and निर्वहण (also called उपसंहृति or उपसंहार). Thus *Mukha saṃdhi* is the combination of the Bīja and Ārambha, *i.e.* wherein the seed is sown, so to speak, with all its *Rasas*. In the *Pratimukha* there is the means (*yatna*) to the chief end, as originally implied by the Bīja in the Mukha which herein sprouts up. In the *Garbha* there is attainment and non-attainment of the desired end, implying a further sprouting up of the original Bīja. There are impediments, but the main plot gains ground under resistance. The *Avamarśa saṃdhi* is that in which the seed attains a more luxuriant growth than in the *Garbha*, being accompanied by *Niyatâpti* of the end, but whose final result is postponed further off by fresh impediments of various sorts (as in the *Ś*ākuntala the king's forgetting Śakuntalā after marriage owing to Durvāsa's curse). The *Nirvahaṇa* or consummation is the harmonious combination of all the aforesaid parts in the final catastrophe.

The subject-matter, whether historical, fictitious or mixed, is, from its inherent nature, capable of a twofold division. It is divided into—(I) सूच्य deserving to be suggested or implied only, as being of a dry or otherwise unfit character; and (2) दृश्यश्रव्य fit to be represented and heard as being highly sentimental and pleasing. The suggestions or implications are made in five ways, विष्कम्भचूलिकाङ्कास्याङ्कावतारप्रवेशकैः॥ (1) *Vishkambha*[1] is an interlude which shows the connection between the parts of the story gone and future, by means of a conversation between characters other than the chief ones. It

1 वृत्तवर्तिष्यमाणानां कथांशानां निदर्शकः।
संक्षिप्तार्थस्तु विष्कम्भो मध्यपात्रप्रयोजितः॥
एकानेककृतः शुद्धः संकीर्णो नीचमध्यमैः॥

is pure when carried on by one or more minor characters, and mixed when introduced by characters minor as well as low. (2) *Chūlika* is the suggestion of some incident from behind the scenes (नेपथ्ये). An (3) अङ्कास्य[1] is one wherein is suggested by the actors at the time of their departure the connexion between the Act finished and the one to be commenced, which otherwise would look disconnected, as the speech of Kāmandakī and others at the end of the 3rd Act of the Māl.-Mādh. (4) अङ्कावतार[2] consists in casting the seed of the subject-matter of an Act in the previous Act before it has drawn to its close, so that the following is a continuation of the one preceding; *e.g.*, the sixth Act of the Śāk., the germ of which is implanted at the end of the fifth Act; *cf.* also Mālav. II. and Māl-Mādh. II. (5) For प्रवेशक see notes p. 68. According to Jagaddhara, the language in a प्रवेशक is generally Śaurasenī or any similar dialect as opposed to the Sanskrit found in a Śuddhavishkambhaka.

The subject-matter is further divided into three kinds— सर्वश्राव्यम् or प्रकाशम्, अश्राव्यम् or स्वगतम् and नियतश्राव्यम्. The terms are explanatory of themselves. The last is of two kinds- जनान्तिकम् and अपवारितकम्. Independent of these divisions, there is one called आकाशभाषितम् (आकाशे) or Speech from the void (which is explained in the Notes).

(B) NETĀ' OR THE HERO.

The Hero is required to be modest, decorous, comely, munificent, civil, of sweet address, eloquent, sprung from a noble family &c.[3] Heroes are mentioned to be of four kinds; *Viz.*

---

1. अङ्कान्तपात्रैरङ्कास्यं छिन्नाङ्कस्यार्थसूचनात् ।

2. अङ्कावतारस्त्वङ्कान्ते पातोऽङ्कस्याविभागतः । The distinction, however, between an Aṅkāsya and an Aṅkāvatāra is considered by some to be merely imaginary. Viśvanātha actually supplants the latter by Aṅkamukha which he defines as that where, in one Act, the substance of all the other Acts is suggested.

3 नेता विनीतो मधुरस्त्यागी दक्षः प्रियंवदः । रक्तलोकः शुचिर्वाग्मी रूढवंशः स्थिरो युवा ॥ बुद्ध्युत्साहस्मृतिप्रज्ञाकलामानसमन्वितः । शूरो दृढश्च तेजस्वी शास्त्रचक्षुश्च धार्मिकः ॥ भेदैश्चतुर्धा ललितशान्तोदात्तोद्धतैरयम् ॥

धीरोदात्त, धीरललित, धीरशान्त and **धीरोद्धत.** '*Dhiroddtta*' or the Hero of sublime qualities is one who is magnanimous, patient not given to boasting, self-possessed, of firm resolve, whose high spirit is concealed and who is true to his engagements. We are not concerned with the other three classes of Heros here. Each of these Heroes may be of one or other of four sorts. He may be **दक्षिण** or 'gallant', *i.e.* equally devoted to many women though principally attached to one; or **शठ** 'sly' *i. e.* one, who being attached to one lady, covertly acts in a way unpleasant to her; or he may be **धृष्ट** 'bold', openly making his professions to another; or lastly, he may be **अनुकूल** 'favourable', devoted to one Heroine only. The **धीरोदात्त** hero has eight manly qualities—**शोभा, विलास, माधुर्य, गाम्भीर्य, धैर्य, तेजस्, लालित्य** and **औदार्य.**[1]

(C) Rasa or Sentiment.

Rasa is that lasting impression or feeling of love or the like produced in and made enjoyable to a man of poetic sensibility by the operation of the *Vibhāvas*, and *Anubhāvas*, as also *Sāttvika* and the *Vyabhichāri Bhāvas*.[2] Bhāva or feeling is the complete pervasion of the heart by any emotion, whether of pleasure or pain, arising from the object under sight. Vibhāva or an Excitant is that which being perceived nourishes the main sentiment. It is divided into *Ālambana*, or that which is, as it were, the support or substratum of the *Rasa*—the person or thing with reference to which a sentiment arises, such as the Hero or the Heroine—and *Uddīpana* or what

---

1. The usual companions of the Hero, viz. the **पीठमर्द, विदूषक** and **विट** as well the Nāyika or the Heroine, are not introduced in the Mudrārākshasa. So the sections about them have been dropped.

2. विभावैरनुभावैश्च सात्त्विकैर्व्यभिचारिभिः । आनीयमानः स्वाद्यत्वं स्थायी भावो रसः स्मृतः ॥ सुखदुःखादिकैर्भावैर्भावस्तद्भावभावनम् । ज्ञायमानतया तत्र विभावो भावपोषकृत् ॥ आलंबनोद्दीपनत्वप्रभेदेन स च द्विधा । अनुभावो विकारस्तु भावसंसूचनात्मकः ॥

excites or enhances (adds to the development of) the sentiment, such as the moon, the beauties of the vernal season, &c., beauty, decorations, &c., of the principal characters, in the case of शृङ्गार. *Anubhāva* or an Ensuant is the outward manifestation of internal feelings through the eyes, face, &c. The Sāttvika or natural *bhāvās* are a subdivision of *Anubhāva, and* are mentioned as eight in number—स्तम्भप्रलयरोमाञ्चाः स्वेदो वैवर्ण्यवेपथुः अश्रुवैस्वर्यमित्यष्टौ ।. The *Vyabhichāris* or the Accessaries are those Bhāvas which are not strictly confined to any *Rasa*, but appearing and disappearing, like waves in the ocean they serve as feeders to the prevailing sentiment and strengthen it in different ways. *Sthāyibhāva* (स्थायिभाव) or the Permanent Sentiment of a composition is one—the ocean melting all salt into water—which, not being interrupted by any sentiment contrary or akin to its nature occurring at intervals converts all of them into its own nature[1]. Now a *Rasa* would prove contrary to another if the आश्रय or substratum of both were the same. But as अङ्गी (principal) and अङ्ग (subordinate) a रस may be mixed with one or more of others.

There are eight Sthāyibhāvas, रति, हास, शोक, क्रोध, उत्साह, भय, जुगुप्सा and विस्मय, on which are based respectively the eight sentiments—शृङ्गार the Erotic, हास्य the Comic, करुण the Pathetic, रौद्र the Furious, वीर the Heroic, भयानक the Terrible, बीभत्स the Loathsome, and अद्भुत the Marvellous. There is a ninth sentiment, that of शान्त the Quietistic, having शम or tranquillity for its Sthāyibhāva. Vīra is the chief Rasa of the Mudrā.; it is of three kinds, (1) as it is characterised by mercy as in the case of Jīmūtavāhana in the Nāgānanda; (2) or by valour as in the case of Rāma in the Mah. ch.; (3) or by generosity as in the case of Chandragupta, the hero of this play.

---

1. विरुद्धैरविरुद्धैर्वा भावैर्विच्छिद्यते न यः । आत्मभावं नयत्यन्यान्स स्थायी लवणाकरः ॥

(D) The General Conduct of the Nāṭaka

Every dramatic piece opens with a prelude or prologue (प्रस्तावना) which is itself introduced by what is called the *Nāndī*. This Nāndī, according to some, suggests the gist of the whole plot. The Sūtradhāra may sometimes retire after the recital of the Nāndī, in which case another actor, called स्थापक (for he *establishes* as it were the topic of the play), takes his place. In the Prelude, which may begin with a brief allusion to the poet's literary attainments, his genealogy &c., the Sūtradhāra or the Sthāpaka suggests the subject in the form of the Bīja, or by a simple beginning, or by naming the character about to enter (as in the present play). He must please the audience with sweet songs descriptive of some season and couched in the Bhāratī Vṛitti. The प्रस्तावना is of two kinds=(1) प्ररोचना as in the Ratn., and (2) आमुख in which the Sūtradhāra holds conversation with the actress or his assistants, bearing on the subject to be introduced. This latter is of three kinds, of which one is प्रयोगातिशय. When the entry of a character is directly indicated by the Sūtradhāra saying 'Here he enters', that is Prayogāṭiśaya.

The Prelude being over the piece is commenced, being hereafter arranged and exhibited in the manner indicated in the three foregoing Sections. The whole matter should be well determined and divided into Acts and Scenes. A Nāṭaka may consists of from five to ten Acts. The Hero should be Dhīrodātta. The prevailing sentiment should be शृङ्गार or वीर (or sometimes करुण), others being introduced as conducive to its development. Nothing should be introduced in the play which either misbeseems the Hero or is discordant with the main sentiment. An Act must not be tiresomely long, should be full of *Rasa*, and introduced by *Vishkambhaka* &c., according to necessity. Its close is marked by the exit of all characters. Such incidents as journeys, massacres, wars, &c., should not be represented in a play; they may only be indicated. The death of the Hero must never be exhibited. This accounts for the somewhat monotonous character of

Sanskrit plays, and the absence of tragedies in Sanskrit.[1] The play should end, as it began, with a benediction or prayer, called the Bharatavākya, as it is repeated by the principal personage in his character of an actor, and contains an expression of wishes for general prosperity and happiness. The Unity of interest or action must be maintained throughout. As regards the language to be used in a piece, the Hero and the higher characters speak in classical Sanskrit, while females and other minor characters speak in the different Prakrit dialects.

The student will have seen from the foregoing sketch, that the characteristic peculiarities of the Indian drama are mainly three:—(1) Its peculiar structure; (2) the absence of the distinction between Comedy and Tragedy; and (3) the diversity of languages to be spoken by the characters. The above-mentioned general characteristics of a Náṭaka belong with certain modifications to the other divisions of the Rūpaka as well. Of these we may notice the Prakaraṇa and the Troṭaka. The plot of a प्रकरण should be fictitious and drawn from real life in a respectable class of society. The Hero, who must be धीरप्रशान्त, may be of ministerial rank, or a Brāhmaṇa, or a merchant (Vaiśya). The Heroine may be a maiden of a noble family, or a courtesan. The most appropriate sentiment is the Erotic. Gamblers and other low characters should be introduced. There should be ten Acts. The Māl.-Mādh. and the Mṛich. belong to this species. A

---

1 Wilson observes—They (the Hindu plays) never offer a calamitous conclusion, which, as Johnson remarks, was enough to constitute. Tragedy in Shakespear's days; and although they propose to excite all the emotions of the human breast, terror and pity included, they never effect this object by leaving a painful impression upon the mind of the spectator. The Hindus in fact have no Tragedy........... The absence of tragic catastrophe in the Hindu dramas is not merely an unconscious omission; such catastrophe is prohibited by a positive rule. The conduct of what may be termed the classical drama of the Hindus is exemplary and dignified. Nor is its moral purport neglected and one of their writers declares in an illustration, familiar to ancient and modern poetry, that the chief end of the Theatre is to disguise, by the insidious sweet, the unpalatable, but salutary bitter, of the cup.

Troṭaka may consist of 5, 7, 8, or 9 Acts. The characters to be represented should be celestial as well as human (as in the Vik.). The Vidūshaka should take a prominent part in it and be present in every Act. The prevailing sentiment should be शृङ्गार. In other particulars it does not differ from the Nāṭaka.

II. THE POET.

The author of this play is Viśākhadatta. Nothing definite is known about this poet or his family, beyond what little is contained in his introduction to the present work. He was the grandson of Vaṭeśvara, who was a mere Sāmanta or petty chief, and the son of Pṛthu, who was honoured with the prouder title of Mahārāja. He himself had the high title of Deva as appears from his name, Viśākhadeva, found in some manuscripts. His patron was king Avantivarman, as is clear from the substitution of his name for that of Chandragupta in the concluding stanza of our play in some MSS. Now, there are two kings of this name mentioned in ancient documents. One is a king of Kāśmîra, but he could not have been the poet's patron (see Telang's Intro., p. 21). The style of the play which is Gauḍî for the most part also shows that the poet belonged to the Gauda country and not to Kāśmîra. The other is the Maukharî king of Kanauj or ancient Kānyakubja; and he is the king meant here. His eldest son, Grahavarman, was married to Rājyaśrī, the sister of king Harshavardhana, or Śrī Harsha of Sthāneśvara, whose era dates from A. D. 606. Before Harsha came to the throne Grahavarman was slain by the king of Mālavā. King Avantivarman, cannot, therefore, be placed later than the close of the sixth century. The reference to the Mlechchhas in the concluding stanza as म्लेच्छैरुद्विज्यमाना (भूतधात्री) also points to the same period. For the म्लेच्छ referred to are the white Huns whose activities were a source of trouble to the people of Northern India in 5th and 6th centuries A.D. Viśākhadatta then must be assigned to the sixth century A. D. But if the reading चन्द्रगुप्तः found in the majority of MSS. be accepted as the original one (and which seems to be so; see Notes) this date will have to be pushed back by one century. The play could not have been written in the reign of Chandragupta, the founder of the Maurya dynasty, as the post does not paint his character as a hero and conqueror in very bright colours in it. So the Chandragupta here referred to must be Chandragupta II of the Gupta dynasty of Magadha also styled Vikramāditya (whose reign extended from 375 to 413 A.D.). This was a very powerful king, able to undertake and complete 'the extension of the wide dominion bequeathed to him by his ever-victorious father. (See V. Smith's Hist. pp. 290-293). And as he brought almost the whole of India under his sway and effectively put a stop to the inroads of the foreigners, it is natural that our poet should pay such a high tribute to him as he does in the Bharatavákya by representing the earth as 'clinging to the pair of his arms for protection'. This, coupled with the fact that there are references to the growth of paddy and the women of Gauḍa in the play, leads us to the conclusion that our poet lived in the fifth century A.D. and was the ruler of some small kingdom in Bengal under Chandragupta II of Magadha. Other circumstances pointing to the high antiquity of the play are—(1) There is a quotation from the play and a reference to its incidents in the Daśarūpakāvaloka of Dhanika, a Com. on the Daśarūpaka composed by his brother Dhạnañjaya; and the Daś. Avaloka belongs to the first half of the tenth century.[1] According to Mr. Dhruva, there is an imitation by Muktāpīḍa of a verse from the Mud. (VII. 3) in a verse[2] ascribed to him in the Paddhati of Śārṅgadhara. Muktāpīḍa *alias* Lalitāditya reigned in Kāshmīra from A.D. 726—753; (for a full discussion of this point see Mr. Dhruva's Intro. pp. 1-4, 20, 21). Even Mr. Telang comes to the conclusion that the 7th or the 8th century A.D. was the probable date of the drama (see his Intro. p. 25).

As a poet Viśākhadatta is certainly inferior to Kālidāsa or Bhavabhūti. Wilson remarks—" The author of the Mud. was

---

1. For, the grant of a village made to Vasantāchārya, son of Dhanika, by king Muñja *alias* Vākpatirāja of Ujjayinī, is dated A. D. 975.

2. वसन्त्यरण्येषु चरन्ति दूर्वां पिबन्ति तोयान्यपरिग्रहाणि ।
तथापि वध्या हरिणा नराणां को लोकमाराधयितुं समर्थः ॥

not a poet of the sphere of Bhav. or Kālidāsa. His imagination rises not to their level, and there is scarcely a brilliant or beautiful thought in the play. As some equivalent for the want of imagination, he has a vigorous perception of character and a manly strain of sentiment, that are inferior only to elevated conception and delicate feeling. He is the Massinger of the Hindus." There is no other work of the Poet yet known (although there are two *anushṭubh* verses[1]—not found in the Mud.—quoted as his in the Subhâshitâvâli of Vallabhadeva) and therefore we cannot form a proper estimate of him as a poet. But as a dramatist, having the faculty which creates requisite situations and circumstances, he takes a high rank. Being a consummate politician himself, he naturally chose a political subject for his drama, such as would give great scope to his creative power but would leave little room for high flights of fancy or imagination. His style is vigorous and expression clear and impressive. The poet was also deeply read in the Nyāyaśāstra of Gotama and the ancient Jyotiḥśāstra in all its 64 parts (See pp. 100, 101 &c.) He appears to have taken great pains to make his drama conform to the cannons of dramaturgy, as he himself tells us in IV.3, and a perfect pattern of dramatic art, as is clear from his observation तत्किंनिमित्तं कुकविकृतनाटकस्येव &c. at p. 127.

III. THE PLAY.

(1) The Nanda Dynasty and Chandragupta.

The *Mudrārākshasa* is a historical play and is mainly concerned with Chandragupta's elevation to the throne of Magadha or South Bihar, on the fall of the Nanda dynasty, and the adoption of measures to strengthen his rule by Chāṇakya, the

---

1. तत्त्रिविष्टपमाख्यातं तन्वङ्गया यद्वलित्रयम् ।
येनानिमिषदृष्टित्वं नृणामप्युपजायते ।। (1548)
सेन्द्रचापैः श्रिता मेघैर्निपतन्निर्झरा नगाः ।
वर्णकम्बलसंवीता बभुर्मत्तद्विपा इव ।। (1728)

renowed politician of his time. The events represented in the play cover a period of about a year, as shown further on, and it is necessary, for a clear understanding of the intricate policy of Chāṇakya during this period, that the reader should have an insight into the history of the time.

A race of kings, designated 'the Śaiśunāgas' from Śiśunāga the first king, reigned in Magadha, according to R. C. Datta, from 637—370 B. C. Their capital was Pāṭaliputra also called Kusumapura. Mahānandin was the last monarch of this dynasty. He had a son named Nanda, otherwise called Mahāpadma by a woman of the Śūdra class. He was a powerful and ambitious king but was exceedingly avaricious. He had by one wife eight sons, Sumālya and others, who, together with their father, were known as the 'Nine Nandas'; and according to tradition he had a son, named Chandragupta, by another wife of low extraction (see also the Commentator's Introduction further on) named Murā. Hence the prince is often called in the play, Maurya, Mauryaputra, Vṛishala &c. The Nandas reigned, according to V. Smith, for fifty years, from 372—322 B. C. (according to the Purāṇas for one hundred years).

The reign of Chandragupta marks a new epoch in the ancient history of India. He reigned from 322—298 B. C. His son was Bindusāra and his grandson the great Aśoka, who ruled from 260—222 B. C. When he came to the throne, Buddhism had made considerable advance in Northern India and spread from Magadha to the surrounding kingdoms.[1] He was nearly a contemporary of Alexander the Great of Macedonia. He is

1. The student is strongly recommended to read Chapter V of Vincent Smith's *Early History of India*, which gives a connected and detailed account of Chandragupta's reign, and also a review of his civil and military system of Government, including some account of Chāṇakya's recently discovered *Arthaśāstra*; that work is of inestimable value as shedding light on the political administration of ancient India, especially of the pre-Mauryan period.

the *Sandrocottus*[1] of the Greeks—also called Xandrames ; a name which is traced to Chandramas or Chandra, by which apellation Chandragupta was also called. When firmly established on the throne of Magadha, Chandragupta turned his attention to the North-Western provinces, forced the Greek and Hindu occupants of them to acknowledge his sovereignty, and thus brought the whole Northern India, from the Panjab to Bihar, under the one rule of Magadha. Even the Greek Satrap, Seleucus, allied himself with him, gave his daughter in marriage to him and placed his ambassador, Megasthenes, at his court, receiving in return a present of five hundred elephants.

(2) Pauraṇic Accounts of Chandragupta.

(*As given by H. H. Wilson*).

The son of *Mahānandī*, born of a *Śūdra* woman, a powerful prince named *Mahāpadma*, shall put an end to the *Kshatriya* rule, and from his time the kings will be mostly *Śūdras* void of piety. He will bring the earth under one umbrella, his rule being irresistible, and he will reign like another *Bhārgava*. He will have eight sons, *Sumālya* and others, who will be kings of the earth for one hundred years. A Brāhmaṇa will destroy these nine *Nandas*, and after their disappearance the *Mauryas* will reign in tha *Kali* age. That Brāhmaṇa will inaugurate Chandragupta as king—(*Bhāgavata*, 12th *Skandha*).

Mahānandī will be the last of the ten *Śāiśunāga* princes, whose joint reigns will be three hundred and sixty-two years. The son of *Mahānandī* or *Nanda*, named *Mahāpadma*, will be

1. It (the identification of Chandra. and Sandro.) is the only point on which we can rest with anything like confidence in the history of the Hindus, and is therefore of vital importance in all our attempts to reduce the reigns of their kings to a rational and consistent chronology..........We find in Diodorus Siculus, the king of Gangaridae (the kingdoms situated along the Ganges), whose power alarms the Macedonian, is there named Xandrames. (Wilson).

born from a *Śūdra* mother. He will be avaricious, and like another *Paraśurāma* will exterminate the *Kshatriya* race, as from him onwards the kings will be all *Śūdras*. He, *Mahāpadma*, will bring the whole earth under one umbrella, his rule being irresistible. He will have eight sons, *Sumālya* and others, who after him will govern the world. He, and these sons, will reign for a period of one hundred years, until *Kauṭilya*, a Brāhmaṇa, shall destroy the nine *Nandas*. After their destruction the *Mauryas* will possess the earth, *Kauṭilya* inaugurating Chandragupta in the kingdom.— (*Vishṇu-Purāṇa*).

(3) Previous History.

(*As given by the Commentator*).

The Nandas, the last Kshatriya dynasty, ruled over Magadha in the beginning of the Kali age. One king of the race, named Sarvārthasiddhi, ruled the country for a number of years, ably assisted by his ministers, Vakranāsa and others, in the administration. The most famous of these, and the one most devoted to his master, was Rākshasa, a Brāhmaṇa of consummate ability and skill in diplomacy. Sarvārthasiddhi had two wives one, a *Kshatriya*, named Sunandā, and the other, a Śūdrā, named Murā. The latter was the favourite of the king, being of great beauty and amiable character. Once the king entertained, with the rites of hospitality, a venerable ascetic, and sprinkled over his queens the water of his feet. Nine drops fell on the head of Sunandā and one on that of Murā. This she received with reverence and the sage was pleased by her piety. Murā gave birth to a son of amiable qualities, who was named Maurya after her. Sunandā brought forth a fleshy lump containing nine undeveloped embryos which Rākshasa placed in an oil-vessel and carefully tended. Nine infants were evolved out of the fleshy mass who were called Nandas by their father. Leaving the cares of state to them when sufficiently grown old, and appointing Maurya the general of their forces, the old king retired to a life of peace. Maurya got a hundred sons, the ablest of whom was Chandragupta. He was gifted with all the marks of royalty, such as the arms reaching to the knees &c., and was popular, liberal and brave.

The Nandas, so far as can be gathered, had no progeny; they hated Maurya who had now become all-powerful, and confined him and all his sons in a cellar, with a daily allowance of one gram and a few drops of water per head. The prisoners, by common consent, agreed that the eldest son, Chandragupta, should have the share of them all on condition that he should avenge their death, and died of starvation in a few days. Chandragupta alone survived and was rescued from his cell to see if he could solve a riddle which was sent to the Nandas by the king of Laṅkā. It was a cage with the figure of a fierce-looking lion in it, and the figure was to be removed from it without opening its bars. Chandragupta, on seeing the cage, at once concluded the figure to be of wax, and holding a red-hot iron bar before it, caused it to melt away in no time. His success and qualities made him an object of deeper suspicion and hatred than before, but the Nandas dared not do away with him on account of his and his father's popularity.

Chandragupta, one day, saw a Brāhmaṇa named Vishṇugupta, son of Chaṇaka, a writer on politics, digging out and burning down to the roots a cluster of *darbha* grass that had hurt his foot, and thinking him to be a proper guide in the eradication of his enemies, became his pupil and told him all that he had suffered at the hands of the Nandas. Chāṇakya, by which alias Vishṇugupta was also known, was well-versed in the science of government taught by Uśanas and was a great diplomatist. He promised to assist Chandragupta in securing the throne of the Nandas. One day he went to a feast given by the Nandas, and occupied the principal post of honour from which he was rejected by the Nandas in spite of the protests of his ministers, whereupon he vowed vengeance on the royal house and plotted for its overthrow. He set a Brāhmaṇa named Induśarman, disguised as a Kshapaṇaka, as a spy upon the actions of Rākshasa and other ministers, and induced the Mlechchha king Parvataka to rise in arms against the Nandas by promising him one half of their kingdom. A battle was fought between the invading army and the army of the Nandas, in which the latter were killed and their party utterly routed. The capital, Kusumapura, fell into the hands of Chandragupta and Parvataka. After the fall of the capital, Rākshasa conducted Sarvārthasiddhi, the father of the Nandas, through a subterranean passage to a safe retreat (where he was subsequently put to death by Chāṇakya's orders) and himself remained for some time in Kusumapura, planning against the life of Chandragupta, without the least success however, on account of the shrewdness of Chāṇakya. Thus the poison-maid sent by Rākshasa to kill Chandragupta was diverted to the camp of Parvataka, who fell a victim to her. Assassins in various disguises were likewise foiled in their nefarious purpose by Chāṇakya; and Rākshasa had ultimately to flee to Malayaketu, the son of Parvataka, whom Chāṇakya had frightened away by having it represented to him that his father was murdered by himself. Rākshasa thus became the chief adviser and guide of Malayaketu and they planned the conquest of Magadha to wreak their vengeance on Chandragupta and Chāṇakya.

It is at this point that the play opens. It has become known to the public that Rākshasa, as the supporter of Malayaketu, is going to invade Magadha.

(4) The Plot.

The Mudrārākshasa is a drama in seven Acts based on the political intrigues of Chāṇakya, the minister of king Chandrragupta of Pāṭaliputra, to win over Rākshasa to his side. It was not an easy task, since Rākshasa was a former minister of the Nandas, by whose destruction Chāṇakya had secured the throne for Chandra. and to whom Rākshasa still professed loyalty. But it was accomplished through a certain signet-ring of Rākshasa coming into the possession of Chāṇakya; hence the title of the play (Mudrārākshasa or 'Rākshasa won over by means of the signet-ring'). For the convenience of the student we summarize below the plot of the play for ready reference :—

ACT I.—By means of a Prastāvanā, wherein the Stage manager (Sūtradhára) converses with his wife, the author hints succinctly at the plot of the play, and prepares the way for the entrance of Chāṇakya. Chāṇakya in a long soliloquy briefly outlines his plan of action, stating what has been done and what remains to be achieved. He has employed spies everywhere, for finding out what is going on in the city, one of these, Nipuṇaka by name, enters and relates his discoveries during the course of his wanderings. Disguised as a mendicant he had gone to the house of the merchant Chandanadāsa, with whom the wife and son of Rākshasa were staying; there he happened to pick up a ring belonging to Rákshasa, which he hands over to Chāṇakya and which is the pivot on which the plot of the story hangs. In pursuance of his plans Chāṇakya gets a certain letter written by Śakaṭadāsa (—professional writer and a friend of Rākshasa—) then seals it with Rākshasa's ring, and gives both the letter and the ring to Siddhārthaka, one of his trusted emissaries, with certain secret instructions. He next tries to induce Chandanadāsa to deliver over the family of Rākshasa but Chand. declines and remains firm in his loyalty, even though threatened with capital punishment. For the present Chāṇakya orders him to be kept under arrest.

ACT II.—Rākshasa is introduced and is shown as plotting variously for the overthrow of Chandragupta: he, too, has employed spies to wander about in Pāṭaliputra and collect information. One of these, Virādhagupta by name, who was disguised as a snake-charmer, comes in and narrates how all the plans of Rákshasa had gone wrong, how all his schemes to kill Chandragupta had been invariably foiled by the vigilance of Chāṇakya, and how all his allies and friends, including Śakaṭadāsa, had been arrested by Chāṇakya on a suspicion of being involved in the attempts on the life of Chandragupta. In the meanwhile, Śakaṭadāsa has been rescued by Siddhárthaka acting upon Cháṇakya's private instructions and brought to Rākshasa. Rākshasa takes off some ornaments from his person and gives them as a reward to Siddhárthaka, (These ornaments were given to Rākshasa by his ally, prince Malayaketu, and will be referred to further in Act V.).

Siddharthāka takes out a ring—Rākshasa's signet-ring— for sealing up the ornaments in a box, and being questioned about it states that he found it near the house of Chandanadāsa, and then restores it at his desire to Rákshasa who gives it in Śakatadāsa's keeping. Siddhārthaka outwardly takes service under Rákshasa while inwardly he remains Chāṇakya's spy.

ACT III—Chāṇakya secretly arranges a sham quarrel with Chandragupta, meant as a ruse to mislead Rākshasa. Chandra. was to order the celebration of the Kaumudī festival, Chāṇakya was to forbid it. This being done, Chandra. sends for Chāṇ. to know why the festivities were forbidden. A fine scene ensues between them in which the monarch reproves Chāṇ. and the latter taunts him as being ungrateful and insolent. Chān. resigns office and leaves the king in high dudgeon, and the king also proclaims that he would rule independently of him—thus to all appearance that they are thoroughly estranged.

ACT IV—The news of the (feigned) quarrel is brought by Rākshasa's agent to his master who is highly pleased at it and believes that it would be easier to overthrow Chandra. now that he has no longer Chāṇakya to advise him. In the meantime Malayaketu, accompanied by Bhāguráyaṇa comes to see Rákshasa who was reported to be suffering from headache. Bhāg. seizes this opportunity to create a suspicion about Rāk.'s sincerity in his master's mind by telling him that the deserters from Chandra. came to him wishing directly to deal with him and not through Rākshasa; the latter, he further suggests, is not so much the foe of Chandragupta; and in case Chāṇ. were somehow dismissed, there would be nothing to prevent him from allying himself with Chandragupta. Malayaketu overhears the conversation between Rāk. and his agent to see Rākshasa, who advises him to lead an expedition against Pāṭaliputra at once.

ACT V.—The scene now shifts to the camp of Malayaketu near Chandragupta's capital. One Jīvasiddhi, who was known as a friend of Rākshasa but was in reality a spy of Chāṇakya, enters into the presence of Bhāgurāyaṇa, Mala. Minister ostensibly with a request for a permit to leave the camp. When pressed to give the reason for doing so, he says he is disgusted with the conduct of Rāk. and wants to leave him before it is too late. Malayaketu is overhearing Jīva.'s speech, and the latter succeeds in poisoning the mind of the prince against Rāk. by his allegation that it was Rāk. and not Chāṇ., who employed the poison-maid against Malaya's father and killed him. After he has left, the guards bring in Siddhārthaka, whom they had caught leaving the camp *without* a permit on the plea that he was a servant of Rāk. On his person are found that old letter which Chāṇ. had given him (in Act I.) and a box of ornaments, both sealed with Rāk.'s seal. The letter is couched in such terms as incriminate Rāk. while the ornaments are easily recognized by Malayaketu to be the same that he had formerly given to Rākshasa. So it was apparently clear that Rāk., was in secret communication with Chandra., which deduction is further corroborated by the oral testimony of Siddhārthaka. When charged with treachery, Rāk. denies it *in toto* as being the fabrication of the enemy. But he is at a loss to explain the fact of the letter being in the handwriting of his friend Śakaṭadāsa. Further, he happened to be wearing at that time an ornament which he had bought unsuspectingly from a person who was in reality an agent of Chāṇakya; that ornament had originally belonged to Malayaketu's deceased father and was later in the possession of Chandragupta. Malaya. recognizes the ornament, and Rāk. finds himself in a fix; he cannot well say that he *bought* it, since Chandra. was hardly likely to sell it. Finally, Malaya. taxes him with having murdered his father by means of the poison-maid. All this circumstantial evidence completely overwhelms Rāk, whom Malaya. now disowns and who thus finds himself without an ally. Mala. has also the indiscretion to order five kings under him to be put to death.

ACT VI.—Malayaketu's expedition proves a failure owing to dissensions among his own followers, and he is taken captive by Bhagurāyaṇa, Bhadrabhaṭa and others. Rākshasa goes to Pāṭaliputra to save his friend Chandanadāsa who was ordered to be impaled by Chāṇakya for sheltering his (Rāk.'s) family.

ACT VII.—Chandanadāsa is being led to the place of execution by the Chaṇḍālas. Rákshasa arrives on the scene; he announces himself to the Chaṇḍālas who take him into the presence of Cháṇakya. The latter explains to him how all his plans, including the forged letter, were intended to bring matters to that particular culmination, it being his (Chāṇakya's) desire to induce Rāk. to take up the post of the chief minister of Chandragupta. After some hesitation Rākshasa accepts it, the life of his friend Chandanadāsa is saved; and all ends happily as originally designed by Cháṇakya.

The student will note that the chief points in the development of the plot are—(1) The fortuitous acquisition of Rākshasa's ring by Chāṇakya; (2) the forged letter and the verbal message; (3) the imprisonment of Chandanadása; (4) the successful flight of Śakaṭadāsa to Rākshasa's camp with Siddhārthaka, Chāṇkya's spy and the admissioṇ of the latter into the service of Rākshasa; (5) the bestowal of the newly received ornament from Malayaketu on Siddh. by Rāk; and the restoration of the signet-ring by Siddh. to Rāk.; (6) the palming off of the ornaments of Parvataka on Rāk.; (7) the feigned quarrel between Chāṇakya and Chandragupta; (8) the arousing of suspicion in the mind of Malayaketu against Rākshasa, and the final rupture between the princes; and that statesman; (9) the unjust murder of the five princes; (10) Malayaketu's precipitate resolve on war and his consequent defeat; (11) the resolve of Rākshasa to surrender himself up to Chandragupta for the sake of his friend; and (12) the final consent of Rākshasa, though given with reluctance, to become the minister of Chandragupta.

(5) The Time of Action.

The events represented in the play seem to cover a period of nearly one year. The play opens shortly after the destruction of the house of Nanda in battle and the accession of Chandragupta to the throne, the murder of Parvataka and the removal of Sarvārthasiddhi from the scene of action and the flight of Rākshasa to Malayaketu's camp, and ends with the reclamation of that minister of the Nanda family. From the temporary cessation of hostilities to the reclamation is a period of about a year, as it was after the assassination of Parvataka that Rākshasa fled to Malayaketu, and the play closes only a few days after the time referred to in the speech of Malayaketu (*viz.* अद्य दशमो मासस्तातस्योपरतस्य at p. 206). When Malayaketu makes the remarks it was the middle of the month of Mārgaśīrsha, as shown in the Notes to the 4th Act. So, counting back, we get the middle of Phālguna as the approximate date of Parvataka's death. The full-moon day seems to be a favourite day with our poet. The opening scene of the last Act is laid in the morning of the full-moon day, as is clear from the Naṭī's talk of a lunar eclipse on that day, and that must be, in all probability, the Pūrṇimā of Chaitra, as at least a month's interval is necessary between the entry of Chandragupta into Pāṭaliputra and the events mentioned in the first Act. So the funeral rite which Chandragupta wanted to perform for Parvataka (see the message brought by the Pratīhārī at p. 48) was that relating to the first *Māsika* (a kind of *Śráddha* performed every month for one year after a person's death). The second Act begins probably a month after, as Siddhārthaka with Śakaṭadāsa is said to have gone over to Rākshasa after having fled from Kusumapura, according to Chāṇakya's direction, and the journey from Kus. to Mala.'s camp was long and tedious (see Karabhaka's speech at the opening of the fourth Act and the reading योजनशताधिक &c.). The third Act opens after the cessation of the rains, as the *Kaumudī* festival falling on the full-moon day of Kārttika is mentioned in it. The incidents of the fourth and fifth Acts occur by the middle ol Márgraśīrsha, and allowing the maximum limit of time to the events mentioned in the last two Acts, the occurrences of the incidents in the play may well be taken to have occupied nearly a year.

(6) Technical Remarks.

The Mudrārākshasa is a *Nāṭaka*, as already remarked, in seven Acts, and it meets almost all the condition of dramaturgy, as the Commentator has taken great pains to show. The hero is Chandragupta, possessed of the qualities of the *Dhīrodātta Nāyaka*. The prevailing sentiment is *Vīra* or heroism. The *Bîja* is cast where Chāṇakya gives expression to his design and his firm resolve to make efforts to force Rākshasa to accept ministerial officer under Chandragupta and thereby to give stability to his rule. (see com. pp. 6-7). The *Bindu* is the gaining of Rākshasa's seal-ring by Chāṇakya which enables him to forge a letter to entrap Rākshasa. This circumstance, together with the *Kārya*, gives our play its name. (See Notes, p. 1). The *Pátāká* in our play is the long dialogue between Rākshasa and Virādhagupta (commencing at p. 100) indicative of the utter failure of the counter-efforts of Rākshasa and the success of his adversary. The *Prakarī* or the fourth element of the plot is, in the present play, the report brought by Karabhaka about the sham quarrel between Chāṇakya and his pupil. The *Kārya* is the final surrender of Rākshasa with the words का गतिः। एष प्रह्वोऽस्मि। (p. 364). The various Saṁdhis with their proper *aṅgas* are indicated by the Com. and need not be dwelt on here.

(7) Critical and General Remarks.

The Mudrārakshasa, unlike the majority of Sanskrit plays, is purely a political drama, and as such derives its subject-matter from history. It belongs to the species of dramatic writing styled 'Nāṭaka'. It has for its theme the winning over of Rākshasa, the hostile minister of the Nanda dynasty in Magadh, to the side of Chandragupta, the new king, set on the throne of the Nandas by Chāṇakya. The language is in perfect keeping with the political character of the play. It lacks, as it should, the beauty and delicacy of Kālidāsa's plays, but it is business-like and vigorous throughout. It is lucid, forcible where necessary, and free from intricate or misleading compounds. It is sometimes terse or even laconic, and yet not without feeling and pathos where occasion requires them. The dialogues are marked by a pleasing simplicity often enlivened by wit and pithy sayings. It is true that the style sometimes becomes laboured and heavy, especially in the more elaborate metrical parts, but it is a defect not easily avoidable in such cases.[1] A singular feature of the present play is that no female appears among its principal *dramatis personae*. "The business of the play," remarks Mr. Telang, "accordingly is diplomacy and politics, to the entire exclusion of love. There is, in truth, but one female character, with one little child, introduced into the play, and these are Chandanadāsa's wife and son, who come in at the beginning of the last Act. But even their appearance introduces no passages suggestive of tenderness or the purely domestic virtues, but only of sacrifice—a stern sense of duty."

As regards its *dénouement* the Mudrārākshasa is second to the Mṛchchakaṭika only. The plot is arranged and developed with a masterly skill not displayed in any other play save the one mentioned. The unity of action is admirably maintained, all the events being made to converge to one end, *viz*. the conciliation of Rākshasa. It is clearly announced at the very beginning; all the means are directed to secure this end; and the various occurrences, in part accidental and unforeseen but most of them deliberately planned and effected, are with great skill made subservient to it. Chāṇakya, with a whole host of spies around his victim—his political opponent, Rākshasa—watches every one of his movements, foils him in his efforts and ultimately succeeds in throwing him into so desperate a condition, that he has to yield, seeing no alternative but either base ingratitude towards a heroic friend or the office of minister under his accursed foe. Well designed at the beginning, vigorously pushed on now under cover, now on open track, though resisted yet ever advancing straight towards the goal, and turning to profit the incidental events

1. Viśākhadatta's diction is admirably forcible and direct; the martial character of his drama reflects itself in the clearness and rapidity of his style. An artist in essentials he uses images, metaphors and similes with tasteful moderation ; alone of the later dramatists, he realises that he is writing a drama, not composing acts of elegant extracts.

The Sanskrit of the Mudra. is classical and the Prakrits number three; for in addition to the normal Śaurasenī and Mahārāshtrī, Māgadhi is used by the Jain monk, by Siddhārthaka and Samiddhārthaka as Chandālas, by a servant and an envoy.

Dr. Keith.

on the way, and rapidly developing into complete success, the plot possesses the chief requisites of a piece of art—unity in variety, entire subordination of the individual factors to one idea and plan, and the harmonious co-operation of the parts to one crowning effect. "It may be difficult," says Wilson, "in the whole range of dramatic literature to find a more successful illustration of the rule."

The play commends itself further on the point of interest which, once awakened, is continually kept up by change of scenery, of persons, opposing views and conflicting events and by a variety of life-like descriptions, some of them highly poetic and stirring.

This drama is objected to on the ground of its bad moral.[1] A good drama ought to teach a moral lesson. Virtue should always succeed in the long run, and vice and cruelty be punished, as they deserve. But here the order seems to have been reversed, inasmuch as vice is represented as gaining the upper hand over virtue—fraud triumphing over honesty of purpose. But to those who will read the drama in its true spirit this objection will not appear to be just. Fraud is used no doubt, but it is used only as a means to achieve a noble end. Chāṇakya, the principal character in the play, has used several stratagems to win over Rākshasa to Chandragupta's side. But this he did because he knew that Rāk. was a firm and devoted minister of his master—a man of sterling virtue and high administrative talent. He also knew that he (Rāk.) was the champion of a lost cause. To allow him to have his own way would have entailed needless and untold suffering and misery, not only on him but also on the innocent people. To avoid all this and to see that virtue was properly

1. It is a historical or political drama, and represents a curious state of public morals, in which fraud and assassination are the simple means by which inconvenient obligations are acquitted, and troublesome friends or open enemies removed. It is not, however, that such acts are not held in themselves as crimes, or that their perpetrators, if instigated by vulgar vice or ferocity, are not condemned as culprits; it is only when the commission of the crime proposes a political end that it is represented as venial, and is compatible with the possession of great virtues, and even with an amiable character.

H. H. Wilson.

rewarded Chāṇkya directed all his efforts. He could have retained office as chief minister for himself had he chosen it and done very well without Rākshasa. But this was not his object; he never meant to seek self-elevation. Thus we can show that fraud is not used here to satisfy a selfish end. Chandanadāsa's fidelity to his friend is also adequately rewarded. The course of policy followed by Chāṇakya is that of crookedness, no doubt. But then he was driven to adopt such a course by the exceptional circumstances of the time. The Nandas had became unpopular and a political revolution had threatened Magadha. Chandragupta had appealed to him for help : and Chān. knew that in helping him he would be helping the right man. Now the question before him was—now to accomplish his object with the least possible bloodshed or trouble to the people—whether to be guilty of innocent fraud and the adoption of extreme means for the removal of a few political adversaries or to plunge the country into general warfare and carnage; and he chose the lesser of two evils. Not that he did not know the sinfulness of his doings but that he could not help it. Thus the murders of Parvataka and Sarvārthasiddhi as also of the five allies of Malayaketu were political necessities. The unsuspecting Malayaketu was treacherously betrayed and made a captive, but this end accomplished, Chān. restored him to his original possessions. Beyond the few incidents mentioned above, there is not a single case of homicide for which Chāṇakya is directly responsible. The threatened executions of Śakaṭ and Chandanadāsa were meant more as political expedients than facts to be accomplished. And the decapitations of the executioners of Śakaṭadāsa, is, as remarked by Mr. Dhruva, a political lie; and not a fact. For had it been a fact Sidh. and Sami. would not have so readily agreed the fact as the executioners of Chāndanadāsa. Thus we see that the immorality of the policy of Chāṇakya is greatly redeemed by his desire to avoid general bloodshed (*cf.* दग्ध्वा संभ्रान्तपौरद्विजगणरहितान् &c. I) and the utter absence of selfishness. The same may be said of the policy of Rākshasa. In judging of the actions of statesmen we must remember that theirs are the ethics of politics and not of ordinary life. It would be certainly wrong to judge and form an estimate of the morals of a society from the doing of a few individuals under political exigencies. How difficult the statesman's task is the poet tells us in IV. 3 (**कर्ता वा नाटकानां···क्लेशमस्मद्विधो वा.**)

(8) The Principal Characters.

Of the characters represented in the play, Chāṇakya and Chandragupta are real historical personages. Rākshasa, too, must be so. For such an important character in the play could not have been a creation of the poet's fancy. Again, had it been a fictitious name, the poet could not have chosen such a reprehensible name as Rākshasa. Malayaketu may also be a historical person. Nipuṇaka, Virādhagupta, &c. as their names indicate, are, no doubt, fictitious characters.

Chāṇakya was the son of the sage Chaṇaka. His own name was Vishṇugupta. Owing to his crooked policy he was nick-named Kautilya. He is also identified by some with Vátsyāyana,[1] the writer of the well-known Kāmasūtras. He was profoundly learned in the Vedic lore and was well versed in the occult charms and mystic rites taught in the Atharva Veda. He was a thorough master of state-craft, so great that Kāmandaka speaks reverentially of him at the beginning of his work, the Nītisāra, and pays his tribute of respect to him. (See com. P. 7.) He is said to have compiled an epitome of the science of politics for Chandragupta[2]. He was the advocate of doctrine of Sukritya or thoroughness of action **सुकृत्यं विष्णुगुप्तस्य** Pt. II.). Nothing is historically known

1. His different names as given by Sanskrit lexicographers are—

विष्णुगुप्तस्तु कौटिल्यश्चाणक्यो द्रामिलोऽङ्गुलः ।
वात्स्यायनो मल्लनागपक्षिलस्वामिनावपि ॥

त्रिकाण्डशेष as quoted by Mr. Dhruva.

2. अधीष्व तावद्दण्डनीतिम् । इयमिदानीमाचार्यविष्णुगुप्तेन मौर्यार्थे षड्भिः श्लोकसहस्रैः संक्षिप्ता । D. K. VIII. p. 191.

about Rākshasa. According to tradition he lived, at first unknown to fame, near the residence of Chandanadāsa in Kusumapura. His name was Subuddhiśarman. One day the king Nanda had a riddle sent to him which no one at his court could solve.[1] Upon this the king sent for Subuddhiśarman. He solved it at once and the king was so much pleased with his ready wit and acuteness of intellect that he immediately appointed him his prime-minister. He was also a good swordsman and as he fought with the strength and fierceness of a giant. He soon came to be called Rākshasa. See II. 14, wherein his feats on the battle-field are described.

The principal characters in the play are the pairs—Chāṇakya and Rākshasa, Chandragupta and Malayaketu, Chāṇakya being the most important of them all. Chāṇakya and Rákshasa are both introduced in the play in their official characters. Both are distinguished by an utter absence of all idea of self-interest.[2] Both have an ultimate end to gain and both are intriguing politicians; but here ends all that is common to them. The poet has been successful in finely drawing the contrast between the characters of these two politicians Chāṇakya is represented as a clear-sighted statesman of sound

1. It was this—Some kings, who were hostilely disposed towards Nanda and wanted to attack his territory, were told by their ministers that so long as Nanda had wise ministers to guide him it would be vain to expect to conquer him. To ascertain whether there was a clever and ready-witted minister at the court of Nanda they got a piece of wood well planed and of perfectly equal thickness, put it in a gold box and sent it to king Nanda with a letter requesting him to mark the root-end of the piece. Neither Nanda nor his ministers could find out that. So the king entered the inner apartment and asked one of the maids, Sumaṅgalā by name to bring the Brāhmaṇa Subuddhiśarman, whom she knew, to him. He on coming said to the king—'Sire, what is puzzling in this ?' Put the piece in water and that end which will sink a little lower in the water is the end towards the root of the tree, as it must be comparatively heavier."

2. *Cf.* Chāṇakya has to fulfil a vow, but that accomplished, relinquishes rank and power; and Rākshasa, whilst he pursues Chandragupta with hostility, seeks only to revenge the death of his former sovereign without the thought of acquiring fortune of dignity for himself.—Wilson.

judgment, never erring in his estimate of men or selection of proper agents. He is firm of resolve and cool-headed and resourceful even under trying circumstances. By his foresight he not only frustrated the plans of his enemies, but by his wisdom and vigilance turned them to his own advantage. And who will say that the praise bestowed on him by his servants Bhāgurāyaṇa and Siddarthaka was not bestowed rightly; see V. 3 and VI 1. Rākshasa on the other hand, is represented as a better soldier than a politician, blundering in his schemes and not a proper judge of means or the characters of men. He is too noble-hearted to distrust any one about him. His faithfulness to his masters is exemplary. The destruction of the house of the Nandas weighed heavily upon his mind and consequently his judgment was often warped by his over-zeal in their cause. The one thought that took complete possession of his mind was how to wreak vengeance for his master's destruction on Cháṇakya and Chandragupta. This led him to engage even persons of untried integrity into his service and to confide his secrets to them. That a man was a deserter from the enemy's camp was enough to gain his confidence. To turn to Chaṇakya, he is wrongly called the Machiaveli of India. Though some of his actions look Machiavelian-like, his guiding principle was not *expediency* as opposed to *right.* He had a noble mission before him and the whole tenor of his life was self-less. Nor was pride of caste the ruling principle with him, as remarked by Wilson. True that he addresses Chand. as Vṛśala, but that was out of his almost paternal affection for him and not owing to the pride of caste, else Chandragupta could not but have resented it. The play does not speak of his having raised any of his Brāhmaṇa accomplices to eminence. Wilson's remark that Chāṇakya revenges wrongs done to himself is also unwarranted by anything in the play. For the play begins after the fall of the Nandas and Chāṇakya's personal wrong had been avenged The avowed object of Chānk's policy, clearly stated at the beginning, is giving stability to his pupil's sovereignty by the consolidation of his empire (pp. 24. 28). The following traits of his character are well brought out in the play. (1) He is self-confident;

see his speech at pp. 22, 76. (2) He is a kind-hearted preceptor (p. 20). He is a harsh but generous master, else his servants could not have loved him so well. (3) His magnanimity is exceptional. (4) He is always ready to praise his enemies for their noble qualities : see pp. 12, 352, 354 (where he calls Rāk. महात्मा), 70 (where he praises Chandanadāsa) (5) the simplicity of his life and his utter disregard of earthly grandeur do ample credit to him as the scion of a saintly family; see Kanch.'s description of his house at p. 158. (6) His mastery over his mind. Even the cleverest of his servants were not able properly to guage his mind or to comprehend his policy. (7) He is haughty and overbearing, but it was owing to this that he was feared by all. And if he boasts of his doings it was not an idle boast as remarked by Chandanadāsa (see p. 66). (8) He is a staunch advocate of industry and has no confidence in the working of fate; p 192. (दैवमविद्वांसः प्रमाणयन्ति). His policy is thorough.

His adversary Rāk. has no perfect mastery over his mind. He is unable to keep his secrets from his servants. He betrays the name of Virādhagupta, although he had at first concealed it from his servant (pp. 98, 126). He is somewhat superstitious, see p. 96 (वामाक्षिस्पन्दनं-सर्पदर्शनं); p. 240 (क्षपणकदर्शनं); p. 236 where he consults astrologers. He fails to impress Malaya. or his own servants with his personality. The servants of Chāṇ. stand in awe of him, while Siddhārthaka openly defies him. Rāk., however, is generous and straightforward. He is also a loving friend. His love for Chandanadāsa was unbounded. He also shows a just appreciation of his adversary's merits (p. 354). The iron sinews of Chāṇ. do not bend before difficulty. Rāk. loses heart when he meets with the reverses of fortune; see his soliloquy in the 6th Act.

Of the other two rivals Chandragupta is represented as having a proper regard, nay veneration, for his Guru (III 33) while Malayaketu's regard for Rākshasa is very scanty, Chandragupta is a very competent (III. 3.) prince who has the good sense to put absolute confidence in the ability and diplomatic skill of his preceptor and entirely submits to his counsels (pp. 144, 146, 356). Malayaketu has no confidence in

Rākshasa (p. 230), but regards him with suspicion (IV. 8.). He not only allows his faith in him to be easily shaken but actually dismisses him from his service (Acts 4—5). He is capricious and thoughtless as proved by his execution of the five princes. He has no strength of character and lends an easy ear to the insinuations of the agents of his enemy. Rāk. himself gives the contrast in his complaint against Malaya. in VII. 14.

Of the minor characters Chandanadāsa stands out as a noble example of friendly affection. He would rather lose all than be treacherous to a trusting friend. Even. Chāṇa. is impressed by this trait of his character and admires him inwardly. See p. 70. A devoted faithfulness to their master marks the other characters. They subordinate the consideration of right or wrong to the cause of their chief and adhere to it with a singular tenacity. They neither betray trust nor grow remiss in the discharge of their duty, although treated with indignity or subjected to physical punishment.

APPENDIX TO INTRODUCTION.

(*Taken from Wilson's Hindu Theatre*).

EXTRACTS FROM CLASSICAL WRITERS RELATING TO THE HISTORY OF SANDRACOTTUS.

He (Alexander) had learned from Phigaeus that beyond the *Indus* was a vast desert of twelve days' journey and at the farthest borders hereof ran the Ganges. Beyond this river dwell the *Tabresians* and the *Gandaritae* whose king's name was *Xandrames*, who had an army of 20,000 horse, 200,000 foot, 2,000 chariots and 4,000 elephants. The king could not believe this to be true, sent for *Porus*, and inquired of him whether it was so or not. He told him all was certainly true but that the present king of the *Gandaritae* was but of a mean and obscure extraction, accounted to be a barber's son; for his father being a very handsome man, the queen fell in love with him and murdered her husband, and so the kingdom devolved upon the present king :—*Diodorus Siculus*.

At the confluence of the Ganges and another river is situated *Palibothra* : it is the capital of the *Prasii*, a people superior to other. The king, besides his birth-name and his appellation from the city, is also named *Sandracottus*. *Megasthenes* was sent to him.

Megasthenes relates that he visited the camp of *Sandracottus* in which 400,000 people were assembled.

Seleucus Nicator relinquished the country beyond the *Indus* to *Sandracottus*, receiving in its stead fifty elephants and contracting an alliance with that prince (contractâ cum eo affinitate).—*Strabo*.

Phegelas informed him, that eleven days from the river the road lay over vast deserts to the Ganges, the largest stream in India, the opposite bank of which the *Gangaridae* and *Parrhasii* inhabited. Their King was named *Aggramen*, who could bring into the field 20,000 horse and 200,000 foot, 2,000 chariots and 3,000 elephants. As these things appeared incredible to the king he referred to *Porus*, who confirmed what he heard. He added, however, that the king was not only of low, but of extremely base origin, for his father was a barber, whose personal merits recommended him to the queen. Being introduced by her to the king then reigning he contrived his death, and under pretence of acting as guardian to his sons, got them into his power and put them to death. After their extermination he begot the son who was now king, and who, more worthy of his father's condition than his own, was odious and contemptible to his subjects.—*Quintus Curtius*.

Megasthenes tells us he was at the court of *Sandracottus*.

The capital city of India is *Palembothrā* on the confines of the *Prasii* where is the confluence of the two great rivers, *Erranoboas* and *Ganges*. The first is inferior only to the *Indus* and *Ganges*.

Megasthenese assures us he frequently visited *Sandracottus*, king of India.—*Arrian*.

Sandracottus was the author of the liberty of India after Alexander's retreat, but soon converted the name of liberty into servitude after his success, subjecting those whom he rescued from foreign dominion to his authority. This prince was of humble origin, but was called to royalty by the power of the gods; for, having offended Alexander by his impertinent language he was ordered to be put to death, and escaped only by flight. Fatigued with his journey he laid down to rest, when a lion of large size came and licked off the perspiration with his tongue retiring without doing him any harm. The prodigy inspired him with ambitious hopes and collecting bands of robbers he roused the Indians to renew the empire. In the wars which he waged with the captains of Alexander he was distinguished in the van, mounted on an elephant of great size and strenth. Having thus acquired power, *Sandracottus* reigned at the same time that *Seleucus* laid the foundation of his dominion, and *Seleucus* entered into a treaty with him, and settling affairs on the side of India directed his march against Antigonus.—*Justin*—15—4.

The kings of the *Gandarites* and *Prasians* were said to be waiting for them there (*on the Ganges*) with 80,000 horse, 200,000 foot, 8,000 chariots and 6,000 elephants. Nor is this number at all magnified, for *Sandrocottus*, who reigned not long after, made *Seleucus* a present of 500 elephants at one time, and with an army of 600,000 men traversed India and conquered the whole.

Sandracottus who was then very young, had a sight of Alexander and he is reported to have said, that Alexander was within a little of making himself master of those countries; with such hatred and contempt was the reigning prince looked upon on account of his profligacy of manner and meanness of birth.—*Plutarch*.—Life of Alexander.

Important Abbreviations

A.G.-Apte's Guide to Sanskrit Composition.
A.-K.—Amarakośa.
AMARU.—Amaruśataka.
BG.—Bhagavadgītā.
BH.—Bhartṛihari's Śatakas.*
BHATTI.—Bhaṭṭikāvya (I-V)*
BHAV. P.—Bhavishya Purāṇa.
CF(cf.), COMP.—Compare.
COM.—Commentary; commentator.
DHU.—Dhuṇḍirāja (com. on the Mud.)
D.-K.—Daśakumāracharita.*
D.-R.—Daśarūpaka.
GIT.—Gītagovinda.
HITOP.—Hitopadeśa.
KAD.—Kādambarī.
KATHA's—Kathāsaritsāgara.
KA'V.—Kāvyādarśa of Dandin.
KIR.—Kirātārjunīya (I.III).
K. N.—Kāmandak's Nîtisāra Triv. edition.
K.-P.—Kāvya-Prakāśa.
KUM.—Kumārasaṃbhava.
MAH.-BH.—Mahā-Bhārata.
MALAV.—Mālavikāgnimitra.
MALLI.—Mallinātha.
MAL.-MADH—Mālatī-Mādhavā.
MEGH.—Meghadūta.
MRICH.—Mṛichchhakaṭika.
M.-S.—Manusmṛiti.
MUDRA.—Mudrārākshasa.
NAG.—Nāgānanda
N-CH.—Naishadhiyacharita.
PAN.—Pāṇini's Ashṭādhyāyī
PRA.-CH—Prabodhachandrodaya.
Pt.—Pañchatantra.
RAGH—Raghuvaṁśa.
RAM.—Rāmāyaṇa
RATN.—Ratnāvali.
Ṛ-V.—Ṛig-Veda.
ṚITUS.—Ṛitusaṃhāra.
ŚAK.—Śākuntala.
S.-D.—Sāhitya darpaṇa.
SID.-K.—Siddhānta-kaumudi
ŚIŚ.—Śiśupālavadha.
UP.—Upanishad.
UTTAR.—Uttararāmacharita.
VART.—Vārttika.
VENI.—Veṇīsaṁhāra.
VIK.-CH—Vikramānkadevacharita of Bīthaṇa.
VIK.—Vikramorvaśīya.
VISHP.—Vishṇu-Purāṇa.

★ Annotated by the Editor.

DRAMATIS PERSONAE.

MALES

चन्द्रगुप्त—The new king of Pāṭaliputra, set on the throne by Chāṇakyā, also called Vṛśala and Maurya—the hero.

चाणक्य—A Brāhmaṇa politician, also called Vishṇugupta—the helper of Chaṇdragupta in gaining the throne of the Nandas and his prime minister until Rākshasa was over.

राक्षस—The Brāhmaṇa minister of the late king and hostile to Chandra., whom it was Chānakya's policy to win over to the side of the new king.

मलयकेतु—Son of Parvataka, king of Mountaineers, allying himself with whom Rāk. wanted to invade Pátaliputṛa.

भागुरायण—Malayaketu's secretary and friend, but really an agent of Chāṇakya.

निपुणक, जीवसिद्धि, सिद्धार्थक, समिद्धार्थक—Chāṇakya's agents and emissaries.

शार्ङ्गरव—A pupil of Chāṇakya.

चन्दनदास, शकटदास—Friends of Rākshasa. Chandandāsa's son.

विराधगुप्त, प्रियंवदक—Servants and agents of Rākshasa.

वैहीनरी—Chandragupta's chamberlain.

जाजालि—A chamberlain in attendance upon Malayaketu.

FEMALES.

Wife of Chandandāsa.

शोणोत्तरा—An attendant on Chandragupta.

विजया—An attendant on Malayaketu.

OTHER PERSONS MENTIONED.

नन्द—King of Pāṭaliputra, destroyed by Chāṇakya.

पर्वतक or पर्वतेश्वर—A mountain king, whose alliance with Chandragupta was secured by Chāṇakya by promising to him half of the kīndom of the Nandas.

सर्वार्थसिद्धि—A relation of Nanda placed on the throne by Rākshasa after the fall of the Nandas but who retired to a forest life.

वैरोचक—Brother of Parvataka to whom the promised half of the kingdom was to be given but who was slain by Rākshasa's emissaries by being mistaken for Chandragupta.

SCENES.

Pātliputra in Acts., I., III., VI. VII., the capital of Parvatakadeśa in Acts II and IV.; and the camp of Malayaketu in Act V.

THE SUBHĀSHITAS OCCURRING IN THE PLAY

I. Sentences

———

II. Ślokas

	Act	No.
अत्युच्छ्रिते मन्त्रिणि पार्थिवे च विष्टभ्य पादावुपतिष्ठते श्रीः । सा स्त्रीस्वभावादसहा भरस्य तयोर्द्वयोरेकतरं जहाति ॥	४	१३
अप्राज्ञेन च कातरेण च गुणः स्याद्भक्तियुक्तेन कः प्रज्ञाविक्रमशालिनोऽपि हि भवेत्किं भक्तिहीनात्फलम् । प्रज्ञाविक्रमभक्तयः समुदिता येषां गुणा भूतये ते भृत्या नृपतेः कलत्रमितरे संपत्सु चापत्सु च ॥	१	१५
उपरि घनं घनरटितं दूरे दयिता किमेतदापतितम् । हिमवति दिव्यौषधयः शीर्षे सर्पः समाविष्टः ॥	(पृ.	६६)
किं शेषस्य भरव्यथा न वपुषि क्ष्मां न क्षिपत्येष यत् किं वा नास्ति परिश्रमो दिनपतेरास्ते न यन्निश्चलः । किं त्वङ्गीकृतमुत्सृजन्कृपणवत् श्लाघ्यो जनो लज्जते निर्व्यूढं प्रतिपन्नवस्तुषु सतामेतद्धि गोत्रव्रतम् ॥	२	१८
चीयते बालिशस्यापि सत्क्षेत्रपतिता कृषिः । न शालेः स्तम्बकरिता वप्तुर्गुणमपेक्षते ॥	१	३
तीक्ष्णादुद्विजते मृदौ परिभवत्रासान्न संतिष्ठते मूर्खान्द्वेष्टि न गच्छति प्रणयितामत्यन्तविद्वत्स्वपि । शूरेभ्योऽप्यधिकं बिभेत्युपहसत्येकान्तभीरूनहो श्रीर्लब्धप्रसरेव वेशवनिता दुःखोपचर्या भृशम् ॥	३	५
परार्थानुष्ठाने रहयति नृपं स्वार्थपरता परित्यक्तस्वार्थो नियतमयथार्थः क्षितिपतिः । परार्थश्चेत्स्वार्थादभिमततरो हन्त परवान् परायत्तः प्रीतेः कथमिव रसं वेत्ति पुरुषः ॥	३	४
प्रारभ्यते न खलु विघ्नभयेन नीचैः प्रारभ्य विघ्नविहता विरमन्ति मध्याः । विघ्नैः पुनः पुनरपि प्रतिहन्यमानाः प्रारब्धमुत्तमजना न परित्यजन्ति ॥	२	१७
भूषणाद्युपभोगेन (ह्युपचारेण) प्रभुर्भवति न प्रभुः । परैरपरिभूताज्ञस्त्वमिव प्रभुरुच्यते ॥	३	२३
मित्राणि शत्रुत्वमुपानयन्ती मित्रत्वमर्थस्य वशाच्च शत्रून् । नीतिर्नयत्यस्मृतपूर्ववृत्तं जन्मान्तरं जीवत एव पुंसः ॥	५	८
स दोषः सचिवस्यैव यदसत्कुरुते नृपः । याति यन्तुः प्रमादेन गजो व्यालत्ववाच्यताम् ॥	३	३२
स्वयमाहृत्य भुञ्जाना बलिनोऽपि स्वभावतः । गजेन्द्राश्च नरेन्द्राश्च प्रायः सीदन्ति दुःखिताः ॥	१	१६

टीकाकृत

उपोद्घातः ।

सिन्दूरारुणगण्डमण्डलमदामोदभ्रमद्भृङ्गिका-
झङ्कारेण कलेन कर्णमुरजध्वानेन मन्द्रेण च ।
तत्तौर्यत्रिकरीतिमेति शिरसः शश्वन्मदान्दोलनं
यस्य श्रीगणनायकः स दिशतु श्रेयांसि भूयांसि वः ॥ १ ॥
षड्भिरङ्गैरुपेताय पुमर्थामरभूरुहे ।
शङ्कराय नमस्कुर्मो निगमाय नयाय च ॥

स्ववंशवर्णनम् ।

श्रीमद्भोसलवंशभूपतिकुलामात्येषु विख्यातिमा-
न्भारद्वाजकुलार्णवेन्दुरुदभूद्धावाजिरद्ध्याहितः ।
पुत्रस्तस्य किलैकभूपतिमणेर्मन्त्री सदैवादृत-
स्तेनासीद्गुरुतत्प्रगल्भधिषणो गङ्गाधराख्योध्वरी ॥ २ ॥
तस्य द्वौ तनयावुदारचरितौ कृष्णाम्बिकागर्भजा-
वेकक्ष्मापतिलालितौ गुरुपदे चारोप्य संमानितौ ।
तत्पुत्रेण च शाहजीक्षितिभृता ज्येष्ठानुवृत्त्यादृतौ
तस्माद्विविधाग्रहारकरणाद्विद्वत्प्रतिष्ठापकौ ॥ ३ ॥
ज्येष्ठस्तत्र सदावदातचरितः श्रीमान्नृसिंहाध्वरी
गायत्रीसमुपासनादिभिरपि श्रौतैश्च सत्कर्मभिः ।
आत्मानं परिपूय तं सुचरितैः पुत्रे प्रतिष्ठाप्य च
त्रेधा ब्रह्महिताय सत्कृतिचितान्स ब्रह्मलोकानगात् ॥ ४ ॥
तस्यात्मत्रितयेग्रजस्तु धृतिमानानन्दरायाध्वरी
कौमारात्प्रभृति प्रगल्भधिषणः श्रीशाहराजादृतः ।
इष्टापूर्त्तसदन्नदानसुहितत्रैविद्यवृद्धैः सह
श्रुत्युक्तार्थपरिष्क्रियापटुमतिः सत्कर्मनिष्णातधीः ॥ ५ ॥
श्रीसाम्बं त्रिपुरेश्वरीमपि कुलाराध्यं नृसिंहं यज-
न्मिष्टान्नैर्जपहोमपूजनमहैर्वासन्तिकैः शारदैः ।
सोयं भक्त्युपपादितैः स्मृतिगतैः श्रौतैश्च सत्कर्मभिः
श्लाघ्यः श्रीप्रभुरिष्टदैवतदयादृष्ट्या चिरं जीवतात् ॥ ६ ॥
युग्मम्

ज्येष्ठे तत्र नृसिंहयज्वनि दिवं यातेनुजस्तत्सुता-
न्पश्यन्पुत्रनदग्रजापचितिमप्यानन्दराये दधत् ।

वैतानानि च कारयन्सुचरितान्येतैः स्वपुत्रेण च
श्रीमानत्र महाग्निचिद्विजयते श्रीत्र्यम्बकार्योध्वरी ॥ ७ ॥
यो गङ्गामवगाहकः पथि महायासं दवीयस्यय-
न्वृद्धां मातरमिष्टदैवततया शुश्रूषमाणोनिशम् ।
धन्यः श्रेयसि गाङ्गपाथसि मुहुर्भक्त्या निमज्ज्य स्वयं
हन्त स्वाऽदुदमज्जयत्पितृगणान्सर्वान्भवाम्भोनिधेः ॥ ८ ॥
वोढुं शाहमहीभृता निजधुरां संछन्द्यमानोपि त-
च्छ्रौतोपास्तिविरोधि नाचकमत प्रज्ञावतामग्रणीः ।
मन्त्रे धर्मनयेथ तेन गुरुवन्नित्यादृतस्तत्कृपा-
लब्धैर्भूरिधनैरयष्ट विबुधान्यज्ञैर्महादक्षिणैः ॥ ९ ॥
तन्त्रे कुत्रचन प्रवृत्य बहुधा राजानुरोधादयं
तत्सिद्ध्यै वसुनो व्ययेन बहुना जातोधमर्णो भृशम् ।
राजा प्राज्यमृणं तदस्य स निराकर्तुं विलम्बं व्यधा-
न्निर्वेदादयमाधमर्ण्यविहतस्तीर्थाटनायाव्रजत् ॥ १० ॥
तत्रोच्चैरुपचार्य नीवृदधिपैरेनं स्वयं चादरा
त्प्रत्युद्गम्य समादधाद्गुणविदामग्रेसरः शाहराट् ।
स त्यागेशसरूपतामथ गतस्तत्पादपद्मार्चना-
यत्तस्वान्ततया ययातिनलमान्धात्रादिभिर्दुर्लभाम् ॥ ११ ॥
भ्राता तस्य महोन्नतिः शरभजीराजः प्रशास्ति क्षितिं
विश्वानन्दविधायिभिर्गुणगणैरावर्जयन्विष्टपम् ।
व्यस्तीर्त्रेब्रह्महिताय शाहजिमहाराजार्पिताः पालय-
न्नाधिक्येन सदादृतद्विजवराशीर्वर्द्धितप्राभवः ॥ १२ ॥
नित्यं वर्षति वासवो जनपदामोदाय वृष्टिं शुभां
कावेरीसलिलैश्च चोलधरणिः स्वच्छन्दमाप्यायते ।
यस्मिन्राज्यमिदं प्रशासति निराबाधं जगन्मोदते
स श्रीमाञ्छरभः क्षितीन्दुरवनीं शासचिरं जीवतु ॥ १३ ॥
एतं ज्येष्ठपुरस्क्रियोपचरितं मन्त्रिप्रवीरं दया-
नावा प्रार्णमहार्णवादुदधरद्दाक्षिण्यशाली नृपः ।
वृत्तिं चातनुतास्य सह्यगिरिजाकूले सुकूले श्रुति-
स्मृत्युक्ताखिलकर्मणां श्रितपरित्राणप्रवीणस्य सः ॥ १४ ॥
यः कौमारिलतन्त्रतः समतनोत्कर्मस्थितिं पावनीं
ब्रह्मोपादिशदाद्य शोकधुतये यो नारदाय स्फुटम् ।
तं स्कन्दं परिचर्य साधु परया भक्त्या तदासुं मह-
त्कर्म ब्रह्मफलं सुधीः कलयते यः स्वामिशैले स्थितिम् ॥ १५ ॥
विष्णुर्मेरुर्विशाखाभिधसुडुयुगलं मध्यरत्नं यदीयं
सैषा चन्द्रार्कनिष्का लघुमणिभिरिवालंकृता चोपहोमैः ।
स्पूताहोरात्रसत्रे विधिवदुपचिताधानतः सप्तविंशे
वर्षे नक्षत्रसत्रस्रगखिलमखभुक्प्रीतये येन पुण्या ॥ १६ ॥
सोयं स्वामिगिरौ गिरीशकृपया प्राप्य स्थितिं सुस्थिरां
विद्वद्वैदिकबान्धवैः सह सदा संभुक्तसंपद्भरः ।

श्रौतैः सचरितैरुपास्तिसुभगैराराधयन्नीश्वर
श्लाघ्यः श्रोत्रियपुत्रपौत्रसहितो जीयात्सहस्रं समाः ॥ १७ ॥
परिष्कुर्वन्नेतत्पुरमभिजनश्रोत्रियबुधा-
श्रितागारैरुद्दाममभिरुपवनाभोगसुभगैः ।
सुमेधोभिर्वेदत्रयत्रिविधशास्त्राभ्यसनतः
समुत्कृष्टं छात्रैरशनवसनाभ्यङ्गसहितैः ॥ १८ ॥
कुमारेशं भक्त्या चिरमुपचरन्भूषणगणै-
रुदारैस्तैस्तैरप्युपचिततरैरुत्सवभरैः ।
प्रसादात्तस्योच्चैः श्रियमनुभवन्भव्यविभव-
श्चिरं जीवन्नव्याद्भुवनमखिलं त्र्यम्बकसखः ॥ १९ ॥
तदीयायाः पात्रं निरुपधिदयायाः श्रितगणै-
र्गणेयस्तैनैवार्पितवसुकृतैः कैश्च सुकृतैः ।
समाराध्य श्रीशं विधुतपितृदेवाघृणतया
कृतार्थस्तस्याज्ञादरवशतया जातकुतुकः ॥ २० ॥
बुधो ढुण्ढिर्नाम्ना जगति विदितो लक्ष्मणसुधी-
मणेः श्रीमद्व्यासान्वयजलधिचन्द्रस्य तनयः ।
दधन्मुद्राङ्कं राक्षसमिति नवं नाम शुभसं-
विधानं व्याचष्टेऽद्भुतरसमयं नाटकवरम् ॥ २१ ॥

कथोपोद्घातः ।

श्रीमद्विशाखदत्तीये मुद्राराक्षसनाटके ।
कथोपोद्घातमाचक्षे संविधानावबुद्धये ॥ २२ ॥
नन्दान्तं क्षत्रियकुलमिति पौराणशासनात् ।
कल्यादौ नन्दनामानः केचिदासन्महीभुजः ॥ २३ ॥
सर्वार्थसिद्धिनामासीत्तेषु विख्यातपौरुषः ।
स चिरादाशिषत्पृथ्वीं नवकोटिशतेश्वरः ॥ २४ ॥
वक्रनामादयस्तस्य कुलामात्या द्विजातयः ।
बभूवुस्तेषु विख्यातो राक्षसो नाम भूसुरः ॥ २५ ॥
दण्डनीतिप्रवीणः स षाड्गुण्यप्रविभागवित् ।
शुचिः शूरतमो नन्दैर्मान्यो राज्यधुरामधात् ॥ २६ ॥
राज्ञः पत्नी सुनन्दासीज्ज्येष्ठान्या वृषलात्मजा ।
मुराख्या सा प्रिया भर्तुः शीललावण्यसंपदा ॥ २७ ॥
स कदाचित्तपोनिष्ठमतिथिं गृहमागतम् ।
अर्घ्यपाद्यादिभिर्भक्त्या सभार्यः समपूपुजत् ॥ २८ ॥
तस्य पादोदकं पत्न्योरुपर्युक्षांबभूव सः ।
ज्येष्ठाया न्यपतन्मूर्ध्नि नवपादोदबिन्दवः ॥ २९ ॥
एको मुरायास्तं भक्त्या मूर्ध्ना प्रह्वेण साग्रहीत् ।
तदादरं वीक्ष्य तस्यां प्रससादाधिकं द्विजः ॥ ३० ॥
मुरा प्रासूत तनयं मौर्याख्यं गुणवत्तरम् ।
सुनन्दा बहुगर्भाक्यां मांसपेशीमसूत सा ॥ ३१ ॥

नवास्यां गर्भशकलान्यासंस्तानि तु राक्षसः ।
तैलद्रोणीषु निक्षिप्य यत्नेन समपूपुषत् ॥ ३२ ॥
बभूवुर्नव ते वीरा राक्षसेनाभिवर्धिताः ।
नन्दा इत्येव ते पित्रा व्यपदिष्टा महौजसः ॥ ३३ ॥
तेषु राज्यं समासज्य तत्सेनान्यं महामतिम् ।
विधाय मौर्यं राजासौ वृद्धः शमरतोऽभवत् ॥ ३४ ॥
चन्द्रगुप्तोत्तमास्तस्य मौर्यस्यासञ्शतं सुताः ।
अत्यशेतेव तान्नन्दान्मौर्यः पुत्रैर्महाबलैः ॥ ३५ ॥
ततो नन्दा दुरात्मानः सपुत्रं तमसूयया ।
प्रवेश्यान्तर्भूमिगृहं मन्त्रव्याजादजीघतन् ॥ ३६ ॥
मधूच्छिष्टमयं जातु जीवन्तमिव पञ्जरे ।
सिंहमाधाय नन्देभ्यः प्राहिणोत्सिंहलाधिपः ॥ ३७ ॥
यो द्रावयेदिमं क्रूरं द्रागनुद्घाट्य पञ्जरम् ।
स वोऽस्ति कश्चित्सुमतिरित्येवं सन्दिदेश च ॥ ३८ ॥
वाक्छलं तदजानद्भिर्मन्दैर्नन्दैर्विलोभितः ।
कथंचिदवशिष्टासुः समुत्तार्य समाहितः ॥ ३९ ॥
चन्द्रगुप्तस्तु मेधावी प्रतप्तायःशलाकया ।
व्यलापयत्पञ्जरस्थं व्यस्मयन्त ततोऽखिलाः ॥ ४० ॥
जिघांसितोऽपि भूच्छिद्रान्नन्दैरेतेन हेतुना ।
निष्कासितो जिजीवासौ भाविन्या दैवसम्पदा ॥ ४१ ॥
आजानुबाहुरित्यादिराजलक्षणलक्षितः ।
औदार्यशौर्यगाम्भीर्यनिधिर्विनयवारिधिः ॥ ४२ ॥
ईदृशोऽपि स तैर्दुष्टैर्नेर्ष्यालुभिरसह्यत ।
पुनश्छद्मवधे तस्य प्रायतन्त दुराशयाः ॥ ४३ ॥
अन्नसत्राधिकारे तैर्नियुक्तः कालपर्ययम् ।
प्रतीक्षमाणस्तत्रास्थात्स नन्दापचिकीर्षया ॥ ४४ ॥
स कदाचित् द्विजं कंचिदद्राक्षीदतिकोपनम् ।
पादलग्नकुशोन्मूलदाहे कृतमहोद्यमम् ॥ ४५ ॥
मत्वातिक्रोधनं मौर्यस्तं नन्दोन्मूलनक्षमम् ।
उपेत्य शरणं स्वेष्टसिद्धये समुपाचरत् ॥ ४६ ॥
विष्णुगुप्ताभिधानः स बाल एव द्विजोत्तमः ।
औशनस्यां दण्डनीत्यां ज्योतिःशास्त्रे च पारगः ॥ ४७ ॥
नीतिशास्त्रप्रणेता यश्चणकस्तस्य नन्दनः ।
चाणक्य इति विख्यातः श्रोत्रियः सर्वधर्मवित् ॥ ४८ ॥
गुणाढ्ये चन्द्रगुप्तस्य पक्षपातो महानभूत् ।
स च नन्दकृतं तस्मै व्यसनं स्वं न्यवेदयत् ॥ ४९ ॥
नन्दराज्यं तदा तस्मै प्रतिश्रुत्य बुभुक्षितः ।
भुक्तिशालां स नन्दानां प्रविश्याग्रासने स्थितः ॥ ५० ॥
नन्दाः क्रुद्धा महात्मानं कालोपहतचेतसः ।
बटुरित्यवमत्यैनमासनादुदतिष्ठिपन् ॥ ५१ ॥

धिग्धिग्मा मैवमित्थंवं वादिष्वखिलमन्त्रिषु ।
अग्रासनात्ते चाणक्यं क्रोधाकुलमचीकृषन् ॥ ५२ ॥
मध्येशालं स रोषान्धः शिखामुन्मुच्य पाणिना ।
प्रतिज्ञामकरोत्तीव्रां नन्दवंशदिधक्षया ॥ ५३ ॥
दर्पान्धान्दुर्मतीनेतानेवं मामवजानतः ।
नन्दाधमाननुत्खाय न बध्नामि शिखामिमाम् ॥ ५४ ॥
इत्युक्त्वा निर्ययौ तूर्णं पुरात्क्षुभितमानसः ।
गताश्रियश्च ते क्रुद्धं न समादधतोद्धताः ॥ ५५ ॥
चन्द्रगुप्तोपि स तदा स्वनिग्रहभयाकुलः ।
निर्यायोपांशु नगराच्चाणक्यं समुपाश्रयत् ॥ ५६ ॥

नाटकीयवस्तुनिर्देशः ।

मौर्येन्दुमुपसंगृह्य कौटिल्यः कुटिलं नयम् ।
अनुसन्दधदातिष्ठद्यत्नं नन्दकुलोद्धृतौ ॥ ५७ ॥
स्वमित्रमिन्दुशर्माणं कृत्वा क्षपणकाकृतिम् ।
तेनाभिचारिकविदा राक्षसादीनवञ्चयत् ॥ ५८ ॥
नन्दराज्यार्धपणनात्समुत्थाप्य महाबलम् ।
पर्वतेन्द्रं म्लेच्छबलैर्न्यरुणत्कुसुमं पुरम् ॥ ५९ ॥
नन्दाः सर्वे सुसंरब्धा निरुद्धाः प्रबलारिभिः ।
दृप्ता राक्षसवीर्येण युद्धायैव मनो दधुः ॥ ६० ॥
घटमानोपि बहुधा दुर्जयं वीक्ष्य तद्बलम् ।
राक्षसश्छद्मना हन्तुं मौर्यं तेनाथ सन्दधे ॥ ६१ ॥
सर्वे नन्दाः पर्वतेन्द्रबलानिलसमेधिते ।
चाणक्यक्रोधदहने घोरे शलभतामयुः ॥ ६२ ॥
ततः स राक्षसः क्लिष्टः प्रक्षीणबलपौरुषः ।
निरुद्धान्नविधासारमसारं क्षीणसञ्चयम् ॥ ६३ ॥
असुरक्ष्यं पुरं पश्यन्नसुरक्षणतत्परः ।
नन्दवृद्धस्य सर्वार्थसिद्धेरेनं सुरङ्गया ॥ ६४ ॥
पुरान्निःसार्य निभृतं पौरैर्नन्दानुरागिभिः ।
पुरं मौर्यवशीकृत्य तत्सख्यमिव नाटयन् ॥ ६५ ॥
अभिचारकृतां मौर्यायादिशद्विषकन्यकाम् ।
तच्छद्मवित्पर्वतेशं कौटिल्योघातयत्तया ॥ ६६ ॥
स्वच्छद्म बोधयित्वा तत्सुतं मलयकेतुकम् ।
उपांशु भीषयित्वाप्तैः पलाययत कूटधीः ॥ ६७ ॥
अराजकं वशीकृत्य कौटिल्यः कुसुमं पुरम् ।
नन्दानुरक्तपौराढ्यं सहसा न विवेश तत् ॥ ६८ ॥
पुरं प्रविष्टमप्याशु जिघांसू राक्षसो रिपुम् ।
सुहृद्भिर्दारुवर्माद्यैः कूटयन्त्राद्ययूयुजत् ॥ ६९ ॥
कौटिल्यः कुटिलप्रज्ञस्तत्सर्वमरिकल्पितम् ।
विषकन्याकूटयन्त्रगरदादि व्यबुध्यत ॥ ७० ॥

क्रूरेण राक्षसेनैव ह्यस्मत्पक्षजिघांसया।
विषकन्या पर्वतेशे योजितेति समादधत् ॥ ७१ ॥

वैरोचकं पर्वतेशभ्रातरं चकिताशयम्।
अस्थापयज्जिगमिषुं शपथैश्छलगर्भितैः ॥ ७२ ॥

स्वापवादं निह्नुवानः पर्वतेशवधोत्थितम्।
प्राग्दित्सितार्धराज्येन शठः प्रालोभयच्च तम् ॥ ७३ ॥

सर्वार्थसिद्धिरगमत्तपस्तप्तुं क्वचिद्वने।
तत्रापि चारदृक्क्रूरः कौटिल्यस्तमजीघनत् ॥ ७४ ॥

सर्वार्थसिद्धिं निहतं श्रुत्वा शोचन्स राक्षसः।
गत्वा मलयकेतुं तं प्रोत्साहयितुमूचिवान् ॥ ७५ ॥

अरूढमूलं मौर्यं द्रागुन्मूल्य सहसा बलात्।
आनृण्यं गन्तुमिच्छामि स्वामिनां नाकवासिनाम् ॥ ७६ ॥

सर्वेस्मास्वनुरज्यन्ते पौरा गूढाभिसन्धयः।
तस्योपांशु वधायासाः पुरे जाग्रति मामकाः ॥ ७७ ॥

सर्वोपायैर्विक्रमैश्च घटेमहि हिताय ते।
जहि मौर्यं सकौटिल्यं नन्दराज्यं तवास्तु तत् ॥ ७८ ॥

विषकन्यां योजयित्वा चाणक्येनैव पापिना।
पिता ते मौर्यराज्यार्द्धहारी विनिहतश्छलात् ॥ ७९ ॥

सर्वथैव निहत्यैनमुपायेन बलेन वा।
त्वय्यासज्याखिलं राज्यमानृण्यं स्वामिनामये ॥ ८० ॥

इति प्रोत्साह्य बहुधा धीमात्साहसिकाग्रणीः।
मौर्यं जेतुं म्लेच्छबलैः समनह्यत राक्षसः ॥ ८१ ॥

उपोद्घातोत्र वृत्तायाः कथाया एवमीरितः।
अतः परं कविर्वस्तु नाटकीयं प्रयोक्ष्यते ॥ ८२ ॥

क्रूरग्रहः स इत्यन्मिस्पद्ये प्रस्तावनामुखे।
उक्तमर्थं श्लेषदिशा कविरन्ववदन्मनाक् ॥ ८३ ॥

इत्युपोद्घातप्रकरणम्।

अथ

मुद्राराक्षसम् ।

प्रथमोऽङ्कः ।

धन्या केयं स्थिता ते शिरसि शशिकला किं नु नामैतदस्या
नामैवास्यास्तदेतत्परिचितमपि ते विस्मृतं कस्य हेतोः ।
नारीं पृच्छामि नेन्दुं कथयतु विजया न प्रमाणं यदीन्दु-
र्देव्यानिह्नोतुमिच्छोरिति सुरसरितं शाठ्यमव्याद्विभोर्वः ॥ १ ॥

अथेदं नाटकं साङ्गं लक्षणपुरःसरं व्याख्यायते । तत्र तावन्नान्दीपद्यद्वयं धन्या केयमित्यादि । अत्र श्रीमान्विशाखदत्तनामा महाकविः प्रारिप्सितस्य नाटकस्य निर्विघ्नपरिसमाप्तिप्रचयसिद्ध्यर्थं स्वेष्टदेवतागुणसंकीर्तनपूर्वकाशीर्वचनरूपं मङ्गलं शिष्य-शिक्षायै नान्द्या निबध्नन्नर्थतः शब्दतश्च नाटकीयं वस्तु ध्वनयति । नान्दीलक्षणमग्रे वक्ष्यते । तत्राद्ये नान्दीपद्ये धन्या केयं स्थिता ते शिरसि इति जटाजूटकुहर-निलीनां दिव्ययुवतिरूपधारिणीं गङ्गामवलोक्य सेर्ष्यायाः शिवायाः शिवं प्रति प्रश्नः । परमप्रेयस्यहं वामाङ्केवतिष्ठामि मत्तोप्युपरि उत्तमाङ्गे श्लाध्ये स्थाने केयं स्थितेति ईर्ष्यास्फोटको धन्याशब्दः । किं च धन्या योषित्प्रलोभिकेति वचनादेवं प्रलोभनशीलायाः कथं वश्योसीति उपालम्भोपि ध्वन्यते । यद्वा । व्यतिरे-कलक्षणया धन्याशब्दोऽधन्यावचनः । पूज्यस्य भर्त्तुर्या शिरः समारूढवती साधन्या अश्लाध्या तस्याः कथं वश्योसीति ध्वन्यते । स्त्रियं तां निह्नोतुकामः शिवः शिरस्थमेव शशिनं कलाशब्दशिरस्कतया स्त्रीलिङ्गेन निर्दिश्य छलेनोत्तरयति । शशिकलेति । पुनरपि मया पृष्टाया एव युवत्याः शशिकलेति नाम स्यादिति मन्वानाया देव्या ऋजूक्तिः किं नु नामैतदस्या इति । पुनश्च शशिकलामेवोद्दिश्य अस्या इत्युभयसाधारण्येन शिवस्य छलोत्तरं नामैवास्यास्तदेतत्परिचितमित्यादिना । कस्य हेतोरिति केन हेतुनेत्यर्थः । निमित्तपर्यायप्रयोगे सर्वासां प्रायोदर्श-नमिति षष्ठी । ते इति शेषे षष्ठी । अथ परिचितशशिकलानामकथनव्याजेन

अपि च ।

पादस्याविर्भवन्तीमवनतिमवने रक्षतः स्वैरपातैः
सङ्कोचेनैव दोष्णां मुहुरभिनयतः सर्वलोकातिगानाम् ।
दृष्टिं लक्ष्येषु नोग्रज्वलनकणमुचं बध्नतो दाहभीते-
रित्याधारानुरोधात्त्रिपुरविजयिनः पातु वो दुःखनृत्तम् ॥ २ ॥

मया बुभुत्सितां युवतिं निह्नुत इति शिवस्य कैतवं ज्ञात्वा जटाजूटनिलीनापरिचितनारीविषयकः प्रश्नः क्रियते न परिचितेन्दुविषय इति देव्याह नारीं पृच्छामि नेन्दुमिति । तत्र नारीमिति एकस्मिन्नेव पदे पृच्छतेरप्रधानकर्मत्वं देव्यभिमतत्वेनापाद्य वाक्छलेन पुनरपि शिव उत्तरयति । यदि नारीं प्रति प्रश्नः क्रियते न तु मां प्रति इन्दुप्रधानकर्मकः तर्हि सजातीयत्वाद्विश्रम्भपात्रं ते सखी पृष्टा सती कथयतु विजया न प्रमाणं यदीन्दुरिति । सुयोज्यमानोपीन्दुरूपोर्थः न प्रमाणं यदि तथ्यत्वेन न संमतश्चेदित्यर्थः । यद्वा । उभयोः कर्मकारकयोः सन्निहितयोः सतोरेकस्य त्यागायोगात् नारीमिन्दुमित्युभयमपि अप्रधानकर्मत्वेनापाद्य शिव एवमाह । यदि नारीं प्रति प्रश्नः क्रियते नेन्दुं प्रति तर्हि कथयतु विजया । न प्रमाणं यदीन्दुर्विजातीयत्वादिन्दुः प्रष्टव्यत्वेन न संमतश्चेदित्यर्थः । देव्या निह्नोतुमिच्छोरिति सुरसरितं शाठ्यमव्याद्विभोर्वः इत्येवं प्रकारेण देव्याः सकाशाद्बुद्धिकृतापादानत्वविवक्षया पञ्चमी । सुरसरितं गङ्गां निह्नोतुमपलपितुमिच्छोर्वाक्छलेन देवीं वञ्चयत इति यावत् विभोः परमेश्वरस्य शाठ्यं छलोक्तिरव्यात्पायादिति पद्यस्य वाच्योर्थः । अत्र वक्रोक्तिरलङ्कारः । यदुक्तमन्यथावाक्यमन्यथात्वेन योज्यते । श्लेषेण काक्वा विज्ञेया सा वक्रोक्तिस्तथा द्विधेति लक्षणात् ॥ तेन च वक्ष्यमाणं नाटकीयं वस्तु व्यज्यते अतोलङ्कारेण वस्तुध्वनिः ॥ १ ॥

द्वितीयं नान्दीपद्यं पादस्येति । पादस्य स्वैरपातैः स्वच्छन्दस्फालनैराविर्भवन्तीमाविर्भविष्यन्तीं । वर्त्तमानसामीप्ये वर्त्तमानवद्वेति लट् । अवनेः पृथिव्याः अवनतिं न्यग्भावं भङ्गमिति यावत् । रक्षतः परिहरतः अवनिभङ्गभीत्या शनैः पादौ निक्षिपत इत्यर्थः । चोरं रक्षतीत्यत्र चोरस्य स्वच्छन्दचारनिषेधवदत्रावनेरवनत्याविर्भावनिषेधो रक्षतेरर्थः । सङ्कोचेनेति । सर्पान् लोकानूर्ध्वं तिरश्चातिक्रम्य गन्तुं समर्थानाम् । अतिविस्तारभाजां दोष्णां भुजानां सङ्कोचेनैव भुजाघातेन लोकाः संहता मा भूवन्निति भुजानां क्रोडीकरणेनैव मुहुर-

---

१ नोग्रं. २ नः इति पाठः.

भिनयतः अङ्गविक्षेपं कुर्वतः । 'अङ्गहारोऽङ्गविक्षेपो व्यञ्जकाभिनयौ समौ' इत्यमरः । दृष्टिमिति । उग्रज्वलनकणमुचं तीव्रविस्फुलिङ्गकिरं दृष्टिं भाललोचनं लक्ष्येषु दृगभिनयदर्शनीयेषु वस्तुषु दाहभीतेर्दग्धानि मा भूवन्निति न बध्नतः न निक्षिपतः । इतीति । इत्याधारानुरोधादित्येवमुक्तस्याधारस्य नृत्तक्रियाश्रयस्य पृथिव्यादेरनुरोधाद्यथाक्रमं भङ्गसंहरणदाहा मा भूवन्निति अनुक्रोशात् त्रिपुरविजयिनः शिवस्य दुःखनृत्तं दुःखेन कृच्छ्रेण यथाकथंचित्सायन्तनावश्यकविधितयाङ्गवैकल्येनाप्यनुष्ठीयमानं नृत्तं वः पातु इति पद्यस्य वाच्योर्थः । नन्वत्र तृतीयलोचनाभिनयासंभवान्नृत्तवैकल्यप्रसञ्जनमयुक्तं तत्पिधायापि द्वाभ्यामेव लोचनाभ्यां लक्ष्याभिनयस्य सुकरत्वादिति चेन्मैवम् । द्विलोचनस्यैकस्मिंल्लोचने विकलेऽन्येनाभिनयवैकल्यवत्त्रिलोचनस्यापि तथात्वोपपत्तेः । तस्मादुक्तं दृगभिनयवैकल्यप्रयुक्तदुःखनृत्तत्वप्रसञ्जनं समञ्जसमिति सन्तोष्टव्यम् । अत्र त्रिपुरविजयिन इति पदेन मया त्रिपुरविजयिना विशिखवह्निना त्रिपुरं दग्धं एवं क्रोधाग्निना नन्दवंशवत्सराक्षसं मलयकेतुं दग्धुं समर्थस्यापि चाणक्यस्य राक्षससञ्जिघृक्षानुरोधात्कृच्छ्रेण कुटिलनीतिप्रयोगाभिनिवेश इति ध्वनितम् । अत्र अवन्यादीनामवनत्याद्ययोगेपि योगकल्पनात्संबन्धातिशयोक्तिरलङ्कारः । संबन्धातिशयोक्तिः स्यादयोगे योगकल्पनमिति तल्लक्षणात् । त्रिपुरविजयिन इति साभिप्रायविशेषणात्परिकरालङ्कारश्च । ताभ्यां कौटिल्यनीतिरूपवस्तुध्वनिः । अनयैव रीत्या गणपतिस्तुतिपरमस्मदीयं पद्यम् ।

शेषाहेः फणभङ्गभीरुरवनौ मन्दं निधत्ते पदं
चीत्कारं जगदण्डसंपुटभिदाभीत्या विधत्ते मनाक् ।
नोड्डीयेत जगज्जवादिति शनैः कर्णाञ्चलं दोलय-
त्येवं योखिललोकरक्षणचणः पायाद्गणेशः स वः ॥

अत्र पूर्वनान्दीपद्ये

नान्दीपद्येऽभिधातव्यं चन्द्रनामेति शासनात् ।
इन्दुरित्यमृतं बीजमायुःप्रदमुदीरितम् ॥
सनामा सूचितस्तेन चन्द्रगुप्तोपि नायकः ।
लक्ष्मीकृन्मगणश्चोक्तस्तल्लक्ष्मीस्थैर्यसूचनम् ॥
नान्दीपद्येषु कुर्वीत मनाक्काव्यार्थसूचनम् ।
इति शास्त्रात्कविः किंचिद्वस्त्वेवं समसूसुचत् ॥
शृङ्गारो वाथवा वीरो मुख्यः स्यान्नाटके रसः ।
करुणाद्भुतहास्याद्यास्तयोरङ्गतया मताः ॥

वीरो रसः प्रधानं स्यान्मुद्राराक्षसनाटके ।
अत्यद्भुतकरी शाठ्यनीतिरत्राङ्गमिष्यते ॥
नीतिर्द्विधेरिता धर्मशाठ्यप्राधान्यभेदतः ।
धर्मशाठ्ये सन्दधतो द्विविधा सा यथायथम् ॥
आद्या युधिष्ठिरादिभ्यो विदुरादिभिरीरिता ।
अन्योक्ता धृतराष्ट्राय दुर्दान्तैः कणिकादिभिः ॥
अत्यद्भुतविधादत्र संविधानान्महाकविः ।
प्रपञ्चयति चाणक्यमुखेन कुटिलं नयम् ॥
दण्डनीतिर्विनयनाल्लोकस्थितिविधायिनी ।
ऐशी तनुर्द्विधा सा स्याच्छिवा घोरा विभेदतः ॥
शिवा धर्मानुविद्धा स्याद्घोरा कौटिल्यगर्भिता ।
साध्वाचारः साधुनेति न्यायायोज्या द्वयोर्द्वयोः ॥
उमा सत्त्वप्रधानत्वादृजुनीतितयेष्यते ।
गङ्गा कुटिलगामित्वात्कुटिला नीतिरिष्यते ॥
तां धर्मनीतेर्निह्नुत्य प्रपञ्चयितुमुत्सुकः ।
चाणक्योद्धतधीरत्र विभुशब्देन सूचितः ॥
आधारवशतो दुःखनृत्तमि युत्तरेण च ।
पद्येन ध्वनितं कृच्छ्राच्छाठ्यनीतिप्रकल्पनम् ॥
आधारो राक्षसो मौर्यराज्यनिर्वाहकत्वतः ।
तत्संजिघृक्षयाधत्त कौटिल्यः कुटिलं नयम् ॥
कलौ पापिनि कौटिल्यनीतिः सद्यः फलप्रदा ।
इत्यभिप्रेत्य कौटिल्यस्तामेवात्र प्रयुक्तवान् ॥
इत्याराधानुरोधादित्युक्त्या राक्षसरक्षणम् ।
यत्नाद्विधेयं ध्वनितं क्रुद्धान्मलयकेतुतः ॥
भागुरायणवाक्येन तदेतत्स्फुटयिष्यते ।
रक्षणीया राक्षसस्य प्राणा इत्यादिना पुरः ॥
सचिवायत्तसिद्धित्वात्पौरुषं स्वमदर्शयन् ।
गभीरात्मा चन्द्रगुप्तो धीरोदात्तोत्र नायकः ॥
तद्राज्याङ्गधुरं वोढुं धृतिमान्राक्षसोर्हति ।
तत्संग्रहोत एवात्र साध्यो नीतिस्तु साधनम् ॥

एवमत्रार्थत इन्दुः शाठ्यमिति शब्दतश्च मनाक्काव्यार्थो ध्वनितः

उदीरितस्त्र्यम्बकार्यैर्नान्दीपद्यध्वनिः शुभः ।
स एष ढुण्ढिनाकारि कारिकाडिण्डिमैः स्फुटः ॥

अथ नाटकादिलक्षणानि निरूप्यन्ते ।

रूप्यतेभिनयैर्यत्र वस्तु तद्रूपकं विदुः ।
नाटकाद्यैर्दशविधं तदित्यन्यत्र विस्तरः ॥

तदुक्तं दशरूपके ।

नाटकं सप्रकरणं भाणः प्रहसनं डिमः ।
व्यायोगसमवकारौ वीथ्यङ्केहा मृगा इति ॥

एतेषां लक्षाणानि विस्तरभयान्नेहोच्यन्ते । अथैषां सामग्री निरूप्यते । तत्र पञ्च सन्धयः ।

मुखं प्रतिमुखं गर्भः सविमर्शो निबर्हणम् ॥ इति ॥

सन्धिर्नाम एकेन प्रयोजनेनान्वितानां कथांशानामवन्तरप्रयोजनसंबन्धः । तत्रारम्भबीजसंबन्धो मुखसन्धिः ॥ यत्नबिन्दुसंबन्धः प्रतिमुखसन्धिः । प्राप्त्याशापताकयोः संबन्धो गर्भसन्धिः । नियताप्तिप्रकर्षसंबन्धो विमर्शसन्धिः । फलागमकार्ययोः संबन्धो निर्वहणसन्धिः ।

बीजबिन्दुपताकाख्यप्रकरीकार्यलक्षणाः ।
आरम्भयत्नप्राप्त्याशानियताप्तिफलागमाः ॥
अर्थप्रकृतयः पञ्च पञ्चावस्थासमन्विताः ।
यथासंख्येन जायन्ते मुखाद्याः पञ्च सन्धयः ॥ इति ॥

अर्थप्रकृतयः कार्यसिद्धिहेतवः बीजादयः पञ्चारम्भादिपञ्चावस्थासमन्विताः सन्तः यथासंख्यं मुखाद्याः पञ्चसन्धयो जायन्त इत्यर्थः । आरम्भादीनां लक्षणं निरूपितं दशरूपके ।

औत्सुक्यमात्रमारम्भः फललाभाय भूयसे ।
प्रयत्नस्तु तदप्राप्तौ व्यापारोतित्वरान्वितः ॥
उपायापायशङ्काभ्यां प्राप्त्याशा प्राप्तिसंभवः ।
अपायाभावतः प्राप्तिर्नियताप्तिः सुनिश्चिता ॥
समग्रफलसंपत्तिः फलयोग उदाहृतः ।

अथ बीजादिपञ्चकं निरूप्यते ।

स्तोकोद्दिष्टः कार्यहेतुर्बीजं विस्तार्यनेकधा ।
अवान्तरार्थविच्छेदे बिन्दुरच्छेदकारणम् ॥
प्रतिपाद्यकथाङ्गं स्यात्पताका व्यापिनी कथा ।
अव्यापिनी प्रकरिका कार्यं निर्वाहकृत्फले ॥
इति लक्षणसंग्रहः ।

अथ नान्दीस्वरूपं निरूप्यते।

अर्थतः शब्दतो वापि मनाक्काव्यार्थसूचनम्।
यत्राष्टभिर्द्वादशभिरष्टादशभिरेव वा॥
द्वाविंशत्या पदैर्वापि सा नान्दी परिकीर्तिता॥

नाटकादिरूपकाणामादौ विहितं पद्यं नान्दीत्युच्यते। केश्चिन्नान्द्यां परानियमो नाभ्युपगम्यते अतोऽत्र नाटके पदनियमो नादृतः। यद्वा पदशब्दः पादवचनः। तथा च पद्यद्वयेनाष्टपदा नान्दी कृतेति ज्ञेयम्। अत्र नाटके वीरो रसः। अतिगहनकौटिल्यनीतिरूपोद्भुतरसः प्रधानमङ्गं। अन्ये शृङ्गारकरुणादयो यथायथं द्रष्टव्याः। धीरोदात्तो नायकः। प्रख्यातमितिवृत्तम्। इतिहासनिबन्धनं प्रख्यातमिति लक्षणात्। चाणक्यकृतस्य नन्दवंशोद्धरणस्य चन्द्रगुप्ताभिषेकस्य च विष्णुपुराणबृहत्कथाकामन्दकादिषु संक्षेपेणोक्तत्वात्।

विष्णुपुराणे।

नव चैतान्नन्दान्कौटिल्यो ब्राह्मणः समुद्धरिष्यति। कौटिल्य एव चन्द्रगुप्तं राज्येऽभिषेक्ष्यति। अतःपरं शूद्राः पृथिवीं भोक्ष्यन्तीति।

बृहत्कथायाम्।

चाणक्यनाम्ना तेनाथ शकटारगृहे रहः।
कृत्यां विधाय सप्ताहात्सपुत्रो निहतो नृपः॥

शकटार क्षपणकलिङ्गधारी चाणक्यमित्रमिन्दुशर्मा।

योगानन्दे यशःशेषे पूर्वनन्दसुतस्ततः।
चन्द्रगुप्तः कृतो राज्ये चाणक्येन महौजसा॥

कामन्दके।

वंशे विशालवंशानामृषीणामिव भूयसाम्।
अप्रतिग्राहकाणां यो बभूव भुवि विश्रुतः॥
जातवेदा इवार्चिष्मान्वेदान्वेदविदांवरः।
योऽधीतवान्सुचतुरश्चतुरोऽप्येकवेदवत्॥
यस्याभिचारवज्रेण वज्रज्वलनतेजसः।
पपात मूलतः श्रीमान्सुपर्वा नन्दपर्वतः॥
एकाकी मन्त्रशक्त्या यः शक्तः शक्तिधरोपमः।
आजहार नृचन्द्राय चन्द्रगुप्ताय मेदिनीम्॥
नीतिशास्त्रामृतं धीमानर्थशास्त्रमहोदधेः।
य उद्दध्रे नमस्तस्मै विष्णुगुप्ताय वेधसे॥ इति॥

(नान्द्यन्ते ।)

सूत्रधारः—अलमतिप्रसङ्गेन । आज्ञापितोस्मि परिषदा यथाद्य त्वया सामन्तवटेश्वरदत्तपौत्रस्य महाराजपदभाक्पृथुसूनोः कवेर्विशाखदत्तस्य कृतिरभिनवं मुद्राराक्षसं नाम नाटकं नाटयितव्यमिति । यत्सत्यं काव्यविशेषवेदिन्यां परिषदि प्रयुञ्जानस्य ममापि चेतसि सुमहान्परितोषः प्रादुर्भवति । कुतः ।

चीयते बालिशस्यापि सत्क्षेत्रपतिता कृषिः ।
न शालेः स्तम्बकरिता वप्तुर्गुणमपेक्षते ॥ ३ ॥

तद्यावदिदानीं गृहं गत्वा गृहिणीमाहूय गृहजनेन सह सङ्गीतकमनुतिष्ठामि । (परिक्रम्यावलोक्य च ।) इमे नो गृहाः । तद्यावत्प्रविशामि । (नाट्येन प्रविश्यावलोक्य च ।) अये तत्किमिदम-

---

नान्द्यनन्तरप्रविष्टेन सूत्रधारेण रङ्गप्रसादनपुरःसरं मृदुमधुरपदैः पद्यैः भारतीवृत्त्याश्रयणेन काव्यार्थः सूचनीयस्तदुक्तम् ।

रङ्गं प्रसाद्य मधुरैः श्लोकैः काव्यार्थसूचकैः ।
ऋतुं कंचिदुपादाय भारतीं वृत्तिमाश्रयेत् ॥ इति ॥

तदेतदाह नान्द्यन्त इति । परिषदा सन्दिष्टार्थस्य क्षिप्रं कर्तव्यत्वाद्वाचामतिप्रसङ्गो वारणीय इत्यर्थः । 'अलं भूषणपर्याप्तिशक्तिवारणवाचकम्' इत्यमरः । यत्सत्यमिति सञ्जातो ध्रुवमित्यर्थे । अत्र भारतीवृत्तेरङ्गं परिषदभिमुखीकरणफला कविकाव्यनटादीनां प्रशंसारूपा प्ररोचना कृता । तथा हि । सामन्तवटेश्वरेति महाकुलप्रसूतत्वकथनेन कविप्रशंसा काव्यविशेषवेदिन्यामिति काव्यपारिषदोः प्रशंसा ।

बालिशस्येति । स्वस्य बालिशकृषीवलदृष्टान्ताद्विनयप्रदर्शनेनात्मश्लाघापराङ्मुखत्वरूपमहागुणकथनान्नटस्तुतिः । बालिशस्य बीजावापानभिज्ञस्यापि सुक्षेत्रपतिता कृषिः कर्षणं कृषिर्लक्षणया तत्संबन्धि बीजमित्यर्थः । चीयते उपचिता अभिवृद्धा भवति । शालेः एकस्य शाल्यङ्कुरस्य स्तम्बकरिता सुक्षेत्रगुणकृतनिबिडीभवनशीलता वप्तुः बीजावापकर्तुः गुणं दक्षत्वादिकं नापेक्षते किंतु स्वयमेव भूसारगुणेनोपचिता भवतीत्यर्थः अत्र सुक्षेत्रदृष्टान्तोपि परिषत्प्रशंसैव । स्तम्बं स्तोमं करोतीति स्तम्बकरिः । स्तम्बशकृतोरिन्व्रीहिवत्सयोरिति वक्तव्यमित्यनुशासनात्स्त-

---

१ अतिविस्तरेण. २ वत्सेश्वर. ३ देवस्य. ४ अपूर्वं. ५ सक्षे० इति पाठः.

स्मद्गृहेषु महोत्सव इव दृश्यते । स्वस्वकर्मण्यधिकतरमभियुक्तः परिजनः । तथा हि ।

वहति जलमियं पिनष्टि गन्धा-

नियमियमुद्ग्रथते स्रजो विचित्राः ।

म्बशब्दे उपपदे कृञ् इन्प्रत्ययः ॥ ३ ॥ अनुतिष्ठामि अनुष्ठास्यामीत्यर्थः । यावत्पुरानिपातयोरिति लट् । इदमामुखम् । तदुक्तम् ।

सूत्रधारो नटीं ब्रूते मारिषं वा विदूषकम् ।
स्वकार्यं प्रस्तुताक्षेपि चित्रोक्त्या यत्तदामुखम् ॥
प्रस्तावना वा तत्र स्यात्कथोद्घातः प्रवृत्तकम् ।
प्रयोगातिशयश्चेति त्रीण्यङ्गान्यामुखस्य हि ॥ इति ॥

एषामङ्गानां स्वरूपं निरूपितं दशरूपके ।

स्वेतिवृत्तसमं वाक्यमर्थं वा यत्र सूत्रिणः ।
गृहीत्वा प्रविशेत्पात्रं कथोद्घातो द्विधैव सः ॥
प्रस्तूयमानपात्रस्य गुणवर्णनया स्वतः ।
प्रविशेत्सुचितं पात्रं यत्र तत्स्यात्प्रवृत्तकम् ॥
एषोऽयमित्युपक्षेपात्सूत्रधारप्रयोगतः ।
पात्रप्रवेशो यत्राय प्रयोगातिशयो मतः ॥ इति ॥
वीथ्यङ्गान्यामुखाङ्गत्वादुच्यन्तेऽत्र स्वभावतः ।
उद्घात्यकावलगिते प्रपञ्चत्रिगते छलम् ॥
वाक्केल्यधिबले गण्डमवस्यन्दितनालिके ।
असत्प्रलापव्याहारमृदवानि त्रयोदश ॥ इति ॥

एषां लक्षणानि । गूढार्थपदपर्यायमालारूपेण प्रश्नोत्तरमालारूपेण च द्विविधमुद्घात्यकम् । अवलगितमपि द्विविधम् । अन्यकार्यच्छद्मनान्यकार्यकरणम् । अन्यकार्यप्रसङ्गात्प्रकृतकार्यसिद्धिश्चेति । असद्भूतं मिथःस्तोत्रं प्रपञ्चः । पूर्वरङ्गे नटादिभिः साम्यादनेकार्थप्रयोजनं त्रिगतम् । प्रियसदृशैर्वाक्यैरप्रियैर्लोभनं छलम् । साकाङ्क्षस्य वाक्यस्य निवर्तनमुक्तिप्रत्युक्तिर्वा वाक्केलिः । स्पर्द्धयान्योन्यवाक्याधिक्यमधिबलम् । सहसोदितं प्रस्तुतविरोधि गण्डम् । रसावेशादुक्तान्यथाव्याख्यानमवस्यन्दितम् । सोपहासनिगूढार्थप्रहेलिका नालिका । प्रहेलिकावहेलनवचनम् । असंबद्धकथाप्रायः प्रलापोऽसत्प्रलापः । अन्यार्थं हास्यप्रलोभनकरवचनं व्याहारः । दोषाणां गुणवत्प्रतिपादनं मृदवमिति । एषां यथासंभवं कतिचित्प्रस्तावनायां प्रयोक्तव्यानि । अत्र अये

१ एतत्क्वचिन्नास्ति.

मुसलमिदमियं च पातकाले
मुहुरनुयाति कलेन हुंकृतेन ॥ ४ ॥

भवतु कुटुम्बिनीं तावदाहूय पृच्छामि । (नेपथ्याभिमुखमवलोक्य ।)

गुणवत्युपायनिलये स्थितिहेतोः साधिके त्रिवर्गस्य ।
मद्भवननीतिविद्ये कार्याचार्ये द्रुतमुपेहि ॥ ५ ॥

(प्रविश्य ।) **नटी**—आर्य इयमस्मि । आज्ञानियोगेन मामार्योनुगृह्णातु । (अज्ज इअह्मि । अण्णाणिओएण मं अज्जो अणुगेह्णदु ।)

सूत्र०—आर्ये तिष्ठतु तावदाज्ञानियोगः । कथम क्रिमद्य भवत्या

तत्किमिदमित्यादिना गृहकृत्यप्रसङ्गेन क्रूरग्रहः स केतुरिति प्रस्तावनारूपकार्यसिद्धेरवलगनादवलगितं नाम आमुखाङ्गम् । वहति जलमिति स्वभावोक्तिरलङ्कारः ॥४॥

गुणवत्युपायेत्यार्या । अल्पसमासा ऋजुपदा भारती वृत्तिः । अत्र भार्याविषये सौशील्यगृहकृत्यदक्षत्वादयो गुणा उपायश्च । नीतिविषये गुणाः सन्धिविग्रहादयः षट् सामादय उपायाश्चत्वारः । विहितकार्योपदेष्टृत्वात्कार्याचार्यत्वमुभयत्र समम् । गार्हस्थ्यस्थितिहेतुत्रिवर्गसाधकत्वं पत्न्याः श्रुतिस्मृतिषु प्रसिद्धम् । नीतिविषये क्षयः स्थानं च वृद्धिश्च त्रिवर्गो नीतिवेदिनामित्युक्तलक्षणस्त्रिवर्गो राज्यस्थितिहेतुः । अत्र ऋतुं कंचिदुपादाय भारतीं वृत्तिमाश्रयेदिति वचनात्तृतीयाङ्के वर्णयिष्यमाणशरदृतूपादानं कृतमिति बोद्धव्यम् तथाहि अम्भःप्रसादादिगुणवति विजिगीषूणां सामाद्युपायनिलये तेषामेव दिग्विजयावसरप्रदायित्वनार्थसाधिके तन्निबन्धनत्वाद्धर्मकामयोस्तत्साधिके च । एवं लोकस्थितिहेतुत्रिवर्गस्य साधिके जैत्रयात्रादिकार्याणामाचार्येनुकूलत्वेन प्रवर्तिके भोः शरद् द्रुतमुपेहीति विजिगीषुणा चन्द्रगुप्तेन शरदागमः प्रार्थ्यते तन्मन्त्रिणा चाणक्येन राक्षसातिसन्धानार्थं स्वकुलविद्यानीतिरभिमुखीक्रियत इति च ध्वनितम् । उपायनिलये इत्यत्र निलीयतेत्रेति योगेन निलयशब्दो विशेष्यनिघ्नः । शरदृतोर्विजयानुकूलत्वं सरितः कुर्वती गाधाः पथश्चाश्यानकर्दमान् । यात्रायै नोदयामास तं शक्तेः प्रथमं शरदित्यादि सर्वैर्महाकविभिः बहुशः प्रपञ्चितम् । अत्र श्लेषोलङ्कारः । ' नानार्थसंशयः श्लेषो वर्ण्यावर्ण्योभयास्पद ' इति तल्लक्षणात् । अत्रासद्भूतभार्यास्तोत्रं प्रपञ्चः । साम्यादनेकार्थप्रयोजनं त्रिगतं चामुखाङ्गं त्रिष्वनुगतत्वादन्वर्थम् ॥ ५ ॥

आर्ये तिष्ठत्विति । इयं साकाङ्क्षस्य वाक्यस्य निर्वर्तनरूपा वाकेलिः । कथ-

---

१ हेतो. २ कार्यादा.

भगवतां ब्राह्मणानामुपनिमन्त्रणेन कुटुम्बकमनुगृहीतमभिमता वा भवनमतिथयः संप्राप्ता यत एष पाकविशेषारम्भः ।

नटी—आर्य आमन्त्रिता मया भगवन्तो ब्राह्मणाः । (अज्ज आमन्तिदा मए भअवन्तो बह्मणा ।)

सूत्र०—कथय कस्मिन्निमित्ते ।

नटी—उपरज्यते किल भगवान् चन्द्र इति । (उवरज्जदि किल भअवं चन्दो त्ति ।)

सूत्र०—आर्ये क एवमाह ।

नटी—एवं खलु नगरवासी जनो मन्त्रयते । (एवं खु णअरवासी जणो मन्तेदि ।)

सूत्र०—आर्ये कृतश्रमोस्मि चतुःषष्ट्यङ्गे ज्योतिःशास्त्रे । तत्प्रवर्त्यतां भगवतो ब्राह्मणानुद्दिश्य पाकः । चन्द्रोपरागं प्रति तु केनापि विप्रलब्धासि । पश्य ।

क्रूरग्रहः स केतुश्चन्द्रं संपूर्णमण्डलमिदानीम् ।
अभिभवितुमिच्छति बलात्

येत्यादि । इदमन्यार्थं पाकक्रियासाफल्यार्थं कुटुम्बकमनुगृहीतमिति प्रलोभनकरं वचनं व्याहारः ॥

कस्मिन्निति । केन निमित्तेनेत्यर्थः । सर्वासां प्रायोदर्शनस्योक्तत्वात् ॥

उपरज्यतीति । इदं प्रियसदृशैर्वाक्यैर्विलोभनं छलम् । वक्ष्यति च विप्रलब्धासीति ॥ एवमिति अयं असंबद्धकथाप्रायः प्रलापः असत्प्रलापः । [उपरागो ग्रहग्रस्तत्वम् ।] अत्र वृथा पाकारम्भरूपदोषस्य तत्प्रवर्त्यतामिति गुणवत्प्रतिपादनं मृदवं नामाङ्गम् ।

क्रूरग्रह इति । नेपथ्ये स्थितस्य चाणक्यस्येदं सहसोदितं प्रस्तुतस्य चन्द्रग्रहस्य विरोधि गण्डम् । क्रूरग्रहः स प्रसिद्धः केतुः राहुरित्यर्थः । उभयोरेकशरीरत्वेनाभेदव्यपदेशः । चन्द्रमसमिदानीमद्य पौर्णमास्यां पूर्णमण्डलमभिभवितुं

---

१ तत्रभवताम् इति पाठः. २ परिश्रमः. ३ चन्द्रमसंपूर्ण इति पाठः.

(नेपथ्ये)

आः क एष मयि स्थिते चन्द्रमभिभवितुमिच्छति ।

सूत्र०— रक्षत्येनं तु बुधयोगः ॥ ६ ॥

नटी०—आर्य कः पुनरेष धरणीगोचरो भूत्वा चन्द्रं ग्रहाभियोगाद्रक्षितुमिच्छति । (अज्ज को उण एसो धरणीगोअरो भविअ चन्दं ग्गहाभिजोआदो रक्खिदुं इच्छदि ।)

सूत्र०—आर्ये यत्सत्यं मयापि नोपलक्षितः । भवतु भूयोभियुक्तः स्वरव्यक्तिमुपलप्स्ये । (क्रूरग्रह इत्यादि पुनस्तदेव पठति ।)

(नेपथ्ये)

आः क एष मयि स्थिते चन्द्रगुप्तमभिभवितुमिच्छति ।

सूत्र०—(आकर्ण्य ।) आं ज्ञातम् । कौटिल्यः ।

नटी०—(भयं नाटयति ।)

ग्रसितुं बलादिच्छति परन्तु बुधस्य ग्रहस्य योगः संबन्ध एनं चन्द्रमसं रक्षतीति । तथा च ज्योतिःशास्त्रे व्याससंहितायां गर्गवचनम् ।

ग्रहपञ्चकसंयोगं दृष्ट्वा न ग्रहणं वदेत् ।
यदि न स्याद्बुधस्तत्र तं दृष्ट्वा ग्रहणं वदेत् ॥ इति ॥

चाणक्यावगतार्थस्तु क्रूरो घोरः ग्रहः चन्द्रगुप्ताभिभवं प्रति आग्रहो यस्य स क्रूरग्रहो राक्षसः केतुना मलयकेतुना सहितः सकेतुः भीमो भीमसेन इतिवत् । चन्द्रम् असंपूर्णमण्डलमिति छेदः । चन्द्रं चन्द्रगुप्तमिदानीमसंपूर्णमण्डलमवशीकृतसर्वराष्ट्रमव्याप्यरूढमूलमिति यावत् । बलान्महता म्लेच्छबलेनाभिभवितुं पराभवितुमिच्छतीति । एनं तु बुधस्य नयज्ञस्य चाणक्यस्य योग उपायो रक्षतीति प्रस्तावनार्थः । प्रस्तावना तु तत्र स्यात्कथोद्धातप्रवर्तिकेति लक्षणात् इयं प्रस्तावना । अत्र वाशब्दस्य समुच्चयार्थत्वात् आमुखप्रस्तावनयोः समुच्चयः कृत इति बोध्यम् । अत्र मुद्रानामालङ्कारः । सूच्यार्थसूचनं मुद्रा प्रकृतार्थपरैः पदैरिति लक्षणात् ॥ ६ ॥

[अभियुक्तः निपुणं दत्तावधान इत्यर्थः । स्वरव्यक्त्या कस्यायं स्वर इति ज्ञास्यामीत्यर्थः ।]

आर्य इति । इदं सोपहासं निगूढार्थप्रहेलिका नालिका । क एष इति । इदं स्पर्धयान्योन्यवाक्याधिक्यरूपमधिबलम् ।

सूत्र०—

कौटिल्यः कुटिलमतिः स एष येन
क्रोधाग्नौ प्रसभमदाहि नन्दवंशः ।
चन्द्रस्य ग्रहणमिति श्रुतेः सनाम्नो
मौर्येन्दोर्द्विषदभियोग इत्यवैति ॥ ७ ॥

कौटिल्य इति । चन्द्रस्य ग्रहणमिति श्रुतेः श्रवणात्सनाम्नः समाननामकस्य मौर्येन्दोश्चन्द्रगुप्तस्य द्विषदभियोगः द्विषता मलयकेतुनाभियोगो निरोधः अभिषेणनमिति यावत् । इत्यवैति एवं जानातीत्यर्थः । अत्र सनाम्नो मौर्येन्दोः द्विषदभियोग इत्यवैतीति रसावेशादुक्तान्यथाव्याख्यानमवस्यन्दितं नामामुखाङ्गम् । गूढार्थपरपर्यायमालारूपं प्रश्नोत्तरमालारूपं च द्विविधमप्युद्घात्यकं नामाद्यमङ्गमाद्ये नान्दीपद्ये कृतमामुखाङ्गत्वेन संग्राह्यम् । नान्दीपद्यस्याप्यामुखप्राक्कालिकत्वेनामुखान्तर्भूतस्याप्युचितत्वात् । यदि नान्दी आमुखबहिर्भूतैवेत्याग्रहस्तर्हि क्रूरग्रहः सकेतुरित्यत्रैव गूढार्थपरपर्यायरूपमुद्घात्यकं बोध्यम् । अत्र रक्षत्येनं तु बुधयोग इति स्वेतिवृत्तसमं वाक्यमर्थं वा यत्र सूत्रिण इति लक्षणात्कथोद्घातः । येन क्रोधाग्नौ प्रसभमदाहि नन्दवंश इति प्रस्तूयमानकार्यस्य गुणवर्णनया स्वत इति लक्षणसत्त्वात्प्रवृत्तकम् । स एष इति पदाभ्यां एषोयमित्युपक्षेपात्सूत्रधारप्रयोगत इति लक्षणस्य च सत्त्वात्प्रयोगातिशयश्चेति त्रीण्यङ्गानि प्रस्तावनाया उक्तानि । इति वीथ्यङ्गैस्त्रयोदशभिः स्वाङ्गैश्च त्रिभिः सहिता षोडशाङ्गा प्रस्तावना निरूपिता । अत्र प्रथमाङ्के वृत्तवर्तिष्यमाणानां कथांशानां निदर्शकः । संक्षेपार्थस्तु विष्कम्भो मध्यपात्रप्रयोजितः । इत्युक्तलक्षणो विष्कम्भो न कृतः । प्रस्तावनयैव क्रोधाग्नौ प्रसभमदाहि नन्दवंश इति वृत्तकथांशस्य मौर्येन्दोः द्विषदभियोग इति वर्तिष्यमाणकथांशस्य च निदर्शनात् । यद्वा । अन्तर्जवनिकासंस्थैश्चूलिकार्थस्य सूचनेति लक्षणान्नेपथ्यगतेनैव चाणक्येन नाटकीयार्थस्य सूचनात् प्रस्तावनान्तर्गतैव चूलिका कृतेति बोध्यम् । अथ प्रकृते नाटके मुखसन्धिरारभ्यते । सन्धेः सामान्यलक्षणानि दशरूपके—अवान्तरार्थसंबन्धः सन्धिरेकान्वये सतीति । एकेन प्रयोजनेनान्वितानां कथांशानां अवान्तरप्रयोजनेन संबन्धः सन्धिः । तत्रारम्भबीजसंबन्धो मुखसन्धिः ॥ ७ ॥

यत्र बीजसमुत्पत्तिर्नानार्थरससंभवा ।
प्रारम्भेण समायुक्ता तन्मुखं परिकीर्तितम् ।

इति मुखसन्धिलक्षणम् ।

तदित आवां गच्छावः । (इति निष्क्रान्तौ ।)

इति प्रस्तावना ।

(ततः प्रविशति मुक्तां शिखां परामृशन्कुपितश्चाणक्यः ।)

चाण०——कथय क एष मयि स्थिते चन्द्रगुप्तमभिभवितुमिच्छति । पश्य ।

आस्वादितद्विरदशोणितशोणशोभां
सन्ध्यारुणामिव कलां शशलाञ्छनस्य ।
जृम्भाविदारितमुखस्य मुखात्स्फुरन्तीं
को हर्तुमिच्छति हरेः परिभूय दंष्ट्राम् ॥ ८ ॥

ततः प्रविशति इत्यादिसन्दर्भो मुखसन्धिः । मौर्यलक्ष्मीस्थैर्यहेतुराक्षससंग्रहरूपमुख्यप्रयोजनार्थायाश्चाणक्योपायविचारकथाया अनुकूलदैवकृतराक्षसमुद्रालाभाद्यवान्तरप्रयोजनेन सह संबन्धस्य सामान्यलक्षणस्यारम्भबीजसंबन्धस्य च वक्ष्यमाणविशेषलक्षणस्य वक्ष्यमाणाया बीजसमुत्पत्तेश्च सत्त्वात् ।

मुक्तां शिखामिति । नन्दकुलप्रतिज्ञावसरे मुक्ता शिखा न बद्धा चन्द्रगुप्तलक्ष्मीस्थैर्यस्याद्याप्यनिष्पन्नत्वात् । अत्र सिंहवदतिक्रूरमपि मां परिभूय मया महता संरम्भेण साधितां मौर्यलक्ष्मीं राक्षसो हर्तुमिच्छतीति रूपकातिशयोक्त्या ध्वनितम् । रूपकातिशयोक्तिः स्यान्निगीर्याध्यवसानतः । इति लक्षणात् । को नामेति राक्षसस्य साहसिकत्वदुःसाध्यसाधकत्वादयो गुणाः सूचिताः । हरेर्दंष्ट्रामिति मौर्यश्रियो दुरुद्धरत्वं सूचितम् । **आस्वादितेति** । अचिरकृतनन्दवंशवधरोषः अद्यापि न शान्त इति सूचितम् । सन्ध्यारुणचन्द्रकलादृष्टान्तेन मौर्यश्रीरभिनवा वर्द्धिष्णुर्विश्वाभिनन्द्येति च सूचितम् । जृम्भाविदारितमुखस्येति स्वस्यास्मिन्विषयेऽतिजाग्रता ध्वनिता । स्फुरन्तीमिति समग्राङ्गतया लक्ष्म्या वैरिदुःसाध्यत्वमुक्तम् । एवं जाग्रतोऽपि मम पौरुषं परिभूय अवज्ञाय मौर्यलक्ष्मीं हर्तुं यतत इत्यहोऽतिशूरो दण्डनीतिपारदृश्वा स्वाभिकार्यधुर्यो राक्षसोऽवश्यं संग्राह्य इति चाणक्यौत्सुक्यमात्ररूपा बीजस्यारम्भावस्थार्थतः सूचिता । चन्द्रगुप्तलक्ष्मीस्थैर्यफलकस्य राक्षससंग्रहरूपकार्यस्य हेतुरनुकूलदैवश्चाणक्यनीतिप्रयोगो बीजम् । यथा रत्नावल्यां वत्सराजस्य सागरिकाप्राप्तिहेतुरनुकूलदैवो यौगन्धरायणोद्योगः । यथा वा वेणीसंहारे द्रौपदीकेशसंयमनहेतुर्भीमक्रोधोपचितो युधिष्ठिरोत्साहो बीजम् । तच्च बीजं महाकार्यावान्तरकार्यभेदादनेकप्रकारमित्यनकधाविस्तारीत्युक्तम् । राक्षससंग्रहश्च मलयकेतुनिग्रहं विना न घटत इति निग्रहोऽप्य-

अपि च ।

नन्दकुलकालभुजगीं कोपानलबहलनीलधूमलताम् ।
अद्यापि बध्यमानां वध्यः को नेच्छति शिखां मे ॥ ९ ॥

अपि च ।

उल्लङ्घयन्मम समुज्ज्वलतः प्रतापं
कोपस्य नन्दकुलकाननधूमकेतोः ।
सद्यः परात्मपरिमाणविवेकमूढः
कः शालभेन विधिना लभतां विनाशम् ॥ १० ॥

शार्ङ्गरव शार्ङ्गरव ।

(प्रविश्य ।) शिष्यः । उपाध्याय आज्ञापय ।

चाण०—वत्स उपवेष्टुमिच्छामि ।

शिष्यः—उपाध्याय नन्वियं सन्निहितवेत्रासनैव द्वारप्रकोष्ठशाला । तदस्यामुपवेष्टुमर्हत्युपाध्यायः ।

चाण०—वत्स कार्याभिनियोग एवास्मान्व्याकुलयति न पुनरुपाध्यायसमभूः शिष्यजने दुःशीलता । (नाट्येनोपविश्यात्मगतम् ।)

वान्तरप्रयोजनत्वेन सूचनीयः ॥ ८ ॥ तदेतदाह नन्देति । नैल्यकौटिल्यगुणेन कालभुजगीधूमलतात्वेन निरूपणम् । बध्यो मलयकेतुरित्यर्थः । मलयकेतुनिग्रहं विना शिखां न बध्नामीति पद्यस्य निष्कृष्टोर्थः ॥ ९ ॥

इममेव संरम्भं वीररसेनोपोद्बलयति । उल्लङ्घयन्निति । मम मदीयस्य समुज्ज्वलतः प्रदीप्तस्य नन्दकुलदाहकवह्निरूपस्य कोपस्य प्रतापमुग्रत्वं ज्वालां चोल्लङ्घयन्नतिक्रमिष्यन्नित्यर्थः । कः मलयकेतुः परात्मनोः परिमाणं तारतम्यं तद्विवेकशून्यः शालभेन विधिना दहनज्वालापतयालुशलभरीत्या विनाशं लभताम् । [अत्र कामन्दकः-आत्मानं च पांश्चैव ज्ञात्वा धीरः समुत्पतेत् । एतदेव हि विज्ञानं यदात्मपरवेदनम् ॥ अन्यत्र च नाग्निं पतङ्गवद्गच्छेत् स्पृश्यमेव हि संस्पृशेत् । किमन्यत्स्याहते दाहात्पतङ्गस्याग्निमृच्छतः ॥ इति ।] अत्र पद्यद्वयेनुभयताद्रूप्यरूपकालङ्कारः । विषय्यभेदताद्रूप्यं रञ्जनं विषयस्य यत् । रूपकं तु त्रिधाधिक्यन्यूनत्वानुभयोक्तिभिः । इति लक्षणात् ॥ १० ॥

कार्यसंरम्भवैयग्र्येण द्विरुक्तिः शार्ङ्गरवेति । वत्सेति । इदमुपालम्भगर्भवचनम् । अधुनाप्यासनं त्वया न सज्जीकृतमित्याशयः । वत्स कार्याभि-

---

१ लोल. २ को नाम इति पाठः. ३ परिणाम.

कथं प्रकाशतां गतोयमर्थः पौरेषु यथा किल नन्दकुलविनाशजनितरोषो राक्षसः पितृवधामर्षितेन सकलनन्दराज्यपरिपणनप्रोत्साहितेन पर्वतकपुत्रेण मलयकेतुना सह सन्धाय तदुपगृहीतेन च महता म्लेच्छराजबलेन परिवृतो वृषलमभियोक्तुमुद्यत इति । (विचिन्त्य ।) अथवा येन मया सर्वलोकप्रकाशं नन्दवंशवधं प्रतिज्ञाय निस्तीर्णा दुस्तरा प्रतिज्ञासरित्सोहमिदानीं प्रकाशीभवन्तमप्येनमर्थं समर्थः प्रशमयितुम् । कुतः—यस्य मम

श्यामीकृत्याननेन्दूनरियुवतिदिशां सन्ततैः शोकधूमैः
कामं मन्त्रिद्रुमेभ्यो नयपवनहृतं मोहभस्म प्रकीर्य ।
दग्ध्वा संभ्रान्तपौरद्विजगणरहितान्नन्दवंशप्ररोहान्
दाह्याभावान्न खेदाज्ज्वलन इव वने शाम्यति क्रोधवह्निः ॥ ११ ॥

नियोग इति । कार्ये राक्षससंग्रहं प्रति अभिनियोगः अभिनिवेश एवं त्वदुपालम्भत्वेनास्मान्व्याकुलयति । न पुनरुपाध्यायसहभूरुपाध्यायत्वव्याप्येत्यर्थः । शिष्यजने विषये दुःशीलता उपालम्भनशीलता । अल्पेप्यपराधे शिष्यजनं प्रति उपालम्भनमुपाध्यायानां सहजो दोष इत्यर्थः । त्वं तु सेवायामत्यन्तं समवहितोसि कार्यव्यग्रत्वादहं त्वामुपालब्धवानस्मीत्यर्थः । अत्र कार्याभिनियोग इत्यनेनानिर्वाहणाद्बिन्द्वादिरूपेणानेकधा विस्तारिणः कार्यहेतोश्चाणक्ययोयोगस्य बीजस्य स्तोकोद्देशः कृत इति बोध्यम् । अथास्य सन्धेरङ्गान्युच्यन्ते । अङ्गानि द्वादशैतस्य बीजारम्भसमन्वयात् । बीजारम्भानुगुण्येन मुखसन्धेरङ्गानि प्रयोक्तव्यानि ।

उपक्षेपः परिकरः परिन्यासो विलोभनम् ।
युक्तिः प्राप्तिः समाधानं विधानं परिभावना ॥
उद्भेदभेदकरणान्यन्वर्थानि यथाक्रमम् ॥ इति ॥

कथमित्यादि । अयमाशयः । पुरं सर्वं नन्दमौलबलाक्रान्तं प्रकृतयश्च सर्वा नन्दकुलामात्ये राक्षसेनुरक्ताः । अतस्तदुद्यममुपश्रुत्य महान्तमन्तःकोपमुत्पादयेयुस्ततश्च महत्सङ्कटमापतितं कथं कर्तव्यमिति चिन्ता । अथ वेति चिन्तापरिहारः । समागतमप्येनं दण्डेन निग्रहीतुं समर्थः इत्यर्थः ।

सामर्थ्यमेवोद्भावयति द्वाभ्याम् । **श्यामीकृत्येति** । अरियुवतय एव दिश इत्यादिरूपकम् । मन्त्रिद्रुमेभ्य इति क्रियया यमभिप्रैति स संप्रदानमिति मोह-

---

१ रोषामर्षः. २ असमर्थः-न समर्थः, किं प्रश०. ३ रिपु. इति पाठः.

अपि च ।

शोचन्तोऽवनतैर्नराधिपभयाद्धिक्शब्दगर्भैर्मुखै-
र्मामग्रासनतोऽवकृष्टमवशं ये दृष्टवन्तः पुरा ।
ते पश्यन्ति तथैव संप्रति जना नन्दं मया सान्वयं
सिंहेनेव गजेन्द्रमद्रिशिखरात्सिंहासनात्पातितम् ॥ १२ ॥

सोऽहमिदानीमवसितप्रतिज्ञाभारोऽपि वृषलापेक्षया शस्त्रं धारयामि येन मया

समुत्खाता नन्दा नव हृदयशल्या इव भुवः
कृता मौर्ये लक्ष्मीः सरसि नलिनीव स्थिरपदा ।
द्वयोः सारं तुल्यं द्वितयमभियुक्तेन मनसा
फलं कोपप्रीत्योर्द्विषति च विभक्तं सुहृदि च ॥ १३ ॥

अथवा अगृहीते राक्षसे किमुत्खातं नन्दवंशस्य किं वा स्थैर्य-

भस्मविक्षेपक्रिययाभिप्रेतानां मन्त्रिद्रुमाणां संप्रदानत्वं पत्ये शेत इतिवत् । राक्षस-वक्रनासादीन्मन्त्रिणः स्वमन्त्रशक्त्या मोहयित्वा प्रतिविधातुमसमर्थान् कृत्वत्यर्थः पौरद्विजेति । वेणुवनदाहे द्विजगणाः पक्षिगणा उड्डीय पलायन्त इति भावः ॥ मन्त्रिणः पौरांश्च हित्वा यत्प्रतिज्ञातं नन्दसंहरणं तदेव मया कृतमिति स्वस्यो-चितकारित्वं सूचितम् । न खेदान्न निर्वेदात् । संप्रति दाह्यो वध्यो मलयकेतुः प्राप्तस्तस्मिन् क्रोधवह्निर्ज्वलिष्यतीति भावः ॥ ११ ॥

शोचन्त इति । अवशं तदानीं प्रतिकर्तुमसमर्थं तथैव यथाग्रासनतोऽहम-वकृष्टस्तथैवेत्यर्थः । ते पश्यन्तीति । ईदृशो मदीयः क्रोधः सर्वलोकप्रत्यक्ष इति भावः ॥ १२ ॥

शस्त्रं उद्योगम् । अयं बीजन्यास उपक्षेपः अङ्गम् । काव्यार्थस्य समुत्पत्ति-रुपक्षेप इति स्मृतः । राक्षससंग्रहरूपकार्यबीजस्य स्वोद्योगस्य बीजन्यासादुपक्षेपात् । शस्त्रधारणमावश्यकमित्याह । येनेति । सारं न्याय्यं । 'सारो बले स्थिरांशे च न्याय्ये क्लीबं वरे त्रिषु' इत्यमरः । फलं निग्रहानुग्रहरूपमभियुक्तेन निग्रहानुग्रहा भिनिवेशवता मनसा द्विषत्सुहृदोस्तुल्यं युगपद्विभक्तं विभज्य स्थापितमित्यर्थः ॥ १३ ॥ सोऽहमिति पूर्वेणान्वयः । इदं बीजस्य बहुलीकरणं परिकरः । चन्द्रगुप्तलक्ष्मीस्थैर्यो-त्पादनहेतोर्बीजस्यावश्यं कर्तव्यत्वेन प्रचुरीकरणाद्द्वितीयमङ्गम् । अहो इति । इयं बीज-

---

१ अग्रया०. २ भरः ३ रोगाः.

मुत्पादितं चन्द्रगुप्तलक्ष्याः । (विचिन्त्य ।) अहो राक्षसस्य नन्दवंशे निरतिशयो भक्तिगुणः । स खलु कस्मिंश्चिदपि जीवति नन्दान्वयावयवे वृषलस्य साचिव्यं ग्राहयितुं न शक्यते । तदभियोगं प्रति निरुद्योगः शक्योवस्थापयितुमस्माभिः । अनयैव बुद्ध्या तपोवनगतोपि घातितस्तपस्वी नन्दवंशीयः सर्वार्थसिद्धिः । यावदसौ मलयकेतुमङ्गीकृत्यास्मदुच्छेदाय विपुलतरं प्रयत्नमुपदर्शयत्येव । (प्रत्यक्षवदाकाशे लक्ष्यं बद्ध्वा ।) साधु अमात्य राक्षस साधु । श्रोत्रिय साधु । साधु मन्त्रिबृहस्पते साधु । कुतः ।

ऐश्वर्यादनपेतमीश्वरमयं लोकोर्थतः सेवते
तं गच्छन्त्यनु ये विपत्तिषु पुनस्ते तत्प्रतिष्ठाशया ।
भर्तुर्ये प्रलयेपि पूर्वसुकृतासङ्गेन निःसङ्गया
भक्त्या कार्यधुरां वहन्ति कृतिनस्ते दुर्लभास्त्वादृशाः ॥ १४ ॥

अत एवास्माकं त्वत्संग्रहे यत्नः कथमसौ वृषलस्य साचिव्यग्रहणेन सानुग्रहः स्यादिति । कुतः ।

विषये आश्चर्यावेशः परिभावना तृतीयमङ्गम् । राक्षसभक्तिगुणविषयकाश्चर्यावेशस्य तत्संग्रहबीजविषयत्वोपपत्तेः । अहो एवं श्लाघ्यो मदीयोद्योग इति । स खल्विति । तस्य नन्दान्वयावयवस्याभियोगं प्रति प्रतिष्ठापनाभिमानं प्रति निरुद्योगो व्यवसायहीनश्चद्वशे स्थापयितुं शक्य इत्यर्थः । तदभियोगं प्रति निरुद्यमो वावस्थाप्येत इति पाठान्तरम् । वा अथवा तदभियोगं प्रति निरुद्यमो व्यवसायहीनोवस्थाप्येत वशीक्रियेतेत्यर्थः । अस्माभिरिति । इदं गूढबीजप्रकाशनमुद्भेदः । पूर्वं गूढतया कृतस्य बीजस्य प्रकाशनात् । यावदेवं सत्यपि नन्दान्वये समूलमुन्मूलिते पीत्यर्थः ।

साधुत्वमेवाह ऐश्वर्यादिति । बहवो दुर्लभा भवानेको जगति दिष्ट्योपलब्धोस्माभिरित्यर्थः कृतिन इति कतिरपाठः । कुशला इत्यर्थः । [प्रशस्तं कृतं कर्म येषां ते कृतपवित्रकार्या धन्या इत्यर्थः ।] तस्य भर्तुः पुनःप्रतिष्ठाशयानुगच्छन्तीत्यनुषज्यते । पूर्वसुकृतासङ्गेन पुराकृतसंरक्षणादिसुकृताविस्मरणेनेत्यर्थः । निःसङ्गया सम्प्रति निरुपाधिकया फलाशारहितयेत्यर्थः । इदं बीजगुणवर्णनं विलोभननामाङ्गम् । कार्यगुणवर्णनेन कारणगुणवर्णनस्यार्थसिद्धत्वात् ॥ १४ ॥ अत एवेति । अत्रात्सुक्यमारम्भः ।

---

१ नन्दवंशोयमं ; निरुद्योगैरस्माभिरवस्थातुमग्रुक्ताभिरनमैव इति पाठः. २ अङ्गीकृत्य, उरीकृत्य. ३ बहवः इति पाठः.

अप्राज्ञेन च कातरेण च गुणः स्याद्भक्तियुक्तेन कः
प्रज्ञाविक्रमशालिनोपि हि भवेत्किं भक्तिहीनात्फलम् ।
प्रज्ञाविक्रमभक्तयः समुदिता येषां गुणा भूतये
ते भृत्या नृपतेः कलत्रमितरे संपत्सु चापत्सु च ॥ १५ ॥

तन्मयाप्यस्मिन्वस्तुनि नशयानेन स्थीयते यथाशक्ति क्रियते तद्ग्रहणं प्रति यत्नः । कथमिव । अत्र तावद्वृषलपर्वतकयोरन्यतरविनाशेनापि चाणक्यस्यापकृतं भवतीति विषकन्यया राक्षसेनास्माकमत्यन्तोपकारि मित्रं घातितस्तपस्वी पर्वतक इति सञ्चारितो जगति जनापवादः । लोकप्रत्ययार्थमस्यैवार्थस्याभिव्यक्तये पिता ते चाणक्येन घातित इति रहसि त्रासयित्वा भागुरायणेनापवाहितः पर्वतकपुत्रो मलयकेतुः । शक्यः खल्वेष राक्षसमतिपरिगृहीतोपि व्युत्तिष्ठमानः प्रज्ञया निग्रहीतुम् । न पुनरस्य निग्रहात्पर्वतकवधोत्पन्नं राक्षसस्यायशः प्रकाशीभवत्प्रमार्ष्टुमिच्छामि । प्रयुक्ताश्च स्वपक्षपरपक्षयोरनुरक्तापरक्तजनजिज्ञासया बहु-

---

अप्राज्ञेनेति । [प्रज्ञाविक्रमाभ्यां शालते स तथोक्तस्तस्मात् ।] ते भृत्या नृपतेर्भूतये भवन्ति इतरे उक्तविलक्षणाः संपत्सु चापत्सु च कलत्रं कुटुम्बवत् केवलं पोष्याः । न क्वापि तैः स्वामिकार्यसिद्धिरिति भावः । इदं बीजगुणप्रोत्साहनं भेदः अङ्गम् । कार्यगुणैः स्वोद्योगस्य बीजस्य प्रोत्साहनादुपबृंहणात् ॥ १५ ॥

नशयानेनेति । नशब्देन समासः । सावधानेन स्थीयत इत्यर्थः । इदं बीजसंविधानं समाधानमङ्गं बीजस्य सम्यग्विधानात् । [विषमयी कन्या विषकन्या । लावण्यभूषणां कान्तां योषितं क्रमशो विषैः । युवतीं योजयेत्कामिरिपुभूपालघातने ॥ इत्युक्तत्वात् ।] लोक इति । लोका अयमेवार्थस्तथ्य इति यथा मन्येरन् यथा चास्मासु विश्वस्युस्तदर्थम् । किंचास्यैव लोकप्रतीतस्यार्थस्याभिव्यक्तये निर्वहणसन्धौ कथं राक्षसेन घातितस्तातो न चाणक्येनेत्येवं मलयकेतुं प्रत्ययमुमेवार्थमभिव्यञ्जयितुं प्रत्यापयितुमित्यर्थः । भागुरायणनाम्ना स्वाप्ततमेन मलयकेतोः कृतकाप्तीकृतेन गूढप्रणिधिना अपवाहितः कटकान्निःसारितः । मलयकेतुरर्धराज्यप्रदानेनात्रैव स्थापितश्चेद्राक्षस उदासीनः अन्यत्र क्वापि गच्छेत् । अमर्षाद्वान्यं कंचित्प्रबलं प्रतिपक्षमुत्थाप्य प्रत्यवतिष्ठेत नास्मद्वशमेयात् । अपवाहिते

---

१ विनाशेपि. २ पर्वतेश्वरः इति पाठः.

विधदेशवेषभाषाचारसञ्चारवेदिनो नानाव्यञ्जनाः प्रणिधयः । अन्विष्यते च कुसुमपुरवासिनां नन्दामात्यसुहृदां निपुणं[1] प्रचारगतम् । तत्तत्कारणमुत्पाद्य कृतकृत्यतामापादिताश्चन्द्रगुप्तसहोत्थायिनो[2] भद्रभटप्रभृतयः प्रधानपुरुषाः । शत्रुप्रयुक्तानां च तीक्ष्णरसदायिनां प्रतिविधानं प्रत्यप्रमादिनः परीक्षितभक्तयः क्षितिपतिप्रत्यासन्ना नियोजितास्तत्र तत्राप्तपुरुषाः । अस्ति चास्माकं सहाध्यायि मित्रमिन्दुशर्मा[3] नाम ब्राह्मणः । स चौशनस्यां दण्डनीत्यां चतुःषष्ट्यङ्गे ज्योतिःशास्त्रे च परं प्रावीण्यमुपगतः । स मया क्षपणकलिङ्गधारी नन्दवंशवधप्रतिज्ञानन्तरमेव कुसुमपुरमुपनीय सर्वनन्दामात्यैः सह सख्यं ग्राहितो विशेषतश्च तस्मिन् राक्षसः समुत्पन्नविश्रम्भः । तेनेदानीं महत्प्रयोजनमनुष्ठेयं भविष्यति । तदेवमस्मत्तो न किंचित्परिहीयते । वृषल एव केवलं प्रधानप्रकृतिष्व[4]स्मास्वारोपितराज्यतन्त्रभारः सतत-

---

तु मलयकेतौ प्राय एनमेव परिगृह्य प्रत्यवतिष्ठेत । तदानेनैव जनापवादेन निर्वहणे जीवसिद्धिप्रत्यायितेन राक्षसमलयकेत्वोर्विरोधं संपाद्य कार्यप्रनाड्या राक्षसो वशयितुं शक्यः स्यादिति भावः । वक्ष्यति चैतद्वनगज इव तस्मात्सोऽभ्युपायैर्विनेय इति । प्रज्ञयेति । प्रज्ञया निर्वहणे संपत्स्यमानयाधुनैव निग्रहीतुं शक्यः । तन्न युक्तमित्याह । न पुनरस्येति । मलयकेतुर्निगृहीतश्चेत् पर्वतकवधोऽपि मयैव कृत इति स्यात् । ततश्च राक्षसोपरि पातितमयशः परिमार्जितं स्यात्तथा सति निर्वहणे कुटिलनयेन संविधास्यमानो राक्षसमलयकेतुविरोधो न सिध्येदिति भावः । निपुणेति । निपुणं गूढत्वेन क्रियमाणं प्रचारगतं कपटाचरणप्रकारः तत्तत्कारणं स्त्रीमद्यमृगयाशीलावित्यादि तृतीयाङ्के वक्ष्यमाणमुत्पाद्य इतो निःसार्य मलयकेतुना सह सन्धाय कृतकृत्यतां एते वयं देवकार्येवहिताः स्म इत्येवंरूपां वक्ष्यमाणां आपादिताः सहोत्थायिनो बाल्यात्प्रभृति स्वसमानतया दानमानादिभिर्वर्धिता इत्यर्थः । इदानीं कार्यनिर्वहणप्रसङ्गसमय इत्यर्थः । यथाशक्ति क्रियत इत्यारभ्य भविष्यतीत्यन्तं बीजानुगुणप्रस्तुतकार्यारम्भःकरणम् अत्रैव करणे अत्र तावद्वृषलेत्यारभ्य प्रमार्ष्टुमिच्छामीत्यन्तः सन्दर्भः बीजानुकूलसङ्घटनप्रयोजनविचारो युक्तिः । शत्रुप्रयुक्तानामित्यादि तत्राप्तपुरुषा इत्यन्तं बीजसुखदुःखहेतुर्विधानम् । सुखदुःखहेतोर्विचारस्यात्र विधानात् । तीक्ष्णरसदायिनो दुःखहेतवः तत्प्रतिविधानं प्रति अप्रमादिनः सुखहेतवः । न किंचित्परिहास्यत इति । परिहीनं न्यूनं न भविष्यतीत्यर्थः । इयं

---

१ निपुणतरम्. २ तत्तत्कृत्यताम्. ३ विष्णु. ४ मिथ्वस्मा.

मुदास्ते । अथवा यत्स्वयमभियोगदुःखैरसाधारणैरपाकृतं तदेव राज्यं सुखयति । कुतः ।)

स्वयमाहृत्य भुञ्जाना बलिनोपि स्वभावतः ।
गजेन्द्राश्च नरेन्द्राश्च प्रायः सीदन्ति दुःखिताः ॥ १६ ॥

(ततः प्रविशति यमपटेन चरः ।)

प्रणमत यमस्य चरणौ किं कार्यं दैवतैरन्यैः ।
एष खल्वन्यभक्तानां हरति जीवं परिस्फुरन्तम् ॥ १७ ॥

पणमह जमस्स चलणे किं कज्जं देवएहि अण्णेहिं ।
एसो खु अण्णभत्ताणं हरइ जीअं चडंफडन्तं[1] ॥

अपि च । (अवि अ ।)

पुरुषस्य जीवितव्यं विषमाद्भवति भक्तिगृहीतात् ।
मारयति सर्वलोकं यस्तेन यमेन जीवामः ॥ १८ ॥

पुरिसस्स जीविदव्वं विसमादो होइ भत्तिगहिआदो ।
मारेइ सव्वलोअं जो तेण जमेण जीआमो ॥

बीजनिष्पत्तिः परिन्यासः । न किंचित्परिहास्यते सर्वं समाहितमिति परितः सर्वैरुपायैर्बीजस्य न्यासात् ।

अभियोगदुःखैः कार्याभिनिवेशजनितखेदैरित्यर्थः । अयं बीजसुखागमः प्राप्तिर्नामाङ्गम् । बीजेन स्वनीतिप्रयोगेण वृषलस्य सुखागमात्सुखप्राप्तेः । इत्थं मुखसन्धेर्द्वादशाङ्गानि निरूपितानि । अतः परं यमपटचरवृत्तान्तः सर्वोपि अवान्तरार्थसंबन्धः सन्धिरेकान्वये सतीत्युक्तस्य स्वपरपक्षानुरक्तापरक्तजनजिज्ञासाराक्षसमुद्रालाभाद्यवान्तरप्रयोजनसंबन्धस्य कथनार्थः । प्रयुक्ताश्च परपक्षेत्यनेन सूचितस्य यमपटचरस्य प्रवेशः ।

परिस्फुरन्तमिति । देशीयं क्रियमाणमित्यर्थः ।

विषमादपि क्रूरादपि यमाद्भक्तिगृहीताद्भक्तिवशीकृताद्भक्तितोषितादिति यावत् । पुरुषस्य जीवितव्यं जीवनं भवतीत्यर्थः । यमभक्तिरपमृत्युहारिणीति तात्पर्यम् । अनेन गीतिद्वयेन चाणक्यस्य यमवत्क्रूरस्य स्वपक्षपरपक्षानुग्रहनिग्रहसामर्थ्यं द्योतयन् स्वस्य गूढचरत्वं सूचयति ।

---

१ तडफडन्तम्.

यावदिदं गृहं प्रविश्य यमपटं दर्शयन् गीतानि गायामि । (जाव एदं गेहं पविसिअ जमपडं दंसअन्तो गीआइं गाआमि ।)

(इति परिक्रामति ।)

शिष्यः—(विलोक्य ।) भद्र न प्रवेष्टव्यम् ।

चरः—अहो ब्राह्मण कस्येदं गृहम् । (हंहो बह्मण कस्स एदं गेहं ।)

शिष्यः—अस्माकमुपाध्यायस्य सुगृहीतनाम्न आर्यचाणक्यस्य ।

चरः—(विहस्य ।) अहो ब्राह्मण आत्मीयस्यैव मम धर्मभ्रातुर्गृहं भवति । तस्माद्देहि मे प्रवेशं यावत्तवोपाध्यायस्य यमपटं प्रसार्य धर्ममुपदिशामि । (हंहो बह्मण अत्तकेरअस्स जेव्व मह धम्मभादुणो घरं होदि । ता देहि मे पवेसं जाव दे उवज्झाअस्स जमपडं पसारिअ धम्मं उपदिसामि ।)

शिष्यः—(सक्रोधम् ।) धिङ् मूर्ख किं भवानस्मदुपाध्यायादपि धर्मवित्तरः ।

चरः—अहो ब्राह्मण मा कुप्य । न हि सर्वः सर्वं जानाति । तत्किमपि ते उपाध्यायो जानाति किमपि अस्मादृशा जानन्ति । (हंहो बह्मण मा कुप्प । ण हि सव्वो सव्वं जाणादि । ता किंवि ते उवज्झाओ जाणादि किंवि अह्मारिसा जाणन्दि ।)

शिष्यः—मूर्ख सर्वज्ञतामुपाध्यायस्य चोरयितुमिच्छसि ।

चरः—अहो ब्राह्मण यदि तवोपाध्यायः सर्वं जानाति तर्हि जानातु तावत्कस्य चन्द्रोऽनभिप्रेत इति । (हंहो बह्मण जइ तव उवज्झाओ सव्वं जाणादि ता जाणादु दाव कस्स चन्द्रो अणभिप्पेदो त्ति ।)

[सुगृहीतं शुभावहत्वान्नाम यस्य । तदुक्तं–' स सुगृहीतनामा स्यात्प्रातर्यः स्मर्यते जनैः ।']

धर्मस्य राजकार्यस्य भ्राता प्रवर्तकः धर्मं पुरवृत्तान्तं निवेदयामीति गूढाभिसन्धानवचनम् । याचकस्य सर्वेऽपि धर्मतो भ्रातर एवेति बहिरर्थः ।

चोरयितुमपलपितुम् चन्द्रगुप्तोऽनभिप्रेत इति गूढम् ।

---

१ नामधेयस्य. २ तमः. ३ अणभिमदो, अणप्पेक्खिदो.

शिष्यः—मूर्ख किमनेन ज्ञातेनाज्ञातेन वा[१]।

चरः—तवोपाध्याय एव ज्ञास्यति यदेतेन ज्ञातेन भवति। त्वं तावदेतावत् जानासि कमलानां चन्द्रोनभिप्रेत इति। ननु पश्य (तव उवज्झाओ एव्व जाणिस्सदि जं इमिणा जाणिदेव होदि। तुमं दाव एत्तिअं जाणासि कमलाणं चन्दो अणभिप्पेदो त्ति। णं पेक्ख।)

कमलानां मनोहरणामपिरूपाद्विसंवदति शीलम्।
सम्पूर्णमण्डलेपि यानि चन्द्रे विरुद्धानि॥ १९॥
कमलाण मणहराण वि रूवाहिंतो विसंवदई शीलं।
संपुण्णमण्डलम्मि वि जाइं चन्दे विरुद्धाइं॥

चाण०—(आकर्ण्यात्मगतम्।) अये चन्द्रगुप्तादपरक्तान् पुरुषान् जानामीत्युपक्षिप्तमनेन।

शिष्यः—मूर्ख किमिदमसंबद्धमभिधीयते।

चरः—अहो ब्राह्मण सुसंबद्धमेवैतद्भवेत्। (हंहो बह्मण सुसंबद्धं ज्जेव्व एदं भवे।)

शिष्यः—यदि किं स्यात्।

चरः—यदि श्रोतुं जानन्तं लभे। (जदि सुणिदुं[२] जाणन्तं लहे।)

चाण०—भद्र विश्रब्धं प्रविश लप्स्यसे श्रोतारं ज्ञातारं च।

चरः—एष प्रविशामि। (प्रविश्योपसृत्य च।) जयतु आर्यः। (एसो पविसामि। जेदु अज्जो।)

चाण०—(विलोक्यात्मगतम्।) [३]कथमयं प्रकृतिचित्तपरिज्ञाने नियुक्तो निपुणकः। (प्रकाशम्।) भद्र स्वागतमुपविश।

[कमलानि सूर्यविकासीनि। न ह्याकृतिः सुसदृशं विजहाति वृत्तमित्यन्यत्रोक्तत्वाद् मनोहरणामपि गुणग्राहकत्वाभात् शीलस्य विसंवादिता।] कमलानामित्यनेन पद्येन मनोहरगुणस्यापि राक्षसपक्षपातिजनस्य स्वरूपाननुगुणं शीलमसम्पूर्णमण्डले चन्द्रगुप्ते विरुद्धमाचरतीति गूढार्थः सूचितः। चन्द्रगुप्तस्य भाविसंपूर्णमण्डलत्वं न सहत इति यावत्॥ १९॥

---

१ गुरोर्भविष्यति इत्यधिकं क्वचित्. २ सुणितारं जाणिचारं अ. ३ अतः प्राक् 'कथं प्रभूतत्वात्कार्याणां कस्य परिज्ञाने नियुक्तो निपुणक इति न ज्ञायते, आः ज्ञातम् अये तत्कथ इत्यधिकं क्वचित्.

चरः—यदार्य आज्ञापयति। (जं अज्जो आणवेदि।) (भूमावुपविष्टः ।)

चाण०—भद्र वर्णयेदानीं स्वनियोगवृत्तान्तम्। अपि वृषलमनुरक्ताः प्रकृतयः।

चरः—अथ किम्। आर्येण खलु तेषु तेषु विरागकारणेषु परिहृतेषु सुगृहीतनामधेये देवे चन्द्रगुप्ते दृढमनुरक्ताः प्रकृतयः। किंतु पुनरस्त्यत्र नगरे अमात्यराक्षसेन सह प्रथमं समुत्पन्नस्नेहबहुमानास्त्रयः पुरुषा देवस्य चन्द्रश्रियः श्रियं न सहन्ते। (अह इं। अज्जेण खु तेसु तेसु विराअकारणेसु परिहरिदेसुं सुगहीदणामहेए देवे चन्दउत्ते दिढं अणुरत्ताओ पकिदिओ। किंदु उण अत्थि एत्थ णअरे अमच्चरक्खसेण सह पढमं समुप्पण्णसिणेहबहुमाणा तिण्णि पुरीसा देवस्स चन्दसिरिणो सिरिं ण सहन्दि।)

चाण०—(सक्रोधम्।) ननु वक्तव्यं स्वजीवितं न सहन्त इति। भद्र अपि ज्ञायन्ते नामधेयतः।

चरः—कथमज्ञातनामधेया आर्यस्य निवेद्यन्ते। (कहं अजाणिअणामहेआ अज्जस्स णिवेदीअन्ति।)

चाण०—तेन हि श्रोतुमिच्छामि।

चरः—शृणोत्वार्यः। प्रथमं तावदार्यस्य रिपुपक्षे बद्धपक्षपातः क्षपणको— (सुणादु अज्जो। पढमं दाव अज्जस्स रिपुपक्खे बद्धपक्खवादो खवणओ—)

चाण०—(आत्मगतम्।) अस्माद्रिपुपक्षे बद्धपक्षपातः क्षपणकः।

[चन्द्रश्रियः श्रीमतः चन्द्रगुप्तस्य श्रियं राज्यम्।] न सहन्ते यत्तदस्तीति वाक्यार्थः कर्ता। चरवाक्ये। आर्यस्य रिपुपक्ष इति तव शत्रुष्वित्यर्थः। [बद्ध पक्षपाता दृढमनुरक्ताः।] क्षपणको जैनाकृतिः।

सहर्षमात्मगतमिति। अयमभिसन्धिः अस्मत्सहाध्यायि मित्रमिन्दुशर्मा नाम ब्राह्मणः। तेनेदानीं महाप्रयोजनमनुष्ठेयं भविष्यतीति पूर्वोक्तः क्षपणको रिपुपक्षपातित्वेन दृढां प्रसिद्धिं गतः। अतस्तन्मुखेनास्माकं इष्टसिद्धिर्भविष्यतीति

---

१ हरिअन्तेसु. २ जीवसिद्धी इत्य. पु०. ३ सहर्षमा. ४ अस्मात्परं—(प्रकाशम्) किन्नामधेयो हि सः. चरः—जीवसिद्धी णाम. चाण०—अस्मद्रिपुपक्षे बद्धपक्षपात इति कथमवगतं भवता. चरः—जेण सा अमच्चरक्खसेण पउत्ता—इति पाठः.

चरः—जीवसिद्धिर्नाम स येन सा अमात्यराक्षसप्रयुक्ता विषकन्या देवे पर्वतेश्वरे समावेशिता। (जीवसिद्धी णाम सो जेण सा अमच्चरक्खसप्पउत्ता विसकण्णा देवे पव्वदीसरे समावेसिदा।)

चाण०—(स्वगतम्।) जीवसिद्धिः। एष तावदस्मत्प्रणिधिः। (प्रकाशम्।) भद्र अथापरः कः।

चरः—आर्य अपरः खल्वमात्यराक्षसस्य प्रियवयस्यः कायस्थः शकटदासो नाम। (अज्ज अवरो अमच्चरक्खसस्स पिअवअस्सो काअत्थो सअडदासो णाम।)

चाण०—(विहस्यात्मगतम्।) कायस्थ इति लघ्वी मात्रा। तथापि न युक्तं प्राकृतमपि रिपुमवज्ञातुम्। तस्मिन्मया सुहृच्छद्मना सिद्धार्थको विनिक्षिप्तः। (प्रकाशम्।) भद्र तृतीयमपि श्रोतुमिच्छामि।

चरः—तृतीयोऽपि अमात्यराक्षसस्य द्वितीयमिव हृदयं पुष्पपुरनिवासी मणिकारश्रेष्ठी चन्दनदासो नाम यस्य गेहे कलत्रं न्यासीकृत्य अमात्यराक्षसो नगरादपक्रान्तः। (तिदीओ वि अमच्चरक्खसस्स दुदीअं हिअअं पुप्फउरणिवासी मणिआरसेट्ठी चन्दणदासो णाम। जस्स गेहे कलत्तं णासीकदुअ अमच्चरक्खसो णअरादो अवक्कन्तो।)

चाण०—(आत्मगतम्।) नूनं सुहृत्तमः। न ह्यनात्मसदृशेषु राक्षसः कलत्रं न्यासीकरिष्यति। (प्रकाशम्।) भद्र चन्दनदासस्य गृहे राक्षसेन कलत्रं न्यासीकृतमिति कथमवगम्यते।

हर्षकारणम्। जीवसिद्धौ निवेदिते तमजानन्तमिव तूष्णीभूतं चाणक्यं जगति तत्तत्कर्मकथनेन ज्ञापयति जीवसिद्धिर्नाम स इति।

अस्मादिति। अस्माकं प्रणिधिर्गूढचरः राक्षसमित्रीभूतः सन्निमं जनापवादं निर्वहणे मलयकेतुं प्रत्यायपिष्यतीति भावः। कायस्थो लेखकः लघ्वी मात्रा फाल्गुस्तस्मादस्माकं नात्याहितं तथापि नोपेक्षणीयः। [तदुक्तं—'अल्पायसोऽप्यरेर्वृद्धिर्महानर्थाय रोगवत्।']

[द्वितीयमिव हृदयं सर्वविश्रम्भस्थानमित्यर्थः।]

---

१ छद्मा. २ (विहस्य) इत्यधिकम्.

चरः—आर्य इयमङ्गुलिमुद्रा आर्यमवगतार्थं करिष्यति । (अज्ज इअं अङ्गुलिमुद्दा अज्जं अवगदत्थं करिस्सदि ।) (इति मुद्रामर्पयति ।)

चाण०—(मुद्रामवलोक्य गृहीत्वा राक्षसस्य नाम वाचयति । सहर्षं स्वगतम् ।) ननु वक्तव्यं राक्षस एवास्मदङ्गुलिप्रणयी संवृत्त इति । (प्रकाशम् ।) भद्र अङ्गुलिमुद्राधिगमं विस्तरेण श्रोतुमिच्छामि ।

चरः—शृणोत्वार्यः । अस्ति तावदहमार्येण पौरजनचरितान्वेषणे नियुक्तः परगृहप्रवेशे परस्यानाशङ्कनीयेन अनेन यमपटेन हिण्डमानो मणिकारश्रेष्ठिनश्चन्दनदासस्य गृहं प्रविष्टोस्मि । तत्र यमपटं प्रसार्य प्रवृत्तोस्मि गीतानि गातुम् । (सुणादु अज्जो । अत्थि दाव अहं अज्जेण पौरजणचरिदअण्णेसणे णिउत्तो परघरप्पवेसे परस्स अणासङ्कणिज्जेण इमिणा जमपडेण हिण्डन्तो[3] मणिआरसेट्ठिणो चन्दणदासस्स गेहं पविठ्ठोह्मि । तहिं जमपडं पसारिअ पउत्तोह्मि गीदाइं गाइदुं ।)

चाण०—ततः किम् ।

चरः—ततश्च एकस्मादपवरकात्पञ्चवर्षदेशीयः प्रियदर्शनीयशरीराकृतिः कुमारको बालत्वसुलभकौतूहलोत्फुल्लनयनो निष्क्रमितुं प्रवृत्तः । ततो हा निर्गतो हा निर्गत इति शङ्कापरिग्रहनिवेदयिता तस्यैवापवरकस्याभ्यन्तरे स्त्रीजनस्योत्थितो महान् कलकलः । (तदो एक्कादो अवैवरकादो पञ्चवरिसदेसीओ पिअदंसणीअसरीराकिदी कुमॉरओ बालत्तणसुलहकोदुहलोप्फुल्लणॲणो णिक्कमिदुं पउत्तो । तदो हा णिग्गदो हा णिग्गदोत्ति सङ्कापरिग्गहँणिवेदइत्तिओ तस्स एव्व अववरकस्स अब्भन्तरे इत्थिआजणस्स उट्ठिदो महन्तो कलअलो ।)

अङ्गुलिप्रणयी इति प्रणयी हस्तगतः इत्यर्थः [वशे यात इति यावत् । अपवरकादत्प्रकोष्ठात् ०देशीयः । ईषदसमाप्तौ कल्पब्देश्यदेशीयरः । पा. ५. ३. ६७.]

बालत्वसुलभं कौमारसहभु ।

---

१ गम्यते भवता. २ अवगमइस्सादि (अवगमयिष्यति). ३ ०न्तो अज्ज (अद्य). ४ आवरकादो. ५ सुउमारो कु०. ६ णअणजुअलो (युगलः). ७ परिग्गहणिभूदगुरुओ (निभृतगुरुकः) इति पाठः.

तत ईषद्द्वारदेशदापितमुख्या एकया स्त्रिया स कुमारको निष्क्रामन्नेव निर्भर्त्स्यावलम्बितः कोमलया बाहुलतया । तस्याः कुमारसंरोधसंभ्रमप्रचलिताङ्गुलेः करात्पुरुषाङ्गुलिपरिणाहप्रमाणघटिता विगलितेयमङ्गुलिमुद्रिका देहलीबन्धे पतिता उत्थिता तया अनवबुद्धैव मम चरणपार्श्वे समागत्य प्रणामनिभृता कुलवधूरिव निश्चला संवृत्ता । मयापि अमात्यराक्षसस्य नामाङ्कितेति आर्यस्य पादमूलं प्रापिता । तस्मादेषोस्या मुद्राया आगमः । (तदो ईसि दारदेशदाविदमुहीए एक्काए इत्थिआए सो कुमारओ णिक्कमन्तो एव्व णिब्भच्छिअ अवलम्बिदो कोमलाए बाहुलदाए । तस्साए कुमारसंरोधसंभमप्पचलिदङ्गुलिदो करादो पुरिसअङ्गुलिपरिणाहप्पमाणघडिआ विअलिआ इअं अङ्गुलिमुद्दिआ देहलीबन्धम्मि पाडिआ उठ्ठिदा ताए अणवबुद्धा एव्व मम चलणपासं समागच्छिअ पणामणिहुदा कुलवहु[1] विह णिच्चला संवुत्ता । मए वि अमच्चरक्खसस्स णामङ्किदेत्ति अज्जस्स पादमूलं पाविदा । ता एसो इमाए आअमो ।)

चाण०—भद्र श्रुतम् । अपसर । नचिरादस्य परिश्रमस्यानुरूपं फलमधिगमिष्यसि ।

चरः—यदार्य आज्ञापयति । (जं अज्जो आणवेदि ।) (इति निष्क्रान्तः ।)

चाण०—शार्ङ्गरव शार्ङ्गरव ।

[कुमारस्य संरोधस्तत्र संभ्रमस्त्वरा । परिणाहो विस्तारः । देहली उदुम्बरः । उत्थिता उत्पतिता । अनवबुद्धा अज्ञाता ।]

इत्थं नानार्थरससंभवा बीजसमुत्पत्तिर्निरूपिता । अतोयं मुखसन्धिः साङ्गो व्याख्यातः । अतः परं प्रतिमुखसन्धिः । 'लक्ष्यालक्ष्यस्य बीजस्य व्यक्तिः प्रतिमुखं मतम्' इति लक्षणात् । पूर्वं लक्ष्यस्य व्यक्तस्य मध्ये यमपटचरवृत्तान्तेनालक्षितचाणक्यनीतियोगबीजस्य पुनरत्र व्यक्तेरुद्भेदात् । यत्नबिन्दुसंबन्धस्य च सत्त्वात् । बिन्दुयत्नौ चाग्रे वक्ष्येते । बिन्दुप्रयत्नानुगमादङ्गान्यस्य त्रयोदश ।

---

१ णववहु (नववधु०) इति पाठः.

(प्रविश्य ।)

शिष्यः—उपाध्याय आज्ञापय ।

चाण०—वत्स मसीभाजनं पत्रं चोपानय ।

शिष्यः—(तथा करोति ।)

चाण०—(पत्रं गृहीत्वा स्वगतम् ।) किमत्र लिखामि । अनेन खलु लेखेन राक्षसो जेतव्यः ।

(प्रविश्य ।)

प्रतीहारी—जयत्वार्यः । (जेदु अज्जो ।)

चाण०—(सहर्षमात्मगतम् ।) गृहीतो जयशब्दः । (प्रकाशम् ।) शोणोत्तरे किमागमनप्रयोजनम्[२] ।

प्रती०—आर्य देवश्चन्द्रश्रीः शीर्षे कमलमुकुलाकारमञ्जलिं निवेश्य आर्यं विज्ञापयति । इच्छाम्यार्येणाभ्यनुज्ञातो देवस्य पर्वतेश्वरस्य पारलौकिकं कर्तुम् । तेन च धारितपूर्वाणि आभरणानि ब्राह्मणेभ्यः प्रतिपादयामीति । (अज्ज देवो चन्द्रसिरी सीसे कमलमुउलाआरम-ञ्जलिं णिवेसिअ अज्जं विण्णवेदि । इच्छामि अज्जेण अब्भणुण्णादो देवस्स पव्वदीसरस्स पारलोइअं कादुं तेण अ धारिदपुव्वाइं आहरणाइं बह्मणाणं[३] पडिवादिमित्ति ।)

बिन्दुप्रयत्नानुगुण्येनास्य सन्धेस्त्रयोदशाङ्गानि प्रयोक्तव्यानि । 'विलासः परिसर्पश्च विधूतं शमनर्मणी । नर्मद्युतिः प्रशमनं विरोधः पर्युपासनम् । वज्रं पुष्पं परि-न्यासो वर्णसंहार इत्यपि ।'

किमत्रेति । अयं चाणक्यस्य पुनरुद्योगो बिन्दुः । अवान्तरार्थविच्छेदे बिन्दुरच्छेदकारणमिति लक्षणात् । अवान्तरार्थेन यमपटचरवृत्तान्तेन विच्छिन्न-स्यान्तरितस्य बीजस्य पुनः प्रवर्तनात् । तदुक्तं दशरूपके— 'अवान्तरितस्य बीजस्य संज्ञान्तरमाह ।' अवान्तरार्थेति । बिन्दुवद्बिन्दुः । जले तैलबिन्दुवत्प्रसृतत्वात् । प्रतीहारीलक्षणं तु— 'सन्धिविग्रहसम्बद्धनानाचारसमुत्थितम् । निवेदयन्ति याः कार्यं प्रतीहार्यस्तु ता मताः ॥ इति ॥ गृहीत इति । अयं कार्यसिद्धिविषयमनोरथो विलासः । प्रथममङ्गम् ।

---

१ यदाज्ञापयत्युपाध्यायः । इति निष्क्रम्य पुनः प्रविश्य । उपाध्याय इदं मसीभाजनं पत्रं च. २ कारणम्. ३ गुणवन्ताणं (गुणवतां), भअवन्ताणं इत्यधिकम्.

चाण०—(सहर्षमात्मगतम्।) साधु वृषल ममैव हृदयेन सह संमन्त्र्य सन्दिष्टवानसि। (प्रकाशम्।) शोणोत्तरे उच्यतामस्मद्वचनाद्वृषलः-साधु वत्स अभिज्ञः खल्वसि लोकव्यवहाराणां तदनुष्ठीयतामात्मनोभिप्रायः। किंतु पर्वतेश्वरधृतपूर्वाणि गुणवन्ति भूषणानि गुणवद्भ्य एव प्रतिपादनीयानि। तदहं स्वयमेव परीक्षितगुणान् ब्राह्मणान् प्रेषयामीति।

प्रति०—यत् आर्य आज्ञापयति। (जं अज्जो आणवेदि।) (इति निष्क्रान्ता।)

चाण०—शार्ङ्गरव उच्यन्तामस्मद्वचनाद्विश्वावसुप्रभृतयस्त्रयो भ्रातरः वृषलात्प्रतिगृह्याभरणानि भवद्भिरहं द्रष्टव्य इति।

शिष्यः—तथेति[2] (निष्क्रान्तः।)

चाण०—उत्तरोयं लेखार्थः। पूर्वः कथमस्तु (विचिन्त्य।) आः ज्ञातम्। उपलब्धवानस्मि प्रणिधिभ्यो यथा तस्य म्लेच्छराजलोकस्य मध्यात्प्रधानतमाः पञ्च राजानः परया सुहृत्तया राक्षसमनुवर्तन्ते। ते यथा।

कौलूतश्चित्रवर्मा मलयनरपतिः सिंहनादो नृसिंहः
काश्मीरः पुष्कराक्षः क्षतरिपुमहिमा सैन्धवः सिन्धुषेणः।

साधु वृषल इति। मन्मनोनुगतमेव त्वया चिकीर्षितमित्यर्थः। वृषलादिति। अलङ्कारत्रयस्य पृथक् पृथक् प्रतिग्रहाय त्रयो भ्रातर इत्युक्तम्। अलङ्कारत्रयं च सत्यवता यदनुप्रेषितं तदुपगतमिति निर्वहणे वाचयिष्यमाण इत्यर्थः। इह दृष्टनष्टबीजानुसरणं परिसर्पः पूर्वसङ्गो दृष्टस्य मध्ये नष्टस्य बीजस्यानुसन्धानात्।

[गुणवन्ति प्रकृष्टगुणानि महार्घाणीति यावत् प्रतिपादयितव्यानि दातव्यानि। प्रणिधयश्चराः।

[कौलूतेति। कौलूतः कुलूतदेशाधिपतिः। चित्रं वर्म सन्नाहो यस्य। सिंहस्येव नादो यस्य। क्षतो नाशितो रिपूणां महिमा येन शत्रुंदम इत्यर्थः।]

---

१ ब्राह्मणेभ्यः इत्यधिकम्. २ यदाज्ञापयत्युपाध्याय इति पाठः. ३ अस्मात्पूर्वं-विचिन्त्य इत्यधिकम्. ४ बलस्य इति पाठः. ५ भक्त्या.

मेघाख्यः पञ्चमोस्मिन्पृथुतुरगबलः पारसीकाधिराजो
नामान्येषां लिखामि ध्रुवमहमधुना चित्रगुप्तः प्रमार्ष्टु ॥ २० ॥

(विचिन्त्य ।) अथवा न लिखामि पूर्वमनभिव्यक्तमेवास्ताम् । (नाट्येन लिखित्वा ।) शार्ङ्गरव ।

(प्रविश्य ।) **शिष्यः**—उपाध्याय आज्ञापय ।

चाण०—वत्स श्रोत्रियाक्षराणि प्रयत्नलिखितान्यपि नियतमस्फुटानि भवन्ति । तदुच्यतामस्मद्वचनात्सिद्धार्थकः । एभिरक्षरैः केनापि कस्यापि स्वयं वाच्यमिति अदत्तवाह्यनामानं लेखं शकटदासेन लेखयित्वा मामुपतिष्ठस्व । न चाख्येयमस्मै चाणक्यो लेखयतीति ।

शिष्यः—तथा (इति निष्क्रान्तः ।)

चाण०—(स्वगतम् ।) हन्त जितो मलयकेतुः ।

(प्रविश्य लेखहस्तः ।) **सिद्धार्थकः**—जयत्वार्यः । आर्य अयं स शकटदासेन लिखितो लेखः । (जेदु अज्जो । अज्ज अअं सो सअडदासेण लिहिदो लेहो ।)

चाण०—(गृहीत्वा) अहो दर्शनीयान्यक्षराणि । (अनुवाच्य ।) भद्र अनया मुद्रया मुद्रयैनम् ।

सिद्धा०—(तथा कृत्वा ।) आर्यायं मुद्रितो लेखः । किमपरमनुष्ठीयताम् । (अज्ज अअं मुद्दिदो लेहो । किं अवरं अणुचिट्ठीअदु ।)

नामान्येषामिति । अस्मिन् पत्रे मदीयेन लेखनेनैते मरिष्यन्ति अतश्चित्रगुप्तः स्वगणिताकरपत्रे जीवितत्वेन लिखितानामेषां नामानि प्रमार्क्ष्यतीति भावः ॥ २० ॥

अथवेति । नामानि लिखितानि चेच्छकटदासोस्माभिश्छलेन लेखयिष्यमाणं पत्रं न लेखिष्यतीत्याशयः । इदमनिष्टवस्तुक्षेपरूपं विधूतम् । अनिष्टवस्तुनि नामलेखने क्षेपान्निषेधात् । विक्षेप इति पाठे स एवार्थः ।

अदत्तानि वाह्यानां कौलूतराक्षसादीनां नामानि यस्मिन् । [वाह्यस्य यस्मै लेखः प्रेष्यते तस्य नाम]

---

१ मेघाक्षः. २ यजनलिखितानि इति पाठः. ३ अस्मात्प्राक्-(कर्णे कथयित्वा) इत्य०. ४ यदाज्ञापयत्युपाध्याय इति पाठः. ५ दर्शनीयताक्षराणाम् इति पाठः. ६ अस्मात्प्राक्-ता आणवेदु अज्जो इत्यधिकम्.

चाण०—भद्र कस्मिंश्चिदाप्तजनानुष्ठेये कर्मणि त्वां व्यापारयितुमिच्छामि ।

सिद्धा०—(सहर्षम् ।) आर्य अनुगृहीतोस्मि । आज्ञापयत्वार्यः किमनेन दासजनेनार्यस्यानुष्ठातव्यम् । (अज्ज अणुग्गिहिदोह्मि । आणवेदु अज्जो किं इमिणा दासजणेण अज्जस्य अणुचिट्ठिदव्वं ।)

चाण०—प्रथमं तावद्वध्यस्थानं गत्वा घातकाः सरोषदक्षिणाक्षिसङ्कोचसंज्ञां ग्राहयितव्यास्ततस्तेषु गृहीतसंज्ञेषु भयापदेशादितस्ततः प्रद्रुतेषु शकटदासो वध्यस्थानादपनीय राक्षसं प्रापयितव्यः । तस्माच्च सुहृत्प्राणपरितुष्टात्पारितोषिकं ग्राह्यम् । राक्षस एव कंचित्कालं सेवितव्यः । ततः प्रत्यासन्नेषु परेषु प्रयोजनमिदमनुष्ठेयम् । (कर्णे एवमेवम् ।)

सिद्धा०—यदार्य आज्ञापयति । (जं अज्जो आणवेदि ।)

चाण०—शार्ङ्गरव शार्ङ्गरव ।

(प्रविश्य ।) **शिष्यः**—उपाध्याय आज्ञापय ।

चाण०—उच्यतामस्मद्वचनात्कालपाशिको दण्डपाशिकश्च यथा वृषलः समाज्ञापयति य एष क्षपणको जीवसिद्धिर्नाम राक्षसप्रयुक्तो विषकन्यया पर्वतकं घातितवान्स एनमेव दोषं प्रख्याप्य सनिकारं नगरान्निर्वास्यतामिति ।

शिष्यः—तथे (इति परिक्रम्य ।)

कस्मिंश्चिदिति । [आप्तो विश्वसनीयः । 'आप्तः प्रत्ययितस्त्रिषु ।' इत्यमरः । दक्षिणाक्षिसङ्कोचेन संज्ञा ताम् । भयापदेशाद्भयव्याजेन ।] अयमिष्टजनानुनयः पर्युपासनम् । प्रथममिति । अयं भावः । शकटदासशूलः रोपणसमये मया सरोषदक्षिणाक्षिसङ्कोचसंज्ञायां क्रियमाणायां तं विहाय भवद्भिः पलायितव्यमिति सङ्केतयितव्या इत्यर्थः ।

[पारितोषिकं परितोषः प्रयोजनमस्य । प्रयोजनमिति ठञ् । सनिकारं सापमानम् ।]

---

१ आत्मनानु. २ नियोजयितुम्. ३ संङ्केतेषु. ४ परिगृह्य. ५ कालान्तरम्. ६ ०कया. ७ पर्वतेश्वरम्. ८ बहिर्निःसार्यताम्. ९ यदाज्ञापयत्युपाध्याय इति सर्वत्र.

चाण०—वत्स तिष्ठ तिष्ठ। योयमपरः कायस्थः शकटदासो नाम राक्षसप्रयुक्तो नित्यमस्मच्छरीरमभिद्रोग्धुमिह प्रयतते स चाप्येनं दोषं प्रख्याप्य शूलमारोप्यतां गृहजनश्चास्य बन्धनागारं प्रवेश्यतामिति ।

शिष्यः—तथा (इति निष्क्रान्तः ।)

चाण०—(चिन्तां नाटयति । आत्मगतम् ।) अपि नाम दुरात्मा राक्षसो गृह्येत ।

सिद्धा०—आर्य गृहीतः । (अज्ज गहीदो ।)

चाण०—(सहर्षमात्मगतम् ।) हन्त गृहीतो राक्षसः । (प्रकाशम् ।) भद्र कोयं गृहीतः ।

सिद्धा०—गृहीत आर्यसन्देशः । तस्माद्गमिष्यामि कार्यसिद्ध्यै । (गिहीदो अज्जसन्देसो । ता गमिस्सं कज्जसिद्धीए ।)

चाण०—(साङ्गुलिमुद्रं लेखमर्पयित्वा ।) गम्यताम् । अस्तु ते कार्यसिद्धिः ।

सिद्धा०—तथा (तह) (इति निष्क्रान्तः ।)

(प्रविश्य ।) **शिष्यः**—उपाध्याय कालपाशिको दण्डपाशिकश्च उपाध्यायं विज्ञापयतः । इदमनुष्ठीयते देवस्य चन्द्रगुप्तस्य शासनमिति ।

चाण०—शोभनम् । वत्स मणिकारश्रेष्ठिनं चन्दनदासमिदानीं द्रष्टुमिच्छामि ।

गृहजनस्य बन्धनागारप्रवेशनफलमुत्तरत्र चतुर्थेऽङ्के तव च पुत्रदारैः सह समागम इति वक्ष्यमाणेन राक्षसवचनेन मलयकेतुमनसि स्मृतं स्यात्पुत्रदारस्येति राक्षसस्य च मनसि विकल्पापादनमिति सूक्ष्मदृग्भिरवधेयम् ।

शत्रुपक्षमाश्रित इति । रोषावेशेन दुरात्मेति गालनम् । हन्तेति । अयमरत्युपशमनं शमः पञ्चममङ्गम् । अरतेश्चिन्ताया उपशमनात् । साङ्गुलीति । उत्तरोत्तरवाक्यैः कार्यसिद्धिबीजप्रकाशनादिदं प्रशमनम् । मलयकेतुराक्षसयोर्विरोधापादनार्थं लेखरूप उपायः कृतः । अतः परं राक्षसस्य मौर्यसाचिव्यप्रवणीकरणाय सप्तमेऽङ्के करिष्यमाणोपायबीजमुपक्षेप्तव्यमित्याह । चन्दनदासमिदानीं द्रष्टुमिच्छामीति ।

---

१ आरोप्य. २ भद्र सिद्धार्थक. ३ जं अज्जो आणवेदित्ति प्रणम्य.

शिष्यः—तथा (इति निष्क्रम्य चन्दनदासेन सह प्रविश्य ।) इत इतः श्रेष्ठिन् ।

चन्दनदासः—(स्वगतम् ।)

चाणक्येनाकरुणेन सहसा शब्दायितस्यापि जनस्य ।
निर्दोषस्यापि शङ्का किं पुनर्मम जातदोषस्य ॥ २१ ॥

चाणक्कम्मि अकरुणे सहसा सद्दाविदस्स वि जणस्स ।
णिद्दोसस्स वि सङ्का किं उण मह जाददोसस्स ॥

तस्माद्भणिता मया धनसेनप्रमुखा निजनिवेशसंस्थिताः कदापि चाणक्यहतको गेहं मे विचि[१]नोति । तस्मादवहिता । निर्वहत भर्तुरमात्यराक्षसस्य गृहजनम् । मम तावद्यद्भवति तद्भवहत्विति । (ता भणिदा मए धणसेणप्पमुहा णिअणिवेससण्ठिआ[२] कदावि चाणक्कहदओ गेहं मे विचिण्णावेदि । ता अवहिदा णिव्वहेह भट्टिणो अमच्चरक्खसस्स घरअणं । मह दाव जं होदि तं होदि तं होदु त्ति ।)

शिष्यः—भोः श्रेष्ठिन् इत इतः ।

चन्द०—अयमागच्छामि । (अअमाअच्छामि ।) (उभौ परिक्रमतः ।)

शिष्यः—(उपसृत्य ।) उपाध्याय अयं श्रेष्ठी चन्दनदासः ।

चन्द०—जयत्वार्यः । (जेदु अज्जो ।)

चाण०—(नाट्येनावलोक्य ।) श्रेष्ठिन् स्वागतमिदमासनमास्यताम् ।

चन्द०—(प्रणम्य ।) किं न जानात्यार्यः यथानुचित उपचारो हृदयस्य परिभवादपि महद्दुःखमुत्पादयति । तस्मादिहैवोचितायां भूमावुपविशामि । (किं ण जाणादि अज्जो जह अणुचिदो उवआरो हिअ[३]अस्स परिहवादोवि मह[४]न्तं दुःखमुप्पादेदि । ता इह ज्जेव उचिदाए भूमीए उववसामि ।)

चाणक्येऽकरुणत्वेन प्रसिद्धे तेन सहसाकस्माच्छाब्दितस्याहूतस्येत्यर्थः ।

---

१ विचाययति. २ तिण्णि वाणिज्जआ (त्रयो वाणिज्याः), सावकाः इति पाठः. ३ सहिअअस्स (सहृदयस्य). ४ महन्तं इति नास्ति पुस्तके.

चाण०—भोः श्रेष्ठिन् मा मैवम् । संभावितमेवेदमस्मद्विधैः भवतः । तदुपविश्यतामासन एव ।

चन्द०—(स्वगतम् ।) उपक्षिप्तमनेन दुष्टेन किमपि । (प्रकाशम् ।) यदार्य आज्ञापयति । (इत्युपविष्टः ।) (उवक्खित्तमणेण दुट्ठेन किंवि । जं अज्जो आणवेदि ।)

चाण०—भोः श्रेष्ठिन् चन्दनदास अपि प्रचीयन्ते संव्यवहाराणां वृद्धिलाभाः ।

चन्द०—(स्वगतम् ।) अत्यादरः शङ्कनीयः । (प्रकाशम् ।) अथ किम् । आर्यस्य प्रसादेन अखण्डिता मे वणिज्या । (अच्चादरो सङ्कणीओ ।) (अहइं । अज्जस्स प्पसाएण अखण्डिदा मे वणिज्जा)

चाण०—न खलु चन्द्रगुप्तदोषा अतिक्रान्तपार्थिवगुणानधुना स्मरयन्ति प्रकृतीः ।

चन्द०—(कर्णौ पिधाय ।) शान्तं पापम् । शारदनिशासमुद्गतेनेव पूर्णिमाचन्द्रेण चन्द्रश्रियाधिकं नन्दन्ति प्रकृतयः । (सन्तं पावं । सारअणिसासमुग्गएण विअ पुण्णिमाचन्देण चन्दसिरिणा अहिअं णन्दन्ति पकिदिओ ।)

चाण०—भोः श्रेष्ठिन् यद्येवं प्रीताभ्यः प्रकृतिभ्यः प्रतिप्रियमिच्छन्ति राजानः ।

भोः श्रेष्ठिन्निति । एतदादि चन्दनदासातिसन्धानार्थं परिहासवचनं नर्म । संभावितमिति । एतदुपचारकरणं संभावितमेवेति बहिरुपचारः । परिभवकरणमिति तु निगूढ आशयः । [उपक्षिप्तं प्रस्तावेन पुरस्कृतम् । प्रचीयन्ते प्रकर्षेण वर्धन्ते । संव्यवहाराणां वृद्धिलाभाः निर्व्याजवाणिज्यसम्पादिता आयाः । अखण्डिता निष्प्रत्यूहा प्रवर्तते ।]

प्रकृतिभिरिति पाठः साधुः । यद्वा स्मरतिर्ज्ञानसामान्यवचनोतो गतिबुद्धीत्यादिना कर्मत्वम् । चन्द्रश्रिया चन्द्रगुप्तेनेत्यर्थः । इयमनुगुणोद्घाटनार्था प्रीतिर्नर्मस्तुतिरष्टममङ्गम् ।

---

१ उचितमेवैतद०. २ उवक्खिदं. ३ लाभाः. ४ अज्ज अह०. इ. पा. ५ प्रतीताभ्यः.

चन्द०—आज्ञापयतु आर्यः। किं कियदस्माज्जनादिष्यत इति। (आणवेदु अज्जो किं कित्तिअं इमादो जणादो इच्छीअदि त्ति।)

चाण०—भोः श्रेष्ठिन् चन्द्रगुप्तराज्यमिदं न नन्दराज्यम्। यतो नन्दस्यैवार्थरुचेरर्थसम्बन्धः प्रीतिमुत्पादयति चन्द्रगुप्तस्य तु भवतामपरिक्लेश एव।

चन्द०—(सहर्षम्।) आर्य अनुगृहीतोस्मि। (अज्ज अणुग्गहीदोम्हि।)

चाण०—भोः श्रेष्ठिन् स चापरिक्लेशः कथमाविर्भवतीति ननु भवता प्रष्टव्याः स्मः।

चन्द०—आज्ञापयतु आर्यः। (आणवेदु अज्जो।)

चाण०—संक्षेपतो राजनि अविरुद्धाभिर्वृत्तिभिर्वर्तितव्यम्।

चन्द०—आर्य कः पुनरधन्यो राज्ञा विरुद्ध इति आर्येणावगम्यते। (अज्ज को उण अधण्णो रण्णा विरुद्धोति अज्जेण अवगच्छीअदि।)

चाण०—भवानेव तावत्प्रथमम्।

चन्द०—(कर्णौ पिधाय।) शान्तं पापं शान्तं पापम्। कीदृशस्तृणानामग्निना सह विरोधः। (सन्तं पावं सन्तं पावं। कीदिसो तिणाणं अग्गिणा सह विरोहो।)

चाण०—अयमीदृशो विरोधः। यत्त्वमद्यापि राजापथ्यकारिणोमात्यराक्षसस्य गृहजनं स्वगृहे रक्षसि।

[किं कियदिति। कीदृग्द्रव्यं किं परिमाणं च। अर्थरुचेः अर्थलोलुपस्य न तु प्रजाहितैषिणः। अपरिक्लेशः अपरिक्लेशनं दण्डपारुष्याभावात् सुखस्थितिरिति यावत्। अविरुद्धाभिर्वृत्तिभिरिति। राज्ञ आनुकूल्येन वर्तितव्यमित्यर्थः।]

इयं राजानुरागहेतुर्वाक्यरचना उपन्यासः। भवितव्यमिति युष्माभिरिति शेषः। भवानेवेति इदं प्रतिमुखनिष्ठुरवचनं वज्रम्। यस्त्वमद्यापीति। पुरा पुरादपक्रमणसमये रक्षणं भवतु नाम अद्यापि मलयकेतुमाश्रित्य राजापथ्यकरणसमये [राजापथ्यकारिणो राज्ञोऽहितमाचरतः।] तत्कलत्ररक्षणमनुचितमिति भावः।

---

१ भवितव्यम्. २ यस्त्वम्. ३ इमाभि-उपनीयामिर, इति पाठः.

चन्द०—आर्य अलीकमेतत्केनाप्यनभिज्ञेन आर्यस्य निवेदितम् । (अज्ज अलीअं एदं केणावि अणभिण्णेण अज्जस्स णिवेदिदं ।)

चाण०—भोः श्रेष्ठिन् अलमाशङ्कया । भीताः पूर्वराजपुरुषाः पौराणामनिच्छतामपि गृहेषु गृहजनं निक्षिप्य देशान्तरं व्रजन्ति । ततस्तत्प्रच्छादनं दोषमुत्पादयति ।

चन्द०—एवं नु इदम् । तस्मिन् समये आसीदस्मद्गृहे अमात्य राक्षसस्य गृहजन इति । (एवंण्णेदं । तस्सिं समये आसि अह्मघरे अमच्चरक्खसस्स घरअणो त्ति ।)

चाण०—पूर्वमनृतमिदानीमासीदिति परस्परविरोधिनी वचने ।

चन्द०—एतावदेवास्ति मे वाक्छलम् । (एत्तिअं जेव्व अत्थि मे वाआच्छलम् ।)

चाण०—भोः श्रेष्ठिन् चन्द्रगुप्ते राजन्यपरिग्रहश्छलानाम् । तत्समर्पय राक्षसस्य गृहजनम् । अच्छलं भवतु भवतः ।

चन्द०—आर्य ननु विज्ञापयामि आसीदस्मद्गृहे अमात्यराक्षसस्य गृहजन इति । अज्ज णं विण्णवेमि आसी अह्मघरे अमच्चरक्खस्स घरअणो त्ति)

चाण०—अथेदानीं क्व गतः ।

चन्द०—न जानामि । (ण जाणामि ।)

चाण०—(स्मितं कृत्वा ।) कथं न ज्ञायते नाम । भोः श्रेष्ठिन् शिरसि भयमतिदूरे तत्प्रतीकारः । अन्यच्च नन्दमिव विष्णुगुप्तः ।

[अलीकमसत्यम् । अनभिज्ञेन याथार्थ्यमजानता । प्रच्छादनं गुप्तिरपराधतामापद्यते । वाच्छलं न तु परमार्थतो विसंवादि । शिरसिभयं राजदण्डः समापन्न एव । तत्प्रतिविधानं राक्षसश्चन्द्रगुप्तं निपात्य मे रक्षणं करिष्यतीत्याशा

१ अणज्जेन (अनार्येण). २ दनमेव. ३ ननु परस्पर०, परस्परम् इति पाठः ४ जाणीमे. ५ फणी. ६ इत्यस्मात्परं-चन्द०—(स्वगतम् ।)

उपरि घनं घनरटितं दूरे दयिता किमेतदापतितम् ।
हिमवति दिव्यौषधयः शीर्षे सर्पः समाविष्टः ॥
उवरि घणं घणरडिअं दूरे दइदा किमेतदावडिअम् ।
हिमवदि दिव्वोसहिओ सीसे सप्पो समाविट्ठो ॥

(इत्यर्धोक्ते लज्जां नाटयित्वा ।) चन्द्रगुप्तममात्यराक्षसः समुच्छेत्स्यतीति मामैवं मंस्थाः । पश्य ।

विक्रान्तैर्नयशालिभिः सुसचिवैः श्रीवक्रनासादिभि-
र्नन्दे जीवति या तदा न गमिता स्थैर्यं चलन्ती मुहुः ।
तामेकत्वमुपागतां द्युतिमिव प्रह्लादयन्तीं जगत्
कश्चन्द्रादिव चद्रगुप्तनृपतेः कर्तुं व्यवस्येत्पृथक् ॥ २२ ॥

अपि च ।

आस्वादितद्विरदशोणितशोणशोभाम् (इति पूर्वोक्तं पठति ।)

चन्द०—फलेन संवादितमस्य विकत्थितम् । (स्वगतम् ।) (फलेण संवोदिदं से विकत्थिदम् ।)

(नेपथ्ये कलकलः ।)

चाण०—शार्ङ्गरव ज्ञायतां किमेतत् ।

शिष्यः—तथा (इति निष्क्रम्य पुनः प्रविश्य ।) उपाध्याय एष राज्ञश्चन्द्रगुप्तस्याज्ञया राजापथ्यकारी क्षपणको जीवसिद्धिः सनिकारं नगरान्निर्वास्यते ।

चाण०—क्षपणकः अहह । अथवा अनुभव राजापथ्यकारित्वस्य फलम् । भोः श्रेष्ठिन् चन्दनदास एवमयमपथ्यकारिषु तीक्ष्णदण्डो राजा । तत्क्रियतां पथ्यं सुहृद्वचः । समर्प्यतां राक्षसगृहजनः । अनुभूयतां चिरं विचित्रो राजप्रसादः ।

सुरतां दूरापेता इत्यर्थः ।] उपरीति इयमार्या प्रक्षिप्ता । नन्द इति जातावेकवचनम् ।

[नयशालिभिः नीतिकुशलैरित्यर्थः । सुसचिवैः मन्त्रिश्रेष्ठैः ।] नवसु नन्देषु जीवत्सु व्यासज्य स्थितापि या मया चालिता सती स्थैर्यं न गमिता तां चन्द्रगुप्ते एकत्वमुपागत्य दृढतया स्थितामविद्यमानेषु नन्देषु कश्चालयेदिति भावः ॥ २२ ॥ [कः पृथक् कर्तुं व्यवस्येदपृथक्करणव्यवसाये सिद्धिभाग्भवेदित्यर्थः ।]

मुण्डी निष्परिग्रहस्तपस्वी निकारानर्ह इति कारुण्याविष्करणार्थोऽहहशब्दः । अथवेति राजापथ्यकारी यः कश्चिदपि निग्राह्य एवेति समाधानम् ।

---

१ श्रीव०. २ संपादिदं. ३ उत्सारणा क्रियते. ४ देवस्य. ५ कथं क्षपणकः । अहहकष्टम् , अथवानुभवतु. ६ अनुभूयन्तां विचित्रा राजप्रसादाः.

चन्द०—नास्ति मे गेहे अमात्यगृहजनः । (णत्थि मे गेहे अमच्चघरअणो ।)

(नेपथ्ये पुनः कलकलः ।)

चाण०—शार्ङ्गरव ज्ञायतां किमेतत् ।

शिष्य०—तथा (इति निष्क्रम्य पुनः प्रविश्य) उपाध्याय अयमपि राजापथ्यकार्येव कायस्थः शकटदासः शूलमारोपयितुं नीयते ।

चाण०—स्वकर्मफलमनुभवतु । भोः श्रेष्ठिन्[4] एवमयं राजापथ्यकारिषु तीक्ष्णदण्डो राजा न मर्षयिष्यति राक्षसकलत्रप्रच्छादनं भवतः । तद्रक्ष परकलत्रेणात्मनः कलत्रं जीवितं च ।

चन्द०—आर्य किं मे भयं दर्शयसि । सन्तमपि गेहे अमात्यराक्षसस्य गृहजनं न समर्पयामि किं पुनरसन्तम् । (अज्ज[1] किं मे भअं दावेसि । सन्तं वि गेहे अमच्चरक्खसस्स घरअणं ण समप्पेमि किं उण असन्तं ।)

चाण०—चन्दनदास एष ते निश्चयः ।

चन्द०—बाढम् । एष मे निश्चयः । (बाढं । एसो[2] मे णिच्चओ ।)

चाण०—(स्वगतम् ।) साधु चन्दनदास साधु ।

> **सुलभेष्वर्थलाभेषु परसंवेदने जने[3] ।**
> **क इदं दुष्करं कुर्यादिदानीं शिबिना विना ॥ २३ ॥**

(प्रकाशम् ।) चन्दनदास एष ते निश्चयः ।

चन्द०—बाढम् । (बाढम्)

सुलभेष्विति । परस्य परकीयार्थस्य संवेदने समर्पणे कृते सति स्वस्यार्थलाभेषु सत्सु स्वार्थं तृणीकृत्य परसंरक्षणरूपमेवं दुष्करम् कर्म जने लोके एकेन शिबिना विना त्वदन्यः कः कुर्यात् । शिबिरपि कृते पुरा कृतयुगे कृतवान् । त्वं तु इदानीं पापिनि कलौ करोषीति ततोऽप्यतिशयितसुचरितस्त्वमिति भावः । इदमपि पुष्पम् ॥ २३ ॥

---

१ अज्ज गेहे सन्तं समप्पेमि कुदो असन्तं समप्पआदि इति पाठः. २ स्थिरो. धीरो. ३ जनः ४ श्रेष्ठिन्

चाण०—(सक्रोधम्।) दुरात्मन् दुष्टवणिक् अनुभूयतां तर्हि नरपतिक्रोधः।

चन्द०—सज्जोस्मि। अनुतिष्ठतु आर्यः आत्मनोधिकारसदृशम्। (सज्जोह्मि। अणुचिट्ठदु अज्जो अत्तणो अहिआरसरिसं।)

चाण०—शार्ङ्गरवोच्यतामस्मद्वचनात्कालाशिको दण्डपाशिकश्च। शीघ्रमयं दुष्टवणिक् निगृह्यताम्। अथवा तिष्ठतु। उच्यतां दुर्गपालो विजयपालः गृहीतगृहसारमेनं सपुत्रकलत्रं संयम्य तावद्रक्ष यावन्मया वृषलाय कथ्यते। वृषल एवास्य प्राणहरं दण्डमाज्ञापयिष्यति।

शिष्यः—यदाज्ञापयत्युपाध्यायः। श्रेष्ठिन् इत इतः।

चन्द०—आर्य अयमागच्छामि। (स्वगतम्।) दिष्ट्या मित्रकार्येण मे विनाशो न पुरुषदोषेण। (अज्ज अअमाअच्छामि। दिट्ठिआ मित्तकज्जेण मे विणासो ण पुरिसदोसेण।)

(परिक्रम्य शिष्येण सह निष्क्रान्तः।)

चाण०—(सहर्षम्।) हन्त लब्ध इदानीं राक्षसः। कुतः।

त्यजत्यप्रियवत्प्राणान्यथा तस्यायमापदि।
तथैवास्यापदि प्राणा नूनं तस्यापि न प्रियाः॥ २४॥

(नेपथ्ये कलकलः।)

चाण०—शार्ङ्गरव शार्ङ्गरव।

वृषल एवेति। इदं छद्मना हितागमननिरोधनं निरोधः। छद्मना कपटेन हितागमनाय स्वेष्टसिद्धये चन्दनदासनिरोधात्। यद्वा हितं राक्षसमागमयतीति हितागमः हितागमनस्य हितराक्षसागमनहेतुभूतस्य चन्दनदासस्य निरोधात्।

[पुरुषदोषान्मानुषतासुलभापराधात्। त्यजतीति। तस्य राक्षसस्यापदि तत्पुत्रकलत्रादीनां समर्पणे उत्पत्स्यमानायामापदि तन्निवारणार्थमित्यर्थः। अप्रियवदनिष्टवस्तुत्यागवत्। तथा अस्यापदि प्राणहानिरूपायामुत्पत्स्यमानायां तद्वारणाय।]

---

१ ०त्मन् तिष्ठ. २ नरपतेः-राज-कोपः. ३ बाहू प्रसार्य. ४ अनुरूपं. ५ सक्रोधं खड्गमाकृष्य दुरात्मन् दुष्ट इत्यधिकम्. ६ उच्यतामस्मद्वचनात् दुर्गपालको विजयपालकः; पालश्च. ६ प्राणहरणं, सर्वस्वहरं. ७ अणिदो इत्यधिकम्. ८ ध्रुवम् इति पाठः.

(प्रविश्य ।)

शिष्यः—उपाध्याय आज्ञापय ।

चाण०—किमेष कलकलः[1] ।

शिष्यः—(निष्क्रम्य विभाव्य पुनः प्रविश्य ।) उपाध्याय एष खलु शकटदासं वध्यमानं वध्यभूमेः[2]रादाय समपक्रान्तः सिद्धार्थकः ।

चाण०—(स्वगतम् ।) साधु सिद्धार्थक कृतः कार्यारम्भैः[3] । (प्रकाशम् ।) प्रसह्य किमपक्रान्तः । (सक्रोधम्[4] ।) वत्स उच्यतां भागुरायणो यथा त्वरितं संभावयेति ।

(निष्क्रम्य प्रविश्य च ।)

शिष्यः—(सविषादम् ।) उपाध्याय हा धिक् कष्टमपक्रान्तो भागुरायणोपि ।

चाण०—(स्वगतम् ।) व्रजतु कार्यसिद्धये । (प्रकाशम् । सक्रोधमिव ।) वत्स उच्यन्तामस्मद्वचनाद्भद्रभटपुरुषदत्तडिङ्गरातबलगुप्तराजसेनरोहिताक्षविजयवर्माणः शीघ्रमनुसृत्य गृह्यतां दुरात्मा भागुरायण इति ।

शिष्यः—तथा (इति निष्क्रम्य पुनः प्रविश्य सविषादम् ।) हा धिक् कष्टं सर्वमेव तन्त्रमाकुलीभूतम् । तेपि खलुभद्रभटप्रभृतयः प्रथमतरमुषस्येवापक्रान्ताः[5] ।

चाण०—(स्वगतम् ।) सर्वेषामेव[6] शिवाः पन्थानः सन्तु । (प्रकाशम् ।) वत्सालं विषादेन । पश्य ।

कृतः कार्यारम्भ इति । अयमपि बिन्दुः । त्वरितं सम्भावयेति निगृह्य समाधाय वा सिद्धार्थकमानयेति बाह्योर्थः । त्वमपि तेन सह गत्वा कार्यं साधयेति आन्तरो गूढार्थः ।

[अपक्रान्तो गूढं पलायितः । तन्त्रं प्रकृतिमण्डलमाकुलीभूतं व्यत्यस्तम् । अनिष्टं सर्वतः प्रसक्तमित्यर्थः ।]

---

१ ज्ञायतां किमेतत्. २ वध्यस्थानात्. ३ त्वयेत्यधिकम्. ४ सक्रोधमिव. ५ अप्रभातायामिव रजन्याम्. ६ सर्वथा.

ये याताः किमपि प्रधार्य हृदये पूर्वं गता एव ते
ये तिष्ठन्ति भवन्तु तेपि गमने कामं प्रकामोद्यमाः ।
एका केवलमेव साधनविधौ सेनाशते भ्योधिका
नन्दोन्मूलनदृष्टवीर्यमहिमा बुद्धिस्तु मा गान्मम ॥ २५ ॥

(उत्थाय) एष दुरात्मनो भद्रभटप्रभृतीनाहरामि । (प्रत्यक्षवदाकाशे लक्ष्यं बद्ध्वा । आत्मगतम् ।) दुरात्मन् राक्षस क्वेदानीं गमिष्यसि । एषोहमचिराद्भवन्तम् ।

स्वच्छन्दमेकचरमुज्ज्वलदानशक्ति-
मुत्सेकिना मदबलेन विगाहमानम् ।
बुद्ध्या निगृह्य वृषलस्य कृते क्रियाया-
मारण्यकं गजमिव प्रगुणी करोमि ॥ २६ ॥

(इति निष्क्रान्ताः सर्वे ।)

इति मुद्रालाभो नाम प्रथमोऽङ्कः ।

ये इति । किमपि प्रधार्य हृदये अस्मद्विरोधं मनसि कृत्वेति बहिः । अस्मत्कार्यमेव साधयितुमिति गूढम् । सर्वा अपि प्रकृतयः सुखेन यान्तु न हि तदवलम्बेनाहं कार्यं साधये बुद्धिबलेनैव सर्वं साधयामीत्यर्थः । अयं चतुर्वर्णनिवर्णनं वर्णसंहारः । ब्राह्मणादिचतुर्वर्णान्तःपातिनीनां प्रकृतीनां ये याता इत्यादिना निर्वर्णनान्निर्देशात् त्रयोदशमङ्गम् । तृतीयाङ्के वक्ष्यमाणं तेषामुदन्तमानेष्यामीति गूढाशयः ॥ २५ ॥

स्वच्छन्दमिति । स्वच्छन्दं निरङ्कुशं स्वपक्षमनाश्रित्य विजातीयं परपक्षं कथमाश्रितोसीति तव कोपि नियन्ता नास्तीत्यर्थः । एकचरमिति । वयमत्र नन्दवंशसंबन्धिनः सर्वे स्वजना वर्तामहे तान्विहाय तत्रैकश्चरसीति भावः । उज्ज्वलदानशक्ति परकृत्योपजापार्थं महता कोशसञ्चयेन स्थापितः शकटदास इति वक्ष्यमाणबहुव्ययकारिणम् उत्सेको दुरभिमानः । अरातिहस्तगतो विनश्येत्र तु चन्द्रगुप्तेन सन्दधीतेति षष्ठाङ्के वक्ष्यमाणदुरभिमानवता मदबलेन विगाहमानमस्मदपकाराय चेष्टमानं त्वामारण्यकं गजमिव प्रगुणीकरोमि । यथा आरण्यको दुष्टगजः शनैर्गर्तपातदृढरज्जुबन्धनादिनोपायेन संवाहना-

---

१ सका०. २ नन्दोत्पाटन. ३ उत्थाय प्रत्यक्षवदाका०. ४ उत्सेकिनम्. ५ बलमदेन. ६ विगाह्यमानम्. ७ ०प्रवणं, ०णीकरोमि. ८ इति मुद्राराक्षसे प्रथमोऽङ्कः.

दिक्रियायां प्रगुणीक्रियत एवं त्वामतिसङ्कटे पातयित्वागतिकतया यथा स्वयमेव प्रवणो भवसि तथा क्रियायां वृषलसाचिव्यक्रियायां वशीकरोमीत्यर्थः । एष यत्नः । 'प्रयत्नस्तु तदप्राप्तौ व्यापारोतित्वरान्वित' इति लक्षणात् । इत्थं यत्न-बिन्दुसंबन्धरूपप्रतिमुखसन्धिः । बिन्दुप्रयत्नानुगुण्येनास्य सन्धेः त्रयोदशान्य-प्यङ्गानि च यथामति योजितानीति सूक्ष्मदृष्टिभिरवधार्य सन्तोष्टव्यम् ॥ २६ ॥

प्रथमोऽङ्क इति । अङ्कलक्षणं निरूपितं दशरूपके–'प्रत्यक्षनेतृचरितो बीजव्य-क्तिपुरस्कृतः । अङ्को नानाप्रकारार्थः संविधानरसाश्रयः' ॥ इति ॥

कर्तैतन्नाटकस्याद्भुतरसविलसत्संविधानप्रवीणः
क्लेशं चाणक्यनीतौ बहुविधमतनोल्लक्षणाद्यैर्वचोभिः ।
तत्तल्लक्ष्ये तदङ्गानुसरणविषयक्लेशमस्मद्विधानां
राजश्रीत्र्यम्बकार्यानुमतिसुविहितं वीक्ष्य तुष्यन्तु सन्तः ॥ १ ॥

इति त्र्यम्बकयज्वप्रभुवर्याश्रित दुण्ढिराजव्यासयज्वविरचिते
मुद्राराक्षसनाटकव्याख्याने प्रथमोऽङ्कः समाप्तः ॥

द्वितीयोऽङ्कः ।

(ततः प्रविशत्याहितुण्डिकः ।)

आहितुदण्डिकः—

जानन्ति तन्त्रयुक्तिं यथास्थितं मण्डलमभिलिखन्ति ।
ये मन्त्ररक्षणपरास्ते सर्पनराधिप उपचरन्ति ॥ १ ॥

जाणन्ति तन्तजुत्तिं जहट्ठिअं मण्डलं अहिलिहन्ति ।
जे मन्तरक्खणपरा ते सप्पणराहिवे उवअरन्ति ॥

(आकाशे ।) आर्य किं त्वं भणसि कस्त्वमिति । आर्य अहं खलु आहितुण्डिको जीर्णविषो नाम । किं भणासि अहमपि अहिना खेलितुमिच्छामीति । (अज्ज किं तुमं भणासि को तुमं त्ति । अज्ज अहं खु आहितुण्डिओ जिण्णविसो णाम । किं भणासि । अहं वि अहिणा खेलिदुं इच्छामि त्ति ।)

अथ राक्षसकृतोपायवृत्तान्तकथनाय प्राप्त्याशापताकासंबन्धरूपो गर्भसन्धिर्द्वितीयेनाङ्केनारभ्यते । 'गर्भस्तु दृष्टनष्टस्य बीजस्यान्वेषणं मुहुः ।' इति लक्षणात् । पूर्वाङ्के दृष्टस्यात्र राक्षसाहितुण्डिकसंवादरूपया व्यापिन्या कथया पताकाख्यया नष्टस्यादृष्टस्य चाणक्यनीतिरूपस्य बीजस्याग्रे मुहुरन्वेषणात् । पताकाप्राप्त्याशानुगुण्येन गर्भसन्धेरङ्गानि । 'अभूताहरणं मार्गो रूपोदाहरणे क्रमः । संग्रहश्चानुमानं च तोटकाधिबले तथा ॥ उद्वेगसंभ्रमाक्षेपा द्वादशाङ्गानुन्यक्रमात् ॥' तत्राहितुण्डिकच्छद्मधारिणो विराधगुप्तस्य सर्वं प्राकृतं वचनं प्रस्तुतोपयोगिच्छद्माचरणमभूताहरणम् । प्रस्तुतस्य राक्षसं प्रति कुसुमपुरवृत्तान्तकथनस्योपयोगे छद्माचरणात् ।

जानन्तीति । तन्त्रं स्वराष्ट्रचिन्तायां शास्त्रौषधमखेष्वपीति वैजयन्ती । तन्त्रे स्वराष्ट्रचिन्तायां विषौषधविशेषे च युक्तिं यथावज्जानन्ति । मण्डलं [सप्तप्रकृतिकं] राष्ट्रं [द्वादशविधर जमण्डलं वा] माहेन्द्रादिदेवतायन्त्रं चाभिलषन्ति चिन्तयन्ति रेखाकारेण लिखन्ति च । [सर्प एव नराधिपः । पक्षे सर्प इव नराधिपः ।] तन्त्रमन्त्रादिष्वत्यन्तमवहितात्मना सर्पनराधिपोपचरणं कर्तव्यमितिमीत्यर्थः ॥ १ ॥

किं ब्रवीष्येवमित्यादि विना पात्रं ब्रवीति यत् । श्रुत्वेवानुक्तमप्येकस्तत्स्यादाकाशभाषणम् । 'अप्रविष्टैः सहालापो भवेदाकाशभाषणम् ।' तदाह आकाश इति ।

अथ कतरां पुनरार्यो वृत्तिमुपजीवति । किं भणसि राजकुलसेवक इति । ननु खेलति एव आर्योऽहिना । कथमिव । अमन्त्रौषधिकुशलो व्यालग्राही प्रमत्तो मतङ्गजारोही लब्धाधिकारो जितकाशी राजसेवक इत्येते त्रयोऽप्यवश्यं विनाशमनुभवन्ति । कथं दृष्टमात्रोऽतिक्रान्त एषः । (पुनराकाशे ।) आर्य किं त्वं भणसि किमेतेषु पेटकसमुद्गकेष्विति । आर्य जीविकायाः संपादकाः सर्पाः । किं भणसि प्रेक्षितुमिच्छामीति । प्रसीदत्वार्यः अस्थानं खलु एतत् । तद्यदि कौतूहलं एहि एतस्मिन्नावासे दर्शयामि । किं भणसि इदं खलु भर्तुरमात्यराक्षसस्य गृहं नास्त्यस्मादृशानामिह प्रवेश इति । तेन हि गच्छत्वार्यः । मम पुनर्जीविकायाः प्रसादेन अस्तीह प्रवेशः । कथमेषोपि अतिक्रान्तः । (अह कदरं उण अज्जो वित्तिं उवजविदि । किं भणासि राअउलसेवकोह्मि त्ति । णं खेलदि एव्व अज्जो अहिणा । कहं विअ । अमन्तोसहिकुसलो वालग्गाही पमत्तो मतङ्गआरोही लद्धाहिआरो जिदकासी राअसेवओ त्ति एदे तिण्णि वि अवस्सं विणासमणुहोन्ति । कहं दिट्ठमेत्तो अदिक्कन्तो एसो । अज्ज किं तुमं भणासि किं एदेसु पेडालससुग्गएसु त्ति । अज्ज जीविआए संपादआ सप्पा । किं भणासि पेक्खिदुमिच्छामित्ति । पसीददु अज्जो । अट्ठाणं खु एदं । ता जइ कोदूहलं एहि एदस्सिं आवासे दंसेमि । किं भणासि एदं खु भट्टिणो अमच्चरक्खसस्स गेहं णत्थि अह्मारिसाणं इह पवेसो त्ति । तेण हि गच्छदु अज्जो । मम उण जीविआए पसादेण अत्थि एत्थ पवेसो । कधं एसोवि अतिक्कन्तो ।)

(स्वगतम् । संस्कृतमाश्रित्य ।) अहो आश्चर्यम् । चाणक्यमतिपरिगृहीतं

[नन्विति । राजसेवाया दुष्करत्वात्क्वापि स्खलने प्राणनाशस्यापि प्रसक्तादहिना खेलत्येवार्य इत्युक्तम् । एतदेव विशदीकरोति अमन्त्रौषधीत्यादिना । व्यालः सर्पः । जितकाशी अवलिप्तोनात्मज्ञ इत्यर्थः । पेटकानां समुद्गकाः संपुटकाश्चास्तेषु पेटकान्तरेषु इत्यर्थः । यद्वा पेटकाश्चसमुद्गकाः संपुटकाश्च तेषु ।]
संस्कृतमाश्रित्येति । वस्तुतः स्वस्योत्तमत्वात्स्वगतं संस्कृतवचनम् ।

१ मत्तमतङ्गा., अग्गिहदक्कुसा; मत्तगअवरारोही इति पाठः २ अपवर्जी (आत्मजो).
३ दिशोवलोक्य संस्कृतमाश्रित्य स्वगतम इति पाठः

चन्द्रगुप्तमवलोक्य विफलमिव राक्षसप्रयत्नमवगच्छामि । राक्षसमतिपरिगृहीतं मलयकेतुमवलोक्य चलितमिवाधिराज्याच्चन्द्रगुप्तमवगच्छामि । कुतः ।

कौटिल्यधीरज्जुनिबद्धमूर्तिं
मन्ये स्थिरां मौर्यनृपस्य लक्ष्मीम् ।
उपायहस्तैरपि[2] राक्षसेन
निकृष्यमाणामिव लक्षयामि ॥ २ ॥

तदेवमनयोः बुद्धिशालिनोः सुसचिवयोर्विरोधे संशयितेव नन्दकुलैलक्ष्मीः ।

विरुद्धयोर्भृशमिह मन्त्रिमुख्ययो-
र्महावने वनगजयोरिवान्तरे ।
अनिश्चयाद्गजवशयेव भीतया
गतागतैर्ध्रुवमिह खिद्यते श्रिया ॥ ३ ॥

तद्यावदमात्यराक्षसं पश्यामि । (इति परिक्रम्य स्थितः ।)

(ततः प्रविशत्यासनस्थः स्वभवनगतः पुरुषेणानुगम्यमानः सचिन्तो राक्षसः ।)

राक्ष०---(सबाष्पम् ।) कष्टं भोः कष्टम् ।

[कौटिल्यस्य धीरेव रज्जुस्तया निबद्धा दृढं बद्धा मूर्तिर्यस्यास्तादृशीम् ।] कौटिल्यधीरज्जुनिबद्धमूर्तिमित्यत्र रूपकानुप्राणिता उत्प्रेक्षा ॥ २ ॥

अनिश्चयादिति । अनिश्चयादन्यतरविजयानिर्धारणात् । अत्रोपमानुप्राणितोत्प्रेक्षा । इयं प्राप्त्याशा । उपायापायशङ्काभ्यां प्राप्त्याशा कार्यसंभव इति लक्षणात । कौटिल्यधीरज्जुनिबद्धेति उपायशङ्का राक्षसेन निकृष्यमाणा इति अपायशङ्का ताभ्यां कार्यस्य मौर्यश्रीस्थैर्यस्य संभवः कादाचित्कत्वेन संभावना । विराधरक्षसयोर्महती संवादकथा पताका । प्रतिपाद्यकथाङ्गं स्यात्पताका व्यापिनी कथेति लक्षणात । अनयोः सबन्धादयं गर्भसन्धिः ॥ ३ ॥

तद्यावदिति । इदमङ्कास्यम् । अङ्कान्तपात्रैरङ्कास्यमुत्तराङ्कार्थसूचनेति लक्षणात् । पूर्वाङ्कान्ते चाणक्येन मदबलेन विगाहमानमिति राक्षसकृतस्य विगाहनस्य नीतिप्रयोगस्यास्मिन्नङ्के वक्ष्यमाणस्य सूचनात् । यद्वा अङ्कावतरणम् । 'यत्र स्यादुत्तराङ्कार्थः पूर्वाङ्कार्थानुसङ्गतः । असूचिताङ्गपात्रं तदङ्कावतरणं मतम् ।' इति लक्षणात् । अत्र वक्ष्यमाणस्य क्षपणकशकटदासादिनिग्रहस्य पूर्वाङ्कार्थानुसङ्गतत्वादाहितुण्डिकप्रवेशस्यासूचनाच्च ।

---

१ कुलस्य. २ इह. ३ लक्ष्यते इत्यधिकम. ४ भृशम. ५ द्वारि स्थित इति पाठः. ६ ऊर्ध्वमवलोक्य इत्यधिकम.

वृष्णीनामिव नीतिविक्रमगुणव्यापारशान्तद्विषां
नन्दानां विपुले कुलेकरुणया नीते नियत्या क्षयम् ।
चिन्तावेशसमाकुलेन मनसा रात्रिंदिवं जाग्रतः
सैवेयं मम चित्रकर्मरचना भित्तिं विना वर्तते ॥ ४ ॥

अथवा ।

नेदं विस्मृतभक्तिना न विषयव्यासङ्गरूढात्मना
प्राणप्रच्युतिभीरुणा न च मया नात्मप्रतिष्ठार्थिना ।
अत्यर्थं परदास्यमेत्य निपुणं नीतौ मनो दीयते
देवः स्वर्गगतोपि शात्रववधेनाराधितः स्यादिति ॥ ५ ॥

(आकाशमवलोकयन् सास्रम् ।) भगवति कमलालये भृशमगुणज्ञासि कुतः ।

आनन्दहेतुमपि देवमपास्य नन्दं
सक्तासि किं कथय वैरिणि मौर्यपुत्रे ।
दानाम्बुराजिरिव गन्धगजस्य नाशे
तत्रैव किं न चपले प्रलयं गतासि ॥ ६ ॥

अपि च अनभिजाते ।

पृथिव्यां किं दग्धाः प्रथितकुलजा भूमिपतयः
पतिं पापे मौर्यं यदसि कुलहीनं वृतवती ।

वृष्णीनामिति । नीतिविक्रमरूपौ गुणौ तयोर्व्यापारेण प्रयोगेण शान्ता गमिताः । व्यर्थोन्तर्भावितः । द्विषो यैरिति बहुव्रीहिः । अकरुणया नियत्या दैवेन । सैवेयं नन्देषु जीवत्सु यादृशी तादृश्येव चित्रकर्मरचना विचित्रपौरुषव्यापारः भित्तिमाश्रयं विना वर्तते । स्वामिनो विनैव मुधा व्याप्रिय इति खेदः ॥ ४ ॥

नेदमिति । विषयव्यासङ्गो विषयोपभोगप्रवणता । [तत्ररूढो बद्ध आत्मा मनो यस्य । नीतौ सामादिप्रयोगे । किंतु परदास्यमप्येत्य] स्वर्गगतस्वाम्याराधनेच्छया नीतौ मनो दीयते न पूर्वोक्तहेतुभिरित्यर्थः । इदं तत्त्वानुकीर्तनं मार्गः ॥ ५ ॥

आनन्दहेतुमिति । स्पष्टम् [गन्धप्रधानो गजो गन्धगजस्तस्य नाशे तस्य मदजलधारेव । प्रलयं गतासि अत्यन्तानुचिताचरणान्मरणमपिश्रेय इति भावः ॥ ६ ॥

दुःखावेशेन अनभिजाते इत्यादि गालनम् । अभिजाताः कुलीनाः ।

पृथिव्यामिति । [प्रथितं विख्यातं कुलं तत्र जायन्ते इति । यद्यस्मात्कारणात् । पापे असत्कुलजातत्वात्पापाचरणप्रवृत्ते ।] पुरन्ध्रीणामित्यर्थान्तरन्या-

---

१ व्यापार०; रूढ, मूढ. २ ०प्रेप्सुना ३ रक्तासि. ४ दुःकुलमौ०. ५ पापं. ६ कृत.

प्रकृत्यां वा काशप्रभवकुसुमप्रान्तचपला

पुरन्ध्रीणां प्रज्ञा पुरुषगुणविज्ञानविमुखी ॥ ७ ॥

अयि अविनीते तदहमाश्रयोन्मूलनेनैव त्वामकामां करोमि । (विचिन्त्य ।) मया तावत्सुहृत्तमस्य चन्दनदासस्य गृहे गृहजनं निक्षिप्य नगरान्निर्गच्छता न्याय्यमनुष्ठितम् । कुतः । कुसुमपुराभियोगं प्रति अनुदासीनो राक्षस इति तत्रस्थानामस्माभिः सहैककार्याणां देवपादोपजीविनां नोद्यमः शिथिलीभविष्यति । चन्द्रगुप्तशरीरमभिद्रोग्धुमस्मत्प्रयुक्तानां तीक्ष्णरसदायिनामुपसंग्रहार्थं परकृत्योपजापार्थं च महता कोशसञ्चयेन स्थापितः शकटदासः । प्रतिक्षणमरातिवृत्तान्तोपलब्धये तत्संहतिभेदनाय च व्यापारिताः सुहृदो जीवसिद्धिप्रभृतयः । तत्किमत्र बहुना ।

इष्टात्मजः सपदि सान्वय एव देवः

शार्दूलपोतमिव यं परिपोष्य नष्टः ।

तस्यैव बुद्धिविशिखेन भिनद्मि मर्म

वर्मीभवेद्यदि न दैवमदृश्यरूपम् ॥ ८ ॥

सोलङ्कारः । 'उक्तिरर्थान्तरन्यासः स्यात्सामान्यविशेषयोः' इति । भगवति कमलालय इत्यादि राक्षसस्य वितर्कप्रतिपादनं वाक्यरूपं नामाङ्गम् ॥ ७ ॥

विचिन्त्येति । आश्रयोन्मूलनहेतुमुपायं विचिन्त्य तमेव प्रपञ्चयति । मया तावदित्यादिना । [न्यायादनपेतं न्याय्यमुचितम् । अभियोगोभियानम् ।]

चन्द्रगुप्तेत्यादि । तत्संहतयो भद्रभटादयः जीवसिद्धिना भेदिता इत्यस्य भ्रमः । इदं प्रकृतोत्कर्षाभिधानमुदाहरणं राक्षसेन प्रकृतकार्यस्योत्कर्षाभिधानात् ।

इष्टात्मज इति । इष्टा आत्मजा यस्येति हेतुगर्भविशेषणम् । निकृष्टक्षेत्रजातमपि यं मौर्यं इष्टात्मजत्वात्प्रियापत्यत्वादुत्तमक्षेत्रजापत्यवत् परिपोष्य नष्टः । स्वपोषकघातकत्वेन शार्दूलपोतदृष्टान्तः । तस्यैव मौर्यस्य मर्म बुद्धिविशिखेन भिनद्मि भेत्स्यामि यदि दैवं न वर्मीभवेत् । वर्मरूपं रक्षकं न भवेद्यदि तदा भिनद्मीत्यन्वयः । अदृश्येति । दैवं दृश्यं चेत्तदपि प्रतिकर्तुं शक्नुयामिति भावः । अत्र मया तावदित्यारभ्यादृश्यरूपमित्यन्तेन राक्षसस्योपायापायशङ्के ॥ ८ ॥

---

१ प्रकृत्यैवाकाश. २ किंकारणमिति. ३ उदासीनः. ४ कृत्योपक्षेपसंग्रहार्थम ५ अदृष्ट०, अमृष्यमानम् इति पाठः.

(ततः प्रविशति कञ्चुकी ।)

कञ्चुकी—

कामं नन्दमिव प्रमथ्य जरया चाणक्यनीत्या यथा
धर्मो मौर्य इव क्रमेण नगरे नीतः प्रतिष्ठां मयि ।
तं संप्रत्युपचीयमानमनु मे लब्धान्तरः सेवया
लोभो राक्षसवज्जयाय यतते जेतुं न शक्नोति च ॥ ९ ॥

(परिक्रम्योपसृत्य च ।) इदममात्यराक्षसस्य गृहम् । प्रविशामि । (प्रविश्यावलोक्य च ।) स्वस्ति भवते ।

राक्ष०—आर्य अभिवादये । प्रियंवदक आसनमानीयताम् ।

पुरु०—इदमासनमुपविशतु आर्यः । (एदं आसणं । उपविसदु अज्जो ।)

कञ्चु०—(उपविश्य ।) कुमारो मलयकेतुरमात्यं विज्ञापयति । चिरात्प्रभृत्यार्यः परित्यक्तोचितशरीरसंस्कार इति पीड्यते मे हृदयम् । यद्यपि सहसा स्वामिगुणा न शक्यन्ते विस्मर्तुं तथापि मद्विज्ञापनां मानयितुमर्हत्यार्यः । (इत्याभरणानि प्रदर्श्य ।) इमान्याभरणानि कुमारेण स्वशरीरादवतार्य प्रेषितानि धारयितुमर्हत्यार्यः ।

कामं नन्दमिति । यथा चाणक्यनीत्या नन्दं प्रमथ्य कुसुमपुरे मौर्यः प्रतिष्ठापितः तद्वज्जरसा कामं विषयाभिलाषमुपमर्द्य मयि धर्मः प्रतिष्ठापितः । वार्द्धके विषयवैराग्ये कामं विहाय धर्ममेव सेवितुमुत्सहे इति भावः । संप्रति मलयकेतुसेवया लब्धान्तरः लब्धावसरः राक्षसः यथा तमुपचीयमानं वर्द्धिष्णु मौर्यमनुलक्ष्यीकृत्य जयाय मौर्यजयायेत्यर्थः । लक्षणेत्थंभूतेति कर्मप्रवचनीयेनानुना योगे द्वितीया । यतते जेतुं च न शक्नोति न शक्ष्यति चाणक्यनीतेः प्रबलत्वात् । एवं सेवया कुलाचारादावश्यकत्वेन गले पतितया राजकुलसेवया लब्धावसरः मे मम लोभः सेवाविषयोभिलाषः वार्द्धकोचितस्य धर्मस्य जयाय यतते जेतुं न शक्नोति च । कुलाचारतया यथाशक्ति राजकुलं सेवमानोपि वार्द्धकोचितं शमदमादिकं धर्मं नोपेक्षे इति भावः । उपचीयमानमपीति पाठे उपचीयमानं जेतुं यतते जयाय न शक्नोतीति व्यवहितान्वयः क्लिष्टः । अनेन कञ्चुकिनिर्वेदेन राक्षसोद्यमस्य चाणक्यनीत्या भावी उपमर्दः सूचितः ॥ ९ ॥

---

१ प्रसह्य. २ अपि. ३ नाट्येन परिक्रम्य. ४ दृष्ट्वा । अयममात्यराक्षसः । परिक्रम्योपसृत्य च. ५ आसनमत्रभवतः. ६ अस्मात्प्राक् नाट्येन इति. ७ अमात्य कु०. ८ इदमाभ.

राक्ष०—आर्य जाजले विज्ञाप्यतामस्मद्वचनात्कुमारः । विस्मृता एव भवद्गुणपक्षपातेन स्वामिगुणाः । किंतु ।

न तावन्निर्वीर्यैः परपरिभवाक्रान्तिकृपणै-
र्वहाम्यङ्गैरेभिः प्रतनुमपि संस्कारचनाम् ।
न यावन्निःशेषक्षपितरिपुचक्रस्य निहितं
सुगाङ्गे हेमाङ्कं नृवर तव सिंहासनमिदम् ॥ १० ॥

कञ्चु०—अमात्ये नेतरि सुलभमेतत्कुमारस्य । तत्प्रतिमान्यतां कुमारस्य प्रथमः प्रणयः ।

राक्ष०—आर्य कुमार इवानतिक्रमणीयवचनो भवानपि । तदनुष्ठीयतां कुमारस्याज्ञा ।

कञ्चु०—(नाट्येन भूषणानि परिधाप्य ।) स्वस्ति भवते साधयाम्यहम् ।

राक्ष०—आर्य अभिवादये ।

कञ्चुकी०—(निष्क्रान्तः ।)

राक्ष०— प्रियंवदक ज्ञायतां कोऽस्मद्दर्शनार्थी द्वारि तिष्ठतीति ।

[भवद्गुणपक्षपातेन भवद्गुणानुरागेण । न तावदिति । निर्वीर्यैः तेजोहीनैः ।] सुगाङ्गेति । सुगाङ्गनामकप्रासादे परपरिभवकर्तृकाक्रान्तिराक्रमणं तेन कृपणैर्दीनैरित्यर्थः । [प्रतनुमत्यल्पामपि संस्काररचनां देहमार्जनालङ्कारधारणादिरूपाम् । निःशेषं यथा तथा क्षपितं क्षयं प्रापितं रिपुचक्रं यस्य । तस्य तव सिंहासनं यावन्नस्थापितं तावदित्यन्वयः । नेतरि कार्यधुरन्धरे सतीत्यर्थः । अनतिक्रमणीयमलङ्घ्यं वचनं यस्य ।] इदमितिबुद्धिस्थपरामर्शः ॥ १० ॥

साधयामीति । प्रायेण ण्यन्तकः साधिर्गमेरर्थे प्रयुज्यते ।

निष्क्रान्त इति । इदं प्रस्तुतोपयोगि समाधानवचनं संग्रहः । प्रस्तुतस्य राक्षसस्योत्साहस्योपयोगित्वात् । यद्वा प्रस्तुतस्य चाणक्योपायरूपस्य बीजस्योपयोगि इदं भूषणदानं समाधानवचनम् । अनुपदमेव राक्षसेन सिद्धार्थकाय पारितोषिकतया दास्यमानानामेषामेव भूषणानां निर्वहणे कूटलेखे उपयोक्ष्यमाणत्वात् ।

---

१ विस्मृता मया स्वामिगुणास्तव पक्षपातिना इति पाठः. २ अनुष्ठीयते. ३ स्वनियोगसाधयाम्यहमिति कञ्चुकी निष्क्रान्तः ।

पुरु०—यदमात्य आज्ञापयति । (इति परिक्रम्य आहितुण्डिकं दृष्ट्वा ।) आर्य कस्त्वम् । (जं अमच्चो आणवेदि । अज्ज को तुमं ।)

आहि०—भद्र अहं खल्वाहितुण्डिको जीर्णविषो नाम । इच्छाम्यमात्यस्य पुरतः सर्पैः खेलितुम् । (भद्द अहं खु आहितुण्डिओ जिण्णविसो णाम । इच्छामि अमच्चस्स पुरदो सप्पेहिं खेलिदुं ।)

पुरु०—तिष्ठ यावदमात्याय निवेदयामि । (राक्षसमुपसृत्य ।) अमात्य एष खलु सर्पोपजीवी इच्छति सर्पं दर्शयितुम् । (चिट्ठ जाव अमच्चस्स णिवेदेमि । अमच्च एसो खु सप्पोपजीवी इच्छदि सप्पं दंसेदुं ।)

राक्ष०—(वामाक्षिस्पन्दनं सूचयित्वा आत्मगतम् ।) कथं प्रथममेव सर्पदर्शनम् । (प्रकाशम् ।) प्रियंवदक न नः कौतूहलं सर्पदर्शने तत्परितोष्य विसर्जयैनम् ।

प्रियं०—तथा (इत्याहितुण्डिकमुपसृत्य ।) आर्य एष खलु ते दर्शनकार्येणामात्यः प्रसादं करोति । न पुनः सर्पदर्शनेन । (अज्ज एसो खु दे दंसणकज्जेण अमच्चो पसादं करेदि । ण उण सप्पदंसणेण ।)

आहि०—भद्रमुख विज्ञापयामात्यं न केवलमहं सर्पोपजीवी प्राकृतकविः खल्वहम् । तस्माद्यदि मे दर्शनेनामात्यः प्रसादं न करोति तदा एतत्पत्रकं वाचयितुं प्रसीदत्विति । (भद्दमुह विण्णवेहि अमच्चं ण केवलं अहं सप्पोपजीवी पाउडकवी क्खु अहं । ता जइ मे दंसणेण अमच्चो पसादं ण करेदि ता एदं पत्तअं वाचेदुं पसीददु त्ति ।)

प्रियं०—(पत्रं गृहीत्वा राक्षसमुपसृत्य ।) आर्य एष खल्वमात्यं विज्ञापयति न केवलमहं सर्पोपजीवी प्राकृतकविः खल्वहम् । तस्माद्यदि

[जीर्णविषः जीर्णं निराबाधं कृतं विषं येन । वामाक्षिस्पन्दनं पुरुषाणां तस्यानिष्टत्वात् ।] कथं प्रथममेव सर्पदर्शनमिति शङ्कारूपः संभ्रमः । [दर्शनकार्येण दर्शनस्य सर्पदर्शनस्य यत्कार्यं पारितोषिकलाभादि तेन तद्दत्वेत्यर्थः । प्राकृतकविः प्राकृते प्राकृतो वा कविः । प्रकृतिभ्यो यल्लब्धं तत्र कविः पण्डितः । कुसुमपुरवासिजनकृत्यज्ञ इति च ध्वनिः ।]

सप्पेहिं अमच्चस्य पुरदो खेलितुम्. २ सर्पेषु. ३ जं अज्जो-अमच्चो आणवेदि त्ति निष्क्रम्य. ४ अमच्चो अदंसणेण फलं देदि न उण दंसणेण. ५ गाथेदुत्ति.

मे अमात्यो दर्शनेन प्रसादं न करोति तदा एतदपि तावत्पत्रकं वाचयत्विति । (अज्ज एसो खु अमच्चं विण्णवेदि ण केवलं अहं सप्पोपजीवी पाउडकवी खु अहं । ता जइ मे अमच्चो दंसणेण पसादं ण करेदि तदो एदं वि दाव पत्तअं वाचेदुं पसीददु त्ति ।

राक्ष०—(पत्रं गृहीत्वा वाचयति ।)

पीत्वा निरवशेषं कुसुमरसमात्मनः कुशलतया ।
यदुद्गिरति भ्रमरः अन्येषां करोति तत्कार्यम् ॥ ११ ॥

पाऊण निरवसेसं कुसुमरसं अत्तणो कुसलदाए ।
जं उग्गिरेइ भमरो अण्णाणं कुणइ तं कज्जं ॥

(विचिन्त्य स्वगतम् ।) अये कुसुमपुरवृत्तान्तज्ञो भवत्प्रणिधिरिति गाथार्थः । कार्यव्यग्रत्वान्मनसः प्रभूतत्वाच्च प्रणिधीनां विस्मृतम् । इदानीं स्मृतिरुपलब्धा । व्यक्तमाहितुण्डिकच्छद्मनो विराधगुप्तेनानेन भवितव्यम् । (प्रकाशम् ।) प्रियंवदक प्रवेशयैनं सुकविरेष श्रोतव्यमस्मात्सुभाषितम् ।

प्रियं०—(तथेति आहितुण्डिकमुपसृत्य ।) उपसर्पतु आर्यः । (उपसप्पदु अज्जो ।)

आहि०—(नाट्येनोपसृत्य विलोक्य च स्वगतम् । संस्कृतमाश्रित्य ।) अयममात्यराक्षसः । स एषः ।

[पीत्वेति । आत्मनः कुशलतया नैपुण्येन समग्रं कुसुमरसं कुसुमपुरवृत्तान्तं पीत्वा सम्यग्ज्ञात्वा भ्रमरः भ्रमणशीलः स्पशः यदुद्गिरति कथयति तदन्येषां तज्जिज्ञासूनां स्वाम्यादीनां कार्यं करोति इति गूढोर्थः ॥ ११ ॥]

अये कुसुमपुरवृत्तान्तज्ञ इति । इयं सञ्चिन्तितार्थप्राप्तिः क्रमः । पूर्वं द्वारि कस्तिष्ठतीति कुसुमपुरवृत्तान्तहरचारगमनस्य सञ्चिन्तितस्य प्राप्तेः । कार्यव्यग्रत्वादिति । इष्टजनानुसन्धानरूपमाधिबलमङ्गम् । व्यक्तमाहितुण्डिकेति [आहितुण्डिकलिङ्गधारिणा ।] इदं लिङ्गादभ्यूहनमनुमानमङ्गम् ।

---

१ उग्गिरन्दि भमरा. २ अस्मात्परं-कुसुमपुरादागतेन.

वामां बाहुलतां निवेश्य शिथिलं कण्ठे विवृत्तानना
स्कन्धे दक्षिणया बलान्निहितयाप्यङ्के पतन्त्या मुहुः ।
गाढालिङ्गनसङ्गपीडितमुखं यस्योद्यमाशङ्किनी
मौर्यस्योरसि नाधुनापि कुरुते वामेतरं श्रीः स्तनम् ॥ १२ ॥

(प्रकाशम् ।) जयतु अमात्यः । (जेदु अमच्चो[3]) ।

राक्ष०—(विलोक्य ।) अये विराध । (इत्यर्धोक्ते ।) ननु प्ररूढश्मश्रुः । प्रियंवदक भुजङ्गैरिदानीं विनोदयितव्यम् । तद्विश्रम्यतामितः परिजनेन । त्वमपि स्वाधिकारमशून्यं कुरु ।

प्रियं०—तथेति । (सपरिवारो निष्क्रान्तः ।)

राक्ष०—सखे विराधगुप्त इदमासनमास्यताम् ।

विरा०—(नाट्येनोपविष्टः ।)

राक्ष०—(निर्वर्ण्य ।) अये देवपादपद्मोपजीविनोवस्थेयम् । (इति रोदिति ।)

विरा०—अमात्यलं शोकेन । नातिचिरादमात्योस्मान् पुरातनीमवस्थामारोपयिष्यति ।

राक्ष०—सखे[7] वर्णय कुसुमपुरवृत्तान्तम् ।

वामामिति । [वामां स्त्रीणां वामभागस्य श्रेष्ठत्वात्] अनुरागबलात्स्कन्धे निहितयापि यदुद्यमभयान्मुहुरङ्के पतन्त्या दक्षिणया बाहुलतयोपलक्षिता इति शेषः । गाढालिङ्गनसङ्गेनासक्त्या पीडितमुखं चिपिटीकृतचूचुकं यथा तथा चन्द्रगुप्तेत्यन्तमनुरक्तापि राक्षसोद्यमाशङ्किनी [राक्षसः स्वोद्यमेन चन्द्रगुप्तं राज्याद्भ्रंशयेदिति शङ्कया मौर्यस्योरसि दक्षिणं स्तनं न करोति । गाढालिङ्गनं न ददातीत्यर्थः ।] सती स्वाभिलषितं गाढालिङ्गनरूपमुपभोगं न संपादयतीति संभोगाभिलाषः शृङ्गारः । अत्र गाढालिङ्गनाकरणस्य यदुद्यमाशङ्कित्वेन समर्थनात्काव्यलिङ्गमलङ्कारः । समर्थनीयस्यार्थस्य काव्यलिङ्गं समर्थनमिति लक्षणात् ॥ १२ ॥

अये विराध इति परिजनं प्रति रहस्यगोपनार्थमर्धोक्तिः । प्ररूढश्मश्रुरिति चोक्तवाक्यस्यान्यथाकरणेन पूरणम् । विराधप्ररूढश्मश्रुरित्येककरणम् । विकृतो राधो वेषः तद्रूपाणि प्ररूढानि श्मश्रूणि यस्य ।

स्वाधिकारमशून्यमिति । [स्वनियोगानुष्ठानपरो भव] परप्रवेशनमदत्वा द्वारि अवहितस्तिष्ठेत्यर्थः । सखे वर्णय इति । इयं व्यापिनी कथा पताका । [तीक्ष्णरसोविषम् ।]

---

१ शिथिलाम्. २ निवृ०. ३ जअदु जअदु अमच्चो; अज्जो. ४ विरूढस्मृतिः विरूढश्मश्रुः इति पाठः. ५ विनोदयामः, न विनो०. ६ अस्मात्पाक्–यदाज्ञापयत्यमात्य इति. ७ विराधगुप्त इत्यधिकम्.

विरा०—अमात्य विस्तीर्णः कुसुमपुरवृत्तान्तस्तत्कुतः प्रभृति वर्णयामि ।

राक्ष०—सखे चन्द्रगुप्तस्यैव तावन्नगरप्रवेशात्प्रभृति अस्मत्प्रयुक्तैः तीक्ष्णरसदायिभिः किमनुष्ठितमित्याद्यादितः श्रोतुमिच्छामि ।

विरा०—एष कथयामि । अस्ति तावच्छकयवनकिरातकाम्बोजपारसीकबाह्लीकप्रभृतिभिः चाणक्यमतिपरिगृहीतैश्चन्द्रगुप्तपर्वतेश्वरबलैरुदधिभिरिव प्रलयोच्चलितसलिलैः समन्तादुपरुद्धं कुसुमपुरम् ।

राक्ष०—(शस्त्रमाकृष्य ससम्भ्रमम् ।) अयि मयि स्थिते कः कुसुमपुरमुपरोत्स्यति । प्रवीरक प्रवीरक क्षिप्रमिदानीम् ।

प्राकारं परितः शरासनधरैः क्षिप्रं परिक्रम्यतां
द्वारेषु द्विरदैः प्रतिद्विपघटाभेदक्षमैः स्थीयताम् ।
त्यक्त्वा मृत्युभयं प्रहर्तुमनसः शत्रोर्बले दुर्बले
ते निर्यान्तु मया सहैकमनसो येषामभीष्टं यशः ॥ १३ ॥

विरा०—अमात्यालमावेगेन । वृत्तमिदं वर्ण्यते ।

राक्ष०—(निःश्वस्य ।) कष्टं वृत्तमिदम् । मया पुनर्ज्ञातं स एवायं काल इति । (शस्त्रमुत्सृज्य ।) हा देव नन्द स्मरामि ते राक्षसं प्रति प्रसादातिशयम् । त्वमत्र सङ्ग्रामकाले

अस्तीति क्रियाया वाक्यार्थः कर्ता । [चाणक्यमतिपरिगृहीतैश्चाणक्यबुद्ध्यनुवर्तिभिः । प्रलये उच्चलितानि सलिलानि येषां तैः उददिभिरिवेत्यनेन बलानां विस्तीर्णत्वमुक्तम्] प्रवीरकस्तदानीन्तनः सन्निहितोनुचरः ।

प्राकारमिति । [शरा अस्यन्ते क्षिप्यन्ते अनेनेति शरासनं धनुस्तस्य धरैः धानुष्कैः प्राकारं परितः परिक्रम्यताम् । प्रतिगता द्विपाः परगजास्तेषां घटानां भेदने क्षमैः । येषां यशोऽभीष्टं । न तु नश्वरो देहः । ये यशोर्थिन इत्यर्थः । ये च त्यक्तमृत्युभयाः शत्रोर्दुर्बले बले प्रहर्तुं मनो येषां ते तथा । इत्यर्थः ।] शत्रुबलस्य दुर्बलत्वकथनं सहानुयायिनां प्रोत्साहनार्थम् । इदं रोषसंभ्रमवचनं तोटकम् । अयं वीररसः स्थायीभावः । विभावैरनुभावैश्च सात्त्विकैर्व्यभिचारिभिः । आनीयमानः स्वादुत्वं स्थायीभावो रसः स्मृतः ॥ १३ ॥

---

१ खलु इत्यधिकम्; तत्कुतः; तदाज्ञापय कुतः. २ प्रलयकालचलितसलिलसञ्चयैः. ३ पर. ४ स्मरामि ते राक्षसः प्रसादानाम्.

यत्रैषा मेघनीला चरति गजघटा राक्षसस्तत्र याया-
देतत्पारिप्लुवाम्भः प्लुति तुरगबलं वार्यतां राक्षसेन।
पत्तीनां राक्षसोऽन्तं नयतु बलमिति प्रेषयन्मह्यमाज्ञा-
मज्ञासीः प्रीतियोगात्स्थितमिव नगरे राक्षसानां सहस्रम्॥१४॥

ततस्ततः।

विरा०—ततः समन्तादुपरुद्धं कुसुमपुरमवलोक्य बहुदिवसप्रवृत्तमतिमहदुपरोधवैशसमुपरि पौराणां परिवर्तमानमसहमाने तस्यामप्यवस्थायां पौरजनापेक्षया सुरङ्गामेत्यापक्रान्ते तपोवनाय देवे सर्वार्थसिद्धौ स्वामिविरहात्प्रशिथिलीकृतप्रयत्नेषु युष्मद्बलेषु,जयघोषणाव्याघातादिसाहसानुमितेऽन्तर्नगरवासिषु पुनरपि नन्दराज्यप्रत्यानयनाय सुरङ्गया बहिरपगतेषु युष्मासु चन्द्रगुप्तनिधनाय युष्मत्प्रयुक्तया विषकन्यका घातिते तपस्विनि पर्वतेश्वरे।

राक्ष०—सखे पश्याश्चर्यम्।

कर्णेनेव विषाङ्गनैकपुरुषव्यापादिनी रक्षिता
हन्तुं शक्तिरिवार्जुनं बलवती या चन्द्रगुप्तं मया।
सा विष्णोरिव विष्णुगुप्तहतकस्यात्यन्तिकश्रेयसे
हैडिम्बेयमिवेत्य पर्वतनृपं तद्वध्यमेवावधीत्॥ १५॥

[यत्रेति। एषा मेघवत् श्यामला शत्रुगजघटा यत्र चलति तत्र राक्षसो यातु। तद्वारणायेतिशेषः।] पारिप्लवाम्भोवत्समीरणलोलसागरकल्लोलवत् प्लुतिरुड्डीयनं यस्य तत् [एवं स्नेहयोगात्कार्यसहस्रकरणाय मामादिशन् राक्षसानां सहस्रं स्थितमिवामंस्थाः]॥ १४॥

[उपरोधवैशसं पुरपरिवेष्टनजनितक्लेशान्।] जयघोषणेति। पौरजनापेक्ष अनुमतिः। जयस्याघोषणा डिण्डिमाघातरूपा कर्तव्येत्याज्ञापिते तदकरणं जयघोषणाव्याघातः। तदादिसाहसे राजाज्ञाभङ्गादिरूपैरनिष्टाचरणैरनुमितेषु शत्रूपजापदूषिता इत्येवमुन्नीतेषु अन्तर्नगरवासिषु युष्मद्बलेषु सत्सु इत्यन्वयः। अतः परमत्रावस्थानमनुचितमिति बहिर्गत्वा सुहृद्बलोत्थापनादिना नन्दराज्यप्रत्यानयनाय युष्मासु बहिरपगतेष्वित्यन्वयः तपस्विनीति। दीने इत्यर्थः।

कर्णेनेति। कर्णेनार्जुनं हन्तुं बलवती एकपुरुषव्यापादिनी शक्तिरिव चन्द्रगुप्तं हन्तुं या विषाङ्गना मया रक्षितेति व्यवहितान्वयः। [विष्णुगुप्तहततस्य चाणक्यबटोः आत्यन्तिकं श्रेयसे समधिकाभीष्टसिद्धये।] श्रीकृष्णवध्यं [हिडिम्बासुतं] हैडिम्बेयं घटोत्कचमिव पर्वतकमेत्य प्राप्य तद्वध्यं तेन विष्णुगुप्तेन परिपणितराज्यार्द्धलुब्धेन वध्यमेवावधीत्॥ १५॥

---

१ स्नेह. २ ०नुमितान्तर्नगरवासिषु. ३ प्रीतये, अत्यन्तनिःश्रेयसे.

विरा०—अमात्य दैवस्यात्र कामचारः किं क्रियताम् ।

राक्ष०—ततस्ततः ।

विरा०—ततः पितृवधत्रासादपक्रान्ते कुमारे मलयकेतौ विश्वासिते पर्वतकभ्रातरि वैरोचके प्रकाशिते च चन्द्रगुप्तस्य नन्दभवनप्रवेशे चाणक्यहतकेन आहूयाभिहिताः सर्व एव कुसुमपुरनिवासिनः सूत्रधाराः यथा सांवत्सरिकादेशादर्धरात्रसमये चन्द्रगुप्तस्य नन्दभवनप्रवेशो भविष्यति । ततः पूर्वद्वारात्प्रभृति संस्क्रियतां राजभवनमिति । ततः सूत्रधारैरभिहितमार्य प्रथममेव देवस्य चन्द्रगुप्तस्य नन्दभवनप्रवेशमुपलभ्य सुत्रधारेण दारुवर्मणा कनकतोरणन्यासादिभिः संस्कारविशेषैः संस्कृतं प्रथमराजभवनद्वारम् । अस्माभिरिदानीमभ्यन्तरे संस्कार आधेय इति । ततश्चाणक्यबटुना अनादिष्टेनैव सूत्रधारेण दारुवर्मणा संस्कृतं राजभवनद्वारमिति परितुष्टेनेव सुचिरं दारुवर्मणो दाक्ष्यं प्रशस्याभिहितम् । अचिरादस्य दाक्ष्यस्यानुरूपं फलमधिगमिष्यसि दारुवर्मन्निति ।

राक्ष०—(सोद्वेगम् ।) सखे कुतश्चाणक्यबटोः परितोषः । अफलमनिष्टफलं वा दारुवर्मणः प्रयत्नमवगच्छामि । यदनेन बुद्धिमोहादथवा राजभक्तिप्रकर्षान्नियोगकालमप्रतीक्षमाणेन जनितश्चाणक्यबटोश्चेतसि बलवान्विकल्पः । ततस्ततः ।

विरा०—ततश्चाणक्यहतकेनानुकूललग्नवशादर्धरात्रसमये चन्द्रगुप्तस्य नन्दभवनप्रवेशो भविष्यतीति शिल्पिनः पौरांश्च गृहीतार्थान्

[कामेन चारः कामचारः] सूत्रधाराः शिल्पिनः । संस्कारविशेषैरिति । चन्द्रगुप्तोपरि तोरणपातनोद्यमादिरूपैः । अभ्यन्तरे संस्कार इति । तीक्ष्णरसदानशयनगृहशायितहननादिरूप इति गूढोभिसन्धिः । [दाक्ष्यं दक्षतां] अनुरूपं फलमिदं वधरूपं फलमिति गूढम् ।

राजभक्तीति । राज्ञि सर्वार्थसिद्धौ भक्तिप्रकर्षः वैरिनिधनेन भक्त्यातिशयप्रदर्शनम् । अयमपकारिजनाद्भयमुद्वेगः । [नियोगकालमाज्ञाकालमप्रतिपालयता] ततश्चाणक्यहतकेनेत्यादि । [लग्नवशाल्लग्नानुरोधात्] इदं चाणक्यस्येष्टार्थोपायानुसरणमाक्षेपो नामान्त्यमङ्गम् ।]

---

१ किमत्र क्रियते. २ वचनात् दत्तलग्नवशात्. ३ एव अभिमतः चन्द्रगुप्तस्य. ४ पूर्वपुर-द्वार-प्रवेशात्. ५ अभिनन्द्य. ६ प्रकर्षनया; नियोग-अभियोग.

कृत्वा तस्मिन्नेव क्षणे पर्वतेश्वरभ्रातरं वैरोचकमेकासनं चन्द्रगुप्तेन सहोपवेश्य कृतः पृथ्वीराज्यविभागः।

राक्ष०—किं वातिसृष्टः पर्वतकभ्रात्रे वैरोचकाय पूर्वप्रतिश्रुतः राज्यार्धविभागः।

विरा०—अथ किम्।

राक्ष०—(स्वगतम्।) नियतमतिधूर्तेन चाणक्यबटुना तस्यापि तपस्विनः कमप्युपांशुवधमाकलय्य पर्वतेश्वरविनाशेन जनितमयशः प्रमाष्टुमेषा लोकप्रसिद्धिरुपचिता। (प्रकाशम्।) ततस्ततः।

विरा०—ततः प्रथममेव प्रकाशिते रात्रौ चन्द्रगुप्तस्य नन्दभवनप्रवेशे कृताभिषेके किल वैरोचके विमलमुक्तामणिपरिक्षेपविरचितचित्रपटमयवारबाणप्रच्छादितशरीरे मणिमयमुकुटनिबिडनियमितरुचिरतरमौलौ सुरभिकुसुमदामवैकक्ष्यावभासितविपुलवक्षःस्थले परिचिततमैरप्यनभिज्ञायमानाकृतौ चाणक्यहतकादेशाच्चन्द्रगुप्तोपवाह्यां चन्द्रलेखां नाम गजवशामारुह्य चन्द्रगुप्तानुयायिना राजलोकेनानुगम्यमाने देवस्य नन्दस्य भवनं प्रविशति वैरोचके युष्मत्प्रयुक्तेन दारुवर्मणा सूत्रधारेण चन्द्रगुप्तोयमिति मत्वा तस्योपरि पातनाय सज्जीकृतं यन्त्रतोरणम्। अत्रान्तरे बहिर्निगृहीतवाहनेषु स्थितेषु चन्द्रगुप्तानुयायिषु नृपेषु युष्मत्प्रयुक्तेनैव चन्द्रगुप्त-

---

[अतिसृष्टो दत्तः। उपांशुवधो रहसि हननम्। उपचितेति। अभिवर्धितेत्यर्थः। किलेत्यलीके। चित्रपटमयेति। [विमलमुक्तामणीनां परिक्षेपेण परितः स्थापनेन विरचितः। चित्रपटमयः वारबाणः कञ्चुकसदृशरचनाविशेष इत्यर्थस्तेन प्रच्छादितं शरीरं यस्य तस्मिन्। 'कञ्चुको वारबाणोऽस्त्री' इत्यमरः। मौलयः संयताः कचाः। ते मुकुटे निबिडं नियमिता यस्य। कुसुमदाम्नो वैकक्ष्यमुपवीतत्वेन निधानम्। ['कण्ठाद्वैकक्षिकं तु तद्यत्तिर्यक्क्षिप्तमुरसि।' इत्यमरः। चन्द्रगुप्त उपवाह्यो यस्यास्तां चन्द्रगुप्तवाहनभूताम्।] राक्षसेनैव चन्द्रगुप्तोपांशुवधार्थं तस्य निषादित्वेन हास्तिपकत्वेन बर्बरकनामा स्वपुरुषो नियोजितः इत्यर्थः।

---

१ पृथक्, ०राज्यार्धविभागः इति पाठः. २ पर्वतेश्वरभ्रात्रे अतिसृष्टं राज्यार्धम्. ३ अयशसः परिहारार्थम्. ४ चरिता. ५ हिमविमलमुक्तागुणपरिक्षेपोपरचितपट्टवार०. ६ वैकक्षक. ७ मन्यमानेन वैरोचकस्योपरि. ८ भूमिपालेषु.

निषादिना वर्वरकेण कनकदण्डिकान्तर्निहितामसिपुत्रिकामाक्रष्टुकामेनावलम्बिता करेण कनकशृङ्खलावलम्बिनी कनकदण्डिका।

राक्ष०—उभयोरप्यस्थाने यत्नः।

विरा०—अथ जघनाभिघातमुत्प्रेक्षमाणा गजवधूरतिजवनतया गत्यन्तरमारूढवती। प्रथमगत्यनुरोधप्रत्याकलितमुक्तेन प्रभ्रष्टलक्ष्यं पतता यन्त्रतोरणेनाकृष्टकृपाणीव्यग्रपाणिरनासादयन्नेव चन्द्रगुप्ताशया वैरोचकं हतस्तपस्वी वर्वरकः। ततो दारुवर्मणा यन्त्रतोरणनिपातनादात्मवधमाकलय्य पूर्वमेवोत्तुङ्गतोरणस्थलमारूढेन यन्त्रघट्टनबीजं लोहकीलकमादाय हस्तिनीगत एव हतस्तपस्वी वैरोचकः।

राक्ष०—कष्टमनर्थद्वयमापतितम्। न हतश्चन्द्रगुप्तो हतौ वैरोचकवर्वरकौ दैवेन। अथ सूत्रधारो दारुवर्मा कथम्।

विरा०—वैरोचकपुरःसरेण पदातिलोकेनैव लोष्टघातं हतः।

राक्ष०—(सास्रम्।) कष्टम्। अहो वत्सलेन सुहृदा दारुवर्मणा वियुक्ताः स्मः। अथ तत्रत्येन भिषजा अभयदत्तेन किमनुष्ठितम्।

विरा०—सर्वमनुष्ठितम्।

राक्ष०—(सहर्षम्।) किं हतो दुरात्मा चन्द्रगुप्तः।

विरा०—अमात्य दैवान्न हतः।

राक्ष०—(सविषादम्।) तत्किमिदानीं कथयसि सर्वमनुष्ठितमिति।

[असिपुत्रिका छुरिका। उत्प्रेक्षमाणा वितर्कयन्ती। आरूढवती आश्रितवती। प्रथमगत्यनुरोधाद्गत्यनुसारेण आदौ प्रत्याकलितं पश्चान्मुक्तं च तेन। प्रभ्रष्टं लक्ष्यं यस्मिन्कर्मणि तद्यथा तथा। आकृष्टा या कृपाणी असिलता तया व्यग्रः पाणिर्यस्य।] व्यग्रपाणिरनासादयन्निति। वैरोचकं हन्तुमवकाशमनासादयन्नित्यर्थः। लोष्टघातमिति। लोष्टैर्हत्वा लोष्टघातं हन्तेर्णमुल्। [अथ भिषजाभयदत्तेनेति-तदुक्तं कामन्दकेन। भिषग्भेदेन वा शत्रुं रसदानेन साधयेत्।]

---

१ ०लामुखाव. २ (स्वगतम्). ३ ०पातमात्मविनाशफलमवधार्य. ४ अस्मात्प्राक्—(सा वेगमात्मगतम्।) न एतावुभौ हतौ दैवेन वयमेव हताः। (प्रकाशम्). ५ तत्र तेन. ६ अमात्य सर्व० ७ अपि सखे हतश्चन्द्रगुप्तहतकः. ८ परितुष्टः सर्व.

विरा०—अमात्य कल्पितमनेन योगचूर्णमिश्रितमौषधं चन्द्रगुप्ताय । तत्प्रत्यक्षीकुर्वता चाणक्यहतकेन कनकभाजने वर्णान्तरमुपलभ्याभिहितश्चन्द्रगुप्तः । वृषल सविषमिदमौषधं न पातव्यमिति ।

राक्ष०—शठः खल्वसौ बटुः । अथ स वैद्यः कथम् ।

विरा०—तदेवौषधं पायितो मृतश्च ।

राक्ष०—(सविषादम् ।) अहो महान्विज्ञानराशिरुपरतः । अथ तस्य शयनाधिकृतस्य प्रमोदकस्य किं वृत्तम् ।

विरा०—यदितरेषाम् ।

राक्ष०—(सोद्वेगम् ।) कथमिव ।

विरा०—स खलु मूर्खस्तं युष्माभिरतिसृष्टं महान्तमर्थराशिमवाप्य महता व्ययेनोपभोक्तुमारब्धवान् । ततः कुतोऽयं भूयान्धनागम इति पृच्छ्यमानो यदा वाक्यभेदान्बहूनगमत्तदा चाणक्यहतकेन विचित्रवधेन व्यापादितः ।

राक्ष०(सोद्वेगम् ।) कथमत्रापि दैवेनोपहता वयम् । अथ शयितस्य चन्द्रगुप्तस्य शरीरे प्रहर्तुमस्मत्प्रयुक्तानां राजगृहस्यान्तर्भित्तिसुरङ्गामेत्य प्रथममेव निवसतां बीभत्सकादीनां को वृत्तान्तः ।

विरा०—अमात्य दारुणो वृत्तान्तः ।

राक्ष०—(सावेगम् ।) कथं दारुणो वृत्तान्तः । न खलु विदितास्ते तत्र निवसन्तश्चाणक्यहतकेन ।

विरा०—अमात्य अथ किम् । प्राक् चन्द्रगुप्तप्रवेशाच्छयनगृहं

[प्रत्यक्षीकुर्वता पातुं योग्यं न वेति विमृशता । तदेवौषधं पायितः कदाचित्परप्रेरिता भिषजो नृपाय सविषमौषधं दद्युरिति तैः प्रथमं पीतं तदाज्ञा पातव्यमिति नीतिविदुपदेशात् । तदुक्तं कामन्दकेन–'औषधानि च सर्वाणि पानं पानीयमेव च । तत्कल्पकैः समास्वाद्य प्राश्नीयाद्भोजनानि च ।' इति] अथ तस्येति । शयनाधिकृतस्य शयनगृहसंस्कारादिना राजप्रलोभनेधिकृतस्येत्यर्थः । [वाक्यभेदानिति यदा परस्परविरोधीनि वाक्यान्याह तदा ।]

---

१ विषयोगचर्णमी०. २ उपरतः. ३ अहह इति पाठः. ४ आत्मविनाशः. ५ ०हतकादेशाद्विचित्रेण व०. ६ सविषादम्. ७ नरपतिशयनगृहस्यान्तःसुरङ्गायां निव०.

प्रविष्टमात्रेणैवं निपुणमवलोकयता दुरात्मना चाणक्यहतकेन कस्माच्चिद्भित्तिच्छिद्राद्गृहीतभक्तावयवैवां निष्क्रामन्तीं पिपीलिकापङ्क्तिमवलोक्य पुरुषगर्भमेतद्गृहमिति गृहीतार्थेन दाहितं तच्छयनगृहम् । तस्मिंश्च दह्यमाने धूमावरुद्धदृष्टयः प्रथमविहितनिर्गमनमार्गमनधिगम्य द्वारं सर्व एव बीभत्सकादयो ज्वलनमुपगम्य तत्रैव नष्टाः ।

राक्ष०—(सास्रम् ।) कष्टं भोः कष्टम् । सखे पश्य दैवसंपदं दुरात्मनश्चन्द्रगुप्तहतकस्य । कुतः ।

कन्या तस्य वधाय या विषमयी गूढं प्रयुक्ता मया
दैवात्पर्वतकस्तया स निहतो यस्तस्य राज्यार्द्धहृत् ।
ये शस्त्रेषु रसेषु च प्रणिहितास्तैरेव ते घातिता
मौर्यस्यैव फलन्ति पश्य विविधश्रेयांसि मन्त्रीतयः ॥ १६ ॥

विरा०—अमात्य तथापि खलु प्रारब्धमपरित्याज्यमेव । पश्य ।

प्रारभ्यते न खलु विघ्नभयेन नीचैः
प्रारभ्य विघ्नविहता विरमन्ति मध्याः ।
विघ्नैः पुनः पुनरपि प्रतिहन्यमानाः
प्रारब्धमुत्तमजना न परित्यजन्ति ॥ १७ ॥

अपि च ।

किं शेषस्य भरव्यथा न वपुषि क्ष्मां न क्षिपत्येष यत्
किं वा नास्ति परिश्रमो दिनपतेरास्ते न यन्निश्चलः ।

[गृहीता भक्तावयवा अन्नकणा यया तां ।] कन्या तस्येति । रसेषु विषेषु । 'शृङ्गारादौ विषे वीर्ये गुणे रागे जले रसे ।' इत्यमरः । मौर्यस्य नाशार्थं प्रणीता मन्त्रीतयः प्रत्युत तस्यैव श्रेयांसि फलन्तीति पश्य दैवसंपदं चन्द्रगुप्तस्येति पूर्वेणान्वयः ॥ १६ ॥

[प्रारभ्यत इति । । नीचाः कार्यं नैवारभन्ते । मध्या आरभ्य जातविघ्नास्ततपरित्यजन्ति । इ०] ॥ १७ ॥ किं शेषस्येति [शेषस्यानन्तस्य वपुषि भरव्यथा भूधारणजनिता न जायते किं यस्मात्कारणादि० । अपि तु जायते एव । किंतु] कृपण-

---

१ ०णैव चाणक्यहतकेन शयनगृहं समन्तादवलोकितम् । ततोन्यस्मात्. २ ०यवानां पिपीलिकानां निष्क्रामन्तीं. ३ ०दृष्टिविषयाः ४ पिहित. ५ उपगता उपरताश्च ६ मे नीतयः इति पाठः. ७ सहरुगुणितैरपि हन्यमानाः. ८ गुणाः,—त्वमिवोद्वहन्ति.

किं त्वङ्गीकृतमुत्सृजन्कृपणवच्छ्लाघ्यो जनो लज्जते
निर्व्यूढं प्रतिपन्नवस्तुषु सतामेतद्धि गोत्रव्रतम् ॥ १८ ॥

राक्ष०—सखे प्रारब्धमपरित्याज्यमिति प्रत्यक्षमेवैतद्भवताम् । ततस्ततः ।

विरा०—ततः प्रभृति चन्द्रगुप्तशरीरे सहस्रगुणमप्रमत्तश्चाणक्यहतक एभ्य एतदीदृशं भवतीत्यन्विष्य निगृहीतवान्पुरनिवासिनो युष्मदीयानाप्तपुरुषान् ।

राक्ष०—(सोद्वेगम् ।) कथय कथय के के निगृहीताः ।

विरा०—प्रथमं तावत्क्षपणको जीवसिद्धिः सनिकारं नगरान्निर्वासितः ।

राक्ष०—(स्वगतम् ।) एतावत्सह्यम् । न निष्परिग्रहं स्थानभ्रंशः पीडयिष्यति । (प्रकाशम् ।) वयस्य कमपराधमुद्दिश्य निर्वासितः ।

विरा०—एष राक्षसप्रयुक्तया विषकन्यया पर्वतेश्वरं व्यापादितवानिति ।

राक्ष०—(स्वगतम् ।) साधु कौटिल्य साधु । स्वस्मिन् ।

परिहृतमयशः पातितमस्मासु च घातितोऽर्धराज्यहरः ।
एकमपि नीतिबीजं बहुफलतामेति यस्य तव ॥ १९ ॥

(प्रकाशम् ।) ततस्ततः ।

विरा०—ततश्चन्द्रगुप्तशरीरमभिद्रोग्धुमनेन व्यापारिता दारुवर्मादय इति नगरे प्रख्याप्य शकटदासः शूलमारोपितः ।

वत् [कृपणेन प्राकृतजनेन तुल्यम् । अङ्गीकृतं कार्यम् ।] उत्सृजन्निति पूर्वेणान्वयः । प्रतिपन्नवस्तुषु अङ्गीकृतवस्तुषु । निर्व्यूढं निर्वाहः भावे क्तः । निर्व्यूढमिति । यदेतत्सतां कुलव्रतमित्यर्थः । निर्व्यूढिः प्रतिपन्नवस्तुषु सतामेकं हि गोत्रव्रतमिति क्वचित्पाठः । निर्व्यूढिरूपमेवं मुख्यं गोत्रव्रतमित्यर्थः ॥ १८ ॥

[प्रारब्धमपरित्याज्यमहं न परित्यजामिति । आप्ता हिताः । निष्परिग्रहं परिवाररहितम् ।]

[परिहृतमिति । अयशः पर्वतेश्वरविनाशजनिताऽकीर्तिः । परिहृतमिति एकं फलं । अस्मासु तत्पातितं संक्रामितमिति द्वितीयं । अर्धराज्यहरो घातितः । अर्धराज्यं च रक्षितमिति तृतीयम् । एवं] एकमपि नीतिबीजमिति । इदमेकं बीजान्वेषणम् ॥ १९ ॥

---

१ आर्याः. २ निर्वाहः ३ कुसुमपुरनिवासिनोः. ४ एष दुरात्मा.

राक्ष०—(सास्रम् ।) हा सखे शकटदास अयुक्तरूपस्तवायमीदृशो मृत्युः । अथवा स्वाम्यर्थमुपरतो न शोच्यस्त्वम् । वयमेवात्र शोच्या ये नन्दकुलविनाशेपि जीवितुमिच्छामः ।

विरा०—अमात्य स्वाम्यर्थ एव साधयितव्य इति प्रयतसे ।

राक्ष०—सखे ।

अस्माभिरमुमेवार्थमालम्ब्य न जिजीविषाम् ।
परलोकगतो देवः कृतघ्नैर्नानुगम्यते ॥ २० ॥

कथ्यतामपरस्यापि सुहृद्व्यसनस्य श्रवणे सज्जोस्मि ।

विरा०—एतदुपलभ्य चन्दनदासेनापवाहितममात्यकलत्रम् ।

राक्ष०—सखे क्रूरस्य चाणक्यबटोर्विरुद्धमयुक्तमनुष्ठितं तेन ।

विरा०—अमात्य अन्वयुक्ततरः सुहृद्द्रोहः ।

राक्ष०—ततस्ततः ।

विरा०—ततो याच्यमानेनाप्यनेन न समर्पितममात्यकलत्रं यदा तदातिकुपितेन चाणक्यबटुना—

राक्ष०—(सोद्वेगम् ।) न खलु व्यापादितः ।

विरा०—न हि । गृहीतगृहसारः सपुत्रकलत्रो बन्धनागारे निक्षिप्तः ।

राक्ष०—तत्किं परितुष्टः कथयसि अपवाहितं राक्षसकलत्रमिति । ननु वक्तव्यं संयमितः सपुत्रकलत्रो राक्षस इति ।

(प्रविश्य ।) पुरुषः—जयतु अमात्यः । एष खलु शकटदासः प्रतीहारभूमिमुपस्थितः । (जेदु अमच्चो एसो खु सअडदासो पडिहारभूमिमुवट्ठिदो ।)

राक्ष०—भद्र अपि सत्यम् ।

[अयुक्तरूपोऽनुचितः । अस्माभिरिति । स्वामी सर्वथानुगन्तव्योऽस्माभिस्तथा न कृतमिति कृतघ्नैरस्माभिरमुमेवार्थं स्वाम्यर्थ एव साधयितव्य इत्येतद्रूपमवलम्ब्य न जीवितुमिच्छामि जिजीविषा तामवलम्ब्य इत्यर्थः ।] न खलु व्यापादित इति । एतदप्यपकारिजनाद्भयमुद्वेगः ।

---

१ अस्माकममुमेवार्थमवलम्ब्य जिजीविषा । इति पाठः. २ अस्मात्परं विरा०-अमात्य नैतदेवम् । युष्माभिरमुमेवा...।......कृतघ्नैर्नानुगम्यते ॥ इत्य० क्वचित्. ३ ०सेनोपरूद्धसाध्वसेन, दृढसौहार्देन. ४ चन्दनदासेन.इत्य. ५ गृहीतोनेन. ६ प्रविश्य पटाक्षेपेण. ७ प्रियंवदक.

पुरु०—किमलीकममात्यपादेषु विनिवेदयामि । (किं अलिअं अमच्चपादेसु विणिवेदेमि ।)

राक्ष०—सखे विराधगुप्त कथमेतत् ।

विरा०—अमात्य स्यादेतदेवं यतो भव्यं रक्षति भवितव्यता ।

राक्ष०—प्रियंवदक किमद्यापि चिरयसि । क्षिप्रं प्रवेशयैनम् ।

पुरु०—यदमात्य आज्ञापयति । (इति निष्क्रान्तः ।) (जं अमच्चो आणवेदि ।)

(ततः प्रविशति सिद्धार्थकेनानुगम्यमानः शकटदासः ।)

शक०—(स्वगतम् ।)

दृष्ट्वा मौर्यमिव प्रतिष्ठितपदं शूलं धरित्र्यास्तले
तल्लक्ष्मीमिव चेतनाप्रमथिनीं मूर्द्धावबद्धस्रजम् ।
श्रुत्वा स्वाम्युपरोपरौद्रविषमानाघाततूर्यस्वनान्
न ध्वस्तं प्रथमाभिघातकठिनं मन्ये मदीयं मनः ॥ २१ ॥

(अवलोक्य सहर्षम् ।) अयममात्यराक्षसस्तिष्ठति य एषः ।

अक्षीणभक्तिः क्षीणेपि नन्दे स्वाम्यर्थमुद्वहन् ।
पृथिव्यां स्वामिभक्तानां प्रमाणे परमे स्थितः ॥ २२ ॥

(उपसृत्य ।) यजत्वमात्यः ।

राक्ष०—(विलोक्य सहर्षम् ।) सखे शकटदास दिष्ट्या कौटिल्यगोचरगतोपि त्वं दृष्टोसि । तत्परिष्वजस्व माम् ।

दृष्ट्वा मौर्यमिति । [प्रतिष्ठितपदं निखातमूलं जातप्रतिष्ठं च । चेतनाप्रमथिनीमन्तःकरणविदारिणीं मनोरुजमावहन्तीं च ।] अत्र वध्यभूमिखातशूलस्य वध्यस्रजश्च मौर्यतल्लक्ष्मीदृष्टान्तः मत्सरातिशयजनितासूयाकृतः । जीवकर्मेन्द्रियवृत्तीनां मनोवृत्त्यधीनतया प्रकृते दर्शनश्रवणबन्धनक्रियाणां मन एव कर्तृ । अतो ध्वंसनक्रिययैककर्तृत्वात् क्त्वाप्रत्ययः । स्वामिनां नन्दानामपरोपो राज्यभ्रंशस्तद्वद्रौद्रविषमानसह्यानित्यर्थः । यद्यस्मात्प्रथमाभिघातेन पूर्वानुभूतानर्थपरंपरासहनेन कठिनमभूत्तस्मान्न ध्वस्तमित्यन्वयः । स्वामिपुरोपरोधविषमानिति क्वचित्पाठः ॥ २१ ॥

अक्षीणभक्तिरिति । परमे प्रमाणे प्रथमकोटौ स्थितः । [अत्युत्कटस्वामिभक्तिशालिनामप्यग्रेसर इत्यर्थः ॥ २२ ॥]

---

१ अमच्चपादोपजीविणो जना न अलिअं मन्तिदुं जाणन्ति. २ ०स्याः स्थले. ३ चेतसः. ४ मूर्ध्नावबद्ध्य, उन्मुच्य वध्य ५ स्वाम्युपरोध. ६ यतन.

शक०—(तथा करोति ।)

राक्ष०—(चिरं परिष्वज्य ।) इदमासनमास्यताम् ।

शक०—(नाट्येनोपविष्टः ।)

राक्ष०—सखे शकटदास अथ कोयं मे ईदृशस्य हृदयानन्दस्य हेतुः ।

शक०—(सिद्धार्थकं निर्दिश्य ।) अनेन प्रियसुहृदा सिद्धार्थकेन घातकान्विद्राव्य वध्यस्थानादपहृतोस्मि ।

राक्ष०—(सहर्षम् ।) भद्र सिद्धार्थक किं पर्याप्तमिदमस्य प्रियस्य । तथापि गृह्यताम् । (इति स्वगात्रादवतार्य भूषणानि प्रयच्छति ।)

सिद्धा०—(गृहीत्वा पादयोर्निपत्य स्वगतम् ।) अयं खलु आर्योपदेशः । भवतु तथा करिष्यामि । (प्रकाशम् ।) अमात्य अत्र मे प्रथमप्रविष्टस्य नास्ति कोपि परिचितः यत्रेममसात्यस्य प्रसादं निक्षिप्य निर्वृतो भवामि । तस्मादिच्छाम्यहमेतया मुद्रया मुद्रितममात्यस्यैव भाण्डागारे स्थापयितुम् । यदा मे प्रयोजनं तदा ग्रहीष्यामि । (अंअं खु अज्जोवदेसो । होदु तह करिस्सं । अमच्च एत्थमे पढमपविठ्ठस्स णत्थि कोवि परिचिदो जत्थ एदं अमच्चस्स पसादं णिक्खिविअ णिव्वुदो भविस्सं । ता इच्छामि अहं इमाए मुद्दाए मुद्दिदं अमच्चस्स एव्व भण्डाआगे ठाविदुं । जदा मे पेओअणं तदा गेह्निस्सं ।)

राक्ष०—भद्र को दोषः । शकटदास एवं क्रियताम् ।

शक०—यदाज्ञापयत्यमात्यः । (मुद्रां विलोक्य जनान्तिकम् ।) अमात्य भवन्नामाङ्कितेयं मुद्रा ।

आर्योपदेश इति । तस्माच्च सुहृत्प्राणपरिरक्षणपरितुष्टादित्यादिः कर्णे एवमेवेति अतः पूर्वोक्त आर्योपदेश इत्यर्थः । इदमपरं बीजान्वेषणम् ।

ग्रहीष्यामीति । भवतोतिसन्धानार्थं यदा कटकान्निर्गमिष्यामि तदा ग्रहीष्यामीति कुटिलो गूढाशयः पयत्यमात्यः । इति ।

---

१ यदाज्ञापयत्यमात्य इति. २ अपवाहितः. ३ काममपर्याप्तम्. ४ पदं खु अज्जोणवदेसेण करिस्सं. ५ एदिणा पओ

राक्ष०—(विलोक्यात्मगतम् ।) सत्यं नगरान्निष्क्रामतो मम हस्ताद्ब्राह्मण्या उत्कण्ठाविनोदार्थं गृहीता । तत्कथमस्य हस्तमुपागता । (प्रकाशम् ।) भद्र सिद्धार्थक कुतस्त्वयेयमधिगता ।

सिद्धा०—अस्ति कुसुमपुरे मणिकारश्रेष्ठी चन्दनदासो नाम । तस्य गेहद्वारपरिसरे पतिता मया आसादिता । (अत्थि कुसुमपुरे मणिआरसेठ्ठी चन्दनदासो णाम । तस्स गेहदुआरपडिसरे पडिदा मए आसादिदा ।)

राक्ष०—युज्यते ।

सिद्धा०—अमात्य अत्र किं युज्यते । (अमच्च एत्थ किं युज्जइ ।)

राक्ष०—भद्र यन्महाधनानां गृहे पतितस्यैवंविधस्योपलब्धिरिति ।

शक०—सखे सिद्धार्थक अमात्यनामाङ्कितेयं मुद्रा । तदितो बहुतरेणार्थेन भवन्तममात्यस्तोषयिष्यति । दीयतामेषा ।

सिद्धा०—आर्य ननु प्रसाद एष यदस्या मुद्राया अमात्यः परिग्रहं करोति । (अज्ज णं पसादो एसो जं इमाए मुद्दाए अमच्चो परिग्गहं करेदि ।) (इति मुद्रामर्पयति ।)

[उत्कण्ठाविनोदार्थम् । उत्कण्ठा इष्टजनस्य सस्पृहं स्मरणं । चिन्ता तु स्मृतिराध्यानं स्मरणं सस्पृहे पुनः । उत्कण्ठोत्कलिके । इति शब्दार्णवः ।]

किमत्र युज्यत इति । मुद्रायाः स्वकीयत्वनिह्नवोनेन क्रियत इति जानन्नप्यजानन्निव पृच्छति । भद्र यदिति । अस्मद्गृहजनस्तत्र वर्तत इत्यस्यार्थस्य गोपनार्थमियमुक्तिः ।

तदितो बहुतरेणेति । इतो मुद्रामूल्यादप्यधिकतरेणेत्यर्थः । परिग्रहमित्यादि । यदर्थमियमानीता तत्सिद्धमित्यर्थो गूढः ।

---

१ सविषादं सवितर्कमा०. २ गृहिण्या. ३ पुरतिवासी. ४ गेहुद्दुआरे भूमिए. ५ एसो मे परितोषो. ६ परिग्गहप्पसादं.

राक्ष०—सखे शकटदास अनयैव मुद्रया स्वाधिकारे व्यवहर्तव्यं भवता।

शक०—यदाज्ञापयत्यमात्यः।

सिद्धा०—अमात्य किमपि विज्ञापयामि। (अमच्च किंपि विण्णवेमि।)

राक्ष०—ब्रूहि[1] विश्रब्धम्।

सिद्धा०—जानात्येवामात्यो यथा चाणक्यबटुकस्य विप्रियं कृत्वा नास्ति पुनः पाटलिपुत्रे प्रवेश इति इच्छाम्यहममात्यस्य चरणे एव शुश्रूषितुम्। (जाणादि एव्व अमच्चो जह चाणक्कबडुअस्स विप्पिअं कदुअ णत्थि पुणो पाडलिउत्ते पवेसो त्ति इच्छामि अहं अमच्चचलणे[2] एव्व सुस्सूसिदुम्।)

राक्ष०—भद्र प्रियं नः। किंतु त्वदभिप्रायापरिज्ञानान्तरितोय-मस्मदनुनयः। तदेवं क्रियताम्।

सिद्धा०—(सहर्षम्।) अनुगृहीतोस्मि। (अनुगिहिदोह्मि।)

राक्ष०—सखे शकटदास विश्रामय सिद्धार्थकम्।

शक०—तथा (इति सिद्धार्थकेन सह निष्क्रान्तः।)

राक्ष०—सखे विराधगुप्त वर्णय[3] वृत्तशेषम्। अपि क्षमन्तेस्मदुपजापं[4] चन्द्रगुप्तप्रकृतयः।

विरा०—अमात्य बाढं क्षमन्ते यथाप्रकाशमनुगच्छन्त्येव[5]।

त्वदभिप्राय इति। त्वदभिप्रायापरिज्ञानेन [पृष्टोऽस्मत्सेवामङ्गीकरिष्यसि न वेतित्वदभिप्रायाज्ञानेन] अन्तरितो विलम्बितः। [अन्यथा] पूर्वमेवास्माभिरेवं भवाननुनेय इत्यर्थः॥

अनुगच्छन्त्येवेति। चन्द्रगुप्तप्रकृतयः भद्रभटादयः मलयकेतूपेक्षणात्कृतघ्न-श्चाणक्यबटुर्न विश्वसनीय इत्येवमस्मदुपजापं यथाप्रकाशमनुगच्छन्त्येव। [यथा प्रकाशं प्रकाशीभवन्तमर्थमनतिक्रम्य तदनुसारेणास्मदुक्तं कर्तुं प्रवर्तन्ते।] अ-त्राप्यागन्तुमुद्युक्त एवेति भावः। वक्ष्यति चैतत्पञ्चमेङ्के। प्राक्परिगृहीतो-पजापैरित्यादि।

---

१ भद्रं ब्रूहि. २ अज्जस्स ज्जेव सुप्पसण्णे पादे सेविदुम्. ३ वर्णयेदानीं कुसुम-पुरवृत्तान्तशेषम्. ४ कुसुमपुरनिवासिनोऽस्म. ५ ननु यथा प्रधानं.

राक्ष०—सखे किं तत्र प्रकाशम्।

विरा०—अमात्य इदं तत्र प्रकाशम्। मलयकेतोरपक्रमणात्प्रभृति कुपितैश्चन्द्रगुप्तश्चाणक्यस्योपरीति चाणक्योप्यतिजितकाशितयासहमानश्च न्द्रगुप्तं तैस्तैराज्ञाभङ्गैश्चन्द्रगुप्तस्य चेतःपीडामुपचिनोति। इत्थमपि ममानुभवः।

राक्ष०—(सहर्षम्।) सखे विराधगुप्त गच्छ त्वमनेनैवाहितुण्डिकच्छद्मना पुनः कुसुमपुरम्। तत्र मे प्रियसुहृद्वैतालिकव्यञ्जनः स्तनकलशो नाम प्रतिवसति। स त्वया मद्वचनाद्वाच्यः यथा चाणक्येन क्रियमाणेष्वाज्ञाभङ्गेषु चन्द्रगुप्तः समुत्तेजनसमर्थैः श्लोकैरुपश्लोकयितव्यः कार्यं चातिनिभृतं करभकहस्तेन सन्देष्टव्यमिति।

विरा०—यदाज्ञापयत्यमात्यः। (इति निष्क्रान्तः।)

(प्रविश्य।)

पुरुषः—जयतु अमात्यः। अमात्य शकटदासो विज्ञापयति एते खलु त्रयोलङ्कारसंयोगा विक्रीयन्ते। तान् प्रत्यक्षीकरोत्वमात्य इति। (जेदु अमच्चो। अमच्च सअडदासो विण्णवेदि एदे खु तिण्णि अलङ्कारसंजोआ विक्कीअन्दि। ते पच्चक्खीकरेदु अमच्चो।)

राक्ष०—(विलोक्यात्मगतम्।) अहो महार्हाण्याभरणानि। (प्रकाशम्।) भद्र उच्यतामस्मद्वचनाच्छकटदासः परितोष्य विक्रेतारं गृह्यतामिति।

जितेन आत्मनो जयेन काशते असौ जितकाशी अतिशयेन जितकाशी अति० तस्य भावः जितकाशिता तया। आत्मनो जयेन अति दृप्त इत्यर्थः। उपचिनोति पुनः पुनः कृतैराज्ञाभङ्गैर्वर्धयति।] ममानुभव इति। इत्थं तत्रत्यवृत्तं मयानुभूयैवागतमित्यर्थः। इदमपि बीजान्वेषणम्॥ [-व्यञ्जनः वैतालिकच्छद्मना वर्तमानः। उपश्लोकयितव्यः श्लोकैः स्तोतव्यः।]

अलङ्कारसंयोगा इति। अलङ्कारसंयोगाः सम्यग्घटिता अलङ्कारा इत्यर्थः।

---

१ कारणम्. २ पाडितश्चन्द्रगुप्तेन चाणक्यः. ३ रूपैः. ४ जअदु जअदु अमच्चो. ५ पसीद स अद० ६ विसेस।

पुरु०—तथा (तह ।) (इति निष्क्रान्तः ।)

राक्ष०—यावदहमपि कुसुमपुराय करभकं प्रेषयामि । (उत्थाय) अपि नाम दुरात्मनश्चाणक्याच्चन्द्रगुप्तो भिद्येत । अथवा सिद्धमेव नः समीहितं पश्यामि । कुतः

मौर्यस्तेजसि सर्वभूतलभुजामाज्ञापको वर्तते
चाणक्योऽपि मदाश्रयादयमभूद्राजेति जातस्मयः ।
राज्यप्राप्तिकृतार्थमेकमपरं तीर्णप्रतिज्ञार्णवं
सौहार्दात्कृतकृत्यतैव नियतं लब्धान्तरा भेत्स्यति ॥ २३ ॥

(इति निष्क्रान्ताः सर्वे ।)

इति राक्षसविचारो नाम द्वितीयोऽङ्कः ।

चन्द्रगुप्तो भिद्येतेति । ततःप्रभृति चन्द्रगुप्तशरीरे सहस्रगुणमप्रमत्तश्चाणक्य इति श्रुत्वा तद्वधोपाये निराशः सन्राक्षसः—आशा बलवती राजन् शल्यो जेष्यति पाण्डवानितिन्यायेन—अतः परं स्तनकलशद्वारा मौर्यचाणक्ययोर्मिथो विरोधेन स्वेष्टसिद्धिं समाशंसते अपि नामेति ॥

मौर्यस्तेजसीति [तेजसि राजतेजसि वर्तते । राजदर्पाध्मात इत्यर्थः । जातस्मयो जातगर्वः ।] राज्यप्राप्त्या प्रतिज्ञार्णवतरणेन च लब्धान्तरा [भेदविधौ] प्राप्तावसरा कृतकृत्यतैव । उभौ सौहार्दाद्भेत्स्यति उभयोः सौहार्दं विघटयिष्यतीत्यर्थः । उभौ कृतकृत्यतया परस्परं निरपेक्षौ मन्तौ केनचिन्निमित्तेन विरोधे सति पुनर्न सन्धास्येते इति भावः । इत्थं पताकाप्राप्त्याशानुगुण्येन गर्भसन्धेर्द्वादशाङ्गानि निरूपितानि गर्भसन्धिश्च समाप्तः ॥

इति त्र्यम्बकयज्वप्रभुवर्याश्रितढुण्ढिराजव्यासयज्वविरचिते ।
मुद्राराक्षसनाटकव्याख्याने द्वितीयोऽङ्कः समाप्तः ॥

तृतीयोऽङ्कः ।

(ततः प्रविशति कञ्चुकी ।)

कञ्चुकी—(सनिर्वेदम् ।)

रूपादीन्विषयान्निरूप्य करणैर्यैरात्मलाभस्त्वया
लब्धस्तेष्वपि चक्षुरादिषु हताः स्वार्थावबोधक्रियाः ।
अङ्गानि प्रसभं त्यजन्ति पटुतामाज्ञाविधेयानि ते
न्यस्तं मूर्ध्नि पदं तवैव जरया तृष्णे मुधा[1] ताम्यसि ॥ १ ॥

(परिक्रम्याकाशे ।) भो भोः सुगाङ्गप्रासादाधिकृताः पुरुषाः सुगृहीतनामा देवश्चन्द्रगुप्तो वः समाज्ञापयति । प्रवृत्तकौमुदीमहोत्सवरमणीयतरं[2] कुसुमपुरमवलोकयितुमिच्छामि । तत्संस्क्रियन्तामस्मद्दर्शन-[3][4]

अथ राक्षसाभिलष्यमाणचाणक्यचन्द्रगुप्तविरोधकथनार्थं विमर्शसन्धिरारभ्यते । तृतीयचतुर्थावङ्कौ विमर्शसन्धिः । 'गर्भसन्धौ प्रसिद्धस्य बीजार्थस्यावमर्शनम् । हेतुना येन केनापि विमर्शः सन्धिरुच्यते ॥' इति लक्षणात् । गर्भसन्धौ प्रसिद्धस्य मुहुरुन्मिषस्य चाणक्यनीतिरूपस्य बीजस्य कौमुदीमहोत्सवप्रतिषेधादिना प्रकरीनाम्न्याल्पया कथया चावमर्शनात् अनुसन्धानात् नियताप्तिप्रकर्योः संबन्धस्य चात्र सत्त्वात् । तृतीयेऽङ्के नियताप्तिः ॥ चतुर्थेऽङ्के राक्षसचारसंवादरूपा कथा प्रकरी वर्ण्यते ॥ नियताप्तिप्रकर्यानुगुण्येनास्य सन्धेस्त्रयोदशाङ्गानि ॥ तत्रापवादसंफेटौ विद्रवद्रवशक्तयः । द्युतिः प्रसङ्गश्छलनं व्यवसायो विरोधनम् । प्ररोचनाविचलनमादानं च त्रयोदश ॥

रूपादीति । [यैः करणैः ज्ञानेन्द्रियैः शब्दादीन् विषयान् निरूप्य भोग्यतयावधार्य त्वयात्मलाभः स्ववृत्तिलाभः कृतस्तेष्वपि चक्षुरादिषु स्वार्थावबोधक्रियाः स्वस्वविषयग्रहणव्यापारा हता नष्टाः । ते आज्ञाविधेयानि निदेशानुवर्तीनि अङ्गानि प्रसभं प्रसह्य पटुतां स्वव्यापारसामर्थ्यं त्यजन्ति । एवमित्यादि ।] यैश्चक्षुरादिभी रूपादिषु विषयेषु गृह्यमाणेषु तत्तद्विषये तृष्णा अभिवर्धते तानीन्द्रियाणि विकलानि सन्ति विषयान्न गृह्णन्ति । यौवने तृष्णावशात् हस्तपादादीन्यङ्गानि स्वक्रियायां व्यापृतान्यासन् तान्यपि संप्रति जरया पटुतां स्वकार्यक्षमतां त्यजन्तीति जरया क्रियमाणं स्वाङ्गवैकल्यं तृष्णायामुपचर्यते ॥ न्यस्तं मूर्ध्नि पदं तवेति । अथापि तृष्णया मुधा ताम्यामीति भावः । कञ्चुकिनिर्वेदो नाटके वर्णनीय इति संप्रदायविदः ॥ १ ॥

---

१ मुधोत्ता०. २ यथा प्र०. ३ ०णीयं. ४ तत् क्रियन्ता.

योग्याः सुगाङ्गप्रासादोपरिभूमय इति । (पुनराकाशे ।) किं ब्रूथ । आर्य किमविदित एवायं देवस्य कौमुदीमहोत्सवप्रतिषेध इति । आः दैवोपहताः किमनेन वः सद्यःप्राणहरेण कथोपोद्घातेन । शीघ्रमिदानीम् ।

आलिङ्गन्तु गृहीतधूपसुरभीन्स्तम्भान्पिनद्धस्रजः
संपूर्णेन्दुमयूखसंहतिरुचां सच्चामराणां श्रियः ।
सिंहाङ्कासनधारणाच्च सुचिरं सञ्जातमूर्च्छामिव
क्षिप्रं चन्दनवारिणा सकुसुमः सेकोऽनुगृह्णातु गाम् ॥ २ ॥

किं ब्रूथ । आर्य इदमनुष्ठीयते देवस्य शासनमिति । भद्रास्त्वरध्वम् । अयमागत एव देवश्चन्द्रगुप्तः । य एषः ।

सुविश्रब्धैरङ्गैः पथिषु विषमेष्वप्यचलता
चिरं धुर्येणोढा गुरुरपि भुवो यास्य गुरुणा ।
धुरं तामेवोच्चैर्नववयसि वोढुं व्यवसितो
मनस्वी दम्यत्वात्स्खलति च न दुःखं वहति च ॥ ३ ॥

(नेपथ्ये ।) इत इतो देवः । (इदो इदो देवो ।)

अविदित एवायमिति । अयं चाणक्येन क्रियमाण इत्यर्थः । अयं बीजस्य चाणक्यनीतेरवमर्शनम् ।

आलिङ्गन्त्विति । [सम्पूर्णेन्दोः मयूखानां किरणानां संहतेः समूहस्येव रुग् येषां तेषां सच्चामराणां शोभाः पिनद्धा बद्धाः स्रजो येषु तान् स्तंभानालिङ्गन्तु । चन्दनवारिणा मूर्च्छाहारिणा । सेको गामनुगृह्णातु सोच्छ्वासां करोतु ।] अत्र चामराणां श्रियः स्तम्भानालिङ्गन्तु इत्युक्त्या कामिनामुपभोगः परिस्फुरतीति समासोक्तिरलङ्कारः । अतिगौरवशालि राजसिंहासनं सुगाङ्गभूमौ तिष्ठतीति तद्धारणात्सञ्जातमूर्छामिवेति वस्तूत्प्रेक्षा ॥ २ ॥

सुविश्रब्धैरिति । सुविश्रब्धैर्दृढैः सुप्रयुक्ततया कार्यक्षमैश्चाङ्गैरवयवैः स्वाम्यमात्यादिभिश्च ।विषमेषु गहनेषु । पथिषु मार्गेषु । राज्यतन्त्रेषु चाचलता अस्खलता धुर्येण राज्यभारनिर्वहणक्षमेणास्य गुरुणा तातेन या भुवो धूश्चिरमूढेत्यन्वयः । दम्यत्वादनतिप्रौढत्वात्स्खलति किंचित्खिद्यते मनस्वित्वादुत्साहवत्त्वाद्दुःखं च न वहति ॥ ३ ॥

इत इत इति । इयं चूलिका । अन्तर्जवनिकासंस्थैश्चूलिकार्थस्य सूचनेति लक्षणात् ।

---

१ उपरितन. २ देवस्य चन्द्रगुप्तस्य. ३ आकाशे किं कथयन्ति भवन्तः एते त्वरामहे इति.

(ततः प्रविशति राजा प्रतीहारी च ।)

राजा—(स्वगतम् ।) राज्यं हि नाम राजधर्मानुवृत्तिपरस्य नृपतेर्महदप्रीतिस्थानम् । कुतः ।

परार्थानुष्ठाने रहयति नृपं स्वार्थपरता
परित्यक्तस्वार्थो नियतमयथार्थः क्षितिपतिः ।
परार्थश्चेत्स्वार्थादभिमततरो हन्त परवान्
परायत्तः प्रीतेः कथमिव रसं वेत्ति पुरुषः ॥ ४ ॥

अपि च ।

दुराराध्या हि राजलक्ष्मीरात्मवद्भिरपि राजभिः । कुतः ।

तीक्ष्णादुद्विजते मृदौ परिभवत्रासान्न सन्तिष्ठते
मूर्खान्द्वेष्टि न गच्छति प्रणयितामत्यन्तविद्वत्स्वपि ।
शूरेभ्योऽभ्यधिकं बिभेत्युपहसत्येकान्तभीरूनहो
श्रीर्लब्धप्रसरेव वेशवनिता दुःखोपचर्या भृशम् ॥ ५ ॥

अन्यच्च कृतककलहं कृत्वा स्वतन्त्रेण किञ्चित्कालान्तरं व्यवहर्तव्यमित्यार्यादेशः । स च कथमपि मया पातकमिवाभ्युपगतः ।

[राजधर्मानुवृत्तिपरस्य राजधर्माननुवर्तमानस्य ।] अप्रीतिस्थानं क्लेशावहमित्यर्थः ॥

परार्थानुष्ठान इति । परार्थानुष्ठाने धर्मतः षष्ठांशदानादिप्रकृतिकार्यपरतन्त्रत्वे स्वार्थपरता स्वच्छन्दविहारादिविषयभोगः नृपं रहयति त्यजति । परित्यक्तस्वार्थः राजा नियतमयथार्थः क्षितिपतिः । ईदृशस्य राजत्वमयथार्थं निष्फलं स्वसुखोपभोगाभावादित्यर्थः । अथापि राजधर्मतया स्वार्थं विहाय प्रजार्थ एवानुष्ठेय इति चेदाग्रहस्तदा राजा पराधीनो जातः । पराधीनस्य भृत्यादेः सौख्यलेशः कुत्रापि नास्तीति लोकानुभवसिद्धमिति भावः ॥ ४ ॥

आत्मवद्भिरिति । समाहितचित्तैरित्यर्थः । [यद्वा कामन्दकोक्तात्मगुणसम्पन्नैः ।]

तीक्ष्णादिति । [तीक्ष्णादुग्रस्वभावाद् उद्विजते मामयं कदाचित्प्रभ्रंशयेदित्युद्विग्ना भवति ।] मृदौ परिभवत्रासान्मृदौ स्थितां मामन्यो बलवान्पराभविष्यतीति तत्र सम्यङ् न तिष्ठति । समवप्रविभ्यः स्थ इति तङ् । लब्धप्रसरा कामुकवशीकरणेन लब्धप्रागल्भ्या वेशवनितेव श्रीर्दुराराध्येत्यर्थः ॥ ५ ॥

---

१ वृत्तस्य. वृत्तिपरतन्त्रस्य   २ जडयति.   ३ वेत्तु.   ४ विद्भिः.   ५ मूर्खं.   ६ ऽप्यधिकं
७ कंचित्कालम्.   ८ उपदेशः.   ९ महापातक०.

अथ वा शश्वदार्योपदेशसंस्क्रियमाणमतयः सदैव स्वतन्त्रा वयम् । कुतः ।

इह विरचयन्साध्वीं शिष्यः क्रियां न निवार्यते
त्यजति तु यदा मार्गं मोहात्तदा गुरुरङ्कुशः ।
विनयरुचयस्तस्मात्सन्तः सदैव निरङ्कुशाः
परतरमतः स्वातन्त्र्येभ्यो वयं हि पराङ्मुखाः ॥ ६ ॥

(प्रकाशम् ।) आर्य वैहीनरे सुगाङ्गमार्गमादेशय ।

कञ्चु०—इत इतो देवः । (नाट्येन परिक्रम्य ।) अयं सुगाङ्गप्रासादः । शनैरारोहतु देवः ।

राजा—(नाट्येनारुह्य दिशोवलोक्य ।) अहो शरत्समयसंभृतशोभानां दिशामतिरमणीयता । कुतः ।

शनैः श्यानीभूताः सितजलधरच्छेदपुलिनाः
समन्तादाकीर्णाः कलविरुतिभिः सारसकुलैः ।

आर्योपदेश इति । आर्योपदेशेन संस्क्रियमाणमतयः शिक्ष्यमाणा इत्यर्थः ॥ इह विरचयन्निति । साध्वाचारः शिष्यः गुरुभिर्न नियम्यते अपि त्वनुमोद्यते । त्यक्तसन्मार्गस्य गुरुरङ्कुशः शिक्षकः । विनये गुरुकृतशिक्षणे रुचिर्येषां ते सदाचारास्तु सदा निरङ्कुशाः स्वतन्त्रा एव वयम् । हिशब्दस्त्वर्थे उक्तवैलक्षण्यद्योतकः । एवं स्वातन्त्र्ये सिद्धेपि वयं त्वत एभ्यः । पञ्चम्यास्तसिल् । उक्तविधेभ्यः कंचित्कालं स्वातन्त्र्येण व्यवहर्तव्यमित्यादिरूपेभ्यः स्वातन्त्र्येभ्यः परतरमत्यन्तं पराङ्मुखाः सर्वथा ईदृशं स्वातन्त्र्यं नेच्छामः । किंचित्कार्यानुरोधात्त्वार्योदेशेनेदं स्वातन्त्र्यमात्मन्यध्यस्य स्वतन्त्रवद्व्यवहराम इति भावः । यद्वा आर्यानुरोधादिदं स्वातन्त्र्यं कथंचिभ्युपगतम् । अतः परतरं अत उत्तरे काले । कालाध्वनोरत्यन्तसंयोगे द्वितीया । स्वातन्त्र्येभ्यो वयं पराङ्मुखाः । अतः परं कदापि स्वातन्त्र्यं नेच्छामः । आर्याधीना एव सर्वदा वर्तामहे इति भावः ॥ ६ ॥

शनैरिति । शनैः क्रमेण श्यानीभूताः कृशीभूताः । संयोगादेरातो धातोर्यण्वत इति श्यायतेर्निष्ठानत्वम् । विरलतया प्रतीयमाना दिशः सरितश्च नभस्तः वियत्तः श्रावणमासाच्च । 'नभाः श्रावणिकश्च स' इत्यमरः । स्यन्दन्ते निःसृता इव दृश्यन्ते । प्रावृषि दिशः सरितश्च घनावृततया सर्वत उत्कूलसलि-

---

१ मनसः. २ विचार्यते. ३ शोभां बिभ्रतीनां, शोभाविभूतीनां. ४ संप्रति हि. ५ श्यामी०, शान्ताः. ६ पुरस्तात्.

चिताश्चिन्नाकारैर्निशि विकचनक्षत्रकुमुदै-
नर्भस्तः स्यन्दन्ते सरित इव दीर्घा दश दिशः ॥ ७ ॥

अपि च ।

अपामुद्वृत्तानां निजमुपदिशन्त्या स्थितिपदं
दधत्या शालीनामवनतिमुदारे सति फले ।
मयूराणामुग्रं विषमिव हरन्त्या मदमहो
कृतः कृत्स्नस्यायं विनय इव लोकस्य शरदा ॥ ८ ॥

इमामपि ।

भर्तुस्तथा कलुषितां बहुवल्लभस्य
मार्गे कथंचिदवतार्य तनूभवन्तीम् ।
सर्वात्मना रतिकथाचतुरेव दूती
गङ्गां शरन्नयति सिन्धुपतिं प्रसन्नाम् ॥ ९ ॥

च्छाप्लुततया च विविक्तत्वेन न गृह्यन्ते शरदि तु विरलाः स्फुटं प्रतीयन्ते इति भावः । अत्र शरदि दिशां सरितां च वर्ण्यत्वादिवशब्दमावर्त्य दिशः सरित इव सरितश्च दिश इवेति च परस्परमुपमानोपमेयभावः । सितजलधरच्छन्दपुलिनाः विकचनक्षत्रकुमुदैरित्यत्र चोपमितसमासः । एवं च पर्यायेण द्वयोस्तच्चेदुपमेयोपमा मता इत्युपमेयोपमालङ्कारः । धर्मोऽर्थ इव पूर्णश्रीरर्थो धर्म इव त्वयीति अत्र पूर्णश्रीत्ववत् । श्यानीभूता इत्यादिसाधारणधर्मोपादानम् । अतः पूर्णेयमुपमा । सा च नमस्त इति श्लेषानुप्राणता । अनेन शरद्गुणकथनेन स्वस्य जैत्रयात्रासन्नाहसमय इति ध्वनितम् । वक्ष्यति च चाणक्यः सोऽयं व्यायामकालो नोत्सवकाल इति ॥ ७ ॥

अपामिति । [उद्वृत्तानां प्रवृद्धानामुद्धतानां च । स्थितिपदमवस्थानभूमिं मर्यादां च । स्थितिपथमिति पाठान्तरम् । शालीनां लक्षणया संभृतसंपदामवनतिं नम्रताम् ।] स्पष्टोऽर्थः । अनेन पद्येनोद्वृत्तस्य मलयकेतोर्भावी निग्रहः राक्षसस्य विषवदत्युग्रविक्रमनीतिविषयकमदापहरणं साम्राज्यफलशालिनो महोन्नतेश्चन्द्रगुप्तस्य विनयसंपच्च समासोक्त्या सूचिता ॥ ८ ॥

भर्तुरिति । बहुवल्लभस्येति हेतुगर्भविशेषणम् । बहुवल्लभत्वादिव कलुषितामिति कालुष्यहेतूत्प्रेक्षा । सा च वाचकाभावाद्गम्या । वर्षात्ययेन कृशीभवन्तीं स्वच्छसलिलां गङ्गां भर्तुः समुद्रस्य मार्गे कथंजिदवतार्य शरत् सिन्धुपतिं नयति । अत्रोपमा । रथिकथाचतुरा दूतीवेति दूतीदृष्टान्तानुरोधान्नायकापराधकुपितां विरहकृशां नायिकां प्रसादमुखीं कृत्वा नायकं प्रति यथा चतुरदूती प्रापयति तद्वदिति गम्यते ।

(समन्तान्नाट्येनावलोक्य ।) अये कथमप्रवृत्तकौमुदीमहोत्सवं कुसुमपुरम् । आर्य वैहीनरे अथास्मद्वचनादाघोषितः कुसुमपुरे कौमुदीमहोत्सवः ।

कञ्चुकी०—अथ किम् ।

राजा—तत्किं न गृहीतमस्मद्वचनं पौरैः ।

कञ्चु०—(कर्णौ पिधाय ।) शान्तं पापं शान्तं पापम् । पृथिव्यामस्खलितपूर्वं देवस्य शासनं कथं पौरेषु स्खलिष्यति ।

राजा—तत्कथमप्रवृत्तकौमुदीमहोत्सवमद्यापि कुसुमपुरम् ।

धूर्तैरन्वीयमानाः स्फुटचतुरकथाकोविदैर्वेशनार्यो
नालङ्कुर्वन्ति रथ्याः पृथुजघनभराक्रान्तिमन्दैः प्रयातैः ।
अन्योन्यं स्पर्द्धमाना न च गृहविभवैः स्वामिनो मुक्तशङ्काः
साकं स्त्रीभिर्भजन्ते विधिमभिलषितं पार्वणं पौरमुख्याः ॥ १० ॥

अनेन पद्येन राक्षसमतिपरिगृहीततया कलुषितां संशयितामिव नन्दकुललक्ष्मीं चतुरदूतीवातिगभीरा चाणक्यनीतिः सागरवदतिगभीराशयं चन्द्रगुप्तं सर्वात्मना सर्वप्रकारेण प्रापयतीति रूपकातिशयोक्त्या सूचितम् । अयमपि बीजामवर्शः ॥ ९ ॥

धूर्तैरिति । [वेशनार्यो वारस्त्रियः स्फुटाश्च चतुराश्च कथास्तासु कोविदैर्पाण्डितैर्धूर्तैर्विटैरन्वीयमानाः अनुगम्यमानाः पृथुजघनभराक्रान्तिमन्दैः गुरुजघनभरालसैः प्रयातैर्गमनैः ।] स्वामिनो गृहस्वामिनो वसनभूषणादिसमृद्धिं स्पर्धयान्योन्यमाधिक्येन दर्शयन्तः पौरमुख्याः स्वस्त्रीभिः सार्धं राजानुमतत्वान्मुक्तशङ्का अत एव बहिः क्रीडनं विगीतमपि पावनं राजानुमत्या प्रशस्तमित्यर्थः । चिरादीप्सितं क्रीडाविधिं कुतो न भजन्त इति कञ्चुकिनं प्रति प्रश्नः । पार्वणमिति क्वचित्पाठः । पर्वणि कार्तिक्यां पौर्णमास्यां भवं क्रीडाविधिमित्यर्थः ॥ १० ॥

एवमेतदिति । चाणक्यकृतं प्रतिषेधं सहसा स्फुटं वक्तुमतिभीतस्येदमस्फुटं सचकितं प्रतिवचनम् ।

---

१ देव आघोषितो देवस्याज्ञया कुसुमपुरे कौमुदीमहोत्सवः. २ पौरजनेन. ३ आर्य वैहीनरे इत्यधिकम्. ४ दूतैः. ५ सायं.

कञ्चु०—एवमेवैतत् ।

राजा—किमेतत् ।

कञ्चु०—देव इदम् ।

राजा—स्फुटं कथय ।

कञ्चु०—प्रतिषिद्धः कौमुदीमहोत्सवः ।

राजा—(सक्रोधम् ।) आः केन ।

कञ्चु०—देव नातः परं विज्ञापयितुं शक्यम् ।

राजा—न खलु आर्यचाणक्येनापहृतः प्रेक्षकाणामतिशय रमणीयश्चक्षुषोः विषयः ।

कञ्चु०—देव कोन्यो जीवितुकामो देवस्य शासनमतिवर्तेत ।

राजा—शोणोत्तरे उपवेष्टुमिच्छामि ।

प्रति०—देव इदं सिंहासनम् । उपविशतु देवः । (देव एदं सिंहासणं । उवविसद देवो ।)

राजा—(नोत्थेनोपविश्य ।) आर्य वैहीनरे आर्यचाणक्यं द्रष्टुमिच्छामि ।

कञ्चु०—यदाज्ञापयति देवः । (इति निष्क्रान्तः ।)

(ततः प्रविशति आसनस्थः स्वभवनगतः
कोपानुविद्धां चिन्तां नाटयंश्चाणक्यः ।)

चाण०—कथं स्पर्द्धते मया सह दुरात्मा राक्षसः ।

कृतागाः कौटिल्यो भुजग इव निर्याय नगरा-
द्यथा नन्दान्हत्वा नृपतिमकरोन्मौर्यवृषलम् ।

महात्मत्वात्संग्राह्यः । स्वशत्रुपक्षमाश्रित इति रोषावेशाद्दुरात्मेति गालनम् ।

कृतागा इति । नन्दैः कृतमागोऽग्रासनाकर्षणरूपं यस्य सः । अत्र दृष्टान्तानुरोधेन तथाहं मौर्यं हत्वा मलयकेतुं राज्ये स्थापयिष्यामीत्येतावति वक्तव्ये श्रियमपहरामीत्येतावन्मात्रं राक्षससाहसं अनुवदतश्चाणक्यस्यायं भावः । ममेव नास्य बुद्धिबलं परन्तु मत्सरमात्रेण अशक्तोहं गृहारम्भे शक्तोहं

---

१ देव इत्यधिकम्. २ आर्य स्फुटमभिधीयताम् इति पाठः. ३ परमस्माभिर्देवो विज्ञापयितुं शक्यते. ४ उल्लङ्घयिष्यति. ५ अस्मात्प्राक्–सक्रोधमित्यधिकम्. ६ आत्मगतम् इत्यधिकम्.

तथाहं मौर्येन्दोः श्रियमपहरामीति कृतधीः
प्रकर्षं मद्बुद्धेरतिशयितुमेष व्यवसितः ॥ ११ ॥

(आकाशे लक्ष्यं बद्ध्वा ।) राक्षस राक्षस वि म्यतामस्माद्दुर्व्यसनात् ।

उत्सिक्तः कुसचिवदृष्टराज्यभारो
नन्दोसौ न भवति चन्द्रगुप्त एषः ।
चाणक्यस्त्वमपि च नैव केवलं ते
साधर्म्यं मदनुकृतेः प्रधानवैरम् ॥ १२ ॥

(विचिन्त्य ।) अथ वा नातिमात्रमत्र वस्तुनि मया मनः खेदयितव्यम् कुतः ।

मद्भृत्यैः किल सोपि पर्वतसुतो व्याप्तः प्रविष्टान्तरै-
रुद्युक्ताः स्वनियोगसाधनविधौ सिद्धार्थकाद्याः स्पशाः ।
कृत्वा संप्रति कैतवेन कलहं मौर्येन्दुना राक्षसं
भेत्स्यामि स्वमतेन भेदकुशलं ह्येष प्रतीपं द्विषः ॥ १३ ॥

गृहभञ्जन इति न्यायेन मौर्यापकारमात्राय प्रयतमानः सन्केवलं पौरुषबलमवष्टभ्य मद्बुद्धेः प्रकर्षमतिशयितुं व्यवसित इति अहो राक्षसस्य दुर्व्यवसितमिति । वक्ष्यति च केवलं प्रधानवैरं मदनुकृतेः साधर्म्यमिति ॥ ११ ॥

[दुर्व्यसनाद्दुःसाध्येऽर्थेभिनिवेशात् ।]

उत्सिक्त इति । उद्रिक्त इत्यर्थः । प्रधानवैरं परिवृढद्वेषः केवलं ते तव मदनुकृतेः मदनुकरणस्य संबन्धि मत्स्पर्धाविषयकमिति यावत् । साधर्म्यं समानो धर्मः स्वार्थे ष्यञ् बहुव्रीहेर्भावे वा । न तु बुद्धिप्रकर्षादिः मत्सादृश्ये तव समानो धर्मोस्ति । अनेन यथा नन्दा उन्मूलितास्तथाहमपि मौर्यमुन्मूलयामीति प्रधानवैरमात्रेण मया सह स्पर्धते न तु बुद्धिप्रकर्षेणेति भावः । मदनुकृताविति विषयसप्तम्यन्तः पाठः साधुः ॥ १२ ॥

मद्भृत्यैरिति । प्रविष्टान्तरैर्वशीकृतशत्रुहृदयैर्भागुरायणादिभिः । स्पशा गूढप्रणिधयः । 'अपसर्पश्चरः स्पशः' इत्यमरः । सिद्धार्थकादयो भेदकर्मणि उद्युक्ता एव वर्तन्ते । अहमपि संप्रति चन्द्रगुप्तेन सह कृतककलहं कृत्वा तेनोपायेन प्रतीपमस्मासु प्रतिकूलचारिणं राक्षसं द्विषः सपत्नान्मलयकेतोः सकाशात् भेत्स्यामि तयोर्विरोधं संपादयिष्यमीत्यर्थः । यद्वा प्रतीपमिति विधेयं विशेषणं

---

१ हत २ प्रभावम् ३ प्रत्यक्षवदा० ४ व्यवसितात्. ५ तन्त्रः ६ च. ७ कुशलस्त्वेष.

(प्रविश्य ।) **कञ्चुकी**—कष्टं खलु सेवा ।

भेतव्यं नृपतेस्ततः सचिवतो राज्ञस्ततो वल्लभा-
दन्येभ्यश्च वसन्ति यस्य भवने लब्धप्रसादा विटाः ।
दैन्यादुन्मुखदर्शनोपलपनैः पिण्डार्थमायस्यतः
सेवां लाघवकारिणीं कृतधियः स्थाने श्ववृत्तिं विदुः ॥ १४ ॥

(प्रक्रम्यावलोक्य च ।) इदमार्यचाणक्यगृहम् । यावत्प्रविशामि । (प्रविश्यावलोक्य च ।) अहो राजाधिराजमन्त्रिणो विभूतिः । तथाहि ।

उपलशकलमेतद्भेदकं गोमयानां
वटुभि रुपहृतानां बर्हिषां स्तूपमेतत् ।
शरणमपि समिद्भिः शुष्यमाणाभिराभि-
र्विनमितपटलान्तं दृश्यते जीर्णकुड्यम् ॥ १५ ॥

द्विष इति षष्ठी । राक्षसं द्विषः प्रतीपं सन्तं भेत्स्यामि प्रतिकूलत्वेनापाद्य विघटयिष्यामीत्यर्थः । एष राक्षसः स्वमतेन स्वसंमत्या भेदकुशलोऽस्तु चन्द्रगुप्ताच्चाणक्यं भेत्स्यामीति स्वस्मिन्कुशलं मन्योऽस्तु न त्वस्य ममेव सामग्रीपौष्कल्यं बुद्धिबलं चास्तीति भावः । इयं नियताप्तिः । अपायाभावतः कार्यनिश्चयो नियताप्तिकेति लक्षणात् ॥ १३ ॥

कष्टमिति । सामान्ये नपुंसकम् ।

भेतव्यमिति । दैन्याद्धेतोः उन्मुखदर्शनानि च अपलपनानि च राजरहस्यगोपनानि च तैः पिण्डार्थमुदरभरणार्थमायस्यतः क्लिश्यमानस्य सेवकजनस्य सेवामित्यन्वयः । [कृतधियः शिक्षितमतयः पण्डिता इत्यर्थः ।] श्वविषये अपलपनं ताडनभयेन गात्रसङ्कोचनम् । सिषाधयिषितकार्यानुरोधादिदमाहितम् । चाणक्यमौर्ययोः कपटवैमत्यं तथ्यत्वेनैव गृह्णतः कञ्चुकिनोयं निर्वेदः ॥ १४ ॥

उपलशकलमेतदिति । त्रेताग्निसंभरणसामिन्धनाद्यर्थं शुष्कगोमयगोलकचूर्णनार्थमुपलशकलम् । उपलोपि सकलो न संगृहीत इति विभूतिनैरपेक्ष्यमस्योपलशकलजीर्णकुड्यादिभिरुक्तम् । बर्हिषां दर्भाणां स्तूपं निधननामकमुष्टिसमूहः । शरणं गृहं समिद्भारेण विनमितपटलान्तमतिजीर्णत्वाद्विभुग्नतृणमयछदिप्रान्तं । 'वलीकनीध्रे पटलप्रान्तेथ पटलं छदिः' इत्यमरः । अनेनास्याप्रतिग्रहत्वकर्मठत्वादयः

---

१ कष्टा. २ ०नेन नटनैः. ३ स्तोमः.

तत्स्थाने खल्वस्य वृषलो देवश्चन्द्रगुप्तः। कुतः।

स्तुवन्ति श्रान्तास्याः क्षितिपतिमभूतैरपि गुणैः
प्रवाचः कार्पण्याद्यदवितथवाचोपि पुरुषाः।
प्रभावस्तृष्णायाः स खलु सकलः स्यादितरथा
निरीहाणामीशस्तृणमिव तिरस्कारविषयः॥ १६॥

(विलोक्य सभयम्) अये तदयमार्यचाणक्यास्तिष्ठति।

यो नन्दमौर्यनृपयोः परिभूय लोक-
मस्तोदयौ प्रतिदिशन्नविभिन्नकालम्।
पर्यायपातितहिमोष्णमसर्वगामि
धाम्नातिशाययति धाम सहस्रधाम्नः॥ १७॥

श्रोत्रियगुणा उक्ताः। तथोक्तं पुरस्तात्। वंशे विशालवंशानामृषीणामिव भूयसाम्। अप्रतिग्राहकाणां यो बभूव भुवि विश्रुतः॥ इति॥ १५॥

वृषलोत्र इति। वृषलशब्देन वदितुमर्हः। सुपि क्यप् चेति क्यप् प्रत्ययः। निस्पृहत्वाद्राजानमपि तृणीकृत्य भृत्यवद्व्यपदिशतीत्यर्थः।

तदेव विवृणोति। स्तुवन्तीति। अवितथवाचः सत्यवचनशीला अपि कार्पण्यात्प्रवाचः उद्दण्डवचनाः सन्तः [श्रान्तास्याः आस्यश्रान्ति यावदित्यर्थः। क्षितिपतिं] अभूतैरसत्यैर्गुणैः स्तुवन्तीति यत्स खलु तृष्णायाः प्रभाव इति योजना॥ १६॥

अये तदयमिति। तदयमिति कर्मधारयसमासः सोयमित्यर्थः।

यो नन्देति। लोकं नन्दामात्यादिकं परिभूय स्वमन्त्रशक्त्या मोहयित्वा नन्दमौर्ययोरभिन्नकालं युगपदस्तोदयौ दत्तवान्। अत एव सर्वशत्रुव्यापिना स्वेन धाम्ना असर्वगामि पर्यायेण कालक्रमेण पातितं नाशितं हिममुष्णं वा येन तत्सहस्रधाम्नः सूर्यस्य धाम तेजः अतिशाययति अतिक्रामयति। धामातिशेते तेन धाम्ना स्वयं अतिशाययति। सोयमार्यश्चाणक्यस्तिष्ठतीति पूर्वेणान्वयः। अतिपूर्वकाच्छीङो हेतुमण्णिच्। अत्र लोकशब्देन लोकालोकपर्वतो लक्ष्यते। असर्वगामीत्यनेन सूर्यतेजसस्तदनतिक्रमणमुक्तम्। एवं च लोकं परिभूयातिक्रम्य नन्दमौर्ययोर्युगपदस्तोदयौ दिशच्चाणक्यतेजः लोकमनतिक्रामतोत एवासर्वगामिनः क्रमेण हिमोष्णयोरुदयास्तमयौ दिशतः सूर्यतेजसोप्यतिशायितमिति व्यतिरेकालङ्कारः लोकमिति श्लेषानुप्राणितः॥ १७॥

---

१ वृषलोत्र. २ स्तुवन्तः. ३ कृतिनः. ४ स्वगतम्. ५ दयावदिशदप्रति. ६ ०ष्णिम.

(जानुभ्यां भूमौ निपत्य ।) जयत्वार्यः ।

चाण०—वैहीनरे किमागमनप्रयोजनम् ।

कञ्चु०—आर्य प्रणतिससंभ्रमोच्चलितभूमिपालमौलिमालामाणिक्यशकलशिखापिशङ्गीकृतपादपद्मयुगलः सुगृहीतनामधेयो देवश्चन्द्रगुप्त आर्यं शिरसा प्रणम्य विज्ञापयति । अकृतक्रियान्तरायमार्यं द्रष्टुमिच्छामीति ।

चाण०—वृषलो मां द्रष्टुमिच्छति । वैहीनरे न खलु वृषलस्य श्रवणपथं गतोयं मत्कृतः कौमुदीमहोत्सवप्रतिषेधः ।

कञ्चु०—आर्य अथ किम् ।

चाण०—(सक्रोधम् ।) आः केन कथितम् ।

कञ्चु०—(सभयम् ।) प्रसीदत्वार्यः । स्वयमेव सुगाङ्गप्रासादगतेन देवेनावलोकितमप्रवृत्तकौमुदीमहोत्सवं पुरम् ।

चाण०—आः ज्ञातम् । ततो भवद्भिरन्तरा प्रोत्साह्य कोपितो वृषलः । किमन्यत् ।

कञ्चु०—(भयं नाटयंस्तूष्णीमधोमुखस्तिष्ठति ।)

चाण०—अहो राजपरिजनस्य चाणक्यस्योपरि प्रद्वेषपक्षपातः । अथ क्व वृषलः ।

कञ्चु०—(भयं नाटयन् ।) आर्य सुगाङ्गगतेन देवेनाहमार्यपादमूलं प्रेषितः ।

चाण०—(उत्थाय ।) सुगाङ्गमार्गमादेशय ।

कञ्चु०—इत इत आर्यः । (उभौ परिक्रामतः ।)

कञ्चु०—एष सुगाङ्गप्रासादः । शनैरारोहत्वार्यः ।

चाण०—(नाट्येनावरुह्यावलोक्य च ।) अये सिंहासनमध्यास्ते वृषलः । साधु साधु ।

[प्रणतीति । प्रणतौ प्रणामक्रियायां यः संभ्रमस्त्वरा तेनोच्चलिता ये भूमिपालास्तेषां मौलिमालासु यानि माणिक्यशकलानि तेषां शिखाभिर्दीप्तिभिः पिशङ्गीकृतं पादपद्मयोर्युगलं यस्य । अन्तरायो विघ्नः । अन्तरा मध्ये ।]

---

१ पादपद्मयोरार्यं प्रणिपत्य. २ क्रियन्तारान्तरायमन्तरेण. ३ भयं नाटयन्. ४ सुगाङ्गप्रसाद. ५ आरोढुमर्हत्यार्यः.

नन्दैर्वियुक्तमनपेक्षितराजराजै-
रध्यासितं च वृषलेन वृषेण राज्ञाम्।
सिंहासनं सदृशपार्थिवसङ्गतं च
प्रीतिं परां प्रगुणयन्ति गुणा ममैते ॥ १८॥

(उपसृत्य ।) विजयतां वृषलः ।

राजा—(आसनादुत्थाय ।) आर्य चन्द्रगुप्तः प्रणमति । (इति पादयोः पतति ।)

चाण०—(पाणौ गृहीत्वा ।) उत्तिष्ठोत्तिष्ठ वत्स ।

आ शैलेन्द्राच्छिलान्तस्खलितसुरनदीशीकरासारशीता-
त्तीरान्तान्नैकरागस्फुरितमणिरुचो दक्षिणस्यार्णवस्य ।
आगत्यागत्य भीतिप्रणतनृपशतैः शश्वदेव क्रियन्तां
चूडारत्नांशुगर्भास्तव चरणयुगस्याङ्गुलीरन्ध्रभागाः ॥ १९ ॥

राजा—आर्यप्रसादादनुभूयत एव सर्वम् । तदुपविशत्वार्यः । (उभौ यथोचितमुपविष्टौ ।)

चाण०—वृषल किमर्थं वयमाहूताः ।

राजा—आर्यस्य दर्शनेनात्मानमनुग्राहयितुम् ।

चाण०—(सस्मितम् ।) अलमनेन प्रश्रयेण । न निष्प्रयोजनमधिकारवन्तः प्रभुभिराहूयन्ते ।

नन्दैर्वियुक्तमिति । अनपेक्षितराजराजैस्तृणीकृतकुबेरैः । [यद्वा तिरस्कृतप्रधाननृपैः ।] राज्ञां वृषेण श्रेष्ठेन कुबेरवदतिधनाढ्यानपि नन्दान्हत्वा तत्पदे यः कश्चिदयोग्यो न स्थापितः किंतु नन्देभ्योप्यतिशयितो धीरोदात्तत्वादिमहाराजगुणोत्तरश्चन्द्रगुप्तोभिषेचितः । अतः सिंहासनं योग्यपार्थिवसङ्गतं जातमिति शेषः । इति स्वस्योचितकारित्वादिगुणैः स्वयंमन्तस्तुष्यति । प्रीतिं परां प्रगुणयन्ति गुणा ममैत इति । एतेन नन्दोद्धारणादिसाधका मम गुणा ममं प्रीतिं प्रगुणयन्ति वर्धयन्ति ॥१८॥

आ शैलेन्द्रादिति । [शिलान्तः प्रस्तरान्तरेषु स्खलिता या सुरनदी गङ्गा तस्याः सीकरासारेणाम्बुकणवर्षेण शीतात् । नैके अनेके रागा यत्र तद्यथा तथा मकरागं ता नेकरागा इति वा । स्फुरिता मणिरुचो रत्नतेजांसि यस्मिन् तस्मात् तीराचागत्यागत्य] शिलान्तस्खलितेत्यादिविशेषणात् शैलेन्द्रो हिमवान्गम्यते । आ हिमाचलादासेतोश्च समागत्य सर्वे नृपतयः त्वां प्रणमन्त्वित्याशीः ॥ १९ ॥

१ ०वृत्तेः. २ भृशम्. ३ सिंहासनात्. ४ धुनी ५ युष्मत्प्र०. ६ सर्वमेतन्नाशास्यते. ७ स्मितं कृत्वा. ८ तत्प्रयोजनमभिधीयताम् इत्यधिकम्.

राजा—आर्य कौमुदीमहोत्सवप्रतिषेधस्य किं फलमार्यः पश्यति ।

चाण०—(स्मितं कृत्वा ।) उपालब्धुं तर्हि वयमाहूताः ।

राजा—शान्तं पापं शान्तं पापम् । न हि न हि । विज्ञापयितुम् ।

चाण०—यद्येवं तर्हि विज्ञापनीयानामवश्यं शिष्येण स्वैररुचयो न निरोद्धव्याः ।

राजा—एवमेतत्कः सन्देहः । किं तु न कदाचिदार्यस्य निष्प्रयोजना [2]प्रवृत्तिरित्यस्ति नः प्रश्नावकाशः ।

चाण०—वृषल सम्यग्गृहीतवानसि[3] न प्रयोजनमन्तरा चाणक्यः स्वप्नेपि चेष्टत इति ।

राजा—आर्य अत एव शुश्रूषा मां मुखरयति ।

चाण०—वृषल श्रूयताम् । इह खल्वर्थशास्त्रकारास्त्रिविधां सिद्धिमुपवर्णयन्ति [6]राजायत्तां सचिवायत्तामुभयायत्तां चेति । ततः सचिवायत्तसिद्धेस्तव किं प्रयोजनान्वेषणेन । यतो वयमेवात्र नियुक्ता वर्त्स्यामः ।

राजा—(संकोपं मुखं परावर्तयति ।)

(नेपथ्ये वैतालिकौ पठतः ।)

स्मितमिति । इत्यादिदोषप्रख्यापनमपवादः । चाणक्येन स्वोपालम्भस्य दोषस्य प्रख्यापनात् ।

स्वैररुचय इति । स्वैररुचयः [न निरोद्धव्या न व्याहन्तव्याः ।] स्वतन्त्रा गुरवो न निर्बन्धनीया भृत्यवन्नानुयोज्या इति ।

वर्त्स्याम इति । वृतुधातोर्भविष्यति लृटि उत्तमपुरुषबहुवचनम् । न वृद्भ्यश्चतुर्भ्यं इतीण्निषेधः । वृद्भ्यः स्यसनोरिति परस्मैपदम् । तत्तत्कार्यानुगुण्येन वर्तिष्यामह इत्यर्थः ॥

---

१ रुचयः स्वतन्त्राः ; रुचयोनुरोद्धव्याः. २ रुचिः प्रवर्तिष्यत इति. ३ मदाशयामित्यधिकम्. ४ अनवेक्षमाणः. ५ प्रयोजनशु०. ६ अस्मात्प्राक्—तद्यथा. ७ अभियुक्ताः. ८ वेत्स्यामः. ९ सकोप इव.

एकः—

आकाशं काशपुष्पच्छविमभिभवता भस्मना शुक्लयन्ती
शीतांशोरंशुजालैर्जलधरमलिनां क्लिश्नती कृत्तिमैभीम् ।
कापालीमुद्वहन्ती स्रजमिव धवलां कौमुदीमित्यपूर्वा
हास्यश्रीराजहंसा हरतु तनुरिव क्लेशमैशी शरद्वः ॥ २० ॥

अपि च ।

प्रत्यग्रोन्मेषजिह्मा क्षणमनभिमुखी रत्नदीपप्रभाणा-
मात्मव्यापारगुर्वी जनितजललवा जृम्भितैः साङ्गभङ्गैः ।
नागाङ्कं मोक्तुमिच्छोः शयनमुरु फणाचक्रवालोपधानं
निद्राच्छेदाभिताम्रा चिरमवतु हरेर्दृष्टिराकेकरा वः ॥ २१ ॥

आकाशमिति । अपूर्वा कापि लोकोत्तरगुणाभिरामा ऐशी तनुरिव शरद् वः क्लेशं मलयकेतुराक्षसाभियोगजनितं क्लेशं हरतु । कीदृशी ईशतनुः काशपुष्पच्छविमभिभवता तच्छविसदृशेन भस्मना आकाशं शुक्लं कुर्वती शीतांशोश्चूडायां वर्तमानस्यांशुजालैर्जलधरमलिनां जलधरसदृशीं ऐभीं गजासुरसंबन्धिनीं कृत्तीं क्लिश्नती क्लिष्टां कुर्वती तन्नैल्यमभिभवन्तीत्यर्थः । कौमुदीमिव धवलां कापालीं स्रजमुद्वहन्ती शरद्विषये भस्मधवलया काशपुष्पच्छव्याकाशं शुक्लयन्तीत्यादि योज्यम् । हास्यश्रीरिव राजहंस्यो यस्यां शरदि राजहंसीव हास्यश्रीर्यस्यां तनावित्युभयत्र विग्रहः । उपमालङ्कारः ॥ २० ॥

प्रत्यग्रोन्मेष इति । शरदि क्षीरनिधौ शेषशयनादुत्थितस्य हरेराकेकरदृष्टिप्रतिपादकानि प्रत्यग्रेत्यादिविशेषणानि । [तदुक्तं-शेते विष्णुः सदाषाढे कार्तिके च विबुध्यते ।] प्रत्यग्रेण निद्राच्छेदानन्तरोदितेनोन्मेषणेनोन्मीलनेन जिह्मा कूणितप्रान्ता । [क्षणं रत्नानि शेषफणामणय एव दीपास्तेषां प्रभाणामि० । आत्मव्यापारे स्वविषयग्रहणरूपे गुर्वी अलसा । अङ्गभङ्गसहितैः जृम्भितैर्मुखविदारणव्यापारैरुत्पन्नाश्रुकणा । 'आकुञ्चितपुटापाङ्गा सङ्गतार्धनिमेषिणी । मुहुर्व्यावृत्ततारा च दृष्टिराकेकरामता ।' इति भरतः ।] स्पष्टमन्यत् । नागाङ्कं शेषपर्यङ्करूपम् । अत्र स्वभावोक्तिरलङ्कारः ॥ २१ ॥

आकाशमिति प्रत्यग्रोन्मेष इति चन्द्रगुप्तवैतालिकेन पठितम् । उत्तरपद्यद्वयं सत्त्वोत्कर्षस्येति भूषणाद्युपभोगेनेति च राक्षसगूढप्रणिधिना वैतालिकवेषधारिणा स्तनकलशनाम्ना चन्द्रगुप्ततेजःसमुत्तेजनार्थं पठितमिति ज्ञेयम् ।

---

१ प्रथमः. २ क्लिन्दतीम्. ३ नागाङ्कम्.

द्वितीयः—

सत्त्वोत्कर्षस्य धाम्रा निधय इव कृताः केपि कस्यापि हेतो-
र्जेतारः स्वेन धाम्रा मदसलिलमुचां नागयूथेश्वराणाम् ।
दंष्ट्राभङ्गं मृगाणामधिपतय इव व्यक्तमानावलेपा
नाज्ञाभङ्गं सहन्ते नृवर नृपतयस्त्वादृशाः सार्वभौमाः ॥ २२ ॥

अपि च ।

भूषणाद्युपभोगेन प्रभुर्भवति न प्रभुः
परैरपरिभूताज्ञस्त्वमिव प्रभुरुच्यते ॥ २३ ॥

चाण०—(आकर्ण्य स्वगतम् ।) प्रथमं तावद्विशिष्टदेवतास्तुतिरूपेण प्रवृत्तशरद्गुणप्रख्यापनमाशीर्वचनम् । इदमपरं किमिति नावधारयामि । (विचिन्त्य ।) आः ज्ञातम् । राक्षसस्यायं प्रयोगः । दुरात्मन् राक्षस दृश्यसे भोः जागर्ति खलु कौटिल्यः ।

राजा—आर्य वैहीनरे आभ्यां वैतालिकाभ्यां सुवर्णशतसहस्रं दापय ।

कञ्चु०—यदाज्ञापयति देवः । (इति उत्थाय परिक्रामति ।)

चाण०—(सक्रोधम् ।) वैहीनरे तिष्ठ न गतव्यम् । वृषल किमय-मस्थाने महानर्थोत्सर्गः ।

राजा—(सकोपम् ।) आर्येणैवं सर्वत्र निरुद्धचेष्टाप्रसरस्य मे बन्धन-मिव राज्यं न राज्यमिव ।

चाण०—वृषल स्वयमनभियुक्तानां राज्ञामेते दोषाः संभवन्ति । तद्यदि न सहसे ततः स्वयमभियुज्यस्व ।

सत्त्वोत्कर्षेति । सत्त्वोत्कर्षस्य बलातिशयस्य केपि लोकोत्तरमहिमानः कस्यापि हेतोः विपक्षक्षपणायेत्यर्थः । [यद्वा कस्यापि हेतोः केनापि हेतुना कृतमाज्ञाभङ्गं न सहन्त इति योजना ।] व्यक्तौ प्रसिद्धौ मानावलेपौ येषां ते ॥ २२ ॥

सक्रोधमित्यादि । एतदादि राजचाणक्ययो रोषसंभाषणं संफेटः । वृषले-त्यादि । स्वयमनभियुक्तानां [राज्यतन्त्रे अदत्तावधानानां] स्वातन्त्र्यमल-भमानानामेते दोषा गुरुजनगौरवासहनरूपाः संभवन्ति । स्वस्वातन्त्र्यलिप्सया गुरुजनस्वातन्त्र्यं न सहन्त इति भावः । स्वयमभियुज्यस्व स्वातन्त्र्यमवलम्बस्व । [राज्यतन्त्राधिकारं प्रतिपद्यस्वेत्यर्थः ।]

---

१ उपचारेण. २ राक्षसहतक. ३ अर्थव्ययः ; ०त्सर्गः क्रियते.

राजा—एते स्वकर्मण्यभियुज्यामहे ।

चाण०—प्रियं नः । वयमपि स्वकर्मण्यभियुज्यामहे ।

राजा—यद्येवं तर्हि कौमुदीमहोत्सवप्रतिषेधस्य तावत्प्रयोजनं श्रोतुमिच्छामि ।

चाण०—वृषल कौमुदीमहोत्सवानुष्ठानस्य किं प्रयोजनमित्यहमपि श्रोतुमिच्छामि ।

राजा—प्रथमं तावन्ममाज्ञाऽव्याघातः

चाण०—वृषल ममापि तवाज्ञाव्याघात एव कौमुदीमहोत्सवप्रतिषेधस्य प्रथमं प्रयोजनम् । कुतः ।

अम्भोधीनां तमालप्रभवकिसलयश्यामवेलावनाना-
मा पारेभ्यश्चतुर्णां चटुलतिमिकुलक्षोभितान्तर्जलानाम् ।
मालेवाम्लानपुष्पा तव नृपतिशतैरुह्यते या शिरोभिः
सा मय्येव स्खलन्ती कथयति विनयालंकृतं ते प्रभुत्वम् ॥ २४ ॥

अथ त्वमपरमपि प्रयोजनं श्रोतुमिच्छसि तदपि कथयामि ।

राजा—कथ्यताम् ।

चाण०—शोणोत्तरे मद्वचनात्कायस्थमचलं ब्रूहि यत्तद्भद्रभटप्रभृतीनां [इतोपरागादपक्रम्य मलयकेतुमाश्रितानां] लेख्यपत्रं दीयतामिति ।

एते स्वकर्मणीति । इदं गुरोरवमाननं छलम् । वयमपि स्वकर्मण्यभियुज्यामह इति । स्वकर्मण्यग्निहोत्रादाविति बहिरर्थः । अनेन कपटकलहेन राक्षसवशीकरणकर्मणि व्याप्रियामह इति गूढम् । प्रथममिति । ममाज्ञायाव्याघातजनितो मनस्ताप एव प्रथमफलत्वेन पर्यवसित इति सोल्लुण्ठनं वचनम् ।

इदमेव मुख्यप्रयोजनत्वेन श्लाघ्यतया त्वयानुमन्तव्यमिति समाधत्ते अम्भोधीनामिति । चटुलतिमिकुलेति अम्भोधीनां दुस्तरत्वमुक्तम् । पारेभ्यः परतीरेभ्यः आ पारान्प्राप्नुवद्भिः पारङ्गतैरित्यर्थः । अभिविधावाङ् । नृपतिशतैर्या तवाज्ञा शिरोभिरुह्यते वक्ष्यते । वर्तमानसामीप्ये वर्तमानवत् । मदाशिषा मन्नीतिबलेन चाम्भोधिपारगानपि द्वीपाधिपानाज्ञाविधेयान्करिष्यसीत्यर्थः । सा मय्येव स्खलति चेत्तव विनयातिशयः प्रभुत्वस्यालंकरणायैवेति भावः । इत्यादि चाणक्यवचनजातं गुरुकीर्तनं प्रसङ्गः । गुरोः कीर्तनं गुरु बहु वा कीर्तनमित्यन्वर्थात् ॥ २४ ॥

---

१ कल्याणम्. २ नत. ३ प्रथ०. ४ अविहतोस्मि इत्यादि०. ५ तत्तावद्दीय०.

प्रती०—यदार्य आज्ञापयति । (इति निष्क्रम्य पुनः प्रविश्य ।) आर्य इदं पत्रकम् । (जं अज्जो आणवेदि । अज्ज इमं पत्तअम् ।)

चाण०—(गृहीत्वा ।) वृषल श्रूयताम्[1] ।

राजा—दत्तावधानोस्मि ।

चाण०—(वाचयति ।) स्वस्ति सुगृहीतनामधेयस्य देवस्य चन्द्रगुप्तस्य सहोत्थायिनां प्रधानपुरुषाणामितोपक्रम्य वध्यमलयकेतुमाश्रितानां प्रमाणलेख्यपत्रमिदम् । तत्र प्रथमं तावद्गजाध्यक्षो भद्रभटः अश्वाध्यक्षः पुरुषदत्तः महाप्रतीहारस्य चन्द्रभानोर्भागिनेयो डिङ्गरातः देवस्य स्वजनसंबन्धी महाराजो बलगुप्तः देवस्यैव कुमारसेवको राजसेनः सेनापतेः सिंहबलस्य[2] कनीयान्भ्राता भागुरायणो मालवराजपुत्रो लोहिताक्षः क्षत्रगणमुख्यो विजयवर्मेति[3] ।

राजा—अथैतेषामपरागहेतून्विज्ञातुमिच्छामि[4] ।

चाण०—वृषल श्रूयताम् । अत्र यावेतौ गजाध्यक्षाश्वाध्यक्षौ भद्रभटपुरुषदत्तनामानौ तौ खलु स्त्रीमद्यमृगयाशीलौ हस्त्यश्वावेक्षणेनभियुक्तौ[5] मयाधिकाराभ्यामवरोप्य स्वजीवनमात्रेणैव स्थापिताविति परपक्षे स्वेन स्वेनाधिकारेण गत्वा मलयकेतुमाश्रितौ । यावेतौ डिङ्गरातबलगुप्तौ तावप्यत्यन्तलोभाभिभूतौ[6] त्वद्दत्तं जीवनमबहु मन्यमानौ तत्र बहु लभ्यत इत्यपक्रम्य मलयकेतुमाश्रितौ । योप्यसौ भवतः कुमारसेवको राजसेन इति सोपि तव प्रसादादतिप्रभूतकोशहस्त्यश्वं सहसैव तन्महदैश्वर्यमवाप्य पुनरुच्छेदशङ्कयापक्रम्य मलयकेतुमाश्रितः । योयमपरः सेनापतेः सिंहबलस्य

श्रूयतामिति । रहस्यत्वाद् दृश्यतां न तु स्फुटं वाच्यतामित्यर्थः ।

कुमारसेवक इति । देवं कौमारमारभ्य सेवत इति कुमारसेवकः ।

सादरमात्मगतं वाचयित्वा बहिर्लोकान्प्रत्यवहेलयति । **एतावदिति** । इतोपरागादपक्रम्य विपक्षमाश्रितानां किमनेन पत्रदर्शनेनेति भावः । [स्वजीवनं वृत्तिस्तदेव जीवनमात्रं तेन । अति प्रभूताः कोशः हस्तिनोश्वाश्च यस्मिन् ।]

---

१ दृश्यतामिदम्. **राजा**–आत्मगतं वाचयति. २ सिंहपालस्य. सिंहबलदत्तस्य ३ एते वयं देवस्य कार्ये अवहिताः स्म इति । (प्रकाशम्) आर्य एतावदेतत्पत्रकम् इत्यधिकम्. ४ श्रोतुम्. ५ इन्यपरक्तौ. ६ लुब्धप्रकृती, अतिलोभाभिभूतत्वात्.

कनीयान्भ्राता भागुरायणोऽसावपि तत्र काले पर्वतकेन सह समुत्पन्नसौहार्दस्तत्प्रीत्या च पिता ते चाणक्येन व्यापादित[1] इत्युत्पाद्य रहसि त्रासयित्वा मलयकेतुमपवाहितवान् । ततो भवदपथ्यकारिषु चन्दनदासादिषु[2] निगृहीतेषु स्वदोषाशङ्कयापक्रम्य मलयकेतुमाश्रितः । तेनाप्यसौ मम[3] प्राणरक्षक इति कृतज्ञतामनुवर्तमानेनात्मनोनन्तरममात्यपदं ग्राहितः । यौ तौ लोहिताक्षविजयवर्माणौ तावप्यतिमानित्वात्स्वदायादेभ्यस्त्वया[4] दीयमानं मानमसहमानौ मलयकेतुमाश्रितौ । इत्येषामपरागहेतवः ।

राजा—एवमेतेषु[5] परिज्ञातापरागहेतुषु क्षिप्रमेव कस्मान्न प्रतिविहितमार्येण ।

चाण०—वृषल न पारितं प्रतिविधातुम्[6] ।

राजा—किमकौशलादुत प्रयोजनापेक्षया ।

चाण०—कथमकौशलं भविष्यति । प्रयोजनापेक्षयैव ।

राजा—प्रयोजनमिदानीं[7] श्रोतुमिच्छामि ।

चाण०—श्रूयतामवधार्यतां च इह[8] खलु विरक्तानां प्रकृतीनां द्विविधं प्रतिविधानमनुग्रहो निग्रहश्च । अनुग्रहस्तावदाक्षिप्ताधिकारयोर्भद्रभटपुरुषदत्तयोः पुनरधिकारारोपणमेव । अधिकारश्च तादृशेषु व्यसनयोगादनभियुक्तेषु[9] पुनरारोप्यमाणः सकलमेव राज्यस्य मूलं हस्त्यश्वमवादयेत् । डिङ्गरातबलगुप्तयोरतिलुब्धयोः[10] सकलराज्यप्रदानेनाप्यपरितुष्यतोरनुग्रहः कथं शक्यः[11] । राजसेनभागुरायणयोस्तु धनप्राणनाशभीतयोः[12] कुतोनुग्रहस्यावकाशः ।

इत्युत्पाद्येति । तथ्यमपि तन्मिथ्यात्वेन लोकप्रत्ययनार्थं उत्पाद्येत्युक्तिः । [आत्मनोनन्तरं स्वामिपदानन्तरवर्ति ।] कथमकौशलमित्यादि वचनं विरोधशमनं शक्तिः । किमकौशलादिति कार्याविरोधे पृष्टे तस्य विरोधस्य शमनात् ।

[आक्षिप्त आच्छिन्नोधिकारो ययोः । व्यसनयोगात्स्त्रीमद्याद्यासक्ततया स्वकर्म-

---

१ घातितः. २ दासप्रभृतिषु. ३ ममानेन प्राणाः परिरक्षिता इति. ४ पैतृकं च परिचयमित्यधिकम्. ५ अस्मात्प्राक्-आर्य. ६ अप्रतिविधानप्रयोजनम्. ७ अस्मात्प्राक्-**राजा**—उभयमपि क्रियते । कथ्यताम् । चाण०-वृषल-इत्यधिकम्. ८ तद्यथानुग्रहो. ९ दोष. १० लुब्धप्रकृत्योः. ११ कर्तुं शक्यते. १२ प्राणनाश.

लोहिताक्षविजयवर्मणोरपि दायादमानमसहमानयोरतिमानिनोः कीदृशोनुग्रहः[1] प्रीतिं जनयिष्यतीति परिहृतः पूर्वः पक्षः । उत्तरोपि खलु वयमचिरादधिगतनन्दैश्वर्याः सहोत्थायिनं प्रधानपुरुषवर्गमुग्रेण दण्डेन पीडयन्तो नन्दकुलानुरक्तानां प्रकृतीनामविश्वास्या एव भवाम इत्यतः परिहृत एव । तदेवमनुगृहीतास्मत्पक्षो राक्षसोपदेशप्रवणो महीयसा म्लेच्छबलेन परिवृतः पितृवधामर्षी[2] पर्वतकपुत्रो मलयकेतुरस्मानभियोक्तुमुद्यतः । सोयं व्यायामकालो नोत्सवकाल इति दुर्गसंस्कारे प्रारब्धव्ये किं कौमुदीमहोत्सवेनेति प्रतिषिद्धः ।

राजा—आर्य बहु प्रष्टव्यमत्र ।

चाण०—वृपल विश्रब्धं पृच्छ । ममापि बहाख्येयमत्र ।

राजा—सोप्यस्य[3] सर्वस्यानर्थस्य हेतुर्मलयकेतुः कस्मादपक्रामन्नुपेक्षितः ।

चाण०—वृपल अनुपेक्षणे[4] द्वयी गतिः । निगृह्येत वा प्रतिश्रुतं राज्यार्द्धं प्रतिपाद्येत वा । निग्रहे तावत्पर्वतकोस्माभिरेव व्यापादित इति कृतघ्नतायाः स्वहस्तो[5] दत्तः स्यात् । प्रतिश्रुतराज्यार्द्धप्रतिपादनेपि पर्वतकविनाशः[6] केवलं कृतघ्नतामात्रफलः स्यादिति मलयकेतुरपक्रामन्नुपेक्षितः ।

राजा—अत्र तावदेवम् । राक्षसः पुनरिहैव वर्तमान आर्येणोपेक्षित इत्यत्र किमुत्तरमार्यस्य ।

व्यनवहितेषु । परिहृतोशक्य इति निराकृतः । अनुगृहीतोऽस्माकं पक्षः अस्मत्पक्षीयवर्गो येन । उपदेशप्रवण उपदेशानुवर्ती । पितृवधामर्षी पितृवधजनितक्रोधः ।]

कृतघ्नतायाः स्वहस्त इति । कृतघ्नता दृढा [अस्माभिरेव दृढीकृता] स्यात् । तथा च राक्षसोपरि पातितं तदयशः परिहृतं स्यात् । तच्चानिष्टम् । राज्यार्द्धप्रदाने तव कृत्स्ननन्दराज्यलाभार्थमुपांशुकृतोपि पर्वतकवधो व्यर्थः स्यात् । कृतघ्नतामात्रं फलं यस्य तथोक्तः केवलं स्यात् । किं तया राक्षससाचिव्यलाभविकलया कृतघ्नतया फलम् । अतो मलयकेतूपेक्षणमेव वरम् । अनया प्रकृतया राजकार्यसंविधानप्रणाल्या राक्षसोपसंग्रहसाधकमित्याशयः । कृतघ्नतामात्रफलः स्यादिति । तव संपूर्णनन्दराज्यफलो न स्यादिति भावः ।

अत्र तावदेवमिति । अत्र मलयकेतूपेक्षणे तावदेवमुत्तरं भवतु । राक्षसोपेक्षणं

---

१ दायादमानप्रदानपीडितयोर्मानमप्यपमानं मन्यमानयोरत्यन्तमानिनोः. २ मर्षितः. ३ ०स्यैव. ४ मलयकेतोरपक्रमणानु०. ५ स्वयं हस्तः. ६ विनाशे कृतघ्नतामात्रपरिहारः स्यात्.

चाण०—राक्षसोपि स्वामिनि स्थिरानुरागित्वात्सुचिरमेकत्र वासाच्च शीलज्ञानां नन्दानुरक्तानां प्रकृतीनामत्यन्तविश्वास्यः प्रज्ञापुरुषकाराभ्यामुपेतः सहायसंपदाभियुक्तः कोशवानिहैवान्तर्नगरे वर्तमानः खलु महान्तमन्तःकोपमुत्पादयेत्। दूरीकृतस्तु बाह्यकोपमुत्पादयन्नपि कथमप्युपायैर्वशयितुं शक्य इत्ययमत्रस्थ एव हृदयेशयः शङ्कुरिवोद्धृत्य दूरीकृतः।

राजा—आर्य कस्माद्विक्रम्य न गृहीतः।

चाण०—राक्षसः खल्वसौ। विक्रम्य गृह्यमाणो युष्मद्बलानि बहूनि नाशयेत्स्वयं वा विनश्येत्। एवं सत्युभयथापि दोषः। पश्य।

स हि भृशमभियुक्तो यद्युपेयाद्विनाशं
ननु वृषल वियुक्तस्तादृशेनासि पुंसा।
अथ तव बलमुख्यान्घातयेत्सापि पीडा
वनगज इव तस्मात्सोभ्युपायैर्विनेय॥ २५॥

राजा—न शक्नुमो वयमार्यस्य वाचं वाचमतिशयितुम्। सर्वथा अमात्यराक्षस एवात्र प्रशस्यतरः।

चाण०—(सक्रोधम्।) न भवानिति वाक्यशेषः। मा तावत्। भो वृषल तेन किं कृतम्॥

तु सर्वथानुचितमिति राक्षसपक्षपातं दर्शयन्निवाह। अत्रेत्यादि। [शीलज्ञानां सच्चरितं जानतां। सहायसंपत्पुरुषबलम्। अन्तः प्रकोपमन्तर्वर्तिनां पुरोहितामात्यादीनां सेनापत्यादीनां चानुरक्तैर्भ्रंशनम्।]

[स इति। स राक्षसोत्यन्तं पीडितः सन्। हे वृषल तादृशेन तादृग्गुणवता कार्यधुरन्धरेण पुरुषेण वियुक्तोसि भविष्यसि। यदस्माकमनिष्टतमम्। अथेति पक्षान्तरे। तव प्रधानयोधान् घातयेत् सापि पीडास्माकं हानिकारिणीत्यर्थः॥ २५॥]

न शक्नुम इति। मया क्वचित्कार्यविरोधे पृष्टे मतिबलेन केवलं समाधत्से राक्षसोपेक्षणं तु सर्वथानुचितमिति भावः। न भवानिति। वाक्यशेषो मास्तु नाम। तस्मिन्को गुणो दृष्ट इति पृच्छति मा तावदिति।

---

१ वृषल, रा०. २ एवात्र ३ कोशबलवान् ४ बाह्यार्थं विकुर्वन्नपि ५ न दुःखसाध्यो भविष्यतीत्यतोपक्राममनुपेक्षितः। राजा—तत्किमर्थमिहस्थ एवोपायैर्नोपक्रान्तः॥ चाण०-अथ कथमपक्रान्तो भविष्यति। ननूपायैरेवासौ हृदयेशयः शङ्कुरिवोद्धृत्य दूरीकृतः। दूरीकरण्यस्य चोक्तं प्रयोजनम् ६ अस्मात्ताक्—वृषल ७ उपयुक्त. ८ नाशयन्. ९ नवगज. १० मतिम्.

राजा—यदि न ज्ञायते तदा श्रूयताम् । तेन खलु महात्मना ।

लब्धायां पुरि यावदिच्छमुषितं कृत्वा पदं नो गले
व्याघातो जयघोषणादिषु बलादस्मद्बलानां कृतः ।
अत्यर्थं विपुलैः स्वनीतिविभवैः संमोहमापादिता
विश्वास्येष्वपि विश्वसन्ति मतयो न स्वेषु वर्गेषु नः ॥ २६ ॥

चाण०—(विहस्य ।) एतत्कृतं राक्षसेन । वृषल मया पुनर्ज्ञातं नन्दमिव भवन्तमुद्धृत्य भवानिव भूतले मलयकेतू राजाधिराजपदे नियोजित इति ।

राजा—अन्येनैवेदमनुष्ठितं किमत्रार्यस्य ।

चाण०—हे मत्सरिन् ।

आरुह्यारूढकोपस्फुरणविषमिताग्राङ्गुलीमुक्तचूडां
लोकप्रत्यक्षमुग्रां सकलरिपुकुलोत्साददीर्घां प्रतिज्ञाम् ।

लब्धायामिति । अत्यायमर्थः । अस्माभिर्निरुद्धासारप्रसारतया बलवदुपनिरुद्धं पुरमसुरक्षं पश्यन्नभयमस्मत्तो याचमान इव पुरमस्मदधीनं कर्तुमस्मद्बलान्यन्तः प्रवेश्याभिलब्धायां वशीकृतायां पुर्यस्मदीयजयापादनघोषणाय प्रवृत्तान्यपि तानि बलानि बलाद्व्याहत्य निगृह्य बहिः स्थितान्बलवतोऽप्यस्मानगणयन्नस्मदुपांशुवधाय विषकन्यानियोजनकूटतोरणशयनगृहनिर्माणादिस्वकार्यसाधनपर्यन्तमन्तर्नगर एव कंचितत्कालं स्वच्छन्दमुषितवान् । अनन्तरमुपांशु सुरङ्गया सर्वार्थसिद्धिमपवाह्य स्वयमपि निर्गत्य बहिः सुहृद्बलमुत्थाप्य पुनरप्यस्मानभियोक्तुमुद्यतः । एवं स्वनीतिविभवैरनेन संमोहिता अस्मन्मतयो विश्वास्येष्वपि जीवसिद्धिभागुरायणप्रभृतिषु स्वेषु वर्गेषु न विश्वसन्ति यतो वयं तानपि पुरान्निःसारितवन्त इत्यहो मतिमानतिशूरः साहसी महात्मा राक्षस इति ॥ २६ ॥

* विहस्येत्यादि । इदं राक्षसनीतिविभवाधिक्षेपार्थं सोत्प्रासवचनं स्वशक्तिशंसनं व्यवसायः । नन्दोद्धरणमौर्याधिराज्यस्थापनहेतोः स्वशक्तेः प्रशंसनात् ।

अन्येनैवेदमिति । इदं नन्दोद्धरणमित्यर्थः । इयं गुरुतिरस्कृतिर्द्रवः । हे मत्सरिन्निति । मत्सरः परोत्कर्षासहनम् ।

आरुह्यारूढेति । [आरूढः यः कोपस्तस्य स्फुरणेन] प्रवृद्धकोपावेशेन विषमिताभिर्विसंष्ठुलं प्रचलिताभिरग्राङ्गुलीभिरङ्गुल्यग्रैर्मुक्ता चूडा शिखा यस्याम् । सकलानां रिपूणामुत्सादनाय कालविलम्बात्प्रतिज्ञाया दीर्घत्वम् । [यद्वा दीर्घां महतीं कठिनामिति

---

१ वर्गेषु २ एतदनन्तरं-**राजा**-अथ किम् । एतत्कृतममात्यराक्षसेन । **चाण०**-वृषल.
३ च्छेद.

केनान्येनावलिप्ता नवनवतिशतद्रव्यकोटीश्वरास्ते
नन्दाः पर्यायभूताः पशव इव हताः पश्यतो राक्षसस्य ॥ २७ ॥

अपि च ।

गृध्रैराबद्धचक्रं वियति विचलितैर्दीर्घनिष्कम्पपक्षै-
र्धूमैर्ध्वस्तार्कभासां सघनमिव दिशां मण्डलं दर्शयन्तः ।
नन्दैरानन्दयन्तः पितृवननिलयान्प्राणिनः पश्य चैतान्
निर्वान्त्यद्यापि नैते स्रुतबहलवसावाहिनो हव्यवाहाः ॥ २८ ॥

राजा—अन्येनैवेदमनुष्ठितम् ।

चाण०—आः केन ।

राजा—नन्दकुलविद्वेषिणा दैवेन ।

चाण०—दैवमविद्वांसः प्रमाणयन्ति ।

राजा—विद्वांसोऽप्यविकत्थना भवन्ति ।

चाण०—(सकोपम्[1] ।) वृषल भृत्यमिव मामारोढुमिच्छसि ।

शिखां मोक्तुं बद्धामपि पुनरयं धावति करः

(भूमौ पादं प्रहृत्य[2] ।)

यावत् ।] ईदृशीमुग्रां प्रतिज्ञामारुह्य कृत्वा केनान्येन नन्दाः पर्यायभूता एकस्यां तस्यां दामनिबद्धाः पशव इव क्रमेण हता इत्यन्वयः । पश्यतो राक्षसस्य पश्यन्तं राक्षसमनादृत्येत्यर्थः । षष्ठी चानादर इति षष्ठी ॥ २७ ॥

गृध्रैरिति । वियति आबद्धचक्रं विरचितमण्डलं यथा तथा विचलितैर्दीर्घा निष्कम्पाः पक्षा येषां तैर्गृध्रैरेव धूमैरिति व्यस्तरूपकम् । चिताग्नीनां ज्वलदङ्गारमात्र-शेषतया सहजधूमाभावात् गृध्रा एव धूमत्वेन निरूपिताः । तैर्गृध्रधूमैर्ध्वस्तार्कभासां तिरोहितसूर्यतेजसां दिशां मण्डलं सघनमिव मेघमण्डलप्रच्छादितमिवेत्युत्प्रेक्षा दर्शयन्तः बहलवसावशेषैर्नन्दैः श्मशाननिलयान्प्रेतवृकादीन् । एतान्प्राणिनः प्रीणयन्तः एते परितः श्मशानेषु दृश्यमाना हव्यवाहा अद्यापि न निर्वान्ति न शाम्यन्ति । पश्य चेति वाक्यार्थः कर्म । अतिक्रान्तेऽपि विषये रोषावेशवशादेतानेत इति च बुद्धौ प्रत्यक्षीकृत्य निर्देशः । नन्दकुलनिर्दहनक्रोधोऽद्यापि न शान्त इत्यर्थः । अयं वधरूपो विद्रवः ॥ २८ ॥

आः केनेति । इयं तर्जनरूपा द्युतिः । नन्दकुलविद्वेषिणा दैवेनेति । एतदादि क्रोध-संरब्धयोरन्योन्याधिक्षेपे विरोधनम् । आरोढुमिच्छसीति । अधिक्षेप्तुं प्रवर्तसे इत्यर्थः ।

शिखामिति । तीर्णप्रतिज्ञत्वाद्बद्धुमिष्टामपि न बध्नामीत्यर्थः । शिखाया अद्यापि

---

१ कोपं नाटयन्. २ पादप्रहारं दत्त्वा.

प्रतिज्ञामारोढुं पुनरपि चलत्येष चरणः ।
प्रणाशान्नन्दानां प्रशममुपयातं त्वमधुना
परीतः कालेन ज्वलयसि मम क्रोधदहनम् ॥ २९ ॥

राजा—(सावेगमात्मगतम् ।) अये कथं सत्यमेवार्यः कुपितः । तथाहि ।

संरम्भस्पन्दिपक्ष्मक्षरदमलजलक्षालनक्षामयापि
भ्रूभङ्गोद्भेदधूमं ज्वलितमिव पुरः पिङ्गया नेत्रभासा ।
मन्ये रुद्रस्य रौद्रं रसमभिनयतस्ताण्डवेषु स्मरन्त्या
सञ्जातोग्रप्रकम्पं कथमपि धरया धारितः पादघातः ॥ ३० ॥

चाण०—(कृतककोपं संहृत्य ।) वृषल वृषल अलमुत्तरोत्तरेण । यद्यस्मत्तो गरीयान्राक्षसोऽवगम्यते तदिदं शस्त्रं तस्मै दीयताम् । (इति शस्त्रमुत्सृज्योत्थाय चाकाशे लक्ष्यं बद्ध्वा स्वगतम् ।) राक्षस राक्षस एष भवतः कौटिल्यबुद्धिविजिगीषोर्बुद्धेः प्रकर्षः ।

न बद्धत्वान्निर्वहणान्ते भत्स्यमानत्वात् । तीर्णप्रतिज्ञेन मया केवलं बध्यते शिखेति वक्ष्यति । प्रतिज्ञामारोढुमिति । कालेन मृत्युना परीतः वशीकृत इवेति लुप्तोपमा । न तु त्वं कालपरीतः चिरंजीवित्वेन वर्धिष्णुत्वादितिभावः । अत्रवीरो रसः स्थायी क्रोधेनानुभावेन पौष्कल्यं नीतः ॥ २९ ॥

अये कथं सत्यमेवार्यः कुपित इति । मया तदाज्ञयैव कार्यानुरोधकैतवेन कोपितोपीति शेषः ।

संरम्भोत्स्पन्दीति संरम्भेण क्रोधावेशेनोत्स्पन्दीन्युच्चलितानि पक्ष्माणि यस्याः । अत एव क्षरता गलतामलजलेन क्रोधाश्रूणा यत्क्षालनं तेन क्षामया रूक्षयापि क्रोधावेशात्पिङ्गयारुणया नेत्रभासा कर्त्र्या भ्रूभङ्गोद्भेदः क्रोधजनितभ्रूविकारविशेषः स एव धूमो यस्मिन्कर्मणि तद्यथा तथा पुरोभागे ज्वलितमिव दीप्तमिव । भावे क्तः । वह्नेर्ज्वलदवस्थायां धूम उद्गच्छतीति वस्तुस्थितिः । ताण्डवेषु पुरुषकर्तृकनृत्यविशेषेषु रौद्रं रसमभिनयतः अभिनीय दर्शयतः रुद्रस्य स्मरन्त्याः । अधीगर्थदयेशां कर्मणीति षष्ठी । धरया पृथिव्या सञ्जातोग्रप्रकम्पं यथा तथा कथमपि कृच्छ्रादार्यस्य पादघातो धारित इत्यन्वयः । रौद्रताण्डवकारिणो रुद्रस्य पादघात इवातिक्रूरश्चाणक्यपादघात इति रौद्रो रसः । वीररसोऽङ्गम् । इयमुद्वेजनरूपा द्युतिः ॥ ३० ॥

---

१ पुनः २ सोद्वेगम ३ ०म्भास्पन्दि. ४ तोदग्रक. ५ वरीयान.

चाणक्यतश्चलितभक्तिमहं सुखेन
जेष्यामि मौर्यमिति संप्रति यः प्रयुक्तः ।
भेदः किलैष भवता सकलः स एव
संपत्स्यते शठ तवैव हि दूषणाय ॥ ३१ ॥

(इति निष्क्रान्तः ।)

राजा—आर्य वैहीनरं अतःप्रभृत्यनादृत्य चाणक्यं चन्द्रगुप्तः स्वयमेव राज्यं करिष्यतीति गृहीतार्थाः क्रियन्तां प्रकृतयः ।

कञ्चु०—(आत्मगतम् ।) कथं निरुपपदमेव चाणक्यमिति नार्यचाणक्यमिति । हन्त संगृहीतोधिकारः । अथ वा न खल्वत्र वस्तुनि देवदोषः । कुतः ।

स दोषः सचिवस्यैव यदसत्कुरुते नृपः ।
याति यन्तुः प्रमादेन गजो व्यालत्ववाच्यताम् ॥ ३२ ॥

राजा—आर्य किं विचारयसि ।

कञ्चु०—देव न किंचित् । दिष्ट्या देव इदानीं देवः संवृत्तः । (निष्क्रान्तः ।)

राजा—(आत्मगतम् ।) एवमस्मासु गृह्यमाणेषु स्वकार्यसिद्धिकामः सकामो भवत्वार्यः । (प्रकाशम् ।) शोणोत्तरे अनेन शुष्ककलहेन शिरोवेदनां मां बाधते । शयनगृहमादेशय ।

प्रती०—एतु एतु देवः । (एदु एदु देवो ।)

राजा—(आत्मगतम् ।)

चाणक्यत इति । दूषणायानिष्टायेत्यर्थः । इदं स्वगुणाविष्करणं विचलनम् ॥ ३१ ॥

स दोष इति । नृपः सचिवमसत्कुरुते नाद्रियते । आदरानादरयोः सदसती । इति यत्स सचिवस्यैव दोषः न नृपस्य । व्यालत्वेन दुष्टगजत्वेन गजः वाच्यतां निन्द्यतां यन्तुः प्रमादेनैव याति न स्वतः । यन्ता शिक्षणेवहितश्चेद्गजोपि विनीतो वशीभवतीत्यर्थः ॥ ३२ ॥

एवमिति । एवमावयोः कृतेपि विरोधे लोकैस्तथ्यत्वेन गृहीते आर्यचिकीर्षितो मलयकेतुराक्षसयोर्विरोधः सुष्ठु संपत्स्यत इति भावः । इदं सिद्धवद्भाविश्रेयःकथनं प्ररोचना ।

---

१ स्वव०. २ वत. ३ राज्यकार्याणि, राजकार्याणि. ४ संहृताधिकारः. ५ देवं दोषेणावगन्तुमर्हामि. ६ किंचिद्विचारयामि । किन्त्वेतच्चिन्तयामि । दिष्ट्या. ७ शिरोव्यथा. ८ आसनादुत्थायात्म०.

आर्याज्ञयैव मम लङ्घितगौरवस्य
बुद्धिः प्रवेष्टुमिव भूविवरं प्रवृत्ता ।
ये सत्यमेव हि[1] गुरूनतिपातयन्ति
तेषां कथं नु हृदयं न भिनत्ति लज्जा ॥ ३३ ॥

(इति निष्क्रान्ताः सर्वे ।)

इति कृतककलहो नाम तृतीयोऽङ्कः ।

चतुर्थोऽङ्कः ।

(ततः प्रविशत्यध्वगवेषः पुरुषः ।)

पुरु०—आश्चर्यमाश्चर्यम् । (ही हीमाणहे हीमाणहे ।)

राजनियोगो महीयान्को नाम गतागतमिह करोति ।
अस्थानगमनगुर्वी प्रभोराज्ञा यदि न भवति ॥ १ ॥

राअणिओओ महिओ को णाम गआगअमिह करेइ ।
अट्ठाणगमणगुव्वी पहुणो अण्णा जइ ण होइ ॥ १ ॥

यावदमात्यराक्षसस्यैतद्गेहं गच्छामि । (श्रान्तवत्परिक्रम्य ।) कोऽत्र दौवारिकाणाम् । निवेदय भर्त्रेऽमात्यराक्षसाय एष करभकस्त्वरयन्पाटलिपुत्रादागत इति । (जाव अमच्चरक्खसस्स एदं गेहं गच्छामि । को एत्थ दुवारिआणं । णिवेदेह भट्टिणो अमच्चरक्खसस्स एसो करभओ तुवरन्तो पाटलिपुत्तआदो आगदोत्ति ।)

(प्रविश्य ।) दौवारिकः—भद्र मा उच्चैः मन्त्रयस्व । एषोऽमात्यः कार्यचिन्ताजनितेन जागरेण समुत्पन्नशीर्षवेदनोऽद्यापि शयनं न मुञ्चति । तस्मात्तिष्ठ मुहूर्तम् । लब्धावसरस्तव आगमनं निवेदयामि । (भद्द

आर्याज्ञयैवेति । भूविवरं प्रवेष्टुं लज्जातिशयेन स्वविलयमभ्युपगन्तुमिव प्रवृत्तेत्यर्थः । इत्थमत्र नियताप्तिः प्रदर्शिता ॥ ३३ ॥

इति श्रीत्र्यम्बकयज्वप्रभुवर्याश्रितढुण्ढिराजव्यासयज्वविरचिते
मुद्राराक्षसनाटकव्याख्याने तृतीयोऽङ्कः समाप्तः ।

अथ चतुर्थेऽङ्के राक्षसचारसंवादरूपाल्पा कथा प्रकरी कथ्यते । ही हीमाणहे इति । अयं निपातसमुदाय आश्चर्यद्योतकः । जोअणसअसमहिअं इति क्वचित्प्रथमपादे पाठः । योजनशतसमधिकं यथा तथेति क्रियाविशेषणम् । अस्थानगमन इति । अस्थाने अकाण्डे एव गमने प्रस्थानविषये गुर्वी अनतिक्रमणीया ॥ १ ॥

---

१ न गुरून्प्रतिमानयन्ति. २ भोः को. ३ सञ्ज.

मीं उच्चं मन्तेहि। एसो अमच्चो कज्जचिन्ताजणिदेण जाअरेण समुप्पण्णसीसवेअणो अज्जवि सअणं ण मुञ्चदि। ता चिट्ठ मुहुत्तअं। लद्धावसरो तुह आअमणं णिवेदेमि।)

करभकः—भद्रमुख तथा कुरु (भद्दमुह तह करेहि।)

(ततः प्रविशति शयनगृहगत आसनस्थः शकटदासेन सह सचिन्तो राक्षसः।)

राक्ष०—(आत्मगतम्।)

मम विमृशतः कार्यारम्भे विधेरविधेयता-
मपि च कुटिलां कौटिल्यस्य प्रचिन्तयतो मतिम्।
अथ च विहिते मत्कृत्यानां निकाममुपग्रहे
कथमिदमिहेत्युन्निद्रस्य प्रयात्यनिशं निशा॥ २॥

अपि च।

कार्योपक्षेपमादौ तनुमपि रचयंस्तस्य विस्तारमिच्छ-
न्बीजानां गर्भितानां फलमतिगहनं गूढमुद्भेदयंश्च।
कुर्वन्बुद्ध्या विमर्शं प्रसृतमपि पुनः संहरन्कार्यजातं।
कर्ता वा नाटकानामिममनुभवति क्लेशमस्मद्विधो वा॥ ३॥

ममेति। मम कार्यारम्भे कार्यारम्भप्रभृति विधेर्दैवस्याविधेयतां [अवशंवदतां] प्रतिकूलतां विमृशतः [चिन्तयतः। तथा च चाणक्यस्य कुटिलां वक्रतया दुरधिगमां मतिं बुद्धिप्रभावं च विशेषेण चिन्तयतः।] मत्कृत्यानां विषकन्यादिकपटकार्याणामुपग्रहे निरोधे अन्यथाभावे [विहिते] कथमिदमिह राजकार्यं भविष्यतीत्युन्निद्रस्य [उद्गता निद्रा यस्य गतनिद्रस्य मम] अनिशं निशा प्रयातीत्यन्वयः॥ २॥

कविरत्राद्भुततरनीतिविषयकस्वसंविधानक्लेशं राक्षसवचनव्याजेन प्रस्तौति कार्योपक्षेपमिति। कार्योपक्षेपं बीजन्यासं तनुं स्तोकोद्दिष्टमादौ मुखसन्धौ रचयंस्तस्य बीजस्य विस्तारं व्यक्तिं प्रतिमुखसन्धाविच्छन्कुर्वन् गर्भितस्य दृष्टनष्टस्य बीजस्य गहनं फलं गूढं यथा तथा गर्भसन्धावुद्भेदयन् अन्विष्यन्विमर्शसन्धौ तस्यैव बीजस्य बुद्ध्या विमर्शमनुसन्धानं कुर्वन् प्रसृतमपि यथायथं विप्रकीर्णमपि कार्यजातं मुखसन्ध्याद्यर्थजातं निर्वहणसन्धौ संहरन्नैकार्थ्यमुपनयन् नाटकानां कर्ता वा तथा आदौ गूढमारब्धं राजकार्यजातं अन्तरान्तरा विस्तारयन्गर्भितानां गूढानां बीजानां मन्त्राणां फलं साध्यं मुहुरुद्भेदयन् उन्नयन् बुद्ध्या विमृशंश्च आयतौ प्रसृतं शुभोदर्कं संहरन्नुपसंहरन् अस्मद्विधो मन्त्री वा महान्तमायासमनुभवतीत्यर्थः॥ ३॥

१ सणेहि. २ एसो क्खु भट्टा अमच्चरक्खसो. ३ अपि संविहिते नत्कृ०:-विहिते नत्कृत्वा०. ४ प्रयान्ति निशाः

तदपि नाम दुरात्मा चाणक्यबटुः—

(उपसृत्य ।) **दौवारिकः**—जयतु (जेदु ।)

राक्ष०—अतिसन्धातुं शक्यः स्यात् ।

दौवा०—अमात्यः । (अमच्चो ।)

राक्ष०—(वामाक्षिस्पन्दनं सूचयित्वा आत्मगतम् ।) दुरात्मा चाणक्यबटुर्जयत्वतिसन्धातुं शक्यः स्यादमात्य इति वागीश्वरी वामाक्षिस्पन्दनेन प्रस्तावगतां प्रतिपादयति । तथापि नोद्यमस्त्याज्यः । (प्रकाशम् ।) भद्र किमसि वक्तुकामः ।

दौवा०—अमात्य करभको द्वारि तिष्ठति । (अमच्चे करभओ दुआरे चिट्ठदि ।)

राक्ष०—शीघ्रं प्रवेशय ।

दौवा०—तथा (इति निष्क्रम्य पुरुषमुपसृत्य ।) भद्र उपसर्प अमात्यम् (। तह । भद्द उपसप्प अमच्चम् ।) (इति निष्क्रान्तः ।)

कर०—(उपसृत्य ।) जयत्वमात्यः (जेदु अमच्चो ।)

राक्ष०—भद्र उपविश ।

कर०—यदमात्य आज्ञापयति । (जं अमच्चो आणवेदि ।) (इति भूमावुपविष्टः ।)

राक्ष०—(आत्मगतम् ।) कस्मिन्प्रयोजने मयायं प्रहित इति प्रयोजनानां बाहुल्यान्न खल्ववधारयामि ।

(इति चिन्तां नाटयति ।)

[अतिसन्धातुं प्रतारयितुम् ।] वागीश्वरीति । वागीश्वरी उपश्रुतिरूपा [वागीश्वरी वाग्देवता यद्वा ईश्वरी वाक्] वामाक्षिस्पन्दनेन प्रस्तावं संवादं गता प्राप्ता सती पूर्वोक्तमर्थं सूचयतीत्यर्थः । इदं कार्यसंग्रहणमादानं नाम विमर्शसन्धेरन्त्यमङ्गम् । चाणक्यकर्तृकस्य राक्षसातिसन्धानरूपस्य कार्यस्य राक्षसेनैव दुरूपश्रुतिदुःशकुनप्रतिपादनद्वारा संग्रहणात् ।

आत्मगतमिति । राक्षसकरभकसंवादावसरे भागुरायणेन मलयकेतुमतिसन्धातुं

---

१ प्रस्तावगतम्. २ एसो क्खु कर०. ३ अविलम्बितं, अवारितम्. ४ भद्द एसो क्खु अमच्चो चिट्ठदि ता. ५ दौवारिकः इत्यधिकम्. ६ जयदु जयदु. ७ (नाट्येनावलोक्य ।) करभक स्वागतम् । उपविश्यताम्. ८ कार्याणाम्.

(ततः प्रविशति वेत्रपाणिर्द्वितीयः पुरुषः ।)

पुरु०—अपसरत आर्या अपसरत । अपेत मानवा अपेत । किं न पश्यथ । (ओसलेह अज्जा ओसलेह । अवेह माणहे अवेह । किं ण पेक्खह ।)

दूरे प्रत्यासत्तिर्दर्शनमपि दुर्लभमधन्यैः ।
कल्याणकुलधराणां देवानामिव मनुष्यदेवानाम् ॥ ४ ॥
दूले पच्चासत्ती दंसणमवि दुल्लहं अधण्णेहिं ।
कल्लाणकुलहलाणं देआणं विअ मणुस्सदेआणं ॥ ४ ॥

(आकाशे ।) आर्याः किं भणथ किं निमित्तमपसारणा क्रियते इति । आर्याः एष खलु कुमारो मलयकेतुः समुत्पन्नशीर्षवेदनममात्यराक्षसं प्रेक्षितुमित एवागच्छति । तस्मादपसारणा क्रियते । (इति निःष्क्रान्तः पुरुषः ।) (अज्जा किं भणाह किं णिमित्तं ओसालणा करीअदित्ति । अज्जा एसो क्खु कुमालो मलयकेदू समुप्पण्णसीसवेअणं अमच्चरक्खसं पेक्खिदुं इदो एव आअच्छदि । ता ओसालणा करीअदि ।)

(ततः प्रविशति भागुरायणेन कञ्चुकिना चानुगम्यमानो मलयकेतुः ।)

मल०—(निःश्वस्यात्मगतम् ।) अद्य दशमो मासस्तातस्योपरतस्य न चास्माभिर्वृथापुरुषाभिमानमुद्वहद्भिस्तमुद्दिश्य तोयाञ्जलिरप्यावर्जितः । प्रतिज्ञातमेतत्पुरस्तात् ।

वक्षस्ताडनभिन्नरत्नवलयं भ्रष्टोत्तरीयांशुकं
हा हेत्युच्चरितार्तनादकरुणं भूरेणुरूक्षालकम् ।
तादृङ् मातृजनस्य शोकजनितं संप्रत्यवस्थान्तरं
शत्रुस्त्रीषु मया विधाय गुरवे देयो निवापाञ्जलिः ॥ ५ ॥

तयोः प्रवेशावसरदानाय राक्षसचिन्तानाटनं कविनोपनिबद्धमिति द्रष्टव्यम् । इदमङ्कावतारम् । अत्र राक्षसं प्रति करभकेण वक्ष्यमाणस्य मौर्यचाणक्ययोर्मिथो विरोधस्य पूर्वकार्यानुसङ्गतत्वात् । लक्षणं तु पूर्वमेवोक्तम् । यत्र स्यादुक्तराङ्कार्थ इत्यादिना ।

राज्ञो गमनत्वरासंभ्रमादपसरतापसरतेति पुनरुक्तिः ।

कल्याणकुलधराणामिति । कल्याणकुलं धरन्तीति कल्याणकुलधरा महोन्नतवंशा मनुष्यदेवा राजानः । देवास्तु कल्याणः सुवर्णमयः कुलधरः कुलपर्वतो मेरुर्येषां तथोक्ताः ॥ ४ ॥ आकाशेति । आकाशलक्षणं पूर्वमुक्तम् ।

वक्ष इति । [वक्षसस्ताडनेन भिन्नानि रत्नवलयानि यस्मिन् । भूरेणुभी रूक्षा

---

१ देवाणं च भूमिदेवाणम्. २ देक्खिदुं. ३ अस्मात्प्राक्-अथवा.

किमत्र बहुना ।

उद्यच्छता धुरमकापुरुषानुरूपां
गन्तव्यमाजिनिधनेन पितुः पथा वा ।
आच्छिद्य वा स्वजननीजनलोचनेभ्यो
नेयो मया रिपुवधूनयनानि बाष्पः ॥ ६ ॥

(प्रकाशम्।) आर्य जाजले एक एवाहममात्यराक्षसस्यातर्कितगमनेन प्रीतिमुत्पादयितुमिच्छामि । तदुच्यन्तामस्मद्वचनादनुयायिनो राजानः कृतमनुगमनक्लेशेनेति ।

कञ्चु०—यदाज्ञापयति कुमारः । (इति परिक्रम्याकाशे।) भो भो राजानः कुमारः समाज्ञापयति न खल्वहं केनाचिदनुगन्तव्य इति । (विलोक्य सहर्षम्।) कुमारस्याज्ञानन्तरमेव सर्वे राजानः प्रतिनिवृत्ताः । पश्यतु कुमारः ।

सोत्सेधैः स्कन्धदेशैः खरतरकविकाकर्षणात्यर्थभुग्नै-
रश्वाः कैश्चिन्निरुद्धाः खमिव खुरपुटैः खण्डयन्तः पुरस्तात् ।
केचिन्मातङ्गमुख्यैर्विहतजवतया मूकघण्टैर्निवृत्ता
मर्यादां भूमिपाला जलधय इव ते देव नोल्लङ्घयन्ति ॥ ७ ॥

अलकाश्चूर्णकुन्तला यस्मिन् ।] निवापाञ्जलिः श्राद्धतर्पणमिति भावः । पितृदानं निवापः स्यादिति त्रिकाण्डी । वक्षस्ताडनेत्यादि जातिवर्णनम् ॥ ५ ॥

उद्यच्छतेति । उद्यच्छतेत्यत्र यद्यपि समुदाङ्भ्यो यमोऽग्रन्थे इत्यात्मनेपदेन भवितव्यं तथापि स्वरितञितः कर्त्रभिप्राये क्रियाफले इत्यतः सूत्रात्कर्त्रभिप्राय इत्यनुवर्तनात्स्वपौरुषोद्यमनक्रियाफलस्य स्वजननीजनलोचनबाष्पापनयनस्य रिपुवधूलोचनगामित्वाभिप्रायेण परस्मैपदं कविना प्रयुक्तमित्यवधार्य सन्तोष्टव्यं वैय्याकरणवर्यैः । आच्छिद्यापनीय रिपुवधेन तन्नयनबाष्प उत्पादिते स्वजननीजनदुःखमपमार्जितप्रायं स्यादित्यर्थः । सुगममवशिष्टम् ॥ ६ ॥ कृतमिति । कृतमित्यव्ययं अलमित्यर्थे ।

सोत्सेधैरिति । खरतराणां तीक्ष्णलोहकण्टककीलितानां कविकानां खलीनानामाकर्षणादत्यर्थं भुग्नैर्नमितैरत एव सोत्सेधैर्मध्यभागोन्नतैः स्कन्धदेशैर्ग्रीवाभागैरुपलक्षिता अश्वाः कैश्चिन्निरुद्धाः । केचित् योधाः । सहसा जवनिरोधे सति मूकघण्टैरिति स्वभावोक्तिः । मातङ्गमुख्यैर्निवृत्ताः जवनान्मातङ्गान्सहसा सन्निगृह्य निवृत्ता इत्यर्थः ॥ ७ ॥

---

१ कुमार कुमार एते भवदाज्ञासमन्तरमेव प्रतिनिवृत्ताः सर्व एव राजनः. २ सोत्सेकैः ३ मुखरकविकया. ४ खरपदैः.

मल०—आर्य त्वमपि सपरिजनो निवर्तस्व । भागुरायण एको मामनुगच्छतु ।

कञ्चु०—यदाज्ञापयति कुमारः । (इति सपरिजनो निष्क्रान्तः ।)

मल०—सखे भागुरायण विज्ञप्तोहमिहागच्छद्भिर्भद्रभटप्रभृतिभिर्यथा न वयममात्यराक्षसद्वारेण कुमारमाश्रयणीयमाश्रयामहे किंतु कुमारस्य सेनापतिं शिखरसेनं द्वारीकृत्य दुष्टामात्यपरिगृहाच्चन्द्रगुप्तादपरक्ताः कुमारमाभिरामिकगुणयोगादाश्रयणीयमाश्रयामह इति । तत्र मया सुचिरमपि विचारयता तेषां वाक्यार्थोवधारितः ।

भागु०—कुमार न दुर्बोधोयमर्थः । विजिगीषुमात्मगुणसंपन्नं प्रियहितद्वारेणाश्रयणीयमाश्रयेदिति ननु न्याय्य एवायमर्थः ।

मल०—सखे भागुरायण नन्वमात्यराक्षसोस्माकं प्रियतमो हिततमश्च ।

भागु०—एवमेतत् । किंत्वमात्यराक्षसश्चाणक्ये बद्धवैरो न चन्द्रगुप्ते । तद्यदि कदाचिच्चाणक्यमतिजितकाशिनमसहमानः स साचिव्यादवरोपयेत्ततो नन्दकुलभक्त्या नन्दान्वय एवायमिति सुहृज्जनापेक्षया चामात्यराक्षसश्चन्द्रगुप्तेन सह सन्दधीत । चन्द्रगुप्तोपि पितृपर्यायागत एवायमिति सन्धिमनुमन्येत । एवं सत्यस्मासु कुमारो न विश्वसेदित्ययमेषां वाक्यार्थः ।

मल०—युज्यते । अमात्यस्य गृहमादेशय ।

भागु०—इत इतः कुमारः । (उभौ परिक्रामतः)

भागु०—इदममात्यगृहम् । प्रविशतु कुमारः ।

मल०—एष प्रविशामि ।

आश्रयामह इति । राक्षसस्य दुष्टत्वं ध्वनयितुं दुष्टामात्येति चाणक्यविशेषणम् । आभिरामिकगुणेति च मौर्यदूषणाय । अवधारित इति । अतःपरं भागुरायणस्य मलयकेत्वतिसन्धानवचनं सर्वं बीजार्थस्यावमर्शनम् । सुहृज्जनेति । सुहृज्जनाश्चन्दनदासशकटदासादयः ।

---

१ शिखरक. २ उर्गा-उरगा-कृत्य. ३ मानिक. ४ कुमार एव. ५ अमात्यराक्षसस्य.

राक्ष०—(आत्मगतम् ।) अये स्मृतम् । (प्रकाशम् ।) भद्र अपि दृष्टस्त्वया कुसुमपुरे स्तनकलशः ।

पुरु०—अमात्य अथ किम् । (अमच्च अह इं ।)

मल०—(आकर्ण्य ।) भागुरायण कुसुमपुरवृत्तान्तः प्रस्तूयते । न तत्र तावदुपसर्पामः । शृणुमस्तावत् । कुतः ।

> **सत्त्वभङ्गभयाद्राज्ञां कथयन्त्यन्यथा पुरः ।**
> **अन्यथा विवृतार्थेषु स्वैरालापेषु मन्त्रिणः ॥ ८ ॥**

भागु०—यदाज्ञापयति कुमारः ।

राक्ष०—भद्र अपि तत्कार्यं सिद्धम् ।

पुरु०—अमात्यप्रसादेन सिद्धम् । (अमच्चप्पसाएण सिद्धम् ।

मल०—सखे भागुरायण किं तत्कार्यम् ।

भागु०—कुमार गहनः सचिववृत्तान्तः । नैतावता परिच्छेत्तुं शक्यते । अवहितस्तावच्छ्रोतुमर्हति कुमारः ।

राक्ष०—भद्र विस्तरेण श्रोतुमिच्छामि ।

पुरु०—शृणोत्वमात्यः । अस्ति तावदहममात्येनाज्ञप्तो यथा करभक कुसुमपुरं गच्छ मम वचनेन भण वैतालिकं स्तनकलशं यथा चाणक्यहतकेन तेषु तेष्वाआज्ञाभङ्गेष्वनुष्ठीयमानेषु चन्द्रगुप्त उत्तेजनसमर्थैः श्लोकैरुपश्लोकयितव्य इति । (सुणादु अमच्चो । अत्थि दाव अहं अमच्चेणाण्णत्तो जह करभअ कुसुमपुरं गच्छ मह वअणेण भण वेआलिअं त्थणकलसं जह चाणक्कहदएण तेसु तेसु अण्णाभङ्गेसु अणुचिट्ठीअमाणेसु चन्दउत्तो उत्तेअणसमत्थेहिं सिलोएहिं उवसिलोअइदव्वो त्ति ।)

राक्ष०—भद्र ततस्ततः ।

कर०—ततो मया पाटलिपुत्रं गत्वा श्रावितः अमात्यसन्देशं वैतालिकः स्तनकलशः । अत्रान्तरे नन्दकुलविनाशदूनस्य पौरजनस्य परितोषं समुत्पादयता राज्ञाघोषितः कौमुदीमहोत्सवः । स च चिरकालपरि-

---

सत्त्वभङ्गभयादिति । सत्वभङ्गो मनोभङ्गः । विवृतार्थेषु परस्परविस्पष्टार्थेषु ॥ ८ ॥

---

१ किं कारणमिति. २ गहनः खलु. ३ गच्छिअ...भणिदव्वो तुए ..ओ थणकलसो.

वर्तमानो जनितपरिचयोभिमतवधूजनसमागम इव सस्नेहं बहुमानितो नगरजनेन। (तदो मए पाडलिउत्तं गदुअ सुणाविदो अमच्चसन्देसं वेआलिओ त्थणकलसो। एत्थन्तरे णन्दउलविणासदूणस्स मोरजणस्स परितोसं समुप्पादअन्तेण रण्णा आघोसिदो कौमुदीमहोस्सवो। सो अ चिरकालपरिवट्टमाणो जणिदपरिचओ अभिमदवधूजणसमागमो विअ ससिणेहं बहु माणिदो णअरजणेण।)

राक्ष०—(सबाष्पम्।) हा देव नन्द।

> **कौमुदी कुमुदानन्दे जगदानन्दहेतुना।**
> **कीदृशी सति चन्द्रेपि नृपचन्द्र त्वया विना॥ ९॥**

कर०—ततः स लोकलोचनानन्भूतोनिच्छत एव तस्य निवारितश्चाणक्यहतकेन। अत्रान्तरे स्तनकलशेन चन्द्रगुप्तसमुत्तेजिका श्लोकपरिपाटी प्रवर्तिता। (तदो सो लोअलोअणाणन्दभूदो अणिच्छन्तस्स एव तस्स णिवारिदो चाणक्कहदएण। एत्थन्तरे त्थणकलसेण चन्दउत्तसमुत्तेजिआ सिलोअपरिपाटी पवट्टिदा।)

राक्ष०—कीदृशी सा।

पुरु०—(सत्त्वोद्रेकस्येत्यादि पूर्वोक्तं पठति।)

राक्ष०—(सहर्षम्।) साधु स्तनकलश साधु। काले भेदबीजमुप्तमवश्यं फलमुपदर्शयेति। कुतः।

> **सद्यः क्रीडारसच्छेदं प्राकृतोपि न मर्षयेत्।**
> **किं नु लोकाधिकं तेजो बिभ्राणः पृथिवीपतिः॥ १०॥**

मल०—एवमेतत्। (सद्यः क्रीडेत्यादिपुनः पठति।)

चिरकालेति। चिरकालाद्बहोः कालात्परिवर्तमानः परितो वर्तमानो जायमानः। जनितपरिचयः परिचितपूर्व इत्यर्थः।

कौमुदीति। कौमुदीमहोत्सवः कुमुदानन्दे कुमुदानां कुवलयानामानन्दजनके चन्द्रे कोः पृथिव्या मुदमानन्दयति समर्धयति कुमुदानन्दे चन्द्रगुप्ते सत्यपि ताभ्यामप्यतिशयितेन सकलजगदानन्दहेतुना त्वया विना कीदृशी व्यर्थेत्यर्थः। व्यतिरेकालङ्कारः॥ ९॥

अनिच्छत इति। अनिच्छन्तमनादृत्येत्यर्थः। षष्ठीचानादर इति षष्ठी। न

---

१ चन्दउत्तेण. २ बन्धु. ३ अस्मात्परं—भद्र ततस्ततः. ४ अमत्र इत्यधिकम्. ५ दर्शयिष्यति. ६ किमु…धाम बिभ्राणाः पृथिवीभुजः.

राक्ष०—ततस्ततः ।

कर०—ततश्चन्द्रगुप्तेनाज्ञाभङ्गकलुषितेन प्रसङ्गसूचितममात्यगुणं प्रशस्यापभ्रंशितोधिकाराच्चाणक्यहतकः । (तदो चन्दउत्तेण अण्णाभङ्ग-कलुसिदेण पसङ्गसूचिदं अमच्चगुणं पसंसिअ अपब्भंसिदो अहिआरादो चाणक्कहदओ ।)

मल०—सखे भागुरायण गुणप्रशंसया दर्शितश्चन्द्रगुप्तेन राक्षसे भक्तिपक्षपातः ।

भागु०—न तथा गुणप्रशंसया यथा चाणक्यबटोर्निराकरणेन ।

राक्ष०—किमयमेवैकः कौमुदीमहोत्सवप्रतिषेधश्चन्द्रगुप्तस्य चाणक्यं प्रति कोपकारणमुतान्यदप्यस्ति ।

मल०—सखे चन्द्रगुप्तस्यापरकोपकारणान्वेषणेन किं फलमेष पश्यति ।

भागु०—कुमार मतिमांश्चाणक्यो न निष्प्रयोजनमेव चन्द्रगुप्तं कोपयिष्यति न च कृतवेदी चन्द्रगुप्त एतावता गौरवमुल्लङ्घयिष्यति । सर्वथा चाणक्यचन्द्रगुप्तयोः पुष्कलात्कारणाद्यो विश्लेष उत्पद्येत स आत्यन्तिको भविष्यतीति ।

कर०—अस्त्यन्यदपि चन्द्रगुप्तस्य कोपकारणम् । उपेक्षितोनेनापक्रामन्मलयकेतुः अमात्यराक्षसश्चेति । (अत्थि अण्णं वि चन्दउत्तस्स कोवकारणं । उवेक्खिदो अणेण अवक्कमन्तो मलअकेदू अमच्चरक्खसो अ त्ति ।)

राक्ष०—(सहर्षम् ।) सखे शकटदास हस्ततलगतो मे संप्रति चन्द्रगुप्तो भविष्यति । इदानीं चन्दनदासस्य बन्धनान्मोक्षस्तत्र च पुत्रदारैः सह समागमः ।

मल०—सखे भागुरायण हस्ततलगत इति व्याहरतः कोस्याभिप्रायः ।

न तथेति । गुणवन्तमेनं संग्रहीतुमेव चाणक्यबटुरनेन निराकृत इत्यर्थः । आत्यन्तिक इति । दृढः अप्रतीकार्य इति यावत् ।

---

१ कुमार न. २ अमच्च अत्थि. ३ अस्मादनन्तरं-जीवसिद्धिप्रभृतीनां क्लेशच्छेदः ॥ भागु०-आत्मगतम् । जातः सत्यं जीवसिद्धेः क्लेशच्छेदः ।

भागु०—किमन्यत् । चाणक्यादपकृष्टस्य चन्द्रगुप्तस्योद्धरणान्न किंचित्कार्यमवश्यं पश्यति ।

राक्ष०—भद्र हृताधिकारः क्व सांप्रतमसौ बटुः ।

कर०—तदेव पाटलिपुत्रमधिवसति । (तहिं एव्व पाडलिउत्ते अहिवसदि ।)

राक्ष०—(सावेगम् ।) भद्र तत्रैव प्रतिवसति । तपोवनं न गतः प्रतिज्ञां वा पुनर्न समारूढवान् ।

कर०—अमात्य तपोवनं गच्छतीति श्रूयते । (अमच्च तपोवणं गच्छेदि त्ति सुणीअदि ।)

राक्ष०—शकटदास नेदमुपपद्यते । पश्य ।

देवस्य येन पृथिवीतलवासवस्य
स्वाग्रासनापनयनान्निकृतिर्न सोढा ।
सोयं स्वयंकृतनराधिपतेर्मनस्वी
मौर्यात्कथं नु परिभूतिमिमां सहेत ॥ ११ ॥

मल०—सखे चाणक्यस्य वनगमने पुनः प्रतिज्ञारोहणे वा कास्य स्वार्थसिद्धिः ।

भागु०—नात्यन्तदुर्बोधोयमर्थः । यावद्यावच्चाणक्यहतकश्चन्द्रगुप्ताद्दूरीभवति तावत्तावदस्य स्वार्थसिद्धिः ।

शक०—अमात्य अलमन्यथा विकल्प्य । उपपद्यत एतत् । पश्यत्वमात्यः ।

चाणक्यादिति । सचिवायत्तसिद्धिः सचिववियोगे हस्ततलगतः सुखेन जेयो भविष्यतीति राक्षसस्य निष्कपटोभिप्रायो भागुरायणेनान्यथा बोध्यते । चन्द्रगुप्तस्योद्धरणादुन्मूलनान्न किंचित्कार्यमवश्यं पश्यति नास्त्यात्यन्तिकाभीष्टसिद्धिः । हस्ततलकरणाद्वशीकरणात्तु स्वस्य साचिव्यप्राप्त्या चन्दनदासादीनामापन्निवृत्तिरात्यन्तिकी स्वार्थसिद्धिरित्यस्याभिप्राय इत्यर्थः ।

सावेगमिति । तत्रैवावस्थाने मौर्योन्मूलनप्रतिज्ञाया अकरणे वा कदाचित्पुनः सन्दधीतेत्यावेगः । मनस्वी मानशीलः ॥ ११ ॥ स्वार्थसिद्धिरिति । स्वस्य साचिव्यपदलाभ इत्यर्थः ।

---

१ गमिस्सदि. २ ०पनयजा. ३ भागुरायण इत्य०. ४ कार्य. ५ कुमार नास्यन्त०.

राज्ञां चूडामणीन्दुद्युतिखचितशिखे मूर्ध्नि विन्यस्तपादः
स्वैरेवोत्पाद्यमानं किमिति विषहते मौर्य आज्ञाविघातम् ।
कौटिल्यः कोपनोऽपि स्वमयभिचरणे[1] ज्ञातदुःखः प्रतिज्ञाम्
दैवात्तीर्णप्रतिज्ञः[2] पुनरपि न करोत्यायतिग्लानिभीतः[3] ॥ १२ ॥

राक्ष०—सखे शकटदास एवमेतत् । गच्छ विश्रामय करभकम् ।

शक०—यथाज्ञापयत्यमात्यः । (इति करभकेण सह निष्क्रान्तः ।)

राक्ष०—अहमपि कुमारं द्रष्टुमिच्छामि ।

मल०—(उपसृत्य ।) अहमेवार्यं द्रष्टुमागतः ।

राक्ष०—(नाट्येनावलोक्य ।) अये कुमारः । (आसनादुत्थाय ।) इदमासनम् । उपवेष्टुमर्हति कुमारः ।

मल०—अयमुपविशामि । उपविशत्वार्यः । (यथार्हमुपविष्टः ।) आर्य अपि सह्या शिरोवेदना ।

राक्ष०—कुमार कुमारस्याधिराजशब्देनातिरस्कृते कुमारशब्दे कुतो मे शिरोवेदनायाः सह्यता ।

मल०—ऊरीकृतमेतदार्येण न दुष्प्रापं भविष्यति । तत्कियन्तं कालमस्माभिरेवं संभृतबलैरपि शत्रुव्यसनमुदीक्षमाणैरुदासितव्यम् ।

राक्ष०—कुमार कुतोऽद्यापि कालहरणस्यावकाशः । प्रतिष्ठस्व विजयाय ।

मल०—आर्य शत्रुव्यसनमुपलब्धम् ।

[राज्ञामिति । चूडायां निबद्धा मणयः चूडामणय इन्दव इव तेषां द्युतिभिः खचिता शिखा यस्य तादृशमूर्ध्नि विन्यस्तपादः । तेषां शासिता सार्वभौम इति यावत् । मौर्यः] स्वैरेव स्वकीयैः सेवकैरित्यर्थः । स्वयमभिचरणेन—चाणक्य-नाम्ना तेनाथ शकटारगृहे रहः । कृत्यां विधाय सप्ताहात्सपुत्रो निहतो नृपः ॥ इति पूर्वोक्तेनाभिचारकर्मणा ज्ञातं अनुभूतं दुःखं क्लेशो यस्यां तादृशी प्रतिज्ञा यस्येति बहुव्रीहिगर्भो बहुव्रीहिः । आयतिग्लानिभीतः प्रतिज्ञातार्थनिर्वहण-क्लेशासहिष्णुः प्रतिज्ञाक्लेशं बहुधानुभूय पुनः प्रतिज्ञां कर्तुं बिभीयादित्यर्थः ॥ १२ ॥ [अतिरस्कृतेऽतिरोहिते । यावत्कुमारोऽधिराजपदं न लभेत ताव-दित्यर्थः । ऊरीकृतमङ्गीकृतम् ।]

---

१ अतिचरणं, अभिचरणे दृष्टदोषः; अभिचरणज्ञातदुःखप्रतिज्ञः. २ पूर्ण. ३ ध्या।नि ४ यथासनम ५ अवेक्षमाणैः ६ अपि श०.

राक्ष०—उपलब्धम् ।

मल०—कीदृशं तत् ।

राक्ष०—सचिवव्यसनं किमन्यत् । अपकृष्टश्चाणक्याच्चन्द्रगुप्तः ।

मल०—आर्य सचिवव्यसनमव्यसनमेव ।

राक्ष०—[1]अन्येषां भूपतीनां कदाचिदमात्यव्यसनमव्यसनं स्यात् । न पुनश्चन्द्रगुप्तस्य[2] ।

मल०—आर्य नैतदेवम् । चन्द्रगुप्तप्रकृतीनां चाणक्यदोषा एवापरागहेतवस्तस्मिंश्च निराकृते प्रथममपि चन्द्रगुप्तेनुरक्ताः संप्रति सुतरामेव तत्रानुरागं दर्शयिष्यन्ति ।

राक्ष०—मामैवम् । ताः खलुद्विप्रकाराः प्रकृतयश्चन्द्रगुप्तसहोत्थायिन्यो नन्दानुरक्ताश्च । तत्र चन्द्रगुप्तसहोत्थायिनीनां चाणक्यदोषा एव विरागहेतवो न नन्दकुलानुरक्तानाम् । तास्तु खलुनन्दकुलमनेन पितृभूतं घातितमित्यपरागामर्षाभ्यां विप्रकृताः सत्यः स्वाश्रयमलभमानाश्चन्द्रगुप्तमेवानुवर्तन्ते । त्वादृशं पुनः प्रतिपक्षोद्धरणे संभावितशक्तिमभियोक्तारमासाद्य क्षिप्रमेनं परित्यज्य त्वामेवाश्रयिष्यन्ते । अत्र निदर्शनं वयमेव ।

मल०—आर्य किमेतदेकमेव सचिवव्यसनमभियोगकारणं चन्द्रगुप्तस्याहोस्विदन्यदप्यस्ति ।

राक्ष०—किमन्यैर्बहुभिरपि एतद्धि प्रधानतमम् ।

[अव्यसनमेव न महते फलाय तस्य अकिंचित्करत्वादित्यर्थः ।] न पुनश्चन्द्रगुप्तस्येति । एवं राक्षसेन समाहितोप्यमात्यराक्षसश्चाणक्ये बद्धवैरो न चन्द्रगुप्ते इत्यादिपूर्वोक्तेन बहुविधेन भागुरायणोपजापेन कलुषिताशयो मलयकेतुः पुनः शङ्कते । चन्द्रगुप्तप्रकृतीनामिति । राक्षसमेव मनसि विषयीकृत्य चन्द्रगुप्तप्रकृतीनामित्यादि ताटस्थ्येन वचनम् । [अपरागोऽननुरक्तिः अमर्षो क्रोधस्ताभ्यां विप्रकृताः कृतक्षोभाः । स्वाश्रयं शोभनं योग्यमाश्रयम् ।]

---

१ कुमार अन्येषां. २ अस्मात्परम्—मल०—आर्य ननु विशेषतश्चन्द्रगुप्तस्येति । राक्ष०—किंकारणं यदस्यामात्यव्यसनमव्यसनम् । ३ नन्दकुलानु०. ४ ०नुगतानाम्. ५ कृत्स्नं कृतघ्नेन घा०. ६ संभाव्य. ७ अमात्य. ८ अन्यदपि किंचित्.

मल०—आर्य कथमिव प्रधानतमम्। किमिदानीं चन्द्रगुप्तः स्वेकार्यधुरामन्यत्र मन्त्रिण्यात्मनि वा समासज्य स्वयं प्रतिविधातुमसमर्थः।

राक्ष०—बाढमसमर्थः। कुतः स्वायत्तसिद्धिषूभयायत्तसिद्धिषु वा भूमिपालेषु तत्संभवति। चन्द्रगुप्तस्तु दुरात्मा नित्यं सचिवायत्तसिद्धावेव स्थितश्चक्षुर्विकल इवाप्रत्यक्षलोकव्यवहारः कथमिव स्वयं प्रतिविधातुं समर्थः स्यात्।

अत्युच्छ्रिते मन्त्रिणि पार्थिवे च विष्टभ्य पादावुपतिष्ठते श्रीः।
सा स्त्रीस्वभावादसहा भरस्य तयोर्द्वयोरेकतरं जहाति॥ १३॥
नृपोपकृष्टः सचिवात्तदर्पणः स्तनन्धयोत्यन्तशिशुः स्तनादिव।
अदृष्टलोकव्यवहारमन्दधीर्मुहूर्तमप्युत्सहते न वर्तितुम्॥ १४॥

प्रतिविधातुमिति। प्रतिविधातुमस्मदभियोगं प्रतिकर्तुमित्यर्थः।

तत्संभवतीति। संभवतीत्यनेन सामर्थ्यस्य कादाचित्कत्वमुक्तम्। उभयायत्तसिद्धेरेवोत्तरश्लोके प्राशस्त्यकथनात्। [दुरात्मा बुद्धिविकलः। लोकव्यवहारो राज्यतन्त्रं पक्षे लोकेषु व्यवहारो भ्रमणादिव्यापारः।]

यत्पृष्टं स्वकार्यधुरामन्यत्र मन्त्रिणीति तत्परिहरति अत्युच्छ्रित इति। श्रीः राज्यश्रीः अत्युच्छ्रितयोः समस्कन्धतयात्युन्नतिं प्राप्तयोः ऐकमत्ये। नान्यूनाधिकभावेन चैकीभावमिवोपगतयोरिति यावत्। मन्त्रिपार्थिवयोः पादौ मन्त्रशक्तिप्रभुशक्तिरूपौ विष्टभ्य समवस्थाप्योपतिष्ठते सुस्थिरा सती तयोः सङ्गता भवतीत्यर्थः। उपाद्देवपूजासङ्गतिकरणमित्रकरणपथिष्विति तङ्। यद्यपि प्रभुमन्त्रोत्साहरूपास्तिस्रः शक्तयस्तथाप्युत्साहशक्तेरुभयानुकूलत्वेन द्वयोरन्तर्भावाभिप्रायेणात्र सा पृथग्न गृहीता। तयोर्मन्त्रिपार्थिवयोर्द्वयोः सतोर्वैमत्येन न्यूनाधिकभावमुपेत्य द्वैधीभावेन स्थितयोः सा श्रीर्द्वयोः पादयोः सम्यगवष्टम्भासंभवाद्भरस्यासहा राज्यभारं वोढुमसमर्था सती स्त्रीस्वभावाद्दौर्बल्याच्चापल्याच्चैकतरं मन्त्रिणं वा पार्थिवं वा जहाति। कंचित्कालं प्रभुमात्रमाश्रित्य वर्तमानापि मन्त्रवैकल्येन स्वयमपि नश्यत्येवं मन्त्रिणमाश्रित्य वर्तमानापि प्रभुत्ववैकल्येन नश्यतीति भावः। यथा काचन नर्तकी उच्छ्रितौ समौ वंशस्तम्भौ पादाभ्यां दृढमवष्टभ्य सुस्थिरा तिष्ठति तयोर्वैषम्ये विसंष्ठुलपदतया देहभरं वोढुमसहा एकं हित्वान्यतरमवलम्बमाना तेन सह स्वयमपि पतति तद्वत्। अत्र प्रस्तुतेनाप्रस्तुतस्य स्फोरणात्समासोक्तिरलङ्कारः। एवमुच्छ्रितः संश्चन्द्रगुप्तोऽनुच्छ्रितेऽन्यस्मिन्मन्त्रिणि धुरमासज्यासमर्थः स्यादिति प्रतिपादितम्॥१३॥

अथात्मन्यासज्येत्यस्य परिहारमाह। नृप इति। तदर्पणः तस्मिन्नेव सचिवे राज्यतन्त्रं सर्वमर्पयतीति तथाभूतः सचिवायत्तसिद्धिरित्यर्थः। अदृष्टलोकव्यवहारः अत एव मन्दधीरिति विशेषणसमासः। तस्मात्साचिवादपकृष्टः सन् राज्यधुरां वोढुमसमर्थो भवतीत्यर्थः॥ १४॥

---

१ स्वराज्य०. २ मल०-किं कारणम्. राक्ष०-स्वाय०...कदाचिदेतत. ३ श्रीः. ४ मूढ.

मल०—(आत्मगतम्।) दिष्ट्या न सचिवायत्ततन्त्रोऽस्मि। (प्रकाशम्।) यद्यप्येवं तथापि बहुष्वभियोगकारणेषु सत्सु व्यसनमभियुञ्जानस्य शत्रुमभियोक्तुरैकान्तिकी कार्यसिद्धिमवगन्तुमर्हति।

राक्ष०—ऐकान्तिकीमेव कार्यसिद्धिमवगन्तुमर्हति कुमारः। कुतः।

त्वय्युत्कृष्टबलेऽभियोक्तरि नृपे नन्दानुरक्ते पुरे
चाणक्ये चलिताधिकारविमुखे मौर्ये नवे राजनि।
स्वाधीने मयि। (इत्यर्धोक्ते लज्जां नाटयन्।)
मार्गमात्रकथनव्यापारयोगोद्यमे
त्वद्वाञ्छान्तरितानि संप्रति विभो तिष्ठन्ति साध्यानि नः॥ १५॥

मल०—यद्येवमभियोगकालमार्यः पश्यति ततः किमास्यते।

उत्तुङ्गास्तुङ्गकूलं स्रुतमदसलिलाः प्रस्यन्दिसलिलं
श्यामाः श्यामोपकण्ठद्रुममतिमुखराः कल्लोलमुखरम्।
स्रोतःखातावसीदत्तटमुरुदशनैरुत्सादिततटाः
शोणं सिन्दूरशोणा मम गजपतयोऽपास्यन्तु शतशः॥ १६॥

अपि च।

गम्भीरगर्जितरवाः स्वमदाम्बुमिश्र-
मासारवर्षमिव शीकरमुद्गिरन्त्यः।
विन्ध्यं विकीर्णसलिला इव मेघमाला
रुन्धन्तु वारणघटा नगरं मदीयाः॥ १७॥

(इति भागुरायणेन सह निष्क्रान्तो मलयकेतुः।)

दिष्ट्येति। त्वयि विरुद्धवृत्तावपि स्वतन्त्रस्य मे नानिष्टमिति भावः। यद्येवमिति। व्यसनमभियुञ्जानस्य अनुसन्दधानस्य व्यसनमन्विष्य शत्रुमभियोक्तुः अभिषेणयत इत्यर्थः। अन्येषु बहुषु कारणेषु सत्सु सचिवव्यसनमपि साधकं न केवलमिति भावः।

अन्यान्यप्युत्कृष्टबलादीनि कारणानि सन्तीत्याह। त्वयीति। स्वप्रशंसायां लज्जा। प्रशंसामेव निह्नुते। मार्गमात्रकथनव्यापार एव योगः उपायः तत्र उद्यमो यत्नो यस्य सः। त्वद्वाञ्छेति। त्वदाज्ञां प्रतीक्षन्त इत्यर्थः॥ १५॥

उत्तुङ्गा इति। [उत्तुङ्गा अत्युन्नताः मम शतशः गजपतयः शोणं अपास्यन्तु तत्सलिलं विधुन्वन्तु इत्यन्वयः। श्यामा उपकण्ठतरवो यस्य। स्रोतसा जलप्रवाहेण खातमतएव अवसीदत् भ्रश्यत् तटं यस्य तम्।] अत्र उत्तुङ्गास्तुङ्गकूलमित्यादिसाधारणधर्मोपादानाद्गजपतीनां शोणसिन्धोश्चोपमा गम्या। शोणमिति श्लेषानुप्राणिता। अत्र स्रग्धरावृत्तस्य एकाक्षरमात्राद्वयस्य न्यूनतया प्रस्तारविशेषः॥ १६॥ गम्भीरेति। नगरं पुष्पपुरम्। वारणमेघमालयोः पूर्णोपमा॥ १७॥

---

१ अमात्य यद्ये०. २ सचिवव्य०. ३ योग्यो. ४ अलिमु०. ५ गा०, पास्यन्ति ६ रोत्स्यन्ति.

राक्ष०—कः कोत्र भोः।

पुरुषः—(प्रविश्य।) आज्ञापयतु अमात्यः। (आणवेदु अमच्चो।)

राक्ष०—प्रियंवदक ज्ञायतां सांवत्सरिकाणां द्वारि कस्तिष्ठति।

पुरु०—यदमात्य आज्ञापयति। (निष्क्रम्य पुनः प्रविश्य।) अमात्य एष खलु सांवत्सरिकः क्षपणकः—(जं अमच्चो आणवेदि। अमच्च एसो खु संवच्छरिओ क्खवणओ)

राक्ष०—(आत्मगतम्। अनिमित्तं सूचयित्वा।) कथं प्रथममेव क्षपणकः।

पुरु०—जीवसिद्धिः। (जीवसिद्धी।)

राक्ष०—(प्रकाशम्।) अबीभत्सदर्शनं कृत्वा प्रवेशय।

पुरु०—तथा (तह।) (इति निष्क्रान्तः।)

क्षपणकः—(प्रविश्य।)

शासनमर्हतां प्रतिपद्यध्वं मोहव्याधिवैद्यानाम्।
ये मुहूर्तमात्रकटुकं पश्चात्पथ्यमुपदिशन्ति॥ १८॥
सासणमलिहन्ताणं पडिवज्जह मोहवाहिवेज्जाणं।
जे मुत्तमात्तकडुअं पच्छा पत्थं उवदिसन्ति॥ १८॥

(उपसृत्य।) धर्मसिद्धिर्भवतु श्रावकाणाम्। (धम्मसिद्धी होदु सावगाणम्।)

राक्ष०—भदन्त निरूप्यतां तावदस्मत्प्रस्थानदिवसः।

जीवसिद्धीति। प्रथमं क्षपणकसामान्यबुद्ध्या दुर्निमित्तविचिकित्सा। पश्चाज्जीवसिद्धिं ज्ञात्वा प्रस्थानमुहूर्तप्रस्तावार्थं प्रवेशानुमतिः। किंचादौ क्षपणक इति दुरुपश्रुत्या राक्षसस्य प्रकृतनीतितन्त्रव्याकोपः सूचितः। पश्चाज्जीवसिद्धिरिति सूपश्रुत्या मलयकेतौ हन्तुमुद्युक्तोप भागुरायणनयोपायेनास्य जीवनसिद्धिश्च सूचितेति द्रष्टव्यम्।

शासन इति [मोह एव व्याधिस्तस्य वैद्यानां चिकित्सकानां ज्ञानोपदेशेन मोहं निरस्यतामित्यर्थः। शासनमादेशम्।] केशोलुञ्चनतप्तशिलाधिरोहणादितीक्ष्णतपसा मोक्ष इत्यार्हतानां मतम्। अनेन गाथार्थेन संप्रति स्वेन वक्ष्यमाणं वचनमापाततो रूक्षमपि परिणामे राक्षसस्य पथ्यमिति सूचितम्।

श्रावक इति। शुश्रूषुपर्यायशब्दस्तन्मतव्यवहारसिद्धः।

भदन्तेति। ज्यौतिषिकनाम तैरेव व्यवहृतम्। अयमत्राभिप्रायः। आश्वयुज्यां पौर्णमास्यां कौमुदीमहोत्सवप्रतिषेधेन व्यायामकालस्योक्तत्वात्तदारभ्य

---

१ क्षपणकं दृष्ट्वा पुनः. २ कारयित्वा. ३ ततः प्रविशति क्षपणकः. ४ धम्मलाहो. ५ शावगाह, साव-ध-कस्स. ६ भद्र.

क्षप०—(नाट्येन चिन्तयित्वा ।) श्रावक निरूपिता मयामध्याह्ना-न्निर्वृत्तसर्वकल्याणा तिथिः संपूर्णचन्द्रा पौर्णमासी । युष्माकमुत्तरस्या दिशो दक्षिणां दिशं प्रस्थितानां च (अ) दक्षिणं नक्षत्रम् । अपि च । (सावगा णिरूविदा मए आमज्झण्णादो णिव्वुत्तसव्वकल्लाणा तिही संपुण्णचन्दा पुण्णमासी । तुह्माणं उत्तलाए दिसाए दक्खिणां दिसं पत्थिदाणं अदक्खिणे णक्खत्ते । अवि अ ।)

अस्ताभिमुखे सूर्ये उदिते संपूर्णमण्डले चन्द्रे
गमनं बुधस्य लग्ने उदितास्तमिते च केतौ ॥ १९ ॥

अत्थाहिमुहे सूरे उदिए संपुण्णमण्डले चन्दे ।
गमणं बुधस्य लग्गे उदिदत्थमिदे अ केदुम्मि ॥ १९ ॥

मासद्वयमात्रेणोभाभ्यां चाणक्यराक्षसाभ्यामुपजापादिना भेदतन्त्रं प्रसाधितम् । अथ मार्गशीर्ष्यां कुसुमपुरोपरोधाय प्रस्थातुकामेन राक्षसेन प्रस्थानदिवसे पृष्टे जीवसिद्धिस्तस्मै मुहूर्तं कथयति । अद्य पौर्णमासी पञ्चचत्वारिंशन्नाडिकेति मध्याह्नपर्यन्तं भद्राभिधं विष्टिकरणं निवृत्तसमस्तकल्याणं प्रयाणे निषिद्धम् । किं चाद्य पूर्वदिशि वर्तमानं मृगशिरोनक्षत्रं दक्षिणदिशं प्रस्थितानामदक्षिणं वामं प्रतिकूलं च । अथापि त्वरया गन्तव्यमिति चेत्सायं सूर्येस्तमिते चन्द्रोदयसमये लग्नं मिथुनं बुधस्तस्याधिपतिः राहुः केतुर्वा तदा उदितास्तमितो भविष्यति । तस्मिन्बुधस्य लग्ने गमनं कर्तव्यमिति शेषः । राहुकेत्वोः सर्पाकारमेकं शरीरं तत्र शिरो राहुः पुच्छं केतुः शिरस्युदिते पुच्छमस्तमितं भवति । पुच्छ उदिते शिरोस्तमिति ज्योतिःशास्त्रसिद्धम् । उभयोरेकशरीरत्वाद्राहुरिति केतुरिति व्यपदेशः । अत उक्तमुदितास्तमिते च केताविति । एवं च मिथुनं द्विस्वभावं धनुषि सप्तमकेन्द्रे स्थितेन क्रूरेणास्तमितेन सूर्येण दृष्टं केतुना पापग्रहेण च युक्तं प्रयाणेऽनिष्टम् । तथा चोक्तम् । द्विमूर्तिराशावुदयं प्रपन्ने क्रूरग्रहैर्युक्त-निरीक्षिते च । प्रयाति यद्यप्यबुधस्तदानीं निवर्तते शत्रुजनाभिभूतः ॥ इति एवं सन्दिग्धे मुहूर्ते उक्ते । लग्ने इति । द्विस्वभावात्प्रयाणे निषिद्धं मिथुनं यद्यपि दुर्लग्नं तथापि बुधेन सौम्यग्रहेणाधिष्ठितं सत्सुलग्नं भवति । तदा चन्द्रबलेन गच्छन् दीर्घां चिरेण भाविनीं सिद्धिं वक्ष्यसि । अतस्तत्र गन्तव्यमित्यस्य ग्रन्थस्यार्थः । अत्र श्लेषेणाभिप्रेतोर्थो जीवसिद्धिना ध्वनितः । तथाहि । शूरो राक्षसः अर्थाभिमुखः अर्थो मौर्यसाचिव्य रूपोभिमुखो यस्येति बहुव्रीहिः । तस्याभिमुख्यत्वेनोपस्थित इति भावः । चन्द्रगुप्तः संपूर्णराष्ट्रः सन्नुदितो मलयकेतुरुदित एवेदानीमतः परमस्तं पराभवमेष्यतीति उदितास्तमितः । पत्थिदाणं अदक्खिणं ण क्खत्तं । इत्थं

राक्ष०—भदन्त तिथिरेव न शुध्यति ।

क्षप०—श्रावक । (सावगा ।)

एकगुणा भवति तिथिश्चतुर्गुणं भवति नक्षत्रम् ।
चतुःषष्टिगुणं लग्नमेष ज्योतिषतन्त्रसिद्धान्तः २० ॥

एक्कगुणा होइ तिथि चउग्गुणे होइ णक्खत्ते ।
चउसत्तिगुणे लग्गे एसे जोइंसतन्तसिद्धन्ते ।

तस्मात् (ता)

लग्नं भवति सुलग्नं क्रूरं ग्रहं परिहर आशु ।
प्राप्नुहि दीर्घं लाभं चन्द्रस्य बलेन गच्छन् ॥ २१ ॥

लग्गे होइ सुलग्गे कूॅलग्गहं पलिहलिज्जाशु ।
पाॅविहि दीहं लाभं चन्दस्स बलेण गच्छन्ते ॥ २० ॥

राक्ष०—भदन्त अपरैः सांवत्सरिकैः सह संवाद्यताम् ।

क्षप०—संवादयतु श्रावकः । अहं पुनर्गामिष्यामि । (संवादेदु सावगो । अहं उण गमिस्सं ।)

राक्ष०—न खलु कुपितो भदन्तः ।

क्षप०—कुपितो न युष्माकं भदन्तः । (कुविदे ण तुह्माणं भदन्ते ।)

राक्ष०—कस्तर्हि ।

क्षप०—भगवान्कृतान्तः । येनात्मनः पक्षमुज्झित्वा परपक्षः प्रमाणीक्रियते । (भॅअवं कअन्तो । जेण अत्तणो पक्खं उज्झिअ परपक्खो प्पमाणीकरीअदि ।) (इति निष्क्रान्तः क्षपणकः ।)

प्रस्थितानां च क्षत्रं न दक्षिणमिति योजना । एवं प्रस्थितानां च युष्माकं क्षत्रं भद्रभटप्रभृति दक्षिणं न भवति किं तु प्रतिकूलं मलयकेतुनिग्रहोन्मुखमित्यर्थः । अस्मिन्समये बुधस्य चाणक्यस्य लग्ने संबन्धे निमित्तभूते सति चाणक्ये त्वत्संबधार्थमुद्युक्ते सतीति भावः ।

चन्द्रगुप्तस्य बलेन मद्रभटादिना गच्छंस्त्वं दीर्घां चिरमनपायिनीं चन्द्रगुप्तस्य साचिव्यपदसिद्धिं वहसीति राक्षसं प्रति गूढाभिसन्धिवचनम् ॥ २० ॥

येन त्वया आत्मनः पक्षं ज्योतिःसिद्धान्तवेदिनं मां परित्यज्य परे सांवत्स-

---

१ दीसादि जोइससि० (दृश्यते ज्योतिषसिद्धान्ते). . २ सोमम्मि गहम्मि जइवि दुल्लग्गे (सौम्ये ग्रहे यद्यपि दुर्लग्नं). ३ वहेसि दीहं सिद्धिं (वहसि दीर्घां सिद्धिं). ४ अतः- प्राक् (स्वगतम्).

राक्ष०—प्रियंवदक ज्ञायतां का वेला वर्तत इति।

प्रियं०—अस्ताभिलाषी भगवान्सूर्यः। (अंत्थाहिलासी भअवं सूरो।)

राक्ष०—(उत्थाय विलोक्य।) अये अस्ताभिलाषी भगवान्भास्करः। संप्रति हि।

आविर्भूतानुरागाः क्षणमुदयगिरेरुज्जिहानस्य भानोः
पर्णच्छायैः पुरस्तादुपवनतरवो दूरमाश्वेव गत्वा।
एते तस्मिन्निवृत्ताः पुनरपरगिरिप्रान्तपर्यस्तबिम्बे
प्रायो भृत्यास्त्यजन्ति प्रचलितविभवं स्वामिनं सेवमानाः॥२२॥

(इति निष्क्रान्ताः सर्वे।)

इति राक्षसोद्योगो नाम चतुर्थोऽङ्कः।

रिका अपेक्ष्यन्ते। अतस्त्वज्ज्योतिःशास्त्रस्य कृतान्तः सिद्धान्तो व्याकोपित इति मत्वा कृतान्तः कुपित इति निष्ठुरवचनं स्पष्टम्। येन त्वयात्मनः पक्षं नन्दवंशीयं चन्द्रगुप्तमपेक्ष्य परपक्षो मलयकेतुः प्रमाणीक्रियतेतस्तव कालः कुपित इति हृदि गूढम्। 'कृतान्तो यमसिद्धान्तौ' इत्यमरः।

सूर इति। शूरो मलयकेतुरस्तोन्मुखः शूरो राक्षसश्चार्थाभिलाषी इति चोपश्रुतिर्ध्वनिता। उक्तामेव दुरुपश्रुतिमन्यथयति भास्कर इति।

आविर्भूतानुरागा इति। उज्जिहानस्योदयमानस्य पर्णच्छायैः पर्णच्छायारूपेण। इत्थंभावे तृतीया। छायाबाहुल्यमिति नपुंसकत्वम्। पुरस्तात्पुरोभागे पुरोगामिसेवकवत्। आशु शीघ्रमेव गत्वा पूर्वाह्णे वृक्षच्छायाः प्रत्यक्प्रसरन्तीति भानोः पुरोगामिभृत्यत्वेनोत्प्रेक्षिताः पश्चादपराह्णे तस्मिन्नस्तोन्मुखे सति निवृत्तास्तं परित्यज्य परावृत्ता इव दृश्यन्ते। अपककुभः प्रान्तपर्यस्तबिम्बे इति पाठे अपककुप्पश्चिमदिगेव। प्रायो भृत्या इत्यर्थान्तरन्यासः। तेन च मलयकेतुदुरवस्था ध्वन्यते। इत्थं नियताप्तिप्रकरीरूपो विमर्शसन्धिस्तस्याङ्गानि चापवादादीनि निरूपितानि॥ २१॥

इति श्रीत्र्यम्बकयज्वप्रभुवर्याश्रितढुण्ढिराजव्यासयज्वविरचिते मुद्राराक्षसनाटकव्याख्याने चतुर्थोऽङ्कः समाप्तः॥

---

१ अस्मात्प्राक्-अ अमच्चो आणवेदि (इति निष्क्रम्य पुनः प्रविश्य।). २ आसनादुत्थाय. ३ पत्र. ४ पुनरितरककुप्.

पञ्चमोऽङ्कः ।

(ततः प्रविशति लेखमलङ्करणस्थगिकां मुद्रितामादाय सिद्धार्थकः ।)

सिद्धा०—आश्चर्यमाश्चर्यम् । (ही हीमाणहे हीमाणहे ।)

बुद्धिजलनिर्झरैः सिच्यमाना देशकालकलशैः ।
दर्शयिष्यति कार्यफलं गुरुकं चाणक्यनीतिलता ॥ १ ॥

बुद्धिजलणिज्झरेहिं सिञ्चन्ती देसकालकलसेहिं ।
दंसिस्सदि कज्जफलं गुरुअं चाणक्कणीदिलदा ॥ १ ॥

तद्गृहीतो मयार्यचाणक्येन प्रथमलेखितोमात्यराक्षसस्य मुद्रालाञ्छितोयं लेखस्तस्यैव मुद्रालाञ्छितेयमाभरणपेटिका । चलितोस्मि किल पाटलिपुत्रम् । यावद्गच्छामि । (परिक्रम्यावलोक्य च ।) कथं क्षपणक आगच्छति । यावदस्याशकुनभूतं दर्शनं मम संमतमेव तस्मान्न परिहरामि । (ता गहीदो मए अज्जचाणक्केण पढमलिहिदो अमच्चरक्खसस्स मुद्दालंच्छिओ अअं लेहो तस्स ज्जेव्व मुद्दालंछिआ इअं आहरणपेडिआ । चलिदोह्मि किल पाडलिउत्तं । जाव गच्छामि । केहं खवणओ आअच्छदि । जाव से असउणभूदं दंसणं मह संमदं एव्व ता ण पडिहरामि ।)

अथ फलागमकार्ययोः संबन्धो निर्वहणसन्धिस्त्रिभिरङ्कैरारभ्यते ॥ तल्लक्षणमुक्तम् । बीजवन्तो मुखाद्यर्था विप्रकीर्णा यथायथम् । ऐकार्थ्यमुपनीयन्ते यत्र निर्वहणं हि तत् ॥ बीजवन्तोनुस्यूतबीजाः मुखसन्ध्यादीनामर्थाः आरम्भबीजसंबन्धादयः यथायथं तत्तत्प्रसङ्गानुसारेण विप्रकीर्णा विशकलिततया यदर्थमारब्धाः सन्तः ऐकार्थ्यमुपनीयन्ते तस्य फलागमशालिनः कार्यस्य यत्र निर्वाहः सिद्धिर्भवति स निर्वहणसन्धिः । कार्यफलागमौ वक्ष्येते । अस्याङ्गानि फलागमकार्यानुगुण्येन प्रयोक्तव्यानि । यथा । सन्धिर्विरोधो प्रथनं निर्णयः परिभाषणम् । प्रसादानन्दसमयाः कृत्याभाषोपगूहनम् । पूर्वभावोपसंहारौ प्रशस्तिश्च चतुर्दश ॥ स्थगिकामिति । राक्षसमुद्रामुद्रितां स्थगिकां पेटिकाम् । हीहीमाणहे इति आश्चर्यद्योतको निपातसमुदायः ।

किलेत्यलीके गमनमलीकं छद्मरूपमित्यर्थः । इदं बीजोपगमनं सन्धिर्नामाङ्गम् । बीजस्य चाणक्यनीतेरुपगमनात्कार्यसिद्ध्यर्थमभ्युपगमान्निर्वहणात् ॥ १ ॥

---

१ दंसइस्सदि. २ अये कहं. ३ ता जाव मे असउणभूदं इमस्स दंसणं ता आदित्तदंसणेण पडिहणामि.

क्षपणकः—(प्रविश्य ।)

अर्हतः प्रणमामि ये ते गम्भीरतया बुद्धेः ।
लोकोत्तरैर्लोके सिद्धिं मार्गैर्गच्छन्ति ॥ २ ॥

अलहन्ताणं पणममामि जे दे गंभीलदाए बुद्धीए ।
लोउत्तलेहिं लोए सिद्धिं मग्गेहिं गच्छंन्दि ॥ २ ॥

सिद्धा०—भदन्त वन्दे । (भदन्त वन्दामि ।)

क्षप०—श्रावक धर्मसिद्धिर्भवतु । (निर्वर्ण्य ।) श्रावक प्रस्थानसमुद्वहने कृतव्यवसायमिव त्वां पश्यामि । (सावगा धम्मसिद्धी होदु । सावगा पत्थाणसमुव्वहणे किदव्ववसाअं विअ तुमं पेक्खामि ।)

सिद्धा०—कथं भदन्तो जानाति । (कहं भदन्तो जाणादि ।)

क्षप०—श्रावक किमत्र ज्ञातव्यम् । एष ते मार्गादेशकुशलः शकुनः करगतो लेखश्च सूचयति । (सावगा किं एत्थ जाणिदव्वं । ऐसो दे मग्गादेसकुसलो सउणो करगदो लेहो अ सूअदि ।

सिद्धा०—ज्ञातं भदन्तेन । देशान्तरं प्रस्थितोस्मि । तस्मात्कथयतु भदन्तः कीदृशोद्य दिवसः । (जाणिदं भदन्तेण । देसन्तरं पत्थिदोह्मि । ता कहेदु भदन्तो कीदिसो अज्ज दिवसा त्ति ।)

क्षप०—(विहस्य ।) श्रावक मुण्डितमुण्डो नक्षत्राणि पृच्छसि । (सावगा मुण्डिअमुण्डो णक्खत्ताइं पुच्छसि ।)

सिद्धा०—भदन्त सांप्रतमपि किं जातम् । कथय प्रस्थानस्य यद्यनुकूलं भविष्यति तदा गमिष्यामि । अन्यथा निवर्तिष्ये । (भदन्त सप्पदं वि किं जादं । कहेहि पत्थाणस्स जइ अणुकूलं भविस्सदि तदो गमिस्सं । अण्णधा निवत्तिस्सं ।)

परिहरामीति । अनेनाशकुनेन कुसुमपुरं प्रति गमनप्रतिबन्ध इष्ट एवेत्यर्थः ।

आर्हतानामिति कर्मणि षष्ठी । जलनिमज्जितमुक्तालाबुवच्छश्वदुत्प्लुत्योर्ध्वगमनमेव मुक्तिरित्यार्हतानां मतम् । अनेन लोकोत्तरकार्यसिद्धिप्रदं चाणक्यनीतिगाम्भीर्यं ध्वनितम् ॥ २ ॥

---

१ ततः प्रविशति०. २ मग्गन्ति (मार्गयन्ति). ३ प्पणमामि. ४ णं एसो ज्जेव दे मग्गणाओकण्णधोर (मार्गनौकर्णधारः) लेहे.

क्षप०—श्रावक सांप्रतमेतस्मिन्मलयकेतुकटकेनुकूलं भविष्यति । (सावेगा ण संपदं एदस्सिं मलअकेदुकडए अणुकूलं भविस्सदि ।)

सिद्धा०—भदन्त कथय कुत एतत् । (भदन्त कहेहि कुदो एदम् ।)

क्षप०—श्रावक निशामय । प्रथमं तावदत्र कटके लोकस्यानिवारितो निर्गमप्रवेश आसीत् । इदानीमितः प्रत्यासन्ने कुसुमपुरे न कोप्यमुद्रालाञ्छितो निर्गन्तुं प्रवेष्टुं वानुमोद्यते । तद्यदि भागुरायणस्य मुद्रालाञ्छितस्तदा गच्छ विश्रब्धोन्यथा तिष्ठ । मा गुल्माधिकारिकैः संयमितकरचरणो राजकुलं प्रवेश्यसे । (सावगा णिसामेहि । पुढमं दाव एत्थ कडए लोअस्स अणिवारिदो णिग्गमप्पवेसो आसी । दाणीं इदो पच्चासण्णे कुसुमपुले ण कोवि अमुद्दालंच्छिओ णिग्गमिदुं पवेट्ठुं वा अणुमोदीअदि । ता जदि भाउराणस्स मुद्दालंच्छिओ तदो गच्छ विस्सद्धो अण्णहा चिट्ठ । मा गुम्माहिआरिएहिं सञ्जमिअकलचलणो राअकुलं पवेसीअसि ।)

सिद्धा०—किं न जानाति भदन्तो अमात्यराक्षसस्य सन्निहित इति । तदमुद्रालाञ्छितमपि मां निष्क्रामन्तं कस्य शक्तिर्निवारयितुम् । (किं ण जाणादि भदन्तो अमच्चरक्खसस्स सण्णिहिदो त्ति । ता अमुद्दालंच्छिदं वि मं णिक्कमन्तं कस्स सत्ती णिवारेदुं ।)

क्षप०—(सावेगम् ।) श्रावक राक्षसस्य पिशाचस्य वा भव न पुनरमुद्रालाञ्छितस्येतो निष्क्रमणोपायः । (सावगा रक्खसस्स पिसाचस्स वो होहि ण उण अमुद्दालंच्छिदस्स इदो णिक्कमणोवाओ ।)

सिद्धा०—भदन्त मा कुप्य मे कार्यसिद्धिर्भवतु । (भदन्त मा कुप्य मे कज्जसिद्धी होदु ।

क्षप०—श्रावक गच्छ भवतु ते कार्यसिद्धिः । अहमपि भागुरा-

सावेगमिति । कौटिल्यकूटकार्यनिर्वहणार्थं कृतोद्योग इति ज्ञात्वा मनस्यावेग औ-

---

१ सावकाणं । (श्रावकानां ।) ०कडए अणुऊलेण अणणुऊलेन वा अग्गहिदमुद्देण गच्छीअदि (अगृहीतमुद्रेण गम्यते ।) इ. पा. २ मलअकेदुक० ३ अण्णधा णिवत्तिअ णिउक्कण्ठं चिट्ठ, चिट्ठ णिउक्के (तूष्णीकः). ४ ०सस्स केलिअरो अन्तिओ, सेवओ सिद्धत्थओ. ५ वा केलिअरो, शेवगे. ६ भण मे कज्ज०.

यणान्मुद्रां याचे । (सावगा गच्छ । होदु दे कज्जसिद्धि । अहं वि भाउराअणादो मुद्दं जाचेमि ।) (इति निष्क्रान्तौ ।)

इति प्रवेशकः ।

(ततः प्रविशति पुरुषेणानुगम्यमानो भागुरायणः ।)

भागु०—(स्वगतम् ।) अहो वैचित्र्यमार्यचाणक्यनीतेः ।

मुहुर्लक्ष्योद्भेदा मुहुरधिगमाभावगहना
मुहुः संपूर्णाङ्गी मुहुरतिकृशा कार्यवशतः ।
मुहुर्नश्यद्बीजा मुहुरपि बहुप्रापितफले-
त्यहो चित्राकारा नियतिरिव नीतिर्नयविदः ॥ ३ ॥

(प्रकाशम् ।) भद्र भासुरक नमां दूरीभवन्तमिच्छति कुमारः । अतोस्मिन्नेवास्थानमण्डपे न्यस्यतामासनम् ।

पुरु०—एतदासनम् । उपविशत्वार्यः । (एदं आसणं । उपविशदु अज्जो ।)

भागु०—(उपविश्य ।) भद्र[2] यः कश्चिन्मुद्रार्थी मां द्रष्टुमिच्छति स त्वया प्रवेशयितव्यः ।

पुरु०—यदार्य आज्ञापयति । (जं अज्जो[3] आणवेदि ।) (इति निष्क्रान्तः ।)

भागु०—(स्वगतम् ।) कष्टमेवमयमस्मासु स्नेहवान्कुमारो मलयकेतुरतिसन्धातव्य इत्यहो दुष्करम् । अथवा ।

त्सुक्यम् । अहमपि इति । अहमपि चिकीर्षितमहाप्रयोजनसिद्ध्यर्थं मुद्रायाचनव्याजेन भागुरायणं प्रति गमिष्यामीति गूढम् । इदं कार्यमार्गणं विरोधो नामाङ्गम् ॥ २ ॥ प्रवेशक इति । तल्लक्षणमुक्तम् । वृत्तवर्तिष्यमाणानां कथांशानां निदर्शकः । प्रवेशकस्तु नाट्येङ्के नीचपात्रप्रयोजितः ॥ इति ।

मुहुर्लक्ष्योद्भेदा इति । मुहुर्लक्ष्योद्भेदा मुखसन्धौ स्तोकोद्दिष्टा सती बहुधा विस्तारिणीत्यर्थः । प्रतिमुखे लक्ष्यालक्ष्यायाः पुनर्व्यक्तेः गहनातिकृशा च । गर्भे मुहुर्दृष्टनष्टान्वेषणान्नश्यदिव बीजमुद्योगो यस्याः सा तथोक्ता । विमर्शे बीजस्य स्पष्टमेव दर्शनात्संपूर्णाङ्गीत्युक्तम् । निर्वहणे सर्वार्थोपसंहाराद्बहुप्रापितफलेत्युक्तम् । ईदृशी नयविदश्चाणक्यस्य नीतिर्नियतिरिव चित्राकारा । नियतेश्चाणक्यनीतेश्च कार्याणां विचित्राकारता कारणे उपचर्यते ॥ ३ ॥

न्यस्यतामिति । मुद्रादानार्थं कटकद्वार्यवस्थानं दूरीभवनमित्याशयः ।

---

१ भ्रष्टय०. २ भद्र भासुरक ३ अमश्चो.

कुले लज्जायां च स्वयशसि च माने च विमुखः
शरीरं विक्रीय क्षणिकधनलोभाद्धनवति ।
तदाज्ञां कुर्वाणो हितमहितमित्येतदधुना
विचारातिक्रान्तः किमिति परतन्त्रो विमृशति ॥ ४ ॥

(ततः प्रविशति प्रतीहार्यनुगम्यमानो मलयकेतुः ।)

मल०—(स्वगतम् ।) अहो राक्षसं प्रति विकल्पबाहुल्यादाकुला मे बुद्धिर्न निश्चयमधिगच्छति । कुतः ।

भक्त्या नन्दकुलानुरागदृढया नन्दान्वयालम्बिना
किं चाणक्यनिराकृतेन कृतिना मौर्येण सन्धास्यते ।
स्थैर्यं भक्तिगुणस्य वाधिगणयन्किं सत्यसन्धो भवे-
दित्यारूढकुलालचक्रमिव मे चेतश्चिरं भ्राम्यति ॥ ५ ॥

(प्रकाशम् ।) विजये क्व भागुरायणः ।

प्रतीहारी—कुमार एष खलु कटकान्निष्क्रमितुकामानां मुद्रासंप्रदानमनुतिष्ठति । (कुमार एसो खु कडआदो णिक्कमिदुकामाणं मुद्दासंपदाणं अणुचिठ्ठदि ।)

मल०—विजये मुहूर्तमसञ्चारा भव यावदस्य पराङ्मुखस्यैव पाणिभ्यां नयने पिदधामि ।

अतिसन्धातव्य इति । यत्कष्टं पापं दुष्करमित्यन्वयः । उक्तं कष्टं समाधत्ते- अथवेति । कुले इति । विचारातिक्रान्तः अतिक्रान्तविचारसमय इत्यर्थः । इदं कार्योपक्षेपणं ग्रथनम् । कार्यस्य मलयकेत्वतिसन्धानेन राक्षसवशीकरणस्योपक्षेपणात् ॥४॥

भक्त्या इति । [चाणक्यस्य निराकृतं निराकृतिस्तेन कृतिना] नन्दान्वयालम्बिना किं मौर्येण सन्धास्यते किंवा भक्तिगुणस्य मयि मया वा क्रियमाणस्य स्थैर्यं दार्ढ्यं अधिगणयन् आधिक्येन पश्यन् सत्यसन्धः सत्या सन्धा नन्दराज्यं सर्वं तवैवास्त्विति पूर्वं कृता प्रतिज्ञा यस्य स तथोक्तो भवेत् । नन्दवंशत्वेन नन्दकुलानुरागजनिता भक्तिर्मौर्ये दृढा भवितुमर्हति सत्यसन्धत्वानुरोधेन मयि च केवलो भक्तिगुणो दृढो भवितुमर्हतीत्युभयकोटिकः संशयः । तत्रापि मौर्यसन्धानकोटिः प्रबलेति ध्वनयितुं चाणक्यनिराकृतेनेति विशेषणं राक्षसस्य मौर्यसान्निध्याभिलाषहेतुगर्भम् । कृतिनेति च विशेषणं लब्धदुर्लभराज्यत्वात्कृतकृत्यः सन्पुनश्चाणक्येन जितकाशिना दुर्विधेयेन मौर्यो न सन्दधीतेति ध्वनयितुम् ॥ ५ ॥

विजये मुहूर्तमिति । अनेन मलयकेतोरतिबालिशत्वं भागुरायणस्य चैवं

---

१ लाभात्, क्षणिकमपि लोभात्. २ न्निष्क्रा. ३ विगणयन्. ४ संपादनाधिकारे चिठ्ठदि ५ निभृतपदमसञ्चारा.

प्रती०—यत्कुमार आज्ञापयति। (जं कुमारो आणवेदि।)

पुरुषः—(प्रविश्य।) आर्य एष खलु क्षपणको मुद्रानिमित्तमार्यं प्रेक्षितुमिच्छति। (अज्ज एसो खु खवणओ मुद्दाणिमित्तं अज्जं पेक्खिदुमिच्छदि।)

भागु०—प्रवेशय।

पुरुषः—तथा (तहा) (इति निष्क्रान्तः।)

क्षपणकः—(प्रविश्य।) धर्मसिद्धिः श्रावकाणां भवतु। (धम्मसिद्धी सावगाणं होदु।)

भागु०—(अवलोक्य स्वगतम्।) अये राक्षसस्य मित्रं जीवसिद्धिः। (प्रकाशम्।) भदन्त न खलु राक्षसस्य प्रयोजनमेव किंचिदुद्दिश्य गम्यते।

क्षप०—(कर्णौ पिधाय।) शान्तं पापं शान्तं पापम्। श्रावक तत्र गमिष्यामि यत्र राक्षसस्य पिशाचस्य वा नामापि न श्रूयते। (सन्तं पावं सन्तं पावं। सावगा तहिं गमिस्सं जहिं रक्खसस्स पिसाचस्स वा णामं वि ण सुणीअदि।)

भागु०—बलवान्सुहृदि प्रणयकोपः। तत्किमपराद्धं राक्षसेन भदन्तस्य।

क्षप०—श्रावक न मे किमपि राक्षसेनापराद्धम्। स्वयमेव मन्दभाग्य आत्मनोऽपराध्यामि।) सावगा ण मम किंवि रक्खसेण अवरद्धं। सअं जेव्व मन्दभाओ अत्तणो अवलद्धामि।)

भागु०—भदन्त वर्द्धयसि मे कुतूहलम्। श्रोतुमिच्छामि।

मल०—(स्वगतम्।) अहमपि श्रोतुमिच्छामि।

क्षप०—श्रावक किमनेनाश्रोतव्येन श्रुतेन। (सावगा किं अणेण असुणिदव्वेण सुदेण)

भागु०—यदि रहस्यं तत्तिष्ठतु।

तद्वशीकरणप्राविण्यं च सूचितम्। तेनेदानीं महत्प्रयोजनमनुष्ठेयं भविष्यतीति पूर्वमुपक्षिप्तस्य जीवसिद्धिना संप्रति क्रियमाणस्य मलयकेतुवार्तसन्धानरूपस्य महाप्रयोजनस्यावसरदानाय चेदं कविसंविधानमित्यवधेयम्।

राक्षसस्य मित्रमिति। अनेन द्वारेणेदानीं मलयकेतुरतिसन्धातव्य इति भावः।

---

१ नाट्येनावलोक्य. २ एतन्नास्ति क्वचित्. ३ भदन्त बलवांस्ते. ४ हतासो मन्दभाओ अत्तणो कम्मेसु लज्जे.

क्षप०—श्रावक न रहस्यं किंत्वतिनृशंसम् । (सावगा ण रहस्यं किंदु अदिणिसंसं ।)

भागु०—यदि न रहस्यं तत्कथ्यताम् ।

क्षप०—श्रावक न रहस्यमेतत्तथापि न कथयिष्यामि । (सावगाण रहस्सं एदं तहवि ण कहिस्सं ।

भागु०—अहमपि मुद्रां न दास्यामि ।

क्षप०—(स्वगतम् ।) युक्तमिदानीमर्थिने कथयितुम् । (प्रकाशम् ।) का गतिः शृणोतु श्रावकः । अस्ति तावदहं मन्दभाग्यः प्रथमं पाटलिपुत्रे निवसन् राक्षसेन मित्रत्वमुपगतः । तस्मिन्नवसरे राक्षसेन गूढविषकन्यकाप्रयोगमुत्पाद्य घातितो देवः पर्वतेश्वरः । (का गदी सुणादु सावगो । अत्थि दाव अहं मन्दभग्गो पढमं पाडलिउत्ते णिवसमाणे लक्खसेण मित्तत्तणं उवगदे तहिं अवसले लक्खसेण गूढं विसकण्णआपओअं उप्पादिअ घादिदे देवे पव्वदीसले ।)

मल०—(सबाष्पमात्मगतम् ।) कथं राक्षसेन घातितस्तातो न चाणक्येन ।

भागु०—भदन्त ततस्ततः ।

क्षप०—ततोहं राक्षसस्य मित्रमिति कृत्वा चाणक्यहतकेन सनिकारं नगरान्निर्वासितः । इदानीमपि राक्षसेनानेकाकार्यकुशलेन किमपि तादृशमारभ्यते येनाहं जीवलोकान्निष्कासिष्ये । (तदो हगे लक्खसस्स मित्तं त्ति कदुअ चाणक्कहदएण सणिकालं णअरादो णिव्वासिदे । दाणीं वि लक्खसेण अणेअअकज्जकुसलेण किंवि तालिसं आलहीअदि जेण हगे जीअलोआदो णिक्कासिज्जेमि ।)

भागु०—भदन्त प्रतिश्रुतराज्यार्द्धमयच्छता चाणक्यहतकेनेदमकार्यमनुष्ठितं न राक्षसेनेति श्रुतमस्माभिः ।

क्षप०—(कर्णौ पिधाय ।) शान्तं पापम् । चाणक्येन विषकन्याया ना-

अर्थिने इति । अर्थिने आदरवते आदरेण श्रुतं मत्कथितं तथात्वेनैव गृह्णीयादिति भावः । घातित इति मम हस्तेनेति शेषः ।

तादृशमिति । तादृशं पर्वतेश्वरघातनसदृशं । मलयकेतुनिग्रहोपीति गूढो भावः । इदं भागुरायणभदन्तयोर्मिथः परिभाषणं जल्पनम् ।

---

१ भदन्त अहं. २ रक्खसस्स. ३ णिव्वासिज्जामि (निर्वासिष्ये).

मापि न श्रुतम् । (सन्तं पावं । चाणक्केण विसकण्णाए णामं वि ण सुदम् ।)

भागु०—भदंन्त इयं मुद्रा दीयते । एहि कुमारं श्रावय ।

मल०—(उपसृत्य ।)

श्रुतं सखे श्रवणविदारणं वचः
सुहृन्मुखाद्रिपुमधिकृत्य भाषितम् ।
पितुर्वधव्यसनमिदं हि येन मे
चिरादपि द्विगुणमिवाद्य वर्धते ॥ ६ ॥

क्षप०—(स्वगतम् ।) अये श्रुतं मलयकेतुहतकेन । हन्त कृतार्थोस्मि । (इति निष्क्रान्तः ।)

मल०—(प्रत्यक्षवदाकाशे लक्ष्यं बद्ध्वा ।) राक्षस राक्षस युक्तं युक्तम् ।

मित्रं ममायमिति निर्वृतचित्तवृत्तिं
विश्रम्भतस्त्वयि निवेशितसर्वकार्यम् ।
तातं निपात्य सह बन्धुजनाश्रुतोयै-
रन्वर्थतोपि ननु राक्षस राक्षसोसि ॥ ७ ॥

भागु०—(स्वगतम् ।) रक्षणीया राक्षसस्य प्राणा इत्यार्यादेशः । भवत्वेवं तावत् । (प्रकाशम् ।) कुमार अलमावेगेन । आसनस्थं कुमारं किंचिद्विज्ञापयितुमिच्छामि ।

मल०—(उपविश्य ।) सखे किमसि वक्तुकामः ।

भागु०—कुमार इह खल्वर्थशास्त्रव्यवहारिणामर्थवशादरिमित्रो-

श्रुतमिति । चिरादपि चिरज्जातमपि अद्य जातमिव द्विगुणं वर्धत इत्यर्थः । कृतार्थोस्मीति । तेनेदानीं महत्प्रयोजनमनुष्ठेयं भविष्यतीति पूर्वोक्तमहाप्रयोजनानुष्ठानेन कृतार्थोस्मीत्यर्थः । सुहृन्मुखाद्रिपुमधिकृत्येत्यनेन स्वस्य सुहृत्त्वेन विश्वास्यवचनत्वं रिपुत्वं च मलयकेतुना मनसि दृढीकृतमिति च कृतार्थता । इदं बीजानुगुणकार्यप्रख्यापनं निर्णयः ॥ ६ ॥

मित्रं ममेदमिति । अनेन ज्ञायते राक्षसपर्वतकयोः पूर्वं महत्सौहृदमासीदन्तरं चाणक्येन राज्यार्धदानपरिपणनप्रलोभनेन राक्षसाद्विभेद्य स्वकार्यसिद्धये पर्वतकः सहायत्वेन प्रवणीकृत इति । तथाचानुपदमेव कुपितो मलयकेतुर्भागुरायणेन समाधीयते तस्मिन्काले सर्वार्थसिद्धिं राजानमित्यादिना महानरातिरासीदित्यन्तेन ग्रन्थेन ॥ ७ ॥

---

१ चाणक्को जाणादि । तेण ज्जेव दुट्ठबुद्धिणा लक्खसेण एसा अकज्जसिद्धी किदा । २ भदन्त कष्टमिदं । इयं. ३ मिहा. ४ ०र्थचाणक्यः. ५ युक्तमिदम्. ६ ममेदं. ७ कार्यः ८ नाक्षि.

दासीनव्यवस्था न लौकिकानामिव स्वेच्छावशात् । यतस्तस्मिन्काले सर्वार्थसिद्धिं राजानमिच्छतो राक्षसस्य चन्द्रगुप्तादपि बलीयस्तया सुगृहीतनामा देवः पर्वतेश्वर एवार्थपरिपन्थी महानरातिरासीत् । तस्मिंश्च राक्षसेनेदमनुष्ठितमिति नातिदोषमिवात्रेति पश्यामि । पश्यतु कुमारः ।

मित्राणि शत्रुत्वमुवानयन्ती मित्रत्वमर्थस्य वशाच्च शत्रून् ।
नीतिर्नयत्यस्मृतपूर्ववृत्तं जन्मान्तरं जीवत एव पुंसः ॥ ८ ॥

तदत्र वस्तुनि नोपालम्भनीयो राक्षसः । आ नन्दराज्यलाभादुपग्राह्यश्च । परतश्च परिग्रहे वा परित्यागे वा कुमारः प्रमाणम् ।

मल०—एवम् । सखे सम्यग्दृष्टवानसि । यतोमात्यवधे प्रकृतिक्षोभः स्यादेवं च सन्दिग्धो विजयः ।

(प्रविश्य ।) **पुरुषः**—जयतु कुमारः । आर्य गुल्मस्थानाधिकृतो दीर्घरक्षो विज्ञापयति । एष खल्वस्माभिः कटकान्निष्क्रामन्नगृहीतमुद्रः सलेखः पुरुषो गृहीतः । तत्प्रत्यक्षीकरोत्वेनमार्य इति । (जेदु कुमारो । अज्ज गुम्मट्ठाणाधिकिदो दीहरक्खो विण्णवेदि एसो खु अह्मेहिं कडआदो णिक्कमन्तो अगहीदमुद्दो सलेहो पुरिसो गहीदो । ता पच्चक्खीकरेदु णं अज्जोत्ति ।)

भागु०—भद्र प्रवेशय ।

पुरु०—यदार्य आज्ञापयति । (जं अज्जो आणवेदी) । (इति निष्क्रान्तः ।)

सिद्धा०—(स्वगतम् ।)

आनयन्त्यै गुणेषु दोषेषु पराङ्मुखं कुर्वत्यै ।
अस्मादृशजनन्यै प्रणमामः स्वामिभक्त्यै ॥ ९ ॥

मित्राणीति । जन्मान्तरे पूर्वजन्मवृत्तं यथा न स्मर्यते तथा जीवित एव पुंसः राजतन्त्रनीतिवशात्पूर्वापकृतादि विस्मार्यत्वेन प्रसज्यत इति भावः ॥ ८ ॥

तदत्र वस्तुनीति इदं कुपितस्य मलयकेतोः समाधानरूपं पर्युपासनं ।

अतःपरमङ्कसमाप्तिपर्यन्तं प्रथमेऽङ्के किमत्र लिखामीत्यादिना कर्णे एवमेवेत्यन्तेन ग्रन्थेनोपक्षिप्तस्य बीजस्यानेकधा प्रकीर्णस्यैकार्थीकरणबीजोपगमनस्यैव सन्धेरङ्गस्य प्रपञ्चः । आनन्त्यैरिति । दोषवति कार्ये प्रवृत्त्यापि दोषे पराङ्मुखं दोषानगण-

---

१ लोकानां. २ नास्ति दोष एवात्र. ३ ०मिवान०. ४ ०मस्यार्थ—अप्यर्थ. ५ वस्तुन्यनुपालभ्यः. ६ विजयः स्यादस्माकम्. ७ तहा.

आणंतीए गुणेसु दोसेसु परंमुहं कुणन्तीए।
अह्मारिसजणणीए पणमामो सामिभत्तीए॥ ९॥

पुरु०[1]—आर्य अयं स पुरुषः। (अज्ज अअं सो पुरिसो।)

भागु०—(नाट्येनावलोक्य।) भद्र किमयमागन्तुक आहोस्विदिहैव कस्यचित्परिग्रहः।

सिद्धा०—आर्य अहं खलु अमात्यराक्षसस्य सेवकः। (अज्ज अहं खु अमच्चरक्खसस्स सेवओ।)

भागु०—भद्र तत्किम[2]गृहीतमुद्रः कटकान्निष्क्रामसि।

सिद्धा०—आर्य कार्यगौरवेण त्वरायितोस्मि (अज्ज कज्जगोरवेण तुवराविदोह्मि।)

भागु०—कीदृशं तत्कार्यगौरवं यद्राजशासनमुल्लङ्घ[3]यति।

मल०—सखे भागुरायण लेखमर्पे[4]नय।

भागु०—(सिद्धार्थकहस्ताद्गृहीत्वा पत्रमुद्रां दृष्ट्वा।) कुमार अयं लेखः। रा[5]क्षसनामाङ्कितेयं मुद्रा।

मल०—मुद्रां परिपालयन्नुद्घा[6]ट्य दर्शय।

भागु०—(तथा कृत्वा दर्शयति।[7])

मल०—(वाँचयति।) स्वस्ति यथास्थानं कुतोपि कोपि कमपि पुरुषविशेषमवगमयति। अस्मत्प्रतिपक्षं निराकृत्य दर्शिता कापि सत्यता सत्यवादिना। सांप्रतमेतेषामपि प्रथममुपन्यस्तसन्धीनामस्मत्सुहृदां पूर्वप्रतिज्ञातसन्धिपरिप[8]णनप्रोत्साहनेन सत्यसन्धः प्रीतिमुत्पादयितुमर्हति। एतेप्येव-

यत्नं कुर्वन्त्यै प्रत्युत गुणेष्वानयन्त्यै गुणपक्ष एव पातयन्त्यै सर्वतो गरीयस्यै स्वामिभक्त्यै नमः। स्वामिभक्तिवशात्स्वामिकार्यसिद्ध्यर्थमनुचितमपि क्रियमाणं गुणपक्ष एव भवति न पुनर्दोषपक्ष इति भावः। स्वामिभक्त्यै इति। क्रियया यमभिप्रैति स सम्प्रदानमिति सम्प्रदानत्वम्॥ ९॥

मुद्रां परिपालयन्निति। लेखस्य धारणपेटिकायाश्च मुद्रापरिपालनं राक्षसमुद्रया सह संवाददर्शनार्थम्। स्वस्ति यथेति। अस्मत्प्रतिपक्षस्य चाणक्यस्य निराकरणं पूर्वमेव त्वया प्रतिज्ञातमासीत्। किलेति बलादापादानार्थम्। अस्मत्सुहृदां कौलूतादीनामित्यर्थः। सन्धिपरिपणनस्य सन्धिसमये पूर्वदित्सितस्य प्रोत्साहनम्।

१ उपसृत्य इत्यधिकम्. २ किमर्थम०. ३ व्यासि. ४ मुपा०. ५ राक्षसमुद्राङ्कितः, ०नामाङ्कोऽयं. ६ उद्वेश्य. ७ गृहीत्वा वाच०. ८ परिपणवस्तु प्रतिपादन०.

मनुगृहीताः सन्तः स्वाश्रयविनाशेनोपकारिणमाश्रयिष्यन्ति । अविस्मृतमेतत्सत्यवतः स्मारयामः । एतेषां मध्ये केचिदरेः कोषहस्तिभ्यामर्थिनः केचिद्विषयेणेति । अलङ्कारत्रयं च सत्यवता यदनुप्रेषितं तदुपगतम् । मयापि लेखस्याशून्यार्थं किंचिदनुप्रेषितं तदुपगमनीयम् । वाचिकं चाप्ततमादस्माच्छ्रोतव्यमिति । सखे भागुरायण कीदृशो लेखः ।

भागु०—भद्र सिद्धार्थक कस्यायं लेखः ।

सिद्धा०—आर्य न जानामि । (अज्ज ण जाणामि ।)

भागु०—हे धूर्त लेखो नीयते न ज्ञायते कस्यायमिति । सर्वं तावत्तिष्ठतु । वाचिकं त्वत्तः केन श्रोतव्यम् ।

सिद्धा०—(भयं नाटयन् ।) युष्माभिः (तुह्मेहिं)

भागु०—किमस्माभिः ।

सिद्धा०—मिश्रैर्गृहीतो न जानामि किं भणामीति । (मिस्सेहिं गिहीदो ण आणामि किं भणामि त्ति ।)

भागु०—(सरोषम् ।) एष ज्ञानासि । भासुरक बहिर्नीत्वा तावत्ताड्यतां यावत्कथयति ।

पुरु०—यदमात्य आज्ञापयति । (जं अमच्चो आणवेदि ।) (इति तेन सह निष्क्रम्य पुनः प्रविश्य ।) आर्य इयं मुद्रालाञ्छिता पेटिका तस्य ताड्यमानस्य कक्षातो निपतिता । (अज्ज इअं मुद्दालंच्छिदा पेडिआ तस्स ताडिअमाणस्स कक्खादो णिवडिदा ।)

अवश्यं दास्यामीत्याश्वसनम् । अविस्मृतमिति । सत्यवत्त्वात्त्वं न विस्मरस्यथापि स्मारयाम इत्यर्थः । लेखस्येति । रिक्तहस्तेन प्रभुं प्रति लेखो न लेख्य इत्याचाराल्लेखसाद्गुण्यार्थं किंचित्प्रेषितमिति भावः ।

भागुरायण इति । कं प्रति केन लिखितामिति प्रष्टव्यमिति भावः । वाचिकमिति । वाचिकं त्वत्तः केन श्रोतव्यमिति पृष्टे प्रस्तुतत्वाच्चन्द्रगुप्तेनेत्येव वक्तव्यत्वेन प्रसक्तेपि युष्मच्छ्रवणगोचरीकर्तुमेवायं सर्वः समारम्भ इति गूढाभिसन्धिः युष्माभिरित्यर्धोक्त्या उत्तरयति । श्रोतव्यमिति वाक्यशेषो गूढः । उक्तमुत्तरं ताडनव्याजेनान्यथयति मिश्रैरित्यादिना । अत्र युष्माभिरिति पूर्वोक्तमन्वेतव्यम् । मिश्रशब्दः पूज्यवचनः ।

---

१ उपगृहीताः. २ दण्डाभ्याम्. ३ सिद्धार्थकात्. ४ लेखार्थः. ५ तुह्मेहिं. ६ सक्रोधम्. ७ ज्ञास्यासि. ८ सर्वमनेन कथितं भवेत्.

भागु०—(विलोक्य ।) कुमार इयमपि राक्षसमुद्राङ्कितैव ।

मल०—सखे अयं लेखस्याशून्यार्थो भविष्यति । इमामपि मुद्रां परिपालयन्नुद्घाट्य दर्शय ।

भागु०—(तथा कृत्वा दर्शयति ।)

मल०—(विलोक्य ।) अये तदिदमाभरणं मया स्वशरीरादवतार्य राक्षसाय प्रेषितम् । व्यक्तं चन्द्रगुप्तस्य लेखः ।

भागु०—कुमार एष निर्णीयत एव संशयः। भद्र पुनरपि ताड्यताम् ।

पुरु०—यदार्य आज्ञापयति (जं अज्जो आणवेदि) (इति निष्क्रम्य सिद्धार्थकेन सह पुनः प्रविश्य ।) एष खलु ताड्यमानः कुमारस्यैव निवेदयामीति भणति । (एसो क्खु ताडिअमाणो कुमारस्स एव्व [2]णिवेदमित्ति भणादि ।)

मल०—तथा भवतु ।

सिद्धा०—(पादयोर्निपत्य ।) अभयेन मे प्रसादं करोत्वार्यः । (अभएण मे पसादं करेदु अज्जो ।)

मल०—भद्र अभयमेव परवतो जनस्य । निवेद्यतां यथावस्थितम् ।

सिद्धा०—निशामयतु कुमारः । अहं खल्वमात्यराक्षसेनेमं लेखं दत्त्वा चन्द्रगुप्तसकाशं प्रेषितः । (णिसामेदु कुमारो । अहं खु अमच्चरक्खसेण इमं लेहं देइअ चन्दउत्तसआसं पेसिदो ।)

मल०—वाचिकमिदानीं श्रोतुमिच्छामि ।

सिद्धा०—कुमार आदिष्टोस्म्यमात्येन यथैते मम प्रियवयस्याः पञ्च राजानस्त्वया सह समुत्पन्नस्नेहाः । ते यथा कुलूताधिपश्चित्रवर्मा मलयनगराधिपः सिंहनादः काश्मीरदेशनाथः पुष्कराक्षः सिन्धुराजः सिन्धुसेनः पारसीको मेघनाद इति । एतेषु प्रथमगृहीतास्त्रयो राजानो मलयकेतोर्विषयमिच्छन्त्यपरौ हस्तिबलं कोषं च । तद्यथा चाणक्यं निराकृत्य महाभागेन मम प्रीतिः समुत्पादिता तथैतेषामपि प्रथमभणितोर्थः संपादयितव्य इत्येतावान्वाक्सन्देशः । (कुमाल आदिट्ठह्मि

व्यक्तं चन्द्रगुप्तस्येति। राजार्हाभरणप्रेषणाच्चन्द्रगुप्तं प्रति राक्षसेन प्रेषित इत्यर्थः।

---

१ यन्मया. २ विण्णवेमि. ३ प्रवेशय. पुरु०—जं कुमारो अणावेदि (इति निष्क्रम्य सिद्धार्थकेन सह प्रविशति) इत्य०. ४ अस्मात्प्राक्-भद्र.

अमच्चेण जहा एदे मह पिअवअस्सा पञ्च राआणो तुए सह समुप्पण्णसि-णेहा। ते जहा कुलूदाहिवो चित्तवम्मो मलअणराहिवो सिंहणादो कह्मी-रदेसणाहो पुक्खरक्खो सिन्धुराओ सिन्धुसेणो पारसीओ मेहणादोत्ति। एदेसु पढमगिहीदा तिण्णि राआणो मलअकेदुणो विसअं इच्छन्ति अवरे हत्थिबलं कोसं अ। ता जहा चाणक्कं णिराकरिअ महाभाएण मह पीदी समुप्पादिदा तहा एदाणं वि पढमभणिदो अत्थो संपादइदव्वोत्ति एत्तिओ वाआसन्देसो।)

मल०—(स्वगतम्।) कथं चित्रवर्मादयोपि मामभिद्रुह्यन्ति। अथवात एव राक्षसे निरतिशया प्रीतिः। (प्रकाशम्।) विजये राक्षसं द्रष्टुमिच्छामि।)

प्रती०—यत्कुमार आज्ञापयति। (जं कुमारो आणवेदि।) (इति निष्क्रान्ताः।)

(ततः प्रविशत्यासनस्थः स्वभवनगतः पुरुषेण सह सचिन्तो राक्षसः।)

राक्ष०—(आत्मगतम्।) पूर्णमस्मद्बलं चन्द्रगुप्तबलैरिति यत्सत्यं न मे मनसः परिशुद्धिरस्ति। कुतः।

साध्ये निश्चितमन्वयेन घटितं बिभ्रत्सपक्षे स्थितिं
व्यावृत्तं च विपक्षतो भवति यत्तत्साधनं सिद्धये।
यत्साध्यं स्वयमेव तुल्यमुभयोः पक्षे विरुद्धं च य-
त्तस्याङ्गीकरणेन वादिन इव स्यात्स्वामिनो निग्रहः॥ १०॥

पूर्णमस्मद्बलमिति। चन्द्रगुप्तबलैर्भद्रभटप्रभृतिभिरस्मद्बलं व्याप्तमिति कृत्वा मनो मे सन्दिग्धमिति भावः।

साध्ये निश्चितमिति। साध्ये सिद्धिविषये पक्षे निश्चितमसन्दिग्धमन्वयेना-न्वयव्याप्त्या घटितं विशिष्टं सपक्षे महानसादौ विद्यमानं विपक्षाद्ध्रदाद्व्यावृत्तं धूमरूपं साधनं हेतुः सिद्धये वह्न्यनुमितये समर्थं भवति। एवं चाणक्यनीति-रूपं साधनं साध्ये चन्द्रगुप्तलक्ष्मीस्थिरीकरणरूपे निश्चितमवश्यसाधकत्वेनाध्यव-सितमन्वयेन व्यतिरेकव्याप्त्या च घटितं मौर्यप्रतिष्ठापननन्दोन्मूलनादिना दृष्टसार-मिति यावत्। सपक्षे भद्रभटभागुरायणादौ स्थितिं बिभ्रद्विपक्षान्मलयकेतोर्व्यावृत्तं सत्सिद्धये मौर्यलक्ष्मीस्थैर्याय समर्थं भवति इति दार्ष्टान्तिके योजनीयम्। यत्साधनं स्वयमेव साध्यं साध्याभिन्नं यथा ज्ञानं प्रमाणं तद्वति तत्प्रतिकारकत्वात्। अत्र साधनं साध्येन प्रामाण्येनाभिन्नं समम्। यच्च साधनमुभयोः सपक्षवि-पक्षयोः वृत्तिमत्त्वेन व्यावृत्तत्वेन वा तुल्यम्। आद्ये उदाहरणं शब्दपक्ष-कानित्यत्वसाधकप्रमेयत्वं तत्र प्रमेयत्वं सपक्षे घटादौ विपक्षे आकाशादौ च

---

१ ०व्वरक्खसेण. २ सन्धाणा. ३ अहिलसन्ति. ४ मह्यम्. ५ स्वपक्षे.

अथवा विज्ञातापरागहेतुभिः प्राक्परिगृहीतोपजापैरापूर्णमिति न विकल्पयितुमर्हामि। (प्रकाशम्।) भद्र प्रियंवदक उच्यन्तामस्मद्वचनात्कुमारानुयायिनो राजानः। संप्रति दिने दिने प्रत्यासीदति कुसुमपुरम्। तैत्परिकल्पितविभागैर्भवद्भिः प्रयाणे प्रयातव्यम्। कथमिति।

प्रस्थातव्यं पुरस्तात्खसमगधगणैर्मामनु व्यूह्य सैन्यै-
र्गान्धारैर्मध्ययाने सयवनपतिभिः संविधेयः प्रयत्नः।
पश्चात्तिष्ठन्तु वीराः शकनरपतयः संभृताश्चीणहूणैः
कौलूताद्यश्च शिष्टः पथि पथि वृणुयाद्राजलोकः कुमारम्॥११॥

प्रियं०—तथा। (तह।) (इति निष्क्रान्तः।)

(प्रविश्य।) **प्रतीहारी**—जयत्वमात्यः। अमात्य इच्छति त्वां कुमारः प्रेक्षितुम्। (जेदु अमच्चो। अमच्च इच्छदि तुमं कुमारो पेक्खिदुं।)

राक्ष०—भद्रे मुहूर्तं तिष्ठ। कः कोत्र भोः।

(प्रविश्य।) **पुरुषः**—आज्ञापयत्वमात्यः (आणवेदु अमच्चो।)

राक्ष०—उच्यतां शकटदासः। यथा परिधापिताः कुमारेणाभरणानि वयम्। तन्न युक्तमनलंकृतैः कुमारदर्शनमनुभवितुम्। अतो यत्तदलङ्करणत्रयं क्रीतं तन्मध्यादेकं दीयतामिति।

वृत्तिमत्त्वेन तुल्यम्। द्वितीये शब्दपक्षकानित्यत्वसाधकशब्दत्वं सपक्षे घटादौ विपक्षे गगनादौ च व्यावृत्तत्वेन तुल्यम्। यच्च साधनं पक्षे विरुद्धं साध्यासमानाधिकरणम्। यथा शब्दपक्षकनित्यत्वसाधककृतकत्वम्। अत्र कृतकत्वं हेतुः पक्षे विरुद्धः साध्येन नित्यत्वेनासमानाधिकरणः। नित्यत्वविरुद्धस्यानित्यत्वस्य साधक इति यावत्। एवमुक्तप्रकारं त्रिविधं यत्साधनं हेत्वाभासस्तस्याङ्गीकरणेन वादिनो निग्रहा पराभवः स्यात्। एवं प्रकृतेपि मलयकेतुबलं भद्रभटादिभिराक्रान्तत्वादुभयत्र तुल्यवदाभासमानं वस्तुतः पक्षे मलयकेतौ भद्रभटाद्यंशेन विरुद्धमत एव स्वयमेव साध्यकोटिप्रविष्टमस्मदिष्टं साधयेद्वा न वेति सन्दिग्धमिति यावत्। एतादृशबलाभासाङ्गीकरणेन स्वामिनो राक्षसमलयकेत्वोर्निग्रहोवश्यं भावीति दार्ष्टान्तिकेवश्यं योजनीयम्॥ १०॥

एवं सन्दिह्य पुनः समाधत्ते अथवेति। अस्माभिर्विज्ञाताश्चन्द्रगुप्तापरागहेतवो येषां तैः वाक्परिगृहीतः अस्माकमुपजापो यैस्तथाभूतैर्भद्रभटादिभिरापूर्णमिति न संशयितव्यमिति भावः।

---

१ तैस्तैर्विज्ञा०. २ अतः. ३ प्रस्था०. ४ गच्छन्तु. ५ ०द्यो विशि०. ६ परिवृ०. ७ जं अमच्चो आणवेदि.

पुरु०—तथा (इति निष्क्रम्य पुनः प्रविश्य ।) अमात्य इदमाभरणम् । (तहा । अमच्च इदं आहरणं ।)

राक्ष०—(नाट्येनात्मानमलंकृत्योत्थाय च ।) भद्रे राजोपगामिनं मार्गमादेशय ।

प्रती०—एत्वमात्यः । (एदु अमच्चो ।)

राक्ष०—(आत्मगतम् ।) अधिकारपदं नाम निर्दोषस्यापि पुरुषस्य महदाशङ्कास्थानम् । कुतः ।

भयं तावत्सेव्यादभिनिविशते सेवकजनं
ततः प्रत्यासन्नाद्भवति हृदये चैवं निहितम् ।
ततोध्यारूढानां पदमसुजगद्वेषजननं
गतिः सोच्छ्रायाणां पतनमनुकूलं कलयति ॥ १२ ॥

(परिक्रम्य ।) **प्रती०**—अमात्य अयं कुमारः । उपसर्पत्वेनममात्यः । (अमच्च अअं कुमारो । उपसप्पदु णं अमच्चो ।)

राक्ष०—(विलोक्य ।) अयं कुमारस्तिष्ठति य एष ।

पादाग्रे दृशमवधाय निश्चलाङ्गीं
शून्यत्वादपरिगृहीततद्विशेषाम् ।
वक्त्रेन्दुं वहति करेण दुर्वहाणां
कार्याणां कृतमिव गौरवेण नम्रम् ॥ १३ ॥

(उपसृत्य ।) विजयतां कुमारः ।

मल०—आर्य अभिवादये । इदमासनमास्यताम् ।

भयं तावदिति । भयं कर्तृ सेव्याद्राज्ञः सकाशात्सेवकजनभिनिविशते अभितः सर्वतः प्राप्नोति । नेर्विद इति तङ् । ततः राजप्रत्यासन्नद्भयं भवति । अस्मात्कारणादध्यारूढानामधिकारिणां पदमसुजनानां दुर्जनानाम् । यद्वा असुमज्जानानां प्राणिमात्रस्येति यावत् द्वेषजननं भवति । उक्तमर्थमर्थान्तरन्यासेन द्रढयति । गतिरिति । सोच्छ्रायाणमुन्मत्तानां गतिरवस्था अनुकूलमवश्यंभावित्वेनोचितं पतनं कलयति । पतनान्ताः समुच्छ्रया इति भावः । मतिरिति पाठेप्ययमेवार्थः । सर्वदा समुच्छ्रयाद्भीताः पतनमेव चिन्तयीरन्मतिमन्तः इत्यर्थः ॥ १२ ॥

पादाग्रे इति । शून्यत्वान्मनोवृत्तिराहित्यादज्ञाततद्विषयविशेषामित्यर्थः ॥१३॥

इदं मलयकेतोः स्वविषयकदौर्मनस्यमजानन् राजकार्यगौरववैयग्र्येण गृह्णाति ।

---

१ जं अमच्चो आणवेदि. २ राजकुल० ३ भवेत्. ४ अनु०, जनोद्वेगं. ५ मतिः. ७ नाट्येनावलोक्य. ८ ०चलन्तीं.

राक्ष०—(तथा करोति ।)

मल०—आर्य चिरदर्शनेनार्यस्य वयमुद्विग्नाः ।

राक्ष०—कुमार प्रयाणे प्रतिविधानमनुतिष्ठता मया कुमाराद्- यमुपालम्भोऽधिगतः ।

मल०—आर्य प्रयाणे कथं प्रतिविहितमिति श्रोतुमिच्छामि ।

राक्ष०—कुमार एवमादिष्टा कुमारानुयायिनो राजानः (प्रस्थातव्यमिति पूर्वोक्तं पठति ।)

मल०—(स्वगतम् ।) कथं य एव मद्विनाशेन चन्द्रगुप्तमाराधयितुमुद्यतास्त एव मां परिवृण्वन्ति (प्रकाशम् ।) आर्य अस्ति कश्चिद्यः कुसुमपुरं प्रति गच्छति तत आगच्छति वा ।

राक्ष०—अवसितमिदानीं गतागतप्रयोजनम् । अल्पैरहोभिर्वयमेव तत्र गन्तारः ।

मल०—(स्वगतम् ।) विज्ञायते । (प्रकाशम् ।) यद्येवं ततः किमार्येणायं सलेखः पुरुषः प्रेषितः ।

राक्ष०—(विलोक्य ।) अये सिद्धार्थकः । भद्र किमिदम् ।

सिद्धा०—(सबाष्पं लज्जां नाटयनम् ।) प्रसीदत्वमात्यः । ताड्यमानेन मया न पारितं रहस्यं धारयितुम् । (पसीददु अमच्चो । ताडीअन्तेण मए ण पारिदं रहस्सं धारिदुं ।)

राक्ष०—भद्र कीदृशं रहस्यमिति न खल्ववगच्छामि ।

सिद्धा०—ननु विज्ञापयामि ताड्यमानेन मया । (णं विण्णवेमि ताडिअंतेण मए ।) (इत्यर्द्धोक्ते सभयमधोमुखस्तिष्ठति ।)

आर्य चिरदर्शनेति । चिरदर्शनेन दर्शनविलम्बकरणेनोद्विग्नाः कार्यत्वरया व्यग्रा इति वाक्यार्थः । त्वद्दर्शनमिदानीमस्माकमरुन्तुदमिति गूढम् । कुमार प्रयाणे प्रतिविधानमनुतिष्ठतेतीदमजानानस्योत्तरम् ।

परिवृण्वन्तीति । कौलूताद्याः पञ्च राजान इत्यर्थः । विज्ञायत इति । वयमेवात्र चन्द्रगुप्तं निग्रहीतुं गन्तार इति राक्षसस्य ऋजुराशयो मलयकेतुनान्यथा गृहीतः । चन्द्रगुप्तसाचिव्यार्थं गन्तार इति विज्ञायत इति । विज्ञापयामि ताड्यमानेनेति अस्यार्धोक्तस्य पूरणवाक्यमेवमतिताड्यमानेनेति वक्ष्यमाणं द्रष्टव्यम् ।

---

१ उपविशति. २ अमात्य. ३ कुमारस्यानु०. ४ कुमार अत्र०. ५ पञ्चषैः. ६ यास्यामः. ७ कुसुमपुरं प्रस्थापितः. ८ नत्र०. ९ अमच्चस रहस्सं. इत्य०.

मल०—भागुरायण स्वामिनः पुरस्ताद्भीतो लज्जितो वा नैष कथयिष्यति । स्वयमेवार्याय कथय ।

भागु०—यदाज्ञापयति कुमारः । अमात्य एव कथयति यथाहममात्येन लेखं दत्त्वा वाचिकं सन्दिश्य चन्द्रगुप्तसकाशं प्रेषित इति ।

राक्ष०—भद्र सिद्धार्थक अपि सत्यम् ।

सिद्धा०—(लज्जां नाट्यन् ।) एवमतिताड्यमानेन मया निवेदितम् । (एवं अतिताडिअन्तेन मए णिवेदिदं ।)

राक्ष०—अनृतमेतत् । ताड्यमानः पुरुषः किमिव न ब्रूयात् ।

मल०—सखे भागुरायण दर्शय लेखम् । वाचिकमेष भृत्यः कथयिष्यति ।

भागु०—अमात्य अयं लेखः ।

राक्ष०—(वाचयित्वा ।) कुमार शत्रोः प्रयोग एषः ।

मल०—लेखस्याशून्यार्थमार्येणेदमप्याभरणमनुप्रेषितम् । तत्कथं शत्रोः प्रयोग एषः ।

राक्ष०—(आभरणं निर्वर्ण्य ।) कुमारेणैतन्मह्यमनुप्रेषितम् । मयाप्येतत्कस्मिंश्चित्परितोषस्थाने सिद्धार्थकाय दत्तम् ।

भागु०—ईदृशस्यै विशेषतः कुमारेणात्मगात्रादवतार्य प्रसादीकृतस्येयंपरित्यागभूमिः ।

मल०—वाचिकमप्याप्ततमादस्माच्छ्रोतव्यमिति लिखितमार्येण ।

राक्ष०—कुतो वाचिकं कस्य वाचिकम् । लेख एवास्मदीयो न भवति ।

मल०—इयं तर्हि कस्य मुद्रा ।

राक्ष०—कपटमुद्रामुत्पादयितुं शक्नुवन्ति धूर्ताः ।

भागु०—कुमार सम्यगमात्यो विज्ञापयति । भद्र सिद्धार्थक केनायं लिखितो लेखः ।

कुमारेत्यादिना एवं वदता राक्षसेन समाहितेपि सोल्लुण्ठनं तदन्यथयति भागुरायणः । ईदृशस्येत्यादिना । अस्मादिति । वाचिकमप्यस्माच्छ्रोतव्यमित्यार्येण लिखितमिति व्यवहितेनान्वयः ।

---

१ अमात्यराक्षसेन. २ कुमार अनृ०. ३ एष स्यात्. (इत्याभरणं दर्शयति) ४ ०स्याभरणविशेषस्य. ५ सिद्धार्थकात्. ६ कुमार ०मुद्रामपि.

सिद्धा०—(राक्षसमुखमवलोक्य तूष्णीमधोमुखस्तिष्ठति ।)

भागु०—भद्र अलं पुनरात्मानं ताडयितुम्[1] । कथय ।

सिद्धा—आर्य शकटदासेन । (अज्ज सअडदासेण ।)

राक्ष०—कुमार यदि शकटदासेन लिखितस्ततो मयैव लिखितः ।

मल०—विजये शकटदासं द्रष्टुमिच्छामि ।

प्रती०—यत्कुमार आज्ञापयति । (जं कुमारो आणवेदि ।)

भागु०—(स्वगतम् ।) न खल्वनिश्चितार्थमार्यचाणक्यप्रणिधयोभिधास्यन्ति । भवत्वेवम् । (आगत्य शकटदासो वा सोयं लेख इति प्रत्यभिज्ञाय पूर्ववृत्तं प्रकाशयेत् । एवं सति सन्दिहानो मलयकेतुरस्मिन्प्रयोगे श्लथादरो भवेत्* ।) (प्रकाशम् ।) कुमार न कदाचिदपि शकटदासोमात्यस्याग्रतो मया लिखितमिति प्रतिपत्स्यते । अतोन्यैर्लिखितमस्यानीयतां वर्णसंवाद एवैतं विभावयिष्यति ।

मल०—विजये एवं क्रियताम् ।

भागु०—कुमार मुद्रामप्यानयत्वियम्[2] ।

मल०—उभयमप्यानीयताम् ।

प्रती०—यत्कुमार आज्ञापयति । (जं कुमारो आणवेदि ।) (इति निष्क्रम्य पुनः प्रविश्य ।) कुमार इदं तच्छकटदासेन स्वहस्तलिखितं पत्रं मुद्रापि । (कुमार इदं तं सअडदासेण सहत्थलिहिदं पत्तअं मुद्दावि[3] ।)

कुमार यदि शकटदासेनेति । शकटदासः सर्वथा न लेखिष्यतीति तस्मिन्विस्रम्भप्रत्ययादियमुक्तिः । भवत्वेवमिति । पूर्वं शकटदासहस्तेन छलाचाणक्येन लेखितामित्यजानत इयमुक्तिः । आर्यचाणक्येनैव केनचिद्व्याजेन सिद्धार्थकप्रेरणेन शकटदासं वञ्चयित्वा तद्धस्तेनेदं लिखितं स्यात् । अतः परं शकटदास इहानीतश्चेत्कुसुमपुर एवानेन सिद्धार्थकेन मद्धस्ताल्लिखियोयं लेख इति स्पष्टं वदेत् । ततः सर्वोप्ययं चाणक्यकूटनीतिप्रयोगो व्याकोपितः स्यादित्याशयेन प्रत्युत्पन्नमतिर्भागुरायण आह भवत्वेवम् । शकटदासागमनं परिहरामीत्यर्थः ।

कुमार न कदाचिदिति । अमात्येन लेखितमपि स्वेन लिखितमपि स्वामिद्रोहभयान्न कथयिष्यतीत्यर्थः । अतः प्रतिलिखितमिति । एतमर्थं परिच्छेत्स्यतीत्यर्थः । कुमार मुद्रापीति । आनीयतामिति पूर्वेण प्रश्लिष्य प्रश्नः ।

---

१ ताडयित्वा. २ प्रतिलि०. ३ प्रती०—कुमार मुद्दावि. * एतदाधिकं क्वचित्.

मल०—(उभयमपि नाट्येन विलोक्य ।) आर्य संवदन्त्यक्षराणि ।

राक्ष०—(स्वगतम् ।) संवदन्त्यक्षराणि । शकटदासस्तु मित्रमिति च विसंवदन्त्यक्षराणि । किं नु शकटदासेन ।

स्मृतं स्यात्पुत्रदाराणां विस्मृतैस्वामिभक्तिना ।
चलेष्वर्थेषु लुब्धेन न यशःस्वनपायिषु ॥ १४ ॥

अथवा कः सन्देहः ।

मुद्रा तस्य कराङ्गुलिप्रणयिनी सिद्धार्थकस्तत्सुहृ-
त्तस्यैवापरलेख्यसूचितमिदं लेख्यं प्रयोगाश्रयम् ।
सुव्यक्तं शकटेन भेदपटुभिः सन्धाय सार्धं परै-
र्भर्तृस्नेहपराङ्मुखेन कृपणं प्राणार्थिना चेष्टितम् ॥ १५ ॥

मल०—(विलोक्य ।) आर्य अलङ्कारत्रयं श्रीमता यदनुप्रेषितं तदुपगतमिति यल्लिखितं तन्मध्यात्किमिदमेकम् । (निर्वर्ण्यात्मगतम् ।) कँथं तातेन धृतपूर्वमिदमाभरणम् । (प्रकाशम् ।) आर्य कुतोयमलङ्कारः ।

राक्ष०—वणिग्भ्यः क्रयादधिगतः ।

मल०—विजये अपि प्रत्यभिजानासि भूषणमिदम् ।

प्रतीहारी—(निर्वर्ण्य सबाष्पम् ।) कथं न प्रत्यभिजानामि । इदं सुगृहीतनामधेयेन पर्वतेश्वरेण धारितपूर्वम् । (कुमार कहं ण पच्चभिजाणामि । ईदं सुगिहीदणामधेएण पव्वदीसरेण धारिदपुव्वं ।)

मल०—(सबाष्पम् ।) हा तात ।

एतानि तानि तव भूषणवल्लभस्य
गात्रोचितानि कुलभूषण भूषणानि ।
यैः शोभितोसि मुखचन्द्रकृतावभासो
नक्षत्रवानिव शरत्समयप्रदोषः ॥ १६ ॥

संवदन्तीति । शकटदासस्तु मित्रमित्ययमर्थो विसंवदति विरुध्यते । तस्यासतमत्वे संशयो जायत इत्यर्थः ।

स्मृतमिति । पुत्रदारस्येत्यधीगर्थेति कर्मणि षष्ठी । स्वामिभक्तिं यशश्च परिमृज्य चलेषु नश्वरेष्वर्थेषु पुत्रदारादिषु च लुब्धः स्यादित्यर्थः ॥ १४ ॥ मुद्रेति । प्रयोगाश्रयं कूटप्रयोगरचितमित्यर्थः । कृपणं दीनं कृत्यं चेष्टितं व्यवसितम् ॥ १५ ॥

एतानीति । वल्लभानि प्रियाणि भूषणानि यस्येति बहुव्रीहिः । शेषं स्पष्टम् ॥१६॥

---

१ तत्किं नु, किमिदानीम्. २ विस्मृताः स्वामिभक्तयः. ३ पत्रं. ४ कष्टम्. ५ इदं खलु.

राक्ष०—(स्वगतम् ।) कथं पर्वतेश्वरेण धृतपूर्वाणीत्याह । व्यक्तमेवास्य भूषणानि चाणक्यप्रयुक्तेन वणिग्जनेनास्मासु विक्रीतानि ।

मल०—आर्य तातेन धृतपूर्वाणां विशेषतश्चन्द्रगुप्तहस्तगतानां क्रयादधिगमः कथं युज्यते । अथवा युज्यत एवैतत् । कुतः ।

चन्द्रगुप्तस्य विक्रेतुरधिकं लाभमिच्छतैः ।
कल्पिता मूल्यमेतेषां क्रूरेण भवता वयम् ॥ १७ ॥

राक्ष०—(स्वगतम् ।) अहो सुश्लिष्टोभूच्छत्रुप्रयोगः । कुतः ।

लेखोयं न ममेति नोत्तरमिदं मुद्रा मदीया यतः
सौहार्दं शकटेन खण्डितमिति श्रद्धेयमेतत्कथम् ।
मौर्ये भूषणविक्रयं नरपतौ को नाम संभावये-
त्तस्मात्संप्रतिपत्तिरेव हि वरं न ग्राम्यमत्रोत्तरम् ॥ १८ ॥

मल०—एतदार्य पृच्छामि ।

राक्षे०—कुमार य आर्यस्तं पृच्छ । वयमिदानीमनार्याः संवृत्ताः ।

मल०—

मौर्योसौ स्वामिपुत्रः परिचरणपरो मित्रपुत्रस्तवाहं
दाता सोर्थस्य तुभ्यं स्वमतमनुगतैस्त्वं तु मह्यं ददासि ।
दास्यं सत्कारपूर्वं ननु सचिवपदं तत्र ते स्वाभ्यमत्र
स्वार्थे कस्मिन्समीहा पुनरधिकतरे त्वामनार्यं करोति ॥ १९ ॥

राक्ष०—कुमार एवमयुँक्तव्याहारिणा भवतैव निर्णयो दत्तः । भवतु तव को दोषः । (मौर्योसौ स्वामिपुत्र इति युष्मदस्मदोर्व्यत्ययेन पठति ।)

मल०—(लेखमलंकरणस्थगिकां च निर्दिश्य ।) इदमिदानीं किम् ।

राक्ष०—(सबाष्पम् ।) विधिविलसितम् । कुतः ।

लेखोयमिति । शकटदासेन सौहार्दं परित्यज्येदं लिखितमिति ग्राम्ये परिहारे उक्ते कः श्रद्दध्यादित्यर्थः ॥ १८ ॥ [स्वामिपुत्रस्त्वया परिचर्य इति शेषः । स त्वयानुगतः स्वमतं यथा तथा तुभ्यमर्थस्य दाता । अत्र मयानुगतस्त्वं मह्यं स्वमतमर्थं ददासि ।] एवं मौर्यसेनातोप्यतिशयिते मयि तव स्वातन्त्र्ये स्थिते इतोप्यधिकतरं कं स्वार्थमवलम्ब्येमवनार्यो जातोसीतिनिष्ठुर उपालम्भः ॥ १९ ॥

[व्यत्ययेन पठति–मित्रपुत्रो मम त्वं.. मह्यं...गतोहं तु तुभ्यं ददामि इ०]

इदमिदानीं किमिति । अयं कस्य दोष इत्यधिक्षेपः ।

---

१ (प्रकाशम्) एतान्यपि चा०. २ वणिग्भ्य, क्रया, वणिग्विक्रय इति न. ३ इच्छता. ४ पदं. ५ सबाष्पमित्यधिकम्. ६ ०मतभृततनुस्त्वं च. ७ अभियुक्त, व्यवहारिणा.

भृत्यत्वे परिभावधामनि सति स्नेहात्प्रभूणां सतां
पुत्रेभ्यः कृतवेदिनां कृतधियां येषां न भिन्ना वयम्।
ते लोकस्य परीक्षकाः क्षितिभृतः पापेन येन क्षता-
स्तस्येदं विपुलं विधेर्विलसितं पुंसां प्रयत्नच्छिदः ॥ २० ॥

मल०—(सरोषम्।) किमद्यापि निह्नूयते एव विधेः किलैतद्व्यवसितं न लोभस्येति। अनार्य।

कन्यां तीव्रविषप्रयोगविषमां कृत्वा कृतघ्नं त्वया
विश्रम्भप्रवणः पुरा मम पिता नीतः कथाशेषताम्।
संप्रत्याहितगौरवेण भवता मन्त्राधिकारे रिपौ
प्रारब्धाः प्रलयाय मांसवदहो विक्रेतुमेते वयम् ॥ २१ ॥

राक्ष०—(स्वगतम्।) अयमपरो गण्डस्योपरि स्फोटः। (प्रकाशम्। कर्णौ पिधाय।) शान्तं पापं शान्तं पापम्। नाहं पर्वतेश्वरे विषकन्यां प्रयुक्तवान्।

मल०—केन तर्हि व्यापादितस्तातः।

राक्ष०—दैवमत्र प्रष्टव्यम्।

मल०—(सक्रोधम्।) दैवमत्र प्रष्टव्यम्। न क्षपणको जीवसिद्धिः।

राक्ष०—(स्वगतम्।) कथं जीवसिद्धिरपि चाणक्यप्रणिधिः। हन्त रिपुभिर्मे हृदयमपि स्वीकृतम्।

मल०—(सक्रोधम्।) भासुरक आज्ञाप्यतां शिखरसेनः। य एते राक्षसेन सह सुहृत्तामुत्पाद्यास्मच्छरीरद्रोहेण चन्द्रगुप्तमाराधयितुकामाः

भृत्यत्वे इति। परिभवो न्यक्कारः तद्विषयो भृत्योऽप्यहं प्रभुभिर्न्यक्कारं कर्तुं समर्थैरपि यैः कृतज्ञैः सर्वज्ञैः स्वामिभिरपत्यनिर्विशेषतया दृष्टोस्मि ते दैवेन हता इत्यर्थः ॥२०॥

कन्यामिति। मन्त्राधिकारे मौर्यस्य मन्त्रित्वे आहितगौरवेण धृताभिलाषेणेत्यर्थः। रिपौ चन्द्रगुप्ते प्रलयाय नाशाय मांसवद्विक्रेतुमारब्धा नियोजिता इत्यन्वयः। इदानीमपि राक्षसेनानेकराजकार्यकुशलेन किमपि तादृशमारभ्यत इति पूर्वं जीवसिद्धिनोपक्षिप्तस्योपजापदुर्विकल्पस्यायमुद्गार इत्यवधेयम् ॥ २१ ॥

अयमपर इति। मर्मस्थानव्रणस्योपरि व्रणान्तरमित्यर्थः। दैवमत्रेति। चाणक्यनामागृहीत्वा दैवमिति वदन्स्वस्य परदोषानाविष्करणरूपं महामनस्त्वं सूचितवान्।

---

१ कृताधियः. २ प्रयत्नो वृथा. ३ सक्रोधम्. ४ कृतघ्नात्मना. ५ रिपोः. ६ नाहं विषकन्यामारोपितवानपापोहं पर्वतेश्वरे. ७ सेनापतिः इत्य०. ८ मोहादंभ.

पञ्च राजानः कौलूतश्चित्रवर्मा मलयनरपतिः सिंहनादः काश्मीरः पुष्कराक्षः सिन्धुराजः सुषेणः पारसीकाधिपो[1] मेघनाद इति। एतेषु त्रयः प्रथमे मदीयां भूमिं कामयन्ते ते[2] गम्भीरश्वभ्रमभिनीय पांशुभिः पूर्यन्ताम्। इतरौ तु हस्तिबलकामुकौ[3] हस्तिनैव घात्येतामिति।

पुरुषः—तथा। (तहा।) (इति निष्क्रान्तः।)

मल०—(सक्रोधम्।) राक्षस राक्षस नाहं विश्रम्भघाती राक्षसो मलयकेतुः खल्वहम्। तद्गच्छ समाश्रीयतां सर्वात्मना चन्द्रगुप्तः। पश्य।

> **विष्णुगुप्तं च मौर्यं च सममप्यागतौ त्वया।**
> **उन्मूलयितुमीशोऽहं त्रिवर्गमिव दुर्नयः॥ २२॥**

भागु०—कुमार कृतं कालहरणेन। सांप्रतं कुसुमपुरोपरोधायाज्ञाप्यन्ताम[4]स्मद्बलानि।

> **गौडीनां लोध्रधूलीपरिमलबहुलान्धूमयन्तः[5] कपोला-**
> **न्क्लिश्नन्तः कृष्णिमानं भ्रमरकुलरुचः कुञ्चितस्यालकस्य।**
> **पांशुस्तम्बा[6] बलानां तुरगखुरपुटक्षोभलब्धात्मलाभाः**
> **शत्रूणामुत्तमाङ्गे गजमदसलिलच्छिन्नमूलाः पतन्तु॥ २३॥**

(सपरिजनो निष्क्रान्तो मलयकेतुः।)

राक्ष०—(सावेगम्।) हा धिक्कष्टम्। तेऽपि घातिताश्चित्रवर्मादयस्तपस्विनः। तत्कथं सुहृद्विनाशाय राक्षसश्चेष्टते न रिपुविनाशाय। तत्किमिदानीं मन्दभाग्यः करवाणि।

विष्णुगुप्तमिति। दुर्नयदृष्टान्तेन स्वस्य दौरात्म्यं रोषावेशवशादुद्घाटितम्॥२२॥ स्वपक्षबलहीनमेनं भद्रभटादिभिर्निग्राहयितुं त्वरयति। गौडीनामिति। लोध्रपुष्पाणां धूली परागस्तस्य परिमलः लेपजनितो गन्धविशेषस्तेन बहुलान्व्याप्तान् गौडीनां गौडस्त्रीणां कपालान्धूमयन्तः धूमवतः कुर्वतः मलिनयन्त इति यावत्। णाविष्टवद्भावेन मतुपो लोपः। गौडस्त्रियः कपोलान्लोध्ररजोभिरलंकुर्वन्तीत्यतस्तेषां तत्परिमलबहुलत्वम्। तथा तासामेव भ्रमरकुलरुचः नीलस्य कुञ्चितस्य संयमितस्यालकस्य कृष्मिमानं नैल्यं क्लिश्नन्तोऽभिभवन्त इत्यर्थः। बलानां सैन्यानां तुरगखुरपुटक्षोभेण लब्धात्मलाभाः जनिताः पांशुस्तम्बाः गजमदसलिलैश्छिन्नमूलाः सन्तः शत्रूणामुत्तमाङ्गे पतन्तु॥ २३॥

---

१ धिराजो मेघाक्षः. २ तेभ्यो भूमिरेव दीयताम्। ने. ३ कामौ. ४ प्रतिश्रूयन्ताम्. ५ धूम्रयन्तः. ६ व्यूहा.

किं गच्छामि तपोवनं न तपसा शाम्येत्सवैरं मनः
किं भर्तॄननुयामि जीवति रिपौ स्त्रीणामियं योग्यता।
किं वा खड्गसखः पताम्यरिबले नैतच्च युक्तं भवे-
च्चेतश्चन्दनदासमोक्षरभसं रुन्ध्यात्कृतघ्नं न चेत्॥ २४॥

(इति निष्क्रान्ताः सर्वे।)

इति पञ्चमोऽङ्कः।

षष्ठोऽङ्कः।

(ततः प्रविशत्यलंकृतः सहर्षः सिद्धार्थकः।)

सिद्धा०—

जयति जलदनीलः केशवः केशिघाती
जयति च जनदृष्टिचन्द्रमाश्चन्द्रगुप्तः।
जयति जयनकार्यं यावत्कृत्वा च सर्वं
प्रतिहतपरपक्षा आर्यचाणक्यनीतिः॥ १॥

जअदि जलदणीलो केसवो केसिघादी
जअदि अ जणदिट्ठीचन्दमा चन्दउत्तो।

किं गच्छामीति। जीवति रिपाविति शत्रुवैरनिर्यातनमकृत्वा स्त्रीवदनुमरणमयुक्तमिति भावः। खड्गसख इति। खड्गमात्रसहायेनारिबलं कृत्स्नं क्षपयितुं समर्थोऽस्मि अथापि चन्दनदासस्योपकारिणो मोक्षो न भवेदिति रभसं रभसवदुत्सुकं चेतः रुन्ध्यात् अरिबलक्षपणानां रोद्धुं प्रवर्तत इत्यर्थः। प्रवर्तनायां लिङ्। न चेत् न रुन्ध्याच्चेत्कृतघ्नं भवेदित्यन्वयः। पारक्रमपक्षे चन्दनदासविषये कृतघ्नतादोषः स्वस्यापरिहार्यः स्यादिति भावः। अप्यकार्यशतं कृत्वा येन केनाप्युपायेन चन्दनदासमोचनमेव संप्रत्यावश्यकत्वेनापतितमतस्तत्रैव प्रयतिष्य इत्यत्रतात्पर्यम्॥ २४॥

इति श्रीत्र्यम्बकयज्वप्रभुवर्याश्रितढुण्ढिराजव्यासयज्वविरचिते
मुद्राराक्षसनाटकव्याख्याने पञ्चमोऽङ्कः समाप्तः।

इत्थं मलयकेतुनिग्रहरूपमवान्तरकार्यनिर्वहणं कृतम्। अतः परं राक्षससंग्रहणरूपप्रधानकार्यनिर्वाहार्थं चन्द्रगुप्तलक्ष्मीस्थैर्यरूपस्य महाफलस्य च सिद्ध्यर्थं षष्ठसप्तमावङ्कावारभ्येते। जयतीति। कृतकार्यतया चन्द्रगुप्तेन भूषणादिनालंकृतेन सिद्धार्थकेनेष्टदैवतराजचाणक्यनीतीनां जय आघोष्यते। जयत्यनेनेति। जयनं सैन्ययुद्धादि। करणे ल्युट्। जयनेन जयकारणेन सेनादिनैव यत्कार्यं तद्यावत्सर्वं स्वयमेव कृत्वा चाणक्यनीतिर्जयतीत्यन्वयः। सेनासन्नाहयुद्धादिकमनपेक्ष्य नीत्यैव सर्वं राज-

जअदि जअणकज्जं जाव काऊण सव्वं
पडिहदपरपक्खा अज्जचाणक्कणीदी ॥ १ ॥

तावच्चिरस्य कालस्य प्रियवयस्यं समिद्धार्थकं पश्यामि । (परिक्रम्याव-लोक्य च ।) एष मे प्रियवयस्यः समिद्धार्थकः इत एवागच्छति । यावदे-नमुपसर्पामि । (दाव चिरस्स कालस्स पिअवअस्सं समिद्धत्थअं पेक्खामि एसो मे पिअवअस्सओ इदो एव्व आअच्छदि । जाव णं उपसप्पामि ।)

(ततः प्रविशति समिद्धार्थकः ।)

समिद्धा०----

सन्तापे तारेशानां गेहोत्सवे सुखायमानानाम् ।
हृदयस्थितानां विभवा विरहे मित्राणां दूनयन्ति ॥ २ ॥

संदावे तारेसाणं गेहूसवे सुहाअन्ताणं ।
हिअअट्ठिदाणं विहवा विरहे मित्ताणं दूणन्दि ॥ २ ॥

श्रुतं मया मलयकेतुकटकात्प्रियवयस्यः सिद्धार्थक आगत इति । तद्यावदेनमन्वेषयामि । (इति परिक्रामति । विलोक्य ।) एष सिद्धार्थकः । (सुदं मए मलअकेदुकडआदो पिअवअस्सओ सिद्धत्थओ आअदोत्ति । ता जाव णं अण्णेसामि । एसो सिद्धत्थओ ।)

सिद्धा०—(उपसृत्य ।) कथं समिद्धार्थकः । अपि सुखं प्रिय-वयस्यस्य । (कहं समिद्धत्थओ । अवि सुहं पिअवअस्सस्स ।)

(इत्यन्योन्यमालिङ्गतः ।)

समिद्धा०—वयस्य कुतो मे सुखं येन त्वं चिरप्रवासप्रत्यागतोप्यद्य न मे गेहमागच्छसि । (वअस्स कुदो मे सुहं जेण तुमं चिरप्पवासप-च्चागदो वि अज्ज ण मे गेहं आअच्छसि ।)

कार्यं चाणक्यः साधितवानित्यर्थः । बहोः कालात्तस्य दर्शनमावश्यकमित्यर्थः ॥ १ ॥ सन्तापे इति । सन्तापे तारेशानां चन्द्राणां सन्तापहारिणामित्यर्थः । गेहोत्सवे इति । मित्रैर्विना गेहोत्सवा व्यर्था इत्यर्थः । हृदयस्थितानां सर्वदा चिन्त्यमानां मित्राणां विरहे विभवा ऐश्वर्याणि दुःखायैव भवन्ति इति सिद्धार्थकविरहेण क्लिश्यते ॥ २ ॥

---

१ उपसप्पादि सन्तावेन्ता आवाणेसुं महूसवेसुं रुआवेन्ता । हिअआट्ठिदावि विहवा विरहे मित्ताणं दूमेन्ति ॥ (सन्तापयन्त आपानेषु महोत्सवेषु रोदयन्तः (रुजायन्तः ।) हृदयस्थिता आपि विभवा विरहे मित्राणां दुन्वन्ति ॥ २ (विलोक्य ।) कधं इदो ज्जेव पिअवअस्सओ सुसिद्धत्थओ । (उपगम्य ।). ४ उभाव. ५ अआणिअ वुत्तन्तं अण्णदो गदोसि त्ति.

सिद्धा०—प्रसीदतु वयस्यः । दृष्टमात्र एव आर्यचाणक्येनाज्ञप्तोस्मि यथा सिद्धार्थक गच्छ इमं प्रियोदन्तं देवस्य चन्द्रश्रिये निवेदयेति । तत एतस्मै निवेद्यैवमनुभूतपार्थिवप्रसादोहं प्रियवयस्यं प्रेक्षितुं तवैव गेहं चलितोस्मि । (पसीदेदु वअस्सो । दिट्ठमेत्तो एव्व अज्जचाणक्केण आणत्तोह्मि जह सिद्धत्थअ गच्छ एदं पिओदन्त देवस्स चन्दसिरिणो णिवेदेहित्ति । तदो एदस्स णिवेदिअ एव्वं अणुभूदपत्थिवप्पसादो अहं पिअवअस्सं पेक्खिदुं तुह एव्व गेहं चलिदोह्मि ।)

समिद्धा०—वयस्य यदि मे श्रोतव्यं भवति ततः कथय किं तत्प्रियं प्रियदर्शनाय चन्द्रश्रिये निवेदितम् । (वअस्स जदि मे सुणिदव्वं भोदि तदो कहेही किं तं पिअं जं पिअदंसणस्स चन्दसिरिणो णिवेदिदं ।)

सिद्धा०—वयस्य किं तवाप्यश्रोतव्यमस्ति तन्निशामय । अस्ति तावच्चाणक्यनीतिमोहितमतिना मलयकेतुहतकेन निष्कास्य राक्षसं हताश्चित्रवर्मप्रमुखाः प्रधानाः पञ्च पार्थिवाः । ततोसमीक्ष्यकार्ययेषु दुराचार इत्युज्झित्वा मलयकेतुकटकभूमिं कुशलतायै भयविलोलशेषसैनिकपरिवारेषु स्वकं स्वकं विषयं सभयं प्रस्थितेषु पार्थिवेषु निर्विण्णहृदयेषु सकलसामन्तेषु भद्रभटपुरुषदत्तडिङ्गरातबलगुप्तराजसेनभागुरायणरोहिताक्षविजयवर्मप्रमुखैः संयम्य गृहीतो मलयकेतुः । (वअस्स किं तुहवि असुणिदव्वं अत्थि ता णिसामेहि । अत्थि दाव चाणक्कणीदिमोहिदमदिणा मलअकेदुहदएण णिक्कासिअ रक्खसं हदा चित्तवम्मप्पमुहा प्पहाणा पञ्च पत्थिवा । तदो असमिक्खकारी एसो दुराआरोत्ति उज्झिअ मलयकेअकडअभूमिं कुसलदाए भअविलोलसेससेणिकपरिवारेसु सकं सकं विसअं सभअं प्पत्थिदेसु पात्थिवेसु णिव्विण्णहिअएसु सअलसामन्तेसु भद्दभट्टपुरिसदत्तडिङ्गरादबलउत्तराअसणेभागुराअणरोहिदक्खविजअवम्मप्पमुहेहिं संजमिअ गिहीदो अमअकेदु ।)

समिद्धा०—वयस्य भद्रभटप्रमुखाः किल देवाच्चन्द्रगुप्तादपरक्ता मलयकेतुं समाश्रिता इति लोके मन्त्र्यते । तत्किं निमित्तं कुकविकृतनाटकस्येवान्यन्मुखेन्यन्निर्वहणे । (वअस्स भद्दभटप्पमुहा किल देवस्स

१ पसी०पसी०. २ वुत्तन्तं पिअं पिअदंसणस्स ३ ता मं पिं सुणावेहि. ४ अकहिदव्वं ५ णिराकारिअ. ७ कदुअ उ०. ७ हदअ. ८ णिअभूमिकु०. ९ सेण्णतणूकिदप.

चन्दउत्तंस्स अवरत्ता मलअकेदुं समस्सिदा त्ति लोए मन्तीअदि । ता किं णिमितं कुकविकिदणाडअस्स विअ अण्णं मुहे अण्णं णिव्वहणे ।)

सिद्धा०—वयस्य दैवगत्या इवाश्रुतगत्यै नम आर्य चाणक्यनीत्यै । (वअस्स देवगदीए विअ असुणिदगदीए णमो अज्जचाणक्कणीदीए ।

समिद्धा०—ततस्ततः । (तदो तदो ।)

सिद्धा०—ततः प्रभूतसारसाधनसमेतेनेतो निष्क्रम्यार्यचाणक्येन प्रतिपन्नराजलोकमशेषं म्लेच्छबलम् । (तदो पभूदसारसाहणसमेदेणं[2] इदो णिक्कमिअ अज्जचाणक्केण पडिवण्णं अरांअलोअं असेसं मिलेच्छबलं ।)

समिद्धा०—वयस्य कुत्र तत् । (वअस्स कहिं तं ।)

सिद्धा०—यत्रैते (जहिं एदे)

अतिशयगुरुकेण दानदर्पेण दन्तिनः
सजलजलदलीलामुद्वहन्तो नदन्ति ।
कशाप्रहारभयेन जातकम्पोत्तरङ्गाः
गृहीतजयनशब्दाः संपतन्ति (संप्लवन्ते) तुरङ्गाः ।। ३ ॥

अदिसअगुरुएण दाणदप्पेण दन्ती
सजलजलदलीलंमुव्वहन्तो णदन्ति ।
कसपहरभएण जाअकम्पोत्तरंङ्गा
गिहिदजअणसद्दासंपअन्ते[6] तुरङ्गा ॥ ३ ॥

समिद्धा०—वयस्य एतत्तावत्तिष्ठतु । तथा सर्वलोकप्रत्यक्षमुज्झिताधिकारः स्थित्वा आर्यचाणक्यः किं पुनरपि तदेव मन्त्रिपदमारूढः । (वअस्स एदं दाव चिट्ठदु । तहा सव्वलोअपच्चक्खं उज्झिआहिआरो चिट्ठिअ अज्जचाणक्को किं पुणो वि तं एव्व मन्तिपदं आरूढो ।)

चन्द्रगुप्तस्येति । चन्द्रगुप्ते अपरक्ता इत्यर्थः । शेषे षष्ठी ।

अतिशयेति । जातकम्पा अत एवोत्तरङ्गाः । कशाताडनभयेन अत्यन्तं कम्पमानाश्चपला अश्वाः । गृहीतजयनशब्दाः जयनं जयस्तस्य शब्दः गृहीतो ज्ञातो जयनशब्दो यैस्ते तथाभूताः जयघोषणां श्रुत्वा सर्वतः संपतन्तीत्यर्थः ॥ ३ ॥

---

१ सिरिणो. २ समुदाएण. ३ सअलराअलोअसहिअं असेसराअबलं. ४ ०णीलाउब्भमन्तो (उद्भ्रमन्तः). ५ ०म्पा तुरन्ता (त्वरयन्तः). ६ सम्पदन्ते.

सिद्धा०—अतिमुग्धोसीदानीं त्वं यदमात्यराक्षसेनाप्यनवगाहितपूर्वमार्यचाणक्यचरितमवगाहितुमिच्छसि । (अदिइमुद्धोसि दाणीं तुमं जो अमच्चरक्खसेण वि अणवगाहिअपुव्वं अज्जचाणक्कचरिदं अवगाहिदुं इच्छसि ।)

समिद्धा०—वयस्य अमात्यराक्षसः सांप्रतं कुत्र । (वअस्स अमच्चरक्खसो संपदं कहिं ।)

सिद्धा०—तस्मिन्भयविलोले वर्धमाने मलयकेतुकटकान्निष्क्रम्योदुम्बरनामधेयेन चरेणानुसन्धीयमान इदं पाटलीपुत्रमागत इत्यार्यचाणक्याय निवेदितम् । (तस्सिं भअविलोले वड्ढमाणे मलअकेदुकडआदो णिक्कमिअ उदुम्भरणामहेएण चरेण अनुसन्धिज्जमाणो इमं पाडलीउत्तं आअदोत्ति अज्जचाणक्कस्स णिवेदिदं ।)

समिद्धा०—वयस्य तथा नामामात्यराक्षसो नन्दराज्यप्रत्यानयने कृतव्यवसायो निष्क्रम्य सांप्रतमकृतार्थः पुनरपीदं पाटलिपुत्रमागत एव । (वअस्स तहा णाम अमच्चरक्खसो णन्दरज्जपच्चाणअणे किदव्ववसाओ णिक्कमिअ संपदं अकिदत्थो पुणोवि इमं पाडलिउत्तं आअदो एव्व ।)

सिद्धा०—वयस्य तर्कयामि चन्दनदासस्नेहेनेति । (वअस्स तक्केमि चन्दणदाससिणेहेणत्ति ।)

समिद्धा०—वयस्य चन्दनदासस्य मोक्षमिव प्रेक्षे । (वअस्स चन्दणदासस्स मोक्खं विअ पेक्खामि ।)

सिद्धा०—कुतोस्याधन्यस्य मोक्षः । स खलु सांप्रतमार्यचाणक्यस्याज्ञप्त्या द्वाभ्यामावाभ्यां वध्यस्थानं प्रवेश्य व्यापादयितव्यः । (कुदो से अधण्णस्स मोक्खो । सो क्खु संपदं अज्जचाणक्कस्स आणत्तीए दुवेहिं अह्मेहिं वज्झट्ठाणं पवेसिअ वावादइदव्वो ।)

समिद्धा०—(सक्रोधम् ।) किमार्यचाणक्यस्य घातकजनोन्यो नास्ति येनावामीदृशेषु अतिनृशंसेषु नियोगेषु नियोजयति । (किं

आगत एवेति । तस्यागमनमश्लाघ्यमित्यर्थः ।

---

१ बुद्धि. २ सो क्खु तस्सिं. ३ वट्टमाणे (वर्तमाने). ४ अनुसरन्तो इमं कुसुमपुरं. ६ कध इमं एव्व. ६ सच्चं चन्दनदासस्स सिणेहेणत्ति । अध इत्यभिकम्. ७ पि अह्मे०.

अज्जचाणक्कस्स घादअजणो अण्णो णत्थि जेण अह्मे ईदिसेसुं अदि-णिसंसेसु णिओएसु णिओएदि।

सिद्धा०—वयस्य को जीवलोके जीवितुकाम आर्यचाणक्यस्याज्ञप्तिं प्रतिकूलयति। तदेहि चण्डालवेशधारिणौ भूत्वा चन्दनदासं वध्यस्थानं नयावः। (वअस्स को[2] जीवलोए जीविदुकामो अज्जचाणक्कस्स आणतिं पडिऊलेदि। ता एहि चण्डालवेसधारिणा भविअ चन्दणदासं वज्झट्ठाणं णएम। इत्युभौ निष्क्रान्तौ।)

इति प्रवेशकः।

(ततः प्रविशति रज्जुहस्तः पुरुषः।)

पुरु०—

षड्गुणसंयोगदृढा उपायपरिपाटिघटितपाशमुखी।
चाणक्यनीतिरज्जू रिपुसंयमनोद्यता जयति ॥ ४ ॥
छग्गुणसंजोअदिढा उवाअपरिवाडिघडिअपासमुही।
चाणक्कणीतिरज्जू रिपुसंजमणुअज्जआ जअदि ॥ ४ ॥

(परिक्रम्यावलोक्य च।) एष स प्रदेश आर्यचाणक्याय उदुम्बरेण कथितो यत्र मया आर्यचाणक्याज्ञया अमात्यराक्षसः प्रेक्षितव्यः। (विलोक्य।) कथमेष खल्वमात्यराक्षसः कृतशीर्षगुण्ठन इत एवागच्छति। तद्यावदेभिर्जीर्णोद्यानपादपैरन्तरितशरीरः प्रेक्षे कुत्रासनपरिग्रहं करोतीति। (एसो सो पदेसो अज्जचाणक्कस्स उदुम्बरेण कहिदो जहिं मए अज्जचाणक्काणत्तिए अमच्चरक्खसोपेक्खिदव्वो। कहं एसो क्खु अमच्चरक्खसो किदसीसावगुण्ठणो इदो एव्व आअच्छइ। ताजाव इमेहिं जिण्णुज्जाणपादवेहिं अन्तरिदसरीरो पेक्खामि कहिं आसनपरिग्गहं करेदि त्ति। (परिक्रम्य। स्थितः।)

(ततः प्रविशति यथानिर्दिष्टः सशस्त्रो[7] राक्षसः।)

अथ कथंचिगदगतिकतया चन्दनदासमोचनरभसेन समायातो राक्षसः साहसी महावीरः शस्त्रपाणिर्वशयितुमशक्य इति तद्धस्ताच्छस्त्रं त्याजयितुं पुनरपि चाणक्य उपायमारचयति। षड्गुण इति। समागतं राक्षसमतिसन्धातुं चाणक्यादिष्टोपायचिकीर्षया करे गृहीततामुद्बन्धनरज्जुं चाणक्यनीतित्वेन निरूपितवान्।

---

१ इंदिसेसु णिओजिआ (आवां नियोजितौ); ईदिसे निसंसे कम्मे णिजुञ्जीअदि (ईदृशे नृशंसे कर्मणि नियुनक्ति) २ ण, णिवसिदुकामो. ३ ऋजुआ. ४ कस्स पुरदो; उदु०. ५ अववारिद. ६ तथा स्थितः. ७ सशंकः.

राक्ष०—(सास्रम्।) कष्टं भोः कष्टम्।

उच्छिन्नाश्रयकातरेव कुलटा गोत्रान्तरं श्रीर्गता
तामेवानुगता गतानुगतिकास्त्यक्तानुरागाः प्रजाः।
आप्तैरप्यनवाप्तपौरुषफलैः कार्यस्य धूरुज्झिता
किं कुर्वन्त्वथवोत्तमाङ्गरहितैरङ्गैरिव स्थीयते ॥ ५ ॥

अपि च।

पतिं त्यक्त्वा देवं भुवनपतिमुच्चैरभिजनं
गता छिद्रेण श्रीर्वृषलमविनीतेव वृषली।
स्थिरीभूता चास्मिन्किमिह करवाम स्थिरमपि
प्रयत्नं नो येषां विफलयति दैवं द्विषदिव ॥ ६ ॥

मया हि।

देवे गते दिवमतद्विधमृत्युयोग्ये
शैलेश्वरं तमधिकृत्य कृतः प्रयत्नः।
तस्मिन्हते तनयमस्य तथाप्यसिद्धि-
र्दैवं हि नन्दकुलशत्रुरसौ न विप्रः ॥ ७ ॥

अहो विवेकशून्यताम्लेच्छस्य। कुतः।

यो नष्टानपि बीजनाशमधुना शुश्रूषते स्वामिन-
स्तेषां वैरिभिरक्षतः कथमसौ सन्धास्यते राक्षसः।
एतावद्धि विवेकशून्यमनसा म्लेच्छेन नालोचितं
दैवेनोपहतस्य बुद्धिरथवा सर्वा विपर्यस्यति ॥ ८ ॥

उच्छिन्नाश्रय इति। आप्तैरप्यस्माभिर्दैवोपहतपौरुषफलैरुद्योगः परित्यक्तः। अथ अतःपरं कर्तव्यप्रयत्नाभावात्किं वा कुर्मः। वाशब्दो भिन्नक्रमः। उत्तमाङ्गरहितैरङ्गैः शवैरिवेति यावत्स्थीयते स्थातव्यं प्रसक्तमित्यर्थः ॥ ५ ॥

पतिमिति। उच्चैरभिजनः वंशो यस्य। छिद्रेण कपटेन स्थिरं दृढमपि येषां नः प्रयत्नं द्विषदिव शत्रुवद्दैवमेव द्विषद्भूत्वा विफलयति चेत्किं कुर्मः ॥ ६ ॥

देवे गत इति। अतद्विधः तत्स्वरूपानर्हः मृत्युयोगो यस्य तस्मिन्देवे नन्दे दिवं गते सति शैलेश्वरं पर्वतकमधिकृत्यावलम्ब्य सर्वार्थसिद्धिप्रतिष्ठापनार्थं कृतः प्रयत्नः। अनन्तरं चाणक्येन राज्यार्धपरिपणनप्रलोभनेन मत्तो विभेद्य स्वायत्तीकृते छद्मना विषकन्यया तस्मिन्पर्वतके हतस्य तनयं मलयकेतुमधिकृत्य कृतः प्रयत्न इत्यनुषङ्गः। दैवमेव प्रबलं किमनेन ब्राह्मणमात्रेण कर्तुं शक्यमित्यनादरेण विप्र इत्युक्तम् ॥ ७ ॥ यो नष्टानिति। बीजनाशमिति णमुलन्तं समूलं नष्टानित्यर्थः। अक्षतः दृढगात्रः। स्पष्टमन्यत् ॥ ८ ॥

---

१ सबाष्पम्. २ उच्छन्ना. ३ कुर्मस्त्व०. ४ ०लमित्र नीचेव. ५ मलयकेतोरित्यधिकम्. ६ जीव. ७ मूढमतिना. ८ सर्वं, पूर्वं, सर्वात्मना क्षीयते.

तदिदानीमपि तावदरातिहस्तगतो विनश्येन्न तु राक्षसश्चन्द्रगुप्तेन सह सन्दधीत[1]। अथवा मम कामसत्यसन्ध इति वरमयशो न तु शत्रुवञ्चनपराभूत[2] इति। (समन्तादवलोक्य सास्रम्।) एतास्ता[3] देवपादक्रमणपरिचयपवित्रीकृततलाः कुसुमपुरोपकण्ठभूमयः। इह हि।

शार्ङ्गकर्षावमुक्तप्रशिथिलकविकाप्रग्रहेणात्र देशे
देवेनाकारि चित्रं प्रजवितुरगं बाणमोक्षश्चलेषु।
अस्यामुद्यानराजौ स्थितमिह कथितं राजभिस्तैर्विनेत्थं
संप्रत्यालोक्यमानाः कुसुमपुरभुवो भूयसा दुःखयन्ति॥ ९॥

तत्क नु गच्छामि मन्दभाग्यः। (विलोक्य।) भवतु दृष्टमेतज्जीर्णोद्यानम्। अत्र प्रविश्य कुतश्चिच्चन्दनदासप्रवृत्तिमुपलप्स्ये। अहो अलक्षितनिपाताः पुरुषाणां समविषमदशापरिणतयो भवन्ति। कुतः।

पौरैरङ्गुलिभिर्नवेन्दुवदहं निर्दिश्यमानः शनै-
र्यो राजेव पुरा पुरान्निरगमं राज्ञां सहस्रैर्वृतः।
भूयः संप्रति सोऽहमेव नगरे तत्रैव वन्ध्यश्रमो
जीर्णोद्यानकमेष तस्कर इव त्रासाद्विशामि द्रुतम्॥ १०॥

अथवा येषां प्रासादादिदमासीत्त एव न सन्ति। (नाट्येन प्रविश्यावलोक्य च।) अहो जीर्णोद्यानस्यारमणीता। अत्र हि।

सन्दधीतेति। पूर्वोक्तार्थपरित्यागेनासत्यसन्धो जात इति अयशः मम कामं वरं प्रशस्तमत्यर्धाङ्गीकारे अथवाशब्दः। कदाचिद्दैवगत्या चन्द्रगुप्तसन्धानप्रसक्तिर्वरं न तु शत्रुणा चाणक्येन वञ्चनपराभूत इत्ययशो वरम्। वञ्चनेनैवंभूतेन पराभूततया सुहृत्तमचन्दनदासविपद्दुःखानुभवो न वरमिति भावः।

शार्ङ्गकर्षावमुक्त इति। शार्ङ्गकर्षावमुक्तः अत एव प्रशिथिलः कविकाप्रग्रहः खलीनवल्गा यस्य अत एव प्रजवितुरगं यथा तथा चलेषु लक्ष्येषु स्वयमपि तुरङ्गवेगवशादतिचलेन देवेन पूर्वं नन्देन बाणमोक्षः कृतश्चित्रमाश्चर्यमिति चललक्ष्यवेधनकौशलमुक्तम्। स्थितं कथितमिति भावे क्तः। तैस्तदादिभिः राजभिर्नन्दैर्विना संप्रतीत्थं शून्या जीर्णाश्च विलोक्यमाना भूयसा बाहुल्येन दुःखयन्ति दुःखवन्तं कुर्वन्ति। णाविष्ठवद्भावेन मतुपो लोपः॥ ९॥

अलक्षितनिपाता इति अतर्कितागमाः।

---

१ सन्धिं कुर्यात्. २ भूतिः. ३ तावद्देवस्य पादचंक्रम. ४ ०र्ङ्गज्याकृष्टि०. ५ पूर्वं. ६ ०सस्य वृत्तान्तम्. ७ (परिक्रम्य स्वगतम्). ८ शीर्णो०, मेकत०. ९ इथाहि.

विपर्यस्तं सौधं कुलमिव महारम्भरचनं
सरः शुष्कं साधोर्हृदयमिव नाशेन सुहृदाम् ।
फलैर्हीना वृक्षा विगुणविधियोगादिव नया-
स्तृणैश्छन्ना भूमिर्मतिरिव कुनीतैरविदुषः ॥ ११ ॥

अपि च ।

क्षताङ्गीनां[2] तीक्ष्णैः परशुभिरुदग्रैः[3] क्षितिरुहां
रुजा कूजन्तीनामविरतकपोतोपरुदितैः ।
स्वनिर्मोकच्छेदैः परिचितपरिक्लेशकृपया
श्वसन्तः शाखानां व्रणमिव निबध्नन्ति फणिनः ॥ १२ ॥

एते च तपस्विनः[4] ।

अन्तः शरीरपरिशोषमुदश्रयन्तः[5]
कीटक्षतिं शुचमिवातिगुरुं वहन्तः[6] ।
छायावियोगमलिना व्यसने निमग्ना
वृक्षाः श्मशानमुपगन्तुमिव प्रवृत्ताः ॥ १३ ॥

यावदस्मिन्[7] विषमदशापरिणामसुलभे भिन्नशिलातले मुहूर्तमुपविशामि । (उपविश्याकर्ण्य च ।) अये किमयमाकस्मिकः[8] पटुपटहशङ्खमिश्रो नान्दी-नादः श्रूयते । य एषः ।

विपर्यस्तमिति । महारम्भा रचना शिल्पं यस्य सौधस्य महारम्भरचना धर्मादिपुरुषार्थी क्रिया यस्य कुलस्य । अविदुषो मूर्खस्य मतिः कुनीतैः कूटनयैः कपटोपदेशैरिव । अत्र जीर्णोद्यानवर्णनव्याजेन सौधकुलादीनामुपमयां नन्दकुलविनाशस्तेन स्वहृदयपरिशोषः मलयकेतुयोगात्स्वनयवैफल्यं मलयकेतुमतिविमोहकभागुरायणकुनीतिश्चेत्येते अर्थाश्च ध्वनिताः ॥ ११ ॥

क्षताङ्गीनामिति । उदग्रक्रमभृतां अत्यन्तशुष्काणां रुजा कूजन्तीनामिवेति गम्योत्प्रेक्षा । परिचितपरिक्लेशनिमित्तकृपयेवेति फणिनां स्वाभाविकं श्वसनं कृपाहेतुत्वेनोत्प्रेक्ष्यते । यथा केचित्कृपालवः परिचितजनानां रुजा क्रियमाणानां तीक्ष्णशस्त्रव्रणान्कृपया दुःखेन निश्वसन्तः पटच्छेदैर्निबध्नन्ति तद्वदित्युत्प्रेक्षा ॥ १२ ॥

अन्तःशरीरेति । तपस्विनो दीना जलसेकाभावात् अन्तःशोषमुपदर्शयन्तः कीटक्षतिस्रुतिभिः कीटक्षतिरन्ध्रनिर्यासैरस्रमश्रु उद्वमन्त इव । छायावियोगेन निष्पर्णतया छायाभावेन मलिनाः शुष्का इत्यर्थः । वृक्षाच्छायावियोगमलिना आ-आतपक्लिष्टा व्यसने निमग्ना नन्दबन्धव इव नन्दानां श्मशानं तत्रैव विद्यमानमुपगन्तुं प्रवृत्ता इवेत्युत्प्रेक्षा ॥ १३ ॥

यावदिति । विषमदशापरिणामवत्सुलभे विषमदशा संप्रति सुलभा अतर्कितोपनता तथेदं शिलातलं दैवाल्लब्धमित्यर्थः ।

---

१ नृप. २ क्षताङ्गानाम्. ३ उदग्रक्रमभृतां. ४ ०स्विनो वृक्षाः. ५ उपाश्रयन्तः, उदग्रयन्तीं. ६ कीटक्षतिस्रुतिभिरस्रमिवोद्वमन्तः. ७ तद्यावत्. ८ अये किमिदमस्मिन्काले पटुपटहशङ्खमिश्रो.

प्रमृद्नञ्श्रोतॄणां[1] श्रुतिपथमसारं गुरुतया
बहुत्वात्प्रासादैः सपदि परिपीतोज्झित इव।
असौ नान्दीनादः पटुपटहशङ्खध्वनियुतो
दिशां द्रष्टुं दैर्घ्यं प्रसरति सकौतूहल इव॥ १४॥

(विचिन्त्य।) आः ज्ञातम्। एष हि मलयकेतुसंयमनसंजातो[2] राजकुलस्य। (इत्यर्द्धोक्ते सासूयम्।) मौर्यकुलस्याधिकपरितोषं पिशुनयति। (सबाष्पम्।) कष्टं भोः कष्टम्।

आवितोस्मि श्रियं शत्रोरभिनीय च दर्शितः।
अनुभावयितुं मन्ये यत्नः संप्रति मां विधेः॥ १५॥

पुरु०—आसीनोयम्। यावदार्यचाणक्यादेशं संपादयामि। (आसीणो अअं। जाव अज्जचाणक्कादेसं संपादेमि।)

(राक्षसमपश्यन्निव तस्याग्रतो रज्जुपाशेन कण्ठमुद्बध्नाति।)

राक्ष०—(विलोक्य।) अये कथमयमात्मानमुद्बध्नाति। अहमिव दुःखितस्तपस्वी। भवतु पृच्छाम्येनम्। (उपसृत्य।) भद्र किमिदमनुष्ठीयते।

पुरुषः—(सबाष्पम्।) आर्य यत्प्रियवयस्यविनाशदुःखितोस्माद्दृशो मन्दभाग्योनुतिष्ठति। (अज्ज जं पिअवअस्सविणासदुःखिदो अह्मारिसो मन्दभग्गो अणुचिट्ठदि।)

राक्ष०—(आत्मगतम्।) प्रथममेव मया ज्ञातं नूनमहमिवार्तस्तपस्वीति। (प्रकाशम्।) हे व्यसनसब्रह्मचारिन्यदि न गुह्यं नातिभारिकं वा ततः श्रोतुमिच्छामि[3]।

प्रमृद्नन्निति। नान्दीनादो मङ्गलतूर्यध्वनिः। अविद्यमानः सारः प्रसारो विस्तारो यस्य तमसारं सङ्कुचितमित्यर्थः। श्रुतिपथं गुरुतया प्रभूततया प्रमृद्नन्पीडयन्। यथा सङ्कुचिते रन्ध्रे गुरुर्मुद्गरादिः प्रविशंस्तदुपमृद्नाति तद्वदित्यर्थः। बहुपीतं जलादि यथोद्गिरन्ति तथान्तरं नान्दीनादं प्रतिध्वनिव्याजेन सौधा उद्गिरन्तीवेत्युत्प्रेक्षा। दिशां दैर्घ्यं द्रष्टुमिति सकलदिग्व्यापित्वमुक्तम्॥ १४॥

सासूयमिति। एष नान्दीनादः। मौर्ये राजशब्दं वक्तुमसूया। अनुभावयितुमिति। चन्दनदासविपद्विमोक्षानुरोधेनेदमिव विधिबलादागत्य गले पतितमिति भावः॥ हे व्यसन इति। व्यसनसब्रह्मचारिन् समानव्यसन। भारिकं भारवत्।

---

१ प्रकुर्वन्. २ कृतं. ३ अतःपरम्-किं ते प्राणपरित्यागकारणम इत्यधिकम्.

पुरु०—आर्य न रहस्यं नातिगुरुकं किं तु न शक्नोमि प्रियवयस्यविनाशदुःखितहृदय एतावन्मात्रमपि मरणस्य कालहरणं कर्तुम् । (अज्ज ण रहस्सं णादिगुरुअं किंदु ण सक्णोमि पिअवअस्सविणासदुक्खिदहिअओ एत्तिअमेत्तं वि मरणस्स कालहरणं कादुं ।)

राक्ष०—(निःश्वस्यात्मगतम् ।) कष्टमेते सुहृद्व्यसनेषु परवदुदासीनाः प्रत्यादिश्यामहे वयमनेन । (प्रकाशम् ।) भद्र यदि न रहस्यं नातिगुरु वा तच्छ्रोतुमिच्छामि ।

पुरु०—अहो निर्बन्ध आर्यस्य । का गतिः । निवेदयामि अस्ति तावदत्र नगरे मणिकारश्रेष्ठी विष्णुदासो नाम । (अहो णिब्बन्धो अज्जस्स । का गई । [२]णिवेदेमि । अत्थि दाव एत्थ णअरे मणिआरसेठ्ठी विह्नुदासो णाम ।)

राक्ष०—(आत्मगतम् ।) अस्ति विष्णुदासश्चन्दनदासस्य परमसुहृत् । (प्रकाशम् ।) किं तस्य ।

पुरु०—स मम प्रियवयस्यः—(सो मम पिअवअस्सो)

राक्ष०—(सहर्षमात्मगतम् ।) अये प्रियवयस्य इत्याह । अत्यन्तसन्निकृष्टः संबन्धः । हन्त ज्ञास्यति चन्दनदासस्य वृत्तान्तम् ।

पुरु[४]०—संप्रति दीनजनदत्ताभरणादिविभवो ज्वलनं प्रवेष्टुकामो नगरान्निष्क्रान्तः । अहमपि यावत्तस्याश्रोतव्यं न श्रृणोमि तावदात्मानमुद्बध्य व्यापादयितुमिदं जीर्णोद्यानमागतः । (संपदं दीणजणदिण्णाभरणादिविहवो जलणं पवेसिदुकामो णअरादो णिक्कन्तो । अहं वि जाव तस्स असुणिदव्वं ण सुणेमि ताव अत्ताणं उब्बन्धिअ वावादइदुं इमं जिण्णुज्जाणं आअदो ।)

राक्ष०—भद्र अग्निप्रवेशे सुहृदस्ते को हेतुः ।

किमौषधपथातिगैरुपहतो महाव्याधिभिः

मत्वर्थीयष्ठन् । यदि नातिभारिकं नातिमहत्तर्हि कथयेत्यर्थः ।

प्रत्यादिश्यामह इति । प्रत्यादेशः प्रतिषेधः । उपलभ्यामह इति यावत् ।

किमौषधपथातिगैरिति । अचिकित्स्यमहाव्याधी राजक्रोधोऽगम्यगुरुदारादिप्रधर्षणमप्रतीकार्यसुहृद्विनाशश्चैतान्यात्मघातनिमित्तानीति भावः ॥ रोगाक्रान्ततया तस्य न मरणव्यवसाय इत्यर्थः ।

---

१ परम. २ एसो णिवे०. ३ अस्मात्परं (प्रकाशं) भद्र किं तस्य. पु०-सो इत्यधिकम. ४ सबाष्पमित्यधिकम्.

पुरु०—नहि नहि । (णहि णहि ।)

राक्ष०—किमग्निविषकल्पया नरपतेर्निरस्तः क्रुधा ।

पुरु०—आर्य शान्तं पापं शान्तं पापम् । चन्द्रगुप्तस्य जनपदे न नृशंसा प्रतिपत्तिः । (अज्ज सन्तं पावं सन्तं पावं । चन्दउत्तस्स जणवदे ण णिसंसा पडिवत्ती ।

राक्ष०—अलभ्यमनुरक्तवान् किमयमन्यनारीजनम् ।

पुरु०—(कर्णौ पिधाय ।) शान्तं पापम् । अभूमिः खल्वेषोऽविनयस्य । (सन्तं पावं । अभूमी क्खु एसो अविणअस्स ।)

राक्ष०—किमस्य भवतो यथा सुहृद एव नाशोऽवशः ॥ १६ ॥

पुरु०—आर्य अथ किम् । (अज्ज अह इं ।)

राक्ष०—(सावेगमात्मगतम् ।) चन्दनदासस्य प्रियसुहृदिति तस्य प्रियसुहृद्विनाशो हुतभुवप्रवेशहेतुरिति यत्सत्यं चलितमेवास्ते युक्तस्नेहपक्षपाताद्धृदयम् । (प्रकाशम् ।) तद्विनाशं च प्रियसुहृद्वत्सलतया मर्तव्ये व्यवसितस्य सुचरितं च विस्तरेण श्रोतुमिच्छामि ।

पुरु०—आर्य अतोऽपरं न शक्नोमि मन्दभाग्यो मरणस्य विघ्नमुत्पादयितुम् । (अज्ज अदो अवरं ण सक्कोमि मन्दभग्गो मरणस्स विग्घमुप्पादेदुं ।)

राक्ष०—भद्र श्रवणीयां कथां कथय ।

पुरु०—का गतिः । किं कर्तव्यम् । एष खलु निवेदयामि । शृणोत्वार्यः । (का गई । किं कादव्वम् । एसो क्खु णिवेदेमि । सुणोदु अज्जो ।)

राक्ष०—भद्र अवहितोस्मि ।

पुरु०—अस्ति इह नगरे मणिकारश्रेष्ठी चन्दनदासो नाम । (अत्थि एत्थ णअरे मणिआरसेठ्ठी चन्दणदासो णाम ।)

आवशोप्रतीकार्यः । चलितमेवास्त इति । चलितमास्त इति यत्तद्युक्तमेवेति व्यवहितेनान्वयः । तद्विनाशमिति । मृत्युं च सुचरितं च विस्तरेण श्रोतुमिच्छामि ।

---

१ अज्ज णहि० पदं वि णात्थि. २ कथय किं नु. ३ दासोस्य सुहृदः प्रियसुहृत्तमस्तस्य ...नाश एवाग्निप्रवेशहेतुरिति यत्सत्यमाकुलित एवास्मि सुहृत्स्नेहपक्षपातिना हृदयेन. ४ भद्र तस्यापि तव प्रियसुहृदः सुहृद्वत्सलतया श्रोतव्यचरितस्य सुच०. ५ इति नास्ति क्वचित्. ६ ०तु भद्रमुखः. ७ दत्तावधानोस्मि. ८ जाणाति अज्जो अत्थि.

राक्ष०—(सविषादमात्मगतम् ।) एतत्तदपावृतमस्मच्छोकदीक्षाद्वारं दैवेन । हृदय स्थिरीभव किमपि ते कष्टतरमाकर्णनीयमस्ति ।

पुरु०—स एतस्य विष्णुदासस्य प्रियवयस्यो भवति । (सो एदस्स विह्णुदासस्स पिअवअस्सो होदि ।)

राक्ष०—(स्वगतम् ।) सोयमभ्यर्णः शोकवज्रपातो हृदयस्य ।

पुरु०—ततो विष्णुदासेन वयस्यस्नेहसदृशमद्य विज्ञप्तश्चन्द्रगुप्तः । (तदो विह्णुदासेण वअस्ससिणेहसरिसं अज्ज विण्णविदो चन्दउत्तो ।)

राक्ष०—कथय किमिति ।

पुरु०—देव अस्ति मे गेहे कुटुम्बभरणपर्याप्तोर्थः तस्य विनिमयेन मुच्यतां प्रियवयस्यश्चन्दनदास इति । (देव अत्थि मे गेहे कुडुम्बभरणप-ज्जत्तो[2] अत्थो । तस्स विणिमएण मुञ्चिज्जदू पिअवअस्सो चन्दणदासो त्ति ।)

राक्ष०—(स्वगतम् ।) साधु भो विष्णुदास साधु । अहो दर्शितो मित्रस्नेहः । कुतः ।

> **पितॄन्पुत्राः पुत्रान्परवदभिहिंसन्ति[3] पितरो**
> **यदर्थं सौहार्दं सुहृदि च विमुञ्चन्ति[4] सुहृदः ।**
> **प्रियं मोक्तुं तद्यो [तं यो] व्यसनमिव सद्यो व्यवसितः**
> **कृतार्थोयं सोर्थस्तव सति वणिक्त्वेपि वणिजः ॥ १७ ॥**

(प्रकाशम् ।) भद्र ततस्तथाभिहितेन किं प्रतिपन्नं मौर्येण ।

पुरु०—आर्य तत एवं भणितेन चन्द्रगुप्तेन प्रतिभणिमतः श्रेष्ठी विष्णुदासः न मयार्थस्य कारणेन चन्दनदासः संयमितः किंतु प्रच्छादितोनेनामात्यराक्षसस्य गृहजनो बहुशो याचितेनापि न समर्पित इति । तद्यदि तं समर्पयति तदास्त्यस्य मोक्षः । अन्यथा प्राण हरोस्य दण्ड

शोकदीक्षाद्वारमिति । शोकानुभवनियमस्तद्वारमागमनमार्गः ।

पितॄनिति । तदिति सामान्ये नपुंसकं तद्यो सद्यो इति अनुप्रासलोभेन प्रयुक्तमग्रे सोर्थ इति पुल्लिङ्गेन निर्देशात् । तमर्थं व्यसनमिव स्त्रीद्यूतपानादिव्यसनमिव । तद्धि व्यसनिभिरतिप्रियतया दुस्त्यजमिति भावः । वणिक्त्वेपि वणिजामर्थलोभः सहजो दोष इति भावः ॥ १७ ॥

१ शोकद्वा०, दीक्षाप्रवेशः, विनाशदीक्षाप्रकाशः. २ पज्जत्ता अत्थवत्ता ता एदिणा (अर्थवत्ता तदेतेन). ३ अभिसन्धाय. ४ समुज्झन्ति. ५ प्रियं [तं सं] सद्यस्त्यक्तुं व्यसनिनि वयस्ये व्यवसितः

इति । एवं भणित्वा वध्यस्थानमानायितश्चन्दनदासः । ततो यावद्वयस्यचन्दनदासस्याश्रोतव्यं न शृणोमि तावज्ज्वलनं प्रविशामीति श्रेष्ठी विष्णुदासो नगरान्निष्क्रान्तः । अहमपि विष्णुदासस्याश्रोतव्यं यावन्न शृणोमि तावदुद्बध्यात्मानं व्यापादयामीतीदं जीर्णोद्यानमागतः ।) अज्ज तदो एवं भणिदेण चन्दउत्तेण पडिभणिदो सेट्ठी विह्णुदासो ण मए अत्थस्स कालणेण चन्दणदासो संजमितो किंदु पच्छादिदो अणेण अमच्चरक्खसस्स घरअणो बहुसो जाचिदेण वि ण समप्पिदोत्ति । ता जदि[2] तं समप्पेदि तदो अत्थि से मोक्खो । अण्णहा पाणहरो से दंण्डो त्ति । एवं भणिअ वज्झट्ठाणं ओणविदो चन्दणदासो । तदो जावं वअस्सचन्दणदासस्स असुणिदव्वं ण सुणोमि तावं जलणं पविसामित्ति सेट्ठी विह्णुदासो णअरादो णिक्कन्दो । अहं वि[7] विह्णुदासस्स असुणिदव्वं जाव ण सुणोमि ताव उब्बन्धिअ अत्ताणं वावादेमि त्ति इदं जिण्णुज्जाणं आअदो ।)

राक्ष०—भद्र न खलु व्यापादितश्चन्दनदासः ।

पुरु०—अद्य तावद्व्यापाद्यते । स खलु सांप्रतं पुनः पुनरमात्यराक्षसस्य गृहजनं याच्यते । न खलु स मित्रवत्सलतया समर्पयति । तदेतेन कारणेन न करोमि मरणस्य कालहरणम् । (अज्ज दाव वावादीअदि । सो खु संपदं पुणो पुणो अमच्चरक्खसस्स घरअणं जाचीअदि । ण खु सो मित्तवत्सलदाए समप्पेदि ता एदिणाकालणेण ण करेमि मरणस्स कालहरणम् ।)

राक्ष०—(सहर्षमात्मागतम् ।) साधु वयस्य चन्दनदास साधु ।

शिबेरिव समुद्भूतं शरणागतरक्षया ।
निचीयते त्वया साधो यशोपि सुहृदा विना ॥ १८ ॥

शिबेरिवेति । शिबेरिवेतीवशब्दो भिन्नक्रमः यशसा संबध्यते । शरणागतरक्षया हेतुना समुद्भूतं समुत्पन्नं शिबेर्यश इव त्वया यशो निचीयते संपाद्यते । शिबिनेवेति तृतीयान्तपाठः सुगमः । तेन हि शरणागतस्य सन्निधावेव स्वविनाशोभ्युपगतः । त्वया तु सुहृदा विनापि । अपिशब्दो भिन्नक्रमः । ममासान्निधान इदं यशो निचीयत इत्यहो शिबेरपि त्वमधिकगुणः श्लाघ्योसीति भावः ॥ १८ ॥

---

१ णो त्ति बहुसो जाणिदं । तेण वि. २ अमच्चरक्खसस्स घरअणं. ३ दण्डो अह्मकोपं पडिमाणेदुत्ति (अस्मत्कोपं प्रतिमानयत्विति) अण्णो वि जनो एवं ण करइस्सदित्ति इत्यधिकम् ४ आणत्तो (आज्ञप्तः). ५ जाव पिअवअस्सस्स. ६ ताव ज्जेव अत्ताणअं वावादेमित्ति जलणे. पविसिदुकामो. ७ ०वि पिअवअस्सस्स. ८ ०णेण होदि से मर.

(प्रकाशम् ।) भद्र गच्छेदानीं शीघ्रं विष्णुदासं ज्वलनप्रवेशान्निवारय । अहमपि चन्दनदासं मरणान्मोचयामि ।

पुरु०—अथ पुनः केनोपायेनार्यश्चन्दनदासं मरणान्मोचयति । (अह उण केण उवाएण अज्जो चन्दणदासं मरणादो मोचेदि ।)

राक्ष०—(खड्गमाकृष्य ।) नन्वनेन व्यवसायसुहृदा निस्त्रिंशेन । पश्य

निस्त्रिंशोयं सजलजलदव्योमसङ्काशमूर्ति-
र्युद्धश्रद्धापुलकित इव प्राप्तसख्यः करेण ।
सत्त्वोत्कर्षात्समरनिकषे दृष्टसारः परैर्मे
मित्रस्नेहाद्विवशमधुना साहसे मां नियुङ्क्ते ॥ १९ ॥

पुरु०—आर्य एवं श्रेष्ठिचन्दनदासजीवितप्रदानपिशुनितं विषमदशाविपाकनिपतितं साधु न शक्नोमि त्वां निर्णीय प्रतिपत्तुं किं सुगृहीतनामधेया अमात्यराक्षसपादा यूयं दिष्ट्या दृष्टा इति । तत्कुरु मे प्रसादं सन्देहनिर्णयेन । (इति पादयोः पतति ।) अज्ज एवं सेट्ठिचन्दणदासजीविदप्पदाणपिसुणिदं विसमदसाविपाकणिपडिदं साधु ण सक्णोमि तुमं णिण्णीअ पडिवत्तुं किं सुगिहीदणामहेआ अमच्चरक्खसपादा तुम्हे दिट्ठिआ दिट्ठात्ति । ता करेहि मे पसादं सन्देहणिण्णएण ।)

राक्ष०—सोहमनुभूतभर्तृवंशविनाशः सुहृद्विपत्तिहेतुरनार्यो दुर्गृहीतनामधेयो यथार्थो राक्षसः ।

पुरु०—(सहर्षं पुनः पादयोः पतित्वा ।) आश्चर्यं दिष्ट्या दृष्टोसि । (ही हीमाणहे दिट्ठिआ दिट्ठोसि ।)

राक्ष०—भद्र उत्तिष्ठोत्तिष्ठ अलमिदानीं कालहरणेन । निवेद्यतां

निस्त्रिंशोयमिति । व्यवसायः उत्साहः पौरुषमिति यावत् । तदेकसहायेन खड्गेन तत्सर्वं मौर्यबलमुत्साद्य सुहृदं मोचयामीत्यर्थः । सजलः जलधारासहितश्चासौ जलदव्योमसङ्काशमूर्तिश्चेति विशेषणकर्मधारयः । नैल्यनैर्मल्यगुणाभ्यां जलदव्योमदृष्टान्तः । धाराजलसहितत्वादेव युद्धश्रद्धापुलकित इवेत्युत्प्रेक्षा धाराजलकणिकानां पुलकसादृश्यसंभवात् । सत्त्वोत्कर्षान्मम कर इवायमपि सत्त्वोत्कर्षशालीत्यर्थः । परैः समरनिकषे दृष्टसारः बहुशोकुण्ठितशक्तित्वेनानुभूत इत्यर्थः । मित्रस्नेहाद्विवशं मित्रस्नेहाधीनतया कार्याकार्यविचारविमुखं मां साहसे नियुङ्क्ते । हिताहितानपेक्षं यत्कर्म तत्साहसं विदुः ॥ १९ ॥

---

१ भद्र भद्र, भद्र गच्छ गच्छे. २ तुम...मोचेसि. ३ महाप्तु. ४ विगत. ५ किदत्थोह्मि (कृतार्थः). ६ कृतानि.

विष्णुदासाय एष राक्षसश्चन्दनदासं मरणान्मोचयतीति । (इति ।निस्त्रिंशोयमिति पठन्नाकृष्टखड्गः परिक्रामति ।)

पुरु०—(पादयोर्निपत्य ।) प्रसीदन्त्वमात्यपादाः । अस्ति तावदत्र प्रथमं चन्द्रगुप्तहतकेनार्यशकटदासो वध्यस्थानमाज्ञप्तः । स च वध्यस्थानात्केनाप्यपहृत्य देशान्तरं नीतः । ततश्चन्द्रगुप्तहतकेन कस्मादेष प्रमादः कृत इति आर्यशकटदासे समुज्ज्वलितः कोपवह्निर्घातकजननिधनेन निर्वापितः । ततः प्रभृति घातका यं कमपि गृहीतशस्त्रमपूर्वं पुरुषं पृष्ठतो वाऽग्रतो वा प्रेक्षन्ते तदात्मनो जीवितं परिरक्षन्तोप्रमत्ता वध्यस्थाने वध्यं व्यापादयन्ति । तस्मादेवं गृहीतशस्त्रैरमात्यपादैर्गच्छद्भिः श्रेष्ठिचन्दनदासस्य वधस्त्वरायितो भवति । (निष्क्रान्तः ।) (पसीदन्दु अमच्चपादा । अत्थि दाव एत्थ पढमं चन्दउत्तहदएण अज्जसअडदासो वज्झट्ठाणं आणत्तो । सो अ वज्झट्ठाणादो केणवि अवहरिअ देसन्तरं णीदो[3] । तदो चन्दउत्तहदएण कीस एसो प्पमादो किदोत्ति अज्जसअडदासे समुज्जलिदो कोववही घादअजणणिहणेण णिव्वाविदो । तदोपहुदि घादआ जं कंवि गिहिदसत्थं अपुव्वं पिट्ठदो वा अग्गदो वा पेक्खन्ति तदो अत्तणो जीविदं परिरक्खन्तो अप्पमत्ता वज्झट्ठाणे वज्झं वावादेन्ति । ता एवं गिहिदसत्थेहिं अमच्चपादेहिं गच्छन्तेहिं सेट्ठिचन्दणदासस्स वहो तवराइदो होदि ।)

राक्ष०—(स्वगतम् ।) अहो दुर्बोधश्चाणक्यबटोर्नीतिमार्गः । कुतः ।

यदि च शकटो नीतः शत्रोर्मतेन ममान्तिकं
किमिति निहतस्तेन क्रोधाद्वधाधिकृतो जनः ।
अथ न कृतकं तादृक्कष्टं कथं नु विभावये-
दिति मम मतिस्तर्कारूढा न पश्यति निश्चयम् ॥ २० ॥

चन्द्रगुप्तेति । चन्द्रगुप्तहतकेनेति आर्यशकटेति च वचनं स्वस्य नन्दकुलपक्षपातित्वद्योतनार्थम् ।

यदि चेति । शत्रोर्मते मौर्यानुमत्या छद्मना यदि शकटदासो ममान्तिकं प्रापितस्तर्हि घातकवधपर्यवसायी क्रोधावेशो न घटेत । अथ घातकवधान्यथानुपपत्त्या कृतकं नेति तदीयं पलाय्यागमनं कृतकं छद्मरूपं न भवति । परमा-

---

१ यथैष-मोचयति. २ आकृष्य खड्गं. ३ अववाहिदो. ४ ०दासवधवज्झणाए. ५ रोसग्गी (रोषाग्निः). ६ वधजलेण. ७ तदो अह्नपधं ज्जेव...अप्पमत्ता एदं अणत्तासवज्झट्ठाणं ८ स. ९ ताः क्रोधावेशात्...ता जनाः. १० लेखं. ११ चकारूढा.

(विचिन्त्य ।)

नायं निस्त्रिंशकालः प्रथममिह कृते घातकानां विघाते
नीतिः कालान्तरेण प्रकटयति फलं किं तया कार्यमत्र ।
औदासीन्यं न युक्तं प्रियसुहृदि गते मत्कृते चातिघोरां
व्यापत्तिं ज्ञातमस्यै स्वतनुमहमिमां निष्क्रयं कल्पयामि ॥ २१ ॥

(इति निष्क्रान्ताः सर्वे ।)

इति षष्ठोऽङ्कः ।

सप्तमोऽङ्कः ।

(ततः प्रविशति चण्डालः ।)

चण्डा०—अपसरत आर्याः अपसरत । अपेत मनुषा अपेत ।
(ओसलेह अज्जा ओसलेह । अवेहँ माणहे अवेह ।)

यदि इच्छत रक्षितुं स्वान् प्राणान् विभवान्कुलं कलत्रं च ।
तत्परिहरत विषमं राजापथ्यं सुदूरेण ॥ १ ॥

जइं महह लक्खिदुं शे प्पाणे विहवे कुलं कलत्तं अ ।
ता पलिहलेह विसमं लाआपत्थं सुदूलेण ॥ १ ॥

र्थत एव शकटदासः सिद्धार्थकस्य तात्त्विकसाहसोपकारेण पलाय्य गतः स्यात्तदा तादृक्कष्टं कुत्सितं स्वहस्तलेखमुद्राङ्कनादिरूपं स्वामिद्रोहं शकटदासः कथं नु विभावयेत्कर्तव्यत्वेन कथं चिन्तयेत् । आचरेदित्यर्थः । चिन्तनमपि तस्यानुचितं किमुताचरणमिति भावः । इत्यादितर्कारूढो न कमपि निश्चय प्राप्नोमीत्यहो दुर्बोधश्चाणक्यनीतिमार्ग इत्यर्थः । स्वहस्तलेखात्स्वामिद्रोहरूपं कर्मातिकुत्सितं वाचा वक्तुमयोग्यमिति तादृक्कष्टमित्युक्तम् । तादृग्लेखमिति क्वचित्पाठः ॥ २० ॥

नायमिति । प्रथमं पूर्वं छलतः परमार्थतो वा घातकानां विघाते कृते त्वरिततरं चन्दनदासघातनप्रसक्तिभयनिस्त्रिंशधारणमनुचितम् । [यद्वा प्रथमं ममोद्यमात्प्राग् घातकानां । कर्तरि षष्ठी । घातकैः कृते । चन्दनदासस्येतिशेषः । विघाते इति योज्यम् ।] नीत्याचरणं तु शिरसि भयं दूरे तत्प्रतीकार इति न्यायेनानुपपन्नम् । सुहृद्विनाशोपेक्षणं तु कृतघ्नतादिमहादोषमापादयेत् । अतश्चन्द्रगुप्ताय दासीभावेनात्मानं निष्क्रीयैव सुहृद्विमोचनं न्याय्यत्वेन गले पतितमिति ज्ञातं निश्चितमिति भावः ॥ २१ ॥

इति श्रीत्र्यम्बकयज्वप्रभुवर्याश्रितढुण्ढिराजव्यासयज्वविरचिते
मुद्राराक्षसनाटकव्याख्याने षष्ठोऽङ्कः समाप्तः ॥

इत्थं षष्ठेनाङ्केन राक्षसवशीकरणरूपं प्रधानकार्यं बीजवद्धिर्यथायथं विप्रकी-

---

१ मत्कृतामवे घोराम्. २ ०स्मिन्. ३ च०-वज्रलोमा. ४ ओसलध, (माणहे-मान्या), अवेध. ५ जइ मणहं लक्खिदुं निअप्पाणे विहवे कुले कलत्ते च । पलिहलध से विसमिव लाआपत्थं पअत्तेण ॥ (यदि मन्यध्वं रक्षितुं निजप्राणान्कुलानि कलत्राणि च । परिहरत तस्माद्विषमिव राजापथ्यं प्रयत्नेन ॥).

अपि च। (अविअ।)

भवति पुरुषस्य व्याधिर्मरणं वा सेविते अपथ्ये ॥
राजापथ्ये पुनः सेविते सकलमपि कुलं म्रियते ॥ २ ॥

होदि पुलिसस्स वाही मलणं वा सेविदे अपत्थम्मि ।
लाआपत्थे उण सेविदे सअलं वि कुलं मलदि ॥ २ ॥

तद्यदि न प्रतीथ तदत्र प्रेक्षध्वमेनं राजापथ्यकारिणं श्रेष्ठिचन्दनदासं सपुत्रकलत्रं वध्यस्थानं नीयमानम्। (आकाशे श्रुत्वा।) आर्याः किं भणथ। अस्त्यस्य कोपि मोक्षोपाय इति। आर्या अस्त्यमात्यराक्षसस्य गृहजनं यदि समर्पयति। (पुनराकाशे।) किं भणथ। एष शरणागतवत्सल आत्मनो जीवितमात्रस्य कारणेनेदशमकार्यं न करिष्यतीति । आर्याः तेन हि अवधारयतास्य सुखां गतिम्। किमिदानीं युष्माकमत्र प्रतीकारविचारेण। (ता जदि ण पदिज्जह ता एह पेक्खह एअं लाआपत्थकालीणं सेट्ठिचन्दणदासं सउत्तकलत्तं वज्झट्ठाणं णीअमाणं। अज्जा किं भणह। अत्थि से कोवि मोक्खोवाओ त्ति। अज्जा अत्थि अमच्चरक्खसस्स घरअणं जइ समप्पेदि। किं भणह। एसे सलणागदवच्छले अत्तणो जीविदमेतस्स कालणे ईदिसं अकज्जं ण कलिस्सदि त्ति। अज्जा तेण हि अवधालेह से सुहां[३] गदिं। किं दाणिं तुह्माणं एत्थ पडिआरविआरेण।)

(ततः प्रविशति द्वितीयचण्डालानुगतो[४] वध्यवेशधारी शूलं स्कन्धेनादाय कुटुम्बिन्या पुत्रेण चानुगम्यमानश्चन्दनदासः।)

नैरन्त्रैकार्थीभावमुपनीतैर्मुखसन्ध्याद्यर्थैर्निर्व्यूढम्। अथ राक्षसेन चन्द्रगुप्तसाचिव्यग्रहणद्वारा तल्लक्ष्मीस्थिरीकरणरूपस्य नाटकस्य प्रधानतमं फलमुपगमयितुं सप्तमोऽङ्क आरभ्यते। पूर्वाङ्के रज्जुहस्तेन पुरुषेण निवेदितं चन्दनदासस्य वध्यस्थाननयनं श्रुत्वा राक्षसः ससंभ्रमं शस्त्रमुत्सृज्य वध्यस्थानं प्रति निष्क्रान्त इत्युक्तम्। संप्रति स एव चन्दनदासवृत्तान्तोऽस्मिन्नङ्के प्रपञ्च्यत इतीदमङ्कावतरणं यत्र स्यादुत्तराङ्कार्थः पूर्वाङ्कार्थानुसंगत इति तल्लक्षणात्।

शरणागतवत्सलेति। इत्यादिपौरवचनेनास्य शरणागतरक्षणबिरुदं लिखितपठितत्वेन सकललोकप्रसिद्धमित्युक्तं भवति। सुखां गतिं शरणागतरक्षणपुण्येनोत्तमलोकप्राप्तिमिति बहिरर्थः। राक्षसप्राप्त्या बन्धमोचनात्सुखप्राप्तिमिति गूढम्।

---

१ कुतो से अधण्णस्स मोक्खोवावो। एदं उण० इत्यधिकम्। २ अज्जा जइ एवं अवधाणेध से असुभगतिं। पत्तिवे दाणीं तुह्माणं पडीआले. ३ असुहं (अशुभां). ४ चण्डालेन बिल्वकेना ०वद्दन.

चन्द०—(सबाष्पम् ।) हा धिक् हा धिक् । अस्मादृशानामपि नित्यं चारित्रभङ्गभीरूणां चोरजनोचितं मरणं भवतीति नमः कृतान्ताय । अथवा न नृशंसानामुदासीनेष्वितरेषु वा विशेषोस्ति । तथाहि । (हद्धी हद्धी अह्मारिसाणं वि णिच्चं चारित्तभङ्गभीरूणं चोरजेणोचिदं मरणं होदि त्ति णमो किदन्तस्स । अह वा ण णिसंसाणं उदासीणेसु इदरेसु वा विसेसोत्थि । तहहि ।)

मुक्त्वा आमिषाणि मरणभयेन तृणैर्जीवन्तम् ।
व्याधानां मुग्धहरिणं हन्तुं को नाम निर्बन्धः ॥ ३ ॥

मोत्तूण आमिसाइं मरणभएण तिणेहिं जीवन्तम् ।
वाहाणं मुद्धहरिणं हन्तुं को णाम णिब्बन्धो ॥ ३ ॥

(समन्तादवलोक्य ।) भो प्रियवयस्य विष्णुदास कथं प्रतिवचनमपि न मे प्रतिपद्यसे । अथवा दुर्लभास्ते खलु मानुषा य एतस्मिन्काले दृष्टिपथेपि तिष्ठन्ति । (सबाष्पम् ।) एतेस्माकं प्रियवयस्या अश्रुपातमात्रेण कृतप्रतीकाराः स्वशरीरैः कथमपि निवर्तमानाः परिवर्धितशोकदीनवदना बाष्पगुरुकया दृष्ट्या मामनुगच्छन्ति । (भो पिअवअस्स विह्णुदास कहं पडिवअणं वि ण मे पडिवज्जसि । अह वा दुल्लहा ते क्खु माणुसा जे एदस्सिं काले दिट्ठिपथे वि चिट्ठन्ति । एदे अह्मपिअवअस्सा अंसुपादमेत्तकेण किदपदीआरा स्वसरीरेहिं कहंवि णिवत्तमाणा परिवड्ढमाणसोअदीणवअणा वाहगुरुआए दिट्ठीए मं अणुगगच्छन्दि ।)
(इति परिक्रामति ।)

चण्डा०—आर्य चन्दनदास आगतोसि वध्यस्थानं तद्विसर्जय गृहजनम् । (अज्ज चन्दणदास आअदोसि वज्झट्ठाणं ता विसज्जेहि घरजणम् ।)

चन्द०—कुटुम्बिनि निवर्तस्व सांप्रतं सपुत्रा । न युक्तं खल्वतःपरमनुगन्तुम् । (कुडुम्बिणि णिवत्तेहि संपदं सपुत्ता । ण जुत्तं क्खु अदोवरं अणुगच्छिदुम् ।)

कुटु०—(सबाष्पम् ।) परलोकं प्रस्थित आर्यो न देशान्तरम् ।

परलोकं इति । देशान्तरं प्रस्थितं बन्धुं नानुगच्छेदिति शास्त्रम् । परलोकं प्रस्थितस्य त्वनुगमनमुचितमेवेति भावः ।

---

१ कुटु०-. २ चोरजणानं विअ मरणं पत्तं ति णमो णमो किदन्तस्स. ३ जीवन्ति. ४ चन्द०-(स०). ५ इमास्सिं. ६ किदणिवापसलिला विअ कहं वि पाडिणं०णा सोअदीण ७ परि. ८ अज्जे कु०...सपुत्ता । वज्झट्ठाणं क्खु एदं अदो अवरं अभूमि क्खु अणुग०.

(परलोअं पत्थिदो अज्जो ण देसन्तरं ।)

चन्द०—आर्ये अयं मित्रकार्येण मे विनाशो न पुनः पुरुषदोषेण तदलं विषादेन । (अज्जे अअं मित्तकज्जेण मे विणासो ण उण पुरिसदोसेण ता अलं विसादेण ।)

कुटु०—आर्य यद्येवं तदिदानीमकालः कुलजनस्य निवर्तितुम् । (अज्ज जइ एवं ता दाणिं अकालो कुलजणस्स णिवट्टिदुम् ।)

चन्द०—अथ किं व्यवसितं कुटुम्बिन्या । (अह किं ववसिदं कुडुम्बिणीए ।)

कुटु०—भर्तुश्चरणावनुगच्छन्त्या आत्मानुग्रहो भवत्विति । (भैत्तुणो चलणे अणुगच्छन्तीए अप्पाणुग्गहो होदुत्ति ।)

चन्द०—आर्ये दुर्व्यवसितमिदम् । त्वयायं पुत्रकोऽश्रुतलोकसंव्यवहारो बालोनुगृहीतव्यः । (अज्जे दुव्ववसिदं एदं । तुए अअं पुत्तओ असुणिदलोअसंववहारो बालो अणुगेह्णिदव्वो ।)

कुटु०—अनुगृह्णन्त्वेनं प्रसन्ना देवताः । जात पुत्रक पत पश्चिमयाः पितुः पादयोः । (अणुगिह्णन्दु ण पसण्णाआ देवदाओ । जाद पुअत्त पतै पच्छिमेसु पिदुणो पादेसु ।)

पुत्र०—(पादयोर्निपत्य ।) तात किमिदानीं मया तातविरहितेनानुष्ठातव्यम् । (ताद किं दाणिं मए तादविरहिदेण अणुचिट्ठिदव्वम् ।)

चन्द०—पुत्र चाणक्यविरहिते देशे वस्तव्यम् । (पुत्त चाणक्कविरहिदे देसे वसिदव्वम् ।)

चण्डा०—आर्य चन्दनदास निखातः शूलस्तत्सज्जो भव । (अज्ज चन्दणदास णिखादं शूले ता सज्जो होहि ।)

कुटु०—आर्याः परित्रायध्वं परित्रायध्वम् । (अज्जा परित्ताअध परित्ताअध ।)

चन्द०—आर्ये अथ किमत्राक्रन्दसि । स्वर्गं गतानां तावद्देवा दुःखितं परिजनमनुकम्पन्ते । (अन्यच्च मित्रकार्येण मे विनाशः

पश्चिमेष्विति । अतः परं द्रष्टुमशक्येष्वित्यर्थः ।

चाणक्य इति । अनेन चाणक्यस्यात्यन्तं क्रौर्यमुक्तम् । आक्रन्दसीति ।

---

१ ता किं हरिसट्ठाणे वि रोदिसि. २ (सबाष्पम ।). ३ भअवदीओ कुलदे०. ४ पणमअपच्छिमस्स पिदुणो.

नायुक्तकार्येण । तत्किं हर्षस्थानेपि रुद्यते ।) (अज्जे अइ किं एत्थ आक्कन्दसि । समं गदाणं दाव देवा दुक्खिअं परिअणं कणुकम्पन्दि । अण्णं अ मित्तकज्जेण मे विणासो ण अजुत्तकज्जेण । ता किं हरिसट्ठाणे वि रोदीअदि ।)

प्रथमश्चण्डालः—अरे बिल्वपत्र गृहाण चन्दनदासम् । स्वयमेव गृहजनो गमिष्यति । (अले विल्लपैत्त गेह्ण चन्दणदासं । सअं एव्व वलजणो गमिस्सदि ।)

द्वितीयश्चण्डालः—अरे वज्रलोमन् एष गृह्णामि । (अले वज्ज-लोमा एसे गेह्णामि ।)

चन्द०—भद्र मुहूर्तं तिष्ठ यावत्पुत्रकं परिष्वजे । (पुत्रं परिष्वज्य-मूर्ध्न्याघ्राय ।) जात अवश्यं भवितव्ये विनाशे मित्रकार्यं समुद्वहमानो विनाशमनुभव। (भद्द मुहु त्तं चिट्ठ जाव पुत्तअं परिस्सैआमि । जाद अवस्सं भविदव्वे विणासे मित्तकज्जं समुव्वहमाणो विणासमणुभवेहि ।)

पुत्र०—तात किमिदमपि भणितव्यम् । कुलधर्मः खल्वेषोस्माकम् । (इति पादयोः पतति ।) (ताद किं एदं वि भणिदव्वं । कुलधम्मो क्खु एसो अह्माणं ।)

चण्डा०—अरे गृहाणैनम् । (अले गेह्ण एणं ।) (चण्डालौ गृहीतश्चन्दनदासम् ।)

कुटु०—(सोरस्ताडम् ।) आर्या परित्रायध्वं परित्रायध्वम् । (अज्जा परित्ताअध परित्ताअध ।)

(प्रविश्य पटाँक्षेपेण राक्षसः ।) भवति न भेतव्यम् । भो भोः शूलायतनाः न खलु व्यापादयितव्यश्चन्दनदासः ।

शोकावेशेन नीचान्प्रति किमाक्रन्दसि सुचरितानुकम्पिनो देवा एव शरणीकरणीया इत्यर्थः । **मित्रकार्येणेति** । मित्रकार्येण मरणात्स्वस्य स्वर्गो निश्चित इति भावः ।
अनुभवामीति । अतस्त्वया न शोचितव्यमिति भावः । अत्र करुणः स्थायी शोकदीनवचनादिभिर्विभावैरनुभावैश्च पुष्कलः ।
प्रविश्य पटाक्षेपेणेति । असूचितस्य सहसा संभ्रमेण प्रवेशः पटाक्षेपः ।
शूलायतना इति । शूलमायतनं जीवनाश्रयो येषां ते तथोक्ताः ।

---

१ भद्दमुह मुहुत्तअं चिट्ठ । अइ जीविहवच्छले किं पत्थ०. २ गदा क्खु ते देवा णन्दा जं दुक्खिदं जणं अणुकम्पन्ति. ३ वत्ता (वक्र), वेणुवत्तका (वेणुवेत्रक). ४ सन्तआमि मान्त्वयामि). ५ अणुभवामि. मारोपयितुं शूले । इत्यधिकम्. ७ अपटाक्षेपेण.

१४

येन स्वामिकुलं रिपोरिव कुलं दृष्टं विनश्यत्पुरा
मित्राणां व्यसने महोत्सव इव स्वस्थेन येन स्थितम्।
आत्मा यस्य वधाय वः परिभवक्षेत्रीकृतोपि प्रिय-
स्तस्येयं मम मृत्युलोकपदवी वध्यस्रगाबध्यताम् ॥ ४ ॥

चन्द०—(सबाष्पं विलोक्य ।) अमात्य किमिदम् । (अमच्च किं एदं ।)

राक्ष०—त्वदीयसुचरितैकदेशस्यानुकरणं किलैतत् ।

चन्द०—अमात्य सर्वमपीमं प्रयासं निष्फलं कुर्वता त्वया किमनुष्ठितम् । (अमच्च सव्वं वि इमं पआसं णिप्फलं करन्तेण तुए किं अणुचिट्ठिदं ।)

राक्ष०—सखे स्वार्थ एवानुष्ठितः । कृतमुपालम्भेन । भद्रमुखे निवेद्यतां दुरात्मने चाणक्याय ।

वज्र०—किमिति । (किं त्ति)

राक्ष०—

दुष्कालेपि कलावसज्जनरुचौ प्राणैः परं रक्षता
नीतं येन यशस्विनातिलघुतामौशीनरीयं यशः ।
बुद्धानामपि चेष्टितं सुचरितैः क्लिष्टं विशुद्धात्मना
पूजार्होपि स यत्कृते तव गतो वध्यत्वमेषोस्मि सः ॥ ५ ॥

प्रथम०—अरे बिल्वपत्रक त्वं तावच्चन्दनदासं गृहीत्वैहैतस्य श्मशानपादपस्य छायायां मुहूर्तं तिष्ठ यावदहमार्यचाणक्याय निवेदयामि गृहीतोमात्यराक्षस इति । (अले बिल्लपत्तअ तुमं दाव चन्दणदासं गेह्णिअ इह एदस्स मसाणपादपस्स छाआए मुहुत्तं चिट्ठ जाव अहं अज्जचाणक्कस्स णिवेदेमि गिहीदो अमच्चरक्खसो त्ति ।)

येनेति । महोत्सव इवेति सप्तम्यन्तम् । यस्य मम परिभवक्षेत्रीकृतोपि । एतादृशं परिभवमनुभवन्नपि आत्मा शरीरं वपुः युष्मादृशां वधाय बधार्थं प्रियो जातः यदर्थं किल चाणक्येन कौलूतादयः युष्मादृशा घातकाश्च छलेन वृथा व्यापादिताः । एतादृशपातकनिमित्तभूतोप्यात्मा येन मया न परित्यक्त इत्यात्मोपालम्भः ॥ ४ ॥ सखे स्वार्थ एवेति । इदं त्वत्संरक्षणं ममात्मरक्षणादप्यभ्यर्हितं श्रेयस्करमिति भावः ।

दुष्कालेपीति । शिबिना पुण्ये कृतयुगे तत्कृतमिति नात्र चित्रम् । पापे कलियुग ईदृशं कर्म कुर्वाणस्ततोप्यतिशयितो यश्चन्दनदासः स त्वयात्यर्थ-

---

१ सखे चन्दनदास कृतमुपालम्भेन । स्वार्थप्रधानो हि जीवलोकः । २ ०मुख अयमथ निवेद्यतां तावत्. ३ शब्रुत्व. ४ सेट्ठिच.

द्वितीय०—अरे वज्रलोमन् एवं भवतु (अले वज्जलोमा एवं होदु ।)

(इति सपुत्रदारेण चन्दनदासेन सह निष्क्रान्तः ।)

प्रथमः—एत्वमात्यः । (राक्षसेन सह परिक्रम्य ।) अस्त्यत्र कोपि निवेदयत तावन्नन्दकुलनगकुलिशस्य मौर्यकुलप्रतिष्ठापकस्यार्यचाणक्यस्य । (एदु अमच्चो । अत्थि एत्थ कोवि णिवेदेह दाव णन्दकुहणगकुलिसस्स मोलिअकुलपडिट्ठावर्केस्स अज्जचाणक्कस्स ।)

राक्ष०—(स्वगतम् ।) एतदपि नाम श्रोतव्यम् ।

एष आर्यनीतिसंयमितबुद्धिपुरुषकारो गृहीतोमात्यराक्षस इति । (एसो अज्जणीदिसंजमिदबुद्धिपुलिसआले गिहीदे अमच्चरक्खसेत्ति ।)

चण्डा०—भद्र कथय कथय ।

(ततः प्रविशति जवनिकावृतशरीरो मुखमात्रदृश्यश्चाणक्यः ।)

केनोत्तुङ्गशिखाकलापकपिलो बद्धः पटान्ते शिखी
पाशैः केन सदागतेरगतिता सद्यः समासादिता ।
केनानेकपदानवासितसटः सिंहोर्पितः पञ्जरे
भीमः केन च नैकनक्रमकरो दोर्भ्यां प्रतीर्णोर्णवः ॥ ६ ॥

चण्डा०—ननु नीतिनिपुणबुद्धिनार्येण । (णं णीदिणिउणबुद्धिणा अज्जेर्ण ।)

चाण०—मा मैवम् । नन्दकुलविद्वेषिणा दैवेनेति ब्रूहि ।

राक्ष०—(स्वगतम् ।) अयं दुरात्मा अथवा महात्मा कौटिल्यः ।

मर्चनीयोपि यस्य मम कृत ईदृशीं विपत्तिमुपनीतः सोयं तव विधेयोस्मीत्यर्थः । बुद्धा अत्यन्तदयालव इति प्रसिद्धं तेषामपि चेष्टितं दयालुत्वं क्लिष्टं कृशीकृतमित्यर्थः॥ ५ ॥

एष आर्यनीतीति । आर्यचाणक्यस्य नीत्या संयमितः कुण्ठीकृतः बुद्धिपरिसरो यस्य सः ।

केनेति । सदागतेर्वायोरगतिता गतिनिरोधः पाशैः सूक्ष्मरशनाभिः केन समासादितः कृत इत्यर्थः । सोपि झटिति कृत इत्याश्चर्यं भित्तितिरस्करिणीबन्धनादिना क्रमेण चिरात्कथंचित्कर्तुं शक्य इत्यर्थः । एवं दुष्करो राक्षसवशीकारः केन कृत इति रूपकातिशयोक्त्या स्वात्मगुणश्लाघा । इयमद्भुतार्थप्राप्तिरुपगूहनं नामाङ्गम् ॥ ६ ॥ नन्दकुलेति । नन्दकुलं सर्वं दैवेन निपातितमिति निवरलम्बतया निर्व्यवसायोयमेव वशीभूत इत्यर्थः ।

---

१ गच्छ. २ केके एत्थ दुआलिआणं. ३ ०कुलसेणसञ्चअचुण्णणकुलिसस्स. ४ ०डिट्ठाविदग्भमसञ्चअस्स. ५ ०णीदिनिभम. ६ पलिसले (परिसरः). ७ दृश्यः महर्षः. ८ ०ण अज्ज.

अकारः सर्वशास्त्राणां रत्नानामिव सागरः
गुणैर्न परितुष्यामो यस्य मत्सरिणो वयम् ॥ ७ ॥

चाण०—(विलोक्य सहर्षं स्वगतम् ।) अये अयमसावमात्यराक्षसः । येन महात्मना ।

गुरुभिः कल्पनाक्लेशैर्दीर्घजागरहेतुभिः ।
चिरमायासिता सेना वृषलस्य मतिश्च मे ॥ ८ ॥

(जवनिकामपनीयोपसृत्य च ।) भो अमात्यराक्षस विष्णुगुप्तोऽहमभिवादये ।

राक्ष०—(स्वगतम् ।) अमात्य इति लज्जाकरमिदानीं विशेषणम् । (प्रकाशम् ।) विष्णुगुप्त न चाण्डालैस्पर्शदूषितं स्प्रष्टुमर्हसि ।

चाण०—अमात्यराक्षस नेमौ चाण्डालौ । अयं खलु दृष्टपूर्व एव भवता सिद्धार्थको नाम राजपुरुषः । योऽप्यसौ द्वितीयः सोऽपि समिद्धार्थको नाम राजपुरुष एव । शकटदासोऽपि तपस्वी तं तादृशं कपटलेखमजानन्नेव मया लेखितः ।

राक्ष०—(स्वगतम् ।) दिष्ट्या शकटदासं प्रत्यपनीतो विकल्पः ।

चाण०—किंबहुना । एष संक्षेपतः कथयामि ।

भृत्या भद्रभटादयः स च तथा लेखः स सिद्धार्थक-
स्तच्चालङ्करणत्रयं स भवतो मित्रं भदन्तः किल ।
जीर्णोद्यानगतः स चार्तपुरुषः क्लेशः स च श्रेष्ठिनः
सर्वोऽसौ मम (इत्यर्धोक्ते लज्जां नाटयति ।
वृषलस्य वीर भवता संयोगमिच्छोर्नयः ॥ ९ ॥

गुरुभिरिति । सेनायां कल्पनाक्लेशाः सदासन्नहनादयः । मतौ कल्पनाक्लेशा ऊहापोहादयः । यन्मतिपौरुषभयान्मौर्यसैन्येन मया चाहर्निशं जाग्रता महानायासोऽनुभूत इति भावः । इदं दुःखप्रशमनं समयः ॥ ८ ॥

भृत्या इति । भवतो मित्रं किल अलीकमित्यर्थः । सर्वमिति । नपुंसकमनपुंसकेनेत्येकशेषः । जातावेकवचनं च । ते भद्रभटादयो भृत्याः स लेख इत्याद्येवंजातीयं सर्वमुपायजातं वृषलस्य भवत्साचिव्यमिच्छोर्मम नयो नीतिप्रकार इति संक्षेपः । त्वत्संग्रहार्थमेतावान्मया नयः कृत इत्यर्थः । अतिशूरः साहसी भवान्विक्रमादिना मलयकेतुवन्निग्रहीतुं न शक्य इति ध्वनयितुं वीरेति संबोधनम् । इदं बीजवतां मुखाद्यर्थानां विप्रकीर्णानामेकार्थोपनयनं कार्यार्थोपसंहृति संहारो नामाङ्गं नवमम् ॥ ९ ॥

---

१ विद्यानां. २ कां करेण; ०कान्तरेण. ३ °सोऽभिवादयते. ४ श्वपाक. ५ श्वपाकौ. ६ ताभ्यामेव सह सौहार्दमुत्पाद्य शक०. ७ सहर्षमात्मगतम्. ८ ये ते. ९ चापि०. १० सर्वं मे.

तदयं वृषलस्त्वां द्रष्टुमि[1]च्छति । पश्यैनम् ।

राक्ष०—(स्वगतम् ।) का गतिः [2]एष पश्यामि ।

(ततः प्रविशति राजा विभवतश्च परिवारः ।)

राजा०—(स्वगतम् ।) विनैव युद्धादार्येण जितं दुर्जयं परबलमिति [3]लज्जित एवास्मि । मम हि ।

फलयोगमवाप्य सायकानामनि[4]योगेन वि[5]लक्षतां गतानाम् ।
स्व[6]शुचेव भवत्यधोमुखानां निजतूणीशयनव्र[7]तप्रतिष्ठा ॥ १० ॥

अथवा ।

विगुणीकृतकार्मुकोपि जेतुं भुवि जेतव्यमसौ समर्थ एव ।
स्वपतोपि ममेव यस्य तन्त्रे गुरवो जाग्रति कार्यजागरूकाः ॥ ११ ॥

(चाणक्यमुपसृत्य ।) आर्य चन्द्रगुप्तः प्रणमति ।

चाण०—वृषल संपन्नास्ते सर्वाशिषः । अयममात्यराक्षसः प्राप्तः तदभिवादय[8]स्वा[9]त्र भवन्तमम[11]ात्यमुख्यम् ।

राक्ष०—(स्वगतम् ।) योजितोनेन संबन्धै[12]ः ।

चाण०—(राक्षसमुपसृत्य ।) आर्य चन्द्रगुप्तोभि[13]वादयते ।

राक्ष०—(विलोक्य स्वगतम् ।) अये चन्द्रगुप्तः । य एषः

बाल एव हि [14]लोकेस्मिन्संभावितमहोदयः ।
क्रमेणारूढवान्राज्यं युथैश्वर्यमिव द्विपः ॥ १२ ॥

फलयोगमिति । विधियोगेन सुदैवप्रसादेन फलयोगं कार्यसिद्धिप्राप्तिमन्यत्र शल्ययोगं प्राप्यापि विपक्षतां विरोधितां गतानामिति विरोधाभासः । वीनां कङ्कानां पक्षा येषामिति बहुव्रीहिः । तेषां भावस्तत्तां गतानां विशिष्टकङ्कपत्रवतामिति वा । इति विरोधपरिहारः । शुचेव विपक्षताप्राप्तिजातया शुचेवेति हेतूत्प्रेक्षा । अधोमुखानां सायकानां निजतूणीशयनमेव व्रतं सर्वदा तत्रैवावस्थाननियमरूपं प्रतुष्ट्यै सन्तोषाय न भवति । अनियोगेन विलक्षतां गतानामिति पाठे नियोगो युद्धादौ निनिगोगस्तदभावेन लज्जितानामित्यर्थो वर्णनीयः ॥ १० ॥ इत्येवं प्रकारेण लज्जित्वा पुनरपि समाधत्ते । विगुणीकृतेति । विगुणीकृतं ज्यारहितं प्रयोजनाभाववच्च कृतं कार्मुकं यस्य । इयं वाञ्छितार्थप्राप्तिरानन्दः ॥ ११ ॥ बाल एवेति । बाल्यमारभ्यैव राजलक्षणलक्षिततया महोन्नतो भविष्यतीति संभावित इत्यर्थः ॥ १२ ॥

---

१ ०मागच्छति. २ (प्रकाशम् ।) इत्यधिकम्. ३ यत्सत्यं ल०. ४ नां विधियोगेन ५ विपक्षतां. ६ न शु०. ७ व्रतं प्रतुष्ट्यै. ८ अभिवादयते. ९ एतन्नास्तिपुस्त०. १० तत्र. ११ ०त्यराक्षसं । पैतृकस्तवायममात्यमुख्यः इ. पा. १२ अस्मात्परं--**चाण०**—(राजानमुपसृत्य) अयममात्यराक्षसः प्राप्तः प्रणमैनम् इत्याधि०. १३ प्रणमति, ०सोहम्–ये. १४ लोकेन.

(प्रकाशम् ।) राजन्विजयस्व ।

राजा०—आर्य ।

जगतः किं न विजितं[1] मयेति प्रविचिन्त्यताम्[2] ।
गुरौ षाड्गुण्यचिन्तायामार्ये चार्ये च जाग्रति ॥ १३ ॥

राक्ष०—(स्वगतम् ।) स्पृशति मां भृत्यभावेन कौटिल्यशिष्यः । अथवा विनय एवैष चन्द्रगुप्तस्य मत्सरस्तु मे विपरीतं कल्पयति । सर्वथा स्थाने यशस्वी चाणक्यः । कुतः ।

द्रव्यं जिगीषुमधिगम्य जडात्मनोऽपि
नेतुर्यशस्विनि पदे नियता[3] प्रतिष्ठा ।
अद्रव्यमेत्य तु विशुद्धनयोऽपि मन्त्री
शीर्णाश्रयः पतति कूलजवृक्षवृत्त्या ॥ १४ ॥

चाण०—अमात्य राक्षस अपीष्यते चन्दनदासस्य जीवितम् ।

राक्ष०—भो विष्णुगुप्त कः सन्देहः ।

चाण०—अमात्य राक्षस अगृहीतशस्त्रेण भवतानुगृह्यते वृषल इत्यतः सन्देहः । तद्यदि सत्यमेव चन्दनदासस्य जीवितमिष्यते ततो गृह्यतामिदं शस्त्रम्[7] ।

राक्ष०—भो विष्णुगुप्त मा मैवम् । अयोग्य वयमस्य विशेषतस्त्वया गृहीतस्य ग्रहणे ।

चाण०—अमात्य राक्षस योग्योऽहमयोग्यो भवानिति कथमेतत्[8] । पश्य ।

जगत इति । जगत इति शेषे षष्ठी । जगति किं न विजितमित्यर्थः ॥ १३ ॥ कौटिल्यशिष्य इति । स्वाभाविक एवैष विनय इत्यर्थः ।

द्रव्यमिति । द्रव्य भव्य इति निपात्यते । द्रव्यं श्रेयःप्राप्तियोग्यं जिगीषुं जयोद्योगिनमधिगम्य जडात्मना मन्दबुद्धेरपि नेतुरमात्यस्य यशस्विपदे स्थाने प्रतिष्ठा नियमतवश्यं भवति किमुतोदारबुद्धेरमात्यस्य । अयोग्यप्रभोराश्रयेण विशुद्धनयोऽपि मन्त्री अहमिव शीर्णाश्रयः सन्पतति नदीकूलगतवृक्ष इवेत्यर्थः ॥ १४ ॥ एवं मनसि विचारयन्तं राक्षसं चन्द्रगुप्तसाचिव्याभ्युपगमाय प्रवणयति । ममात्येत्यादिना । साचिव्यमनभ्युपगम्य ताटस्थ्येन वृषलानुग्रहः अप्रयोजक इति भावः ।

---

१ जितं किं न मया लोक ऐहिकामुष्मिकद्वयम्. २ त्वयि,-कार्ये प्रशाम्यति. ३ नियतम्. ४ भुवि. ५ कुतः. ६ नानु०. ७ अस्मात्परं (राक्षसश्चिन्तयति) ॥ चाण०· तपोवनं यामि विहाय मौर्य त्वां चाधिकारं ह्यधिकृत्य मुख्यम् । त्वयि स्थिते वाक्यनिबद्धबुद्धौ भुनक्तु गामिन्द्र इवैष चन्द्रः ॥ इत्यधिकम्. ८ योग्योऽहं न त्वं योग्य इति किमनेन.

अश्वैः सार्द्धमजस्रदत्तकविकैः क्षामैरशून्यासनैः
स्नानाहारविहारपानशयनस्वेच्छासुखैर्वर्जितान् ।
माहात्म्यात्तव पौरुषस्य मतिमन्दृप्तारिदर्पच्छिदः
पश्यैतान्परिकल्पनाव्यतिकरप्रोच्छूनवंशान्गजान् ॥ १५ ॥

अथवा किं बहुना । न खलु भवतः शस्त्रग्रहणमन्तरेण चन्दनदासस्य जीवितमस्ति ।

राक्ष०—(स्वगतम् ।)

नन्दस्नेहगुणाः स्पृशन्ति हृदयं भृत्योस्मि तद्विद्विषां
ये सिक्ताः स्वयमेव वृद्धिमगमंच्छिन्नास्त एव द्रुमाः ।
शस्त्रं मित्रशरीररक्षणकृते व्यापारणीयं मया
कार्याणां गतयो विधेरपि न यन्त्याज्ञाकरत्वं चिरात् ॥ १६ ॥

(प्रकाशम् ।) विष्णुगुप्त नमः सर्वकार्यप्रतिपत्तिहेतवे सुहृत्स्नेहाय । का गतिरेष प्रह्वोस्मि ।

चाण०—(सहर्षं शस्त्रमर्पयित्वा ।) वृषल वृषल अमात्यराक्षसेनेदानीमनुगृहीतोसि । दिष्ट्या वर्द्धते भवान् ।

राजा०—आर्यप्रसाद एव चन्द्रगुप्तेनानुभूयते ।

(प्रविश्य ।) **पुरुषः**—जयत्वार्यः । एष खलु भद्रभटभागुरायणप्रमुखैः संयमितकरचरणो मलयकेतुः प्रतिहारभूमिमुपस्थापितः । इदं श्रुत्वा आर्यः

अश्वैरिति । स्नानाहारादिवर्जनादेव क्षामैः कृशैरजस्रक्तकविकैः शून्यासनैरनपनीतखलीनपल्याणैः सदा सन्नद्धैरित्यर्थः । परिकल्पनाव्यतिकरेण सदा सन्नाहप्रसङ्गेन पल्याणापनयावात्प्रोच्छूनाः शोफरुजा व्याप्ता वंशाः पृष्ठास्थिभागा येषां तान्पश्येति । आदरेण पुनः पश्येति प्रयोगः । मतिमतः दृप्तारिदर्पच्छिदः पौरुषशालिनश्च तव माहात्म्यादिति साचिव्याय त्वमेव योग्य इति प्रकटीकर्तुं प्रशंसा ॥ १५ ॥

किं बहुनेति । अस्मत्परिक्लेशकथनेन किं प्रयोजनम् । साचिव्यपदं भवतावश्यमङ्गीकर्तव्यमित्याह । न खल्विति ।

नन्देति । ये नन्दाः स्वयमेव मया सिक्ताः गर्भपतनात्प्रभृति तैलद्रोणीनिधानादिना महता परिक्लेशेन परिपालिताः सन्तः वृद्धिमगमंस्ते संप्रति नष्टाः । तद्गुणाकृष्टहृदयस्यापि मम तेषां विद्विषो मौर्यस्य भृत्यत्वं मित्रशरीररक्षणार्थमवश्यमभ्युपेयत्वेन प्रसक्तमित्यहो कार्याणां गतिवशाद्विधिविलसितमप्यन्यथा भवतीति खिद्यते । कार्याणां गतयः विधेरप्याज्ञाकरत्वं चिरान्न यन्ति । अतिप्रबलोपि विधिः कार्यगतिवैचित्र्यात्कार्यगतिकिंकर इव भवतीत्यर्थः ॥ १६ ॥

एष प्रह्वोस्मीति । इदं प्राप्तकार्यानुमोदनमाभाषणमङ्गम् ॥ आर्यप्रसाद एष इति ।

---

१ कविका. २ किमनेन. ३ पाणिपयसा. ४ ०यान्त्यालोचनागोचरम्. ५ सज्जः. ६ गृहीतशस्त्रेण.

प्रमाणम्। (जदु अज्जो। एसो क्खु भद्दभटभाउराअणप्पमुहेहिं संजमिदकलचलणो मलअकेदू पडिहारभूमिं उवट्ठाविदो। एदं सुणिअ अज्जो प्पमाणम्।)

चाण०—भद्र निवेद्यताममात्यराक्षसाय। सोयमिदानीं जानीते।

राक्ष०—(स्वगतम्।) कथं दासीकृत्य मामिदानीं विज्ञापनायां मुखरीकरोति कौटिल्यः। का गतिः। (प्रकाशम्।) राजन् चन्द्रगुप्त विदितमेव ते यथा वयं मलयकेतौ कंचित्कालमुषितास्तत्परिरक्ष्यन्तामस्य प्राणाः।

राजा०—(चाणक्यमुखमवलोकयति।)

चाण०—वृषल प्रतिमानयितव्योमात्यराक्षसस्य प्रथमः प्रणयः। (पुरुषं प्रति।) भद्र अस्मद्वचनादुच्यन्तां भद्रभटप्रमुखा अमात्यराक्षसेन विज्ञापितो देवश्चन्द्रगुप्तः प्रयच्छति मलयकेतवे पित्र्यमेव विषयम्। अतो गच्छन्तु भवन्तः सहानेन। प्रतिष्ठिते चास्मिन्पुनरागन्तव्यमिति।

पुरु०—यदार्य आज्ञापयति। (जं अज्जो आणवेदि) (इति परिक्रामति।)

चाण०—भद्र तिष्ठ तिष्ठ। अपरं च वक्तव्यो दुर्गपाला विजयपालः। अमात्यराक्षसलाभेन सुप्रीतश्चन्द्रगुप्तः समाज्ञापयति य एष श्रेष्ठी चन्दनदासः स पृथिव्यां सर्वनगरश्रेष्ठिपदमारोप्यतामिति। अपि च विना हस्त्यश्वं क्रियतां सर्वमोक्ष इति। अथवामात्यराक्षसे नेतारि किं हस्त्यश्वेन प्रयोजनम्। तदिदानीम्

विना वाहनहस्तिभ्यो मुच्यतां सर्वबन्धनम्।
पूर्णप्रतिज्ञेन मया केवलं बध्यते शिखा ॥ १७ ॥

इदं लब्धस्थिरीकरणं कृतिर्नामाङ्गम् ॥ भद्र निवेद्यतामिति। इदमिष्टकार्यदर्शनं पूर्वभावो नामाङ्गम् ॥ प्रतिमानयितव्य इति। यद्यपि शत्रुशेषं न शेषयेदिति शास्त्रान्मलयकेतुर्न मोक्षणीय इति तथापि राक्षसस्य साचिव्यग्रहणप्रथमप्रार्थनावश्यं मानयितव्येत्यर्थः। भद्रभटप्रमुखा इति। भद्रभटादयः राक्षसस्य साचिव्यनिर्वाहाध्यवसाये सन्दिहानास्तद्वचनं चन्द्रगुप्तवचनं च न प्रमाणीकरिष्यन्तीत्यस्मद्वचनादित्युक्तम्। किं च अमात्यराक्षसेन विज्ञापित इति वचनं स्वयं तथापकृतेनापि राक्षसेन स्वस्मिन्नेवमुपकृतमिति राक्षससौजन्यं मलयकेतुना ज्ञातव्यमिति। विना वाहनहस्तिभ्य इति। ततः प्रविशति मुक्तां शिखां परामृशन्निति मुखसन्धावपक्षिप्तस्य बीजस्यैवं मया निर्वहणं कृतमित्याह। तीर्णप्रतिज्ञेन मया केवलं बध्यते शिखेति।

---

१ उवट्ठिदो. २ राजकार्यं करिष्यति. ३ किंचित्कालान्तरम्. ४ ०सस्य गृहीतशस्त्रस्य प्रीत्या देवश्च०. ५ वाहनहस्तिभ्यः. ६ हस्त्यश्वेन...सहवाहन०. ७ अस्मात्परं-इति शिखां बध्नाति.

पुरु०—यदार्य आज्ञापयति । (जं अज्जो आणवेदि)(इति निष्क्रान्तः)

चाण०—भो राजन् चन्द्रगुप्त भो अमात्य राक्षस उच्यतां किं वां भूयः प्रियं करोमि ।

राजा[1]**०**—किमतः परमपि प्रियमस्ति ।

राक्षसेन समं मैत्री राज्ये चारोपिता वयम् ।
नन्दाश्चोन्मूलिताः सर्वे किं कर्तव्यमतः प्रियम् ॥ १८ ॥

राक्ष०—तथापीदमस्तु भरतवाक्यम् ।

वाराहीमात्मयोनेस्तनुमवनविधावास्थितस्यानुरूपां[2]
यस्य प्राग्दन्तकोटिं प्रलयपरिगता शिश्रिये भूतधात्री ।
म्लेच्छैरुद्विज्यमाना[3] **भुजयुगमधुना संश्रिता**[4] **राजमूर्तेः**
स श्रीमद्बन्धुभृत्यश्चिरमवतु[5] **महीं पार्थिवश्चन्द्रगुप्तः**[6] **॥ १९ ॥**

(इति निष्क्रान्ताः सर्वे ।)

इति सप्तमोऽङ्कः समाप्तः ।

इति विशाखदत्तविरचितं **मुद्राराक्षसं** नाटकं समाप्तम् ।

भो राजन्निति । इदानीं चन्द्रगुप्तस्य राज्यलक्ष्मीस्थिरीकरणाध्यवसायाद्वृषलव्यब्दमपहाय राजन्निति संबोधम् । किं च मलयकेतुनिग्रहराक्षससंग्रहरूपं चन्द्रगुप्तस्य प्रियं कृत मलयकेतुजीवनदानस्वराज्यप्रतिष्ठापनरूपं चन्दनदासबन्धमोचनसकलनगरश्रेष्ठिपदलाभरूपं च राक्षसस्य गहत्प्रियमनुष्ठितम् । अतोऽप्यधिकं युवयोः प्रिय किं करोमीत्याह । किं वा भूय इति ।

राक्षसेनेति । इदं शुभशंसनं प्रशस्तिर्नाम निर्वहणसन्धेरुत्तममङ्गम् ॥ १८ ॥

वाराहीमिति । भूतधात्री पृथ्वी प्रलयपरिगता प्रलयेनोपप्लुता सती प्राक्कल्पादौ अवनविधौ जगद्रक्षणविधाने अनुरूपां समर्थां वाराहीं तनुमाश्रितस्यात्मयोनेः स्वयंभुवः आदिवराहमूर्तेर्भगवतः श्रीविष्णोर्दन्तकोटिं दंष्ट्राग्रं शिश्रिये आश्रिताभूत् । तस्यैवं संप्रति राजमूर्तेः राजा चन्द्रगुप्त एव मूर्तिः शरीरं यस्य । ना विष्णुः पृथिवीपतिरिति स्मरणात् । तथाभूतस्य भगवतो भुजयुगमधुना म्लेच्छैरुद्विज्यमाना भूतधात्री संश्रितास्ते । श्रीमद्बन्धुभृत्यः श्रीमन्तः बन्धवो भृत्याश्च यस्य स तथाभूतः अनेन बन्धुभृत्येभ्यः संपत्प्रदत्वमस्योक्तम् । पार्थिवश्चन्द्रगुप्तः पार्थिवचन्द्रगुप्तरूपः स श्रीमाननादिविष्णुर्महीमवतु रक्षत्वित्यर्थः । अत्र श्रीविष्णोश्चन्द्रगुप्तस्य चाभेदकथनादनुभयाभेदरूपकमलङ्कारः । अयं हि धूर्जटिः साक्षाद्येन दग्धाः पुर क्षणादितिवत् ॥१९॥

मङ्गलादीनि मङ्गलमध्यानि मङ्गलान्तानि शास्त्राणि प्रथन्ते वीरपुरुषकाणि भवन्ति आयुष्मत्पुरुषकाणि चेत्यादि श्रीमहाभाष्यकारपतञ्जलि भगवत्पादानुशासनात्कविरत्र नाटक आदौ धन्या केयं स्थिता ते शिरसीत्यादिनान्दीपद्यद्वयेन भगवतः सदाशिवस्य गुणसङ्कीर्तनरूपं मङ्गलं कृतवान् । मध्ये च शरद्ध-

---

१ राजा०—राक्षसश्च-किम०-स्ति । तथापि यद्यपरितोषस्तदिदमस्तु भरत० । वाराही०. २ मतन्नुबलामा०. ३ उद्वेज्यमाना. ४ पीवरम्. ५ श्रीमान. ६ ०वां व(र)न्तिवर्मा.

र्णनप्रस्ताव आकाशं काशपुष्पच्छवीति पद्येन भगवतः शिवस्य प्रत्याग्रोन्मेषजिह्मेति पद्येन भगवतो नारायणस्य च गुणसङ्कीर्तनरूपं मङ्गलं विहितवान् । नाटकसमाप्तौ च वाराहीमात्मयोनेरिति पद्येनादिवराहरूपधारिणो भगवतो महापुरुषस्य जगदुद्धरणगुणसङ्कीर्तनरूपं मङ्गलं विरचितवान् । अनेन मङ्गलाचरणेनोपास्योपासकभेदावस्थायामप्युपास्ययोर्हरिहरयोरभेदेनैवोपासनमखिलश्रेयःप्राप्तिसाधनत्वेन श्रुतिस्मृतीतिहासपुराणप्रसिद्धमित्युक्तं भवति । तथा च श्रीमदाचार्यभगवत्पादैः श्रीविष्णुसहस्रनामभाष्ये हरिहरयोरभेदोपासनपराणि महाभारतादिवचनान्युदाहृतानि । नामानि तव गोविन्द यानि लोके महान्ति च । तान्येव मम नामानि नात्र कार्या विचारणा ॥ १ ॥ त्वदुपासा जगन्नाथ सैवास्तु मम गोपते । आवयोरन्तरं नास्ति शब्दैरर्थैर्जगत्पते ॥ २ ॥ यस्त्वां द्वेष्टि स मां द्वेष्टि यस्त्वामनु स मामनु । इत्यादीनि वचनानि द्रष्टव्यानि । गङ्गास्तुतौ च भगवत्पादैरनयोरभेदभक्तिप्रार्थना कृता ॥ भूयाद्भक्तिरविच्युता हरिहराद्वैतात्मिका शाश्वतीति ॥

इति श्रीत्र्यम्बकयज्वप्रभुवर्याश्रितढुण्ढिराजव्यासयज्वविरचिते
मुद्राराक्षसनाटकव्याख्याने सप्तमोऽङ्कः समाप्तिमगमत् ॥

बुधो ढुण्ढिर्नाम्ना जगति विदितो लक्ष्मणसुधी-
मणेः श्रीमद्व्यासान्वयजलधिचन्द्रस्य तनयः ।
स्फुटं साङ्गं व्याख्यन्नयगुणविदस्त्र्यम्बकविभो-
र्नियोगात्प्रौढार्थं बुधगणमुदे नाटकमिदम् ॥ १ ॥

अत्र नाटके चतुर्थेऽङ्के कविरद्भुततरचाणक्यनीतिविषयकस्वसंविधानक्लेशमनुभाव्य प्रमोदभरमनुभवन्तः सरसाः सहृदया जगति दुर्लभा इति मन्वानः स्वयमेव स्वस्य नाटकीयसंविधानक्लेशं राक्षसवचनव्याजेन प्रस्तौति स्म । कार्योपक्षेपमादौ तनुमपि रचयंस्तस्य विस्तारमिच्छन्नित्यादिना । एवं नाटकीयं चतुःषष्ट्यङ्गलक्षणानुसरणकविहृदयाभिमतार्थाविष्करणप्रयासोऽपि व्याख्यातुरनुमोदयितव्यः सहृदयैरिति प्रार्थयामः ।

कर्तैतन्नाटकस्याद्भुतरसविलसत्संविधानप्रवीणः
क्लेशं चाणक्यनीतौ बहुविधमतनोल्लक्षणाढ्यैर्वचोभिः ।
तत्तल्लक्ष्ये तदङ्गानुसरणविषयावासमस्मद्विधानां
राजश्रीत्र्यम्बककार्यानुमतिसुविहितं वीक्ष्य तुष्यन्तु सन्तः ॥ १ ॥

श्रीमद्विशाखकविवर्यकृतिर्मयैषा श्रीत्र्यम्बकानुमतितो विवृता यथावत् ।
श्रीस्वामिशैलवसतिर्भगवान्विशाखो देवोऽनया मुदमुपैतु सनत्कुमारः ॥ २ ॥

बाणाग्न्यृतुमहीसंख्यामितेऽब्दे जयनामके ॥
ढुण्ढिना व्याकृतं जीयान्मुद्राराक्षसनाटकम् ॥ ३ ॥

[१६३५ शालिवाहनशाकेऽब्दे जयसंवत्सरफाल्गुनमासि विरचितमिदं मुद्राराक्षसनाटकव्याख्यानं जीयादित्यर्थः ॥]

श्रीकृष्णाद्रिसुतेशपादजलजे सन्धाय चित्ताम्बुजं
वाणीसौरभशालि भेदतमसः सन्धूननैकाग्रधीः ।
मुद्राराक्षसनाटकं लिखितवान्कौटिल्यनीतेः कलां
गन्तुं यत्र विहारिणः प्लवततो नीत्यम्बुधौ सज्जनाः ॥ १ ॥

श्लोकसूची।

श्लोकसूची

THE

MUDRĀRĀKSHASA.

PROLOGUE.

"Who is this blessed one throned on your head"? "*S'as'ikalá* (the digit of the moon)." "What? Is that her *name*? "That, indeed, is her name (that signifies her). How (lit. for what reason) did you forget it, though it was familiar to you?" "I ask (about) the woman and not the Moon." "If you do not believe in the Moon (lit. if the Moon be no authority) let Vijayâ tell you." May the skill in equivocation of the Lord S'iva, displayed in thus concealing the celestial river (Gaṅgâ) from his consort, protect you! (1)

Moreover,

May the dance of the Conqueror of Tripura, rendered uneasy (uncomfortable or difficult) on account of his regard for (*i. e.* having to accommodate himself to) the place (of dancing) protect you! The Conqueror of Tripura who avoided the bending of the earth (by gentle steps) which (else) would have manifested itself by the wilful fall of the foot; who every now and then gesticulated by the mere contraction of his arms (else) stretching beyond all worlds, and who did not fix on objects his gaze emitting fierce sparks of fire, lest they be scorched (lit. for fear of scorching them). (2)

(*After the recital of the Benediction*).

MANAGER—Enough of prolixity. I am asked by the audience to represent (before them) a new drama, MUDRA'-RA'KS'ASA by name, a composition of the poet Vs'âkhadatta, grandson of the tributary prince, Vaṭe'svaradatta and the son of Pṛthu, bearing the title of Mahârâja. Surely, I too, who am now performing before an audience knowing (*i. e.* appreciating) the excellence of poetry, feel very great satisfaction. For,

The cultivation of (the seed sown by) even a foolish person when bestowed (scattered) on a good field (*i. e.* fertile soil) thrives; the being formed into ears (*i. e.* luxuriant growth) of S'âli stands not in need of (does not depend upon) any excellence on the part of the sower. (3)

I will, therefore, first go home, and having called my wife, will commence singing with the inmates of the house. Here is our house. I will at once enter. (*Entering and looking about*). Holla, what do I see here! There seems to be a festival in it; the attendants are unusually engaged in their respective duties. For, lo!

Here is a woman fetching water; here is one pounding aromatic herbs; and here is another stringing together charming (lit. diversified) garlands; while this lady here is often accompanying the pestle, as it descends, with a soft indistinct *hum* (sound). (4)

Well, I will call my wife and ask her. (*Looking towards the attiring room*).

O you, who are meritorious, who are an abode of expedients (expert in devising expedients), who bring about (or accomplish) the three objects (of human existence) which are the cause of the stability of worldly life, who are the science (or code) of morals (incarnate) of my house, and who are my instructor (or guide) in (all) duties, come here quickly. (5)

The Actress—(*Entering*). Here am I, my lord. May Your Honour favour me with your command (lit. the entrusting with &c.).

Mana.—Lady, let aside for a moment the entrusting-with-my-command. Tell me—has our family been favoured by you by having invited venerable Brâhmaṇas? Or have welcome guests come to our house?—that there are these special preparations of meals?

Actr.—My lord, the worthy Brâhmaṇas have been invited by me.

Mana.—Tell me for what reason.

Actr.—Because they say the moon is to be eclipsed.

Mana.—Lady, who says so?

ACTR.—Such, indeed, is the talk among the townsfolk.

MANA.—Lady, I have spent some labour on (*i. e.* studied carefully). the science of astronomy with its sixty-four branches; let, therererefore, your preparation of meals in honour of the worthy Brâhmaṇas be proceeded with; as for the eclipse of the moon you are deceived by some one. For, see—

That well known Ketu, of malicious resolve, (or the malignant planet) wishes, perforce, to attack (devour) Chandra (the moon) having the full *Maṇḍala* (orb);—

(*Behind the curtains*).

Who is he that, while I live, wishes to overpower *Chandra*?*

MANA.—but the union with (*i. e.* near presence of) Budha (Mercury) saves him.† (6)

ACTR.—But my lord, who is this that, being a denizen of the earth (or having shown himself on the earth), desires to save the moon from the attack of the planet?

MANA.—My lady, to tell you the truth, I too did not observe him. Well, being attentive again, I shall mark the manifestation of his voice (*i. e.* ascertain clearly whose voice it is). [*He repeats*—That well known Ketu &c.

(*Behind the scenes*).

Ah! Who is he that desires to attack Chandragupta while I am alive?

MANA.—(*Listening*). Ah, I see. It is Kauṭilya.

ACTR.—(*Gesticutates fear*).

MANA.—This is that Kauṭilya of crooked intellect, by whom the race of the Nandas was, perforce, burnt up in the fire of his wrath. Having heard the words चन्द्रस्य ग्रहणं (the seizure of the moon) he understands by them (that there is to be) an attack by the enemy on the noble (lit. moon-like) Maurya who bears the same name (Chandra). (7)

Away let us go then from here. [*Exeunt.*

END OF THE PROLOGUE.

---

* The sense understood by Châṇakya is this—He, of wicked resolve (Râkshasa), accompanied by Ketu (Malayaketu), wishes to attack with force Chandra (gupta) whose sovereignty is now fully established.

† But the policy (or plans) of a wise (diplomatic) man (Châṇakya) will save him.

ACT I.

(*Enter* CHA'ṆAKYA *in an angry mood touching with his hand his loosened hair*).

CHA'N.—Tell me who it is that desires to attack Chandragupta while I am yet living. Look here,

Who is it that wishes to snatch away, with force, from the mouth of the lion, with his mouth wide open in the act of yawning, his bright jaw, the colour of which is reddened with the blood of the elephants (just) tasted (by him), and which (consequently) appears like a digit of the moon tinted red by the twilight ? (8)

Besides,

What doomed man (person seeking his death) does not wish even now my tufted-hair tied up, (the hair) which has been the (destructive) black female-serpent to the race of the Nandas, and which is (as though) the thick dark curling mass of smoke of the fire of my anger. (9)

Who, being at a loss to distinguish between th measure of his own strength and that of others, can court instantaneous destruction in the manner of a moth, crossing the intense heat of my blazing anger, acting like fire to the forest (in the form) of the race of the Nandas ? (10)

S'âriṅgarava ! S'âriṅgarava !

PUPIL—(*Entering*). Revered sir, what are your commands ?

CHA'N.—Dear boy, I wish to sit down.

PUPIL—Preceptor, why, there is the hall in the court near the door already provided with a cane-seat. The Preceptor, therefore, will be pleased to take his seat there.

CHA'N.—My boy, it is simply absorption in (or, ardent devotion to) work (management of state affairs) that distracts me, and not the roughness of temper towards pupils naturally to be found in preceptors. (*Sits down*) (*To himself*). How now, has this matter got abroad among the citizens that Râkshasa, whose anger is excited by the destruction of the house of Nanda, having allied himself with Malayaketu, the son of Parvataka, wroth at his father's assassination, and encouraged (to undertake the expedition) by the offer of the entire Kingdom of the Nandas, and assisted (lit. surrounded) by a large force of the Mlechchha princes under him (Mal.) is striving (preparing) to attack Vṛshala? (*Thinking*). Or why, I am able to counteract this matter though it is spreading abroad—I, who, having first, in the presence of all people, vowed the destruction of the Nanda race, crossed the insurmountable river of a solemn vow. For,

The fire of my anger, having by means of the incessant (columns of) smoke of grief darkened the moons in the form of faces, of the directions in the form of the young wives of the enemies, having scattered at will (or profusely) over the trees in the form of ministers, the ashes of stupefaction (or embarrassment) wafted by the wind of my policy, and having burnt down the shoots of the bamboos in the form of the Nandas, excepting the flocks of frightened birds in the form of the citizens, has abated (ceased to burn) like a conflagration in a forest, not owing to weariness, but through the absence of material to be consumed. (11)

Moreover,

Those persons, who, bewailing, with down-cast faces with the words 'fie upon him' stifled within on account of the fear of the king, formerly gazed upon me, helpless, as I was dragged away from the seat of honour, have now seen Nanda, along with his family, pulled down by me just in the same way, from the throne, like a lord of elephants hurled down from the summit of a mountain by a lion. (12)

I then, though I have acquitted myself of the burden of (completely fulfilled) the vow, hold the weapon (retain office as chief minister) out of regard for Vṛshala—I, by whom,

The nine Nandas have been eradicated (*i. e.* extirpated) like so many darts (wrankling) in the heart from (the face) of the Earth; sovereignty has been made firm-footed (firmly established) in the case of Maurya like a lotus-plant in a lake and the twofold, well-deserved fruit of the two things, anger and love, has been equally meted out with a careful mind to the foe and the friend. (13)

Or rather, so long as Râkshasa has not been won over, how can the race of Nanda be said to be extirpated or what stability has been given to the sovereignty of Chandragupta? (*Thinking*). Oh! how unsurpassable is the excellence of devotion of Râkshasa to the house of Nanda. So long as one member (how-so-ever remote) of the race of Nanda is living he cannot, indeed, be made to accept the ministership of Vṛs'ala. If rendered inactive in his work in the interest of (lit. devotion to) that (family), it is possible for us to manage him (*i. e.* win him over). In this very belief, poor Sarvârthasiddhi, of the family of Nanda, was caused to be assassinated, though he had retired to the penance-grove. He is, nevertheless, making still greater efforts for our destruction by having accepted (as his master) Malayaketu. (*Fixing his look on the sky, as if on some tangible object*). Noble, very noble, Oh minister Râkshasa; praiseworthy, Oh, learned Brâhmaṇa; well done, Oh you, Bṛhaspati-like minister, well done! For,

These (*i. e.* ordinary) people serve their lord (so long as he is) not deprived of his sovereignty, for the sake of gain; those who follow him in adversity do so in the hope of his restoration; but rarely are to be found those blessed persons of your type, who undertake the responsibility of duty out of disinterested devotion, remembering past favours, even after the complete ruin of their master. (14)

Hence our attempt to secure you—how he (you) might be disposed to favour (us) by accepting the ministership of Vṛs'ala. For,

What is the use of a servant who is not wise and is timid though possessed of loyalty (or devotion)? Or what good can come out of one, who, though distinguished by his intelligence and bravery, is devoid of loyalty? Those servants contribute to (*i. e.* bring about) the prosperity of their royal master who combine (lit. display) in themselves the qualities of intelligence, bravery and devotion; others are like wives (to be fed by their lords) in prosperity as well as in adversity. (15)

Therefore, I too do not sleep over this matter, but am making an effort, as much as I can, to secure him. How is that? In the first place this (has been done). A scandalous report is caused to be circulated in the world that poor Parvataka, our extremely obliging friend, has been killed by Râkshasa by means of a poison-maid, thinking that harm would be done to Châṇakya by the destruction of either of the two, *viz.*, Vṛshala or Parvataka. In order to make this very matter clear and that people might be convinced (of this), Malayaketu, son of Parvataka has been removed by Bhâgurâyaṇa, having in private inspired fear in him that his father was killed by Châṇakya. Although he were to rise (against us) aided by the talent of Rákshasa, he could, indeed, be subdued by the force of my intellect. I do not, however, wish, by subduing him, to put an end to (*i. e.* suppress) the scandal about Râkshasa in connection with the assassination of Parvataka, which is spreading abroad. I have also employed emissaries in various disguises and conversant with various places, dresses, languages, manners and modes of dealing with (or moving among), strangers with the desire of knowing the people that are attached to or disaffected towards our side or that of the enemy. The doings and actions of the ministers and friends of the Nandas are also being skilfully watched (lit. looked into). The principal persons, Bhadrabhaṭa and others, who rose (against the Nandas) simultaneously with Chandragupta, have been made to further our interests (by fleeing to the camp of the enemy as malcontents) by creating various occasions (for that purpose). Trusted persons, ever careful to take measures against men employed by the enemy to administer poison, and of tried loyalty have been appointed to be near (*i. e.* in attendance upon) the king. There is also a Brâhmaṇa, a friend of ours and a fellow-student, Indus'armâ by name. He has acquired very great proficiency in the science of astronomy in all its sixty-four divisions. That person was, immediately after my vow to destroy the family of Nanda, brought by me to Kusumapura in the disguise of a Jaina mendicant and made to form friendship with all the ministers of Nanda. Râkshasa, in particular, places very great confidence in him. Presently an important service will be rendered by him. Thus, then, nothing is wanting on our side. It is only Vṛshala, the king (lit. the chief personage in the body politic) who entrusts the responsibility of administering the kingdom to me, and always remains apathetic. Or rather, that sovereignty alone gives happiness, which is removed from (*i. e.* devoid of) the peculiar troubles worthy of application to work. For,

Lords of elephants and lords of men, who have to toil for their livelihood, generally give way under affliction, although they are naturally possessed of strength. (16)

(*Then enter a* SPY *with a* YAMAPAṬA).

SPY—Bow to the feet of Yama; what is the use of other deities? For, he takes away the struggling life of those who are devoted to other (deities). (17)

Moreover,

A man can obtain his livelihood from even the dreadful Yama when propitiated by devotion. We live by means of that Yama who kills all people. (18)

I shall therefore enter this house, and exhibiting the *Yamapaṭa*, sing my lays.

(*Walks about*).

PUPIL—(*Seeing him*). Good man, you should not enter.

SPY—Oh Brâhmaṇa, whose house is this?

PUPIL.—Of our preceptor, the venerable Châṇakya, of auspicious name.

SPY—(*Smiling*). O Bráhmana, then it belongs to a relative, my own spiritual brother. Allow me, therefore, to enter, so that I will show the *Yamapaṭa* to your preceptor, and tell him something about Duty (*Dharma*).

PUPIL—(*Angrily*). Fie upon you, fool! Do you pretend to be better conversant with *Dharma* than our preceptor?

SPY—No offence, O Brâhmaṇa. It is not, indeed, that every one knows every thing. Your preceptor knows certain things while people like myself know others.

PUPIL—Blockhead, do you wish to rob our preceptor of (*i. e.* assume) his omniscience.

SPY—O Brâhmaṇa, if your preceptor knows every thing then let him know (*i. e.* ask him if he knows) by whom *Chandra* (the moon,-Chandragupta) is not liked.

PUPIL—You wiseacre! Of what consequence is it, whether it is known or not?

SPY—Your preceptor alone will know the use of its being known. While you simply know this much, that the moon is not liked by lotuses. Just see,

The character of lotuses, howsoever lovely, is inconsistent with their form (or, outward beauty), since they are opposed to the moon though full-orbed. (19)

CHA'N.—(*Listening, to himself*). Ah, he has hinted that he knows the people who are estranged from (or, disaffected towards) Chandragupta.

PUPIL—Fool, what do you talk all this nonsense for?

SPY—O Brâhmaṇa, it will be good sense.

PUPIL—How?

SPY—If I get a person who knows how to hear.

CHA'N.—Good sir, enter freely. You will get a person who will hear and understand.

SPY—Here I enter. (*Entering and approaching*). Victory to Your Honour!

CHA'N.—(*Observing him, to himself*). How now? This is Nipuṇaka appointed by me to know the minds of the people. (*Aloud*). Good sir, you are welcome. Sit down.

SPY—As Your Honour commands. (*Sits down on the ground*).

CHA'N.—Good man, now give an account of your mission. Do the subjects love Vṛshala?

SPY—They do. The various causes of dissatisfaction being removed by Your Honour, the subjects are firmly attached to His Majesty, Chandragupta, of blessed name. But there are three persons in the city who have already conceived affection and great regard for Râkshasa, and who do not bear to see the prosperity of His Majesty, Chandragupta.

CHA'N.—(*Angrily*). Why, rather say, they do not bear (*i. e.* are weary of) their lives. Well, do you know their names?

SPY—How can I inform Your Honour, if I do not know their names?

CHA'N.—Then I wish to hear them.

SPY—May Your Honour hear. Then there is first a Jaina mendicant, who has fixed his affection on the party of Your Honour's enemies—

CHA'N.—(*To himself*). A mendicant who has fixed his affection on the party of our enemies!

SPY—Jîvasiddhi by name, he, by whom the poison-maid employed by Râkshasa was directed against king Parvateshvara.

CHA'N.—(*To himself*). Jîvasiddhi! he is but our spy. (*Aloud*). Good fellow, who is the second man?

SPY—Your Honour, the second man is a Kâyastha, also a friend of Râkshasa, S'akaṭadâsa by name.

CHA'N.—(*With a smile, to himself*). A Kâyastha is a matter of small concern (*i. e.* a negligible quantity). Yet it is not proper to neglect even an insignificant enemy. (*Aloud*). Well, now I wish to hear the third name.

SPY—The third man, the second heart as it were of the minister Râkshasa, is the chief of jewellers, Chandanadâsa by name, and an inhabitant of Pushpapura, in whose house Râkshasa left his family and escaped from the town.

CHA'N.—(*To himself*). Surely, he must be his best friend; for Râkshasa will not leave his family with persons unworthy of himself. (*Aloud*). Good man, how do you know that Râkshasa left his family in the house of Chandanadâsa?

SPY—Sir, this seal-ring will acquaint your honour with every thing. (*With these words, he hands over the ring*).

CHA'N.—(*Looking at the ring, takes it and reads the name of* RA'KSHASA; *and then joyfully to himself*). I should rather say that Râkshasa himself has sought the love of my finger (*i. e.* has come into my possession). (*Aloud*). Good man, I wish to know in detail how you came by the ring.

SPY—May Your Honour hear. Being appointed by Your Honour to spy the actions of the citizens, I wandered about showing this Yamapaṭa, which excites no suspicion when

I enter the house of a stranger. Thus, I entered the house of the jewel-merchant Chandanadâsa. There I unfolded my *Yamapaṭa* and began to sing the songs.

CHA'N.—What next?

SPY—Then from one of the windows of the house a boy about five years old, with a lovely and pleasing form of body and with his eyes dilated through curiosity natural to childhood, began to come out. Then there arose from inside the very window a great confused noise—"Ah, he has gone out! Ah, he has gone out!"—proceeding from women, indicative of the feeling of fright. Then that boy while coming out was caught hold of after chiding with a soft creeper-like hand, by a lady who showed her face slightly at the region of the door. Then this signet-ring, made to suit the measure of the finger of a man slipped off from her hand, the fingers of which moved about in the hurry of restraining the boy and fell down at the threshold; (and thence) rebounding, it reached the vicinity of my feet, quite unnoticed by her, and became steady (remained motionless) like a noble-born girl remaining motionless in the act of salutation. I, too, seeing that it bore the inscription of the name of the minister Râkshasa brought it to Your Honour's feet. This is how the ring came into my possession.

CHA'N.—Good man, I have heard it. You may withdraw. Ere long you will get a reward worthy of your trouble.

SPY—As Your Honour commands. [*Exit.*

CHA'N.—S'ârṅgarava! O S'ârṅgarava!

PUPIL—(*Entering*). What are your commands?

CHA'N.—Boy, get me an inkstand and paper.

PUPIL—(*Does accordingly*).

CHA'N.—(*Taking the paper, to himself*). What shall I write here? For Râkshasa is to be won over by this document.

FEMALE DOORKEEPER—(*Entering*). Victory to Your Excellency!

CHA'N.—(*With joy, to himself*). I accept the word of victory. (*Aloud*). S'oṇottarâ, what brings you here?

FEM. D.—Your Honour, His Majesty, the esteemed Chandragupta, having placed on his forehead his folded hands resembling a lotus bud, begs to inform your honour—"I wish with Your Honour's permission to perform the obsequies of His Highness Parvates'vara, and to present to the Brâhmaṇas the ornaments formerly worn by him."

CHA'N.—(*With joy, to himself*). Well done, O Vṛshala! You have sent this message as if after consulting my very heart. (*Aloud*). Say to him in my name—"Well done, my boy! You are, indeed, well acquainted with the ways of the world. Do as you desire; but the excellent (*i. e.* precious) ornaments formerly worn by Parvateśvara ought to be given to *worthy* Brâhmaṇas. I myself, therefore, will send you Brâhmaṇas of tried merits."

FEM. D.—As Your Honour commands. [*Exit.*

CHA'N.—S'ârṅgarava, say at my command to the three brothers, Vis'vávasu and others—'You should take as a gift the ornaments from Vṛshala and see me.'

PUPIL—Your command will be obeyed. [*Exit.*

CHA'N.—This (*i. e.* the subject of ornaments) shall form the latter part of the letter. What shall be the first? (*Musing*). Ah! I have it. I have learnt from my spies that out of the followers of the Mlechchha prince (*i. e.* Malayaketu) five principal princes follow Râkshasa, on terms of the greatest friendship. They are—

Chitravarman, king of the Kulûtas, the brave Siṁhanâda, lord of Malaya, Pushkarâksha of Kâshmîra, Sindhusheṇa, king of Sindh, who has eclipsed the glory of his enemies, and the Persian Emperor Megha, the fifth of the party, with a large force of cavalry,—I shall indelibly write down their names. Let Chitragupta blot them out (if he can or, from his account book). ·(20)

(*Thinking*). But no, I shall rather not write them. Let the first part be vague. (*Gesticulating writing*). S'ârṅgarava!

PUPIL—(*Entering*). Your commands, Preceptor.

CHA'N.—Child, the handwriting of a S'rotriya Brâhmaṇa (like myself), although written with care, must certainly be illegible. Tell, therefore, my command to Siddha'rthaka—Get letter written in these words by S'akaṭadása, without the one to some one else in person, and then come to me. You should not tell him that Châṇakya wants him to write."

PUPIL—As you command. [*Exit.*

CHA'N.—(*To himself*). Thank God, Malayaketu is subdued.

(*Enter* SIDDHA'RTHAKA, *letter in hand*).

SID.—Victory to Your Honour. Sir, here is the letter written by S'akaṭadâsa.

CHA'N.—(*Taking it and looking at the writing*). Oh, how beautiful is the handwriting! (*Going over it silently*). Good man, seal it with this ring.

SID.—(*Doing so*). Here is the letter with the seal. What else is to be done?

CHA'N.—My good friend, I wish to employ you in a business which can be executed by a trustworthy person only.

SID.—(*With joy*). It is a favour, sir. Your Honour may tell me what this your slave is to do for you.

CHA'N.—In the first place, you go to the place of execution and make the executioners understand the sign, made with the angry contraction of the right eye; and when they, having understood the sign, run here and there under the pretext of fright, S'akaṭadâsa should be carried away (by you) from the place of execution and taken to Râkshasa. You may accept a reward from him (which he will offer you being pleased at your having saved the life of his friend. You should then serve Râkshasa himself for some time and when the enemies are near, you should execute the following business. (*Whispers into his ear*—thus &c.).

SID.—As Your Honour commands.

CHA'N.—S'âr̃ngarava! S'âr̃ngarava!

PUPIL—(*Entering*). Your command, Preceptor!

CHA'N.—Say at my bidding to Kâlapâśika* and Daṇḍapâśika that Vṛshala gives the following order—"You should ignominiously drive out of the city the Jaina mendicant Jivasiddhi, who, being instigated by Râkshasa, killed Parvates'vara by means of the poison-maid, after proclaiming this very crime to the public."

---

* Two principal officers of justice.

PUPIL—So I will do. (*Offers to go*).

CHA'N.—Wait my boy, wait a little.—"And that other man, S'akaṭadâsa, a Kâyastha, who, at Râkshasa's instigation ever tries to plot against our life should also be impaled after the publication of this his guilt, and his household put into prison."

PUPIL—I will execute your command. [*Exit.*

CHA'N.—(*Gesticulates anxiety*; *to himself*). Is it likely that this wicked Râkshasa can be taken?

SID.—Taken sir,—

CHA'N.—(*Joyfully to himself*). Bless me! Râkshasa is taken. (*Aloud*). Friend, what is this that is taken?

SID.—I have taken Your Honour's instructions. I will, therefore, go to accomplish my mission.

CHA'N.—(*Handing over the letter and the seal-ring*). You may go. May you obtain success in your business.

SID.—May it be so! (*Exit.*

PUPIL—(*Entering*). Preceptor, Kâlapâśika and Daṇḍapâśika beg to request Your Honour that they will immediately execute the command of His Majesty Chandragupta.

CHA'N.—Good child, I wish now to see Chandanadâsa, the head-jeweller.

PUPIL—Well. (*Exit, and re-enter with* CHANDANADA'SA). This way, this way, sir.

CHAND.—(*To himself*). In the case of the ruthless Châṇakya, a person, though innocent and but accidentally called, entertains fear; how much more should I, who have committed a crime? (21) I have, therefore, warned Dhanasena and others living in my house thus--Perhaps the vile Châṇakya might search the house. Be careful, then, about the safety of (or to remove) the family of my master, Râkshasa. As to myself let any fate overtake me.

PUPIL,—This way, this way merchant.

CHAND.—Here I am coming. [BOTH *turn round.*

PUPIL—(*Approaching*). Sir, here is the merchant, Chandanadâsa.

CHAND.—Victory to Your Honour!

CHA'N.—(*Looks at him*). Merchant, you are welcome. Take this seat, please.

CHAND.—(*Bowing*). Does not Your Honour know that undeserved courtesy shown to a man grieves the heart even more than an (open) insult? I will, therefore, sit down here on the ground, which is proper for me.

CHA'N.—Oh, do not say so. So much respect is but due to you from persons like me. Pray, therefore, do take the seat.

CHAND.—(*To himself*). Oh, the wretch has set on foot (commenced) something. (*Aloud*). As Your Honour commands. (*Sits down*).

CHA'N.—Oh merchant Chandanadasa, are the emoluments of your honest mercantile transactions on the increase?

CHAND.—(*To himself*). This extreme courtesy raises suspicion. (*Aloud*). Yes, my business goes on uninterrupted by Your Honour's favour.

CHA'N.—Do not the faults of Chandragupta now make the subjects remember the virtues of former kings?

CHAND.—(*Stopping his ears*). God forbid! (On the contrary) the subjects are delighted all the more with the worthy Chandragupta as with the full moon rising in an autumnal evening.

CHA'N.—Oh merchant, if so, the kings expect some benefit (agreeable service) in return from their contented subjects.

CHAND.—Your Honour will be pleased to order what and how much is expected from this person.

CHA'N.—O merchant, this is the reign of Chandragupta and not of Nanda. For, the prospect of money alone pleased Nanda who was greedy of wealth. The good-will (well-being, lit. his being not forced to take harsh measures against) of you (his subjects) alone pleases Chandragupta.

CHAND.—(*Joyfully*). Your Honour, I am highly obliged to you.

CHA'N.—Oh merchant, you ought to have asked me how that good-will is manifested.

CHAND.—Your Honour should explain it.

CHA'N.—In a word, by their (the subjects) acting in a manner not hostile to the king.

CHAND.—Sir, what wretch is he, who is considered by Your Honour as hostile to the King?

CHA'N.—In the first place, you yourself.

CHAND.—(*Stopping his ears*). Heaven forbid such a thing! What kind of hostility can grass bear to fire?

CHA'N.—The hostility is of this nature, that you still keep in your house the family of the minister Râkshasa who acts inimically towards the King.

CHAND.—Sir, this is an untruth told to Your Honour by some one ignorant of facts.

CHA'N.—O merchant, do not be alarmed. It is usual with the servants of ex-kings when overtaken by fear, to leave their families in the houses of the citizens even against their will, and to go to other countries. But then, it is their concealment that constitutes a crime.

CHAND.—It is quite so (just as Your Honour says). The family of the minister Râkshasa was in my house at that time.

CHA'N.—First you said it was an untruth; now you say the family was &c. These are two contradictory assertions.

CHAND.—So far only have I been guitly of seeming dishonesty in words (and not in reality).

CHA'N.—In the reign of Chandragupta, there is no acceptance (toleration) of dishonesty. Deliver up the family of Râkshasa and clear yourself of dishonesty.

CHAND.—Sir, do not I say that there was *formerly* (but not now) the family of Râkshasa in my house.

CHA'N.—Where is it gone to now?

CHAND.—I don't know.

CHA'N.—(*Smiling*). How possibly can you not know it? O merchant, danger stands (immediately) over your head, while its remedy is far away.* Besides, as Vishṇugupta

---

* After this the ed.s read—

CHAND.—(*To himself*).

Overhead is the deep thunder of clouds, the beloved is far away. What is this that has come to pass! On the Himâlayas grow the herbs of supernatural efficacy, whereas the serpent is seated on the head.

eradicated Nanda-(*Gesticulating the feeling of modesty*). So, do not even suppose that the minister Râkshasa will extirpate Chandragupta. Just see—

Who can attempt to separate from king Chandragupta the sovereignty, like moonlight from the moon, (now) consolidated and delighting the whole world, which, unsteady as it often was, could not be made firm (even) at the time when Nanda lived, by good ministers such as Vakranâsa and others who were brave and skilled in politics. (22)

Moreover,

Who desires to snatch away &c. (S'loka 8.)

CHAND.—His bragging has been made consistent with (justified by) the result.

(*A confused noise behind the scenes*).

CHA'N.—S'ârṅgarava, ascertain what noise it is.

PUPIL—As you command. (*Exit and re-enter*). Sir, it is the Jaina mendicant, Jîvasiddhi, a traitor to the King, who is by the command of His Majesty Chandragupta being turned out of the city with disgrace.

CHA'N.—I am sorry for you, oh Kshapaṇaka. Or why, taste (reap) the fruit of being treacherous to the King. O merchant Chandanadâsa, the King thus inflicts a severe punishment upon traitors. Act up, therefore, to the salutary advice of a friend. Surrender the family of Râkshasa and enjoy the manifold royal favours for a long time.

CHAND.—The family of the minister, Râkshasa, is not in my house.

(*Renewed noise behind the curtains*).

CHA'N.—S'ârṅgarava, see what the matter is.

PUPIL—As you command. (*Exit and enter again*). Here is this another felon, the *Kâyastha* S'akaṭadâsa, being taken away for being impaled.

CHA'N.—Let him suffer the consequences of his own acts. Merchant, this king who is thus merciless in his punishment of traitors will not excuse your concealment of the family of Râkshasa. Save, therefore, your wife and life by delivering up the wife of another.

CHAND.—Sir, why do you seek to intimidate me? I would not have delivered up the family of the minister Râkshasa, even if it were in my house. What then, when it is not in my house?

CHA'N.—Chandanadâsa, is that your resolution?

CHAND.—Yes, that is my firm resolve.

CHA'N.—(*To himself*). Bravo, Chandanadâsa, you ought to be praised.

When the acquisition of money is easy by delivering up what belongs to another, who, but S'ibi, can, in this world, now do such a difficult thing? (23)

(*Aloud*). Chandanadâsa, is this your resolve?

CHAND.—Ay, it is.

CHA'N.—(*Wrathfully*). Oh villain, thou wicked merchant experience then the anger of the King.

CHAND.—I am prepared. Your Honour may do what befits your (high) office.

CHA'N.—S'ârṅgarava, say at my bidding to Kâlapâśika and Daṇḍapâśika—Let this rascally merchant be pinioned immediately. Or, wait. Let Vijayapâla, the jail superintendent (or the keeper of the fort) be told to detain him in prison with his wife and sons, after having confiscated all the valuables in his house, till I shall have informed Vṛshala of the matter. Vṛshala himself will pass the sentence of death upon him.

PUPIL—As the Preceptor commands. Merchant, this way.

CHAND.—Here do I follow you, sir. (*To himself*). Fortunately I suffer ruin for the sake of a friend and not for any fault of mine common to man. [*Exit with* PUPIL.

CHA'N.—(*With delight*). I am glad, Râkshasa is now in my hand. For,

Just as this (merchant) sacrifices his life as if it were unwelcome to him when he (Râkshasa) is in calamity, so indeed will life become a burden (lit. not dear) to him (Râkshasa) when this man is in peril. (24)

(*Noise behind the scenes*).

CHA'N.—S'ârṅgarava ! S'ârṅgaraava !

PUPIL—(*Entering*). Your command, Preceptor ?

CHA'N.—What noise is this ?

PUPIL—(*Goes out, ascertains the cause and re-enter*). Sir, it is Siddhârthaka running away from the place of execution having carried with him S'akaṭadâsa who was going to be killed.

CHA'N.—(*Aside*). Well done, Siddhârthaka, you have set yourself about your work. (*Aloud*). What, has he gone away by force ? (*Angrily*). Child, tell Bhâgurâyaṇa that he should immediately overtake him.

PUPIL—(*Having gone out and re-entering, in alarm*). Alas, sir, what a misfortune ! Bhâgurâyaṇa has also run away.

CHÂN.—(*Aside*). Let him go to accomplish his mission. (*Aloud, with feigned anger*). Child, say to Bhadrabhaṭa, Purushadatta, Dingarâta, Balagupta, Râjasena, Rohitâksha, and Vijayavarman that I command them to quickly pursue the villain Bhâgurâyaṇa and arrest him.

PUPIL—I will execute your command, sir. (*Exit and re-enter with dejection*). Alas, what a calamity ! Oh ! the whole machinery is out of gear (*i. e.* the whole arrangement is unhinged or gone out of order). Those persons too, Bhadrabhaṭa and others, were the first to go away this morning.

CHA'N.—(*To himself*). May their way be prosperous in all respects. (*Aloud*). Child, do not be dejected ; for,

Those who have already gone, having formulated some scheme in their mind, are, indeed, gone ; let those also who still remain, by all means try to go away, just as they like. Let only my intellect, which by itself is more than a hundred armies in the accomplishment of desired objects, and the greatness of whose prowess was seen in (*i. e.* proved by) the destruction of the Nandas, not forsake me. (25)

(*Rising*). Here shall I bring back the wicked Bhâgurâyaṇa and others. (*Fixing his glance on something in the air*).

(*To himself*). Oh Râkshasa, of wicked resolve, where can you go now? Here shall I, ere long,

Capture you by (the force of) my intellect and make you apply yourself to work in the interest of Vṛshala, you who are acting alone at will, whose power to give (munificence) is brilliant (great) and who are laying out deep plots in your overbearing pride, just as one should catch by contrivance and break to labour a wild elephant who wanders all alone in full freedom, whose capacity to shed rut is great and who roams (in the woods) through the exuberant strength of youthful vigour. (26)

[*Exeunt Omnes.*

END OF ACT I.

ACT II.

(*Enter a* SNAKE-CATCHER).

SNAKE-CATCHER—Those who know the application of antidotes, (are conversant with the plans or policy to be followed in the administration of a kingdom), who draw the enchanted circle in the right way, (who prescribe the proper course of conduct for or properly mark out, *i. e.* hold in check, the circle of kings), and who are devoted to the observance of spells, (are versed in preserving state secrets), can deal with (manage) a serpent (a king to be cautiously approached like a serpent). (1)

(*Looking at the sky*). What do you say, sir? Do you ask me who I am? I am a serpent-catcher, Jîrṇavisha by name. What say you? That you, too, wish to play with a serpent? Well, what is Your Honour's means of subsistence? What do you say? That you are a servant of the King? Then Your Honour does, indeed, play with a serpent. You want to know how? A snake-catcher who is not well acquainted with charms and medicinal herbs, one who mounts an intoxicated elephant without the knowledge of restraining it, and a servant of the King (an officer of state) invested with authority (and therefore) overbearing (lit. proud of his success)–these three persons assuredly meet with ruin. Oh, he has vanished from my sight the moment he was seen. (*Agai.. looking at the sky*). What does Your Honour say? You ask me as to what these baskets and boxes contain? They contain, sir, snakes, the means of obtaining my livelihood. What say you? That you wish to see them? Please Your Honour, this is not the proper place to exhibit them. If you have a curiosity, come with me. I will show them to you in this house. What does Your Honour say? That the house belongs to the minister Râkshasa, where people of your sort can have no access? Well then, Your Honour may take your departure. I, however, shall have access here, through the favour of my calling. How now? He too has gone away!

(*To himself, speaking in Sanskṛt*).

Oh wonder! Seeing Chandragupta guided by the intellect of Châṇakya I consider the attempt of Râkshasa as futile; considering again (that) Malayaketu (is) aided by the counsel of Râkshasa, I look upon Chandragupta as almost deposed from his Supreme Power. For,

I consider the Royalty of king Maurya as stable, with her form held fast (lit. tied down) by the cord, in the form of the talent of Kauṭilya; but that very Royalty I look upon as being snatched away by Râkshasa with his hands, in the form of plans (*or*, expedients). (2)

So when there is this contest (rivalry) between these two able ministers, eminent for their talents, the sovereign power of the Nanda family is, as it were, in suspense.

The bewildered goddess of wealth is surely much tired by moving backwards and forwards through indecision between these two eminent ministers strongly opposed to each other in this case, like a female-elephant in a large forest between two wild elephants. (3)

I will therefore see minister Râkshasa. (*Turns about and waits*).

(*Then enter* RA'KSHASA *seated in an anxious mood, followed by a* MAN i. e. an ATTENDANT.)

RA'K.—(*Tearfully*). Alas, Oh, alas!

Now that the large family of the Nandas who, like the Vṛshṇis, had vanquished their enemies by the employment of the qualities of prudence and valour, is destroyed by the merciless fate, I, who am watchful night and day, with a mind tossed by intense anxiety, am (as it were) practising painting (using my diplomatic skill) in the same way (as when the Nandas lived but) without a back-ground (a convass *or* wall to paint upon). (4)

Or rather,

It is not because I have forgotten my loyalty (to my old master), not because my heart is engrossed in the enjoyment of the objects of senses, not because I am afraid of the loss of my life, nor because I am desirous of self-glorification, that I have closely and carefully devoted my attention to politics, but because His Majesty (*i. e.* Nanda) though gone to heaven may be propitiated by the destruction of his enemies. (5)

(*Looking towards the sky, with tears in his eyes*). Oh venerable lotus-throned goddess, you are quite incapable of appreciating merits. For,

Tell me why you, having discarded His Majesty Nanda, though a source of delight have become attached to his enemy, the son of Maurya? Why, O wanton one, did you not vanish for ever at that very time, like the line of ichor-water disappearing at the death of a scent-elephant? (6)

Moreover, oh you base-born one!

Are all sovereigns of illustrious descent on earth dead (lit. burnt up) that you, oh wicked one, should have chosen Maurya, of low extraction, for your lord? Or rather, (why should I blame you?) the mind of women, which by nature is as fickle as the edge of a *S'irîśa* flower is averse (has no inclination) to the appreciation (discrimination) of the merits of men. (7)

And now, oh ill-bred one, I will, for that reason, defeat you in your object by destroying your very resting-place. (*Thinking*). I for myself did a right thing in keeping my family in the house of my best friend, Chandanadâsa, when I left the town. For, the energetic work of the adherents of

His Majesty residing in the city who are united in interest with us, will not be slackened, at the thought 'Râkshasa is not indifferent in the matter of the attack on the city of Kusumapura.' S'akaṭadâsa has been kept there with a large treasure in his possession for keeping well-pleased the persons engaged by us to administer poison and to do injury to the body of Chandragupta, and for communicating to us the secret doings of the enemy. And friends like Jîvasiddhi and others have been employed to secure information about the enemy every moment, and to break up their confederacy. Why waste more words on this matter?

I shall pierce with the dart of intellect the vital parts of that very person, whom, His Majesty, fond of sons, having brought up, like a cub of a tiger, suddenly perished along with his family, if invisible Fate will not serve (him) as an armour. (8)

(*Then enter the* CHAMBERLAIN).

CHAM.—Old age, having eradicated passion from within me, just as the policy of Châṇakya destroyed Nanda, has gradually firmly established the feeling of piety (Dharma) in me like Maurya in the city; and now avarice, having got an opportunity through service (accepted by me), is trying to put it down as it (Dharma) is growing, like Râkshasa who having found an opportunity (for his plans) by (accepting) service, is endeavouring to vanquish Chandragupta who is gaining in strength, but does not succeed. (9)

(*Turning round and walkaing forth*). This is the dwelling of the minister Râkshasa. I will enter. (*Entering and looking about*). Prosperity to you!

RA'K.—Venerable man, my respects to you. Priyaṁvadaka, bring a seat.

MAN—Here is a seat. Your Honour may sit down.

CHAM.—(*Sitting down*). Prince Malayaketu requests Your Excellency—My heart is grieved that Your Honour has left off personal decorations for a long time. Although the merits of your master (Nanda) cannot at once be forgotten, yet you will be pleased to honour my request (by accepting the ornaments). (*So saying and showing him the ornaments*).

Your Excellency will please put on these ornaments which have been sent by the Prince after having taken them off from his person.

RA'K.—Worthy Jâjali, respectfully say to the Prince in my name—The merits of my lord have already been forgotten by me through my attachment to Your Highness' merits. However—

I will not wear the slightest decoration on these my limbs which are powerless and pitiable by being subjected to disgrace at the hands of the enemy, so long as, oh best of men, this golden throne of Your Highness has not been placed in the Sugânga palace after Your Highness has completely destroyed the circle of the enemies. (10)

CHAM.—While the minister (*i. e.* you) is the leader (*i. e.* is at the head of affairs) it is easy for the Prince to accomplish this. May, therefore, this first request of the Prince be granted.

RA'K.—Worthy sir, you too are one like the Prince, whose words cannot be transgressed. I, therefore, will act up to the command of the Prince.

CHAM.—(*Gesticulates putting on the ornaments*). Prosperity to Your Excellency. I take my departure.

RA'K.—Venerable man, my respects to you.

[*Exit.* CHAMBERLAIN.

RA'K.—Priyamvadaka, ascertain who waits at the door desirous of an audience with (lit. seeing) me.

MAN—As Your Honour commands. (*Turning round and observing the* SNAKE-CATCHER). Sir, who are you?

SNAKE-CATCHER.—Sir, I am a snake-catcher, Jîrṇavisha by name. I wish to give a performance with my snakes before the Minister.

MAN—Wait, till I inform the Minister. (*Going back to* RA'KSHASA). Minister, it is a snake-catcher (lit. a man who earns his livelihood by snakes) who wishes to exhibit snakes.

RA'K.—*Gesticulating a twitching of the left eye, to himself*). How, at the very beginning, there is the sight of serpents! (*Aloud*). Priyamvadaka, I have no curiosity to see snakes. Therefore satisfy him and let him go.

PRIY.—As Your Honour orders. (*Approaching*). Sir, the Minister shows you his favour by giving you this reward (lit. that which would have resulted from his having actually seen your exhibition); he has no mind, however, to see the serpents.

SNAKE-CATCHER—Good Sir, say to the Minister, that I am not only a professional snake-charmer, but also a versifier in Prâkṛt. If, therefore, the Minister does not wish to favour me with an audience, request him to read this letter.

PRIY.—(*Taking the letter and approaching* RA'KSHASA). Sir, he requests Your Honour, saying "I am not only a snake-catcher by profession but also a versifier in Prâkṛt. If the Minister, therefore, does not grant me the favour of an audience he will at least read this letter."

RA'K.—(*Takes the letter and reads it*). That which the bee gives out after having, by its skill, completely drunk up *Kusumarasa* (honey of flowers; important news from *Kusumapura*) serves the purpose of others. (11)

(*Musing, to himself*). Ah, the verse purports to say that he is my spy and is acquainted with the state of affairs in Kusumapura. I forgot it on account of my mind being engrossed in my work, and of the large number of my spies. Now remembrance comes back to me. He is evidently Virâdhagupta, disguised as a snake-charmer. (*Aloud*). Priyaṁvadaka, usher him in; he is a fine poet; I will hear from him good sayings.

PRIY.—As you command. (*Approaching the* SNAKE-CATCHER). Your Honour may come in.

SNAKE-CATCHER—(*Gesticulates that he goes in. Looking about, to himself, adopting Sanskṛt*). This is minister Râkshasa. He,

Afraid of whose efforts the goddess of wealth, having her creeper-like left arm twined loosely round the neck of Maurya, with her face turned away and her right arm constantly falling down on her lap, though perforce placed on the shoulder, does not even now bring her right breast in contact with the bosom of Maurya, so as to have its nipple hardpressed in the act of close embrace. (12)

(*Aloud*). Victory to the Minister!

RA'K.—(*Looking at him*). Ah, Virâdha—(*Here he breaks off*). I say, what a beard he has got!

Priyaṁvadaka, I wish to have some pastime with the serpents. Let the servants, therefore, retire. You too attend to your duty.

PRIY.—As you command. [*Exit with* ATTENDANTS].

RA'K.—Friend Virâdhagupta, take this seat.

VIRA'DH.—(*Gesticulates that he sits down*).

RA'K.—(*Closely marking him*). Alas! that this should be the condition of a servant of His Majesty! (*Weeps*).

VIR'ADH.—Away with this sorrow, Minister. Ere long Your Honour will restore us to our former position.

RA'K.—Friend, report the state of affairs in Kusumapura.

VIRA'DH.—Minister, the tale of Kusumapura is very long. Where shall I narrate it from?

R'AK.—Friend, I wish to hear from the beginning the doings of the persons employed by us to give poison, after the formal entry of Chandragupta himself into the city.

VIRA'DH.—Here I begin. The city of Kusumapura was blockaded on all sides by the forces belonging to Chandragupta and Parvateśvara, composed of the S'akas, Yavanas, Kirâtas, Kâmbojas, Pârasîkas, Bâlhikas and others guided by the directions of Châṇakya, and resembling the oceans with their water in wild commotion (lit. running high) at the time of the world's final destruction.

RA'K.—(*Drawing his sword in great haste*). Ah, who dares blockade Kusumapura while I am living? Pravîraka! Pravîraka! Quickly now—

Let archers move rapidly round the rampart; let elephants able to break through the lines of the elephants of the enemy stand (be posted) at the gates; and let those united in mind with me who are ambitious of glory, and who, regardless of (lit. dismissing) the fear of death, are bent upon attacking the weak force of the enemy, march out with me. (13)

VIRA'DH.—Your Honour should spare this agitation. It is the past that is being described by me.

RA'K.—(*Sighing*). Alas, it is a past event! I, however, imagined that it was the same time now. (*Dropping down the sword*). Oh King Nanda, I call to my mind your excessive graciousness towards Râkshasa. For, you at the time of battle, seemed to think in your affection (for me) that there were a thousand Râkshasas living in the city when you despatched to me order after order, thus:—Where this line of elephants, dark-blue like (a mass of) clouds, moves, there let Râkshasa go; let this troop of cavalry bounding like heaving waves be warded off by Râkshasa; let Râkshasa destroy the body of infantry; and the like. (14)

What further?

VIRA'DH.—Thereupon, when His Majesty Sarvârthasidhi, seeing Kusumapura besieged on all sides and not bearing to see the great hardships of a siege entailed on the citizens for a long time, came to an underground passage and out of regard for the subjects even in such a state left the city to retire to a penance-grove; when deprived of their king, your forces, slackened their efforts; when your partisans residing in the city were found out to be so by their daring acts, such as their obstruction to the proclamation of (Chandragupta's) victory; when you, too, escaped by the subterranean passage for the restoration of the sovereignty of the Nandas; and when poor Parvataka was killed by the poison-maid employed by you for the destruction of Chandragupta.—

RA'K.—Friend, see the wonder of it.

The efficacious poison-maid, destined to kill one man, whom I had reserved for the destruction of Chandragupta, came in contact with king Parvataka, and to the great good luck of Vishṇugupta, killed him whose very death was sought by him (*i. e.* Vishṇugupta), just as the powerful missile, the oneman-slayer, which was kept in reserve by Karṇa in order to kill Arjuna, smote, to the great interest of Vishṇu (Kṛshṇa), the son of Hidimbâ, whom he (Kṛshṇa) wished to make its victim. (15)

VIRA'DH.—Minister, it was the wanton pastime of fate. What could be done?

RA'K.—Well, proceed with your story.

VIRA'DH.—Then, after prince Malayaketu, frightened at the murder of his father, had fled, and Vairochaka, the brother of Parvataka, had been taken into confidence, the entry of Chandragupta into the palace of the Nandas was publicly announced, when the cursed Chânakya called together all the carpenters ressident in Kusumapura and addressed them thus—"According to the directions of the astrologers the entry of Chandragupta into the abode of the Nandas will take place at midnight. You will, therefore, decorate the royal palace commencing with the (main) eastern entrance." Then the carpenters said—"Sir, the front gate of the royal palace has already been embellished with special decorations, such as the construction of golden arches, by the carpenter Dâruvarman who had learnt that His Majesty Chandragupta would make his entry into the palace of the Nandas. We shall, therefore, make the decorations in the interior." Then the fellow Chânakya, hearing that the carpenter Dâruvarman had, without being ordered, decorated the gate of the palace, bestowed, as if pleased a long eulogy on the foresight of Dâruvarman and said—"O Dâruvarman, before long you will receive a fitting reward for this your foresight."

RA'K.—(*With agitation*). Whence can there be satisfaction in the case of that fellow, Chânakya! I think the labour of Dâruvarman must have been fruitless or even it must have led to an undesirable end; for, by his not waiting till he received the order, be it through foolishness or through the excess of devotion to the King, a strong suspicion must have been aroused in the mind of the devil, Chânakya. What next?

VIRA'DH.—Then that cursed fellow, Chânakya having made the artisans and the citizens understand that the entry of Chandragupta would take place at midnight owing to a favourable juncture of stars, seated Vairochaka, the brother of Parvateshvara, at that very time, on the same throne with Chandragupta and divided between them the sovereignty of the world.

RA'K.—What? Was half the portion of the kingdon that

had already been promised, given away to Vairochaka, brother of Parvateśvara?

VIRA'DH.—Yes, it was.

RA'K.—(*To himself*). The extremely shrewd (or wily) Châṇakya must have assuredly thought of some secret way of doing away with the poor man, and given rise to this report among the public in order to wipe away the ill-repute (scandal) caused by the murder of Parvateśvara. (*Aloud*). And after that?

VIRA'DH.—Then, the entry of Chandragupta having been already proclaimed as taking place at night, Vairochaka was made to go through the semblance of coronation ceremony; and when the same Vairochaka, whose body was covered with an armour-like robe formed of variegated texture of bright pearls and gems woven cross-wise, whose head looked all the more graceful on account of the close fitting diadem richly set with jewels, on whose broad bosom glittered garlands of fragrant flowers placed crosswise, and whose form (being thus hid) could not have been recognised even by those who knew him most, had mounted, at the command of the vile Châṇakya, the female elephant, Chandralekhâ, whom Chandragupta used to ride, and, followed by the princes, the (habitual) attendants of Chandragupta, was entering the palace of Nanda, the carpenter Dâruvarman, as directed by you, kept his mechanical gateway ready to drop down on him, believing him to be Chandragupta. In the meantime the attendant princes of Chandragupta reined in their steeds and remained outside, when Varvaraka, Chandragupta's driver, also employed by Your Honour, caught hold of a hollow gold stick suspended by a gold chain with his hand with the intention of drawing out the poniard that was concealed in it.

RA'K.—The efforts of both were alike misdirected.

VIRA'DH.—Then the she-elephant anticipating a stroke on the hips took to a different gait with very quick steps. Then the arch which was let fall according to a calculation based on her previous speed, but which fell wide of the mark, smashed poor Varvaraka with the drawn poniard clenched in his hand, ere he reached Vairochaka, whom he had taken for Chandragupta. Anticipating his own execution on account of his having let fall the arch, Dâruvarman, who had already got upon the top of a lofty archway, drew out the iron bolt (or pivot) by which the machinery could be moved, and killed poor Vairochaka seated as he was on the female elephant.

RA'K.—Alas! Two undesirable things (misfortunes) have happened. Chandragupta is left unharmed, while Vairochaka and Varvaraka are killed by fate! Now, how fared the carpenter Dâruvarman?

VIRA'DH.—He was stoned to death by the footmen themselves who marched before Vairochaka.

RA'K.—(*With tears in his eyes*). Alas, we are bereaved of our affectionate friend Dâruvarman. Now, what has the physician, Abhayadatta, living there, done?

VIRA'DH.—He did every thing.

RA'K.—(*Joyfully*). What? Is the wicked Chandragupta killed?

VIRA'DH.—No, Minister; he was not killed, as fate would have it.

RA'K.—(*In dismay*). How could you say then that he did every thing.

VIRA'DH.—Minister, he had prepared a medicine mixed with powder of magical virtue for Chanragupta; but the villainous Châṇakya, happening to examine it, observed a change of colour in a gold plate, and said to Chandragupta—Vṛshala, this medicine is poisoned, you should not drink it.

RA'K.—He is a wily fellow indeed. What of the physician?

VIRA'DH.—He was compelled to drink the same medicine and died.

RA'K.—Alas! A great treasure of knowledge is lost! And what became of Praviraka, who had charge of (the King's) bed chamber?

VIRA'DH.—He shared the fate of others.

RA'K.—(*In alarm*). How do you mean?

VIRA'DH.—That fool having obtained the large treasure

given by you began to enjoy pleasures with great extravagance and when questioned as to how he came by so much wealth, he made many contradictory statements, whereupon that rogue Chânakya ordered him to be killed in a fearful (lit. strange) way.

RA'K.—(*Sorrowfully*). How, here too, we have been disappointed by fate! And what news you bring of Bîbhatsaka and others who were charged by us to slay Chandragupta when lying down on his bed, and who lay in wait having already occupied a recess in the wall of the royal palace?

VIRA'DH.—Minister, it is a very heart-rending tale.

RA'K.—(*With uneasiness*). How? A very heart-rending tale! I hope that villain Châṇakya did not find them out when concealed there.

VIRA'DH.—Minister, he did. That wicked soul, the cursed Châṇakya, entered the bed-chamber before Chandragupta's entry, when, the very moment, casting a searching look about, he noticed a line of ants with particles of food in their mouths issuing from some crevice in the wall, whence concluding that there were men (assassins) hidden in the interior of the house, he ordered the bed-chamber to be set on fire. As it was burning, all those, Bibhatsaka and others, with their eyes obstructed by smoke, could not find the outlet through which they had previously arranged to make their exits, and being enveloped in flames perished.

RA'K.—(*Fearfully*). Alas! What a sad end, oh! Friend, behold the tide of the good luck of the wicked Chandragupta, of cursed name. For,

The maid with a poisoned body whom I secretly employed to bring about his death, fortunately for him killed that very Parvataka who was to claim half of his kingdom. Those persons who were employed to use weapons and poisons (against him) were made to suffer death by those very means. Mark, how my schemes yield a rich harvest of blessings to Chandragupta himself. (16)

VIRA'DH.—Minister, still what is undertaken must not be given up. See,

Mean (low-spirited) men set not to work from fear of obstacles: ordinary men begin, but desist, when confronted with difficulties; but men of exalted qualities (best energy) although again and again assailed by difficulties, do not give up what is once undertaken. (17)

Moreover,

Is it because S'esha does not feel the pain caused by the load of the earth on his body that he does not throw it off? Or does not the Sun feel fatigued that he does not sit down motionless? (Not so). But a praiseworthy man is ashamed to lay aside, like a mean-hearted person, what he has once undertaken. To carry their undertakings to their end—this is, indeed, the family-vow of the good. (18)

RA'K.—Friend, you actually see that we are not giving up what we have undertaken. What further?

VIRA'DH.—The cursed Châṇakya who thenceforth grew a thousand times more careful about the life of Chandragupta arrested your friends in the city after learning, on enquiry, that such attempts originated from them.

RA'K.—(*With uneasiness*). Oh, tell me who were arrested.

VIRA'DH.—In the first place the Jaina mendicant, Jîvasiddhi, was banished the city with ignominy.

RA'K.—(*Aside*). So far it is bearable. Loss of place will not pain one who has no earthly connections. (*Aloud*). Friend, on what charge was he expelled?

VIRA'DH.—On the charge that he killed Parvateśvara with the poison-maid employed by you.

RA'K.—(*To himself*). Cleverly done! O Kauṭilya, it was a nice stroke of policy on your part!

Removing the ill-repute from yourself, you have cast it upon us, while at the same time the person who would have claimed half the kingdom is done away with. Thus a single seed of your policy (state-craft) bears multfarious fruit. (19)

(*Aloud*). Who else?

VIRA'DH.—Then he ordered S'akaṭadâsa to be impaled after having it proclaimed throughout the city that Dâruvarman and others were instigated by him to plot against the life of Chandragupta.

RA'K.—(*With tears*). Ah friend S'akaṭadâsa, such an end was quite undeserved by you; or, you who perished for your master, must not be mourned for. But accursed is the life of me who wish to live even after the race of Nanda is destroyed.

VIRA'DH.—(But) Minister, you are working purely in the interest of your master.

RA'K.—Friend,

I, * ungrateful that I am, have not followed His Majesty (*i. e.* have not gone to the other world), having in view this very object (*viz.* the interest of my master) and not through the desire to live (*i, e.* not because I care any thing for life). (20)

Proceed, I am prepared to hear of the misfortunes of other friends also.

VIRA'DH.—On hearing of these occurrences, Chandanadâsa had your family removed.

RA'K.—Friend, he did wrong in thus going against that cruel fellow, Châṇakya.

VIRA'DH.—But, Minister, it would have been worse to betray a friend.

RA'K.—What followed?

VIRA'DH.—When he did not surrender your wife, although requested to do so, the wretched Châṇakya flew into rage.

RA'K.—(*In alarm*). Surely he did not order his execution?

VIRA'DH.—No, he sequestered his property, and sent him to prison with his wife and son.

RA'K.—How do you say then with satisfaction that he had the wife of Râkshasa removed? You had rather said that Râkshasa himself, with wife and son, was put into irons.

A SERVANT—(*Entering*). Victory to the Minister! S'akaṭadâsa is waiting at the door.

RA'K.—Good man, is it true?

---

* If the reading in the foot-note be adopted the meaning is—I who am ungrateful do not follow my lord......putting forth this excuse and not the love of life. *Vir.*—It is not so—

You who are grateful follow not our royal master......having this very object (the cause of our master) in view &c.

SERVANT—Can I report a falsehood to the Minister?

RA'K.—Friend, Viràdhagupta, how is this?

VIRA'DH.—Minister, it may be so. Destiny protects one on whom fortune smiles.

RA'K.—Priyaṁvadaka, why do you tarry now? Quickly usher him in.

SERVANT—As you order. [*Exit.*

(*Enter* S'AKANADA'SA *followed by* SIDDHA'RTHAKA).

S'AK.—(*To himself*).

That my heart, having seen the impaling stake firmly planted in the ground, like Maurya firmly established on the earth, as also the garland tied round the head which destroys one's consciousness, like the sovereignty of Maurya which pains (violently shakes) consciousness, and having heard the sounds of the trumpets of execution sounding as terrific and dismal as at the time of the dethronement of the lord, did not break down, was, meseems, because it was hardened by previous strokes. (21)

(*Going near and seeing* RA'KSHASA ; *with joy*).

This is minister Ràkshasa; he who, with his devotion (to Nanda) unimpaired though Nanda himself has disappeared and bearing up the cause of his master, stands on earth like the highest standard (*i. e.* noblest pattern) of those who are loyal to their masters. (22)

(*Approaching*). Victory to the Minister!

RA'K.—(*Seeing him, rejoicingly*). Friend, S'akaṭadàsa, it is by good luck that I see you, though fallen into the clutches of Kauṭilya. Do you, therefore, embrace me.

RA'K.—(*After a long embrace*). Take this seat, please.

S'AK.—(*Gesticulates that he sits down*).

RA'K.—Friend, S'akaṭadàsa—To whom am I beholden for this delight of the heart (*i. e.* this delightful event)?

S'AK.—(*Pointing to* SIDDHA'RTHAKA). This dear friend, Siddhàrthaka, put the executioners to flight and bore me hither.

RA'K.—(*Joyfully*). Good friend, Siddhàrthaka, what can be an adequate return for this favour? But take these. (*He takes off the ornaments from his body and gives them to* SIDDHA'RTHAKA).

SIDDH.—(*Takes them, and falls at his feet; to himself*). Such, indeed, is the advice of (instructions given me by) my master. I will act accordingly. (*Aloud*). Minister, as I come to this place for the first time, I have no acquaintance here to whom I can entrust this favour of Your Excellency and be free from care (on that score). I should, therefore like to deposit the ornaments after having sealed them with this seal-ring in your treasury. I will take them away when there is an occasion for them.

RA'K.—Friend, what harm is there in that? S'akaṭadâsa do so.

S'AK.—As the Minister commands. (*Looking at the seal-ring; aside*). Minister, the ring has your name inscribed upon it.

R'AK.—(*Looking at it, to himself*). To be sure, this was taken from me by my wife, when I left the city, as a souvenir (lit. the means of beguiling the time of separation) How could it then come into his hands? (*Aloud*). Friend, Siddhârthaka, how did you come by this ring?

SIDDH.—There is in Kusumapura a jeweller, Chandanadâsa by name. I found this ring fallen near the door of his house.

RA'K.—That is right.

SIDDH.—Minister, what is right in this?

RA'K.—Friend, that such a thing should be found fallen somewhere in the houses of very rich men.

S'AK.—Friend Siddhârthaka, the ring bears upon it the stamp of the Minister's name. Give it to him. The Minister will reward you with money exceeding its value.

SIDDH.—I esteem it a favour that the Minister accepts the ring. (*He hands over the ring*).

RA'K.—Friend, S'akaṭadâsa, you are to use this ring in discharging your office.

S'AK.—As the Minister commands.

SIDDH.—Minister, I have a request to make.

RA'K.—Speak out unreservedly.

SIDDH.—The Minister knows full well, that when any one has given offence to the wretch Châṇakya, entry into Pâṭaliputra is prohibited to him. I wish, therefore, to remain in Your Honour's service.

RA'K.—Friend, we are pleased at this. It was our ignorance of your intention that prevented us from making this request to you ourselves. Do so then.

SIDDH.—(*Joyfully*). I feel beholden to Your Honour.

RA'K.—S'akaṭadâsa, see that Siddhârthaka takes rest.

S'AK.—As you command. [*Exit with* SIDDHARTHAKA.

RA'K.—Friend Virâdhagupta, go on with the remainder of your tale. Do the subjects of Chandragupta lend a favourable ear to our overtures?

VIRA'DH.—Minister, they do. They are already acting in pursuance of them as certain things are being revealed.

RA'K.—Friend, what are the things that are being revealed there?

VIRA'DH.—This is what has come to light there, Minister, that Chandragupta has got angry with Châṇakya ever since Malayaketu's escape. Châṇakya, of course, in his extreme arrogance, does not bear this, and pains the heart of Chandragupta with various acts of disobedience. Such is *my* experience too.

RA'K.—(*Delightfully*). Friend Virâdhagupta, go again to Kusumapura in this very disguise of a snake-charmer. There lives a dear friend of mine, Stanakalas'a by name, disguised as a bard. Tell him in my name that as Châṇakya will be committing acts of disobedience he should praise Chandragupta with stanzas calculated to inflame his spirit (*i. e.* excite his jealousy); and that whatever business he will have to transact, he should send me word, under the profoundest secrecy, through Karabhaka.

VIRA'DH.—As the Minister commands. [*Exit.*

SERVANT—(*Entering*). Minister, Sakaṭadâsa informs you that these three ornaments of a set are offered for sale, and that you should examine them yourself.

RA'K.—(*Looking at them*). Oh, these are very precious ornaments. Friend, tell S'akaṭadâsa in my name that he should satisfy the seller and buy them.

SERVANT—As you command. [*Exit.*

RA'K.—I too will immediately send Karabhaka to Kusumapura. (*Rising*). Would there be a split between Chandragupta and the vile Chânakya? Or why? I consider my desire as already fulfilled. For,

Maurya, ruling over (lit. commanding) all the kings of the earth, has become imperious. Chânakya too is full of self-sufficiency at the thought that Maurya became king through his support. The feeling of satisfaction itself, having thus found an opportunity, will certainly alienate them from their friendship—the one happy by his acquisition of the kingdom, the other by his having successfully crossed the ocean of his vow. (23) [*Exeunt Omnes.*

End of Act II.

ACT III.

(*Enter the* Chamberlain).

Cham.—(*Dejectedly*).

The operations of perceiving sensuous objects have been impaired (or suspended) with regard even to those very organs of sense, the eye and others, by means of which thou hadst derived thy being (or gained thy object), by having perceived the objects of sense such as form and others; the organs of action which were (formerly) obedient to thee, have perforce given up their energy (active vigour): thus, O Desire, old age has planted its foot on thy very head; in vain dost thou pine now. (1)

(*Turning round and looking into the air*). Oh you officials of the Sugâṅga palace, His Majesty Chandragupta, of blessed name, commands you thus—"I wish to enjoy a sight of Kusumapura, now the more delightful on account of the commencement of the Kaumudî festival. You should therefore decorate, for our reception, the upper terraces of *Sugâṅga.*" (*Again looking into the air*). What do you say? Do you say "Sir, does not His Majesty know that the festival has been forbidden?" Ah, fie upon you, ill-fated beings! Why should you allude to a subject which will bring about your instantaneous death? Quickly now,

Let beautiful (lit. the beauty of) bright *Châmaras* that

rival in splendour the streaming rays of the full moon embrace (hang round) the pillars, fragrant by being fumigated with incense, and having garlands fastened round them; let also a sprinkling with sandal-water mixed with flowers quickly favour (refresh) the earth that has long been as it were drooping under the weight of the lion-emblemed throne. (2)

What do you say? 'That you are readily obeying the order of the King?' Make haste, friends. His Majesty Chandragupta is at the gates. He,

Who being strong-minded, has resolved to bear up, even in his prime youth, that very yoke of (responsibility of governing) the earth, which, though heavy, was for a long time borne by his sire, like a trained bull (experienced and able), who did not step amiss even on rough paths (trying situations) on account of his firm limbs (trusty assistants); he stumbles on account of his youthfulness (*i. e.* inexperience) but bears it lightly (lit. without feeling pain). (3)

(*Behind the Scenes*).

This way, this way, Your Majesty.

(*Then enter the* King *and a* Female Door-keeper).

King—(*To himself*). Sovereignty is, indeed, a source of great uneasiness to a king, who is intent on conforming to the duties of sovereigns (conscientiously doing his duty as a sovereign). For,

If a king (the protector of the people) devotes himself to the interests of others he has to neglect his own interest (lit. his application to his interest abandons him); and a king who abandons personal interest is not the lord of the earth in the real sense of the term. If moreover, he values more others' interests than his own, then alas, he is dependent (a servant of others); and when a man is dependent, how can he know (enjoy) the flavour of pleasures? (4)

Besides, the goddess of wealth is difficult to be propitiated even by kings possessed of the characteristic excellences of kings (or by self-controlled kings). For,

She shrinks from one who is austere; abides not with one who is meek from fear of insult; hates a fool, but bears no love to the most learned either; she feels exceedingly shy of the brave; but scoffs at those who are always timid: the goddess of wealth is very difficult to please like a harlot, who has gained ascendency (over her lover). (5)

Moreover, it is the advice of my revered preceptor that I should pick a sham quarrel with him and manage matters independently for some time. I accepted it with great difficulty as if it were a sin; or rather, with my mind properly guided by His Honour, I am always independent. For,

In this world a pupil, acting in the right way, experiences no check (from his preceptor); when, however, he strays from the proper path through infatuation, the preceptor becomes a goad to him; hence *good* men who delight in acting according to instruction are ever free from restraint; we for our part are averse to any independence beyond this. (6)

(*Aloud*). Venerable Vaihînari, lead the way to Sugâṅga.

CHAMB.—This way, Sire, this way. (*He gesticulates that he walks on*). This is the palace Sugâṅga. Ascend gently, my lord.

KING—(*Gesticulates ascent, and looks at the quarters*). Oh the extreme loveliness of the directions whose beauty is enhanced by the autumnal season! For,

Gradually shrinking up, having the strips of white clouds for sandbanks, crowded all round with swarms of sweetly gabbling swans, and thick-set at night with asterisms of various forms like so many full-blown lotus flowers, the extensive ten directions flow down from the sky like ten long rivers (flowing in consequence of the rainy season &c.) (7)

Moreover,

Leading back the turbulent waters to their proper basins, making the paddy-stalks bend low being laden with a wealth of grain and depriving the peacocks of their excessive lust as of virulent poison, Autumn seems to have imparted a proper training to the whole world. (8)

Also,

Like a female messenger adept in love-matters, the Autumnal Season, having with great difficulty brought Gaṅgâ who was so much offended (had become turbid in the rainy season) with her husband for his having (professed love to) many wives, to the proper path as she grew leaner and leaner (shrank within its bed), leads her in a completely pleased (serene) mood to the lord of rivers (the sea). (9)

(*Taking a view of the region around*). Ah, how is it that the Kaumudi festival has not yet been commenced in Kusumapura? Venerable Vaihînari, has not the Kaumudî festival been proclaimed in Kusumapura at our command?

CHAMB.—Ay, my lord.

KING—Why then, have not the citizens obeyed our command?

CHAMB.—(*Stopping his ears*). God forbid, God forbid! Your Majesty's order has never been disobeyed in the world. How can it be disobeyed by the citizens?

KING—How is it then that the festivities have not been commenced in Kusumapura?

Courtesans accompanied by gay beaux skilled in free and clever talk do not grace the streets with their gaits slow on account of the weight of their plump hips; nor do the leading (or, rich) citizens vying with one another in the display of the wealth of their houses and being free from misgivings partake, along with their consorts, in the desired festivity falling on the full-moon day. (10)

CHAMB.—It is just this—

KING—What is that?

CHAMB.—My lord, this—

KING—Speak clearly.

CHAMB.—The Kaumudî festival has been prohibited.

KING—(*Angrily*). By whom?

CHAMB.—My lord, beyond this I am not able to say.

KING—I hope the venerable Châna ya has not deprived the spectators of an exceedingly lovely sight.

CHAMB.—Sire, who else that loves life can transgress the command of Your Majesty.

KING—S'oṇottarâ, I wish to sit down.

FEM. DOOR-KEEPER.—Sire, here is the seat of state.

KING—(*Sitting down.*) Venarable Vaihînari, I wish to see the venerable Châṇakya.

CHAMB.—As my lord commands. [*Exit.*

(*Then enter* CHA'NAKYA *seated in his house in an angry and contemplative mood*).

CHAN.—How now! Does the wicked Râkshasa keep up rivalry with me?

" As Kauṭilya, on leaving the town after being insulted, like an (injured) snake, destroyed the Nandas and raised Vṛshala, son of Murâ (or maurya) to the throne, so shall I wrench the sovereignty from the moon-like Maurya—" Thus resolved he is attempting to surpass the excellence of my own genius. (11)

(*Fixing his glance on vacancy*). Râkshasa, Râkhasa, desist from this vain pursuit.

It is not Nanda who was conceited and whose affairs of state were managed by bad ministers; it is Chandragupta (with whom you have to deal). Nor are you Châṇakya; enmity to the principal person is the only point of resemblance in your imitation of myself. (12)

(*Musing*). Or rather, I need not much worry my mind in this matter. For,

That son of Parvataka, as I well know, has been circumvented by my servants who have gained his confidence; my spies, Siddhârthaka and others, are intent on executing the mission entrusted to them. Now by my cunning causing a (sham quarrel) with the moonlike Maurya, I shall, in no time, separate Râkshasa who is plotting against me and who, according to his own idea (estimation) is a master of the art of creating discord, from the enemy. (13)

CHAMB.—(*Entering*). Hard indeed is service!

In the first place a servant has to be afraid of the king, then of his minister, then of his favourite and also of other voluptuous persons who dwell in his palace having gained his favour. It is but right that the wise regard the service, which degrades a man, of one who from penury plods for bread by his entreating looks and the concealment of his feelings, as a dog's life. (14)

(*He walks and looks forward*). This is the house of the venerable Châṇakya; I will enter. (*He enters and take a survey of the house*). Oh! the pomp of the minister of a universal sovereign! This it is—

Here is a piece of stone for breaking cow-dung-cakes; here is a stack of the holy grass brought by his young disciples; and the house too, with its dilapidated walls appears to have the skirts of its roof bent down by the holy sticks exposed for drying. (15)

It is but right, therefore, that Chandragupta should be (simply) Vṛshala to him. For,

That persons who (else always) speak the truth indulge in words through helplessness and praise a king for qualities which he does not even possess, till their tongues are wearied—all that, indeed, is the might (result) of Desire. Otherwise to those who are free from Desire, a king is an object of disregard (little importance) like grass. (16)

(*Looking forward, with awe*). Ah, here is his honour Châṇakya,

Who occupying the world and bringing about, at one and the same time the rise and fall of the kings, Maurya and Nanda by his splendour surpasses the splendour of the thousand-rayed Sun which causes heat and cold in alternate succession and which does not pervade all space! (17)

(*Falling on his knees*). Victory to Your Honour!

CHA'N.—Vaihînari, what brings you here?

CHAMB.—Sir, His Majesty Chandragupta, of blessed name, the couple of whose lotus-like feet is purpled by the rays of the pieces of rubies on the series of the diadems of kings, shaken in the act of their hurried salutation, respectfully bows to your honour and says—" I wish to see Your Honour without causing any interruption in your (other) duties (*i. e.* at your leisure)."

CHA'N.—Vṛshala wants to see me? Vaihînari, the prohibition of the Kaumudi festival made by me has not reached the ears of Vṛshala, I hope?

CHAMB.—It has, sir.

CHA'N.—(*Wrathfully*). Ah, who told him that?

CHAMB —(*In alarm*). Please, Your Honour, His Majesty himself, when he went to the Sugânga palace, saw that the festival was not commenced in the town.

CHA'N.—Ah, I understand it. So you secretly exasperated Vṛshala and provoked his anger. What else?

CHAMB.—(*Shows fear and hangs down his head in silence*).

CHA'N.—Oh the feeling of hatred entertained by the servants of the king towards Châṇakya! Where is Vṛshala now)?

CHAMB.—(*Showing fear*). Sir, His Majesty who was in the Sugânga palace sent me to Your Honour's feet.

CHA'N.—(*Rising*). Lead the way to Sugânga.

CHAMB.—This way Your Honour. (BOTH *walk on*).

CHAMB.—This is the palace Sugânga. Your Honour may gently ascend.

CHA'N.—(*Ascends and looks forward*). Oh, Vṛshala is seated on the throne. Very good, very good.

The throne wrested from the Nandas, who treated with scorn even Kubera (who were exceedingly wealthy), has been occupied by Vṛshala, the foremost among sovereigns and it has thus been united with a worthy king. These good occurrences (brought about by me) produce supreme satisfaction in me. (18)

(*He approaches* VṚSHALA). Victory to you, Vṛshala.

KING—(*Rising from his seat*). Venerable sir, Chandragupta bows to you. (*Falls at his feet*).

CHA'N.—(*Taking him by the hand*). Rise child.

May kings coming again and again from the lord of mountains cooled by the showers of spray of the celestial river (Ganges) playing about among its rocks, as well as from the farthest extremity of the shores of the southern ocean brilliant with gems flashing with divers colours, bow to your feet in awe and ever make the interstices of the toes of your feet filled with the rays of their crestjewels. (19)

KING.—All this I find realized through the favour of

Your Honour. Your Honour may sit down. (*Both sit down according to rank*).

CHA'N.—Vṛshala, why did you summon me?

KING.—To bless myself with Your Honour's sight.

CHA'N.—(*With a smile*). No more compliments, please. Kings do not send for their officers without purpose.

KING—Sir, what good has your honour in view in forbidding the Kaumudî festival.

CHA'N.—(*With a smile*). You have then summoned me to administer me a reproof.

KING—God forbid, God forbid. No, not at all; only to make a respectful representation.

CHA'N.—If so, then the uncontrolled tastes of those who are to be respectfully treated ought by no means to be checked by a pupil.

KING—It is so; there is no doubt. But Your Honour never does a thing without having some object in view. So there is scope for my question.

CHA'N.—Vṛshala, you have well comprehended the fact that *Châṇakya* never does a thing without some aim.

KING—For this very reason, sir, the desire to know (lit. to hear your motive in prohibiting the festival) makes me speak (*i. e.* put you the question).

CHA'N.—Vṛshala, listen. In connection with this topic writers on politics mention three forms of administration:—(I) That dependent (entirely) on the king. (2) that dependent (entirely) on the minister, (3) and that dependent upon both. Now what have you, who are entirely dependent upon your minister, to do with inquiring into the reasons of a thing? Since I who am the responsible officer will alone act in this matter.

KING—(*Turns away his face in anger*).

(*Behind the scenes*—TWO BARDS).

FIRST BARD—Whitening the sky with its ashen hue (with its ashes—in the case of देवी तनु) that surpasses the brightness of Kâs'a flowers, counteracting the impression of the elephant-hide-like space dark with clouds (of the elephant-hide dark like a cloud) by means of the streaming rays of the moon, bearing the bright moon-light like a white garland of skulls (bearing the white moon-light-like garland of skulls) and displaying its swans like beauteous smiles (with its smiles like swans) may the Autumnal Season, thus unusually accoutred, like the body of S'iva, remove your trouble! (20)

Moreover,

May the half-closed eyes of Vishṇu when about to leave his broad serpent-bed having the group of hoods for its pillow grant you protection for ever!—the eyes which look slantingly on account of their recent opening, which are turned away for an instant from the beaming lustre of the jewel-lamps, which are (yet) tardy in performing their function, in which particles of water have been produced on account of yawning accompanied with the movements of the limbs, and which are reddish at the corners from break of sleep. (21)

SECOND BARD—O you best of kings, eminent universal sovereigns like you, who are made by the Creator the receptacles of supreme valour, who, by their peculiar might, subdue kings having a large force of rut-shedding elephants, and who are distinguished by their sense of self-esteem and pride, do not put up with the infringement of their command for any reason whatsoever, just as the lords of beasts who are created by the Creator as the store-houses of strength, who by their fierce vigour conquer the rut-shedding leaders of elephant-herds, and whose dignity and haughtiness are distinctly manifested, do not brook the breaking of their jaws on any account. (22)

Moreover,

A lord does not become a lord by the wearing of ornaments, &c. He is said to be a lord, like you, whose order is not slighted by others. (23)

CHA'N.—(*To himself*). The first is a blessing describing the beauties (lit. qualities) of the autumnal season now set in, in the form of the praise of the supreme deities. What this other is, I do not understand. (*After reflecting*). Ah, I comprehend it now. It is the intrigue of Râkshasa, You are detected (lit. seen), vile Rákshasa! Be sure, Kauṭilya is wide awake.

KING—Venerable Vaihînari, let a hundred thousand gold coins be given to these bards.

CHAMB.—As Your Majesty commands. (*He rises and turns round*).

CHA'N.—(*Angrily*). Stop, Vaihînari, don't go. Vṛshala, why this large expenditure for a paltry thing?

KING—(*In a rage*). Kingship is like bondage to me, when my course of action is thus checked in every case by Your Honour; it is not like kingship at all.

CHA'N.—Vṛshala, such evils are but the lot of those kings who do not attend personally to their own duties. If you cannot bear them, apply yourself to your duties.

KING—Just now do I apply myself to my duties.

CHA'N.—It is agreeable to me. I too shall apply myself to my duties.

KING—Well then I want to know in the first place your object in prohibiting the Kaumudi festival.

CHA'N.—Vṛshala, I too wish to hear your reason for the celebration of the Kaumudi festival.

KING—The first and foremost (the most important) is the obedience of my command.

CHA'N.—Vṛshala, disobedience of your command is *my* first purpose in forbidding the Kaumudi festival. For,

That order of yours, which is borne like a garland of unfaded flowers on their heads by hundreds of kings up to the shores of the four oceans, the forests on the coast-lines of which are darkened by the leaves of *tamâla* trees and the waters of which are inwardly agitated by the collections of *timi* fishes quickly moving about, when failing in me alone, tells of your character as a sovereign graced by humility. (24)

And if you wish to hear the second reason, that too, I will tell you.

KING—Do so.

CHA'N.—S'oṇottarâ, tell the Kâyastha Achala that I command him to send me the document in connection with

Bhadrabhaṭa and his colleagues [who left us through discontent and went over to Malayaketu].

FEM. DOOR KEEPER—As Your Honour commands. (*Exit and re-enter*). Your Honour, here is the writing.

CHA'N.—(*Taking it*). Vṛshala, listen.

KING—I am all attention.

CHA'N.—reads—" Reverence to the lord. This is a document containing the list of those principal persons, who once shared in the prosperity of (or, rose along with) His Majesty Chandragupta, of blessed memory, who having fled from here have gone over to the ill-fated Malayaketu. They are:—In the first place Bhadrabhaṭa, the principal officer of elephant-warriors, Purushadatta, the commander of cavalry, Dingarâta, the nephew of Chandrabhânu, the Principal porter, Balagupta, a kinsman of His Majesty, Râjasena, who was from his boyhood a personal attendant of His Majesty, Bhâgurâyaṇa, the younger brother of general Simhabala, Lohitâksha, the son of the King of Mâlavâ, and Vijayavarman, the head of a class of Kshatriyas."

King—Now I wish to know the cause of this disaffection of these men.

CHA'N.—Vṛshala, here. Those two, by name Bhadrabhaṭa and Purushadatta, respectively the commanders of the elephant and the horse, were addicted to women, wine and chase, and neglected to look after the elephants and the horses; so they were removed by me from their office and kept on mere subsistence-allowance. They, therefore, went over to the enemy and took service under Malayaketu in their respective capacities. As to Dingarâta and Balagupta, they were affected by extreme greed and thinking the salaries given by you insufficient, went over to Malayaketu, believing that they could get more there. As to Râjasena, your young page, he too having suddenly, through your favour, got considerable fortune, consisting of a large treasure, elephants and horses, went and joined Malayaketu from fear of its being taken back. Now about the other fellow, Bhâgurâyaṇa, the younger brother of general Siṁhavarman. He had at that time formed friendship with Parvataka, and out of affection for him frightned Malayaketu in secret by inventing the story that his father was killed by Châṇakya and made him leave the town. When afterwards Chandanadâsa and others who acted perfidiously towards you, were arrested, he entertained fear on account of his own misdeeds and fled for protection to Malayaketu He (Malayaketu) too, thinking that he (Bhâgurâyaṇa) had saved his life out of gratitude, conferred upon him his ministership. a rank next to his own (or appointed him his private secretary.) Lastly, the two, Lohitâksha and Vijayavarman could not bear, in their great vanity, what you gave to their relatives, and went over to Malayaketu. These are the causes of their disaffection.

KING—If the causes of their discontent were known, why did Your Honour not promptly counteract them?

CHA'N.—Vṛshala, it was not possible to counteract.

KING—Why, owing to want of skill (incomptence) or to some purpose (political object) in view?

CHA'N.—How could there have been want of skill? There was a special purpose in view.

KING—That purpose I want now to hear.

CHA'N.—Hear it and bear it well in mind. With regard to the present matter (I have to observe that) there are two ways of dealing with discontented subjects, *viz.* favour or punishment. In the case of Bhadrabhaṭa and Purushadatta who were dismissed from office, to show favour would have meant re-instating them. And if such people, who are careless in the discharge of duty on account of their addiction to vice, be restored to office, they would lead to destruction the whole body of horse and elephant, the main prop of the realm. How could it have been possible to win over those extremely covetous fellows, Dingarâta and Balagupta who would not be pleased even by the gift of the whole kingdom? In the case of Râjasena and Bhâgurâyaṇa who were afraid of losing their property there was not the least scope for a kind treatment. What kind of favour would have won the affection of Lohitâksha and Vijayavarman who are jealous of their relatives and who are extremely proud? For these considerations I had to abandon the first after-native. The other alternative too (*viz.* of adopting severe measures) had to be given up. For after our recent acquisition of the realm of the Nandas, had we inflicted severe punishment upon the influential persons who were our adherents we should have been distrusted by the subjects who are yet attached to the family of the Nandas. Having thus received our partisans into his favour, and guided by the counsels of Râkshasa, Malayaketu, son of Parvataka, incensed at his father's murder, is preparing to attack us with a large force of Mlechchhas. The present is thus the time for exertion and not for festivities. Thinking, therefore, that we had rather put the fortress in order than celebrate the festival, I forbade (the latter).

KING—Sir, I have much to ask in this matter.

CHA'N.—Vṛshala, ask without reserve. I too have much to explain.

KING—Why did you allow Malayaketu, the cause of all this mischief, to escape?

CHA'N.—In case he was not allowed to escape, there were two courses open—to punish him or to give him half the kingdom as promised. To have punished him would have been ourselves giving support to (the supposition) that the murder of Parvataka was an act of ingratitude perpetrated by us. On the other hand, had the promised half of the kingdom been given him, the only result of the assassination of Parvataka would have been the sin of ingratitude. For these reasons I suffered Malayaketu to escape.

KING—This is your explanation in this case. Then again you neglected to take proper steps against Râkshasa who was living here. What has Your Honour to say to this?

CHA'N.—Râkshasa on account of his unswerving devotion to his master and his long stay in one place enjoys the perfect confidence of the subjects who are attached to the Nandas and who know the character of persons; he is endowed with intelligence and valour, is strong in allies and has a large treasure at his command. If, therefore, he had been allowed to remain in the city itself he would, indeed, have caused serious disturbance within. Whereas, if he were suffered to depart from the city, and then he caused disaffection abroad, it would be possible to manage him with efforts. He was therefore pulled off even as he lived here, like a dart rankling in the heart, and removed to a distance.

KING—Sir, why did you not capture him by force?

CHA'N.—He is Râkshasa, mind you. Had we used violence against him, he would have destroyed many of your soldiers, or, found death himself—an unwelcome result in either case. See,

If being hard-pressed he were to meet with his end, then, O Vṛshala, you would indeed lose such a great person (of such sterling worth); if on the other hand, he were to destroy the flower of your army, that too would be a serious injury. He must, therefore, be trained (won over) with statagems like an elephant of the forest. (25)

KING—We are unable to surpass Your Honour in arguing. But after all Râkshasa is more praiseworthy.

CHA'N.—(*In anger*). "Thank you" I should supply. But it must not be so. O Vṛshala, what has he done?

KING—If you cannot know it yourself, then hear it from me. He, a magnanimous soul,

Dwelt in the city, which had been captured by us, as long as he liked, planting his foot on our neck, (*i. e.* quite in defiance of us) and forcibly offered resistance to the proclamation of victory &c. made by our forces. Thus my mind thrown into great bewilderment by the manifold magnificence of his state-craft has no confidence even in our own trusty adherents. (26)

CHA'N.—(*Laughing*). This it was that was done by Râkshasa! I, however, thought he had invested Malayaketu with the post of sovereign of sovereigns on earth like you, having uprooted you as (I did) Nandas.

KING—It was another that did this, what has Your Honour to boast of in this?

CHA'N.—O you malicious creature,

By whom else having made a dreadful vow in the presence of the people, difficult (lit. long) to be performed on account of the *whole race* of enemies having to be destroyed and in which the knot of hair was loosened by the tips of fingers forcibly agitated by the flashing of anger that was rising within, were the proud nine Nandas, the well known lords of ninety-nine crores (of gold coins,) killed in succession like so many beasts under the very eyes of Râkshasa. (27)

Moreover,

Behold, these funeral fires which contain in them a large store of marrow dripped down, do not cease to burn yet, making the circle of directions appear as if overcast with clouds, the rays of the sun being obscured by the smoke-like vultures wheeling round in circles in the sky with their out-stretched and motionless wings, and entertaining the animals that haunt the cemetery with a feast on the Nandas. (28)

KING—All this was brought about by some one else.

CHA'N.—By whom then?

KING—By fate which bore inveterate hatred to the family of the Nandas.

CHA'N.—The illiterate alone believe in fate.

KING—The literate too are not given to boasting.

CHA'N.—(*In anger*). Vṛshala, you wish to lord it over me like a common servant.

My hand again runs to loosen the knot of hair though (wished to be) tied up.

(*Stamping the ground with his foot*).

This foot moves forth to enter upon another pledge. Being doomed by the god of destruction you now inflame the fire of my anger which was extinguished on account of the destruction of the Nandas. (29)

KING—(*In alarm to himself*). How now? His Honour is really angry, For,

His ruddy eyes though dimmed by being washed by the clear water dropping from the eyelids raised up in anger flashed forth, as it were, fire, in which the knittings of the eyebrows appeared like smoke, and, methinks, the stamping of his foot was borne with difficulty and with a fearful quaking by the Earth, who must have remembered Rudra exhibiting in his frantic dances the sentiment of terror. (30)

CHA'N.—(*Checking his pretended anger*). Vṛshala, enough of bandying words. If you think Râkshasa is superior to me give him this sword. (*He throws down the sword* ; *then rising and fixing his eyes on vacancy* ; *to himself*). Râkshasa, Râkshasa, this is indeed the height of your intellect in your desire to outdo the genius of Kauṭilya !

The whole plan of dissension which has now been devised by you, thinking that you would very easily conquer Maurya when he has swerved from his devotion to Châṇakya, will end, O cunning one, in your own conviction. (31) [*Exit*

KING—Venerable Vaihînari, let it be proclaimed to the subjects that henceforward Chandragupta himself will rule independently of Châṇakya.

CHAMB.—(*To himself*). Oh, he calls him Châṇakya, without any epithet of respect, and not as revered Châṇakya. Alas ! Authority has been withdrawn from him. But His Majesty is not to blame in this matter. For, it is the fault of the minister himself if the King does wrong (or does not respect the minister). An elephant comes to be censured as a vicious animal through the carelessness of the driver. (32)

KING—Venerable sir, what are you thinking of ?

CHAMB.—Nothing, sire. I am glad Your Majesty has now become a king in reality.

KING—(*Aside*). By our being looked on in this light (*i. e.* as independent) let His Honour wishing to accomplish his object realize his desire. (*Aloud*). S'oṇottarâ, I have got a headache on account of this useless quarrel. Lead the way to the bed-chamber.

FEM. DOOR-KEEPER—Come, my lord, come.

KING—(*To himself*).

My mind has as it were begun to enter the very cavity of the earth though I overstepped the limits of respectfulness by the command of His Honour himself. How, indeed, does not shame rend the hearts of those who really (wantonly) slight their preceptors ? (33) [*Exeunt Omnes.*

END OF ACT III.

———

ACT IV.

(*Enter a* MAN *in a traveller's costume*).

MAN—What wonder, oh !

All powerful is the royal command ! Who, indeed, would undertake to come and go back, if it were not for the command of the master, inviolable even when one has to go at an unseasonable hour ? (1)

This is the house of minister Râkshasa. I will go there. (*Walks on like one tired.*) Holla, is there any door-keeper here ? Tell your master, minister Râkshasa that Karabhaka has come from Pâṭaliputra in great haste.

DOOR-KEEPER—(*Entering*). Good sir, do not speak so loudly. The minister who has been suffering from headache brought on by sleeplessness caused by the cares of state is yet in bed. Wait therefore for about an hour. When I find a suitable opportunity I shall announce your arrival.

MAN—Good sir, do so.

(*Enter* RA'KSHASA *seated in his bed-chamber, lost in anxious thoughts,* S'AKATADA'SA *at his side*).

RA'K.—(*To himself*).

While I reflect upon the adverseness (or, uncontrollable nature) of fate at the very outset of my scheme, and seriously take into account the crooked policy of Châṇakya and further see how all my plans have been completely frustrated, I remain awake thinking "how is this (*i. e.* the object desired) to succeed in the face of all this ?" and thus the night even passes away. (2)

Moreover,

First of all to cast the tiny seeds of the enterprise, then to look to their development, and when the seeds have shot up, to unfold the secret deep-hidden fruit; then to lay on the plot more definitely by the force of intellect, and finally to make the various incidents converge to the desired issue—such is the trouble which a writer of plays or a person like me (politician) has to undergo. (3)

Would that the wicked fellow Châṇkya can—

DOOR-KEEPER—(*Entering*). Be victorious.

RA'K.—Still be duped?—

DOOR-KEEPER—Minister.

RA'K.—(*Indicating that his left eye throbbed*; *to himself*). The goddess of speech, as manifested in the discourse and coinciding with the throbbing of the left eye, declares that the vile Châṇakya will be successful, and I, the minister, shall be duped. Still I must not give up my effort. (*Aloud*). Good man, what do you want to say?

DOOR-KEEPER—Minister, Karabhaka is waiting at the door.

RA'K.—Quickly introduce him.

OOR KEEPER—As you order. (*He goes and approaching the* MAN). Good sir, you may see the minister. [*Exit*

KAR.—(*Approaching*). Victory to the Minister.

RA'K.—Sit down, friend.

KAR.—As the Minister commands. (*Sits on the ground*).

RA'K.—(*Aside*). I really do not recollect, on account of the multiplicity of affairs, on what errand he was sent.

[*He reflects.*

(*Then enter* ANOTHER MAN *with a cane-staff in his hand*).

MAN—Move away, sirs, move away; off, men. Don't you see?

Let alone their close proximity; even a sight of kings, the representatives of blessed races, is, like that of gods, difficult to be obtained by the unlucky. (4)

(*Looking at vacancy*). What do you say, noble sirs? "Why is the passage being cleared?" Sirs, here is prince Malayaketu, coming this very way, to see the minister Râkshasa who has got a headache. I therefore ask you to move aside. [*Exit* MAN.

(*Enter* MALAYAKETU *followed by* BHA'GURA'YANA *and the* CHAMBRLAIN).

MAL.—(*With a sigh, to himself*). This is the tenth month since my father's death, and yet through the vain pride of self, I have not offered even one handful of water to his memory. I then solemnly pledged myself to this—

That I should first reduce the wives of my foes to that altered condition which was then brought on of my mothers by grief, a condition, in which they beat their breasts till their pearl-necklaces were shattered, their upper garments fell off, cries of 'woe' were piteously uttered, and the hair made rough by the particles of dust, and then I should offer the funeral offerings to my sire. (5)

In short,

Bearing up a yoke worthy of a brave man I will either follow the path of my father by dying in battle, or I shall forcibly take away the tears from the eyes of my mothers and transfer them to the wives of my enemies. (6)

(*Aloud*). Venerable Jâjali, going alone I wish to give delight to the minister Râkshasa by my unexpected visit. Say, therefore, in my name to the princes that (from my suit that) they should not trouble themselves by following me further.

CHAMB.—As Your Highness orders. (*Turning round and looking into the air*). Ye kings, the Prince orders you that none of you should follow him. (*Looking off*; *with joy*). No sooner was the Prince's command proclaimed than the kings have turned back. See my lord.

Some kings have checked (reined in) their coursers whose necks raised up are excessively bent on account of the very harsh bridles being pulled in and who are striking, as it were, with their hoofs against the void in front of them, while others have turned back their stately elephants whose bells are silent on account of their speed being checked—Thus my lord, the kings, like the oceans, do not trespass the boundary assigned to them by your order. (7)

MAL.—Noble Kanchuki, you too retire with your followers. Let Bhâgurâyaṇa alone follow me.

CHAMB.—As Your Highness commands.

[*Exit with his train.*

MAL.—Friend Bhâgurâyaṇa, when Bhadrabhaṭa and others came here, they told me that they sought my desirable service not through the minister Râkshasa, but that, being alienated from Chandragupta who was wholly guided by a vile minister, they approached me through my general Sîkharaka, thinking me to be a worthy master on account of my amiable qualities. But I have not been able to grasp the meaning of their words although I have been long musing on them.

BHA'G.—The meaning of these words is not hard to understand. This is certainly a very proper course of conduct; since one should resort to a master who is ambitious and endowed with personal qualities through the medium of one who is beloved and friendly.

MAL.—But friend Bhâgurâyaṇa, Rakshasa is certainly our dearest and most well-meaning friend.

BHA'G.—Yes, he is. But the minister Râkshasa bears hatred towards Châṇakya and not towards Chandragupta. So if Chandragupta, not brooking the extreme haughtiness of Châṇakya, should ever remove him from the post of minister, then on account of his devotion to the family of Nanda, as well as of his yearning for his friends, Râkshasa might form an alliance with Chandragupta, thinking that he is the scion of the family of the Nandas. Chandragupta too would agree to the alliance thinking him to be the hereditary minister of his father. In that case Your Highness would not trust them (Bhadrabhaṭa and others). This is the import of their words.

MAL.—That is right. Now lead the way to the mansion of the minister.

BHA'G.—This way, this way, Your Highness. (BOTH *walk forth*).

BHA'G.—This is the mansion of the minister. Your Highness may enter.

MAL.—Here I enter.

RA'K.—(*To himself*). Ah, I recollect it. (*Aloud*). Friend, did you see Stanakalas'a in Kusumapura?

MAN—Minister, I did.

MAL.—(*Listening*). Bhâgurâyaṇa, affairs relating to Kusumapura are being talked over. Let us not go forth at once, but overhear them. For,

Ministers speak in one way in the presence of their master for fear of discouraging (lit. causing his courage to fail him), but in another way in confidential talks where matters are freely and openly stated. (8)

BHA'G.—As the Prince commands.

RA'K.—Friend, did the business succeed ?

MAN—Yes, by your favour.

MAL.—Friend, Bhâgurâyaṇa, what might the business be ?

BHA'G.—Prince, the affairs of the minister are mysterious. So it cannot be definitely known at this stage. Your High ness should hear attentively.

RA'K.—Friend, I wish to hear it in detail.

MAN—Your Honour may listen. I was ordered by Your Excellency saying ' Karabhaka, go you to Kusumapura and in my name, tell the bard Stanakalas'a that he should praise Chandragupta in stanzas that might rouse his anger as Châṇakya will be committing various acts of disobedience '.

RA'K.—Friend, what next?

KAR.—Then I went to Pâṭaliputra and communicated Your Honour's message to the minstrel Stanakalas'a. In the meantime the King, desiring to gladden the townsfolk who still lament the destruction of the Nandas, proclaimed the *Kaumudî* festival. That festival, so familiar (with them) returning after a long time, was, like the company of a beloved wife, delightfully welcomed by the citizens.

RA'K.—(*Tearfully*). Alas, Oh, King Nanda !

O moon-like king, what *Kaumudî* (festival) could there be without you, the cause of delight to the whole world, even if there were the moon (Chandragupta) the delight of lotuses (of ordinary men). (9)

KAR.—But the festival, the joy of the eyes of the people, was forbidden by the cursed Châṇakya in spite of the King. Meanwhile Stanakalaśa sang a series of stanzas that exasperated Chandragupta.

RA'K.—What were the verses ?

MAN—(*Repeats*; " O best of kings, &c.").

RA'K.—(*With joy*). Bravo, Stanakalaśa, bravo !

The seed of discord sown in time assuredly bears the desired fruit. For,

Even an ordinary person will not brook an abrupt interruption in his eagerly desired festive pleasure; much less than a king possessed of lustre transcending that of all men. (10)

MAL.—It is just so.

RA'K.—What next?

KAR.—Then Chandragupta enraged at the infringement of his order praised Your Honour's virtues (naturally) suggested by the occasion and dismissed the vile Châṇakya from office.

MAL.—Friend Bhâgurâyaṇa, by this praise of his qualities Chandragupta has shown his leaning through affection towards Râkshasa.

BHA'G.—Not so much by the praise of his qualifications, as by the removal from office of the cursed Châṇakya.

RA'K.—Is this prohibition of the *Kaumudî* festival the only cause of Chandragupta's displeasure towards Châṇakya or is there any other?

MAL.—Friend, what good does he see from inquiring into other causes of Chandragupta's displeasure?

BHA'G.—Prince, the sagacious Châṇakya will not rouse Chandragupta's anger for nothing. Chandragupta too is grateful and will not, for one single reason, transgress (the bounds of) the respect due to him. He then means that if the breach is due to a number of causes then only it will be lasting.

KAR.—Yes, there is another cause of Chandragupta's anger—that he connived at the escape of Malayaketu and of the Minister Râkshasa.

RA'K.—(*Joyfully*). Friend S'akaṭadâsa, Chandragupta will now come into my power. Now Chandanadâsa will be released from prison and you will be united with your wife and sons.

MAL.—Friend, what does he mean by saying "into my power"?

BHA'G.—What else? He does not see any benefit by uprooting Chandragupta when he is estranged from Châṇakya.

RA'K.—Friend, deprived of his office, where is the fellow now?

KAR.—He lives in that very Pâṭaliputra.

RA'K.—(*In great uneasiness*). What, he stays there? Did he not go to a penance-forest or enter upon a second vow?

KAR.—Minister, he means to retire to a penance-grove, hear.

RA'K.—S'akaṭadâsa, this is not explainable. Just think.

How can that proud fellow, who did not put up with the insult offered to him by His Majesty who was the very Indra on earth, in that he was pulled off from the foremost seat occupied by him, suffer this disgrace at the hands of Maurya, a king of his own creation? (11)

MAL.—Friend, what object of his can be accomplished by Châṇakya's retiring to forest or undertaking a new vow?

BHA'G.—The matter is not very difficult to understand. The more Châṇakya is alienated from Chandragupta, the easier is the accomplishment of his object.

S'AK.—Don't take the matter otherwise; it is capable of being explained. Your Ministership should just consider.

How can Maurya, who has planted his foot on the head of kings with their crests adorned with the lustre of their moon-like crest-jewels, put up with the breach of his command committed by his own people? Kauṭilya too, though wrathful, knowing personally from his incantations (practised for the destruction of his foes) the hardships of a solemn vow and having fulfilled one by good luck, does not make another apprehensive of failure in future. (12)

RA'K.—Friend S'akaṭadâsa, go and look to Karabhaka's taking rest.

S'AK.—As the minister commands. [*Exit with* KARABHAKA.

RA'K.—Now I wish to see the Prince.

MAL.—(*stepping forward*). I have myself come to see Your Honour.

RA'K.—(*Looking at him*). O, the prince! (*Rises from his seat*). Here is seat, please sit down, Prince.

MAL.—Here I sit down. Your Honour, too, should do so. (*They sit down according to rank*). Sir, has your headache moderated?

RA'K.—Prince, how can my headache subside, so long as your title of 'Prince' is not supplanted by that of 'Emperor.'

MAL.—This, as it has been undertaken by Your Honour will not be difficult to attain. How long are we to remain inactive, with our forces thus mustered, in expectation of some weak point of the enemy?

Ra'k.—Prince, whence can there be any more time for delay? Start for victory.

Mal.—Sir, have you found out any weak point of the enemy?

Ra'k.—Yes.

Mal.—Of what nature is it?

Ra'k.—A ministerial one, what else? Chandragupta has fallen off from Châṇakya.

Mal.—Sir, a weak point arising from the (loss of a) minister is no weak point.

Ra'k.—A difficulty arising from a minister may be no difficulty in the case of other kings; but with Chandragupta it is so.

Mal.—Sir it is not so. The faults of Châṇakya are the cause of the disaffection of Chandragupta's subjects; since he is removed now, those who were already attached to Chandragupta will manifest a still greater attachment to him.

Ra'k.—Not so at all. The subjects are divided into two classes, the adherents of (lit. those who owe their rise to) Chandragupta, and the followers of (lit. those attached to) Nanda. The misdeeds of Châṇakya are the cause of disaffection of the adherents of Chandragupta and not of those attached to the house of Nanda. These (latter) are indeed affected by dislike and resentment, knowing as they do that Chandragupta destroyed the family of Nanda which bore parental affection to them (or relation to him). But not finding an able leader they follow Chandragupta himself. If on the other hand they get a champion like you who is acknowledged to possess the power to root out the enemy, they will quickly leave him and come over to your side. In proof of this statement I cite my own instance.

Mal.—Sir, is Chandragupta's ministerial difficulty the only reason for acting on the offensive, or is there any other?

Ra'k.—What have you to do with a number more? This is the principal.

Mal.—How do you call it 'the principal?' Is not Chandragupta now able to resist our attack (or to take countermeasures against us) by entrusting the affairs of his kingdom to another minister or having taken them up himself?

RA'K.—Oh, no. For this reason, that it is possible only in the case of those kings the accomplishment of whose object depends upon themselves. The vile Chandragupta, however, is habitually dependent on his minister for success in an undertaking and is, therefore, like a blind man, inconversant with the affairs of the world. How will he be able to resist us by himself?

The goddess of royalty stands with her legs rigidly placed on the King and on the minister (when) grown too powerful; being, as a woman, unable to sustain her weight she abandons one of them. (13)

Just as a very young suckling, drawing suck from (its mother's) breast will not be able to live even for a short time if weaned from its mother's breast, so a king, who entrusts everything to his minister, if drawn away from him, will not be able to act (conduct his affairs) even for a moment, his intellect not being unfolded on account of his inexperience of the affairs of the world. (14)

MAL.—(*Aside*). I am glad that I don't depend on a minister for the management of my affairs. (*Aloud*). Although it is so, still when there are *many* reasons for commencing hostilities, success is certain in the case of one who carefully tries to find out some (particular) misfortune of the enemy and then assails him.

RA'K.—Certain success the Prince should look for (in the present case). For,

When you possessed of an excellent army are the leader, the town is attached to the Nandas, Châṇakya is adversely disposed owing to his removal from office, Maurya is but a new king, and I am at your disposal—(*Here he breaks off through modesty*) whose endeavours to suggest the means will be limited to merely the pointing out of the way, our desired objects are now delayed (lit. separated), O Prince, simply by your will (to march out). (15)

MAL.—If Your Honour thinks that this is the fit time for an attack, why should we sit idle?

Let my lordly elephants, red with red-lead, of towering

height, dripping rut, darkish in colour, sending forth a loud roar, and undermining the banks with their huge tusks, dash in hundreds (or in a hundred ways) the water of the S'oṇa, with its lofty banks, its dripping waters, dark trees lining its sides, its noisy waves and its banks undermined by the current. (16)

Moreover,

Let the rows of my elephants uttering a deep thunderous roar, and pouring down a rain of spray mixed with the water of their rut besiege the city, as trains of clouds sending forth peals of deep thunder and pouring an abundance of rain surround the Vindhya mauntain. (17) [*Exit* MAL. *with* BHA'G.]

RA'K.—Who waits there?

MAN—(*Entering*). Your command, sir.

RA'K.—Which of astrologers is in attendance at the door?

MAN—Kshapaṇaka—

RA'K.—(*Gesticulating that he perceived a bad omen; to himself*). What Kshapaṇaka, at the first sight!

MAN—Jivasiddhi.

RA'K.—(*Aloud*). Let him enter in a dress not loathsome (*i. e.* auspicious).

MAN—As your order. [*Exit*

(*Enter* KSHAPAṆAKA).

KSHAP.—Accept the words of the worthy (Saints), the physicians that heal the disease of delusion; they teach what is bitter only for a moment, but is wholesome afterwards (in its effects). (18)

(*Approaching*). May salvation attend the faithful (*i. e.* the worshippers of Buddha or Jaina).

RA'K.—Bhadanta, ascertain an auspicious day for our expedition.

KSHAP.—(*Meditates*). Pupil, I have ascertained that the full-moon-day on which the moon is full is after noon quite auspicious. The constellation also is propitious to you who are to march from the north to the south.

Moreover,

You should go when the sun* has almost set, and the

---

* There is a double *entendre* on these words. सूर the brave, Râkshasa; चन्द्र—Chandragupta firmly established; बुध—Châṇakya, केतु—Malayaketu.

full-orbed Chandra (moon) risen, in conjuction with Budha (the planet mercury) and when Ketu has risen and set (*i. e.* Râhu's head is rising and its taill disappearing). (19)

RA'K.—Bhadanta, the day itself is not propitious.

KSHAP.—Pupil,

The virtue of the day is one, of the constellation fourfold and of the conjunction sixty-fourfold ; such is the conclusion of the science of astrology. (20)

For,

Thus the conjunction is favourable; quickly give up this cruel thought (of delaying); going by the power of Chandra (the moon,-Chandragupta) secure everlasting benefit. (21)

RA'K.—Bhadanta, compare your decision (see that it agrees) with that of other astrologers.

KSHAP.—Compare it yourself. I go.

RA'K.—I hope you are not angry !

KSHAP.—Bhandanta is not angry with you.

RA'K.—Who then ?

KSHAP.—The worshipful god that reigns over the destinies of creatures. For you have left your own side (despised me) and gone over to that of others (*i. e.* appeal to other persons).

[*Exit* KSHAPANAKA.

RA'K.—Priyaṃvadaka, see what time it is.

PRI.—His reverence the sun is about to set.

RA'K —(*Rising and looking*). Indeed, the divine sun is going to set. For now,

These garden trees, having manifested their affection in the form of red tinge and quickly gone in front of the sun as he rose from the Orient Mountain, by means of the shadows of their leaves, have now turned back, when his disc is pending on the brim of the Western mountain: generally servants who wait upon their masters leave him when he declines in prosperity. (22) [*Exeunt Omnes.*

END OF ACT IV.

ACT V.

(*Enter* SIDDHA'RTHAKA *with a letter and sealed box containing ornaments*).

SID.—Wonderful, wonderful !

Sprinkled with streams of the water of intellect from the

jars of proper place and season, the creeper of Châṇakya's policy is abont to bear the rich fruit of success. (1)

I have, therefore, taken with me this letter stamped with the seal of the minister Râkshasa which was first caused to be written by His Honour Châṇakya, and this box of ornaments also marked with Râkshasa's seal. Now I am ostensibly going to Pâṭaliputra. Let me then set out. (*He moves forth and sees* KSHAPANAKA). Holla, here comes Kshapaṇaka. His sight, though an ill-omen, is favourable to me. I will not, therefore, avoid him.

(*Enter* KSHAPANAKA).

KSHAP.—I bow to the followers of Arhat who by their profound intellect, accomplish their objects in this world by uncommon paths. (2)

SID —Bhadanta, I salute you.

KSHAP.—S'râvaka, salvation to you. (*Eyeing him*). S'râvaka, I find that you are busy in preparing for a journey.

SID.—How do you know it, Bhadanta?

KSHAP.—What is to be known in that? This good omen capable of directing your way properly, and the letter you hold in your hand, tell me that.

SID.—You have rightly guessed. I am going on a journey. Please therefore, tell me what sort of day I have.

KSHAP.—(*With a laugh*). You inquire after the constellations after getting yourself shaved!

SID.—What harm is there even now? Tell me. If the constellations be favourable to my departure I will go; else I will return.

KSHAP.—There will be nothing favourable (*i. e.* nothing favourable will be of any help to one) at present in Malayaketu's camp.

SID.—Pray, tell me, whence is this?

KSHAP.—Listen. Formerly people had free ingress and egrees in this army. But now that Kusumapura is near, nobody is allowed to go out or to come in without a passport, (lit. a seal-impression). If you have a pass from Bhâgurâyaṇa, go in good cheer. Otherwise stay, lest you might be taken to the King's tent by the officers at the out-post, with your hands and feet in irons.

SID.—Do you not know that I am a personal attendant of the minister, Râkshasa? Who will, therefore, have the power to stop me even though I leave without a pass?

KSHAP.—(*With anguish*). You may be a friend of Râkshasa or of the devil; but there is no way for you to get out unless you have a pass.

SID.—Bhadanta, be not angry that I may succeed in the accomplishment of my object.

KSHAP.—S'râvaka, go; may success attend you! I too go to ask for a pass of Bhagurâyaṇa.

END OF THE PRAVEŚAKA.

(*Enter* BHA'GURA'YANA *followed* by a MAN).

BHA'G.—(*To himself*). Oh the manifold nature of the policy of worthy Châṇakya!

Sometimes its manifestation can be clearly discerned, sometimes it is deep, not being comprehended, now full in all its parts and now very subtle, in accordance with the object to be gained; to-day its seed appears to be destroyed, tomorrow laden with an abundance of fruit—Oh, how varied in character, like Destiny, is the strategy of the politician Châṇakya. (3)

(*Aloud*). Friend Bhâsuraka, the Prince does not wish that I should be far off from him. Place my seat, therefore, in this very council-pavilion.

MAN.—Here is the seat; Your Honour may sit down.

BHA'G.—(*Sits down*). Whoever may wish to see me for a pass, bring him to me.

MAN.—As Your Honour commands. [*Exit*

BHA'G.—(*To himself*). Alas! It is hard to have to deceive this prince, Malayaketu, who is kind to me to such an extent. Or rather,

Why should a man in a dependent position, having first turned his back on his pedigree, on the sense of shame, on personal reputation and self-esteem, and sold himself (lit. his body) through the lust of momentary wealth to a rich man, still consider when executing his command, whether a thing is good or bad when he has passed the stage of reflection? (4)

(*Enter* MALAYAKETU, *followed by a* FEMALE DOOR-KEEPER)

MAL.—(*To himself*). Oh, my mind being perplexed by doubts about Râkshasa does not come to a decision. For,

Will he, through his devotion strengthened by his affection for the house of the Nandas, made an alliance with Maurya who is connected with the Nanda family, and who is now happy by his removal of Chânakya? Or will he, counting foremost the firmness of the virtue of fidelity, remain true to his promise?—Thus does my mind whirl about continually as if mounted on a potter's wheel. (5)

(*Aloud*). Vijayâ, where is Bhâgurâyaṇa?

FE. D.-K.—Here he is, engaged in the work of issuing passes to those who desire to leave the camp.

MAL.—Vijayâ, remain motionless for a moment, so that I may approach him from behind and cover his eyes with my hands.

FE. D.-K.—As the Prince commands.

MAN—(*Entering*, to BHA'GURA'YANA). Sir, here is Kshapaṇaka wishing to see you for a pass.

BHA'G.—Let him come in.

MAN—As your order.

KSHAP.—(*Entering*). Salvation to the faithful!

BHA'G.—(*Seeing him, to himself*). Oh! this is Jîvasiddhi, Râkshasa's friend. (*Aloud*). I believe you are going on some business to be done for Râkshasa?

KSHAP.—(*Stopping his ears*). God forbid!! I will go to a place where I may not hear the name of either Râkshasa or of the devil.

BHA'G.—Great is your love-quarrel with your friend. What wrong has Râkshasa done to you?

KSHAP.—Sir, he has done me no wrong. But an unfortunate wretch that I am, I am wronging myself.

BHA'G.—Bhadanta, you rouse my curiosity. I wish to hear what you mean.

MAL.—(*To himself*). I too wish to hear it.

KSHAP.—S'râvaka, why hear a matter which is not worthy of your ear?

BHA'G.—If it is a secret, let it go.

KSHAP.—It is not a secret, but something extremely cruel.

BHA'G.—If it be no secret, then tell it.

KSHAP.—Sir, it is no secret; yet I won't tell it.

BHA'G.—Then I won't give you a pass.

KSHAP.—(*To himself*). It is right that I should tell it as he is much pressing me for it. (*Aloud*). What help is there for me? Listen, I, an unlucky creature, first formed friendship with Râkshasa while residing in Pâṭaliputra. At that time Râkshasa killed Parvates'vara by the mysterious means of a poison-maid.

MAL.—(*Shedding tears, to himself*). What? Râkshasa killed my father, and not Châṇakya!

BHA'G.—What next?

KSHAP.—Then Châṇakya thinking me to be a friend of Râkshasa had me disgracefully expelled from the city. And even now, Râkshasa, who is skilled in doing many bad things, has planned something similar to it by which I shall be turned out of this world of living creatures.

BHA'G.—Sir, we had heard that the cursed Châṇakya, not intending to give the promised half of the kingdom, committed this foul deed.

KSHAP.—(*Stopping his ears*). Heaven forbid! Châṇakya did not even know the name of the poison-maid.

BHA'G.—Bhadanta, here I give you the pass. Come, tell this to the Prince.

MAL.—(*Approaching*).

I have heard, friend, the words rending the ear with regard to the enemy from the mouth of his friend, by which my grief for my father's murder as if increases twofold even to-day though a long time has elapsed. (6)

KSHAP.—(*Aside*). Ah, the wretch Malayaketu has heard it. Hey-day! I have gained my object. [*Exit*

MAL.—(*Looking into space as if he saw* RA'KSHASA *visibly before him*). Râkshasa, Râkshasa, very proper indeed, this!

O Râkshasa, since you caused my father to fall (killed him) along with the tears of his relations, when he, with his mind perfectly at ease at the thought that you were his friend, had trustingly entrusted all his affairs to you, you are indeed, a Râkshasa in the full sense of the word. (7)

BHA'G.—(*Aside*). It is the order of my master that

Râkshasa's life should be saved. Well then, it must be so. (*Aloud*). Prince do not be excited. Pray sit down. I have to say something to Your Highness.

MAL.—(*Sits down*). What do you want to say, friend?

BHA'G.—Prince, in this world, in the case of politicians the consideration of friend, or foe, or neutral, is dependent on interest, and not on personal inclination as with ordinary men. As at that time Râkshasa wished Sarvârthasiddhi to be King, His Highness Parvates'vara, of blessed name, on account of his being more powerful than even Châṇakya, stood as an obstacle in the way of his project, and was consequently his great foe. So Râkshasa acted against him. I therefore, see that there was nothing much wrong in this. The Prince should just consider.—

Turning from considerations of interest friends into foes and foes into friends, policy leads a man, while still living, into another kind of existence in which past conduct (relation) is all forgotten. (8)

Râkshasa, therefore, should not be blamed in this matter, but should be retained in service till you gain the kingdom of Nanda. Afterwards you are free to retain him or to dismiss him from service.

MAL.—Quite so. Your view is right. For if the minister be killed the subjects will be irritated (or will rise into revolt), and thus victory will be rendered dubious.

MAN—(*Entering*). Victory to the Prince! (*To* BHA'G.). Sir, Dîrgharaksha, the superintendent at the out-post, begs to inform you—Here is a person with a letter arrested by us as he was going out of the camp without a pass. Your Honour should be pleased to inspect him personally.

BHA'G.—Good man, introduce him.

MAN—As you command. [*Exit*

(*Enter* SIDDHA'RTHAKA *bound hand and foot, followed by the* MAN).

SID.—(*To himself*). I bow to Loyalty, the mother of people of my sort, that turns (all that is commanded) into virtue and makes us blind to faults. (9)

MAN—Here is the man, Your Honour.

BHA'G.—(*Looking at him*). Is he a stranger or an attendant of some one here?

SID.—Sir, I am attendant of the minister Râkshasa.

BHA'G.—Friend, why do you then leave the camp without a pass?

SID.—Sir, I was obliged to act with despatch owing to the importance of the business.

BHA'G.—What is the important business that makes you transgress the royal order?

MAL.—Friend Bhâgurâyaṇa, take the letter from him.

BHA'G.—(*Taking it from* SID.'s *hand and seeing the seal*). Prince, here is the letter. The seal bears Râkshasa's name.

MAL.—Open the letter preserving the seal, and show it to me.

BHA'G.—(*Does accordingly and shows him the letter*).

MAL.—(*Reads*). After compliments some body from some place informs some important personage in the proper place. The veracious one has shown an indescribable truthfulness in dismissing our adversary. Now, the truthful one will be pleased to secure the pleasure of these our friends with whom an alliance has already been proposed by encouragement, by giving them the already stipulated exchange for the alliance. These on their part, when thus favoured, will come over to their benefactor after destroying their present master. We remind the truthful one of this, though it has not been forgotten. Of these some desire the treasure and elephants of the enemy, and others his territory. I received the three ornaments sent by the truthful one. I have also sent something as an accompaniment to the letter which should be accepted. The verbal message should be heard from this most trusty person.

MAL.—What sort of letter is this?

BHA'G.—Friend, Siddhârthaka, whose is the letter?

SID.—Sir, I don't know.

BHA'G.—You rogue, you carry the letter and don't know whose it is. Never mind other things. By whom is to be heard your oral message?

SID.—(*Showing fear*). By you.—

BHA'G.—What? By us?

SID.—Arrested by you, I don't know what I should say.

BHA'G.—(*Angrily*). You shall soon know it. Bhâsuraka, take him out and beat him till he confesses.

MAN—As the minister commands. (*Going out with him and re-entering*). Sir, this sealed box dropped from his arm-pit, as he was being beaten.

BHA'G.—(*Looking at it*). This too is sealed with Râkshasa's seal.

MAL.—Friend, this must be the present accompanying the letter. Open it also and show it, but preserve the seal.

BHA'G.—(*Does accordingly and show it*).

MAL.—(*Looking at it*). Ah, these are the ornaments which I took from my person and sent to Râkshasa. Clearly the letter is meant for Chandragupta.

BHA'G.—Prince, we shall just have the doubt cleared up. Friend, beat him again.

MAN—As you order. (*Going out and re-entering with* SID.). The fellow, being punished, says that he will confess the matter to the Prince alone.

MAL.—Let him do so.

SID.—(*Falls at his feet*). Your Highness will favour me by granting me amnesty.

MAL.—A dependent person is always exempt from punishment. Tell everytning as it happened.

SID.—Please Your Highness, the Minister Râkshasa gave me this letter and sent me to Chandragupta.

MAL.—I wish to hear the verbal message now.

SID.—The Minister ordered me to say—"Here are my dear friends, five princes, who feel affection for you. They are—Chitravarman, the chief of the Kulûta country, Simhanâda, lord of the city of Malaya, Pushkarâksha, king of Kâshmîra, Sindhusena, sovereign of Sindh, and Meghanâda, of Persia. Out of these, the first mentioned three kings desire the dominion of Malayaketu, and the last two his elephants and treasury. Just as, therefore, the magnanimous one delighted me by dismissing Châṇakya, so he should please them by granting them the aforesaid things." This much is the oral message.

MAL.—(*To himself*). Strange that Chitravarman and the others also conspire against me! Or why? This accounts for their unbounded love for Râkshasa. (*Aloud*). Vijayâ, I want to see Râkshasa.

FE. D.-K.—As the Prince commands. [*Exit*

(*Enter* RA'KSHASA *seated in his mansion with a* FOLLOWER, *full of anxious thoughts*).

RA'K.—(*To himself*). My mind is not really at ease since our army is filled to some extent with Chandragupta's men. For,

That *Sâdhana* (army--middle term) alone leads to *Siddhi* (victory--a conclusion) which has the *Sâdhya* (a particular aim--major term) established, which has *Anvaya* (union,—capability of being joined in an affirmative proposition), which has *Sapaksha* (is faithful to its side--a corroborative instance on the same side), and is turned away from *Vipaksha* (enemy's side *i. e.* has no hostile element in it--negative instance); but where the *Sâdhana* is identical with *Sâdhya* (an army seeks its own interest--the middle term is itself the major term) or is equal to both sides (is indifferent to the result--can be joined in an affirmative proposition with both *Sapaksha* and *Vipaksha*), or is adverse to the *Paksha* (faithless through treachery--it cannot be joined with the minor term), reliance upon it is fatal to the King as it is to the disputant. (10)

Or rather, I ought not to have any misgivings, since our army is nearly full of persons the causes of whose disaffection were fully ascertained, and who had already accepted our overtures. (*Aloud*). Friend, Priyaṁvadaka, tell in my name the kings, the allies of the Prince, that as every day's march brings us in closer and closer proximity to Kusumapura, they should proceed on their march after forming detachments in the following manner.—

Let the troops consisting of the Khasas and the Magadhas follow me in the van, drawn up in battle-array. Let the Gândhâras, along with the Yavana chieftains take care about the march of the central division. After them should march the valiant S'aka kings with the Chinese and the Hûtas; while the other kings, Kaulûta and others, should guard the person of the Prince in every part of the way. (11)

PRIY.—As you command. [*Exit*

FE. D. K.—(*Entering*). Victory to the Minister. Minister—the Prince wishes to see you.

RA'K.—Good woman, wait a little while. Holla, who is here?

MAN—(*Entering*). Your order, Minister?

RA'K —Say to S'akaṭadâsa—The Prince has given me ornaments; it is not, therefore, becoming in me to see him without decoration. Send me, therefore, one of the three ornaments that have been purchased.

MAN—As you command. (*Exit and re-enter*). Minister, here is one of the ornaments.

RA'K.—(*Putting on the decoration and rising*). Good woman, show the way leading to the King.

FE. D. K.—Come, Minister.

RA'K.—(*To himself*). A post of authority is, indeed, a source of great apprehension (or misgivings) even to an innocenent man. For,

In the first place the fear of the master takes entire possession (of the mind) of the servant, and then fear of those about him occupies his heart. Then the position of those who have risen very high provokes the jealousy of the wicked. (Hence) the condition of those occupying a high rank considers a fall to be close at hand. (12)

(*They walk forth*).

FE. D. K.—Minister, here is the Prince. You may approach him.

RA'K.—Here is the Prince, who

With his motionless eyes fixed on the tip of his feet and not perceiving their particular objects through their vacant staring, is supporting by his hand his moon-like face, bent down, as it were, under the weight of his arduous undertakings.

(*Approaching*). Victory to the Prince!

MAL.—Minister, I bow to you. Please take this seat.

RA'K.—(*Does so*).

MAH.—Minister, we felt uneasy since we did not see you so long (to-day).

RA'K.—Prince, I had to arrange the march, so I came to have this taunt from you.

MAL.—Minister, I want to know what arrangements you have made with regard to the march.

RA'K.—Prince, the allied kings who have to follow you, have been thus ordered :—(*He Repeats* "Let the troops" &c.)

MAL.—(*Aside*). What! The very kings surround me who are endeavouring to please Chandragupta by ruining me! (*Aloud*). Minister, is there any one who goes to or comes from Kusumapura?

RA'K.—The purpose of going there and coming back is at an end. We ourselves shall go there in a few days.

MAL.—(*Aside*). I understand it. (*Aloud*). If so, why did you send this man with a letter?

RA'K.—(*Looking at him*). Ah! Siddhârthaka! Friend, what is this?

SID.—(*With tears, and gesticulating shame*). Excuse, Minister. Being beaten I could not keep the secret.

RA'K.—Frind, I don't understand what secret you mean.

SID.—Do not I say that being beaten I—(*He breaks off in fear and casts down his head*).

MAL.—Bhâgurâyaṇa, he will not tell it before his master, either through fear or shame. You yourself tell it to the Minister.

BHA'G.—As the Prince commands. Minister, he says that you sent him to Chandragupta with a letter and an oral message.

RA'K.—Friend, Siddhârthaka, is this true?

SID.—(*Gesticulating shame*). When soundly beaten, I said so.

RA'K.—It is untrue. What will not man say when beaten?

MAL.—Friend Bhâgurâyaṇa, show him the letter. The verbal message the servant will tell.

BHA'G.—Minister, here is the letter.

RA'K.—(*Having read it*). Prince, this is the work of the enemy.

MAL.—You also sent this ornament as a present accompanying the letter. How can it then be the work of the enemy?

RA'K.—(*Closely looking at the ornament*). This was sent to me by you. I too made a present of it to Siddhârthaka on some occasion of joy.

BHA'G.—Is such a costly ornament, especially one sent as a favour by the Prince from his bodily attire, to be given away to such a person?

MAL.—You also write that Siddhârthaka will communicate the verbal message.

RA'K.—What message can there be, and to whom? The letter itself is not mine (from me).

MAL.—Then whose seal is this?

RA'K.—Rogues can manufacture a counterfeit seal.

BHA'G.—Prince, the Minister speaks truly. Friend Siddhârthaka, who wrote this letter?

SID.—(*Looks at* RA'K. *and keeps silent with his face hung down*).

BHA'G.—Friend, do not provoke a second beating. Tell it

SID.—By S'akaṭadâsa, sir.

RAK.—If S'akaṭadâsa wrote it, then it is as good as written by me.

MAL.—Vijayâ, I want to see S'akaṭadâsa.

BHA'G.—(*Aside*). The emissaries of His Honour Châṇakya will not say anything that has not been well ascertained. But S'akaṭadâsa, if he comes here, may recognize the document as the same that he was made to write once and may disclose all that passed between him and Siddhârthaka. In that case Malayaketu will be distrustful and the plan will fail. (*Aloud*). Prince, perhaps S'akaṭadâsa will not admit in the presence of his master that he wrote the letter. Let us therefore get another writing of his. The similarity of letters will at once decide the matter.

MAL.—Vijayâ, do so.

BHA'G.—Prince, let her get the seal-ring also.

MAL.—Get both.

FR. D.-K.—As the Prince commands. (*Exit and re-enter*). Here is a letter written by S'akaṭadâsa, and the ring.

MAL.—(*Looks at both*). Minister, do the characters agree ?

RA'K.—(*Aside*). The letters agree ; but S'akaṭadâsa is my friend ; so they cannot agree. May it be that S'akaṭadâsa—

Forgetting his loyalty, and coveting transitory wealth and not imperishable fame, should have thought only of his wife and children ? (14)

But what doubt is there ?

The ring is ever on his finger and Siddhârthaka is his friend ; the letter, the basis of the plot, is proved to be his, by the other writing ; evidently S'akaṭa wishing to save his life has turned his back on loyalty and stooped to this mean act, having entered into an alliance with the foes who are skilled in causing dissension. (15)

MAL.—(*Looking at* RA'K). Minister, you say in your letter that you duly received the three ornaments sent by His Majesty. Is this (one that you wear) one of them ? (*Looking at it more carefully, to himself*). This is the very ornament that my father wore. (*Aloud*). Minister, where did you get these ornaments from ?

RA'K.—From merchants, by purchase.

MAL.—Vijayâ, do you recognize this decoration ?

VIJA.—(*Marking closely, with tears*). Prince, how can I not recognize it ? It was worn by Parvateśvara, of blessed name.

MAL.—(*Tearfully*). Alas ! Father !

The ornament of the race ! These are the ornaments, worthy of your person who loved ornaments, by which you, with your moon-like face shining, were graced like an autumnal evening with the moon and the stars. (16)

RA'K.—(*To himself*). What ? These were worn by Parvateśvara, he says. Evidently they must be his, sold to us by some merchants set on by Châṇakya.

MAL.—Minister, how can it be possible that these ornaments which were worn by my father, and especially, which were in the possession of Chandragupta, could be got by purchase. Or, this is quite possible. For,

You, a cruel man, have fixed us as the price to be paid for these to Chandragupta who sells them in the hope of making a more valuable acquisition (in return). (17)

RA'K.—(*To himself*). Oh, the snares were skilfully laid by the foe (lit. the enemy's plan turns out to be cleverly arranged). For,

To say that the document is not mine is not a proper reply, since it bears my seal. And how can it be believed that S'akaṭadâsa broke the ties of friendship? Again who will possibly expect King Maurya to sell the ornaments? A fair admission, therefore, is better in this case than a churlish reply. (18)

MA'L.—I ask Your Honour this—

RA'K.—(*With tears*). Prince, ask him who is a man of honour. I am no longer a man of honour.

MAL.—That Maurya is the son of your master (one to be served), while I am the son of our friend, intent upon serving you. He, well served (lit. obeyed), is the giver of wealth to you according to his pleasure, while you, whom I obey, give it to me, according to your pleasure. There you have, indeed, the post of a minister which is but honourable servitude, while here you are the master. What greater interest could there be, the desire for which makes you act in a dishonourable way? (19)

RA'K.—Prince, in uttering these unworthy things, you have yourself given the decisive answer. Well, it is not your fault. (*He repeats the verse* " That Maurya" &c. *substituting the second personal pronoun for the first, and vice versa*).

MAL.—(*Pointing to the letter and the box containing the ornaments*). And what is this here ?

RA'K.—(*Tearfully*). The wanton play of my fate. For,

It is the grand work of that Fate, the frustrator of men's exertions, which, the accursed one, destroyed those kings who were the proper judges of (the characters of) men, and who, masters as they were, being grateful and of refined intellect, did not, out of affection, regard me as different from a son although there was the relation of servitude, which is subject to humiliation. (20)

MAL.—(*Angrily*). You still deny it, calling it the sport

of Fate and not of your greed! You, unworthy of the name of Ârya,

Having employed the maid, dangerous by the use of virulent poison absorbed by her, you, O ungrateful one, formerly consigned my father, trustingly following you, to the domain of history. And now coveting (lit. attaching a high value to) the post of (the enemy's) minister, you have commenced, in order to work my destruction, to sell me off to the enemy like meat. (21)

RA'K.—(*Aside*). This is a pimple on a boil. (*Stopping his ears*). (*Aloud*). God forbid, God forbid! I never set the poison-maid against Parvates'vara.

MAL.—Who then killed my father?

RA'K.—Ask Destiny.

MAL.—(*Angrily*). I should ask Destiny, and not Kshapaṇaka Jîvasiddhi?

RA'K.—(*Aside*). What? Jîvasiddhi too a spy of Châṇakya! Alas! The enemies have captured my very heart.

MAL.—(*In a rage*). Bhâsuraka, give my order to S'ekharasena thus :—The five princes, Chitravarman of Kulûta, Simhanâda, King of Malaya, Pushkarâksha, the Kâshmira King, Sushena, King of Sindhu, and Meghanâda of Persia, having formed a close friendship with Râkshasa wish to gain Chandragupta's favour by designing against our person. Of these the first three covet my territory; they should be taken to a deep pit and buried with earth; the other two who wish to have elephants should be killed by means of an elephant.

MAN.—As Your Highness commands. [*Exit*

MAL.—(*In anger*). Râkshasa, Râkshasa, I am not Râkshasa, a treacherous murderer. I am, indeed, Malayaketu. Go, therefore, and serve Chandragupta with all your heart. See, I am able to uproot Vishṇugupta and Maurya though advancing in combination with you, as improper conduct does the three objects of life. (22)

BHA'G.—Prince, we must no longer delay. Let our forces be now ordered to lay siege to Kusumapura.

Let the columns of dust risen from the tread of the hoofof horses in the army, and having their roots severed by the rut-water of the elephants, fall on the heads of the enemies, imparting a smoky hue to the cheeks of the Gauḍî women richly perfumed with the pollen of *Lodhra* flowers, and obscuring the black colour of their curly hair resembling a swarm of black bees. (23) [*Exit* MALAYAKETU *and suite*

RA'K.—(*With anguish*). Oh, fie! What a misfortune! Poor Chitravarman and the others too are slain! How is it that Râkshasa is working for the destruction of his friends and not of his enemies? What can I do now, an unlucky man!

Shall I go to a penance-grove? There my revengeful mind will feel no relief. Shall I follow my master (in death)? That is a course fit for women, so long as my foe is alive. Or shall I, having the sword for my companion, fall on the forces of the enemy? No. This step too is not proper. My heart which is anxious to bring about the release of Chandanadâsa would not allow me to do that; else it would be ungrateful. (24) [*Exeunt Omnes*

END OF ACT V.

ACT VI.

(*Enter* SIDDHA'RTHAKA *decorated and in high spirits*).

SID.—Glory to the cloud-coloured Kes'ava, the slayer of Kes'in! Glory to Chandragupta, the Moon to the eyes of the people and glory to the Diplomacy of the venerable Châṇakya which has destroyed the party of the enemy, having accomplished all that may be gained by means of an army (lit. the instrument of victory)! (1)

I will now see my dear friend Samiddhârthaka after a long time. (*Walks round and looks forward*). Here comes my dear friend, Samiddhârthaka. I will in the meanwhile approach him.

(*Enter* SAMIDDHA'RTHAKA).

SAMI.—Riches give pain when there is separation from

friends, who are like the moon in times of affliction, who give delight on occasions of household festivals, and who are (ever) present in the heart. (2)

I hear that my dear friend Siddhârthaka has arrived from Malayaketu's camp. I will then find him out. (*He walks forth and looks forward*). Oh, here is Siddhârthaka.

SID.—(*Approaching*). Holla, Siddhârthaka, how do you do, dear friend? (*They embrace each other*).

SAMID.—Friend how can I be happy, when you did not come to my house to-day, though you have returned from your long journey?

SID.—Excuse me, friend. The moment the venerable Châṇakya saw me, he ordered me to communicate the happy tidings to His Majesty the moon-like Chandragupta. Then having communicated the news to him and received this royal favour, I am just on my way to your house to see you, my dear friend.

SAMID.—Friend, if I may hear it, then tell me what the agreeable news is, that you communicated to the worthy Chandragupta of lovely appearance.

SID.—Friend is there anything that I should withhold from you? Listen then. First the cursed Malayaketu, whose mind's eye was bedimmed by the policy of Châṇakya, discarded Râkshasa, and killed five of the principal kings, Chitravarman and others. Then thinking that he was rash and wicked, the allied kings left the camp of Malayaketu for safety and set out in fear for their respective dominions followed by their remaining soldiers and attendants trembling with fear, while all his vassals became sick at heart. Whereupon Bhadrabhaṭa Purushadatta, Dingarâta, Balagupta, Râjasena, Bhâgurâyaṇa, Rohitâksha, Vijayavarman and others seized Malayaketu and made him captive.

SAMID.—Friend, it was talked of among the people, that Bhadrabhaṭa and others, being discontentd with king Chandragupta, had joined the side of Malayaketu. Why is there then one thing in the laying out, and another in the consummation of the plot, as in the play of a bad poet?

SID.—Bow to the state-craft of the venerable Châṇakya, the course of which is inscrutable like that of Destiny.

SAMID.—What next?

SID.—Thereupon the revered Châṇakya marched out from here with a large picked force and encountered the entire army of the Mlechchhas deserted by the chieftains.

SAMID.—Friend, where did he attack them?

SID.—There,

Where the elephants, resembling (imitating) the action of clouds charged with water, are roaring in their excessive pride of rut, and where the horses, bouncing about with a start (resembling waves) from fear of the stroke of the whip and catching the sounds of victory rush forth together. (3)

SAMID.—Friend, let all this aside. How did the venerable Châṇakya having in that manner resigned his post of authority in the presence of all men, accept again the very post of minister?

SID.—You appear to be extremely simple-minded since you wish to fathom the deeds of His Honour Châṇakya, not fathomed before even by the minister Râkshasa.

SAMID.—Friend, where is the minister, Râkshasa now?

SID.—It has been reported to His Honour Châṇakya that as the frightful tumult (of war) thickened, he issued from the camp of Malayaketu and came here to Pâṭaliputra, his steps being dogged by a spy named Udumbara.

SAMID.—Friend, has the minister Râkshasa after all come back to this Pâṭaliputra, with his object unaccomplished, having left it in that manner, resolved to restore the sovereignty of Nanda?

SID.—He came here, I think, out of his affection for Chandanadâsa.

SAMID.—I fancy Chandanadâsa will be set free.

SID.—Whence can the unfortunate man obtain his release? By the order of His Honour Châṇakya we two have ourselves to take him just now to the place of execution and to kill him.

SAMID.—(*Angrily*). Does His Honour Châṇakya find no other hangmen that he appoints us to such exceedingly cruel tasks?

SID.—Who, in this world of mortals, that desires to live, can oppose the order of His Honour Châṇakya? Come, let us dress ourselves as Chaṇḍâlas and take Chandanandâsa to the place of execution. [*Exeunt* BOTH

END OF THE PRAVES'AKA.

(*Enter a* MAN, *rope in hand*).

MAN—

Glory to the rope of Châṇakya's policy, which is strong by the combination of six *guṇas* (strings-expendients), the noose of which is formed with (of) a series of efforts (political tactics or stratagems) and which is ready to capture the enemy ! (4)

(*He walks forth and looks about*). This is the region mentioned to His Honour Châṇakya by Udumbara, where I have to see Râkshasa by the order of His Honour Châṇakya. (*Looking about*). Ah, the minister Râkshasa is coming in this very direction, with his head veiled. Hidden by the trees of the old garden I will just see where he takes his seat. (*He walks forth and waits*).

(*Enter* RA'KSHASA, *armed with a sword, as already described*).

RA'K.—(*Shedding tears*). Alas ! alas !

Like a harlot, Royalty has gone to another house being alarmed as it were at the loss of her support; the subjects forsaking their love (loyalty) have gone just after her, being blind followers; even our trusty friends, not having obtained the reward for their manly efforts, have given up the arduous task (they had undertaken); but what could they do? They have to live like bodies without heads. (5)

Moreover,

The goddess of Sovereignty having abandoned the King, her husband, the lord of the world and of illustrious descent, has, by taking advantage of a weak point, gone to Vṛshala like an immodest wench, and has settled firmly with him. What can we do in the matter since fate, like an enemy, thwarts our efforts, howsoever persistent ? (6)

For I,

When His Majesty had gone to heaven, not at all deserving the kind of fate he met with, made a vigorous effort, having placed Parvateśvara at the head of affairs and after he was killed, his son, but attained no success. Fate, therefore, is the enemy of the house of Nanda, and not that Brâhmaṇa. (7)

Oh the want of judgment betrayed by the Mlechchha!

How can that Râkshasa who still serves his masters even when they are destroyed to the very seed, enter, as long as he is sound in body, into an alliance with the foes? Of this much even, the Mlechchha, his mind being devoid of discrimination, did not think. Or why, the reason of those doomed by destiny, becomes entirely vitiated. (8)

Even now Râkshasa will rather die, falling into the hands of the enemy, than treat with Chandragupta; or I would prefer the disgrace of being false to my word to that of being duped by adversary. (*Looking about, with tears*). These are the border grounds of Kusumapura the surface of which is rendered holy by the frequent treadings of the feet of His Majesty. For, in this place,

His Majesty loosening his grasp of the bridle cast down in drawing his bow, discharged in a wonderful way his arrows at moving marks while his horse galloped at full speed. In this grove of trees the King sat; here he talked with his feudatories; the sight of these grounds of Kusumapura, now bereaved of them, causes very great pain. (9)

Whither can I go then, an ill-starred man? (*Looking about*). Ah, here is the old garden. I will enter it and obtain some tidings about Chandanadâsa from some one. Oh, the favourable and unfavourable turns of life fall to the lot of men without their being foreseen! For,

I, who formerly walked forth with gentle steps from the town like a king surrounded by thousands of feudatory princes, the citizens pointing at me with their fingers as at the new moon, I, the very same person, am now entering with hasty steps the old garden of the very town, in fear, like a thief, all my efforts having become fruitless. (10)

But why, *they* themselves are no more, to whose favour all this was due. (*Entering and looking about*). Oh the sad appearance of the old garden! For here,

The mansion, a grand work of masonry, is in ruins (dilapidated) like a family that once performed mighty deeds; the lake is dried up like the heart of a good man by the destruction of his friends; the trees bear no fruits like political schemes formed under adverse destiny; and the ground is covered with grass like the mind of a foolish man with bad counsels. (11)

Moreover,

The serpents hissing (heaving sighs) are through pity excited by the sufferings of their acquaintances, bandaging, as it were, with the pieces of their sloughs, the wounds of the branches of the trees which are uttering cries of pain in the form of the cooings of the pigeons, being hewn with huge and sharp-edged axes. (12)

Again, these unfortunate

Trees, clearly disclosing the drying up within (their trunks), bearing the holes bored in them by worms like very heavy (corroding) grief, gloomy-looking from want of shade and plunged into misery, are, as it were, proceeding to the cemetery. (13)

In the meanwhile I will sit on this broken stone-slab, easy to be obtained in the adverse condition of life. (*He sits down and hears*). Ah, whence is this sudden sound of rejoicing mixed with the sound of drums and conches?

This tumult of rejoicing blended with the sound of deep-sounding drums and conches, which on account of its heavy swell overpowers (stuns) the narrow cavity of the ear of the hearers, and which on account of its magnitude is drunk in and then vomited forth as it were by the mansions, spreads as if curious to measure the expanse of the quarters. (14)

(*Musing*). Ah, I have it. This sound arising from the capture of Malayaketu indicates the increased joy in the royal place–(*Breaking off through jealousy*) in the palace of Maurya. (*Weeping*). Alas! alas!

I have been made the hearer of the prosperity of my foe; I have been made to see it after being brought here; and I think the effort of Fate is now to make me feel it! (15)

MAN—He has sat down. I shall now execute the command of His Honour Châṇakya. (*He throws the noose of the rope round his neck in front of* RA'K. *feigning not to have noticed him*).

RA'K.—(*Looking at him*). Oh, the man is hanging himself up. The poor fellow must be as miserable as myself! Well, I will ask him. (*Approaching him*). Good man, what are you doing?

MAN—(*Weeping*). Sir, the same that an unlucky man like myself does, when grieved at the loss of his dear friend.

RA'K.—(*To himself*). I already knew that the fellow was miserable like myself. (*Aloud*). O my companion in misery, if it is not a secret, nor very painful, I wish to hear your account.

MAN—Sir, it is neither secret nor very painful; but with my heart afflicted with the loss of a dear friend, I cannot afford to brook even so much delay in death.

RA'K.—(*Breathing a sigh to himself*). Woe to me! Here I am put to shame by this man since I am apathetic like a stranger in the calamity of my friend (*Aloud*). Friend, if it is neither secret nor painful then I wish to hear it.

MAN—Oh, Your Honour is very pressing. What help! I will tell it. There is in this town a jewel-merchant named Vishṇudâsa.

RA'K.—(*To himself*). There is, Vishṇudâsa a great friend of Chandanadâsa. (*Aloud*). What of him?

MAN—That dear friend of mine—

RA'K.—(*With joy, to himself*). Ah, his dear friend, he says That is a very close connection. I am glad he may be knowing Chandanadâsa's account.

MAN—Having given away the ornaments and all other property to poor men, has now gone out of the city with the desire of throwing himself into the fire. I too came to this old garden in order to hang myself up before I should hear of his sad end.

RA'K.—Friend, what is the cause of your friend's entering fire?

Is he attacked by serious diseases that baffle the power of medicine?

MAN—No, no.

RA'K.—Is he smitten with royal displeasure little short (in its dire effects) of fire or poison?

MAN—God forbid, sir, God forbid. No acts of cruelty are committed in the kingdom of Chandragupta.

RA'K.—Did he love some woman that was out of his reach?

MAN—(*Stopping his ears*). Heaven forbid! He is not the man to commit such an act of immodesty.

RA'K.—Did he suffer, like you, from the inevitable loss of a friend? (16)

MAN—So, it is, sir.

RA'K.—(*With anguish, to himself*). On hearing that he is the friend of Chandanadâsa, and that the ruin of a beloved friend is the cause of his entering fire, my heart does but rightly tremble within me through the just feeling of affection. (*Aloud*). I long to hear in detail the account of his friend's destruction and also the noble life of one who is prepared to die out of his affection for his friend.

MAN—Unlucky that I am, I can cause no further delay to my death.

RA'K.—Friend, tell me a tale that is so worth hearing.

MAN—What course? What can I do? I will tell you; listen.

RA'K.—Friend, I am all attention.

MAN—There is a jewel-merchant in this town, by name Chandanadâsa.

RA'K.—(*In alaram, to himself*). Here Fate has opened the door for initiating me into the study of grief. Be firm, my heart, thou hast to hear something very painful. (*Aloud*). Yes, friend, he is known to be a good man and a loving friend. What of him?

MAN—He is the beloved friend of that Vishṇudâsa.

RA'K.—(*Aside*). Now the thunderbolt of grief is about to fall on my heart.

MAN—Then, Vishṇudâsa to-day made a request to Chandragupta, in a manner befitting his affection for his friend.

RA'K.—What request, pray?

MAN—This. He said—"My lord, there is in my house wealth sufficient for the maintenance of a family. Your Majesty should take that in exchange and set my friend, Chandanadâsa, at liberty."

RA'K.—(*To himself*). Bravo, Vishṇudâsa, bravo! You have proved your love for a friend. For,

You are at once resolved to cast off as an evil, in spite of your being a merchant, that wealth for which sons try to kill their parents and parents their sons as if they were enemies, and for which friends relinquish their affection for friends. That wealth, therefore, of you, a merchant, has accomplished its end. (17)

(*Aloud*). Friend, what did Maurya say in reply when thus addressed?

MAN—Sir, thus addressed, Chandragupta replied to the merchant Vishṇudâsa—"I have imprisoned Chandanandâsa not for the sake of money; but because he had concealed the wife of minister Râkshasa, and he did not deliver her up although repeatedly asked to do so. If, therefore, he would deliver her, he might obtain his release; otherwise he would be capitally punished." Having said so, he ordered Chandanandâsa to be taken to the place of execution. Thereupon the merchant Vishṇudâsa left the town intending to enter fire before he heard of the sad end of his friend, Chandanadâsa. I too, came to this old garden in order to hang myself up to death before the melancholy news about Vishṇudâsa reaches my ears.

RA'K.—Friend, I hope Chandanadâsa is not yet put to death.

MAN—He will be executed to-day. He is now repeatedly requested to give up minister Râkshasa's family; he does not deliver it out of his affection for his friend. For this reason I would no longer delay my death.

RA'K.—(*Joyfully, to himself*). Bravo, Chandanadâsa, bravo!

Noble man, you are acquiring a fame like that of S'ibi arising from the protection of those who came to you for protection even in the absence of your friend. (18)

(*Aloud*). Friend, go, go quickly to Vishṇudâsa and prevent him for entering the fire. I, on my part, will rescue Chandanadâsa from death.

MAN—By what means will Your Honour release Chandanadâsa from death?

RA'K.—(*Drawing his sword*). By means of this sword, my companion in any undertaking. Lo,

This my sword, which, dark-blue in appearance like a water-charged-cloud and the sky, appears to be thrilling with eagerness for fight, being grasped in the hand, and the strength of which, in consequence of its high temper has been seen by my enemies tested on the touch-stone of battle, now prompts me, who am overpowered by (have lost control over myself on account of) my affection for my friend, to some act of daring. (19)

MAN—Sir, when you thus betray yourself by offering your life for the merchant Chandanadâsa, but are fallen into an adverse condition of life, I am not able to know you definitely and to recognize in you Minister Râkshasa of blessed name, whose feet I have thus the good luck to see to-day. (*He falls at his feet*). Do you favour me then by clearing my doubt.

RA'K.—I am that man who witnessed the destruction of the race of his masters, who is the cause of his friends' misery, a vallain, of accursed name, and a Râkshasa in the real sense of the term.

MAN—(*Again joyfully falls at his feet*). Oh wonder! I am glad I have seen you.

RA'K.—Arise, arise good friend; no further delay now. Tell Vishṇudâsa that Râkshasa is just going to deliver Chandanadâsa from death. (*He repeats* 'This my sword," &c. *and walks about with the drawn sword in his hand*).

MAN—(*Falling at his feet*). Excuse me, revered Minister. As you know, S'akaṭadâsa was first ordered by the cursed Chandragupta to be taken to the place of execution. From that place he was borne away by some one and taken to some other country. Then the cursed Chandragupta, angry that such a piece of carelessness should have been committed, quenched the blazing fire of his anger against His Honour S'akaṭadâsa with the blood of the executioners. Since that time, whenever the executioners see a stranger armed with a weapon either behind them or in the front, they are on their guard, and wishing to save their own lives, kill the victim on the spot of execution. If Your Honour, therefore, goes there thus armed, the death of Chandanadâsa will only be expedited. [*Exit*

RA'K.—Oh, how inscrutable is the course of the cursed Châṇakya's policy! For,

If S'akaṭadâsa was brought to me with the consent of the enemy then why were the executioners (lit. persons appointed to kill criminals) put to death by him in anger? If he was not, then how could he even think of such a sinful fabrication? Thus my mind being mounted on conjectures arrives at no define conclusion. (20)

(*Reflecting*).

This is not the time for the sword, since the hangmen would put (my friend) to death before (I could rescue) him. Policy bears fruit after an interval of time; what is the use of it in this case? Indifference is not proper, when my dear friend has met with an extremely dreadful calamity on my account. I know now how to act—I will offer this my body as a ransom for him. (21) [*Exeunt Omnes.*

END OF ACT VI.

ACT VII.

(*Enter a* CHANDA'LA).

CHANDA'.—Move away, respectable sirs, move away; be off, ye men, be off.

If you wish to save your life, property, family and wife, then keep very far off from treason to the King which is so dreadful. (1)

Moreover,

If a man has recourse to something unwholesome, he alone is affected by a disease or dies; whereas if he takes to felony against a king, the whole family perishes. (2).

If you don't believe me then see here the merchant Chandanadâsa who is being led to the place of execution with wife and son for acting treacherously towards the King. (*Looking towards the sky*). What do you say, ye respectable citizens? Do you ask me whether there is any means of setting him at liberty or not? There is, sirs, if he delivers up the family of the minister Râkshasa.

(*Again looking into the sky*). What do you say? That he, who is kind to those who seek his protection, will never do a wicked deed like this merely for the sake of his life. Then wish him, ye respectable men, a blissful passage; but no more think of a means of rescue in this case.

(*Then enter* CHANDANADA'SA *in a criminal's dress, followed by a second* CHA'NDA'LA, *with a pale on his shoulder and accompanied by his* WIFE *and* SON).

CHAND.—(*Weeping*). Alas! alas! Bow to the god of Death, that people like us who are afraid of deviation from the path of duty should die the death of a bandit! Or why? Cruel men make no distinction between those who are indifferent or wise. For,

What obstinate desire it is of hunters to kill an innocent deer that leaves flesh and lives on grass through the fear of death? (3)

(*Looking about*). Oh dear friend Vishṇudâsa, how is it that you do not even give me any response. Or rather, rare indeed are those men who will even (care to) stand within the range of sight at such an hour. (*Tearfully*). Those dear friends who are returning with their bodies with great difficulty, having resorted to shedding tears only as the means of averting (my misfortune), are with their faces sad with grief, following me with eyes heavy through rising grief.

CHANDA'.—Revered Chandanadâsa, you have arrived at the place of execution. Dismiss, therefore, your people.

CHAND.—Dear wife, return now with your son. It is not proper to follow me further.

WIFE—(*Weeping*). You leave, my dear, for the next world, not for a distant country.

CHAND.—Dear wife, I die for a friend's sake, and not for a personal crime. Grieve not, therefore.

WIFE—My dear, if that be the case then it is not proper for persons of a respectable family to return.

CHAND.—What has my lady now resolved to do?

WIFE—To bless myself by following my lord's feet (in death).

CHAND.—That is an ill-conceived idea, dear. You should take care of this our son who is young and who has got no experience of wordly affairs.

WIFE—May the deities, taking pity, bless him. Child, my boy, fall at the feet of your father which you see for the last time.

SON—(*Falling at his father's feet*). Papa, what shall I do, bereaved of you?

CHAND.—Child, live in a country where Châṇakya will not be found.

CHANDA'.—Revered Chandanadâsa, the pale has been implanted; be you, therefore, ready.

WIFE—Help, Oh, sirs, help.

CHAND.—Wife, why do you cry now. The gods take compassion on the afflicted families of those who go to heaven. (Besides I suffer death for a friend and not for doing anything wrong. Why do you weep then when you ought to rejoice) ?

FIRST CHANDA'.—O Bilavpatra, seize Chandanadâsa; his family then will go of itself.

SEC. CHANDA'.—O Vajraloman, here I seize him.

CHAND.—Friend, wait for a while, so that I will embrace my son. (*Having embraced and smelt his* SON *on the head*). Child, when death is sure to befall a man, die in doing a service to a friend.

BOY—Need this be said, father? This is our family-rule. (*Falls at his feet*).

CHANDA'.—O, seize him. (The CHANDALAS *seize* CHANDA-NADA'SA).

WIFE—(*Beating her breast*). Save him, O sirs, save him.

Enter RA'KSHASA *with a hurried toss of the curtain*).

RA'K.—Fear not, lady, fear not. Ye hangmen, kill not Chandanadâsa,

Let this execution-garland, the road leading to the world of death, be hung upon me, who formerly witnessed the family of my master suffering destruction before me (*i. e.* in my very presence) as if it were an enemy's family, who remained at ease when my friends were smitten with calamity as if it was an occasion of great festivity, and who loves his soul, though made the object of ignominy, for the destruction of people like you (as on a former occasion). (4)

CHAND.—(*Looking at him with tearful eyes*). Minister, what is this?

RA'K.—Merely an imitation of a portion of your noble conduct.

CHAND.—Minster, what is this that you have done by rendering vain all this my effort?

RA'K.—Friend, I have only attended to my own interest. Do not blame me. (*To one of the* CHA'NDA'LAS). Friend, tell the wicked Châṇakya—

VAJRA.—What is it?

RA'K.—Here am I, the man for whose sake this person, though worthy of veneration, has incurred the penalty of death at your hands, he who, the glorious one, saving another at the cost of his own life in these evil times of the Kali Age in which tastes of the people are wicked, has rendered insignificant even the glory of S'ibi, and who being pure in soul, has by his virtuous conduct eclipsed the course of conduct of the Buddhistic saints. (5)

FIR. CHANDA'.—O Bilvapatra, you take Chandanadâsa in your charge and wait for a while in the shade of this cemetery-tree, while I report to Châṇakya that Ministr Râkshasa is caught.

SEC. CHANDA'.—O Vajraloman, let it be so. [*Exit* F. C. *with* CHANDANADA'SA *followed by his* WIFE *and* SON].

FIR. CHANDA'.—Come Minister. (*They walk on*). Holla, is there any one here? Inform the noble CHâṇakya, the thunderbolt to the mountain of the race of Nanda and the founder of the house of Maurya—

RA'K.—(*To himself*). Oh pity! Even this I must hear!

CHANDA'.—That Minister Râkshasa whose intellect and prowess have been thwarted by His Honour's state-craft is in our hands.

(*Enter* CHA'NAKYA, *his face only visible, the rest of his body covered with a veil*).

CHA'N.—Say, friend say,

Who bound with the skirt of his garment the fire red with the mass of its mighty flames? Who reduced the ever-moving (wind) to a state of stillness with his snares? Who crossed by means of his arms the dreadful ocean, abounding in crocodiles and alligators? (6)

CHANDA'.—Surely by Your Honour whose intellect is adept in state-craft.

CHA'N.—No, no, say not so. Say—by Fate, the inveterate foe of the house of Nanda.

RA'K.—(*Aside*). This is the mean-minded—or rather noble-minded—Kauṭilya.

The mine of all *S'âstras*, as the ocean is of jewels, with whose merits we are not sufficiently pleased, although jealous. (7)

CHA'N.—(*Looking at* RA'K., *joyfully to himself*). Ah, here is the minister Râkshasa, by whom, the great-minded one, the army of Vṛshala and my own intelligence were seriously taxed for a long time with the heavy troubles of preparations, and of the devising of plans, which were the cause of protracted wakefulness. (8)

(*Removing the veil and approaching*).

Oh minister Râkshasa, I, Vishṇugupta, salute you.

RA'K.—(*Aside*). 'Minister' is a humiliating epithet now. (*Aloud*). Vishṇugupta, please do not touch me, polluted by the touch of a Chaṇḍâla.

CHA'N.—O minister Râkshasa, these are not Châṇḍâlas. This one is a royal official named Siddhârthaka whom you have already seen. This other here too is a servant of the King, Samiddhârthaka by name. Poor S'akaṭadâsa, also, was made to write that forged letter by me, he knowing nothing (about its nature).

RA'K.—(*Aside*). I am glad my suspicion about S'akaṭadâsa is removed.

CHA'N.—Why waste more words? I tell you briefly—

Those (your) servants, Bhadrabhaṭa and others, the letter written in that way, that Siddhârthaka, those three sets of decoration, that your friend Bhadanta, the man under affliction you saw in the old garden, and the trouble of the merchant, all these—(*Breaking off through modesty*).—Oh valiant one, were devices of mine through my desire for Vṛshala's union with you. (9)

Here is Vṛshala, therefore, wishing to see you. Please see him.

RA'K.—(*Aside*). What help? I will see him.

(*Enter the* KING *followed by his* SUITE *according to rank*).

KING—(*Aside*). I am indeed ashamed that His Honour has conquered, without a fight, the invincible army of the enemy. For,

My arrows have perpetually to observe the vow of lying down in their own quiver, with their heads hung down, as if through grief for their condition and put to shame (as it were) by their not being used although furnished with sharp-edged points. (10)

Or rather,

One in whose interest, as in mine, his preceptors are wide-awake and attend to all the affairs of his kingdom, though he himself be sleeping, is able even with his bow unstrung, to vanquish, on earth, whatever is desired to be conquered. (11)

(*Approaching* CHA'NAKYA). Venerable sir, Chandragupta bows to you.

CHA'N.—Vṛshala, all your desire have been accomplished. Here we have the minister Râkshasa. Salute, therefore, His Honour, your prime-minister.

RA'K.—(*Aside*). He has established the relationship.

KING—(*Approaching* RA'KSHASA). Sir, Chandragupta bows to you.

RA'K.—(*Looking at him, to himself*). Ah, Chandragupta! He—

Who when yet a boy gave distinct promise of his future exaltation, and who has gradually obtained sovereignty like an elephant obtaining mastery over a herd of elephants. (12)

(*Aloud*). Victory to you, King.

KING—Sir,

Just think—What have I not conquered in the world, when His Honour and Your Honour are, as *gurus*, wide-awake in the proper use of the six expedients? (13)

RA'K.—(*Aside*). Ah, the disciple of Kauṭilya refers to me as a servant! Or rather, this is, indeed, but the humility of

Chandragupta, and it is only jealousy that makes me think otherwise. All things considered, it is but proper that Châṇakya has become victorious. For,

A minister, dull-minded though he be, is sure to rise to an exalted position when he has to serve a proper person (*i. e.* King) who is ambitious, whereas a minister though of unerring policy, falls in the manner of a tree on the bank of a river, when he has to deal with an unworthy master. (14)

CHA'N.—Minister Râkshasa, do you wish that Chandanadâsa should live?

RA'K.—Vishṇugupta, what doubt can there be (about it)?

CHA'N.—Minister Râkshasa, I have some doubt because you are favouring Chandragupta without accepting the sword (the badge of ministerial office). If then you really wish to save Chandanadâsa's life, accept this weapon.

RA'K.—No, Vishṇugupta; not so. I am unworthy to receive the weapon, especially when it was wielded by you.

CHA'N.—Minister Râkshasa, how can it be that I am fit to wield it and you are not. Just see—

Those horses which being continually bridled and saddled have become emaciated, and also look at the elephants which have their spines swollen on account of being kept in continual readiness, and which have been deprived of the pleasures of bathing, feeding, sporting, drinking and sleeping at will. (And all this) O talented one, is owing to the greatness of your prowess which subdues the pride of conceited foes. (15)

Or, to be brief, Chandanadâsa cannot live unless you accept the weapon.

RA'K.—(*Aside*).

The qualities of the kindness of the Nandas touch my heart, yet I am now a servant of their foes. Those trees which being watered by me had attained growth are cut off. So I must wield this weapon for saving the life of my friend. The courses of events do not submit (or, make me submit, नयन्ति) to fate even after a long time. (16)

(*Aloud*). Vishṇugupta, I bow to the affection for a friend which makes one undertake anything whatsoever. There is no alternative. I am willing.

CHA'N.—(*Joyfully giving him the sword*). Vṛshala, Vṛshala you are now favoured by the minister Râkshasa. I congratulate you on your good fortune.

KING—It is Your Honour's favour that Chandragputa is thus enjoying.

(*Enter a* MAN).

MAN—Victory to Your Honour. Here Malayaketu has been placed at the door, with his hands and feet chained, by Bhadrabhaṭa, Bhâgurâyaṇa and others. The future depends upon Your Honour's pleasure.

CHA'N.—Friend, communicate your message to Minister Râkshasa. He knows (what orders to pass) now.

RA'K.—(*Aside*). How no, having made me a slave Kauṭilya now makes me give the order! What help? (*Aloud*). King Chandragupta, you know that I was living with (*i. e.* in dependence upon) Malayaketu for some time. Let therefore his life spared.

KING—(*Looks at* CHA'NAKYA'S *face*).

CHA'N.—King, the first request of Minister Râkshasa must be granted. (*To the* MAN). Tell Bhadrabhaṭa and the others in my name, that King Chandragputa, at the request of Minister Râkshasa, grants Malayaketu his paternal king dom. They should, therefore, accompany him and come back after he is established on his throne.

MAN—As Your Honour commands. (*Going*).

CHA'N.—Stay, friend, stay. I have something more to say. Tell Vijayapâla, the Superintendent of the fort, that Chandragupta, highly pleased at the reconciliation of Râkshasa, orders that the merchant Chandanadâsa should be appointed to the post of the principal merchant in all cities of the world; and further, that all except the war horses and elephants should be set free. Or rather, with minister Râkshasa as the adviser (of the King) where is the need for horses and elephants even! So now,

Unloose every tie except that of (riding) horses and elephants; having fulfilled my solemn declaration, I will (now) tie up my hair only. (17)

MAN.—As Your Honour commands. [*Exit*

CHA'N.—O King Chandragupta, O Minister Râkshasa, tell me what further favour I may confer upon you.

KING—Is there anything dearer than this?

Râkshasa is won over; I have been placed on the throne, and all the Nandas are annihilated; what thing, more to be coveted than this, remains to be accomplished? (18)

RA'K.—Still let there be this word of Bharata—

May King Chandragupta with his prosperous connections and servants long protect the earth—he who is a kingly manifestation of that self-existent God, to whose tusk, when He had assumed the form of the Boar fitted to grant protection, the earth, of yore, clung, amidst universal destruction, and on whose arms she now leans, being frightened by the Mlechchhas. (19) [*Exeunt Omnes*

END OF ACT VII.

END OF THE DRAMA MUDRĀRĀKSHASA COMPOSED BY VISĀKHADATTA.

NOTES.

P. 7. मुद्राराक्षसम्—मुद्रया जितः राक्षसः मुद्राराक्षसः स एव अभेदोपचारात् (by transference of an epithet) तदाख्यं नाटकम् here neither छ (ईय) nor अण् can be affixed; nor can we explain the comp. as a Bah. comp. (मुद्रया जितो राक्षसः यस्मिन्); for in that case we shall have to take recourse to *Lakshaṇâ*, as it is not राक्षस that the work contains but an account of the way in which Râkshasa was won over to his side by Châṇakya; see Bhaṭṭoji on शारीरकं भाष्यं, Kau. on Pâṇ. IV. 3. 87.

धन्या—Pârvatî, who had believed herself to be the most fortunate lady having obtained a place in half the part of S'iva's body, now finds that there is another actually worshipped by her husband being allowed a seat on his head, and, therefore, calles her 'blessed'. The question may also imply taunt as suggested in the com. शशिकला—S'iva pretends to misunderstand the point of Pârvatî's question, and answers 'It is S'as'ikalâ' (also situated on his head). Pârvatî in her simplicity of mind asks किं नु &c. The equivoques and puns are fully explained in the com. नाम—in the second line of the stanza does not mean 'a proper name', but a term that signifies a particular thing (अभिधेयवाचकशब्द). कस्य हेतोः—by Pân. II. 3. 26. षष्ठी हेतुप्रयोगे and सर्वनाम्नस्तृतीया च (II. 3. 27)—when a pronoun and the word हेतु are both used and 'cause or reason' is to be expressed, the Gen. or the Instr. may be used; केन हेतुना कस्य हेतोर्वा वसति । नारीं पृच्छामि—त्वां is understood in the first case, प्रश्नं in the other. विजया—one of the two female friends of Pârvatî. In the Pârvatipariṇaya Nâṭaka (*cf.* also Kum. VIII. 49) she and जया are represented as P.'s attendant companions in her father's house before marriage.

शाठ्य—Does not mean 'fraud' but 'equivocation, skill in *Vakrokti*', being an abstract noun from शठ which has the same meaning as in शठनायक.

The fig. in the stanza according to the Com. is *Vakrokti* (equivoque), which consists in giving quite a different sense to the words of another by means of a pun or an affected change of tone. See K. P. IX. 1 (78). As pointed out by the Com., the equivocations of the stanza are intended to indicate the crooked policy which underlies the plot of the play. Gaṅgâ is the sovereignty of Chandragupta, Pârvatî of Nanda. *Indu* suggests Chandragupta.

P. 8. आविर्भवन्ती—Which would else have manifested itself. Present for immediate future; see com. रक्षतः--avoiding. स्वैरपातैः—if allowed to fall at *i. e.* heedlessly, at random; see com.; had he treaded at will the earth would have sunk down. We may, however, take स्वैरपातैः with रक्षतः स्वैर meaning 'gentle or slow', as better corresponding to the constructions in the 2nd and 3rd lines. मन्दः स्वच्छन्दयोः स्वैरः Amara. लक्ष्य—लक्ष्यत इति an object. त्रिपुर--त्रयाणां धातूनां पुराणि तानि. यद्वा त्र्यवयं पुरं त्रिपुरं (and not त्रयाणां पुराणां समाहारः as some explain it; for that will give त्रिपुरी) तद्विजयतीति. The reference is to the three cities of gold, silver and iron built in the sky, air and on earth by Maya, the architect of the demons which were destroyed by S'iva at the request of the gods. त्रिपुर also came to signify the demon who ruled over these three cities. दुःखनृत्तं—दुःखेन कृतं नृत्तं a Madh. comp. नृत्त is defined as 'नृत्तंताललयाश्रयं' *i. e.* a dance which consists of the mere movements of the body without gesticulation and which is regulated by the marking of the musical intervals or stops. The dance here alluded to is the Tândava dance of which S'iva is represented to be very fond.

This stanza, too, has a bearing on the plot of the play. It foreshadows the difficulties to be experienced by Châṇakya on account of his desire to spare the life and secure the services of Râkshasa, though able to kill him and Malayaketu; see com. There is in the first three lines the fig. *Atis'ayokti* or exaggeration, and *Parikara* or the fig. of the significant epithet in the fourth line.

P. 13. नान्दी—The benedictory stanzas, so called because the deities are supposed to be delighted by it. (नन्दन्ति देवता अत्र). Jagaddhara derives the word as आशीर्योगादिना नन्दयतीति नन्दः । पचाद्यच् । नन्द एव नान्दः । प्रज्ञादित्वादण् । and by adding ङीप् (ई) नान्दी. For the origin *cf.* नन्दी वृषं कोपि महेश्वरस्य रङ्गत्वमादौ किल खे जगाम । तद्रङ्गमुद्दिश्य कृतां तु पूजां नान्दीति तां नाट्यविदो वदन्ति ॥ The Nândî is of four kinds:—नमस्कृतिर्माङ्गलिकी आशीः पत्रावली तथा । नान्दी चतुर्धा निर्दिष्टा नाटकादिषु संमता ॥ The नान्दी here consists of 8 *padas* if *pada* be understood to mean 'a quarter of a stanza' and is of the पत्रावली type, since the plot is slightly hinted in it; see com. and Râghavabhaṭṭa on Nândî in S'âk.

नान्द्यन्ते सूत्रधारः—At the close of the Nândi, the Sûtradhâra. This seems somewhat puzzling. What is the predicate to be supplied? If we supply पठति then two questions would naturally present themselves—who repeats the Nândî? and when does the Sûtradhâra enter? The only possible answer to these is that the Sûtradhâra enters the stage and himself recites the *Nândî*. But as the Nândî contains a blessing or a salutation to some deity it is auspicious and as such must form the first words according to the general usage of Sanskṛt writers. *Cf.* Jagaddhara on Mâl. Mâd. नान्द्यन्ते सूत्रधारस्यैव श्रुतत्वेनेयमपि तेनैव पठनीया । प्रथमं सूत्रधारः प्रविशतीतिनोक्तम् । मङ्गलार्थं देवतानमस्कारादेरेव विधानात् । *Cf.* in this respect Pâṇini who begins his work with वृद्धिरादैच्, (though it should have properly been आदैज्वृद्धिः like the following Sûtra अदेङ्गुणः), by putting in वृद्धि first, as it is indicative of prosperity. Comp. also the words of Patañjali quoted by our Com. on p. 177. Hence it is that the stage direction प्रविश्य सूत्रधारः never introduces a Sanskṛt play, but is usually written after the Nândî as नान्द्यन्ते सूत्रधारः. For other particulars, see our note on these words at S'âk. p. 4 or Vik. p. 5. Bharata's rules also provide that the Sûtradhâra may retire after having repeated the Nândî and then another actor possessing qualities answering to those of the Sûtradhâra and called 'Sthâpaka' should enter and commence the play. But the best writers do not seem to have taken advantage of this option.

सूत्रधारः—The manager or chief actor. It is probable, the exhibitions of puppets and paper figures preceded the drama and that *Sûtradhâra* meant originally the holder of threads or strings by which he moved the figures as he spoke. When the drama was developed Sûtradhâra came to mean the thread of connection running through and holding together the various incidents &c. to be represented in a piece. See com.

सामन्त—सम्यगन्तः समन्तः adjoining region, frontier; तत्र भवः a frontier king paying tribute to an emperor (see Malli. on Rag. IX. 15); hence a tributary prince in general. For वटेश्वर and other names, see introduction. कृति—like क्रिया (Vik. I. 2) is used for a literary action or composition. यत्सत्यं—to tell the truth, forsooth, indeed. This comp. *indec.* is of constant occurrence. *Cf.* यत्सत्यं कम्पितमिव मे हृदयं Ven. Act. I, Mṛch. IV. Kâd. p. 131. प्रयुञ्जानः—the present participle is used intransitively to show a हेतु or cause = यतोहं प्रयुञ्जे.

बालिश—बलिशस्य मत्स्यवेधनस्यायं मूर्खत्वादपूज्यत्वात् । Bhânujî Dikshita on Amara. कृषि—act of ploughing, cultivation; here used in its *Lâkshanika* or secondary sense of 'seeds sown.' स्तम्बकरिता—the capacity to produce sheaves; fr. स्तम्ब (a stalk or a sheaf of corn) + कृ + इ (नु) which is added to कृ, by Pâṇ. III. 2. 24 and the Vârt.

on it (see com.), to स्तम्ब and शकृत् in the sense of 'corn' and 'a calf' respectively; (स्तम्बकारः शकृत्कारः otherwise).

गृहिणीमाहूय—In some editions these words are omitted which is better for brevity. The cons. or meaning of the sentence does not suffer thereby as the Sûtradhâra further on says कुटुम्बिनीं तावदाहूय.

सङ्गीतं—गीतं वाद्यं नर्तनं च त्रयं सङ्गीतमुच्यते ।

गृहाः—*Mas.* and pl. (when it means the house with its environments). The word is by no means of rare occurrence; *cf.* तत्रागारं धनपतिगृहादुत्तरेणास्मदीय Meg., II. 15 ममापि सत्त्वैरभिभूयन्ते गृहाः S'âk. VI. p. 171.

P. 15. हुङ्कृतं—Is a sort of sound resembling हुं which accompanies every effort in such mechanical works as that spoken of here.

कुटुम्बिनी—कुटुम्बमस्यास्तीति कुटिम्बी तस्य भार्या.

गुणवति &c.—An instance of भारती वृत्ति a style of composition which is characterised by simple compounds and words of easy import. The *adjectives* qualify both भार्या (which follows from the context) and नीतिविद्या (the science of policy personified—whose help is invoked as being indispensably necessary for success in the object sought to be accomplished in the piece). The six *gunas* in the case of नीति are (1) सन्धिः (forming an alliance), (2) विग्रहः (war), (3) यानम् an expedition or marching against, (4) आसनं (waiting for a suitable opportunity to attack or to improve one's weakened resources, (5) द्वैधं (duplicity), and (6) आश्रयः (applying to a powerful king for help &c.). उपाय–(1) expedients, to be used in household management; (2) the four *upâyas* are भेदो दण्डः साम दानम् । Amara. स्थिति—(1) a householder's position, (2) stability of a kingdom. त्रिवर्ग in the case of *Nîti* means—the three states of loss, stability and increase (of the collection of the eight things *viz.*—कृषिर्वणिकपथो दुर्गः सेतुः कुञ्जरबन्धनं । खन्याकरबलादानं शून्यायां च निवेशनम् ॥). कार्य—(1) household duties; (2) political ends. मङ्गवन॰, ॰चार्यें—*cf.* the Subhâshita कार्येषु मन्त्री वचनेषु दासी भोज्येषु माता शयनेषु रम्भा । धर्मानुकूला क्षमया धरित्री भार्या च षाड्गुण्यवतीह दुर्लभा ॥ The Com points out also an implied reference to Autumn described in the third act and explains the equivoques in support of his statement. See com. He thus shows the stanza to be an instance of what is technically called '*Trigata*' a minor *anga* of A'mukha or Prelude.

स्थितिहेतोः—The varient स्थितीहेतो is Voc. sing. and means 'You who are the cause of the well regulated domestic life.

कार्याचार्ये--कार्यादार्ये *v. l.* is better for the Sûtra, calls his wife not for some but a special business now as is apparent from his words गृहिणीमाहूय पृच्छामि. Although he had started with the intention of calling her for singing, he had given it up now after seeing the preparations at his house and is anxious to know their reason now. It also explains why he calls her (द्रुतं) quickly.

P. 16. ब्राह्मणानामुपनिमन्त्रणेन—Feeding the Brâhmaṇas is a part of the *Puras'charaṇa* enjoyed at an eclipse. See Dharmasindhu p. 27, also Yâj. Smṛti I. 217, 218 (अमावास्याष्टकावृद्धिः... । ...ग्रहणं चन्द्रसूर्ययोः । &c.). Although a *S'râddha* is usually prohibited at night it is specially enjoined at the time of an eclipse and so may be performed at night on the occasion of a lunar eclipse. It may be confined to the presentation of uncooked food, sweetmeat &c. Mr. Dhruva quotes the following from V. P. राहोश्च दर्शने दत्तं श्राद्धमाचन्द्रतारकम् । गुणवत्सर्वकामीयं पितृणामुपतिष्ठति ॥ अतिथि—अतति गच्छति न तिष्ठति इति; fr. अत् + इथि; or न विद्यते द्वितीया तिथिर्यस्य *Cf.* Manu एकरात्रं तु निवसन्नतिथिर्ब्राह्मणः स्मृतः । अनित्यं हि स्थितो यस्मात्तस्मादतिथिरुच्यते ॥

चतुष्षष्ट्यङ्गे—According to Garga there are 24 *Aṅgas* and 10 *Upâṅgas* of the mixed science of astrology and astronomy all of which are here spoken of without distinction as *Aṅgas*. 64 seems to be a favourite number with the ancient writers. Thus the scenic Art (Nâṭyas'astra) is divided into 64 *Aṅgas*. There are also 64 *Kalas*.

क्रूरग्रहः &c.—The *double entendres* on this stanza are well explained in the com. ०ग्रहः--determined purpose, firm resolve. केतुः (1) for Râhu, to suit the double meaning; (2) it stands for Malayeketu by a sort of convention often resorted to by poets. as भामा does for सत्यभामा राम for परशुराम &c. In separating the words स केतुः we have followed the Com. and translated accordingly. But it is better to read the two words as one सकेतुः क्रूरग्रहः (1) the cruel planet, in combination with the Ketu; (2) Râkshasa &c. as in the foot-note. We need not then take केतु in the sense of Râhu. Similarly चन्द्र stands for चन्द्रगुप्त as भीम does for भीमसेन. The Com. reads चन्द्रमसंपूर्ण० (which is also the reading of the majority of Mss.) and separates the words in the second case as चन्द्रम् असंपूर्ण०. But this goes against Châṇakya's statement further on—कृता मौर्ये लक्ष्मीः...स्थिरपदा, (See sl. 13) and the words of the spy. सम्पूर्णमण्डलेपि चन्द्रे in sl. 19, which require the reading adopted in the text, *viz*. चन्द्रं सम्पूर्ण०. Again, a man of Châṇakya's stamp and high mettle would not himself speak of the Maṇḍala being असंपूर्ण. This is also the reading of S. D. which quotes this sl. see further on, notes on p. 19. Maṇḍala in this case comprehends the seven constituent parts of a kingdom, as given by Kâmandaka in his Nitîsâra, *viz* स्वाम्यमात्यश्च राष्ट्रं च दुर्गं कोशो बलं सुहृत् । परस्परोपकारीदं सप्ताङ्गं राष्ट्रमुच्यते ॥ IV. I. *Cf.* also Amara—स्वाम्यमात्यसुहृत्कोशराष्ट्रदुर्गबलानि च । सप्ताङ्गानि प्रकृतयः । When all the seven members of a kingdom work in perfect harmony it is called सम्पूर्णमण्डल. As for Maṇḍala and the comparison to the moon, comp. also K. n. VIII. 3. Chân.'s fears, however, were roused because Chandragupta's royalty had not taken a firm root yet. *Cf.* अचिराधिष्ठितराज्यः शत्रुः प्रकृतिष्वरूढमूलत्वात् । नवसंरोहणशिथिलस्तरुरिव सुकरः समुद्धर्तुम् ॥ Mâl. I. 8.

P. 17. चन्द्रमभि०—Some Mss. omit these words but they are necessary for the following speech of the Naṭi to be intelligible. Some read चन्द्रगुप्त but this is wrong, as the full name will leave no scope for the Naṭî's question. In his first impulse of anger Châṇakya catches up the word चन्द्र from the Sûtradhâra's speech and so repeats it.

बुधयोगः—बुध (1) the planet Mercury ; (2) the wise Châṇakya. योगः—(1) conjunction ; (2) connection with ; policy, strategy. In Bâlabhârata the planet Mercury is similarly spoken of as preventing a lunar eclipse. *Cf* तन्नन्दनस्तन्मिथुनानुरूपो रूपोस्ति चिद्रूपतया बुधाख्यः यद्योगभाजं न विधुंतुदोपि विधुं तुदत्युग्रविरोधबोध ॥ Bâl. Bhâr. I. 8. (D.). The Com. quotes Bṛ. Garga S. in support of this view. The five Grahas meant are—The Sun, the Moon, Mercury (बुध) Jupiter (गुरु) and Venus (शुक्र). Varâhamihira, in his Bṛ. Saṁ., rejects this theory saying :—पञ्चग्रहसंयोगात्र किल ग्रहणस्य संभवो भवति । (तैलं च जलेष्टम्यां) विचिन्त्यमिदं विपश्चिद्भिः ॥ V. 17.

रक्षति &c.—Is a continuation of the Sût.'s speech and completes the Âryâ क्रूर &c. The fig. is *S'lesha.*

धरणीगोचरो भूत्वा—Being a denizen of this world—for whom the task would be impossible. Or this may be equivalent to धरण्यामात्मानं दर्शयित्वा showing himself on the earth.

अभियुक्तः—Devoted to ; hence attentive ; mark this sense here and the various other senses in which the root अभियुज् is used in this work ; *cf.* p. 14. I. 2, p. 18. I. 5, p. 23. I. 3, p. 26. I. 3. p. 87. I. 19 &c.

चन्द्रगुप्तं—Châṇakya fancying that he was not properly understood utters the full name of Chandragupta.

P. 18. कौटिल्यः &c.—As to कौटिल्यः कुटिलमतिः see *infra* p. 99. प्रसभं—प्रगताः सभा विचारो यस्मिन्कर्मणि; Com. on Amara. It is more probably derived fr. सह to bear or endure, ह being changed to म्. श्रुतेः—usually means श्रुतिवाक्यात् but here—श्रुत्वा. सनाभः—स is substituted for समान by a rule obtained by detaching the syll. समानस्य from the Sûtra समानस्य छन्दसि &c. Pân VI. 3. 84. द्विषदभियोगः—*cf.* pp. 111, 112.

P. 19. The mode in which the principal character is introduced here is technically called *Udghâtyaka.* It consists in giving to the words of one quite a different sense and thus introducing a character on the stage. *Cf.* Sâh. Dar. 289, where the stanza क्रूरग्रह &c. is quoted as an instance of this mode. प्रस्तावना—see com. p. 14.

मुक्तां शिखां &c.—Châṇakya had vowed that he would not tie up his hair until he had completed the task of effecting the total destruction of the Nanda dynasty. That task was not complete as long as Chandragupta's rule was not thoroughly established. Châṇakya, therefore, ties up his hair at the end of the play. The student will remember the similar loosening and tying up of Draupadî's braid in the Veṇisaṁhâra.

परिभूय—'Having defeated,' has here the force of an *adv.*, 'in spite of, with force'. For the implications of the various expressions, see com. Cha'ṇ. will further have an occasion to repeat this sl.; see p. 42.

P. 20. काकभुजगी—Which is well known for the spirit of Vengeance. नील—indicates that the fire is yet smouldering and may burst into a flame again at any time. धूमलता—धूमो लता इव. अद्यापि—though I have fulfilled my vow. *Cf.* कौरव्यवंशदावेऽस्मिन्क एष शलभायते। मुक्तवेणीं स्पृशन्नेनां कृष्णां धूमशिखामिव ॥ Veṇ. I. 19. sl. cited in Al. K. as an instance of *Mâlârûpaka.*

°काननधूमकेतु—Occurs in Uttar. and Chandakaus'ika. शालभ—शलभस्यायं. लभतां—the Imper. indicates the certainty of the destruction. *Cf.* अविदित्वात्मनः शक्तिं परस्य च समुत्सुकः। गच्छन्नभिमुखो वह्नौ नाशं याति पतङ्गवत् ॥ Also Bhar. Vai. S'at. sl. 21.

उपाध्यायः—उपेत्याधीयतेऽस्मात्। a pupil is to so address his Guru. *Cf.* आर्येति ब्राह्मणं ब्रूयान्महाराजेति पार्थिवम्। उपाध्यायेति चाचार्यम् B. Nât. उपवेष्टुमिच्छामि—implies censure cast on the pupil for not having prepared a scat. कार्याभियोगः—indicates the casting of the *Bija*; see com. व्याकुलयति—and hence I did not notice the seat; see com. दुःशीलता—roughness of conduct, petulance.

P. 21. परिपणन—an offer (in consideration of service done). सर्वलोकप्रकाशं—सर्वेषां लोकानां प्रकाशो यथा स्यात्तथा । *cf.* तीर्त्वा जवेनैव नितान्तदुस्तरां नदीं प्रतिज्ञामिव तां गरीयसीम् । Sis. XIV. 74. निस्तीर्णोरुप्रतिज्ञाजलनिधिगहनः । Veṇ V. 37 न (अ) समर्थः *v. l.*—Mr. Telang finds fault with this reading and with reason; for its cuts off the sentence यस्य मम from its correlative. कुतः—from what cause. If you ask how, here is the reason.

श्यामीकृत्य &c.—Notice the vigorous style of and bold metaphors in this s'loka. अरियुवतिदिशां—it is generally a *dik* that is personified as a lady, the moon being regarded as her face. *Cf.* Vik. III. 6; दिग्वधूरथ पुरन्दरसेव्या Vik. ch. XI. 26. But here the order is reversed. The wives of the enemies are compared to quarters and their faces are represented as moons. सम्यान्त &c.—shows that Chāṇakya was not a reckless murderer of men, but duly respected the rights of the citizens. The fig.s are *Rûpaka* (समस्तवस्तु and परंपरित) and *Upamâ* (ज्वलन इव) which, however, detracts from the force of the *Rûpaka.* रिपुवने without ज्वलन इव would have been better.

P. 22. अग्रासन—अग्रे स्थितमासनं । the syntactical construction of these two s'lokas, though somewhat irregular, is not very difficult to understand. अवकृष्टं &c.—see Intro.

वृषलापेक्षया—Out of regard for, because I take interest in the well-being of Vṛshala. शस्त्र—the sword, the symbol of ministerial office. The chief minister of those days, it seems had, in addition to his other duties, to act as commander of the forces in times of war Thus we find both Râkshasa and Chāṇakya as principal in command of the troops of Malayaketu (see p. 133) and of Chandragupta (p. 148) respectively.

शल्याः—रोगाः *V. l.* The former better expresses the idea of the insult rankling in Chāṇ.'s mind and also better agrees with समुत्खात. The reading रागाः is evidently a corruption of रोगाः द्वयोः सारं &c.—The fig. is a fusion of *Upamâ* and यथासख्यं. *Cf.* शत्रु मित्रं विपत्ति च जय रज्जय भञ्जय ।

P. 23. तदभियोग—अभियोगं zealous or devoted work for the Nandas. If अभि० be taken to mean 'an attack,' then तद् must refer to Vṛshala. शक्योवस्थापयितुं—it is possible to manage him; lit. to place in a favourable or subservient position. बुद्धि—belief, intention. or object in view. तपस्वी—poor, helpless; it is generally used as a term of pity; but always in a good sense, while वराक is used in a good or bad sense. It never means miserable or wretched as some dictionaries give it. See our note on तपस्विनी S'âk. p. 99. विपुल—वि + पुल great, fr. पुल् to be great.

आकाशे लक्ष्यं &c.—This is what is technically called आकाशभाषितं. This must, however, be distinguished from the stage direction आकाशे for which, see Act. II. p. 48. In the case of the former the character addressed is absent and beyond hearing but mentally pictured as standing before the addresser's eyes; while in the latter case the person spoken to is within hearing and although not present on the stage is supposed to give replies (uttered by the speaker himself with a clever ventriloquism). This is done to make up for the deficiency of actors. अमात्य—अमा सह वसतीति; fr. अमा+त्य by Vârt. on Pâṇ. IV. 2. 104. श्रोत्रिय—a Brâhmaṇa well versed in the Vedas. छन्दोधीत इति श्रोत्रियः; irregularly derived by Pâṇ. V. 2. 84. *Cf.* जन्मना ब्राह्मणो ज्ञेयः संस्कारैर्द्विज उच्यते । विद्यया याति विप्रत्वं त्रिभिः श्रोत्रिय उच्यते ॥

अर्थतः—तस् shows हेतु; for the sake of. अनु—is a कर्मप्रवचनीय (prep. which can be used by itself in government with a noun or pronoun in the Acc.) in the sense of direction towards (लक्षण) or statement of a particular relation or state (इत्थंभूताख्यान). See Sid. Kau. on लक्षणेत्थंभूताख्यानभागवीप्सासु प्रतिपर्यनवः। Pâṇ. I. 4. 90. भर्तुर्यें &c.—*cf.* एते सत्पुरुषाः परार्थघटकाः &c. Bhar. Nît. S'at. 74. and भृत्या अपि ते एव ये संपत्तेर्विपत्तौ सविशेषं सेवन्ते &c. Kâd. p. 470.

कथमसौ &c.—Explains the यत्न.

P. 24. अप्राज्ञेन च &c.—*Cf.* किं भक्तेनासमर्थेन किं शक्तेनापकारिणा। भक्तं शक्तं च मां विद्धि नावज्ञातुं त्वमर्हसि ॥ Pt. I. 136 ते भृत्याः &c.—Mark the derivation:—भृत्याः fr. भृ to support, are those who deserve to be maintained (from their intrinsic merit); hences excellent, true, servants. कलत्र is derived fr. कड् (ल्) to eat or to protect (कडयन्ते) who must be fed or protected under any circumstances. In interpreting the last two lines we have followed the Commentator and translated accordingly. But that lowers the dignity of women. In this sl. three kinds of servants are mentioned; the first two forming one class (to be awarded) the last a different type of servants. The last two lines should therefore be construed as येषां गुणाः भर्तर्य समुदिताः ते इतरे भृत्याः सम्पत्सु आपत्सु च कलत्रमिव those other servants &c. stick to their lord like a wife, in prosperity as well as in adversity, for such a high ideal of wife, *cf.* यस्मिन्कृत्यं समावेश्य निर्विशङ्केन चेतसा । आस्यते सेवकः स स्यात्कलत्रमिव चापरम ॥ Pt. I. 85.

नशयान—A comp. सुप्सुपा: see Malli. on नातितोष्ण Rag. IV. 8. **तद्ग्रहणं प्रति यत्नः**—Chânakya had a double object to accomplish—to secure the whole kingdom of the Nandas for Chandragupta and to win over Râkshasa to his side. For this purpose he formed the following plan. He procured the death of Parvates'vara, but could not have killed Malayaketu also without risking his popularity. He, therefore, secretly frightened Malayaketu by the suggestion that the murder of his father proceeded from him; but at the same time he spread a report that Râkshasa had killed Parvates'vara. He strengthened the report by suffering Malayaketu quietly to escape from the camp of Chandragupta. He knew that Malayaketu would join Râkshasa and thus place himself in an adverse position to him and that then it would be easy to get rid of him. The rumour circulated was intended to be afterwards the means of destroying the alliance between Malayaketu and Râkshasa and thus to throw each of them into a desperate condition. See the Com.'s remarks. **विषकन्या**—a beautiful maid with a body gradually poisoned to such a degree that intercourse with her would prove to be instantaneously fatal. This artifice of employing the poisoned maid to get an adversary quietly out of the way seems to have been sometimes resorted to in ancient times, as writers on medicine make a reference to it. Mr. Dhruva quotes from S'us'rûta—विषकन्योपयोगाद्वा क्षणाज्जह्यादसून्नरः । तस्माद्वैद्येन सततं विषाद्रक्ष्यो नराधिपः । Kalpasthâna I. 5. and from Vâgbhaṭṭa—आजन्मविषसंयोगात्कन्या विषमयी कृता । स्पर्शोच्छ्वासादिभिर्हन्ति तस्यास्त्वेतत्परीक्षणम् । तन्मस्तकस्य संस्पर्शान्म्लायेते पुष्पपल्लवौ । शय्यायां मत्कुणैर्वस्त्रे यूकाभिः स्नानवारिणा । जन्तुभिर्म्रियते ज्ञात्वा तामेवं दूरतस्त्यजेत् ॥

उत्तिष्ठमानः—उदोऽनूर्ध्वकर्मणि Pân. I. 8. 24. The root स्था preceded by उद् is Atm. when it does not mean 'getting up,' *i. e.* is used in a figurative sense such as (striving for, aspiring to &c.). *Cf.* Kir. XI. 13, S'is. II. 101. XIV. 17. Bhaṭṭi. VIII. 13. **निग्रहीतुं**—to hold in check, to subdue, to secure. **निग्रहान्**—goes with प्रमाद्युम्. **अनुरक्तापरक्त**—a conjunctive Dvandva.

P. 25. **सञ्चार**—'Modes of proceeding or dealing' as Mr. Telang takes it. Or modes of moving in. **बहुविध** &c.-or आचार &c obtaining in various countries. **व्यञ्जन**—external form or appearance, disguise; *cf.* अमात्यव्यञ्जना राज्ञां दूष्यास्ते शत्रुसंशिताः । S'is. II. 56. तपस्विव्यञ्जनोपेतः Hit. **निपुणं**—may beter be taken as an *adv.* **प्रचारगतं**—actual doings, movements. **तत्तत्कारणं**—See com. and Act. III. p. 89. **उत्पाद्य**—shows that the causes were not real but feigned ones. **कृतकृत्यतां**—made to promote our interest or to subserve our object *viz.* to effect a split in the enemy's camp and to alienate Mal. from Râkshasa; see com. also. Mr. Dhruva takes कृत्यतां in the sense of 'Malcontents' (who were made to desert our ranks and to join the enemy under the feigned character of malcontens) and quotes Somadevasûri—स्वामिदोषस्वदोषाभ्यामुपहतवृत्तयः क्रुद्धलुब्धभीतावमानिताः कृत्याः । In this case *cf.* K. n. XII. 22. (कृत्यपक्षोपसंग्रहः) The reading कृतककृत्यतां also seems to be probable. It makes a positive step in Chânakya's plan &c. circumvent Râkshasa. It means 'They have been advised to show themselves) as outwardly disconted and therefore hostile. On p. 175 Chân. refers to भद्रभट and others as विरक्त; this shows that there was कृतककृत्यता. The reading तत्रकृत्यतामा॰ made to execute business of various sorts' is simpler. **सहोत्थायिनः**—adherents; lit. raising against the Nandas along with. *Cf.* सहाध्यायी further on. **तीक्ष्णरस**—poison. Kings were required to be protected also from persons employed by their enemies to administer poison to them secretely; see K. n. VI. 9. On रस meaning poison *cf.* D. K. VIII. शस्त्राग्निरसप्रणिधयः &c.; अस्मकेन्द्रप्रयुक्तास्तीक्ष्णरसदादयः *idem* further on.

औशनसी—Composed by U'sanas or S'ukrâchârya, son of Bhṛgu and preceptor of the *Asuras.* **दण्डनीति**—दण्डो नीयते बोध्यते अनया दण्डं नयतीति वा; science of government or politics. **क्षपणक**—a Jaina mendicant. **लिङ्ग**—an external mark; *cf.* यतिपार्थिवलिङ्गधारिणौ Rag. VIII. 16. वर्णिलिङ्गी Kir. I. 1, Here Chân. pursues the policy of *Dvaidhîbhâva.*

P. 26. **प्रधानप्रकृति**—The chief of, or the central figure in-the Prakṛtis; the King.—Mr. Telang reads प्रधानप्रकृतिषु अस्मासु. But evidently it is not a good reading. In the first place Chânakya would not call himself प्रधान; secondly our reading agrees well with the context further on. See p. 111; *cf.* प्रधानप्रकृति in प्र॰कोपः in Mâl. Mâd. X. p. 217. where it may be taken to mean 'King.' **तन्त्र**—administration, governing. *Cf.* लोकतन्त्राधिकारः, and प्रजाः स्वा इव तन्त्रयित्वा S'âk. V. 5. **उदास्ते**—remains indifferent or apathetic; takes no interest in state matters or politics. **अभियोग**—close application or devotion to; see p. 17.

Sl. 16. Fig.—a mixture of अप्रस्तुतप्रशंसा and तुल्ययोगिता.

यमपट—A roll of cloth (*cf.* प्रसार्य p. 31) containing a series of pictures illustrative of the exploits of Yama or connected with his court. The Instr. is उपलक्षणार्था. The exhibition of Yamapaṭa was one of the sources of making money; see Harshacharita p. 170 where a Yamapatika, exhibiting the scenes in Yamapurî painted on a piece of cloth is described (परलोकव्यतिकरं कथयन्तं यमपटिकं ददर्श ।).

Sl.s. 17. 18. विषम—Fearful, unrelenting. The two Sl.s. have a hidden meaning (वस्तुध्वनि). The first warns the people to pay their homage, and to be loyal to Chânakya; lest it would be a dangerous game to offend him (by professing loyalty to the Nanda family). The second means that the followers of Chânakya alone will be safe. The fig. in sl. 17 is *Kâvyalinga* in the 1st half and *Vyâghâta* in the 2nd.

P. 27. सुगृहीतनामन्—सुखाय शुभाय वा गृह्यते नाम अस्य; lit. one whose name it is auspicious to invoke or utter. It is an epithet to be used when speaking about persons entitled to respect or veneration; see Das'. R. II. 68. धर्मभ्राता—धर्मेण जातो भ्राता one who is in a similar relation to that of a brother, as by learning under the same *Guru* or by professing the same religious creed &c. चोरयितुं—to steal away, hence here, to assume it on one's part, or to deny. This passage (from चरः—हं हो ब्रह्मण........to चाणक्य—चन्द्रगुप्तादपरक्तान्पुरुषाञ्ज्ञामि &c.) is quoted in the Das. R. p.p. 85-6 with different readings as an instance of Nâlikâ, a subdivision of Vîthi which is defined as सोपहासा निगूढार्था नालिकैव प्रहेलिका ।

कस्स चन्दो &c.—The spy insinuates that he knows the people who are dis-attached to Chandragupta and that Chân. would want to know them. The pupil had not the good sense to perceive this hidden meaning and calls the spy 'a fool.'

P. 28. कमलानां &c.—कमल is a lotus blooming at sunrise; *cf.* कुमुदान्येवशशाङ्कः सविता बोधयति पङ्कजान्येव । S'âk. V. 28. उपक्षिप्त—thrown out, hinted, insinuated. प्रकृति—subjects.

P. 29. वृषलमनुरक्ताः—Notice the Acc.; in such cases अनु should be taken separately and treated as a कर्मप्रवचनीय. See *supra*, note on अनु p. 23. and A. G. § 94.

विरागः—Discontent, disaffection. अस्ति—*indec.* used as an introductory particle. ' अस्ति सत्त्वे ' Amara.

नामधेयतः—*Cf.* मातरं नामतः पृच्छेयं S'âk. p. 199. चाणक्यः सहर्षं—see the reason of this explained in the com.

P. 30. कायस्थ—A man of a mixed class (proceeding from a Kshatriya father and a S'udra woman). *Cf.* Yâj. I. 336. Mrch. IX. The Kayasthas, who formed the writer-caste, seem to have been much looked down upon in old days. " The name Sâkatadâsa is to be noted. It seems to belong to Eastern India where the Kâyasthas are still a large and an important class of the population, and Dâs is still a prevailing surname "—Telang.

मात्रा—Lit. measure, hence consideration, significance. **प्राकृतमपि रिपुं**—*cf.* अल्पीयसोप्यरेर्वृद्धिर्महानर्थाय रोगवत् । Malli. on S'is. II 10.

श्रेष्ठी—श्रेष्ठं धनादिकमस्त्यस्य । **चन्दनदास**—may be a Bengalee or a Gujarâthi name, but more probably the former here.

P. 31. **अङ्गुलीप्रणयी**—For a similar, though not identical use *cf.* कृतोक्षसूत्रप्रणयी तया करः । Kum. V. 11. **विस्तरतः**—mark the difference between विस्तर a detailed account and विस्तार expanse. विस्तार is derived from स्तॄ with affix घञ् (अ) by प्रथने वावशब्दे Pân. III. 3. 33 (प्रथने किं तृणविस्तारः अशब्दे किं ग्रन्थविस्तरः); विस्तर is derived with अप् (अ) by ऋदोरप् Pân. III. 3. 57 (roots ending in ऋ and उ take अ); *cf.* विस्तारो विग्रहो व्यासः स च शब्दस्य विस्तरः । Amara; while there is a third word derived from the same root with वि, *viz.* विष्टर in the sense of, 'a seat Pân. VIII. 3. 93.

अस्ति—An Avy. Comp.; you know, as you remember; see *supra* p. 29. **अपवरक**—an air-hole, a widow; fr. अपवृ+अक, also अपवारक. **०देशीयः**—the affixes देश्य, देशीय and कल्प are added in the sense of 'bordering on, little less than;' पञ्चवर्षसमीपे वर्तमानः. देशीय originally derived from देश (पञ्चवर्षाणि देशस्तत्र भवः); *cf.* अष्टादशवर्षदेशीयां कन्यां Kâd. p. 212.

P. 32. **दापित**—Cau. used in the primitive sense (दत्त). **पुरुषाङ्गुलि** &c.-This gives the reason why the ring slipped down so easily. **देहली**—देहं गोमयाद्युपलेपं लातीति । **निभृता**—breathless, motionless; *cf.* निष्कम्पवृक्षं निभृतद्विरेफं; Kum. III. 42. Mr. Apte takes निभृत in the sense of modest humble, (Dic.); *cf.* in this respect अनिभृतकरेषु प्रियेषु । II. 7. **मुद्राया आगमः**—here begins the प्रतिमुखसन्धि. See com. The acquisition of the ring is the incident which gives rise to the Bindu. (see Introduction). For the passage cited in the com. see D. R. pp. 13, 14.

P. 33. **जयशब्दः**—The announcement of victory, *scil.* that in जेदु &c. coming immediately after जेतव्यः. Such an accidental utterance is supposed to indicate future success or otherwise and forms a common device in Sanskrt dramas. It is technically called गण्ड and is classed as a subvariety of *Patâkâsthâna.* It is defined as—गण्डः प्रस्तुतसम्बन्धि भिन्नार्थं सहसोदितम् । *i. e.* an unexpected utterance of words having a distinct bearing, but so put together as to be syntactically connected with the matter hand. Das'. Rûp. III, 18. *Cf.* किमस्या न प्रेयो यदि पुनरसह्योन विरहः । दौ०— देव उपस्थितः । Uttar. I. &c.; also अज्ज गहीदो । &c. p. 37 *infra.**

---

* **Wilson Remarks—**

The Greek plays are full of similar instances, and they are sufficiently abundant in every other department of classical liter-

पारलौकिकं—परलोकाय हितं; परलोक + इक Lit. what is beneficial to one, *i. e.* secures a good position for one, in the next world; hence, the religious rites to be performed on one's demise. ब्राह्मणानं—The Prâkṛta Gen. for the Dative. Parvates'vara being a Mlechchha the question arises—how Chandragupta could perform his obsequies. The probable answer is that these foreigners on coming to India tried to mix with the people by adopting not only their dress and manners but even their religious ceremonies.

P. 34. अस्मद्वचनात्—Is an expression of frequent occurrence. It means—in my name, at my command or direction.

उत्तरो लेखार्थः—अर्थ subject matter. The latter part refers to the ornaments which the three brothers are directed to receive from Chandragupta and to bring them to him (Chânakya). See the letter at p. 122, *infra*.

कौलूतः—King of the Kulûta country. Kulûta is the name of a district (the modern Kulu, according to Mr. A. Boroosh) lying to the south-east of Kâs'mira and to the north-east of the Jâlandar Doab on the right band of the S'atadru (Sutlej). It appears to have been a flourishing kingdom in the 6th and the 7th centuries as it is mentioned by Bâṇa, Varâhamihâra and also by the Chinese pilgrim Hiouen Tsaug (apparently as lying on the way from Jâlandar to Mathurâ and Thanes'var (Telang's Intro. p. 32).

मलयनरपतिः—King of Malaya, the southern portion of the Ghauts running from the south of Mysore and forming the eastern boundary of Travancore. See, however, *N. B.* below. काश्मीर—This province

---

ature. Cicero cities various curious examples in his book "De Divinatione." That related of Lucius Paulus is very analogous to the instance in the text. "Lucius Paulus the consul had been appointed to conduct the war against Perseus. On returning to his house in the evening he found his little daughter Tertia full of grief, and on asking her what was the matter, replied '*Persa* (*a puppy so named*) is no more.' Taking her up in his arms, and kissing her, the codsul exclaimed. "I accept the omen,' and the event correspouded with the expression." The effect of the omen seems also with the Hindus, as well as the Greeks and Romans, to have depended in a great measure upon a person's applying it, and signifying his acceptance of it .....*Oionon* dekesthai, Omen arripere, and Sabdam Grihitum, are terms of similar import in three languages.;

is still known by the same name. सैंधवः—King of Sindhu, the country around the Indus.

P. 35. पारसीकाधिराजः—King of the Pârasîkas. These are supposed to be the ancient Persians, or inhabitants of that part of Persia which borders on the Indu-Afgan frontier.

पृथुतुरगबलः—The ancient Persians were known for their cavalry; *cf.* Rag. IV. 62. It should be observed that with the exception of Malaya, all these names refer to the Northern and North-western part of India.

N. B.—Although it is not clear from the play that all the kings were Mlechchhas, as they are spoken of as only म्लेच्छराजलोकस्य मध्यात्प्रधानतमाः yet it is probable that they were so and belonged all to Northern India. *Cf.* therefore, Mr. Dhruva's note—On its (Malayaketu's kingdom) eastern border should be placed the kingdom of Malayades'a. Its site is roughly indicated by modern Malebhoom (Malayabhumi.) It lay probably between the Rapti and the Gaṇḍakî in Nepâl.

ध्रुवम्—Indelibly; not to be effaced. चित्रगुप्तः—One of Yama's servants, who registers men's virtues and vices. See Muir's Sans. Texts Vol. V. p. 302. One of the duties attaching to Chitragupta's office is to inform Yama as soon as a person's period of life expires. प्रमार्ष्टु—Châṇ. is so sure of the success of his plan that he asks Chi. to take off the names of these kings from his register as he would send them in time to the abode of Yama. Mr. Telang compares Milton's phrase—blotted out from the book of life. See his notes.

अथवा न लिखामि—Châṇ., on a second thought, changed his mind and did not write the names of the princes he wished to destroy in the letter, for the obvious reason that S'akaṭa. would not have copied it but given warning to Râkshasa. It was, however, of prime importance to him to have the letter copied just by S'akaṭa., who enjoyed Râk.'s confidence and who became (as Châṇ. with unmistakable foresight expected him to be) his secretary afterwards. The success of Châṇakya's plan depended on that. The defect in the letter was made up by the oral message.

पूर्वं—We should have adopted the reading सर्वम्. By saying उत्तरार्धं लेखार्थः Chan. does not state what it is; and then he wishes to keep the first part also vague, by saying अथवा &c.; and we see from the letter (see pp. 124-5) that it was not the first part only that was vague but the whole writing. So the reading सर्वं is better.

वाच्यनाम—The name of the addressee. **उपतिष्ठस्व—स्था** with उप is Âtm. in the senses of 'उपाद्देवपूजासंगतिकरणमित्रकरणपथिष्विति वाच्यं Vârt. on Pân. I. 3. 25; here it means—**संगतिकरण अनुवाच्य—अनुवाच्** to read silently or to oneself as distinguished from 'to read aloud' *i. e.* in the hearing of others.

P. 36. **आप्त**—Very friendly, trustworthy. *Cf.* Rag. V. 89, **परेषु** The enemies; see p. 120. **प्रयोजनं**—see p. 119. *et seq.*

कर्णे एव॰—The further part of the communication was more important and therefore Châṇakya, to secure great secrecy whispers it into his ear. The poet also wants to keep up the interest of his audience in the subsequent developement of the plot.

यदार्य आज्ञापयति—We should expect the stage direction **इति निष्कान्तः** after this but that would not serve the poet's purpose. He wanted him there to say **आर्यगृहीतः** (see next page) which forms the **पताकारस्थानं**. So he represents Châṇ. as hastily calling out to his pupil without handing over the writing to him.

कालपा॰—कालपाशः प्रहरणमस्य । Pân. IV. 4. 57; similarly **दण्डपाशो प्रहरणमस्य** (**दाण्डपाशिक** usually) the **अ** not taking Vṛddhi by the exemption given by the maxim **संज्ञापूर्वको विधिरनित्यः ।** Two police officers executing commands. Or **कालपाशिक** may mean (**कालस्य इवः पाशः यस्य**) the officer who gave the command and **दण्ड॰** the officer who executed it. All Mss. (even the one followed by Wilson–see H. T. Vol. II. p. 167.) give these as two different names. Mr. Dhruva, however, reads **काल॰ दण्डपाशिकः** treating the first as the name of the executing officer on the analogy of **दुर्गपाल विजयपालः** further on (see p. 44) and this seems to be a better view. **निकारः**—disgrace, ignominy; *cf.* Kir. I. 43.

P. 37. **अपि नाम**—indicates a wish and introduces a question with respect to that wish being realised It may also mean here 'Is it likely that?' **अज्ज गहीदो**—Sid., who was waiting for the letter Châṇ. had to give him. finds him absorbed in thought and thus exclaims to call his attention to him. Of course the words prove auspicious to Chânakya. This is another instance of a *Patàkàsthana*; see *supra.* note on **जयशब्दः** p. 33.

P. 38. **चाणक्यहतकः—हतक** is a depreciatory term mostly used at the end of compounds and means 'cursed, miserable, vile &c.

See रामहतक Uttar. I. Sometimes it precedes the word with which it is used; हतविधिः ; हतकहिमांशुः Vid.

P. 39. संभावितं—Is here equivalent to संभावना, honour, respect or civility. The other reading is simpler. उपक्षिप्तं &c—Châṇ. sees a sly hint in Châṇakya's word अस्मद्विधे:—that he was honoured in that way by Râkshasa. किमपि the loss of the ring leads Chand. to suppose that Châṇ. might have known about Râk.'s wife and son being in his house.

संव्यवहार—Honest, fair transactions. Châṇakya perhaps pays here a compliment to the merchant. The pl. shows that Chand.'s business was not cofined to jewelry only. वृद्धिलाभ—the earning of interest &c., emoluments. वणिज्या—वणिजः कर्म (भावो वा); fr. वणिज् + य by the rule 'दूतवणिग्भ्यां च (Bha. Dik. and Kas',); but the Sid. Kau. remarks वणिज्यमिति काशिका। माधवस्तु वणिज्याशब्दः स्वभावात् स्त्रीलिंगः। भाव एव चार्थे न तु कर्मणीत्याह। भाष्ये तु दूतवणिग्भ्यामिति नास्त्येव। More correctly, therefore, explain वणिजि साधुः. यत् being affixed by Pâṇ. IV. 4. 38, The form वाणिज्या is incorrect unless we read वाणिज्या लाभाः in which case it will be an *adj.* derived from वणिज्या.

स्मरयन्ति—स्मृ Cau. to cause to remember with regret or longing for the past. (स्मृ आध्याने। आध्यानमुत्कण्ठापूर्वकं स्मरणं। Sid. Kau.). *Cf.* S'is. VI. 56. स्मारयन्ति will simply mean 'to put in mind of, to cause to remember' which does not seem to be intended here.

शान्तं पापं—An expression constantly occurring in plays and expressing one's disapproval of or abhorrence at blasphemous or malevolent words, or indicating a wish that some evil should be averted. पूर्णिमा—पूर्णं चन्द्रस्य पूरणं तेन निर्वृत्ता· (aff. इम). प्रातिप्रियं--प्रतिकृतं प्रियं, प्रतिप्रीणातीति वा· See Rag. V. 56.

P. 40. किं किमिदं &c—Chandanadâsa thought that Châṇ. wanted a money payment from him. नन्दस्यैवार्थरुचेः—Brâhmâṇic and Buddhistic accounts tally in depicting Nanda as very avaricious. The Nandas were said to possess the fabulous amount of 99 crores of gold coins. On the cupidity of the Nandas. Mr. Telang refers to Max Muller's History of A. S. Literature pp. 289-296, and adds 'cupidity seems to be attributed to the Mauryas also.'

अपरिक्लेशः—Lit. non-punishment or not torturing (people like you). The adoption of stringent measures or परिक्लेश is a kind of दण्ड or punishment; *cf.* वधोर्थग्रहणं चैव परिक्लेशस्तथैव च। इति दण्डविधानज्ञैर्दण्डोपि त्रिविधः स्मृतः॥ K. n. XVII. 9. Châṇ. means to suggest that Chandragupta would be happy not to have recourse to harsh measures against his subjects (such as imprisonment, torturing them &c.).

राज्ञा विरुद्धः—Is ungrammatical; it should be राज्ञः or राजनि वि०, unless it means 'opposed by the king.' Or read राज्ञो.

स्वगृहे &c.—The reading **स्वगृहमभिनीय** is rejected as it goes, against the context. For in the next speech Chân. accuses Chand. not of taking the wife and son of Râk. to his house but of giving asylum to them when left there by Râk. himself, which appears to have been the case even from the words of Râk. on p. 52.

P. 41. **वाक्छलं**—Dishonesty (contradiction) in words and not in reality. Chandanadâsa lays stress on Chân.'s अद्यापि and wishes to convey to him the idea that he denied the presence of Râk.'s family in his house at the time he was speaking but does not wish to hide the fact that it was with him before that time. But he admits that he might be charged with seeming dishonesty in words only in as much as he did not state that in plain terms before. **चन्द्रगुप्ते राजनि**—Notice the Loc.; or it may be Loc. Abs.; 'in the reign of Chandragupta.'

(ज्ञायते) नाम—may be here **संभाव्ये** (in the sense of possibility) or कुत्सायां (you are foolish enough to deny knowledge &c). **शिरसि भयं** &c.—He means—dangers easily befall man; but it is very difficult to remedy them. One, therefore, must not tempt them.

उपरि घनं &c.—In the case of men who are away from home, it is a hard calamity to have the rains set in before they return home. For the idea *cf.* Meg. I. 3 and Rag. XIII. 28. **घणाघण** *V. l.* means a cloud ready to burst. **वर्षुकाब्दो घणाघणः ।** Amara. **हिमवति** &c.—The mountain Himâlaya is famous for herbs of great potency and virtue. *Cf.* Kum. I. 10. This stanza (with a variety of readings) is quoted anonymously in the Sar. Kan. as an instance of उत्तरपक्षनिदर्शन.

We have removed this sl. from the text as it is not in accord with the merchant's demeanour in this case. He had come from home prepard to meet with any fate and to make any sacrifice in the cause of his friend. To attribute fear to him goes against the self-possession and firmness of purpose which he displays throughout this scene. Wilson, too, does not seem to have had the sl. in the Mss. consulted by him; *cf.* his trans.—'Beware, The hooded snake hangs over you, and far Your hope of safety lies. As Vishṇugupta Will Nanda &c.

P. 42. **भ्रातृसचिवैः**—Chân. means—Râk. cannot be expected ot do, single handed, what he failed to do when assisted by his brother ministers, and those too, able statesmen. चन्द्रमिव—The comparison to the moon suggests that S'rî must be regarded now as inseparably united to Chandragupta.

आस्वादित &c.—इच्छति must be taken in this case, in the sense of the poten. (इच्छेत् in the sense of impossibility of अनवक्राप्ति)-who will wish to attempt the impossible task &c. संवादितं one of the Mss. consulted by Mr. Dhruva, reads विसंवदिस्सदि (will be proved false) in which case फल would refer to the result of the battle contemplated by Râkshasa. कलकलः—उत्सारणा *V. l.*-driving away of the people by the policemen. But this will leave less room for Chân 's next speech than the word कलकल does. अहह—is used here खेदे.

P. 43. सुलभेष्व०—संवेदन in the sense of समर्पण is unusual; निवेदन is the word used in that sense; *cf.* Rag. XIV. 70. शिबिना—As to S'ibi, see notes on VI. 18.

P. 44. दुर्गपालः—The keeper of the fort or superintendent of the prison. Some read च after विज०, making दुर्ग० a proper name. But the sing. रक्ष farther on shows that one person is meant. See p. 176 also. ०सार—valuables, property. पुरुषदोष—Faults common to humanity.

P. 45. साधु—(I. 7.) may also go with कृतः &c.; you have made an excellent beginning. Chân. says this स्वगतं. The shrewd politician does not want his pupil even to know what his plans are. संभावय—catch or overtake. Mark this sense of the root. *Cf.* अपि नाम जीवन्तीमेनां संभावयेयं Mâl. Mâd. V. तन्त्र—Arrangement. शिवाः पन्थानः सन्तु—I wish them godspeed.

P. 46. प्रभार्यं हृदये—*Cf.* S'âk. किमपि हृदये कृत्वा Act. I. कामं प्रकाम०—One of these is superfluous both being synonymous. (See Amara. II. 9. 57) कामं, however, may be taken to mean, 'If they desire although they do not' (अकामानुमतौ कामं Amar. III. 4 13.) or the reading सकामोद्यमाः should be preferred 'whose effort (to go) is successful.' बुद्धिस्तु मा गान्मम—Chânakya speaks like one quite conscious of the success his plot is to attain. He knows how excellently it was begun.

एकचर—(1) moving about (*i. e.* acting) alone, away from the relatives and friends of Nanda; (2) straying from the herd. *Cf.* Kir. XIII. 3. उत्सेकिन्—from उत्सिच् to overflow or to spout up; excessive. विगाहमान—(2) forming schemes; (2) roaming about. As this is a trans. verb. the object नय in the first case and वन in the second must be supplied; *cf.* in the first case विषमोपि विगाह्यते नयः। Kir. II. 3 मदबलेन विगाह्यमानं। *V. l.* meaning 'affected with the pride of valour or strength' will be better from a grammatical point of view, though less forcible. प्रगुणीकरोमि-(1) force you to yield or to be inclined to, prepare you for; (2) break in for use. The comparison with the elephant implies power but without a proportionate degree of mental vigour or acuteness of intellect. The fig. is repeated at p. 93.

ACT II.

P. 48. With this Act begins the *Garbhasandhi* (see com.) which is a combination of प्राप्त्याशा (a certain hope about the attainment of the final object) and पताका or an episodical dramatical incident. For further particulars see com p. 11. For the passage अमृताहरणं &c. quoted in the com. see D. R. p. 19.

Having depicted in the 1st Act the character of Châṇakya as a sound politician, seeing beforehand with the clear foresight of a statesman the doings and policies of his adversary and promptly taking measures to counteract them with perfect confidence in his own powers and diplomatic skill, the poet proceeds to give in this Act that of his political rival, Râkshasa. He is described as a man unsuccessful in all his undertakings, as one wanting in that keen political insight which enables a statesman to see through incidents the machinations of his enemies that lie behind them. He is thus the reverse prototype of Chânakya.

आहितुण्डिकः—A juggler, a serpent-charmer; अहितुण्डेन दीव्यतीति; fr. तुण्ड+इक (ठक्), Pân. IV. 4. 2. Also अहितुण्डिक, Vṛddhi being optional; see note on दण्डपाशिक p. 36. तुण्ड being the principal part of a serpent's body which attracts attention is used here for the body by लक्षणा. आहितुदण्डिकः in our present text is a mere misprint.

तन्त्र—There is a श्लेष or pun upon the several words of this sl.; the double meanings are explained in the com. तन्त्रयुक्ति—(1). The proper selection and application of drugs that serve as antidotes; (2) the judicious management of state affairs, administration of one's own state (and not of foreign matters). मण्डल—in the case of the snake means the enchanted circle which a serpent-charmer draws round a snake to keep it within its limits. In the case of the king this may mean the circle of the consistuent parts of a kingdom, as the Com. takes it, or the band of the frontier friendly, hostile and neutral kings. For various kinds of Mandalas see K. n. VIII. मन्त्र—(1) charms and (2) state secrets. सप्पणराहिवे—may be translated by सर्पनराधिपान् serve kings and serpents. उपचरन्ति—(1) prescribe remedies, (2) deal with, serve.

आकाशे—This is what is technically called आकाशभाषितं. For its definition see com., where the quotation is from D. R. p. 51. It is a speech addressed to some one not present on the stage but supposed to be behind the curtains and within earshot. See *supra.* note on प्रत्यक्षवदाकशे. In reply to his question the actor pretends to hear something said by the person or persons addressed and repeats it for the audience by asking the question 'what do you say &c.'

खेलत्येवार्योहिना—He means—To serve a king is playing as dangerous a game as playing with serpents. अहि—is a word of Vedic origin and originally meant the malignant influence personified as a demon (also called Vritra) that kept confined the celestical cows (the waters) which Indra liberated by killing the demon. Then it came to signify the malignant snake.

P. 49. मत्तमतंगजारोही—*v. l.*-मत्त is emphatic. A rider who is foolish enough to ride a mad elephant. The reading adopted in the text is better as it keeps up symmerty. जितकाशी-जित is used in the sense of the abstract noun जय (भावे क:) तेन काशते उद्धतो भवतीत्यर्थ: । lit. appearing or behaving like a conqueror, assuming the airs of a conqueror; hence haughty, overbearing. Here the juggler evidently refers to Chânakya as likely to be ruined on account of his haughtiness. This he does to show to the audience that he is a partisan of Râkshasa. पुनराकाशे—The juggler meets with two men, the one a royal servant, the other an ordinary passer by. This second man is brought in, in order to introduce the juggler to the minister's house. समुद्गक—समुद्गच्छति that which rises well (assumes a beautiful form): समुद्गम्+ड (अ) + कन् स्वार्थे

संस्कृतमाश्रित्य—As Virâdhagupta is not speaking in his assumed character he uses the language proper for him; as for the change of language, see D. R. II. 66. ०मतिपरिगृहीत—aided, entirely guided by the counsels of.

P. 50. धीरज्जु—The metaphor is repeated in VI. 4. उपाय—see I. 5.; the fig. is *Rûpaka.*

संशयिता—संशयमापन्ना; p. s. of intran. roots are used actively. *Cf.* संशय्य कर्णादिषु तिष्ठते यः Kir. III. 14. Or we may add इत (च्) in the sense of तदस्य संजातं by Pân. V. 2. 36. as the तारकादि is an आकृतिगण.

वशा—A female elephant, a female (here). गतागतैः—The goddess of wealth is supposed to move to one side or to the other as the one or the other of the ministers proves to be superior for the moment, and hence she gets wearied by these movements. *Cf.* Rag. VII. 93.

स्वभवनगतः—Sitting in the interior of his house.

P. 51. वृष्णीनां—the Yâdavas, so named after Vṛshṇi, an ancestor of Kṛshṇa. When Kṛshṇa, his earthly mission over returned to heaven, the Yâdavas perished by intestine divisions and quarrels among themselves, only a few surviving. See M. Bh. XVI. शान्त—used in the sense of the causal; see com. चित्रकर्म—(1) painting; (2) divers efforts. भित्ति—The back-ground. Divested of the fig. it means support. Râkshasa means that since the Nandas are dead, all his activity is without the main thing which should support it. Fig., a fusion of *Upamâ* and *Atishayokti*.

अथवा &c.—Herein he justifies his activity by saying that though he could not carry out his main object *viz.* the reinstatement of the Nandas, yet he would be doing them a service by being active in that way.

०व्यासङ्गरूढ—Set on the desire for *i. e.* intensely fond of. शात्रव-शत्रुरेव शात्रवः by adding अण् (अ) स्वार्थे which is affixed to the words of the प्रज्ञादि group. See Pân. V. 4. 38.

गन्धगज—A superior species of elephants so called from the strong smell they give out. The possession of such an elephant is supposed to ensure victory to a king गन्धप्रधानो गजः Madhya. comp.; *cf.* यस्य गन्धं समाघ्राय न तिष्ठन्ति प्रतिद्विपाः ॥ स वै गन्धगजो नाम नृपतेर्विजयावहः ॥ The comparison of Nanda to a Gandhagaja is intended to show Nanda's superior excellence as compared to Chaudragupta's inferiority of birth. चपला—Unsteadiness is usually ascribed to Lakshmî *Cf.* Rag. VI. 41.

कुलहीन—Because he was a वृषल (a man of mixed caste being the son of a Kshatriya by a S'udra wife).

P. 52. पुरन्ध्री—A woman having her sons and husband living; here used for a woman in general. The fig. in the last line is *Arthântarnyâsa*.

अकामा—Defeated in your wish to live with a low-born husband. **अनुदासीनः**—उदासीन *V. l.* means—thinking that Râk. is indifferent to *i. e.* does not take interest in, the cause. **उपजाप**-fr. उपजप् to whisper; secret communication *Cf.* this with the kindred but slightly different sense it has at p. 70. This is in accordance with the dicta of politics. *Cf.* Kâmandaka on the work to be done through the agency of the spies:—रागापरागौ जानीयात्प्रकृतीनां च भर्तरि ॥ कृत्यपक्षस्य चोपायं कुर्यादनभिलक्षितः । रिपोः शत्रुपरिच्छेदः सुहृद्बन्धुविभेदनम् (which corresponds to तत्संहतिभेदन of the text) ॥ दुर्गकोषबलज्ञानं कृत्यपक्षोपसंग्रहः ॥ K. n. XII. 8, 9, 22. **सुहृदो जीवसिद्धिप्रभृतयः**—This was the fatal mistake committed by Râkshâsa. He had not the sagacity to look men through, but rashly admitted even strangers to his intimacy. **पोत**—fr. पू to purify, *Cf.* the kindred Latin words *putus, pullus*.

कञ्चुकी—The Kanch. is described as-अन्तःपुरचरो राज्ञां वृद्धो विप्रो गुणान्वितः । सर्वकार्यार्थकुशलः कञ्चुकीत्यभिधीयते ॥ तदुक्तं मातृगुप्ताचार्यैः—ये नित्यं सत्त्वसम्पन्नाः कामदोषविवर्जिताः । ज्ञानविज्ञानकुशलाः कञ्चुकीयास्तु ते स्मृताः ॥ See also p. 73. **प्रतिष्ठा**—being firmly established; *cf. supra* p. 23; and Rag. VIII. 10. **प्रसह्य**—*V. l.* for क्रमेण would mean 'by rigorous or repressive measures,' in Châṇakya's case. But Châṇ. appears to have been anxious to win the affection of the citizens gradually and by gentle means. **अनु**—See p. 29. **लब्धान्तरः**—*Cf. infra.* sl. 22. अन्तरान्वेषी भवामि S'âk. VII. p. 193. **च**—but (पक्षान्तरे) A. G. § 272. **विस्मर्तुं**—an instance of Pass. *inf.*

P. 54. **पक्षपात**—A strong liking, affection; *cf.* भवन्ति भव्येषु हि पक्षपाताः । Kir. III. 12. and अहेतुः पक्षपातो यस्तस्य नास्ति प्रतिक्रिया Uttar. V. 17 and *Supra* p. 20. It, however, often means partiality as in Mâl. p. 22. &c.

सुगाङ्गः—Name of the palace of the Nandas at Pâṭaliputra, so called probably because it commanded a good view of the Ganges. **सिंहासनमिदम्**—of course Râk. is speaking as if the throne of Malayaketu is before his eyes. *Simhâsana* does not mean here a throne of gold as it usually does (*Cf.* सिंहासनं तु तद् हैमं Amara) but simply an excellent *i. e.* costly throne.

प्रतिमान्यताम्—*i. e.* honour it by accepting the ornaments. **कुमार इव** &c.—The Canch. not only by his age but by the place he held in the palace and his scholarship and other good qualities was always entitled to respect.

P. 55. **सर्पदर्शन**—The sight of such cruel animals as snakes &c. is held to be inauspicious. *Cf.* Mṛch. IX. 12. **दर्शनकार्य**-What would have accrued from his having seen the show *viz*. some present, remuneration. प्राकृतकवि—may mean 'a poet composing songs in the Prâkṛta languages, or a petty poet.'

इति गाथार्थः—The hidden meaning is suggested by कुसुमरस which means the talk of the people (रस from रस् which also means to sound) and भ्रमर also meaning a spy. (fr. भ्रम् to wander). अपणारां—may also stand for अज्ञानां (as suggested by Mr. Dhruva) and mean 'those who are in need of such information.'

P. 57. विराध—Râkshasa unmindfully half utters the name of Virâdhagupta, but suddency checking himself tries to give the term a different meaning (of fantastic dress or appearance) by adding प्रकटवपुः. See com. This he does to conceal from his servants the real character and name of the snake-charmer. भुजङ्गैरिदानीं &c.—This is contrary to the purpose for which the apparent juggler was called in. Râkshasa does not purposely allude to his *Subhâshitas* lest the servants might desire to wait there; at least he could not have unceremoniously asked them to withdraw and thus deprived them of the pleasure of listening to the songs. The sight of serpents was not such an unusual thing.

स्वं नियोगं &c.—This is the usual form used when a servant is to be asked to withdraw. *Cf.* S'âk. p. 51 &c.

P. 58. आदितः—Virâd. understands this to mean—from the beginning of the whole affair *i. e.* the attack on Kus. by the enemy.

शकयवन &c.—The S'akas appear to be a tribe inhabiting central India, who came in the first century preceding the Christian era and settled on the North-western frontier of India between the Indus and the sea—the Sacæ of the classical writers and generally identified with the Scythians. The Marâthi word शक is derived from this name. The Yavanas referred to here were probably the frontier tribes, inhabitants of Afghanistan and the neighbouring districts. They could not have been Greeks as Prof. Wilson supposes. *Kira'tas*—a savage tribe which, according to Mr. A. Boroosh, inhabited the hilly tracts just below the Himalayas, near Kumaon and Nepal. The Kambojas were a people that inhabited the Hindukush mountain which separates the Giljit valley from Balkh and probably extended upto little Thibet and Ladak. Their country was famous for handsome horses and shawls, and abounded in walnut trees. See Rag. IV. 69 and our note thereon. The Pâras'ikas were doubtless the people that inhabited Persia and the adjoining regions. Their country was also famous for the best breed of horses. See Rag. IV. 60, where the horses are mentioned as coming from the Vanâyu country. Bâlhîka is the name of the tribes that inhabited the Punjab. Their country is the modern Bactria or Balkh. In the Mah. Bhâr. they are said to have inhabited the country watered by the Indus and the five rivers of the Punjab outside 'holy India'. Their country was noted for its breed of horses and asafœtida.

क्षिप्रं—One क्षिप्रं is redundant. To avoid tautology take the other क्षिप्रं as modifying the परिक्रमणाक्रिया or omit the first. **प्रहर्तुमनसः**-हृ with प्र is generally construed with the Loc.; *cf.* न प्रहर्तुमनागसि S'âk. I. 11; ऋषिप्रभावान्मयि नान्तकोपि प्रभुः प्रहर्तुं &c. Rag. II. 62; also II. 54. &c. **ज्ञातं**—Believed, thought.

P. 59. **वैशस**—Hardships, troubles; fr. शस् with वि to kill &c. **अन्तर्नगरवासिषु**—These were the adherents of the Nandas.

कर्णेनेव &c.—Karṇa obtained from Indra, who was pleased at his having given him his divine armour and ear rings, the *S'akti* here mentioned, which was destined to kill *one* warrior, whoever he may be. See Mah. Bhâr. Droṇap. Ads. 179-180. **विष्णोः**—*i. e.* of Kṛshṇa and Chân. **आत्यन्तिक**०-अतिक्रान्तोऽन्तमत्यन्तः तत्र भवः (ठञ्)- **श्रेयसे**--because the *S'akti* and the maid not only did not kill the *protegees* of Kṛshṇa and Châṇakya but killed the very persons whom they wished to get rid of. **हैडिम्बेय**-is Ghatotkacha, the son of Bhîma by Hidimbâ (the daughter of the demon Hidimba). The possession of the *S'akti* by *Karna* was a source of great anxiety to Kṛshṇa who did not allow his *protegee* Arjuna to fight with Karṇa until the dangerous missile had passed out of the latter's hands. Sl. quoted in Al. Kau. as an instance of समस्तवस्तुविषया सावयवा उपमा.

P. 60. **प्रकाशित**—Publicly announced. **सांवत्सरिक**—संवत्सरं वेत्तीति aff. (ठक्), an astrologer.

परितुष्टेनेव--Omit इव. For Châṇakya was too shrewd to show that his satisfaction was feigned or was not real. Again the prsence of इव would leave no room for Râk.'s remark कुतश्चाणक्यबटोः परितोषः। **चाणक्यबटु**-बटु at the end of a comp. is used as a depreciatory term. **विकल्प**—optionality of thought, hence suspicion.

P. 61. **राज्यार्धविभागः**—अर्धश्चासौ विभागश्च अर्ध०, राज्यस्य अर्ध०. **उपांशु**—in secret. In many cases an *adv.* stands as the first member of a Karm. comp. उपनिवृत्ता अंशवो यस्मात्, that from which the rays have departed; hence, hidden, secret. This speech shows that Râkshasa was ignorant of the rumour circulated by Chânakya whom he believed to be the author of Parvates'vara's murder. उपचिता—see com. In translating, the reading उपचरिता has been followed.

किल—is used here अलीके 'only a semblance of coronation; or वार्तायां 'as was reported'. चित्रपट—not a variegated cloth, but a texture formed of pearls and diamonds woven together. वैकक्ष्य—wearing in the manner of the sacred thread; see com. चन्द्रगुप्तोपवाह्या—the riding she-elephant of Chandragupta. प्रविशति वैरोचके &c.—Notice the vigilance and shrewdness of Chânakya apparent from this. arrangement. यन्त्रतोरण—a gateway that moved by some mechanical contrivance.

P. 62. कनकदण्डिका—A hollow gold stick or rod that served as a sheath and hung from his belt. असिपुत्रिका—असेः पुत्रिका इव; पुत्रिका is here treated as a diminutive.

प्रभ्रष्टलक्ष्य—In which the mark was missed, wide of the mark. यन्त्रघट्टनबीज—the means (a bolt or axle) by which the machine was moved. कोष्ठघातं—see com.; 'करणे हनः' Pâṇ. III. 4. 31. The Namul of हन् is used with a noun signifying the instrument of the action and compounded with it as its first member, provided some form of the root हन् is used as the principal predicate.

वत्सलं—वत्से अभिलाषोऽस्यास्तीति; from वत्स + ल (a possessive affix added to वत्स and अंस in the sense of 'affection' and 'strength' respectively, by Pân. V. 2. 98).

P. 63. योगचूर्ण—A powder having the specific virtue (of causing a man's death). औषध—ओषधेरिदम् fr. ओषधि + अण् which is added in any other sense than *jâti* or species (Pâṇ. V. 4. 37). 'According to the Buddhistic accounts Chandragupta was fed on poison and thus made proof against it by Chânakya. See Max Muller's Ancient Sanskṛt Literature pp. 294-95.' Telang. कनकभाजने वर्णान्तरं &c.—*Cf.* लोहानां (सुवर्णादीनां) च मणीनां च मलपङ्कोपदिग्धता । प्रभावस्नेहगुरुता वर्णस्पर्शवधस्तथा ॥ औषधानि च सर्वाणि पानं पानीयमेव च । तत्कल्पकैः समास्वाद्य प्राश्नीयाद्भोजनानि च ॥ K. n. VII. 24. 27.

वाक्यभेदान्—Divergent accounts, contradictory statements. विचित्रवध—means death in an unusual way, *e. g.*–by being tied to the foot of an elephant or being hurled down from a precipice, or cut peacemeal,–by such and various other tortures; and occurs in Dk. Ull. I. (चित्रवधवार्ताप्रेषणेन); also चित्रमेनं हनिष्यसि Ull. 2; *cf.* also Mal. Mâd. p. 168. लवशो लवश एनां निकृत्य &c.

कथमत्रापि दैवेनोपहता वयम्--Râk. attributes the failure of his plans to Fate, but it was due to Châṇakya's foresight and to the folly or want of judgment of his own accomplices.

P. 64. निपुणमवलोकयता &c.—*cf.* कारयेन्भवनशोधनमादौ &c. K. n. VII. 37. विहित—made *i. e.* fixed upon. Another reading is अभिहित spoken to *i. e.* agreed upon. The reading अपिहित or पिहित means 'closed up.' मन्त्रीतयः—my schemes or plots, devices of policy. Sl. quoted in Al. Kau. as an instance of *Vishama*.

प्रारभ्यते &c.—This stanza is quoted in the com. on the D. R- (p. 44.) as from Bhar. with the reading in the fourth line—जनास्त्व. मिवोद्वहन्ति—a reading which is more appropriate, if so at all, in the Mud. It is probable, therefore, thinks Mr. Telang, that the author of the Das'arûpakâvaloka, quoting from memory, quoted the text of his copy of the Mud., wrongly attributing it to Bhar.'s S'at. The following stanza too occurs in some Mss. of Bhar.'s S'atakas. The probable explanation of such occurrences is to be sought in what may be called the *Subhâshita* theory—that the stanzas already existed as Subhâshitas and were borrowed by the authors of both the works as suited their purpose. The reading त्वमिवो &c., however, is not appropriate to the context, which requires the stanza to be a general statement. With our reading only Virâdhagupta's introductory speech and the following words of Râk. सखे प्रारब्धमपरित्याज्यं &c. are intelligible. *Cf.* Kathâs. XVIII. 188.

P. 65. कृपणवत्—Like a mean-hearted person, a coward (who has no sense of personal honour); opp. to श्लाघ्य. *Cf.* कार्पण्य III. 16; कृपणं V. 15. निर्व्यूढ—*p. p.* noun, same as निर्वाह *V. l.* carrying to their completion or end. गोत्रव्रते-*cf.* कुलधर्म p. 167. Sl. quoted in the Al. Kau. as an instance of *Mâlârûpaka*.

Wilson remarks on the above two Sl.s.-It may be doubted if perseverance is any where recommended in a more manly and spirited tone.

एतदीदृशं—Such attempts, *viz.* to poison Chandragupta &c. निष्परिग्रह—one without earthly belongings or ties.

परिहृत &c.—This A'ryâ is variously read as स्वस्मिन्, 'परि०-त्रप०' omiting च; ननं परि &c.; परिहृतमयशः स्वपिं &c. But in all these cases the metre is violated. Mr. Telang who reads स्वस्मिन्परिहृत० remarks—It is possible that the stanza was intended to be of the Aryâgiti sort;... but this stanza differs from that in having 20 instead of 19 *mâtrâs* in the 2nd line while the 3rd and 4th are here as in an ordinary A'ryâ...But see Mâgha IV. 48.

अर्धराज्य—is generally considered to be a grammatical anomaly; it shou.d be राज्यार्धः, as it was exactly half of the revenue of the kingdom and not of the land. The comp. is correct if exactly half of the land be meant. Sl. quoted in Al. Kau. as an instance of the fig. *Vishama.*

P. 66. **अयुक्तरूपः**—Exceedingly undeserved or unworthy. The aff. रूप is added in the sense of प्रशंसा which here lies in the excess of युक्तता, by प्रशंसायां रूपप्' Pân. V. 5. 66. युक्तरूपो न भवतीति अयुक्तरूपः। *Cf.* S'âk. युक्तरूपमिदं तव p. 14. युक्तरूपं सन्देष्टव्यं p. 110.

कृतघ्नैः—Although he had a laudable object in view, Râk., overpowered by emotion calls himself ungrateful in as much as he did not immediately follow his master in death. If the additional reading given in the foot-note be original, आलम्ब्य in the first sl. will have to be translated by 'taking my stand upon, putting forth this' as an excuse, (and not जिजीविषा) and Râk. taken to mean—I am really ungrateful and wish to live but under the pretext of doing a service to my master, &c. This would necessitate the following speech of Virâdhagupta who could not be expected to allow this unmerited self-censure on the part of his master. In some Mss. we have स्वार्थमवलम्ब्य जि०; if then अर्थ be taken in apposition with जिजीविषा the meaning will be 'I am not following my master on account of this very thing *viz.* the desire to live long.' This reading, followed by Virâdhagupta's अमात्य नैतदेवं &c. will also do very well.

ननु वक्तव्यं &c.—Râkshasa knew quite well what the result of Chandanadâsa's imprisonment would be. He felt that his future was bound up with the lot of his friend.

P. 67, **भव्यं**—Fortunate, not condemned by fate, destined to live; *cf.* अरक्षितं तिष्ठति दैवरक्षितम् Pt. I. 20. **भवितव्यता**—The state of what is destined to happen, personified into Destiny. *Cf.* Kir. XI. 47, Mâl. Mâd. I. 23.

प्रतिष्ठितपदं—(1) firmly planted, fixed; (2) established on the throne. **चेतनाप्रमथिनी**—(1) destroying consciousness; (2) violently irritating the mind. **मूर्द्धाव०**—a strange comp. This must be taken as an object to दृष्ट्वा. The reading मूर्ध्निवबध्य स्रजम appears better as it well harmonises with दृष्ट्वा and श्रुत्वा; but then अवबध्य does not apply to लक्ष्मीं. The reading of the German Ed. तल्लक्ष्मीमिव चेतसः प्रमथिनीमूढ्वाच वध्यस्रजम् । would solve all difficulties as it has a verb to correspond to दृष्ट्वा &c.

which can also be taken with लक्ष्मीं. As to the स्रज् *cf.* वध्यस्रज् VII. 4; Mṛch. X. 21. and p. 478, where Chârudatta wears a similar garland. **रौद्रविषमान्**—रौद्र refers to the feeling of terror roused; विषम harsh or fearful to the ear. **आघात॰**—आघातार्थं तू॰; trumpets sounded at the time of his execution. Mr. Telang takes आघा॰ in the sense of 'musical instruments to be beaten like a drum &c.' **प्रथमाभिघात**—previous strokes of misfortune. S'akaṭadâsa means that he could bear the sight of the pale, listen to the dismal music &c. simply because his heart had grown callous by previous calamities Fig. *Upamâ*.

मन्ये—यत्तद् *V. l.*; see com. With the reading मन्ये there is no difficulty of construction. But with the reading यत्तद् we have an clumsy construction; for we must construe यत्प्रथमाभि॰ तन्मदीयं मनः &c.; and even if यत्तद् be taken in the sense of 'since' the construction becomes equally awkward.

अक्षीणभक्तिः &c.—Here the poet gives his own estimate of Râkshasa's character. **स्वाम्यर्थसुद्वहन्**—Upholding the cause of his master.

॰गोचरगत—Fallen into his clutches, gone into his power. Mark the meaning of गो in such instances where it means an इन्द्रिय though it generally refers to the eye.

P. 68. **किं**—काममपर्याप्तं *v. l.* I admit that this is inadequate to the favour done by you—is also a good reading.

सखे विराधगुप्त—Transported with joy Râk. forgets the precaution he had taken to keep off his spy's name from his servants and addresses him here by his name. Chân. could not have been guilty of such a blunder. **इदं**—*scil.* his gift of the ornaments. **अस्य प्रियस्य**—this favour, this aggreeable service rendered by you, *viz.* the rescue of S'akaṭadâsa. **अर्थं**—*scil.* that he should receive the ornaments, keep them with Râkshasa, &c.; see com.

P. 69. **ब्राह्मण्या**—His wife. **उत्कण्ठाविनोदार्थं**—to drive away her longing, as a means of alleviating the pain of separation. This appears to be a common thing with ladies; *cf.* the similar use of the ring in the S'âk.

गेह—is derived by Bhânujî Dîkshita as गेनं गणेशेन ईह्यते काम्यते, गो गणेशो गन्धर्वो वा ईहा ईप्सिता यस्मिन् वा. But these explanations seem far-fetched. गेह is probably the Prâkṛta form of गृह afterwards re-sanskritised. **अमात्य अत्र किं युज्यते**—Siddhârthaka of course intends by this question to elicit, if he can, some further information about Râkshasa's family and friends. He is, however, disappointed in this.

तद्दीयतामेषा—Chânakya had the ring restored to Râkshasa, it seems, for the following reasons. First, that Siddhârthaka, by promptly delivering the ring, would make a favourable impression upon Râkshasa, as a man that could intend no evil, and thereby secure his confidence the more easily. Secondly, it would be impossible for Râkshasa to allege against the letter being imputed to him that the ring was no longer in his possession and had probably fallen into the hands of his enemy. Thirdly Malayaketu would not believe any statement of Râkshasa to the contrary when he saw the ring actually in his possession.

P. 70. **स्वाधिकार**—What this अधिकार was, is not clearly stated. It appears, however, that S'akaṭadâsa had the management of Râkshasa's private affairs. See p. 71. ll. 15, 16 and *cf.* p. 139. *infra.* **पाटलिपुत्र**—The capital of Magadha (or South Behar) situated near the confluence of the Ganges and the S'oṇa. It was also called Kusumapura (Palibothra, referred to in the classical accounts of India). It is said to have been destroyed by a river inundation about the middle of the 8th century A. D. The legend accounting for the origin of the name given in the Kathâs. is briefly this— Putraka, an exiled king, secretly married Pâṭali, the princess of A'karshikâ, and to avoid the dreadful consequences of her father's anger, fled with her to the banks of the Ganges. At the request of his wife he founded there, by his magical power, a city which was called Pàtaliputra:—अथ गङ्गातटनिकटे गङ्गामवतीर्य स प्रियां श्रान्ताम् । पात्र (a magical utensil in his possession) प्रभावजातैराहारैर्नन्दयामास ॥ आलोकितप्रभावः पाटल्या सोर्थितश्च ततः । यष्टया (a stick with magical virtue) लिलेख तत्र स नगरं चतुरङ्गबलयुक्तम् । तदिदं दिव्यं मायारचितं सपौरमत एव । नाम्ना पाटलिपुत्रं क्षेत्रं लक्ष्मीसरस्वत्योः । See Kathâs. I. 3.

अनुनयः—Request. **विश्रामय**—make arrangements about his taking rest; see that he is refreshed being well lodged and fed.

उपजाप—Overtures. secret negotiations; instigation to rebellion ; *cf.* उपजापः कृतस्तेन S'is. II. 99; उपजापसहान् विलङ्घयन् &c. Kir. II. 47; also XVI. 42. तेषु तेषु च कृत्येषु प्रासरन्परोपजापाः । D. K.

यथाप्रकाशं—They are emboldened to act according to our secret instructions as things are disclosing themselves. This is explained in the context.

P. 71. **जितकाशितया**—See p. 49. *supra.* **उपचिनोति**—Adds to his vexation, constantly pains his mind. *Cf.* the use of the word at p. 61. (उपचिता). **उपश्लोकयितव्यः**—उपश्लोकय् a Denom. meaning to praise in stanzas or songs. ०हस्तेन-हस्त simply means here 'instrumentality or means of communication and so stands for ०मुखेन.

अलङ्कारसंयोगाः—Ornaments forming a set; articles of decoration to be worn on the person together (संयुज्य धार्यन्ते इति).

P. 72. तेजसि—*i. e.* क्षात्रतेजसि वर्तते reigns in full majesty, hence is arrogant. स्मयः—pride, self-sufficiently. *Cf.* तस्मै स्मयावेशविवर्जिताय Rag. V. 19; प्रभवः स्मयदूषिताः Bhar. Vai. 2. कृतकृत्यता &c.—Because they are no longer in need of each other's help. लब्धान्तरा—For the meaning of अन्तर see II. 9. भेत्स्यति will make them break away from each other. The Fig. is *Anumâna.* Here end the *Patàkâ* and the *Garbhasandhi.*

ACT III.

P. 73. The Third Act embodies the *Avamarshasandhi.* See com- कञ्चुकी-सनिर्वेदम्—Kâñchukin (so called from his long thin robe) is a respectable attendant of the harem. He is generally represented as an old man, a Brâhmaṇa, endowed with many good qualities, such as truthfulness &c. The Sanskṛt plays represent him as always full of despondency, In fact the Kañchukin's character is surrounded by a dignity and air which make the impression about the effects of old age he makes on the minds of the audience more vivid and telling.

करण—An instrument of knowledge; an organ of perception. आत्मलाभ—its own being, birth; *cf.* Kâd. II. sl. 3. or the gaining of one's object. स्वार्थ—their proper object. अङ्ग.—is used here in the sense of 'an organ of action (कर्मेन्द्रिय). मुधा ताम्यसि—Because the powers of action and perception being enfeebled by age, your cravings cannot be satisfied; they will only cause pain. Fig. *Kâvyaliṅga.*

कौमुदीमहोत्सव—This, as generally understood, falls on the full-moon day of *A'svina.* Jagadhara, commenting on the word at Mâl. Mâd. Act VII. p. 141, however, says—कौमुद्याश्विनपूर्णिमाव्रतं यद्वा कार्तिक्यां चन्द्रमण्डलपूजा कौमुदीव्रतम् । It is this latter festival, *viz.* that on the full-moon day of Kârtika that seems to be meant here as is clear from the 21st sloka which makes a reference to Vishṇu's awakening from his long sleep of four months which takes place on the 11th day of Kârtika. कौमुद also is the name of the month of Kârtika. कौमुदः स्यात्कार्तिकके ।

P. 74. भूमयः—Floors. दैवोपहत—doomed by fate, ill-fated. कथोपोद्घात—mentioning or alluding to a topic or subject.

पिनद्ध०—The अ of अपि is optionally dropped. सिंहाङ्कासन—the throne of Chandragupta, distinguished by a lion's picture. संजातमूर्छा—The earth is supposed to be languishing under the load of the throne. Fig.—*Samâsokti* and *Utprekshâ*.

सुविश्रब्ध—Well-confident, showing no nervous tottering, firm; (2) trusty. अङ्गैः—(1) limbs; (2) the members of the political body. पथिषु—(1) paths; (2) political situations. धुर्य—धुरं वहतीति (accustomed to bear the yoke); opposed to दम्य (दमनार्हः to be trained to bear the yoke). The comparison is common enough; *cf.* Rag. V. 66 &c. The bull was considered a noble animal in ancient times, and the word वृषभ expressed 'excellence' when at the end of a compound, like सिंह, शार्दूल &c. Mark the antithesis between गुरु and नववयस्, धुर्य and दम्य and अचलता and स्खलति. दुःख—may be a noun.

P. 75. रहयति—जडयाति *v. l.* seems to be a better reading. In this case the second line becomes a different alternative. परवान्-Because he is not at liberty to attend to personal comforts, since he must devote his attention first to the interests of others. आत्मवत्—self-restrained: *Cf.* आत्मवत्तया *v. l.* Rag. VIII. 10; commenting on which Malli. says—निर्विकारमनस्कतयेत्यर्थः । उदयादिष्वविकृतिर्मनसः सत्त्वमुच्यते । आत्मवान्सत्त्ववानुक्तः । इत्युत्पलमालायाम् । or आत्मवत् may mean आत्मसम्पन्न endowed with आत्मसम्पत् or the characteristic qualities of a king. These Kâmandaka describes as—वाग्मी प्रगल्भः स्मृतिमानुदग्रो बलवान्वशी । नेता दण्डस्य निपुणः कृतशिल्पः सुविग्रहः ॥ पराभियोगप्रसहो दृष्टसर्वप्रतिक्रियः । परच्छिद्रान्वेषी च सन्धिविग्रहतत्त्ववित् ॥ गूढमन्त्रप्रचारश्च देशकालविभागवित् । आदाता सम्यगर्थानां विनियोक्ता च पात्रवित् ॥ क्रोधलोभभयद्रोहस्तम्भचापलवर्जितः । परोपतापपैशुन्यमात्सर्येर्ष्यानृतातिगः । वृद्धोपदेशसम्पन्नः शक्तो मधुरदर्शनः । गुणानुरागी स्मितवागात्मसंपत्प्रकीर्तिता । Nît. IV. 15-19. सन्तिष्ठते—स्था with सम्, अव, प्र and sometimes वि is Âtm. (Pân. I. 3. 32). एकान्तभीरु-exceedingly timid, or always timid, as Mr. Telang takes it. लब्धप्रसरा—(1) who has got a considerable scope for occupation; (2) who has got considerable ascendancy. *Cf.* Malli. on S'is. III. 35. वेशवनिता—वेशे वेश्याजनसमाश्रये वर्तमाना वनिता or वेशेन (by hire, D. R. p. 90) लभ्या वनिता.

कृतक—Artificial; hence pretended or sham. कालान्तरं—not a Nityasamâsa but a Gen. Tat.

P. 76. संस्क्रियमाणमतयः—*cf.* for a similar thought चंद्रापीडस्ताभिरमलाभिरुपदेशवाग्भिः प्रक्षालित इवोन्मीलित इव निर्मृष्ट इवाभिषिक्त इवाभिलिप्त इवालंकृत इव पवित्रीकृत इवोद्भासित इव प्रीतहृदयः &c. Kâd.

परतरमतः &c.—Independence beyond this *i. e.* independence guided by विनय as mentioned in the third line. The commentator's explanation does not seem to be accurate. By making the observation अथवा &c. which is explained in the present stanza, Chandragupta is trying to satisfy his mind as to the *Pa'taka* he thought he was guilty of, by supposing that he is always independent in a way and that his present conduct is in conformity with that स्वातंत्र्य.

श्यानीभूताः—The epithets refer to both दिशः and सरितः. सितजलधर—सितजलधरच्छेदा एव पुलिनानि यासां; पक्षे ०च्छेदा इव पुलिनानि यासां. सारसकुलैः—Swans are described as returning in Autumn from the Mânasa lake, moving gaily through the atmosphere and uttering sweet notes. सरित इव—like *i. e.* as well as; (as the speaker here describes both, the rivers and the directions).

P. 77. विकच०—०नक्षत्राणीव कुमुदानि नक्षत्राणि कुमुदानि च । पक्षे नक्षत्राण्येव कुमुदानि तैः । The double meanings are explained in the com. नभस्तः—(1) From the sky; (2) From the time of the rainy season नभस्; *cf.* Latin *mebula.* The description of Autumn here is very beautiful and can compare well with similar descriptions by Kâlidâsa and other great poets. As to the commentator's remark अनेन शरद्गुणकथनेन ' &c. *cf.* Rag. IV. 24.

उद्वृत्तानां—The epithets are used in a literal and a figurative sense; (1) overflowing their boundaries,; in flood; (2) going astray. *Cf.* उद्वृत्तः क इव सुखावहः परेषाम् । S'is. VII. 18 Rs. III. 3. स्थितिपद—(1) the proper bed for their flow; (2) the right path of conduct. अवनति—(1) bending posture; (2) humility. उदारे—&c. (1) a rich crop; (2) abundance of wealth. *Cf.* भवन्ति नम्रास्तरवः &c. S'âk. V. 12. मयूराणां &c. *Cf.* मयूरमदमुषि शरत्समयारम्भे Har. शरादि हंसरवाः परुषीकृतस्वरमयूरमयूरमणीयताम् । S'is. VI. 44: also 45. पश्यन्ति नोन्नतमुखा गगनं मयूराः । Rs. III. 12; also 13. विनय—training, regulation; for it teaches propriety of conduct to those who go astray, modesty to the rich and humility to the arrogant. *Cf.* Rag. II. 8; and *infra* III. 25. The fig.s in the sl. are *S'lesha, Upamâ* and *Utpreksha.*

कलुषितां—(1) rendered turbid during the rains; (2) offended, jealous. *Cf.* Rag. V. 64 (where some take कलुषा in this sense. बहुवल्लभ—The sea is often poetically spoken of as the husband of rivers: *cf.* Rag. IV. 45. XIII. 9. तन्नभवन्तीं—*Cf.* Rag. IV. 24.

सर्वात्मना—doing her best; goes with नयति; or it may better be taken with प्रसन्ना completely pleased. **गङ्गां**—Here Gaṅgâ is represented as a *Khaṇḍita* Nâyikâ. See D. R. II. 25. **प्रसन्नां**—Waters resume their lucidity in the winter. *Cf.* Rag. IV. 21; XIII. 46. This simple idea is clothed here in rich poetic imagery. As remarked by the Com. the बीजावमर्श is visible in these three s'lokas.

P. 78. **गृहीतं**—Obeyed, acted on. **स्खलिष्यति**—will be disobeyed. *Cf.* Lat. *Sceuls, eris.*

धूर्त—Gay, licentious people; beaux. It generally means gamblers, gamesters &c.; a deceitful lover &c., see. D. R. p. 92. com. **पृथुजघन०**—For the idea comp. यातं यत्र नितम्बयोर्गुरुतया मन्दं विलासादिव S'âk. II. 2. **मुक्तशङ्का:**—Because of the permission granted by the king. This may be taken with वेशनार्य: also. **अभिलषितं**—The festival seems to have been time-honoured and held in great esteem by the citizens. See p. 105. **पार्वणं**—falling on the Parvaṇ or full-moon-day (of Kârtika as remarked by the Com.). See note on कौमुदीमहोत्सव p. 73. *Cf.* the description of the spring festival at Rat. I. 11. 12.

P. 79. **अनुविद्धा**—Mixed with, full of. *Cf.* S'âk. I. 18 and com. thereon. **दुरात्मा**—perverse-minded, of wicked resolve. **कृतागा:**—here means 'one against whom an offence was committed,' injured or insulted (कृतमागो यस्य).

P. 80. **मौर्येन्दो:**—Mark the propriety of इन्दु in connection with श्री. **दुर्व्यसन**—persistence in an evil pursuit.

उत्सिक्त:—Vain, conceited; from उत्सिच् to spout out; hence to be swelled or puffed up with pride; *cf.* S'âk. IV. 17; Rag. IV. 70; स्तूयमाना नोत्सिच्यन्ते Kâd. p. 470. **कुसचिव**—*Cf.* दौर्मन्त्र्यान्नृपतिर्विनश्यति Bhart. Nît. 42; and the Subh. दुर्मन्त्री राज्यनाशाय. **मदनुकृते:**—Better read मदनुकृते or ०कृतौ (Loc. sing.). **प्रधानवैरं**—प्रधानस्य वैरं enmity to the principal person (the king). See sl. 11. **किल**—Assuredly, verily.

प्रविष्टान्तरै:—Who have entered into the heart *i. e.* dived into the secrets of the enemy. **स्वमतेन** The Com. reads भेदकुशलोऽस्त्वेष: let him be, according to his own estimation, a master of &c. **प्रतीपं**—The commentator takes this in the sense of (1) 'acting adversely towards us;' and (2) 'I shall so alienate him as to act adversely towards our enemy (Malayaketu). The second sense is not justified by the context; for Râkshasa does not leave Malayaketu or act adversely towards him; it is Malaya. who casts away Râkshasa. The first sense is not also good. So it seems better to take प्रतीप to mean 'on the contrary, contray to his expectation (*i. e.* instead of his separating me from Chandragupta, I shall separate him from Malayaketu). प्रतीप fr. प्रती + अप्; प्रतिगता आपो अत्र, the अ of अप् being changed to ई and अ (अच्) added.

P. 81. विटाः—Voluptuous companions, whose duty it is to please by flattery. अपलपन—see com.; it rather means 'concealment of one's real feelings and thoughts,' lest the declaration of truth might give offence; hence flattery. *Cf.* ये च विद्यमानेपि स्वात्मनि अस्वाधीनसकलेन्द्रियवृत्तयः पश्यन्तोप्यन्धा इव शृण्वन्तोपि बधिरा इव वाग्मिनोपि मूका इव स्वामिचित्तादर्शे प्रतिबिंबवद्वर्तन्ते Kâd. p. 471; Bhar. Vai. S'at. 6; Nit. S'at. 31.

कृतधियः—Those of refined or cultivated intellect (शिक्षितबुद्धयः Malli. on S'is II. 79). It may also mean those who have fixed notions about a subject. श्ववृत्तिः—(1) शुन इव वृत्तिः (or शुनः वृत्तिरिव;) (2) शुनः वृत्तिः । a canine mode of living; *cf.* सेवा श्ववृत्तिराख्याता तस्मात्तां परिवर्जयेत् Manu. IV. 6. राजाधिराज०—अधिको राजा अधिराजः ।

विभूति—Grandeur, pomp. The sentence is of course ironical as remarked by Mr. Telang. गोमय—means here dry cow-dung cakes or balls. Chânakya, therefore, was an Agnihotrin. स्तूप—a heap; from स्तूप् 10 cl. to raise. 'This is the word used for the Buddhist 'Tope', but is not confined to that sense.'—Telang. पटल—roof. This stanza clearly shows how simple was the private life of Chânakya and greatly redeems his character as an ambitious statesman. See Introduction, Fig. *Svabhâvokti.*

P. 82 वृषलः—The reading वृषलोद्य does not so forcibly express the contratst intended. It is also difficult to explain it grammatically. For by the rule 'वदः सुपि क्यप् च' Pân. III. 1. 106. क्यप् or यत् (य) may be added to the root वद्; so ब्रह्मोद्यं or ब्रह्मवद्यं 'recital of Veda.' वृषलोद्य (according to Bhattoji who would have the aff. भावे) means वृषलशब्दस्य वदनं the act of uttering the word वृषल; and then by affixing अच् including the word in the अर्श आदि group, we get वृषलशब्दस्य वदनमस्यास्तीति वृषलोद्यः; *cf.* सत्यवद्यः Bhatti. V. 60. But then it must go with चाणक्यः and not चन्द्रगुप्तः. And even if we add the aff. कर्मणि (as some grammarians would have it—See Kau. on the above Sûtra) the same difficulty confronts us. This, therefore, is a grammatical anomaly. अस्य—For the Gen. Mr. Telang compares वीरो न यस्य भगवान्भृगुनन्दनोपि Uttar. V. 34.

अभूतै:—not really existing, imaginary. भूत means what exists, what is really present ; *cf.* भूतार्थं S'âk. p. 6; and भूतार्थव्याहृति Rag. X. 33. **प्रवाच: कार्पण्यात्**—may also mean on account of the absence of plain speaking (प्रकृष्टा वाक् तस्या:), since they cannot speak out plainly. **वितथ**—विगतं तथा सत्यं तस्मात् । **निरीहाणां**—*cf.* तृणमिव लघुलक्ष्मीर्नैव तान्संरुणद्धि । Bhar. Nît. 17 ; and the Subbhâshita निस्पृहस्य तृणं जगत् ।

परिभूय—Mark the meaning of this:-having overpowered *i. e.* pervaded or filled up; stands in contrast with असर्वगामि.-**पर्याय**—in succession or turns. **असर्वगामि**—Because sunlight is not all reaching; *e. g.* it does not dispel गुहागतं तम: &c. ; again it covers only half the globe at a time ; but the influence of Châṇakya was universally felt. **अतिशाययति**—Here the Caus. aff. (णिच्) is added स्वार्थे. To take it in the sense of the Cau. as धाम्ना अतिशाययति makes his lustre (might) surpass that of the sun, (see com.) is to make the cons. clumsy. Notice the व्यतिरेकालं. in this which consists in representing the *upameya* as superior to the *upamâna* in some particular respect. There is also the fig. *Yathâsankhya*.

P. 83. **प्रणति॰**—Mr. Telang has adopted the reading—प्रणतसंभ्रम॰, though he pronounces in favour of the reading adopted by us. In that case प्रणत must be taken as a separate *adj*. qualifying भूमिपाल्स or as equivalent to प्रणमन. **अन्तरा**—Secretly. **प्रद्वेषपक्षपात:**—feeling of hatred ; (lit.) a strong (leaning towards,) liking for hatred.

P. 84. **॰राजराज**—is Kubera. For the enormous riches of the Nandas see *infra*. sl. 23. Mr. Telang suggests that राजराज may also mean 'principal kings under ths Nandas ; who did not care for (despised) the principal kings under them'. *Cf* in this respect उपजापसहान् विलङ्घयन् स विधाता नृपतीन् मदोद्धत: । सहते न जनोऽप्यध: क्रियां किमु लोकाधिकधाम राजकम् ॥ Kir. II. 47. The reading in the foot-note (राजवृत्तै:), however, is preferable, as राजराजै: conveys no censure to the Nandas but ॰वृत्तै: does. **परं**—we should have noticed the reading त्रय: which is also good. **गुणा:**—excellences; good results. मम should be construed with प्रीतिं. Fig.—a mixture of समुच्चय and परिकर.

मणिरुच:—The southern ocean is known for its pearls ; see Rag. IV. 50 ; *cf.* however Bilhaṇa, रत्नोत्करग्राहिषु यद्गदेषु तदग्रुक्मौक्तिशुक्तिमङ्गया । Vikramâ. I. 108. **आगत्यागत्य** coming every day. The repetition shows नित्यत्व.

न निष्प्रयोजनं &c.—The student will see here the first glimpse of the sham quarrel between Chân. and the king.

P. 85. विज्ञापयितुं—To make a respectful representation. Mark the contrast between विज्ञापय् and आज्ञापय्. Both mean to represent, to inform &c.; but the first carries with it the additional sense of respect or humility, the second that of authority or command, and hence these are used with respect to inferior and superior persons when making a representation. See our note on आज्ञापय् Vik. p 30.

विज्ञापनीयानां—The pl. shows the respect due to the preceptor.

स्वैररुचयः—Independent tendencies or tastes. गृहीतवान्—*cf. supra* p. 37.

शुश्रूषा &c.—Notice the respectful tone of Chandra. in his earlier speeches. His unwillingness to disrespeet his *Guru* (even at his suggestion) is distinctly seen in this. Châṇakya, however, assumes an apparant tone of arrogance which fills his pupil with disgust and gradually rouses his anger and finally leads to the intended rupture between the two.

अर्थशास्त्र—अर्यते गम्यते इत्यर्थः (fr. ऋ + थ by Uṇâdi. II. 3.) भूम्यादिस्तस्य शास्त्रं means here the science of polity, politicst It also means the science of practical life and is often contrasted with धर्मशास्त्र. सिद्धि—lit. the accomplishment of object; hence, the execution of state business, administration. 'The distinction is,' remarks Mr. Telang, " in essence the same as that between a despotic monarch, a consti tutional monarch, and a monarch who regins but does not govern." वत्स्यामः—The reading वेत्स्यामः would perhaps have better suited the context, but it is grammatically wrong: it should be वेदिष्यामः since the *Anit* विद् obtainable in the 4th and 7th conjugations does not mean 'to know.'

वैतालिकौ—विविधेन तालेन चरति इति वैतालिकः one who sings in different *tâlas.* A kind of poetical warder or bard whose duty it was to announce fixed periods of time, to awaken kings from their sleep &c. The bards are generally introduced in pairs in Sanskṛt plays. The bards herein mentioned do not seem to have been in the king's employ as they are asked to be remunerated further on.

P. 86. काशपुष्प—The *Kâs'a* flower is represented by Sanskṛt poets as one of the types of whiteness. *Cf.* ०काशनिकाशमूर्त्यां D. K.; also Ṛt. III. 1, 2, Rag. IV. 17. अभिभवता—*i. e.* which resembles it. भस्मना—It is difficult to see what this means in the case of शरत्. Mr. Telang understands by it the white clouds of Autumn and compares Ṛt. III. 4. ऐभी कृतिः—(1) seems to refer to the impression of the

4

elephant-hide-like space (the clear dark-blue Autumnal sky); (2) S'iva is represented as wearing the skin of Gajâsura (the Elephant demon) killed by him. **क्षिभती**—oppressing ; hence ' overpowering or counteracting the impression of' as Mr. Telang takes it. **कापाली**—*Cf.* Kum. V. 78. Vai. S'at. 29. **इति**—Thus, in this way. Mr. Telang remarks—" According to usual course with such stanzas the double meanings in the previous lines should be expressed as they are in the third line. But, as above stated, the construction of those previous lines does not apparently suit this, though the commentator's explanation is based on that view." **हास्यश्री०**—(1) *cf.* Rt. III. 2. Rag. IV. 19.

In this sl. Autumn is described as having attained the high attributes of S'iva's body and is therefore able to grant protection. But since in the next Vishṇu is praised, here too, prominence should have been given to पेशीतनु and the line should have read हरतु शरदिव क्लेशमेशीतनुर्वः ।

जिह्मा—Squint, half-closed ; it may also mean dull or slow. ' जिह्मस्तु कुटिले मन्दे,' Haima Koṣa. **रत्न०**—The jewels may probably be those in the hoods of S'esha ; *cf.* नत्फणामण्डलोदर्चिर्मणिद्योतितविग्रहम् । Rag. X. 17. **नागाङ्कं**—*v. l.* नागचिह्नं in the form of. **आकेकरा**—' आकेकरलक्षणं तु नृत्यविलासे—दृष्टिराकेकरा किंचित्स्फुटापाङ्गे प्रसारिता । मीलितार्धपुटालोके ताराव्यावर्तनोत्तरा ॥ ' Malli. on Kir. VIII. 53. This stanza is quoted in the Sar. .. with the remark अत्र दृष्टेः प्रत्यग्रोन्मेषजिह्मतादिभिः प्रबोधो नाद्यापि निष्पद्यते ति प्रतीयते । The poet, it will be seen, praises S'iva in the first stanza annd Vishṇu in the second, Fig. *Savabhâvokti.*

P. 87. **सत्त्व**—Mental calibre, that peculiar energy of the mind which never allows it to flag, sweeping all obstacles before it, and leads to the completion what is undertaken. **कस्यापि हेतोः**—For some special reason; Com. The suggested sense given by the Com. may be intended. This may better be taken with आज्ञाभङ्ग. Kings should never allow their order to be disobeyed under any circumstances. **दंष्ट्राभङ्ग**—*Cf.* I. 8. **मानावलेप**—may also mean pride of one's dignity. Mr. Telang remarks ' it is difficult to distinguish between मान and अवलेप, if we take the comp., with the Commentator, as a द्वंद्व. Perhaps it might be allowable to take it thus—whose pride about the respect due to them is well-known. ' But we humbly differ from such a high authority. मान and अवलेप are generally used synonymously no doubt. But here they are used in different senses. मान is derived from मन् to think and *has to do with the mind.* It means high opinion about one's-self, self-respect. *Cf.* मानश्चित्तसमुन्नतिः Amara. अवलेप

is derived from लिप with अव—अवलिप्यते अनेन (करणे घञ्) and properly means a paint or a coating. It thus refers *more to the outward bearing* or *external features* than to the mind; it means a behaviour of pride or spirit of resentment. Here the two words mean self-respect and pride or spirit of resentment, and must be supposed to be used in a good sense. It may be necessary for kings to resent an insult for having their commands universally obeyed. **आज्ञाभङ्ग** &c.—For आज्ञाभङ्गो नरेन्द्राणामशस्त्रो वध उच्यते । **सार्वभौमः**—सर्वभूमेः ईश्वरः, सर्व भूमौ विदितो वा । Pân. V. 1. 42, 43.

उपभोगेन—उपचार *v. l.* external appendages; this fits in better with भूषणादि. We have, however, preferred उपभोगेन to उपचारेण as it is likely to touch the heart more effectively than the latter. **अपरिभूताज्ञः**—*Cf.* Bhar. राज्यं किमाज्ञाफलं; Nît. Misc. 2. The student will at once see the bard Stanakalas'a, Râkshasa's agent, speaking through these verses and trying to set the king against his minister.

विशिष्ट—Specific, specially worshipped. **अर्थोत्सर्ग**—expenditure of money. **दोषाः**—evils, misfortunes. **अनभियुक्त**—not applying themselves to work.

अभियुज्यस्व—युज् generally preceded by a *prep.* beginning or ending with a vowel is Atm. except when it does not refer to sacrificial utensils. प्रोपाभ्यां युजेरयज्ञपात्रेषु । Pâṇ. I. 3. 64. **स्वराद्यन्तोपसर्गादिति** वक्तव्यं Vârt.

P. 88. **आज्ञाव्याघातः**—The repetition of the same term in different senses lends a peculiar force to the speeches.

तमालश्याम॰—*Cf.* तमालतालीवनराजिनीला Rag. XIII. 15. **तिमि**—A fabulous fish of monstrous size, said to be a hundred *yojanas* in length; अस्ति मत्स्यस्तिमिर्नाम शतयोजनमायतः । **मालेव** &c.—Which is respectfully obeyed. *Cf.* गुणानुरागेण शिरोभिरुह्यते नराधिपैर्माल्यमिवास्य शासनम् । Kir. I. 21. तथेति शेषामिव भर्तुराज्ञां &c. Kum. III. 22. **उह्यते**—The Com. needlessly and without propriety takes this in the sense of the future. Mr. Telang remarks—If the command was at that time already accepted by all kings, a breach of it by Châṇakya would then properly be spoken of as it is here. **Fig.** *Vyâghâta* (according to Al. Kau.).

P. 89. **प्रमाणलेख्यपत्र**—A document showing the number; or a document to serve as evidence or proof. **कुमारसेवक**—may mean a servant of the king from his (or the king's) boyhood. **एते वयं** &c.–see foot note. Almost all Mss. conclude the document with these words.

But they are quite out of place here as their insertion will make the document an important state paper and it could not have been brought so openly by Vaihînari. Again Chāṇakya would not allow a sentence to be added in the document which would make the real object of the desertes, which he was taking care to keep concealed known. Some editions make the king read the better (आत्मगतम्); see readings. In this case the words एते वयं &c. would show to the king that they were really serving him and would leave no room to the king to ask the question एतेषामपरागहेतून् &c. in the next speech.

स्त्रीमद्य०—Three of the four principal vices mentioned by Manu and alluded to by Kâli. in Rag. IX. 7. स्वजीवनमात्रेण &c.—Not to give them due allowance for their maintenance would have been impolitic. K. n. V. 65.

P. 90. इत्युत्पाद्य—Having fabricated or got up the story. दायाद—lit. those who take a share of the paternal estate, those entitled to inherit; hence relatives (quarrelling with one another for inheritance).

अनुग्रह—Reward, showing favour. निग्रह—punishment. राज्यस्य मूलं—The basis, the main prop of the kingdom. *Cf.* गजेषु नीलाभ्रसमप्रभेषु राज्यं निबद्धं पृथिवीपतीनाम्। K. n. XV. 10., also XIX. 62.

P. 91. पूर्वः पक्षः—The first alternative. उत्तरोपि खलु &c.—"The answer to the second alternative seems to be that the adherents and friends of the Nandas would become disaffected, and would have no confidence of fair treatment by Chandragupta, if Chandragupta's own adherents and friends were punished as suggested, and thus the gradual subsidence of old memories and quieting of the kingdom would be delayed." Telang. प्रवणः—fovourably inclined or disposed towards, ready to act on. व्यायाम—Action, active operations.

द्वयी गतिः—A two-fold course; द्वाववयवौ यस्याः द्वयी or द्वितयी.

स्वहस्तः—One's helping hand; hence a confirmation or corroboration of. Or स्वहस्त may mean one's own handwriting serving as evidence, hence unmistakable or incontrovertible proof.

P. 92. एकत्र—*i. e.* in one place with the subjects of Nanda. पुरुषकारः—पुरुषस्य कारः कर्म manliness, courage. सहाय०-rich in friends. *Cf.* सहायसाध्याः प्रदिशन्ति संपदः; Kir. XIV. 44. Here Râkshasa is represented as talented and resourceful—as possessed of the three powers necessary for an ambitious conqueror. Thus his सहायसं० and the possession of कोष constitute his प्रभुशक्ति, while his political talent (प्रज्ञा) and पुरुषकार indicate his मन्त्रशक्ति and उत्साहशक्ति; *cf.* स प्रभावः

प्रतापश्च यत्तेजः कोषदण्डजम् । Amara, and K. n. मन्त्रस्य शक्तिं सुनयोपचारं सुकोषदण्डौ प्रभुशक्तिमाहुः । उत्साहशक्तिं बलवद्विचेष्टां त्रिशक्तियुक्तो भवतीह जेता ॥ XV. 32. **अन्तःकोप**—internal disturbance or disaffection. For अन्तःकोप and बाह्यकोप see K. n. XV. 19–21. For the disastrous consequences of Antaskopa, *cf.* अणुरप्युपहन्ति विग्रहः प्रभुमन्तःप्रकृतिप्रकोपजः । Kir. II. 51.

राक्षसः खलु असौ—He is Râkshasa, mind you. *Cf.* Marâthi राक्षस तो.

अभियुक्तः—Forcibly assailed, hard-pressed. (**वियुक्तः**) **असि**—stands for स्याः or भविष्यसि. **अथ**—is पक्षान्तरे. **वनगज इव**—For the propriety of the simile *cf.* I. 26. *supra.* **प्रशस्यतर**—Mark how the king chooses his words; he does not say वाग्मितर or मतिमत्तरः. **वनगज इव** &c.—Here Chân. speaks seriously; *cf. supra.* I. 26. **उपायैर्विनेयः**—The remedies used are those of (1) उपेक्षा or conniving at Râkshasa's actions; (2) भेद or alienating Râk. from Malaya. through the instrumentality of Siddhârthaka, Bhâg. and others; (3) दण्ड or punishmant inflicted on his adherents, (4) माया or the fuss about the sentence passed on Chandanadâsa and (5) साम and दान.

P. 93. **कृत्वा पदं नो गले**—is idiomatic for 'quite in defiance of us.' **अस्मद्बलानां**—goes with जयघोष०. **स्वनीतिविभवैः**—विभव implies richness; his various prolific political schemes. **मतयः**—The plural used probably for the metre. **स्वेषु वर्गेषु**—explains why Chânakya may also be distrusted.

आरूढ—Rising within, or rather thrilling through the whole body. **अग्राङ्गुली**—This comp. is generally analysed as अग्रं चासौ अङ्गुली च (see Malli. on Kir. XVII. 38.) समानाधिकरणसमासः । In विशेषण पूर्वपदकर्म० such as नीलोत्पल, उत्पल and नीलत्व are indentical; but in this case अग्रं and अङ्गुली are not indentical. But they may be so regarded by *Lakshaṇâ* through their relation as अवयव and अवयवी. See Râghavabhaṭṭa's remarks on अग्रहस्त, S'âk. p. 92. and Vâmana quoted by him there; also our note *ad. loc.* **०दीर्घा**—The Com. takes this to refer to the length of time taken to destroy the enemy. It rather refers, as Mr. Telang observes, to length of space, the figure in the mind of the poet being probably the same as at p. 21, where the प्रतिज्ञा is compared to a river, and the length of water to be crossed is great owing to the number of enemies sworn to be destroyed.

P. 94. **नवनवतिशत०**—The Nandas were the reputed lords of ninety-nine crores of gold coins, *cf.* एहि राज्ञः सखे नन्दाद्याचितुं गुरुदक्षिणां । गच्छामो नान्यतोऽस्माभिरियत्काञ्चनमाप्यते । नवाधिकाया नवतेः कोटीनामधिपो हि सः ॥ Kathâs. Lambak. I. Tar. IV. 24, 95. But the reading in the text makes them lords of 99 hundreds of crores of gold coins. So the original reading may have been, as conjectured by Mr. Dhruva, नव नवनवतिद्रव्यकोटीश्वराः । पर्यायभूताः—standing in a successive line. पश्यतो राक्षसस्य—When contempt or disregard is to be shown the Genitive Absolute is used; *cf.* Pâṇ. II. 3. 38 quoted in the commentary.

गृध्रैः, धूमैः—The Com. explains this as a व्यस्तरूपक being equivalent to गृध्रधूमैः । नन्दैः—of course means the Nandas and their men that fell with them. पितृवन—The residence of the dead, a cemetery, also called पितृसद्म; Kum. V. 77. ०निकयान्प्राणिनः—*cf.* Mâl. Mâd. V. 11-18. एते—Châṇ. is speaking as if he and Chand. saw the whole scene visibly before them though past.

दैव &c.—*cf.* दैवेन देयमिति कापुरुषा वदन्ति ।

शिखां मोक्तुं—This was Châṇ.'s habit. बद्धामपि—must be taken to mean 'almost tied (बद्धप्रायां).' Or Châṇ. appears to forget in the fury of anger (of course pretended) that the knot had been already untied.

P. 95. आरोढुं—To exercise power on, to get ascendancy over, (hence to treat with contempt or to take to task, as the Com. takes it). परीतः—Lit. surrounded by; hence overpowered, doomed by.

क्षाम—Properly, wasted, grown lean or emaciated (*p. p.* of क्षै); here it means grown turbid (enfeebled, so far as its function of seeing is concerned). रुद्रस्य—Verbs meaning to remember have their object in the Gen. case; अधीगर्थदयेशां कर्मणि (षष्ठी) Pâṇ. II. 3. 52. रौद्रं रसं—the sentiment of fury of which S'iva is the presiding deity. स्याद्रुद्रो रुद्रदैवतः Bharata. ताण्डव—तण्डुना प्रोक्तं । 'तेन प्रोक्तं' (Pâṇ. IV. 3. 101.) इत्यण् । the violent or frantic dance of S'iva. उग्रप्रकम्पं—The reading उदग्रकम्पं is rejected because उदग्र (उद्गतमग्रमस्य) would mean (trembling upwards) while here the trembling was caused all round *cf.* I. 2.

उत्तरोत्तर—Bandying or exchanging words, verbal altercation. शस्त्र—see p. 22.

P. 96. दूषण—Disgrace, conviction. This expectation of Châṇakya is realized. See. pp. 134-136. The sham quarrel which was so deliberately planned and successfully effected had the following effect. It served to throw Râkshasa off his guard by turning his attention to a wrong quarter by making him over-confident of the favourable issue of open warfare and by closing his eyes to the activity of Châṇakya's emissaries. Moreover, it led Malayaketu to believe that the deserters from Chandragupta, Bhâgurâyaṇa, and others came over to him through real discontent. It corroborated the insinuations of the forged letter and of Bhâgurâyana, that Râkshasa aimed at being the minister of Chandragupta. Lastly it helped to produce in Malaya. the fatal belief that the affairs of Chandragupta were really in a state of disorder and that that was the favourable time for striking the blow.

उपपद—An epithet or title of respect. **हन्त**—expresses pity.

असत् कुरुते—असत् 'wrong, an injury' may be taken separately; but the com. is better. **व्याल**—a wicked elephant; व्यालो दुष्टगजे सर्पे इति हैमः। *cf.* Malli. on Kir. XVII. 25.

एवं गृह्यमाणेषु—Understood to be such; looked on in this light. This sense of ग्रह् is common enough; *cf.* एवं जनो गृह्णाति Mâl. I. परमार्थेन न गृह्यतां वचः S'âk. II. 25; मयापि मृत्पिण्डबुद्धिना तथैव गृहीतं *Ibid.* VI. p. 160.

P. 97. **बुद्धिः प्रवेष्टुं** &c.—Chandragupta means that his intelligence is just on the point of leaving him, so much overpowered by shame he is; he is quite beside himself with shame. **अतिपातयन्ति**—अतिपातय् seems to be nsed here synonymously with लङ्घ्. *Cf.* अतिपातितकालसाधना: Kir. II. 42. The sloka clearly shows that Chandragupta duly appreciated the services of Châṇakya and had proper respect for his *Guru.* Contrast this trait of his character with the fickleness of mind of Malayaketu and the readiness with which he insults Râkshasa, his real well-wisher and a man of tested loyalty. (Act V. pp. 134–136).

ACT IV.

अध्वग—अध्वानं गच्छतीति a wayfarer, a traveller. **ही हीमाणहे**—expresses wonder; this occurs in Mṛch. pp. 15, 460 &c. It is made up of ही and माणहे (which stands for मानुषा Voc. pl.).

महीयान्—All-powerful. Cal. Ed.s read योजनशतं समधिकं &c. **अस्थानगमन॰**—seems to mean—great (powerful) enough to force one to go to a place not fit to go to. It may also mean 'important because one has to visit places not easily approachable in order to gather information.'

दौवारिक...द्वारे नियुक्तः। 'तत्र नियुक्तः'। Pâṇ. IV. 4. 69. इति ठक् (इक)। 'द्वारादीनां च' VII. 3. 4. इति औ आगमः। **मा उच्चैः**—शनैः *v. l.* is not appropriate.

P. 98. भद्रमुख—Good sir. Generally used in addressing a stranger. *Cf.* S'âk. p. 197.

अविधेयता—Unmanageableness, uncontrollable nature. Fate was stubbornly adverse to him and would not crown his efforts with success. अपि च—and to add to that. विहते *v. l.*—foiled, frustrated (अस्माभिः कृते तत्कृत्यानामुपग्रहे विहते). निकामं—exceedingly, entirely. अनिशं—*i. e.* night is as it were no night to me.

कार्योपक्षेपं &c.—For the Sanskṛt definitions of the various dramatic terms occurring herein, see p. 11. कार्य—The business or chief object. उपक्षेप—(1) one of the twelve subsidiary parts of *Mukha* (बीजन्यास उपक्षेपः । D. R.); (2) setting on foot, commencing. बीज—(1) the germ or the so-called *seed* of the plot of the story; (2) the primary incidents of an undertaking or political measure. आदौ—*scil.* in what is called मुखसन्धि (that in which the seed sprouts up connected with the various *Rasas* and attended with आरम्भ). विस्तारं—*i. e.* the गर्भसन्धि (wherein the seed that has already struck root has only slightly developed, being aided by the means to the end). गर्भितानां—*i. e.* when the seeds are in what is called गर्भसन्धि (in which the seed or the first cause of the fruit attains a further development and is accompanied by obstructions and search after the end which on the whole help the *denouement* of the plot). बुद्धि—dramatic genius ; (2) political insight, forethought. विमर्शं—The *Sandhi* of that name (generally called अवमर्श wherein the seed attains a more luxuriant growth that in the *garbha* being accompanied by *niyatâpti* of the end, but whose final result is yet postponed by fresh impediments such as a curse, and the like). (2) deliberation as to the chances of success or otherwise. संहरन्—*i. e.* in the निर्वहणसन्धि (wherein the final catastrophe is reached, the various incidents, howsoever scattered, converging to one point *i. e.* the end). There is श्लेषालङ्कार in the first three lines.

कर्ता वा &c.—The poet's task is as arduous as that of a minister. For a similar fig. comp. S'is. XI. 6. (where a poet and a king who is a practical adminstrator are likened); Bhar. Nît. S'at. Misc. sl. 16, and Vai. S'at. 51 where a poet and a *mantrin*, and a man and an actor are compared.

P. 99. तदपि नाम &c.—The whole sentence is चतुरतिसन्धातुं शक्यः स्यात्. The interruption gives another version to it which is explained in Râkshasa's next speech. Râk. of course takes this as an ill omen. See p. 33. *supra* and notes.

वागीश्वरी—Such accidental words are supposed to proceed from some superhuman agency and are considered as divine. Their import was corroborated by the coincident twiching of the left eye. A throbbing sensation in the left part of the body of men is supposed to indicate some future evil. प्रस्ताव—The Com. needlessly takes this in the sense of संवाद 'agreement with' (which is however arbitrary). It is better to take the Inst. करणे. Divine speech expressed or rather established her meaning by means of &c.

P. 100. अज्जा—Mr. Telang reads 'आअदो' but it is out of place. कल्याण—meaning 'gold' is rather unusual, though the Kos'as give the sense; 'कल्याणे हेम्नि मङ्गले'। Cal. Ed.s read कल्याणकुलधराणं (गृहाणां) the abodes of what is auspicious.

पुरुषाभिमान—May mean pride characteristic of man, or pride about one's prowess पौरुष).

भूरेणु०—भुवः रेणुभिः रूक्षा अलका यस्मिन्। मातृजन—the mothers; पितृपत्न्यः सर्वा मातरः). निवापाञ्जलिः—निवापाय अञ्जलिः a comp. सुप्सुपा. न्युप्यते निवपनमिति वा निवापः। करणे भावे वा घञ्। An offering offered to a deceased person after the *Sapîṇḍákaraṇa.* The mention of the *Nivâpa* shows that Malaya. was not a Yavana.

P. 101. उद्यच्छता-Bearing up; यम् with उद् is Atm. when the object is not a literary work; as भारमुद्यच्छते, and it should be so here. But as the fruit of the action goes to his father (*viz.* his satisfaction) the poet uses the Par.; see also com. धुरं-the yoke of; hence doing the onerous duty of a hero. अकापुरुष—not a timid or mean-hearted person; *i. e.* a high-souled or brave man. The whole means—Bearing the brunt of battle and doing deeds of great valour. गन्तव्यमा०—As Parvate. had not fallen on the battle-field but met with his death in his bed chamber while clasping the Poison-maid, this simply means—By dying in the battle I should follow my father to the next world.

प्रतिनिवृत्ताः—Turned back *i. e.* desisted from proceeding further. सोत्सेध—raised high up. उपलक्षणे तृ०. *Cf.* पयोधरोत्सेधविशीर्णसंहतिः। Kum. V. 8. खमिव खण्डयन्तः—"alluding apparently to the manner in which the horse raises his foot very high in moving when his speed is suddenly checked."—Telang. मर्यादां—*Cf.* वेलां समुद्रा इव न व्यतीयुः। Rag. XIV. 2. जलधय इव—The comparison to the sea indicates the vastness of the troops,

P. 102. भद्रभटप्रभृतिभिः—These were the men who came over to Malaya. apparently through discontent, but who were really Chânakya's emissaries. See VII. 9. ०परिगृहीता—*cf.* चाणक्यमति परिगृहीत, राक्षस० p. 49. चन्द्रगुप्तात्—अपरज्ञ is used with the Abl.; *cf.* 'नयहीनादपरज्यते जनः Kir. II. 49. आभिरामिक—अभिराम एवाभिरामिकः। स्वार्थे ठक् (इक).

आत्मगुण०—' Possessed of qualities, tastes, feelings &c. as one's self.' So Mr. Telang. It seems rather to mean endowed with the quali. ties of the soul (आत्मनो गुणाः); *cf.* अत्रभवति सर्वैवात्मसंपदभिजनात्प्रभृत्यन्यूनैव लक्ष्यते। D. K. II. ननु—certainly.

किंतु—Mark how skilfully Bhâg. insinuates as Châṇakya's agent, that Râk.'s devotion to Malaya. is not real and that he (Râk.) may enter into an alliance with Chandragupta towards whom he is not actuated by any feeling of animosity. सुहृज्जन—*i. e.* Râkshasa's friends in the city. पितृ०—पर्यायेणागतः पर्यायागतः। पितृभ्यः पर्यायागतः पितृ०। युज्यते—shows that Bhâg.'s words have produced their effect on Malayaketu. The ground is thus prepared for the future structure of Bhâgurâyaṇa's policy of *Bheda*.

P. 103. सत्वभङ्ग—may mean मनोभङ्ग (giving offence), सत्व being used by *Lakshaṇâ* for the seat of *Satva,* as the Com. takes it. Or it may better be taken with राज्ञाम्. Ministers give a false report to their masters that they may not lose their courage, अन्यथा, अन्यथा—Mark the use of these two words—in one way, in another. स्वैरालापेषु-may also be taken as स्वैः स्वजनैः सह आला०.

गहनः &c.—Not easily to be penetrated or comprehended. Bhâg. is here trying to thicken the suspicion about Râk.'s sincerity which has already gained possession of Malaya.'s mind. परिच्छिद्—To cut all round; hence to grasp fully and accurately. The root constantly occurs in this sense; *cf.* Rag. VI. 77, Mâl. Mâd. I. 33, 34, &c.

P. 104. जनितपरिचयः—जनितः (कालेन) परिचयः यस्य। मानितः-hailed with respect.

कौमुदी &c.—There is a pun on the words कौमुदी, कुमुदानन्द, and चन्द्र. कौमुदी—(1) The festival; (2) moonlight. कुमुदानन्द—the gladdener of a section of people, by *Lakshaṇâ* ; or कुत्सिता मुद् येषां तेषामानन्दः gratifier of people delighting in bad things *i. e.* Châṇakya and people of his type; (2) gladdener of nightlotuses. चन्द्र—(1) Chanbragupta ; (2) the moon. The contrast between कुमुदानन्द and जगदानन्द, चन्द्र and नृपचन्द्र is also intended to be significant. The one Chandra delights a *few people*: the other was the gratifier of *all*. Fig.-see com.; there are also *Kâvyaliṅga* and *S'lesha*.

परिपाटी—A series or succession. This is said simply to please Râk. as the bard had repeated two slokas only.

सद्यः—समाने अहनि *indec.*; momentary. सद्यःक्रीडा may also be taken as one word; 'immediate sport.' *cf.* सहते न जनोप्यधःक्रियां किमु लोकाधिकधाम राजकम्। Kir. II. 47.

P. 105. कलुषित—Properly means-made turbid or foul, and as anger has a pereceptible effect on the mind and also the body of a person, it means angry; *cf.* III. 9. *supra*; also विमलं कलुषीभवच्च चेतः Kir. XIII. 6; anger is considered a *mala* which sullies the mind. न तथा-See Bhâg.'s meaning explained in the com. कृतवेदी—grateful; see XIII. 32. आत्यन्तिक—lasting; see II. 14. हस्ततलगतः—Because no longer aided by the wise counsels of Chânakya.

P. 106. चाणक्यात् &c.—Mark how Bhâg. gives a different version of Râk.'s plain words. He invidiously suggests that Râkshasa's object must be to become minister in Chânkya's place. See com. सावेगं—Because Chân.'s conduct seemed to throw a doubt over the reality of the quarrel.

देवस्य—देवकृता (offence) given by the king. स्वाप्रा०—स्वस्य अप्रासना-पयनात्। स्वयं कृत०—Read स्वयंकृत &c. मनस्वी-a proud man (मानी).

अमलन्यथा &c.—S'akaṭa. means that Râk. should not have unnecessary misgivings but may well believe the news.

P. 107. इन्दु—Moon-like gems (by *Lakshaṇâ*; इन्दवः तत्सदृशा म .यः). कोपनः—कुप्यति तच्छीलः; from कुप्+युच् (अन) added शीलार्थे. 'क्रुधमण्डार्थेभ्यश्च' Pâṇ. III. 2. 151. अन is added to the roots क्रुध् and मण्ड् and their synonyms in this sense; क्रोधन, मण्डन, भूषण, &c. अभिचरण—employment of spells and incantations and the performance of such rites as the S'yenesti, with a view to obtain one's object. (वृष्ट्यायुः-पुष्टिकामो वा तथैवाभिचरन्नपि Yâj. I. 295); but generally for malevolent purposes such as the destruction of one's enemies &c.; *cf.* बभार रम्योपि वपुः स भीषणं गतः क्रियां मन्त्र इवाभिचारिकीम्। Kir. III. 56. अभिचारक्रियाक्रूरैकप्रकृतयः Kâd. p. 177. Such acts are considered *upapâtakas*, as animals like a hawk (*cf.* श्येनेनाभिचरन्यजेत) have to be killed and sacrificed. Chânakya, it is said, performed such destructive rites and encompassed the death of his enemies, the Nandas. Kâmandaka refers to this at the begining of his Nîtisa'ra when paying his tribute of respect to Chânakya—यस्याभिचारवज्रेण &c. I. 4. See *supra*. p. 12. com. ज्ञातदुःखः—For it is not an easy task to perform the Abhichârakriyas as they entail unusual trouble on, and cause a great deal of worry to, the performer. So it is not often that one can do these things. दैवात्—S'akaṭa. suggests that in fulfilling his first vow Chân. was indebted more to his good luck than to his diplomacy.

This he does evidently to please Râkshasa. आयतिः—उत्तरः काल आयतिः । Amara; but it generally means 'a favourable future;' *cf.* रहयत्यापदुपेतमायतिः । Kir. II. 14. केशनखानामायतिभङ्गः । Kâd. p. 26. अनायतिक्षमं (वचः) । Pt. III. 109. ग्लानि—failure; discomfiture in the future; if this means 'failure of energy' then आयति will mean simply future time.

विश्रामय—See p. 70 *supra.* अतिरस्कृत—not screend or thrown into shade, *i. e.* supplanted. डरीकृतमेतदा०—*cf.* नैतत्संस्थास्यते कार्यं दक्षेणोरीकृतं त्वया । Bhaṭṭi. VIII. 11. संभृत—collected, or fully equipped; hence ready for action. उदीक्षमाणैः—uselessly or idly waiting for. This is not the same as अपेक्षमाण.

P. 108. सचिवव्यसनं &c.—*Cf.* स्वशक्त्युपचये केचित्परस्य व्यसने परे । यानमाहुस्तदासीनं त्वामुत्थापयति द्वयम् ॥ S'is. II. 57; and Manu—तदा यायाद्विगृह्यैव व्यसने चोत्थिते रिपोः । See sl. 15. further on. व्यसन is derived as यस्माद्धि व्यस्यति श्रेयस्तस्माद्व्यसनमुच्यते । K. n. XIII. 19. सचिवोत्थितं व्यसनं सचिवव्यसनम्—Mad. comp. A weak point arising from want of an able minister to guide the state affairs. चन्द्रगुप्तप्रकृतीनां—Malaya. cf course is covertly referring to Râkshasa, his mind* being previously poisoned by Bhâgurâyaṇa.

पितृभूतं—'Bearing to him the relation of his paternal family.' Telang. It seems, however, undoubtedly better to take it in connection with the subjects. The अपराग and अमर्ष referred to are explicable only if we suppose the Nandas to have taken fatherly care of their *subjects.* For, what could the subjects have cared for the Nandas, had they been oppressive, even though they bore paternal relation to *Chandragupta*? With our meaning the comp., too, becomes appropriate, पिता इव भूतं (comp. सुप्सुपा); *cf.* प्रजानां विनयाधानाद्रक्षणाद्भरणादपि । स पिता पितरस्तासां केवलं जन्महेतवः ॥ Rag. I. 24. विप्रकृताः—Lit driven from their nature; hence affected or troubled by. Hence also harassed or tormented, as in Kum. II. 1. स्वाश्रय०—सु + आश्रय. संभाव्य०—whose power may be believed as equal to. *Cf.* संभावनीयानुभावास्याकृतिः । S'âk. VII. p. 206; संभाव्यपराक्रमं Kir. XIII. 1. निदर्शन—An instance (which proves what is stated previously); *cf.* Rag. VIII. 45.

P. 109. प्रतिविधातुं—To resist (our attack). The reading 'स्वायत्तसिद्धिषूभयायत्त &c. has been adopted in preference to स्वायत्तसिद्धिषु (भूमि०) as it is in better keeping with Mal.'s previous speech. तत्—*i. e.* स्वयं प्रतिविधानं. सचिवायत्तसिद्धौ स्थितः-see p. 85 *supra.* Râk. is speaking here as Chandragupta's antagonist, but he was inwardly conscious of Chandragupta's great worth and the promise of future greatness he gave early in life. *Cf.* VII. 12.

अत्युच्छ्रिते—Occupying a very elevated place, grown almost as powerful as the king. The figure is taken from the games of dancers and tumblers as remarked by the Com. Lakshmí, unable to keep long in a state of equilibrium which is necessarily unstable, makes her choice soon and clings to one of them. असहा भरस्य—सहते इति सहा, सह् + अच् + आ. भरस्य—कृद्योगे कर्मणि षष्ठी । कर्तृकर्मणोः कृति Pâṇ. II. 3. 65. A. G. § 109. *Cf.* संप्राप्ते वपुषि सहत्वमातपस्य । Kir. VII. 7. हीवि-भूमिरसहा विरहस्य । S'is. X. 81. एकं भूमिपतिः करोति सचिवं राज्ये प्रमाणं यदा &c. Pt. I. 263. Hit. II. 126. Divested of the fig. the meaning is that the joint administration of a state—by the king and his minister—will not continue long, it will either take the autocratic or the ministerial form of government, one of the two losing his unrestrained power.

Sl. 13. &c. *Cf.* स्वायत्तसिद्धे राज्ञो हि प्रज्ञोपकरणं मता । सचिवायत्तसिद्धेस्तु तत्प्र-श्रैवार्थसाधनम् । त एव चेन्निरुत्साहाः श्रियै दत्तो जलाञ्जलिः ॥ Kâthasar. Tar. XV. 58. तदर्पणः—Who makes over or entrusts his affairs to his minister. स्तनंधयः—स्तन धयतीति । नासिकास्तनयोर्ध्माधेटोः Pâṇ. III. 2. 29. Also स्तनंधयी. The nasal comes in by Pâṇ. VI. 3. 67. See our note on परंतप Bhaṭṭi. I. 1. उत्सहते—has the energy to. वर्तितुं—वृत् to act, to perform his royal duties. *Cf.* यः कुर्यात्सचिवायत्तां श्रियं तद्व्यसने सति । सोऽन्धवज्जगतीपालः सीदेत्संचारकैर्विना ॥ Hit. II. 128.

P. 110. अभियुञ्जानस्य—Applying himself to (taking advantage of). ऐकान्तिकी—एकान्ताय हिता प्रभवति वा; lit, leading to *one* end; hence certain.

चलिता०—चलिताधिकारः च (not अतएव) विमुखः (not favourably inclined) च. मौर्ये नवे राजनि—*Cf.* Mâl. I. 8. quoted before (see p. 5. notes). योग—means; see com. ना—Râk. identifies Malaya.'s. interest with his own. In this sl Râk. sums up the circumstances favourable for an immediate march. In the first place his own party is strong enough to act on the offensive; secondly, the prime minister and the subjects of the enemy are disattached to him; thirdly Maurya is inexperienced and fourthly Malaya. has everything favourable to himself. *Cf.* मित्रामात्यसुहृद्वर्गा यदा स्युर्दृढभक्तयः । शत्रूणां विपरी-ताश्च कर्तव्यो विग्रहस्तदा ॥ Hit. III. 65; also K. n. X. 27.

उत्तुङ्गाः &c.—The figures in this stanza are *Upamá*, *S'lesha* and *Anuprása.* There are two sets of adjectives indicating the common qualities on which the comparison is grounded, one set applying to the river S'oṇa, the other to Malaya.'s elephants. मुखरः—निन्दितं मुखमस्य । मुखशब्दो लक्षणयात्र वचनपरः । र shows possession and is affixed to words

5

like ख, मुख &c. Pâṇ. V. 2. 107. खात—*p. p.* used abstractively. शोण—A river rising in Goṇḍavana and joining the Ganges; *cf.* Rag. VI. 36. अपास्यन्तु—*i. e.* on their way to Pâṭaliputra, the elephants will enjoy a bath tossing the current in all directions. *Cf.* Rag. IV. 45. It appears from Kshapaṇaka's speech at p. 112, that Malayaketu's army had to pass from north to south crossing on its way the river S'oṇa. Pâṭaliputra, therefore, appears to have been situated to the south of the S'oṇa.

विन्ध्यं &c.—The Vindhya being the central chain is naturally the resting place of the clouds in their passage from the south and is often referred to by poets ; *cf.* तस्यापतन्मूर्ध्नि जलानि जिष्णोर्विन्ध्यस्य मेघप्रभवा इवापः । Rag. XIV. 8. Ṛt. II. 27. इव मेघमाला—the comparison suggests the huge size of the elephants. Clouds and elephants are often compared ; *cf.* Mṛch. V. 21; Meg. I. 2.

P. 111. सांवत्सरिक—संवत्सरं वेत्ति ; fr. संवत्सर + ठक् ; an astrologer. कथं क्षपणकः—The sight of a Kshapaṇaka (a Buddhist or Jaina mendicant) is considered ominous. *Cf.* p. 115. The mention of Kshap. causes uneasiness to Râk., but the subsequent mention of the name Jiva., which sounds auspicious, quiets his fears and he asks his servant to send him in ; see com.

अबीभत्स—बीभत्स disgusting, revolting to view. The appearance of *Kshapaṇakas* and other Buddhist mendicants is generally represented as loathsome. *Cf.* प्रेक्षस्व प्रेक्षस्व य एष गलन्मलपङ्कपिच्छिलबीभत्सदुःप्रेक्ष्यदेहच्छविः उल्लुञ्चितचिकुरः मुक्तवसनवेषदुर्दर्शनः शिखिशिखण्डकपिच्छिकाहस्त इत एवाभिवर्तते । Prabodhachandrodaya.

अर्हत्—A Buddha of the highest rank ; also the supreme divinity of the Jainas ; सर्वज्ञो जितरागादिदोषस्त्रैलोक्यपूजितः । यथास्थितार्थवादी च देवोऽर्हन्परमेश्वरः ॥ This as well as the words अर्हतः प्रणमामि &c. (V. 2.) show that Kshap. was more probably a Jaina ascetic. The first words of the specific prayer formula of the Jainas are नम आर्हतानां नमः सिद्धानां नम आचार्याणां &c. See Monier Williams' Buddhism, p. 536.

प्रतिपद्यध्वं—Accept, *i. e.* act according to it. This Gâthâ has also a side meaning. अर्हत् refers to Châṇakya. Those who will obey the commands of the worthy Châṇakya, although at times characterised by severity, will profit in the end.

धर्मसिद्धिः—Success in their religious practices ; salvation or Nirvâṇa. *Cf.* Siddhi. V. 2. श्रावकाणां—S'râvaka– lit. a devout or reverent listener; a believer in Buddhism or Jainism ; a Buddhist votary in general ; used as a formal title of address even with reference to persons of different faiths. For a similar blessing *cf.* आर्याः कुरुत धर्मसंचयं Mṛch. p. 311.

भदन्त—A recluse ; (भदन्तः प्रव्रजितः Sid. Kau. on. Uṇâdi III. 130). Used as a title of respect in addressing a Buddhist or Jaina mendicant. *Cf.* Mar. भगत.

P. 112. निवृत्त०—आमध्या०—from mid-day *i. e.* noon onward. निर्वृत्त०–in which blessing of all kinds may be secured (निर्वृत्तानि सर्वाणि कल्याणानि यस्यां). पौर्णमासी—पूर्णो मासो अस्यां ; बहुव्रीहौ कृते स्वार्थे अण् । दक्षिण—southerly (and so favourable). Kshapaṇaka advises Râk. to start the very day in the evening ; see com. The full-moon-day is one of the days called *Purṇâ viz.* 5th, 10th and 15th, which are regarded as auspicious in the bright half of a month. *Cf.* नन्दा च भद्रा च जया च रिक्ता पूर्णेति तिथ्योऽशुभमध्यशस्ताः । Muh. Chin. I. 4. It will be more auspicious towards the evening, just as the sun would be setting and the moon rising. For the lunar mansion पूर्वाफाल्गुनी presiding over the 15th Muhûrta is one of the seven *nakshatras* beginning with *Maghâ* and assigned to the south. And this will be favourable to those going towards the south. *cf.* एवं दक्षिणस्यां मघादिसप्तभैः (यात्रा प्रशस्ततमा); com. on Muh. Chin. XI. 33. The Com. reads निव्वुत्त० *i. e.* निवृत्त० and explains आम०...तिथिः as ' the day ' is not auspicious at all till noon. He also takes अदक्षिण to mean ' not favourable.' For his view see com. But this does not seem to be intended. Jiva. apparently gives a decisive answer considering the question from all points of view. He knows that an undecisive answer would not satisfy Râkshasa. णिवुत्तसमत्तकलणा (करणा) सोहणा तिही *v. l.* means—The day is auspicions after the Karaṇa *i. e.* भद्रा which is unpropitious. See. com.

अस्ताभिमुखे—The circumstances mentioned herein make the evening a very desirable time for the march. The sun, being a *Krûra* graha, is reguired to be set, while the rising moon would exert a favourable influence (what is generally known as चन्द्रबल) according to the maxim ' चन्द्रो लक्षगुणाधिकः '. बुधस्य लग्ने—*Lagna* means the contact of a zodiacal sign and the horizon. Now it was the month of Mârgashîrsha when Râk. asked the question. And in this month the sun is in the zodiacal sign *Dhanus* (Sagitarius). This is the *Lagna* at sunrise. This gives *Mithuna* (Gemini) as the *Lagna* at the time of sunset. And as Budha is the presiding planet of Mithuna, it is called Budha's *Lagna.* The moon too would be in *Mithuna* at that time and is then westerly. So that to those journeying southwards it will be on the right-handside; and such a moon is favourable. **उदितास्त०**—Ketu is another malignant planet; and this too will set at the time of marching after having risen.*

Such is the apparent meaning of this passage. It has also a hidden meaning. Jiva. means—When you go to Pâṭaliputra good fortune will smile upon you fully (**निर्वृत्त०**) as Chandra *i. e.* Chandragupta has his rule firmly established (**संपू०**). But as you will march towards the south, the quarter of Yama, with Malayaketu and his army, the *Kshatriyas*, Bhadrabhaṭṭa and others, will not be favourable to you (**अदक्षिणे**) and destruction will await you. Again, oh brave Râkshasa (**सूरे**) you will be near gaining the high post of chief minister (**अत्थाहिमुदे-अर्थाभिमुखे**) as you will come in contact with the wise Châṇakya (**बुधस्य लग्ने**). And the sovereignty of Chandragupta will be complete after Malayaketu is captured and his army overthrown. See com. where this is fully explained.

P. 113. **न शुद्धयति**—is not propitious or unobjectionable. Râk. means—How can we go when the *day itself* is not favourable? The full-moon day is one of the days on which a journey is forbidden. *Cf.* **न षष्ठी न च द्वादशी नाष्टमी नो सिताद्या तिथिः पूर्णिमामा न रिक्ता ।** Muh. Chin. XI. 9. **प्रत्येकं तिथिफलान्याह वसिष्ठः—× × × विनाशदाथपूर्णिमा यशःक्षयं करोत्यमा ।** Com. on the above.

एकगुणा &c.—Kshap. asserts that the evil influence exerted by the day is more than counteracted by the good influence of the constellation and the zodiacal conjunction.

लग्नम्. Jiva. gently blames Râk. for his indecision. He says—"Do not express unnecessary doubts. The *Lagna* is good; only avoid the planets Sun and Ketu &c." The hidden meaning is—The meeting (of Châṇakya with you) will be blissful; give up the cruel thought of avenging the destruction of the Nandas. You will obtain lasting happiness by going in the company of Bhadrabhaṭṭa and others, the trusted men of Chandragupta, See com. For the meaning of the other reading see. com. p. 112.

संवाद्यतां—Let a consultation be made with; *i. e.* see that your decision agrees with that of other astrologers. **कृतान्तः**—(1) the god of death; (2) the decision or the conclusion *i. e.* the science of astrology. The double meaning is well explained in the com.

---

* For the information contained in the notes on this, I am indebted to Mr. Dhruva who has discussed the whole question ably and learnedly.

P. 114. पर्णच्छायैः—A Tat. ending in छाया is *neu.* when the sense to be expressed is thickness of shade. आद्य—Because in the morning the shadows are the longest; thereafter they go on shortening. During the fore part of the day the shadows keep to the west in which direction also the sun is going. They are therefore compared to devoted servants who go before their masters. In the latter part of the day the shadows recede and gradually lengthen out in the eastern *i. e.* the opposite direction. Hence they are compared with servants who leave their masters in the decline of their fortune. प्रायः &c.—*cf.* सर्वः प्रायो भजति विकृतिं भिद्यमाने प्रतापे । Mv. II. 4.

ACT V.

P. 115. Herewith begins, according to the Com., the *Nirvahaṇasandhi*, which takes up the last three Acts. It has fourteen *Aṅgas*; see com. ततः प्रविशति &c.—Siddhârthaka, as the reader will perceive, now starts on his mission in accordance with his master's instructions.—ततः प्रत्यासन्नेषु &c. (see p. 36.)

बुद्धिजल &c.—Mr. Telang remarks—"The figure in this stanza is criticised by Professor Wilson as not "natural to the style of the compositions of the period to which the drama belongs." But नीतिपादप and its flowers are spoken of in Kâlidâsa (Mâlvikâgnimitra p. 20) and in Bhavabhûti (Vîra-Charita p. 93), and the further elaboration of the figure here is scarcely open to the critism bestowed upon it." *Cf.* also Mâl. IV. 1. where 'Love' is compared to a tree.

देशकाल०—A politician must make a proper choice of the time and place for carrying out his plans; *cf.* परार्थं देशकालज्ञो देशे काले च साधयेत् । स्वार्थं च स्वार्थकुशलः कुशलेनानुकारिणा ॥ K. n. V. 30.

आर्यचाणक्येन &c.—See pp. 36, 68. किल—is used here in the sense of 'a feigned action,' see com.; he did not really want to go to Pâṭaliputra. यावदस्य &c.—Because Siddh. wished that he should not succeed in going out of the camp, but that he should fall into the hands of Malayaketu's men and thus open the door to his future scheme. ता जाव से आदिस्तदंसणेण &c. *v. l.*-Here Siddh. must be supposed to refer to the object of his journey which he apprehends might be frustrated by the Kshapaṇaka's sight. But since he does not avoid the latter's sight this does not seem to be the original reading.

P. 116. अलहन्ताणं (अर्हतः or अर्हद्भ्यः) Buddhist or Jaina saints: lit. the followers of अर्हत्. The Gen. for the Dat. or Acc. In Prâkṛt there is no Dative, and therefore when the idea of the Dative is to be expressed the Gen. is used for it. गम्भीर—profound, acute enough to fathom the truth. लोकोत्तर—uncommon, not followed by the common run of men. लोकेभ्यः लक्षणया लोकप्रतिपन्नमार्गेभ्य उत्तराः। मार्गैः—This may refer to the eightfold path leading to the cessation of suffering first pointed out by Gautama to his five old disciples, *viz.* (1) Right Belief, (2) Right Aspiration; (3) Right Speech; (4) Right Conduct, (5) Right means of livelihood, (6) Right Exertion; (7) Right Mindfulness and (8) Right Meditation (Mahavagga I. 6). "A more perfect system of self-culture" remarks Mr. R. C. Dutt, "was never proclaimed by philosopher or saint." Or मार्ग may signify 'the fourfold roads to saintship.' These are the four means,– the will, the exertion, the preparation and the investigation by which Iddhi is acquired. सिद्धि—called by the Buddhists Iddhi—salvation or a state of perfection. In later Buddhism Iddhi means supernatural powers. For other particulars, see Dutt's Civilisation in Anciant India, ch. XIII. The Com. remarks that according to the A'rhats or Jainas salvation consists in the constant upward tendency of the human soul, resembling the rising of a gourd when immersed in water.

समुद्दहन्—Carrying out or preparing for (a rather peculiar use). Cal. Eds. read समुद्दसन्तलणकिद० (समुद्रसन्तरणकृत०) which means 'bent or intent on some arduous task.'

मुण्डित०—You are locking the stable-door when the steed has been already stolen. Certain days of the month (*tithis*) and constellations (*nakshatras*) are regarded as unpropitious for shaving. Hence the appropriateness of the remark. Kshap. means that he is too late in consulting the constellations as he has already set out on his journey.

P. 117. अनिवारितः—Uncontrolled, free. निर्गम०—read ०प्रवेशो भास्ताम्. The sing. stands for the dual by the maxim प्राकृते लिङ्गवचनमतन्त्रम्। अमुद्रालाञ्छितः—without having a pass (lit. a seal-impression). It is not easy to see whether a paper bearing an impressien of the ring was given or the impression was made on the outer coat. The use of the word लाञ्छित shows, however, that the latter is more likely. मा प्रवेश्यसे—notice the use of मा with the indicative. It is not unusual to find this particle used for the sake of force with other tenses and moods than the Imperative, or the Aorist; *cf.* मा कस्यापि तपस्विनः हस्ते पतिष्यति S'âk. Act II. मा कश्चिन्ममाप्यनर्थो भवेत् Pt. V. मा नाम

देव्याः कादंबर्या एव किमप्यनिष्टमुत्पन्नं भवेत् Kâd. p. 441. भेदानीमेषा परहस्तगता भविष्यति Mâl. Mâd. Act VII.

गुल्मा०—The officers of or in charge of the *Gulmas.* Gulma means a small company or band of soldiers posted at different stations (called *chaukis* in Marâ.) round the camp of an army for keeping guard or giving the signal of danger &c. See Manus. VII. 190, K. n. XV. 6. गुल्मः...सैन्यरक्षणे इति विश्वः । गुल्म also means a subdivision of Akshohini (see Amara II. 8. 81); but that is not meant here.

सन्निहित—अहं is to be supplied from the context. सावेगम्—with agitation, excitedly. We have inserted this from the com.; the Com.'s explanation seems to be quite inappropriate as Kshap. and Siddh. though both emissaries of Châṇakya appear from the context to be ignorant of each other's real character. पिशाचस्य वा—Kshapaṇaka wants to show by this that he is somehow dissatisfied with Râkshasa but Siddh. fails to notice this. मा कुप्य &c.—Siddh. fears lest the mendicant's anger might thwart his wishes.

P. 118. प्रवेशकः—See com. प्रवेशक or 'the Introducer' is an interlude acted by inferior characters and is meant to acquaint the audience with what has occurred in the interval of the Acts and what is going on to happen thereafter. Like विष्कम्भक it serves as a connecting link between two Acts, with this difference that it can never occur at the beginning of the first Act. The प्रवे० here shows that Siddh., according Châṇakya's instructions tries to leave the camp of Malayaketu, that Malayaketu and his army are near the city and that Kshapaṇaku also wishes to leave the camp. This information is necessary to the audience to understand the subsequent events represented in the Act. वैचित्र्य—manifold character. मुहुः &c.—In this sl. the policy of Châṇakya is compared to the course of Fate. The commentator identifies policy with the plot of a drama basing the identification on the use of the terms लक्ष्य, बीज &c. which are common to dramaturgy also. See com. for explanation. उद्भेद—its shooting up *i. e.* its workings. अधिगमा०—०भावेन गहनाः. अधिगम comprehension. कार्यवशतः—as the purpose to be accomplished at a particular time requires it to be.

चित्राकारा नियतिरिव—*Cf.* हतविधिलसितानां ही विचित्रो विपाकः। S'is. XI. 64.

आस्थान०—आतिष्ठन्त्यस्मिन्। अधिकरणे ल्युट् (अन); मण्डप a pavilion or tent for holding a council meeting &c. एवमपि—*v. e.* goes with स्नेहवान्; although kind to me to such an extent Bhâg. feels remorse for his treacherous conduct; but he has sworn fidelity to his master, and the thought soon dispels his uneasiness.

P. 119. **विमुखः**—Mark the force of this word. He consciously does not take notice of the things. **क्षणिक०**—क्षणिकमपि *V. l.* here अपि is without any force. **धन०**—indicates 'want of proper consideration.' Bhâg. means—when a man has rashly sold his independence for pelf which is but momentary, he has passed the stage of reflection, and is thenceforth bound to carry out his master's bidding. The time for consideration was before he entered service.

कुर्वाणः—Habitually carrying out or executing. The affix आन here shows habit; see Pân. III. 2. 129; H. Sans. Gr. § 671. **विमृशति**—stands for विमृशेत् or–तु.

चाणक्यनिराकृतेन—निराकृतः चाणक्यः येन । The परनिपात of निराकृत must be explained by classing it under the आहिताग्नि group; *e. g.* अग्न्याहितः or आहिताग्निः । *Cf.* शरीरबद्धः प्रथमाश्रयो यथा । Kum. V. 30. **कृतिना**—not for his having discarded Chânakya but for having obtained the *râjya*. **स्थैर्ये भक्ति**—for not only Malayaketu, but even his father, Parvataka was deeply attached to Râkshasa. **अधिगणयन्**—counting foremost, setting a high value on or reckoning highly. *Cf.* तां भक्तिमेवागणयत्पुरस्तात् । Rag. V. 20.

विजये मुहूर्ते &c.—Shows the childishness of Malaya. and the hold Bhâg. had on his guileless mind. See com.

P. 120. **अये राक्षसस्य**—From this it appears that Bhâg. did not know that Kshapaṇaka was one of Chânakya's spies and a co-conspirator with him. Chânakya, in order to secure greater secrecy, seems to have taken the precaution to keep his emissaries (with a few exceptions) ignorant of one another's mission or individuality. Such is also the injunction of the science of politics; *cf.* एते ज्ञेयास्तु सञ्चाराः सर्वे नान्योन्यवेदिनः । K. n. XII. 34. **न खलु**—has the force of 'you are going &c. are you not? Or, I believe you are going &c.'

राक्षसस्य पिशाचस्य—Mark how Kshap. uses the same expression again, to show to Bhâgurâyaṇa that he is not on good terms with Râkshasa now. When questioned as to the wrong done to him by Râkshasa he gives an evasive answer thereby adding to the curiosity of Bhâgurâyaṇa. **प्रणयकोप**—प्रणयेन प्रणयकृतो वा कोपः is anger which does not terminate in destroying friendship, but is evanescent and indicative of real affection.

किमपराद्धं भदन्त—अपराध् generally governs the Loc. and sometimes the Gen., as here. *Cf.* किंपुनरसुरावलेपेन भवतीनामपराद्धं Vik. p. 10. and our note thereon.

हताशः—*V. l.*, lit. one who is defeated in his object (generally a wicked one); hence one whose life has been miserable or accursed. It is generally used as a term of abuse. आत्मनः—कर्मसु—*v. l.* will not do as it will be an admission of his own bad deeds by the speaker himself which the context does not justify.

अश्रोतव्यं—Something which is either so hard or so disastrous that the hearing of it will cause disgust or pain, and which therefore must not be heard; hence sometimes, a calamity. *Cf.* p. 147.

P. 121. अर्थिने—To one who solicits it. Kshapaṇaka means that Bhâgurâyana will implicitly believe what he so earnestly wishes to hear, and is likely to turn it to the sort of use desired by him. See com. मलय०-कथं &c.—Mark the ingenuity of the poet in making Malaya. overhear the conversation between Bhâg. and Kshapaṇaka. It helps considerably to poison Malayaketu's mind against Râkshasa.

निष्कासिष्ये—Pass. Fut.: Kshap. means that Râk., situated as he is, is not likely to succeed in his treacherous object and that his own ruin might be involved in the doom that would befall his master.

अकार्यं—अ has the sense of अप्राशस्त्य; कुत्सितं कार्यम् । चाणक्येन विषकन्यायाः &c.—This is at least a falsehood if not a deliberate lie. See p. 24 *supra.*

P. 122. सुहृत्—Mr. Telang understands by this, the friend of the रिपु, and we have followed him in translating the passage. The Com. takes it with reference to Kshap. and we think his way is preferable. Since Malaya. now calls Râkshasa a *Ripu* it is but natural that he should call Kshapaṇaka from whom he obtains the information, a friend. Mark how rash and hasty in his judgment Malayaketu is. In an instant he calls the Kshap. a friend and Râkshasa an enemy (and in the next stanza, a true Râkshasa or demon).

कृतार्थोऽस्मि—Because his object, which is to communicate this account to Malaya., was fulfilled beyond his expectation.

मित्रं &c.—From this it appears that Parvates'vara was a friend of Râk., before he was won over to his side by Châṇakya with the promise of the gift of half of Nanda's kingdom.

सहबन्धु०—*Sahokti*; *cf.* पपात भूमौ सह सैनिकाश्रुभिः । Rag. III. 61. The figure consists in coupling two facts so as to strike poetically; *e. g.* छाया संश्रयते तलं विटपिनां श्रान्तैश्च पान्थैः सह । **अन्वर्थः**—अनुगतार्थः Prep. Tat.; *cf.* तथैव सोऽभूदन्वर्थो राजा प्रकृतिरञ्जनात् । Rag. IV. 12.

भवतु—Mr. Telang quotes Râghavabhaṭṭa भवतु इति निषेधे । अस्तु भवतु पूर्यत इति निषेधे इत्युक्तेः । (see his com. at S'âk. p. 129.) and says it 'indicates something about to be done; contray to that to which things were tending before.'

Bhâg. being a faithful spy of Chāṇakya, sees the necessity for appeasing the anger of Malayaketu, lest Râkshasa's life might be endangered and shapes his following speech accordingly.

अर्थशास्त्र—Lit those who act according to the laws of political science, politicians. **अर्थवशात्**—अर्थ the object or political end to be gained.

P. 123. **व्यवस्था०**—Lit. setting down or looking on as, consideration. **लौकिक**—लोके विदितः प्रसिद्धः हितो वा (aff. ठन्), people acting in private life. **अर्थपरिपन्थी**—अर्थस्य परिपन्थी; परि दोषाख्यानं पन्थयितुं to spread or circulate शीलं यस्य । परिपन्थिन् lit. means who points out faults or speaks against and thus prevents another from gaining his object. Hence, coming in the way of; an obstacle. Some derive it as पन्थानं पर्यवष्टभ्नातीति. In either way it is irregularly derived (निपातनात्). According to Pân. the form is admissible only in the Vedas. But it is sometimes used in *laukika* Sanskṛt also. *Cf.* नामविध्यमहं तत्र यदि तत्परिपन्थिनी । Mâl. Mâd. IX. 52. तौ ह्यस्य परिपन्थिनौ । Bg. III. 34. **नातिदोषमिव**—Bhâg. does not wish to free Râk. entirely from the guilt of having mudered Parvataka but would rather have Malaya.'s suspicion about Râk.'s fidelity grow stronger.

मित्राणि &c.—This sl. gives expression to a great political truth. **अस्मृत०**—A politician led by his interest has to act in a hostile manner towards a friend or *vice versa*, totally ignoring all previous relations; he, in fact, passes from one kind of political existence to another. See K. n. VIII. 73.

उपग्राह्यश्च—Should be retained in service.

एवं सखे &c.—This brings out the levity of Malayaketu's mind. With little consideration he believed in the words of Kshapaṇaka and alienated his heart from Râkshasa his true friend and well-wisher. With as little consideration he now accepts, as proper, the defence of his father's murder made by Bhâgurâyaṇa.

दोषेषु—*i. e.* in one's behaviour or actions. **प्रणमामः** &c.—shows that that was the age when loyalty to one's master was valued above every other virtue.

P. 124. **परिग्रहः**—A servant. Bhâg. it seems, knew Siddhârthaka and the errand on which he was sent (see his speech at p. 132.) but purposely feigns ignorance here.

स्वस्ति—Invariably marks the beginning of letters in Sanskṛt. **यथास्थानं**—Here the names of the place, the writer of the letter and the addressee and the friends are not purposely written; for had they been written S'akaṭadâsa would not have written the letter. The letter is so worded that by कोपि Malayaketu should understand Râkshasa and by कमपि पुरु० Chandragupta, while in प्रति पक्ष he should find a reference to Châṇakya. **अवगमयति**—informs, writes to say. This was the letter which Châṇakya got written by S'akaṭadâsa through Sarvârthasiddhi. **कापि**—indescribable, very great. **उपन्यस्त**—proposed. **परिपणन**—price for.

सत्यसन्धः—Refers to Chandragupta and is calculated to excite Malayaketu's jealousy.

P. 125. **स्वाश्रय**—*i. e.* Malayaketu. **उपकारिणं**—*i. e.* Chandragupta. **सत्यवतः**—Gen. sing. The letter is couched in terms complimentary to Chandragupta, and is intended to show Râkshasa's high regard for him. **कोषदण्डाभ्याम्**—अर्थिन् is used with the Instr.; को वधेन ममार्थी स्यात् । Mah. Bhâr. तुषैरर्थिनः Dk. **अशून्यार्थं**—as an accompaniment; lit. that it should not be unaccompanied by the customary present. **वाचिक**—सन्दिष्टोर्थोनया वाच्यते सा वागेव वाचिकम् । स्वार्थे (ठक्). इक्· 'वाचो व्याहतार्थायां' Pân. V. 4. 35. It means 'an oral message or communication.' Important secrets were transmitted orally.

कीदृशः—&c.—What is the bearing of this letter *i. e.* who may be the writer and who may be the addressee? धूर्त-धुर्व् to kill; धूर्यते स्म or धूर्तमस्यास्तीति ।

युष्माभिः—Siddh. wanted to say युष्माभिर्गृहितो न जानामि &c. But as he pronounced the words very slowly like one frightened, Bhâg. fancies this to be a reply to his querry. Finding that Bhâg. was angry at this, Siddh. changes this for a more pleasing epithet and says मिश्रैः &c. **मिश्रैः**—मिश्र is a term of honour generally used as an affix. पूज्ये मिश्रपदं नित्यं बहुवचनान्तम् । 'मरीचमिश्रैर्दक्षेण' इति विष्णुपुराणात् । Jagad. on Mâl. Mâd. **एष जानासि**—*i. e.* we shall compel you to know it. Bhâg. means that he will receive a sound drubbing and so will have to confess.

P. 126. चन्द्रगुप्तस्य—*i. e* addressed to Chandragupta. कुमारस्य—Gen. for the Dat. परवान्—dependent; lit. one having a master.

मलयनगराधिपः—Malaya is properly the name of a mountain. ०नगर therefore means the capital of the territory around the mountain. The Cal. reading 'मलयजनपदाधिपति,' therefore, seems preferable.

P. 127. मामभिद्रुह्यन्ति—Mr. Telang reads मह्यं &c. But then the construction becomes wrong grammatically. The rule is क्रुधद्रुहोरुपसृष्टयोः कर्म ।

पूर्णमस्मद्बलं &c.—From this it appears that certain facts were revealing themselves, calculated to create a suspicion, howsoever vague, even in the mind of the guileless Râkshasa, about the real motives of the deserters from Chandragupta's camp, though he soon tries to rid his mind of it. परिशुद्धि—Lit. a state of clearness (freedom from misgivings); hence 'ease.'

साध्ये &c.—साध्य and the like words herein mentioned are technical terms of *Nyâya* or logic. As these are explained in the elemenlary treatises on Indian Logic which can be easily referred to, we do not discuss them fully here, but merely indicate their meaning. साध्य is the predicate of a logical proposition corresponding to the major term in the Western Logic; *e. g.* fieriness in the usual syllogism–The mountain is fiery, because it has smoke on it; and all that smokes is fiery. (पर्वतो वह्निमान् धूमवत्वात् । यो यो धूमवान् स स वह्निमान् । यथा महानसम् । तथा चायं *i. e.* अयं पर्वतः धूमवान् । तस्मात्तथा-वह्निमान् ।).

अन्वय—Also called अन्वयव्याप्ति is the assertion of the invariable concomittance of the हेतु (tho middle term) and the साध्य (हेतुसाध्ययोर्व्याप्तिः), as in the above instance—wherever there is smoke there is fire. सपक्ष—A corroborative instance on the same side (निश्चितसाध्यवान् सपक्षः), as a महानस or kitchen where the *Sâdhya* (fieriness) is definitely known to be present. विपक्ष—an instance on the opposite side (*i. e.* contrary) which is characterised by the definite absence of the *Sâdhya* (निश्चितसाध्याभाववान्); *e. g.* a tank (wherein fire cannot exist) साधन—generally called हेतु (sometimes लिङ्ग)—the instrument of proof—is the middle term, as smokiness (the mountain has smoke) in the above instance. Thus these two lines give the conditions which a good हेतु must satisfy that it should lead to a legitimate conclusion; *viz.* that (1) it (as धूम here) should be known to be present on the Sâdhya here used for पक्ष or the mountain) definitely (this includes the tests of अबाधितविषयत्व and असत्प्रतिपक्षत्व); (2) it should have अन्वयव्याप्ति with the साध्य; (3) it should be present on सपक्ष (सपक्षवृत्तित्वं); and lastly it should never be found with विपक्ष विपक्षाद्व्यावृत्तत्वम्. सिद्धि—Arriving at the legitimate conclusion or *anumiti.*

यत्साधनं स्वयमेव साध्यं—Where the middle term is itself the major term (see com.) *i. e.* where, in the language of Western Logic the major premiss is an identical proposition. तुल्यमुभयोः (*i. e.* सपक्षविपक्षयोः) as द्रव्य in the case of पर्वतो धूमवान् द्रव्यत्वात्, which is one of the five हेत्वाभास (and which includes the two fallacies of European Logic, *viz. Illicit process of the major* and the *undistributed middle*). विरुद्ध—(the fallacy of contradiction) is that which proves the absence of the *Sâdhya.*

In the case of स्वामिन् or king, साध्य means the object aimed at, victory. निश्चित—assuredly known to gain victory, of proved valour. अन्वय—allies, forces of friends. स्थिति—attachment to, firmly sticking to the same side. विपक्ष—the enemy's side. The Com. shows that Chandragupta has all these on his side. यत् साधनं स्वयमेव साध्यं may mean (1) which is identical with the ultimate object *i. e.* which is rebellious and desires to secure the power for itself; or (2) whose efficiency is yet to be proved. उभयोस्तुल्यं—*i. e.* indifferent. विरुद्ध—opposed, not true to the cause of its master but ready to side with the enemy. For other particulars see com. and translation.

P. 128. परिगृहीतं—Accepted, received with favour. आपूर्ण—almost or nearly full of. परिकल्पित—properly distributed or arranged; *cf.* परिकल्पितसान्निध्या Rag. IV. 6, also XI. 28. Further on we have कल्पय् in the sense of 'to offer'; see p. 153. sl. 21. प्रयाणे—At the time of every march or when marching.

पुरस्तात्—In the van. खश—The Khas'as appear to be identical with the tribes still dwelling in the Khasias and Garo Hills in the north-eastern parts of Bengal. मगध—The country of the Magadhas, the modern Behar. It was also called कीकट. "If our text on this point is correct, and all our MSS. read the name as Magadha, the reference is probably to the discontented inhabitants of Magadha, who still followed Râkshasa, repudiating all connection with Chandragupta as a usurper. I own, however, that I have a suspicion, though it is nothing more, that मगध is not the correct reading, but that it should be मगर. If our identification of the Khas'as is right, this rectification is strongly suggested by the fact that the Magars tribe inhabits the Himâlaya in tracts near Kumaon in the neighbourhood of the Khas'as. According to Mr. Carleylle, the Goorkhas of Nepâl originally belonged to the twin tribes, Magaras and Khas'as. It must be admitted, however, that the emendation here is a mere suggestion, which cannot be accepted at prestent in the face of the evidence of our MSS. of the Mudrârâkshasa." Telang's Introduction. **गान्धारैः**—The people who had settled in the province to the west of the Indus about the modern Peshâwar, and Kandhar. **प्रयत्नः**—an exertion *i. e.* care should be taken about the march of the central division. *Cf.* महान् हि यत्नस्तव देवदारौ । Rag. II. 56. प्रतिपात्रमाधीयतां यत्नः । S'âk. p. 5.

चीणहूणैः—" The Chînas are the next people who claim attenttion. Mr. A. Baroosh identifies the Chinas mentioned in the Mahâbhârata with the Chinese. The Chînas of our text are probably not to be distinguished from the Chinas mentioned in the great epic. But Professor Max Mûller doubts whether in the Mahâbhârata the name Chînas really does stand for the Chinese. However, whether they are to be identified with the Chinese or not, they would seem to belong to somewhere about the north-eastern quarter of India, whether on this side of the Himâlaya mountain or the further side. The Hûnas come next, and these are probably to be identified with the White Huns, whose inroads into India are said to have occurred in the fifth and sixth centuries A. D. " Telang's Introduction.

P. 129. **अधिकारपदं नाम** &c.—Here Râk. has a vague presentiment of what is coming. *Cf.* राज्यं हि नाम &c. p. 75. *supra.*

भयं तावत् &c.—For similar ideas, comp. III. 14. **अभिनिविशते**—Forcibly enters, firmly takes possession of विश् with अभि and नि is Atm. **उन्नतोच्छ्रायरूढानां**—*Cf.* अत्यारूढिर्भवति महतामप्यपभ्रंशनिष्ठा । See S'âk. IV. Various Readings p. 8; comp. also,

' They that stand high have many blasts to shake them ;
And if they fall, they dash themselves to pieces.'

Shakespeare, King Richard III. Act. I. Sc. 3.

अनुकूलं—Used in its literal sense-near the bank, near at hand.

निश्चलाङ्गी—Going with दृशं is rather peculiar. The reading निश्चलन्तीं, may have same sense. Perhaps the poet wrote निश्चलाङ्गः. **शून्य०**—*Cf.* गमनमलसं शून्या दृष्टिः &c. Mâl. Mâd. I. 20. The figures in the sl. are *Utprekshâ* and *Svabhâvokti.*

P. 130. **प्रतिविधानं**—Simply means here 'arrangement, disposition of.'

ताड्यमानेन मया &c.—Siddhârthaka's conduct in this Act is characterised by the grossest villany. He has the boldness to tell to his late master's face such abominable lies.

P. 131. **आर्यस्य**—The Gen. with कथं is noticeable. **अवृत**—*Cf.* Lat. *ratus* settled, ratified; *irritus*. **ईदृशस्य** &c.—Bhâg. is simply adding fuel to the fire. **०भूमि**—proper place *i. e.* a fit person or worthy recipient.

P. 132. **अलं ताडयितुं**—The use of the *inf.* with अलं is ungrammatical. It should be ताडयित्वा. It is, however, met with now and then. *Cf.* अलं प्रकृतिसुकुमारमात्मानं खेदयितुम् Ven. Act II.; again ०द्रौणायने अलमत्यर्थमात्मानं शोकानले प्रक्षेप्तुम् *Ibid.* Act III.

न खलु &c.—This shows that Bhâg. knew that Siddh. was one of Châṇakya's spies. **आगत्य** &c.—These words are omitted by Mr. Telang. We have inserted these as the context requires them. The words of the Com. also show that he too must have felt the necessity of supplying some such words for a clear understanding of the passage.

प्रतिपत्स्यते—*Cf.* संप्रतिपत्ति sl. 18. *infra*; admission, acknowledgement. **अन्यलि०**—प्रतिलिखित *v. l.* does not seem to be the original reading. In the first place the shrewd Bhâg. cannot be excepted to send for a copy of the letter as that would have created a suspicion in S'akaṭadâsa's mind and led him to suspect some mischief. Secondly, the word अपर occurring in the next sl. shows that it was not a प्रतिलि० that was sent for. **विभावयिष्यति**—विभावय् to cause a thing to be seen; hence to make clear, to prove. *Cf.* विभावितैकदेशेन &c. Vik. IV. 17.

P. 133. **शकटदासस्तु०**—The meaning may simply be—When I compare the two handwritings the characters seem to agree; but when I call to my mind the fact that S'akaṭa. is my friend, I must say that they do not agree. The Com.'s view, however, seems to suit the context better. In this case translate—If so, the words S'akaṭa. and friend do not agree.

पुत्रदारस्य—पुत्राश्च दाराश्च पुत्रदारं Sama. Dvan. **चलेष्वर्थेषु**—The Loc. is वैषयिक 'सप्तम्यधिकरणे च' Pân. II. 3. 36. औपश्लेषिको वैषयिकोभिव्यापकश्चेत्याधारस्त्रिधा । कटे आस्ते, स्थाल्यां पचति, मोक्षे इच्छास्ति । Sid. Kau. **अनपायिषु**—not perishing, everlasting. *Cf.* प्रसादाभिमुखे तस्मिन्श्रीरासीदनपायिनी । Rag. XVII. 46.

कराङ्गुलिप्रणयिनी—*Cf.* p. 31. *supra.* **प्रयोगाश्रय**—Which is the basis of the enemy's scheme. **शकट**—Stands for S'akaṭadâsa used in contempt. **कृपणं**—*Cf.* कृपणवत् II. 18.

भूषणवल्लभ—Notice the comp. which should rather be वल्लभभूषण:. The poet has, it seems, placed वल्लभ: latter following the analogy of प्रिय which may optionally take परनिपात by the rule वा प्रियस्य; प्रियगुड: or गुडप्रिय:. **मुखचन्द्र०**—मुखचन्द्रेण कृतोऽवभासो यस्य । The ornaments are compared to the stars, Parvateshvara's face to the moon and Par. himself to the autumnal evening.

P. 134. **चाणक्यप्र०**—Some read before this—(प्रकाशम्) पतान्यपि; but this is unnecessity after Râk.'s reply 'वणिग्भ्य: कयादधिगत:' on p. 133. **सुश्लिष्ट**—Well arranged, well planned; *cf.* सुश्लिष्टगुणतया and मालत्या अपि स्नेहदर्शनात्सुश्लिष्टमेतत् Mâl. Mâd. pp. 35, 36. **य आर्यः** &c.—Râk. means that in consequence of the accusation brought against him, he no longer deserved to be addressed as Ârya. As to the qualities of an Ârya *Cf.* कुलं शीलं दया दानं धर्मः सत्यं कृतज्ञता । अद्रोह इति येष्वेतत्तानार्यान्संप्रचक्षते ॥ K. n. XVII. 48.

न उत्तरं—Not a fit or reasonable reply. **ग्राम्य**—ग्रामे भवं churlish, hence not weighty or reasonable ; *cf.* the similar admission of guilt by Chârudatta, Mṛch. p. 417.

मौर्योऽसौ &c.—Mark the contrast suggested by the sets of assertions. Malaya. means—there your relation is that of a servant to his master, here the reverse of that &c.

निर्णयो दत्तः—*Viz.* that implied in त्वामनार्यं करोति.

व्यत्ययेन पठति—By repeating the sl. in the manner stated and making the lines questions of appeal, Râkshasa means to suggest that there was no earthly reason for him to act in a treacherous and dishonourable way, as ungenerously supposed by Malayaketu.

P. 135 **परिभावधामनि**—The place of humiliation or insult. See III. 14. By परौ भुवोऽवज्ञाने Pân. III. 3. 55, we have both परिभाव and परिभव in the sense of 'contempt,' though the latter is more generally used. *Cf.* के वा न स्युः परिभवपदं निष्फलारम्भयत्नाः । **कृतधियां**—of fixed opinions, as contrasted with Malayaketu of wavering mind.

प्रयोग—Use. **विषम**—Lit. what is unevenly or not well placed; hence what is surrounded by fear; *cf.* Bhaṭṭi. VI. 8. and Bhag. II. 2. where विषमे is rendered as सभये स्थाने in the Bhâshya of S'aṅkarâchâya. Also कान्ताविश्लेषदुःखव्यतिकरविषमे यौवने विप्रयोग: Bhar. Nît. 38. Here it means dangerous to life, fatal. **विश्रंभप्रवणः**—विश्रंभेण

प्रवण:, well inclined towards, ready to act up to the advice of, through confidence. *Cf.* तपसा तत्प्रवणीकृतो हर: Kum. IV. 42. आहित०– should be properly compounded with मन्त्राधिकारे; but it is a comp. सापेक्षत्वेपि गमकत्वात् (on account of the connection being indicated). प्रलय—utter destruction. This is the greatest height of villainy and ingratitude. Mr. Dhruva compares Bhaṭṭi. XVI. 132. मांसविक्रयिण: कर्म व्याधस्यापि विगर्हितम् ।

गण्डस्योपरि &c.—This is adding misery to misfortune. *Cf.* ततो गण्डस्योपरि पिटक: संवृत्त: । S'âk. p. 44. and Shakespeare 'When sorrows come, they come not single spies, but in battalions'. Hamlet Act IV. Sc. 5. Also 'One woe doth tread upon another's heel, so fast they follow.' *Ibid.* Act IV. Sc. 7.

P. 136. श्वभ्र—A spacious ditch or pit. अभिनीय—अभिनी generally means to gesticulate or act, but here it is used in its literal sense. *Cf.* गुहजनं स्वगृहमभिनीय । &c. p. 40. Here Malaya. is guilty of an error of policy, *viz.* दण्डपारुष्य; he was also guilty of वाक्पारुष्य. It is such errors which lead a man to ruin *cf.* स्त्रियोक्षा मृगया पानं वाक्पारुष्यं च पञ्चमं । महच्च दण्डपारुष्यं...। अष्टौ पूर्वनिमित्तानि नरस्य विनशिष्यत: Mah. Bhâr. Udyog.; K. n. XIII. 61.

सर्वात्मना—Wholly and unreservedly.

त्रिवर्ग—The collection of three. *viz.* धर्म, अर्थ and काम. दुर्नय:—bad conduct, injustic. See the Com.'s remark.

गौडीनां—Gauḍa or Puṇḍra, the ancient nama of Northern Bengal. लोध्रधूली०—The dust of the *lodhra* flowers was applied by ladies to their cheeks to give them a lustrous appearance. परिमल—paint. बहुल-increased in size, by being covered or plastered with. क्लिश्नत:- lit. teasing or troubling, hence diminishing or tempering the deep darkness of. *Cf.* क्लिश्नती कृत्तिमैभीं III. 20, where the meaning is slightly different. आत्मलाभ—*cf.* III. 1. Kir. III. 32, XVII. 29. &c. उत्तमाङ्ग—The head. Rag. VII. 51. Kum. VII. 41. गजमद०—The idea is common enough; *cf.* Rag. VIII. 43. This shows that there were many rut-shedding elephants in Malayaketu's army.

करवाणि—What should I do? (implying a little helplessness on the part of the speaker). This use of the Imperative should be noted. *Cf.* Uttar. किं स वत्स: करोतु ।

P. 137. सवैर—Because the feeling of animosity must needs lead to प्रवृत्ति and not to निवृत्ति. नैतच्च &c. Construe—एतदनयुक्तं भवेत् । यत: कृतघ्नं नचेत् मम चन्दन० चेत: इन्ध्यात्; but this will not be a proper course for me to follow. For, my heart, if it be not ungrateful (which it is not), would prevent me, &c. Or कृतघ्नं न चेत् may be taken separately-न चेत् if it did not कृतघ्नं भवेत्. The reading नैतत्र for नैतच्च makes no sense for in that case the construction will be कृतघ्नं चन्दन० मम चेतः न हन्यात् चेत् पतत्रयुक्तं न भवेत्; but then if the चेतः is कृतघ्न it would not be चन्दन० रमसं. Râkshasa means that gratitude for the splendid service rendered by Chandanadâsa will not allow him to do any thing that will jeopardise his life. For रमस in the sense of a strong or ardent desire *cf.* Kir. V. 1. रमसया नु दिगन्तदिदृक्षया; also Rag. IX. 61.

ACT VI.

जयति &c.—Glory to (my veneration to-impliedly. जयतिशब्देन नमस्कृतिराक्षिप्यते). जलदनीलः केशवः—For the reverse comparison, *cf.* Mrch. V. 3, where the मेघ is described as केशवगात्रश्याम. जयनकार्यं—What can be accomplished by means of the instruments of victory (such as an army, fighting &c.); see com. यावत्—यावत्तावच्च साकल्ये । Amara. The Cal. Ed.s read—जअति जअणसज्जं जा अकाऊण सेणं (जयति जयनसज्जं या अकृत्वा च सैन्यं). But this reading is not satisfactory, as it is not supported by the context; *cf.* pp. 140, 163. Sl. 15. Here Siddhârthaka really means to pay his tribute of respect to and express his admiration of his master Châṇakya, who by his sound statesmanship and wise statecraft accomplished his object without causing much bloodshed and with the least possible trouble to the citizens.

P. 138. तारेशानां—*i. e.* who gladden by dispelling anxiety. सुखायमाना०—who take pleasure in. But here सुखाय seems to be used transitively—who contribute to happiness or pleasure. हृदय०—*i. e.* who are bosom friends. The stanza shows that Samid. too was in prosperous circumstances.

P. 139. एदस्स निवेद्य—The Gen. for the Sanskrt Dat. प्रियोदन्त—gladsome news (प्रियश्चासौ उदन्तश्च).

असमीक्ष्यकारी—असमीक्ष्य कर्तुं शीलमस्य acting rashly. कुशलतायै for safety. कुशलतया *v. l.*—here the Instr. may be हेतौ ; in order to ensure their safety. भयविलोलशेष०—It is difficult to see the propriety of शेष here unless विलोल be taken to mean ' who fled in terror.' Possibly the author wrote अशेष. पार्थिव—means here independent kings in alliance with Malaya.; सामन्त his feudatories. देवस्स चन्दउत्तस्य—

The Gen. is irregular. अपरक्त is construed with the Abl. or Loc.; and it must be so translated into Sanskṛt. It may, however, be explained by the general rule शेषे षष्ठी. मुख, निर्वहण—We have already explained these terms. It is necessary for every good play that there should be perfect harmony between the opening *Sandhi* and the concluding one. Otherwise the play is defective. Here the poet suggests that this play at least is faultless in this respect.

P. 140. सर्वथा &c.—Siddh. means—We can only watch the courses events take, not seek to fathom Châṇakya's policy; so mysterious are its workings. *Cf.* Bhâg.'s speech at p. 118. *supra.*

अश्रुत—Not properly studied *i. e.* comprehended or understood. सारसाधन—The flower of the army, chosen troops. &c.—प्रतिपन्न—approched from the opposite side, hence attacked. अतिशय &c.—This supposes that the fight was still going on. ०जलदलीलां—नीला उद्भ्रमन्तः *v. l.*, उद्भ्रमन्तः moving about. The variant, ०नीलामुद्वहन्तः is rather mysterious. In this case इवं must be supposed to be understood. जात०—जातकम्पा अत एवोत्तरङ्गाः (looking like heaving waves). जयन—abstract noun (जयः).

P. 141. अतिमुग्धः &c.—Very green; *cf.* 'How green are you and fresh in this old world.' King John. अवगाहित—Lit. entered into, fathomed; hence fully comprehended or grasped. ०विलोल—विलोल is used here as a noun; tumult, agitation. अनुसन्धीयमानः—his course being tracked or closely followed. चरेण—*i. e.* a spy in Châṇakya's service. नाम—प्राकाश्ये.

P. 142. जीवितुकामः—The nasal of the *inf.* is dropped before काम and मनस्. तदेहि &c.—Siddh.'s principle is आज्ञा गुरूणां ह्यविचारणीया Rag. XIV. 46.

षड्गुण &c.—Here by a very happily chosen metaphor, the man compares the policy of Châṇakya to a net which so completely entangled Râk. in its meshes. गुण—(1) a string; (2) for the six *guṇas* see p. 15 and notes. उपाय—(1) efforts; (2) means here stratagems or schemes; it does not seem to be used in its technical sense of सामन्, दान &c. *Cf.* II. 2. where Châṇakya's intellect is compared to a rope. ०ऋजुआ (ऋजुका) will mean 'able to catch &c.'

P. 143. ०आश्रयकातरा—Lakshmî is often described as entertaining such a fear; *cf.* III. 5; for आश्रय see p. 52. कुलटा—Mark the Sandhi (कुल + अटा). It is a word of the शकन्ध्वादि group wherein there is पररूपसन्धि. *Cf.* पतिव्रता चैकपती द्वितीये कुलटा स्मृता । Devi Bhâg. IX. 35. गतानुगतिकाः—गतमनु गतिर्येषां blind followers, thoughtlessly doing what others do. कुर्वन्तु—see our note on करवाणि p. 136. उत्तमाङ्ग—the best limb, *i. e.* the head, being the seat of intelligence; hence the principal person (the person for whom to work).

पतिं त्यक्त्वा &c.—Comp. II. 6. 7. उच्चैः—is here treated as an *adj.* and so used as the first member of a Bah. comp. छिद्र—a loop-hole, a weak point. The Com. explains it by कपटेन but that is not a good rendering. Lakshmî is spoken of as रन्ध्रचला; *cf.* 'श्रियमवेक्ष्य स रन्ध्रचलां &c.' Rag. IX. 15. स्थिरमपि—This is more fully explained in the following sloka.

अतद्विष०—The Com.'s reading (अतद्विषमृत्युयोगे) is better and should have been adopted in the text. शैलेश्वर—*i. e.* Parvateshvara. अधिकृत्य—lit. having placed him in the front, accepted him as a leader.

विवेकशून्यता—This complaint of Râk. is just. It is quite borne out by Malaya.'s unjust dismissal of Râkshasa without even hearing him, and his precipitate order to execute the five princes. See Introduction.

बीजनाशं—This reading, though it gives a good sense, is gramalically inaccurate. We should, therefore, have preferred जीवनाशं-a *namul*, (which is used when the same root is used after it. See Pân. III. 4. 43. 46.). For, the present form is not defensible by उपमाने कर्मणि च (Pân. III. 4. 45); चात्कर्तरि Sid. Kau. ; as the intended sense is not बीजं इव नष्टान् but बीजं यावन्नष्टान्. It cannot therefore, be regarded as a namul (as the Com. thinks). It may at best be taken as Acc. (भावकर्मन्) governed by नष्टान् ; or as बीजस्य नाशो यस्मिन्कर्मणितद्यथा तथा, which case we have recourse to a Vyadhikaraṇa Bahuvrîhi.

दैवेनोपहतस्य &c.—*cf.* विवेकभ्रष्टानां भवति विनिपातः शतमुखः । Bhar. Nît. 10. सर्वा विपर्यस्यति—is perverted wholesale. The root विपर्यस् though transitive is used here intransitively ; *cf.* विपर्यस्तं सौधं—further on. Comp. the Latin *adage—Quem deus vult perdere prius dementate.* The reading सर्वं विपर्यस्यति presents no difficulty.

P. 144. अरातिहस्तगतः—Supply चेत् ; if he falls into the hands of. अथवा—is used पक्षान्तरे ; *cf.* Rag. I. 4. कामं—has its proper sense here, *viz.* that of अकामानुमतिः or adopting a course of action against one's will; अकामानुमतौ कामं Amara. असत्यसन्धः &c.—He means to say that if he is forced to do the worst, he may enter into an alliance with Chandragupta independently of Chânakya. See com.

एतास्ताः--This shows that Râk. loved his masters with almost filial piety.

शार्ङ्ग--शृङ्गस्य विकारः; a horny bow. चित्रं and प्रजवितुरगं are adverbs. **चित्रं**—see com.; it may better be taken with बाणमोक्ष. **चलेषु**—Skill in shooting down moving game was considered a mark of high attainment in ancient archery. *Cf.* उत्कर्षः स च धन्विनां यदिषवः सिध्यन्ति लक्ष्ये चले। S'âk. II. 5. and our note thereon Rag. IX. 49. **भूयसा**—greatly. **दुःखयन्ति**—See com.; a Denom. from दुःखवत्, the *matub* aff. being dropped.

कुतश्चित्—From some one. **दशापरिणतयः**—turns or conditions of life.

नवेन्दुवत्—The new moon was looked at, in ancient days, as it is now, with great curiosity by the people. *Cf.* नेत्रैः पपुस्तृप्तिमनाप्नुवद्भि-र्नवोदयं नाथमिवौषधीनाम्। Rag. II. 73. निदर्शयामास विशेषदृश्यमिन्दुं नवो-त्थानमिवेन्दुमत्यै। *Ibid.* VI. 31.

P. 145. **विपर्यस्तं**—Dilapidated; the literal sense is also prominent. **सौध**—सुधा लेपो अस्यास्तीति *m. n.* **महारम्भ**—as applied to कुल means 'great act or deeds. **रचना**—(1) structure; (2) doing. **शुष्क**—parched up. *Cf.* its opp. आर्द्र which is frequently used in connection with हृदय. Mr. Telang compares Wordsworth's--'the hearts are dry as summer dust' **कुनीतैः**—*p. p.* participles are often used abstractively; *cf.* कलमन्यभृतासु भाषितं (भाषणं) कलहंसीषु मदालसं गतं &c. Rag. VII. 59.

उदग्र—Lit. whose raised point can be well seen; hence prominent, large &c. **कूजन्तीनां** &c.—*Cf.* उपास्रोदेवनदत्पतङ्गः कुमुद्वतीं तीरतरुदिनादौ। Bhaṭṭi. II. 4. The reading of the Com. is उदग्रक्रममृतां which if adopted, must be taken as an epithet of शाखानां. The reading क्षताङ्गानां is rejected because as qualifying क्षितिरुहां it will mean 'the branches of which were cut off' which is absured. **उपरुदित**—The plaintive cries. उप has no force; it is used for the sake of metre.

तपस्विनः—Poor, in a pitiable condition. See p. 59. **उदग्रयन्तः**—An unsual word; Denom. fr. उदग्र; उदग्रीकरोति उदग्रयति shows in a prominent way. **छायावियोग**—see the cause of this explained in the com. The trees were left uncared for and were in a decaying condition. They are, therefore, represented as mourning for the loss of the Nandas. परिशोष in the case of mourners means—the parching up of the body owing to grief. छाया means 'bright or lustrous complexion.' The fig. is *Utprekshâ.*

विषम०--The Com.'s way of taking the comp. does not seem to be good; rather dissolve ०परिणामे सुलभं तस्मिन्. सुलभ may better (see trans.) be taken to mean-fit for, suited to; see S'âk. IV. 5. (चरणोपमोगसुलभ:) and Râghavbhaṭṭa on it. नान्दी—नन्दन्त्यस्यामिति a festive occasion, rejoicing. पटु—well sounding.

P. 146. श्रुतिपथ—The tympanum of the ear. असारं—weak, not strong (enough to bear the strain) अत एव प्रसृद्धन. गुरुता—intensity. बहुत्व—magnitude. दिशो द्रष्टुं—*cf.* Kâd. p. 47, where the fig. is applied to the big branches of the *S'âlmali* tree.

सासूयं—Mark the sense of असूया. He does not like to call मौर्य a king yet. 'गुणेषु दोषाविष्करणमसूया' Sid. Kau. पिशुनयति—This is often used in the sense of सूचयति; *cf.* पिशुनयति रथस्ते शीकरक्लिन्ननेमि: S'âk. Act VII. कष्टं कष्टं &c.—Here the poet very skilfully makes the sounds of rejoicing at the royal palace in the distance fall on the ears of Râk. just at the time when he was touched by the melancholy scene presented by the ruined mansion and the neglected garden around it. The impression of loneliness and forlornness made on the mind of Râkshasa is thus deepened and he now feels his possition more miserable and critical than ever.

अभिनीय—is once more used in its literal sense. अनुभावयितुं—To make one feel it.

व्यसनसब्रह्मचारिन्—व्यसनमेव समानं ब्रह्म चरतीति । समान is changed to स by 'चरणे ब्रह्मचारिणि' Pâṇ. VI. 3. 16. ब्रह्म वेद: । तदध्ययनार्थं व्रतमपि उपचाराद्ब्रह्म । तच्चरितुं शीलमस्येति ब्रह्मचारी । Lit. a fellow-student in the school of misfortune; hence a fellow sufferer, one in the same miserable condition as another *Cf.* दु:खसब्रह्मचारिणी तारलिका क्व गता Kâd. p. 279. भारिक—भारो विद्यते अस्य hanging over as a load; hence causing pain, or 'very great or weighty' as the Com. takes it.

P. 147. परमुदासीना—Exceedingly indifferent or apathetic. Mark the effect of the man's words on Râkshasa's mind. Châṇakya's hand is clearly visible in all this. The puppets move as he pulls the strings प्रत्यादिश्—To order back as worthless, to throw into the back ground, to eclipse; see com. निर्बन्ध—urgent request; importunity; *cf.* निर्बन्धपृष्ट: स जगाद सर्वं । Rag. XIV. 32. हन्त—is used here हर्षे. विभव—property, one's belongings; see p. 153.

उद्बध्य—This उद्बन्धन is a common device in Sanskṛt plays. See Rat. Act. III. व्यापादयितुं—For a similar idea comp. D. K. p. 9.

औषध०—Baffling or defying the power of medicine: *cf.* वैद्ययत्नपरिभाविनं गदं । Rag. XIX. 53.

P. 148. अग्नि०—Anger is often compared to fire. ०कल्पया—A little less than, almost equal to. ईषदसमाप्तौ कल्पप्देश्यदेशीयर: । Pân. V. 3. 67.

नरपतेः क्रुधा. *i. e.* नरपतिना क्रुद्धेन । **शान्तं पापं** &c.—Mark how the man seeks to make a good impression about Chandragupta's rule on the mind of Râkshasa. **प्रतिपत्तिः**—(actions, deeds). **चन्द्रगुप्तस्य** &c.—may have a double meaning (1) चन्द्रगुप्तस्य ..प्रतिपत्तिः न नृशंसा Chandragupta's behaviour towards his country (the people) is not cruel ; (2) People's actions are not cruel in Chand.'s kingdom. **नारीजनं**—अनुरञ्ज् sometimes governs the Acc.; *cf.* वृषलमनुरक्ता प्रकृतयः । *supra.* **अवशः**—lit. beyond man's control *i. e.* power to prevent ; to which there is no help.

०च्छेदपक्षपात—*Cf.* चाणकस्योपरि प्रद्वेषपक्षपातः p. 83 *supra.* **मर्तव्य**—*Pot. p.* here used as a noun (मरण); *cf.* अश्रोतव्यं न शृणोमि. **वत्सल**—'वत्सांसाभ्यां कामबले' Pân. V. 2. 98. The *matub*, aff. ल is added to वत्स and अंस in the sense of 'affectionate towards' and 'strong' respectively.

P. 149. **शोकदीक्षां**—दीक्षा properly means 'the initiatory ceremony at a sacrifice'; hence here 'introduction to.' The word is used metaphorically in several senses; *cf.* आपन्नाभयसत्रेषु दीक्षिताः खलु पौरवाः। S'âk. II. 16. विवाहदीक्षा &c. The fig. here is somewhat analogous to that contained in व्यसनब्रह्मचारिन्. **कष्टतर**—is equivalent to अतीव कष्टं, no comparison being meant. तर is added merely in the sense of excess.

अभ्यर्ण—Near. अर्देः सन्निविभ्यः । अभेश्चाविदूर्ये । Pâṇ. VII. 2. 24. 25. इ is not added to the *p. p.* participle in the case of अर्द् after the prepositions सम्, नि, वि and अभि when the sense is nearness or proximity; समर्ण, अभ्यर्ण &c. **अर्थवत्ता**—*V. l.* possesion of wealth, property. The *matub* sense is not prominent here. It is equivalent to अर्थः । Comp. धातुमत्ता Kum. I. 4. See, however, Mallinâtha's remarks there. **विनिमय**—properly exchange (From मे A.; *cf.* Rag. I. 26.) hence here, a ransom.

परवत्—परेण तुल्यं like an enemy. **अभिहिंसन्ति**—अभि adds no force; it is used *metri causa.* **तयो**—should be properly तं यो. The reason of this violation of gender is given in the com. The reading in the foot-note is better (व्यसनिनि वयस्ये makes better sense). **सति वणिक्त्वेपि**—For merchants naturally love money more than others.

प्रतिपन्नं—'Replied.' Mr. Telang. प्रतिपद् properly means to do or say something in response to another; hence here, it rather means अङ्गीकृतं 'what did he agree or undertake to do? **प्राणहरः दण्डः**—capital punishment.

P. 150. **आणविदो**—Mr. Dhruva translates this by आज्ञप्तः which is certainly better. **स गृहजनं याच्यते**—गौणे कर्मणि दुह्यादेः प्रधाने नीहकृष्वहां । ...लादयो मताः । Sid. Kau. *Cf.* याचित Rag. XI. I.

शिबेरिव—शिबिनेव would be a better reading as far as symmetry is concerned. शिबि—name of a king renowned for his generosity, On one occasion Indra and Agni came to him in order to try him, assuming the forms of a hawk and a dove in hot pursuit, when he rescued the supposed dove from the clutches of the hawk by offering an equal quantity of his own flesh weighed in a balance. See Mah. Bhâr. Van. P. Ad. 197. See p. 158. sl. 5. *infra.* "S'ibi's is a common story among Buddhists; see *inter alia* Cunningham's Geography p. 82. Fa. Hian, pp. 29, 206, Burgess and Bhagavânlâl's Cave Inscriptions of Western India, p. 87." Telang. सुहृदा विनापि—see the force of this explained in the com.

P. 151. निस्त्रिंशः—निर्गतः (exceeding) त्रिंशतोऽङ्गुलिभ्यः । सजल०—Cal. Ed.s read विगत० resembling the sky free from clouds. The Com. takes सजल separately ; सजलः full of water, sharp-edged and bright. धाराजल, धाराम्भः &c. are very common expressions ; *cf.* 'निष्ठ्यूतधाराजलबिन्दुदन्तुरेण कृपाणेन' Kâd. p. 12. धाराम्भसः फेनमिव व्यनक्ति । Vik. I. 1. It is, however, better to take सजल with जलद to which a bright sword bears resemblance. The meaning of bright is expressed by the comparison. Mr. Dhruva takes करेण in the second line to mean 'a ray ०श्रद्धा—means here an ardent desire (आदर); *cf.* श्रद्धां विधास्यन्ति सचेतसोत्र । Vik. I. 13. श्रद्धादरे च काङ्क्षायाम् । इति मेदिनी । Here it is used nearly in the sense of hope (in the hope of being engaged in battle). Mr. Telang quotes—कलयसि कलहश्रद्धया किं त्रिशूलं from Bâṇa's Chandakaus'ika, and अपि नाम भवदुपाध्याययजमानस्य निवृत्ता हरचापारोपणश्रद्धा from Prasanna Râghava. सत्त्वोत्कर्ष—Its great virtue. The root-sense of सत्त्व is prominent here. It means that quality which enables a thing to keep up its *existence* and does not allow it to give way. विवश—no longer my own master, but entirely in the power of मित्रस्नेह.

पिशुनितं—See note on पिशुनयति p. 146. प्रतिपत्तुं—to recognise, to know definitely. *Cf.* भेदप्रतिपत्ति Bhar. Vai. S'at. 85. अमात्यपादाः—This is a respectful mode of speaking. *Cf.* आचार्यपादाः, तातपादाः, गुरुपादाः &c. तत्कुरु &c.—We have adopted the order of this and the next two speeches from the Cal Ed.s as that seems to be quite natural.

दुर्गृहीत०—Said in reply to the man's सुग्रहीतनामधेयाः । यथार्थो राक्षसः—*cf.* last line of V. 7. ही हीमाणहे—see p. 115. *supra.*

P. 152. चन्द्रगुप्तहतकेन—This he says to show that he is a partisan of the Nandas, and thereby to lull all suspicion of being Châṇakya's emissary, if any such could have been caused by his previous praise of Chandragupta's rule. घातकजन०—It does not clearly appear from the play whether the hangmen were really put to death by Châṇakya's order. Chân. is not likely to do such a thing. Very probably this a lie and an invention of the spy. Râk., however, does not seem to be inclined to disbelieve him. See sl. 21. जीवितं परिरक्षन्तः--Wishing to save their own lives; for the purpose of saving their own lives (lest they should themselves have to share the fate of S'akaṭadâsa's hangmen). The pre. par. term. has the sense of the object for which an action is done; लक्षणहेत्वोः क्रियायाः। Pân. III. 2. 126. हेतुः फलं कारणं च। Sid. Kau. त्वरायितः—expedited, accelereted, *cf.* p. 124 where it means 'made to make haste.'

शत्रोः—*i. e.* of Châṇakya. मतेन—This he guesses from S'akaṭadâsa's supposed treachery and Siddhârthaka's share in the plot as revealed in the fifth Act. वधाधिकृतः जनः—persons in charge of the execution of criminals; hangmen, executioners. क्रोधावेशात्—Râk. thinks the आवेश to be quite unaccountable in that case. अथ न &c.—The line as it stands is somewhat obscure. The Com. takes अथ पक्षान्तरे and कृतक to qualify तदानयन which follows from the context. Mr. Telang calls this explanation a little forced and takes न with अथ meaning 'But if not—that is to say if he was not brought to me with the assent of the enemy.' He then takes तादृक् कष्टं कृतकम् in the sense of 'a sinful fabrication ' In either explanation we have to take कृतक as a noun (which it is not) and understand it in an obscure (अप्रसिद्ध) sense. The Cal. reading—अथ स कृतकं तादृग्लेखं &c. presents no difficulty of meaning. But it is not supported by the context. For Râk. believed the letter referred to as genuine and not a forged one. On the whole the Com.'s interpretation is the only way out of the difficulty.

तर्कारूढा—Mounted on the wheel of thought, embarking on guesses निश्चयं—निर्णयम्.

P. 153. प्रथमं—On the former occasion. घातकानां-The Gen. must be taken कर्तरि; see com.; since hangmen put a person to death before the rescuer rescues the victim. The Com. arrives at the same sense in a round about way. कालान्तरेण—after an interval of time—while Chandanadâsa's critical condition needed immediate consideration. व्यापत्ति—calamity, ruin. *Cf.* Mṛch. VI. 1. (where the Com. renders व्यापत्ति by विशिष्टापात्ति). व्यापत्तिः स्खलितान्तरेषु नियता सिद्धिर्भवेद्वा न वा। Pt. I. 307. It may also mean danger to life; *cf.* Meg. अव्यापन्नः कुशलमबले पृच्छति त्वां वियुक्तः.' ज्ञातं—I have it, I know how to act. निष्क्रय—purchase value, ransom; *cf.* Rag. XV. 55. II. 55.

ACT VII.

P. 153. **इच्छत**—The Imper. is meaningless; so read **इच्छथ. विषम**—Dreadful or fatal in its consequences. See p. 135.

P. 154. **राजापथ्य**—Lit. what is not wholesome or beneficial to a king; hence felony or treason; *cf.* pp. 42. 43. *supra*. *Cf.* the similar scene in Mṛch. Act. X. where Chârudatta is similarly led to the stake.

वध्यवेश—Such as wearing red garments, red garlands, red marks on the body &c.; *cf.* सर्वगात्रेषु विन्यस्तै रक्तचन्दनहस्तकैः। पिष्टचूर्णावकीर्णश्च पुरुषाहं पशूकृतः॥ रक्तं तदेव वरवस्त्रमियं च माला। &c. Mṛch, X. 5. 44; also 3; **शूलं स्कन्धेनादाय**—The condemned criminal, it seems, was made to carry the stake on which he was to be impaled. *Cf.* अंसेन बिभ्रत्करवीरमालां स्कन्धेन शूलं हृदयेन शोकम्। Mṛch. X. 21. **कुटुंबिनी**—The wife.

P. 155. **चन्द०**—In some Ed.s this speech is put in the mouth of Chandanadâsa's wife, which is decidedly better. For a resolute man like Chandanadâsa cannot be expected to utter such a speech of helplessness. **चारित्रभङ्ग०**—चारित्रं good character, a right course of conduct. चरित्रमेव चारित्रं, स्वार्थे अण्। The word is of no rare occurrence; *cf.* अनृतं नाभिधास्यामि चारित्रभ्रंशकारणं। Mṛch. III. 27; also 26; I. 43. Rag XV. 73. किं चाह चारित्रविलासशून्याः &c. Vik. I. 25. **उदासीन**—*i. e.* those who never meddle with their affairs. **कृतान्तः**—कृतमन्तयतीति.

स्वत्वा आमिषाणि—*i. e.* for fear of offending the hunters who eat meat. **निर्बन्ध**—an obstinate course of conduct. The meaning is that wicked people make no scruple to oppress the innocent; *cf.* व्योमैकान्तविहारिणोपि विहगाः &c. Pt. II. 23. **दुर्लभास्ते** &c.—*cf.* मित्रं न कश्चिद्विषमस्थितस्य। Mṛch. X. 16.

सबाष्पं-एतेऽस्माकं &c.—This speech is properly assigned to Chandanadâsa. **कृतनिवापसलिला**—*v. l.* will not do. For निवापस० is water offered after death, which implies certain death, while the uppermost thought in every one's mind then must have been that Chand. should escape the intended doom and not meet with it. **परिजन**—*v. l.* those that surrounded him (his wife and son). **परलोक**—see com.

P. 156. **व्यवसित**—Determined or resolved upon. **आत्मानुग्रह**—personal benefit. **संव्यवहार**—honest transactions, fair dealings; *cf.* IV. 14.

प्रसन्ना देवताः—*Cf.* Chandanadâsa's speech further on. पश्चिमौ—पश्चाद्भवौ to be seen for the last time. अपश्चिमस्य or योः—*v. l* अपश्चिम as a Bah. (नास्ति पश्चिमो यस्मात्) has the same sense as पश्चिम. *Cf.*—अयमत्र ते जन्मन्यपश्चिमः...मकरन्दबाहुपरिष्वङ्गः Mâl. Mâd. IX; see Apte's Dic.

चाणक्यवि०—For Chânakya might recklessly do any thing, fears the merchant, ignorant of his real character.

P. 157. हर्षस्थाने &c.—For the sentiment comp. I. 48. अवश्यं भवितव्ये विनाशे &c.—*cf.* धनानि जीवितं चैव परार्थे प्राज्ञ उत्सृजेत् । सन्निमित्ते वरं त्यागो विनाशे नियते सति ॥ Hit. I. 44. समुद्वहमानः—taking upon yourself or carrying out courageously (सम्). कुलधर्मः &c—This shows that the noble father had a nobler son. पटाक्षेपेण—With a sudden toss of the curtain. This stage direction is used when a character enters the stage hurriedly and without previous intimation. शूलायतनाः—The executioners; see com.

P. 158. परिभवक्षेत्रीकृतः—Made the object of ignominy or contempt. *Cf.* for a similar use न हि अल्पीयसा शोककारणेन क्षेत्रीक्रियन्ते एवंविधा मूर्तयः । Kâd. p. 217. वः—*i. e.* of people of your profession; see com. This is the greatest degradation. मृत्युलोकपदवी—for, the fastening of the garland prepares the way to the realm of Death.

अमात्य सर्वमपि &c.—A paralel of this will be found in the story of the two Syracusan youths, Damon and Pythias. स्वार्थ एव—care-worn and utterly thwarted in his object by the diplomacy of Chânakya, Râk. felt life to be quite a burden. Chandanadâsa's death would have been the crowning piece of misfortune. So putting an end to his existence was to his gain as giving him relief.

असज्जनरुचौ—असत्यो जनरुचयो यस्मिन् । in which the tastes of the people are quite depraved Mr. Telang takes this differently—'which does not satisfy good persons. The Kali age is not an age with which good people can be satisfied.' औशीनरीय—उशीनरस्यापत्यं पुमान् औशीनरः तस्येदम् of the son of Us'inara *i. e.* S'ibi. S'ibi, son of Us'înara, king of Kâs'î, is mentioned as the author of the first Rk' of Rg. X. 12. 179. See Sâyanâchârya's Introduction to the Ṛk. बुद्धानामपि &c.—Mark this praise of the Buddhist saints. It is due to their life of self—denial and practice of kindness towards all living creatures. See Com.'s remark. This shows that the Buddhists were yet held in high esteem even by the followers of Brâhmâṇism and bears testimony to the antiquity of the play. For a similar thought comp. वन्द्या त्वमेव जगतः स्पृहणीयसिद्धिरेवंविधैर्विलसितैरतिबो-

घिसत्वे: ॥ Mâl. Mâd. X. 21. See also S'is. XI. 58. क्लिष्ट—We have already twice met with this root in this sense. See pp. 86. 136.

P. 159. बुद्धिपुरुष०—परिसर:—*v. l.* (used in its literal sense of extent) is a bad word; it should be प्रसर:.

उत्तुङ्गशिखा—Refers to a fire furiously breaking up. सदागतेरगतिता &c.—For the fig. *cf.* स्थविरे केन देवो मातरिश्वा बद्धपूर्व: । D. K. p. 100. अनेकप—(द्विप) used for poetic beauty. नैक नक्र—Two instances where न is not changed to अ or अन्; *cf.* नशयानेन *supra.* अर्णवः—अर्णांसि अत्र सन्ति; irregular. Mark the *anuprâsa* in the sloka. Châṇakya herein gives expression to the high estimation in which he held Râkshasa's ability.

नन्दकुलविद्वेषिणा &c.—Châṇakya was no beliver in the power of fate. See the contrary stated at p. 94. He says this here merely to please and, magnify the greatness of Râkshasa and thereby to make a favourable impression about him on the minds of his servants.

P. 160. आकर: &c.—Himself trained in the same school of polititians, it is no wonder that Râk. should not find fault with the foul means used by Châṇakya to accomplish his end, but on the contrary should express his admiration for him. मत्सरिण: &c.—The prejudices against Châṇakya being deep rooted in the heart of Râk, he is not expected to manifest the ecstatic joy at the sight of Châṇ. which the latter does at the sight of his political adversary.

कल्पना—(1) devising remedies, forming plans; (2) arrangement. See. sl. 15. *infra.*

अमात्य इति लज्जाकरं &c.—Râk. says this for two reasons. Firstly he was no longer an *amâtya*; secondly, he could not do justice to that title as all the plans devised by him had met with ill success. कपटलेखम्—Mr. Telang who reads तादृशं लेखमजानन्नेव कपटलेखं मया thinks this may be a *namulanta.* But then the *namul* is without propriety. The first ' लेखं ' therefore has been dropped (as in the Cal. Ed.s).

आर्तपुरुष:—This explains, better than स चापि पु०, the feigned character of the man and Châṇ.'s hand in it. इत्यर्धोक्ते &c.—This modesty does great credit to Châṇakya. वीर—Châṇ. here pays a compliment to Râkshasa. नया:—devices of policy.

P. 161. लज्जित एव &c.—Chandragupta is somewhat ashamed to find that he had no opportunity given him to display his valour or to know how far he could rely on his own strength.

फलयोगं &c.—Construe—फलेन शल्येन योगमवाप्यापि अनियोगेन उपयोगाभावात् विलक्षतां गतानां लज्जितानामत एवाधोमुखानां सायकानां स्वशुचेव निजतूणीशयनमेव व्रतं तत्र प्रतिष्ठा भवति। The reading ०व्रतं प्रवृष्टे is abandoned as it implies some dissatisfaction on the part of Chandragupta. **फलयोग** &c.—The double meanings are explained in the com. **फल**—(1) the fruit; (2) the sharp point. **विपक्षतां** *v. l.*—**विपक्ष**—(1) the party of the enemy; (2) birds' feathers. Feathers were attached to the hinder parts of arrows in order to regulate their motion *Cf.* Rag. II. 31; Vikra. X. 3. **अधोमुख**—Their points are called their मुख. **प्रतिष्ठा**—fixed or permanent position. *Cf.* for a similar idea. Kir. XVII. 47.

अथवा—The next moment Chandra. drives away the feeling of uneasiness and shows that he is pleased at his Guru's achievement.

विगुणीकृत—See com. **तन्त्र**—administration of kingdom (राज्यं राज्ञः कर्म); *cf.* Rag. XIV. 85. **जागरूकः**—जागरणशीलः; जागृ + ऊक showing habit; जागुरूकः Pân. III. 3. 165.

आशिषः—Mark the sense of this word here which means 'a desire'; *cf.* जगच्छरण्यस्य निराशिषः (निरभिलाषस्य Malli.) सतः किमेभिराशोपहतात्मवृत्तिभिः। Kum. V. 76. **चाणक्यः राजानं** &c.—see ft. note. This speech is quite out of place here and is, therefore, dropped. **संभावित०**—He gave promise of his future exaltation. **क्रमेण** &c.—*Cf.* I. 1. II. 9, *supra.*

P. 162. **षाड्गुण्य**—षड्गुणा एव षाड्गुण्यं, स्वार्थे ष्यञ् (य). S'is. II. 93. **आर्ये**—The first refers to Chân., the second to Râkshasa. It is but proper that Chandra., knowing the desire of Châṇakya, should pay such a compliment to Râkshasa.

भृत्यभावेन—As a servant or dependent. For, by his foregoing speech, Chandragupta showed that he accepted him as his minister (honourable servitude as Malaya. had put it). **कौटिल्यशिष्य**—This is very significant. At first Râk. thinks that Chandra., as a pupil of Kauṭ. calls him आर्य merely as a political device having some secret object in view. But suddenly he remembers what implicit confidence Chandra. had in his premier that he might have sincerely accepted him as his premier readily acceeding to the will of his preceptor and says अथवा &c. **स्थाने**—may be a *prep.* or a noun in the Loc.

द्रव्य—The fit or proper person. **जिगीषु**—lit. one desirous of conquering; hence one stirred by ambition, aspiring. **नेतुः**—the minister at the head of the management of affairs. See Kir. VI. 42. **प्रतिष्ठा**-

The word has already occurred twice; II. 5, 9. For the idea *cf.* क्रिया हि वस्तूपहिता प्रसीदति । Rag. III. 29. पात्रविशेषन्यस्तं गुणान्तरं व्रजाति शिल्पमाधातुः । Mâl. I. 6. 'क्रिया हि द्रव्यं विनयति नाद्रव्यम्' इति कौटिल्यः । Also Hit., 43. प्रस्ता० शुद्धनयः—Scheming rightly, unerring in his policy. कूलजवृक्ष०—*i. e.* the king by his impolitic meddlings un. does what his minister does, like a stream underming the tree on its bank (which strengthens it).

अगृहीतशस्त्रेण—Without accepting the minister's sword (post). Chân. means to say-we have called you अमात्य and you have merely acquiesed in it. But that is not ratified by my actually delivering over the ministerial sword to you and your accepting it.

गृह्यताम्—Taking the sword was virtually and formally accepting the ministerial office.

P. 163. अशून्या०—अशून्यानि not non-existent. *i. e.* विद्यमानानि व्यासनानि येषु. शयना०—०शयने शयनविषये स्वेच्छासुखैः । माहात्म्य—greatness.

परिकल्पना—Being equipped for battle. व्यतिकर—contact. Here it nearly means 'by reason of.' This word has a variety of meanings according to the context. प्रोच्छून—much swollen; *p. p.* participle of श्वि with प्र and उत्.

स्नेहगुणाः—Many kind acts or excellences of—गुण many mean here, excellence or effect. भृत्योस्मि—For Râk. sees no other way out of the difficulty. व्यापारणीयं—I have to wield, I am forced to accept.

कार्याणां गतयः—See com.; *cf.* नमस्तत्कर्मभ्यो विधिरपि न येभ्यः प्रभवति । Bhar. Nît. 99.; and Shakespere 'Time's glory is to calm contending kings, and turn the giddy round of fortune's wheel'. This may also be taken as—कार्याणां गतयः चिरादपि नरं विधेः आज्ञाकरत्वं नयन्ति—The c urses events take force a man even after a long time (howsoever he may resist them) to yield to fate.

P. 164. आर्यः प्रमाणम्—*i. e.* it rests with your honour to decide what is to be done with him. जानीते—knows what order to pass ; *i. e.* he is the responsible minister now.

मलयकेतौ—in dependence on. For the Loc. Mr. Telang compares Manus. II. 67.

प्रतिष्ठित—Established on the throne. The restoration of the kingdom to Malaya. shows that Chân. wished to represent Chandragupta as a Dharmavijayî king. *Cf.* Rag. IV. 43. हस्त्यश्वं—war-elephants and war-horses (necessary for the protection of the kingdom). सर्वमोक्षः—To order a general release on an exceptional occasion of joy, such as the birth of an heir to the throne, royal inauguration &c., seems to have been a very ancient custom which is still observed in the courts of Indian princes. See Rag. III. 20. **नेतरि**—see sl. 14. *supra.*

P. 165 **राक्षसेन** &c.—It is but meet that Chandragupta should thus express his gratitude to Châṇakya. **नन्दाशी०** &c.—is specially meant to please Châṇakya. The sl. is omitted in the Cal. Ed.s and perhaps with better taste. The reference to the annihilation of the Nandas in the very hearing of Râk., to conciliate whom is the chief object of the drama, is, as remarked by Mr. Dhruva, highly impolitic and unbecoming.

भरतवाक्य—The concluding stanza or stanzas so called in honour of Bharata, the father of Indian drama, (or being enjoned by him) and containing the expression of a wish for general prosperity &c on the part of the actors.

आत्मयोनि—here Vishṇu; see Rag. X. 20. **तनुमास्थितस्य**—*cf.* स्वरूपमास्थाय Kum. V. 84. **यस्य प्राक्** &c.—*Cf.* Taittirîya A'raṇ. उद्धृतासि वराहेण कृष्णेन शतबाहुना । According to the Taitt. Brâhmaṇa it was Prajâpati, afterwards known as Brahmâ, who raised the earth out of the boundless waters. According to the Harivaṁs'a, the Earth, not being able to bear the weight of the mountains upon it, sank into the unfathomable deep from which it was raised by Vishṇu assuming the form of a Boar. भूत्वा यज्ञवराहोसौ द्रागधः प्राविशद् गुरुः । अद्भिः संच्छादितामुर्वी स तामार्च्छत् प्रजापतिः । रसातलतले मग्नां रसातलतले गतः । प्रभुर्लोकहितार्थाय दंष्ट्राग्रेणोज्जहार च ॥ **राजमूर्तिः**—The king is supposed to be an incarnation of Vishṇu. The king meant here is of course Chandragupta. **म्लेच्छैः**—Although apparently putting the verse into the mouth of Râkshasa the poet really refers to the early invasions of India by the white Huns in which they were worsted. **चन्द्रगुप्तः**—Some read **अवन्तिवर्मा** assigning the verse to Chandra. and Râk.; and the poet, no doubt, covertly refers to this king, his patron. In this case we must suppose Chandra. and Râk. to repeat the verse in their characters as actors. See remarks in the Introduction. For the fig. based on the identification of Vishṇu with the king, see commentary.

the birth of an heir to the throne, royal inauguration &c., seems to have been a very ancient custom which is still observed in the courts of Indian princes. See Rag. III. 20. [illegible]—[illegible], 14. *supra*.

P. 166. [illegible] &c.—It is but meet that Chandragupta should thus express his gratitude to Chāṇakya. [illegible] &c.—is specially meant to please Chāṇakya. The śl. is omitted in Ch. It is and perhaps with better taste. The reference to the annihilation of the Nandas in the very hearing of Rāk., to bow[illegible] whom is the other object of the drama, is, as remarked by Mr. Dhruva, highly injudicious and unbecoming.

[illegible]—The concluding stanza of dramas so called in honour of Bharata, the father of Indian drama (or being enjoined by him?) and containing the expression of a wish for general prosperity &c. on the part of the actors.

[illegible]—here Vishṇu, see Rag. X. [illegible]. [illegible]—*of* [illegible] Bhān. V. [illegible] [illegible] &c.—*cf.* Taittirīya Āraṇyaka [illegible] [illegible] According to the Taitt. Brāhmaṇa it was Prajāpati, afterwards known as Brahmā, who raised the earth out of the boundless waters; according to the Harivaṁśa, the Earth not being able to bear the weight of the mountains upon it sank into the unfathomable deep from which it was raised by Vishṇu assuming the form of a boar. [illegible]
[illegible]
[illegible]—The king is supposed to be an incarnation of Vishṇu. The king meant here is of course Chandragupta. [illegible]—Although a [illegible] putting the verse into the mouth of [illegible] really refers to the same [illegible] which they are [illegible]. [illegible]—Some read [illegible] assigning the verse to Chāṇakya; and Telang and the [illegible] correctly give it this place, in the text. In this case we must suppose Chandragupta and Rāk. to remain [illegible] in their characters as actors. See remarks in the Introduction. For the [illegible] based on the identification of Vishṇu with the king, see commentary.

APPENDIX.

——:o:——

I. The Metres Occurring in the Play.

Their Definitions and Schemes.

A short syllable is marked as ⏑, and a long one as —. The following letters are symbols representing different triads (गणs) of light and heavy syllables:—

य ⏑ — —; र — ⏑ —; त — — ⏑; भ — ⏑ ⏑; ज ⏑ — ⏑; स ⏑ ⏑ —; म — — —; न ⏑ ⏑ ⏑ ग represents a heavy syllable and ल a light one.

The following couplet will help the student in remembering the long and short syllables forming each Gaṇa—आदिमध्यावसानेषु यरता यान्ति लाघवम् । भजसा गौरवं यान्ति मनौ तु गुरुलाघवम् ॥

अनुष्टुभ्—This is defined as—पञ्चमं लघु सर्वत्र सप्तमं द्विचतुर्थयोः । गुरुषष्ठं च पादानां शेषेष्वनियमो मतः ॥ In an *Anushṭubh* the fifth syll. ought to be short and the sixth long in all quarters. The seventh should be short in the second and fourth quarters only. Other syllables are governed by no rule.

I. 3, 16, 23, 24; II. 20, 22; III. 23, 32; IV. 8, 9, 10; V. 14, 17, 22; VI. 15. 18; VII. 7, 8, 12, 13, 17, 18.

इन्द्रवज्रा—स्यादिन्द्रवज्रा यदि तौ जगौ गः । Sch. of G. त त ज ग ग. V. 8.

उपजाति—अनन्तरोदीरितलक्ष्मभाजौ पादौ यदीयावुपजातयस्ताः ॥ A mixture of इन्द्र० and उपेन्द्र० forms उपजाति.

II. 2; IV. 13.

वंशस्थ or वंशस्थविल—जतौ तु वंशस्थमुदीरितं जरौ । Sch. of G. ज त ज र. *Vams'astha* is a metre with twelve syllables for a foot. Take off the last syll. and what remains is *Upendravajrā.*

IV. 14.

रुचिरा—जभौ सजौ गिति रुचिरा चतुर्ग्रहैः Sch. of G. ज भ स ज, ग. (4. 9).

II. 3, V. 6.

प्रहर्षिणी—म्याशाभिर्मनजरगाः प्रहर्षिणीयम् । Sch. म न ज र ग (3. 10).

I. 7; III. 12; V. 13.

वसन्ततिलका—उक्ता वसन्ततिलका तभजा जगौ गः । Sch. त, भ, ज, ज, ग, ग

I. 8, 10, 26; II. 6, 8, 17; III. 9, 17, 18, 31, 33; IV. 6, 11, 17; V. 7., 16; VI. 7, 13; VII. 14.

मालिनी—ननमयययुतेयं मालिनी भोगिलोकैः । Sch. न, न, म, य, य. (8. 7).

III. 15, 25; VI. 1, 3.

पृथ्वी—जसौ जसयला वसुग्रहयतिश्च पृथ्वी गुरुः ।

Sch. ज, स, ज, स, य, ल, ग. (8. 9).

VI. 16.

हरिणी—नसमरसला गः षड्वेदैर्हयैर्हरिणी मता । Sch. न, स, म, र, स, ल, ग. (6. 4. 7).

III. 6; IV. 2; VI. 20.

शिखरिणी—रसै रुद्रैश्छिन्ना यमनसभला गः शिखरिणी ।

Sch. य, म, न, स, भ, ल, ग. (6. 11).

I. 13; II. 7, 10; III. 3, 4, 7, 8, 11, 16, 29; V. 3, 4, 12; VI. 6, 11, 12, 14, 17.

मन्दाक्रान्ता—मन्दाक्रान्ता जलधिषडगैर्म्भौ नतौ ताद्गुरू चेत् । Sch. म, भ, न, त, त, ग, ग. (4. 6. 7).

VI. 19.

शार्दूलविक्रीडित—सूर्याश्वैर्यदि मः सजौ सततगाः शार्दूलविक्रीडितम् ।

Sch. म, स, ज, स, त, त, ग. (12. 7).

I. 12. 14, 15. 22, 25; II. 4, 5, 9, 12, 13, 15, 16, 18, 21, 23. III. 1, 2, 5, 13, 14, 26; IV. 5, 15; V. 5, 10, 15, 18, 20, 21, 24; VI. 5, 8, 10; VII. 4, 5, 6, 9, 15, 16.

सुवदना—ज्ञेया सप्ताश्वषड्भिर्मरभनययुता म्लौ गः सुवदना ।

Sch. of G. म, र, भ, न, य, भ, ल, ग (7. 7. 6).

IV. 16.

स्रग्धरा—म्रभ्नैर्यानां त्रयेण त्रिमुनियतियुता स्रग्धरा कीर्तितेयम् ।

Sch. म, र, भ, न, य, य, य. (7. 7. 7).

I. 1. 2, 11, 20; II. 14; III. 10, 19, 20, 21, 22, 24, 27, 28, 30; IV. 3, 7, 12, 22; V. 11, 19, 23; VI. 9. 21; VII. 19.

वैतालीय—षड्विषमेऽष्टौ समे कलास्ताश्च समे स्युर्नोनिरन्तराः । न समात्र पराश्रिता कला वैतालीयेऽन्ते रलौ गुरुः ॥ The first and third quarters contain six *mâtrâs* (syllabic instants) and the second and fourth eight each, followed by a रगण and short and a long syllyble. See also Apte's Dictionary.

VII. 10, 11.

औपच्छंदसिक—The same as Vaitâlîya with a long syll. added as the end of each quarter.

आर्या—This belong the class of metres regulated by the number of *mâtrâs* or syllabic instants.

यस्याः पादे प्रथमे द्वादश मात्रास्तथा तृतीयेपि ।
अष्टादश द्वितीये चतुर्थके पञ्चदश सार्या ॥

The first and third quarters contain 12 *mâtrâs* or syllabic instants, the second 18 and the fourth 15.

I. 5, 6, 9, 17, 18, 19, 21; II. 11, 19; IV. 1, 18, 19, 21; V. 1; VI. 4; VII. 1, 2, 3.

गीति—आर्याप्रथमार्धसमं यस्याः परार्धमीरिता गीतिः । That is Gîti whose third and fourth quarters are like the first and second quarters of an *âryâ i. e.* whose first and third quarters contain 12 *mâtrâs* and second and fourth 18 *mâtrâs* each.

II. 1; IV. 4 (Udgîtî), V. 9; VI. 2 (irregular).

Doubtful Metres. IV. 20, V. 2.

II.

THE MORE IMPORTANT RHETORICAL FIGURES MENTIONED IN THE COMMENTARY OR NOTES.

अतिशयोक्ति—Or Hyperoble is of four kinds, of which one of frequent occurrence is—प्रस्तुतस्ययदन्यत्वं—सातिशयोक्तिर्विज्ञेया; *i. e.* when the thing in hand is described as of a different kind (superior in excellence or beauty) that is *Atis'ayokti.*

अर्थान्तरन्यास—Or Corroboration; सामान्यं वाविशेषो वा तदन्येन समर्थ्यते । यत्र सोर्थान्तरन्यासो साधर्म्येणेतरेण वा ॥ Where general proposition is adduced to support a particular instance, or a particular instance to support a general proposition either under a resemblance or a contrast, that is *Arthântarangâsa.*

उत्प्रेक्षा—Or Poetical Probability; संभावनमथोत्प्रेक्षा प्रकृतस्य समेन यत् ॥ प्रकृतमात्मनः सम करोतिति समसुपमानम् । Apprehending the object under consideration as looking identical with something to which it is compared, is what is termed *Utprekshâ.* It is of two kinds (1) expressed or (2) understood. The expressed is one wherein such words ध्रुवं, मन्ये &c. are used; It is again of three kinds, हेतूत्प्रेक्षा फलोत्प्रेक्षा and वस्तूत्प्रेक्षा or स्वरूपोत्प्रेक्षा.

उपमा—Or Comparison—साधर्म्यमुपमा भेदे, पूर्णा लुप्ता च साऽग्रिमा । श्रौत्यार्थी च भवेद्वाक्ये समासे तद्धिते तथा ॥ The (striking) possession of a common property when there is difference is *Upamâ.*

काव्यलिङ्ग—Or the Poetical Reason; काव्यलिङ्ग हेतोर्वाक्यपदार्थता । *Kâvyaliṅga* is the statement of a reasón in the form of (1) a sentence, or (2) of a word or (3) words. Or to make the definition simpler वाक्यपदार्थयोः हेतुता—that is काव्य० wherein either a sentence or a word (or words) is intended to give a reason for the statement made in the whole sentence. The हेतु according to some must be आर्थ or implied.

परिकर—विशेषणैर्यत्साकूतैरुक्तिः परिकरस्तु सः । साकूतैः साभिप्रायैः । उक्तिरर्थाविशेषस्य । That is *Parikara* where there is description (of course of the subject) with attributes which are significant *i. e.* have an implied meaning (व्यंग्य). Here विशेषण and विशेष्य are dependent on each other. In *Kâvyaliṅga* कार्यकारणभाव is necessary; so here is no व्यंग्य. But परिकर contains a व्यंग्य which produces the charm. According to Jagannâtha the use of oven one significant adjective is sufficient for *Parikara.*

मुद्रा—See Com. I. 6.

रूपक—Or Metaphor—तद्रूपकमभेदो य उपमानोपमेययोः । The identity of उपमान and the उपमेय is *Rûpaka.* When two things known to be different from each other, still to show their great resemblance, are identified together, the fig. is *Rûpaka.* Hence it is plain that in a *Rûpaka* the उपमेय and the उपमान (the प्रकृत and the अप्रकृत) must be mentioned in words.

वक्रोक्ति—See com. I. 1. and notes.

व्यतिरेक—A figure of speech which consists in representing the *Upameya* as superior to the *Upamâua* in some particular respects; उपमानाद्यदन्यस्य व्यतिरेकः स एव सः । K. P. X.

श्लेष—Or Pun. *double entendre,* the susceptibility of a word or words to yield two or more meanings.

समासोक्ति—परोक्तिर्भेदकैः श्लिष्टैः समासोक्तिः । The description of another thing by paronomastic (श्लिष्टैः having many senses) adjecteves (भेदकैः) is *Samâsokti.*

स्वभावोक्ति—Or description according to Nature (also called Jâti by some).—स्वभावोक्तिस्तु डिम्भादेः स्वक्रियारूपवर्णनम् । *Svabhâvokti* is the description of the particular action or appearance, colour or posture (रूपं वर्णः संस्थानं च) of an object such as a child and the like. Of course the action &c. must be striking, such as is perceived by the poet alone.

III.

BOMBAY UNIVERSITY EXAMINATION QUESTIONS.

1871. B. A.

1 (*a*) Give and criticise the character of Râk., supporting your remarks with quotations, or at least references to passages from the drama. (*b*) What defects or excellences, if any, do you see in the character of Malayaketu? 2. Distinguish the fiction from the reality of the Mud., giving shortly your authorities or reasons. 3. Translate closely but idiomatically into English:—(*a*) IV. 22. (*b*) मत्त्या...... विगणयन् &c. V. 5. (*c*) भयं तावत्......अतोध्यारूढानां V. 12. (*d*) उच्छिन्नाश्रय...गोत्रान्तरं...नागेश्चिरं स्थीयते VI. 5. (*e*) पातिं त्यक्त्वा......प्रयातुं नो येषां VI. 6. 4. What figure of speech is involved in *pâda* 4 of (*a*)? Who were the Nandas? Derive the sense of गोत्र in (*d*). A Ms. reads प्रयत्नं for प्रयातुं in (*e*); which reading is preferable and more likely to be the correct one and why? What is the exact force of तावत् in l. 1 of (*e*)?

1877 Sec. B. A.

1. Translate:—(*a*) I. 8. अधैः सार्धं......काविकाक्षामैरशून्यासनान्...... VI. 15. 2. Translate the following passages and name and explain the *alankâras* in them. I. 16; (*b*) II. 1. (*c*) प्रत्यग्रोन्मेष...प्रमाणां... निद्राच्छेदा...राकेकरा वः । p. 36. केनानेक......पञ्जरे p. 159. 3. (A) Do you suspect any mislection in the following? If you do, state why, suggesting the proper reading. If the sense is clear as the passages stand, give it. (*a*) कृतककलहं कृत्वा स्वतन्त्रेण त्वया कंचित्कालं......मित्यार्योपदेश ...अथवा...सदैव स्वतन्त्रा वयम् । कुतः । (*b*) स्तुवन्त्यश्रान्तास्याः......कार्पण्याददतिवितथवाचोपि कृतिनः । (*c*) आसैरप्य......त्तमांगरहितैर्नागैश्चिरं स्थीयते । p. 143. (*d*) श्रावितोस्मि......मां विना ॥ p. 146. (B). Of the two readings in the following which is correct or better and why?—(*a*) किमन्यत्... गुप्तस्योद्धरणेसौ कार्यमवश्यमवगच्छति—द्धरणात्र किंचित्कार्यमवश्यं पश्यति । p. 106. (*b*) भीम...चनैकनक्रमकरो...र्णवः । p. 159. 4. (A). IV. 3. Name the several stages in the development of the plot of a play mentioned by writers on Dramaturgy and indicated in this sloka. Analyse the plot of the Mud., and point out these stages in it. Translate the sloka. (B) What are the logical fallacies alluded to in the following, and why?—p. 127. sl. 10.

1882. Sec. B. A Vol.

1. Translate:—(*a*) राजा—राज्यं हि नाम &c. .. । यतः—परार्थानुष्ठाने जडयति (*v. l.* रहयति)...परित्यक्तस्वार्थो (*v. l.* त्यक्तान्यार्थो)...पुरुषः ॥ p. 75.

Discuss the various readings. (*b*) फलयोगमवाप्य...मनियोगेन विलक्षतां... स्वशुचेव...ग्रतप्रतिष्ठा ॥ p. 161. (2) Explain the following giving the context and translating into Sanskṛt the Prâkṛta passages:*—(*a*) जाणन्ति तन्तजुत्तिं.........उवचरन्ति । (*b*) अत्थाहिमुहे.........अ कहुम्मि ॥ (*c*) विजिगीषुरात्मगुणसंपन्नः०......न्याय्य एवायमर्थः । (*d*) तथा नामामात्यराक्षसः......... कुसुमपुरमागतः । (*e*) स्मृतं स्यात्पुत्रदाराणां विस्मृताः स्वामिभक्तयः । चलेष्वर्थेषु......... स्वनपायिषु ॥ (3) कार्योपक्षेपमादौ &c.........मस्मद्विधो वा. IV. sl. 3. Explain all the terms in this verse which relate to Dramaurgy, and state the portions of the plot which those terms refer to. (4) Annotate on and derive:—स्तम्बकरिता, उपजाप, यमपट, दक्षिणद्वारिकं नक्षत्र, जीवनाशं नष्टाः, अपथ्यकारिन्. (5) What is the date of Chandragupta and how is it determined? Justify the remark that the date of Chandragupta is an important link in the determination of Indian Chronology, and mention the places and persons of Chandragupta's time, alluded to in the Mudrârâkshasa.

1883. Sec. B. A. Vol.

(1). Contrast the style and sentiment displayed in the writings of S'udraka and Vis'âkhadatta and state what you know of the lives of each of those poets. (2) Describe and compare the civil policy of Châṇakya and Râkshasa. What natural advantage had the former on his side? (3) State what you know of the History of Chandragupta from Greek, Roman, Buddhist or other sources, and give a comparison of the historical account of that king with that given in the Mudrârâkshasa. (4) Translate adding a few explanatory notes where necessary. (*a*) I. 2; (*b*) II. 6. (*c*) अस्ति तावत्......कुसुमपुरम् p. 58. (*d*) ततः समन्तात्...तपस्विनि पर्वतेश्वरे—p. 59. (5) Explain the following translating* the Prâkṛta into Sanskṛt. (*a*) सासणमलिह०...धम्मलाहो होदु—p. 111. (*b*) एसो कखु...वत्थिदो p. 66. भअवं ......प्पमाणीकरोसि; p. 113. To what religious sect does Jîvasiddhi belong? Is the author right in calling him as Kshapaṇaka? If not, give reasons.

1184 Sec. B. A. Vol.

1. Who is the author of the Mudrârâkshasa and what materials are there to determine his date? Examine the play as a dramatic work and point out its defects and excellences. 2. Translate:—(*a*) भर्तुस्तथा कुलषितां...III. 9. (*b*) दुष्कालेपि...VII. 5. (*c*) शिबेरिव...VI. 11. Explain fully the allusion in (*c*). 3. Explain, giving the context where necessary:—(*a*) तदुच्यतां...एभिरक्षरै...लेख शकटदासेन लेखयित्वा

---

* **Intermediate students may not expect such questions.**

मामुपतिष्ठस्व. (*b*) अस्माभिर (*v. l.* अस्माकम)...जिर्जाविषां (*v. l.* जिजीविषा)... अनुगम्यते ॥ (*c*) अस्ताभिमुखं सूर्ये...केतौ । (*d*) प्रतिमानयितव्योमात्यराक्षसस्य प्रथमः प्रणयः । (*e*) अनुपेक्षणे द्वयी गतिर्निगृह्येत वा...प्रतिपाद्येत वा । (*f.*) अयं लेखस्याशून्यार्थो भविष्यति । इमामपि...दर्शय (*g*) अलहन्ताणं...गच्छन्दि ॥ p. 116. (*h*) अज्ज ण रहस्सं णादिगुरुअं किंदुः...मरणस्स कालहरणं कादुं. Discuss fully the various readings in (*b*) and translate (*g*) and (*h*) into Sanskṛt. 4. (*a*) What is meant by षड्गुण, उन्मेष, निदर्शन, बजि, विमष and यमपट. (*b*) Sketch briefly the character of Bhâgurâyaṇa, stating the part he is made to play in the drama. (*c*) State all the allusions to the Buddhist religion that occur in the play.

1885 Sec. B. A. Vol.

1. Translate:—(*a*) शक्यः खल्वेष...प्रमार्ष्टुमिच्छामि. p. 24. (*b*) III. 28. (*c*) VII. 19. What is the technical name for the verse and why is it so called? 2. State in what connection the following sentences are used and translate them:—(*a*) अज्ज णं पसादो...करेदि । p. 69. कथं निरुपपद...चाणक्यमिति । p. 96. (*c*) शोणं...शतशः IV. 16. State the metre of this line. (*d*) अतः प्रतिलिखितमस्या.........विभावयिष्यति । p. 132. (*e*) वअस्स भद्दभट...अण्णं मुहे अण्णं णिह्वणे । p. 139. Explain clearly the words underlined in (*e*) and state which portions of the plot in the Mud. are covered by them. 3. What are the different ways in which dramatic writers wind up the प्रस्तावना ? Which of them is used in the Mud. ? 4. Analyse the character of Châṇ. giving quotations where necessary. Do you concur in the remark that the policy of this Brâhmâṇa politician may be regarded as quite Machiavellian ? Give fully your reasons. 5. What relation does Prâkṛta bear to Sanskṛt ? What are the different kinds of Prâkṛta ? Which of them are used in our play ? Give an instance of each. 6. Give the substance of the letter which Chân. made S'akaṭa. write without any address upon it. What part does it play in the *denouement* of Mud. ? 7. What different people are mentioned in the Mud. ? Identify them where you can. Criticise the style of Vis'âkh., stating the merits and demerits and illustrating the latter. To what time does his play refer ? Give the precise meanings of the following:— कल्यवर्त, हस्त्यश्वम्, यमपट, पुरुषकारः, शूलायतनाः, त्रिवर्गः, वाक्छलम्, भूतार्थः.

First B. A.

1. What reference is there in the Mud. to the Buddhas and what trait of character does it illustrate? 2. With what object in view did Châṇ. cause Râk.'s ring to be delivered to the latter and what purpose is served by the feigned quarrel between Châṇ. and

Chandragupta? 3. Translate.—(*a*) p. 86. sl. 21. (*b*) शाङ्गंकर्षा०. VI. sl. 9. 4. Discuss the merits of the different readings in the following Passages:—(*a*) भक्त्या कार्यधुरं (रां *v. l.*) वहन्ति बहवः । (*b*) अथवा न लिखामि पूर्व (सर्व *v. l.*) मनाभिव्यक्तमेवास्ताम् । (*c*) तल्लक्ष्मी......मूर्धा-(मूध्रा *v. l.*) बबध्य स्रजम्. (*d*) चित्रवर्मादयो मह्य(मा) मभिद्रुह्यन्ति । (*e*) अगृहीतशस्त्रेण भवतानु-(ना नु *v. l.*) गृह्यते वृषल इत्यतः संदेहः । (*f.*) अथवा अमात्यराक्षसे नेतरि किमस्माकं (किं हस्त्यश्वेन *v. l.*) प्रयोजनमिदानीम् । (*g*) विना (सह) वाहनहस्तिभ्यां मुच्यतां सर्वबन्धनम्, 5. Explain (*a*) सत्वभङ्गभयाद्राज्ञाम् (*b*) मुण्डितमुण्डो नक्षत्राणि पृच्छसि ; (*c*) शकटदासस्तु......अक्षराणि. (*d*) सर्वज्ञतामुपाध्यायस्य चोरयितुमिच्छसि. 6. Explain the meaning of the following:—पञ्चवर्षदेशीय, परसंवेदन, शात्रव, वाचिक, लोष्ठघातम्, निर्व्यूड, वृषलोद्य, उपश्लोकयितव्य.

1887 Sec. B. A. Vol.

1. Translate inte into Engligh:—(*a*) p. 73. sl. 1. (*b*) p. 99. sl. 3. 2. (*a*) What is a नाटक ? What historical facts do you find embodied in the plot of the Mud.? (*b*) What is a पताका and a प्रकरी ? Refer to any in the Mud. 3. Who were the allies of Malaya. ? What countries were they the sovereigns of? With whom do you identify the Mlechchhas referred to in म्लेच्छैरुद्विज्यमाना &c. in the Bharatavâkya? (4). Explain fully the following—(*a*) p. 56. sl. 11. (*b*) p. 112. sl. 19. (*c*) त्वद्वाग्च्छान्तरितानि संप्रति विभो तिष्ठन्ति साध्यानि नः । (*d*) मयापि लेखस्याशून्यार्थी किमपि प्रेषितम् । अयं लेखस्याशून्यार्थो भविष्यति । (*e*) p. 127. sl. 10. ll. 3. 4. (*f*) संवदन्त्य......विसंवदन्त्यक्षराणि....What is the *alaṅkâra* in (*a*) and (*b*)? 5. What Jaina doctrine is indirectly alluded to in अलहन्ताणं......गच्छन्दि. p. 119. 6. What difference in language do you make in (*a*) and (*b*) in question 4, and the verse given under question 5? What kinds of Prâkṛta do you find in the Mud.? What are the principal distinguishing marks of each? Can you connect any of our modern Indian Vernaculars with these or any other forms of Prâkṛta?

1889. Sec. B. A. Vol.

1. Translate:—(1) p. 159. sl. 6. (2) p. 76. sl. 6. (3) p. 46, sl. 23. Who utters the first verse, on what occasion, and with what object? Explain the comp. नैक in the last line and give another instance from the play of a similar formation. What is the story about शिबि to which allusion is made in (3). 2. Dissolve the following compounds:—विमलमुक्ता......वक्षस्थले p. 61. Explain giving the context:—(1) त्वदीयसुचरितैकदेशस्यानुकरणं किलैतत् (2) अलक्षितनिपाता...... दशपरिणतयो भवन्ति. (3) मुण्डितमुण्डो नक्षत्राणि पृच्छसि. (5) त्वद्वाग्च्छा...... साध्यानि नः (5) फलेन संवादितमस्य विकत्थितम् । 3. With what character

does the Mud. *actually* commence, and how is it introduced on the stage? By what name is this form of introduction known to Hindu critics? What is your opinion regarding the state of public morality as disclosed by the Mud.? Compare the character of Chân. with that of Râkshasa. 4. Give the meaning of the following words as used in the Mud.; अभियोग, उपजाप, विकार, स्पश, व्याल, अपवरक, जितकाशिन्, अभिचार, व्यापत्ति, उत्सेध. 5. What means did Râk. employ to destroy the life of Chandra., and how was he forestalled by Chân. in every one of his efforts? Explain the plot planned by Chân. to bring about a rupture between Râk. and Malayaketu.

1892. F. B. A.

1. Compare the following characters as sketched in the Mudrârâkshasa; (*a*) Châṇakya and Râkshasa; (*b*) Chandra. and Malayaketu. Cite passages to illustrate your remarks. 2. Dissolve the following compounds:—(*a*) अरिमित्रोदासिनव्यवस्था; (*b*) सजलजलदव्योमसंकाशमूर्तिः. 3. Explain the formation of the following words:—(*a*) निर्व्यूढ; (*b*) प्रोच्छून; (*c*) अमात्य. 4. Translate into English:—(*a*) III. 19; (*b*) V. 4; (*c*) VII. 5.

Inter. Ex.

1. Translate:—p. 108. sl. 11.; p. 145. 12. 2. Briefly sketch the character of Bhâgurâyaṇa citing passages to illustrate your remarks. 3. Write notes in English to explain the following passage—कार्योपक्षेप &c. IV. 3.

1893. Sec. B. A.

1. What allusion do you find in Mud. to the *Nâtya-sandhis*? Illustrate these with reference to this play. 2. Give in Sanskṛt the substance of the feigned quarrel between Chan. and Châṇakya. 3. Translate and explain fully giving the context:—(*a*) द्वयोः सातुल्यं द्विषति च विभक्तं सुहृदि च। (*b*) उत्तरोयं लेखार्थः पूर्वः कथमस्तु? (*c*) उवक्खित्तरंमणेण चुट्टेण किंवि। (*d*) शिरसि भयमतिदूरे तत्प्रतीकारः। (*e*) ये याताः किमपि...... गमने कामं प्रकामोद्यमाः। (*f*) अमन्तोसहिकुसलो वालग्गाही.........बिणासणु होन्ति। (*p*) अस्माभिर (अस्माकम) मुमेवार्थमालम्ब्य (मवलम्ब्य)...जिजीविषां (विषा)... कृतघ्नैः। (कृतज्ञैः) नानुगम्यते। (*n*) दुरात्मन् राक्षस द्दश्यसे खलु भोः। जागर्ति खलु कौटिल्यः (*i*) सावगा णिरूविदा......अदक्खिणे नक्खते। (*l*) अहवा ण णिसंसाणं उदासीणेसु इदरेसु वा विसेसोत्थि। (*k*) फलयोगमवाप्य......प्रतुष्टचै। Discuss the readings in (*g*). Describe the scheme of Râk. to baffle the attempts of Chân. and show how the latter either vigilantly nipped them in the bud or turned them to his own advantage.

1894. Sec. B. A.

1. Translate :—sl. 13. p. **111** ; कुले &c......क्षणिकमपि लोभाद्धनवति (*v. l.* क्षणिकधनलोभात्)......विमृशति. p. **119**. 2. Explain the following giving the context :—(*a*) सुलभेष्वर्थलाभेषु......शिखिना विना. Explain the allusion. State in what other connection the same story is alluded to in the drama. (*b*) नामान्येषां लिखामि......चित्रगुप्तः प्रमार्ष्टु. (*c*) वनराज इव......विनेयः । Quote the verse from the Mud. in which the same idea is expressed. (*d*) पर्यायपातितः......सहस्रधाम्नः । (*e*) विजिगीषुमात्मगुणसंपन्नं ......न्याय्य एवायमर्थः । (*f*) संवादे तारेसाणं......दूणन्ति ॥ (*g*) वअस्स भद्दभट-प्पमुहा किल......अण्णं मुहे अण्णं निव्वहणे (*h*) कार्याणां गतयो......आज्ञाकरत्वं चिरात् । 3. Write in Sanskṛt a commentary on either of the following :—(*a*) अपामुद्वृत्तानां.........शरदा । (*b*) मुहुर्लक्ष्योद्भेदा नीतिर्नयविदः । 4. What do you understand by the dramatic terms पताका and प्रकरी. Explain them fully with special reference to the Mud. 5. Discuss the date of Vis'akhadatta.

1895. Sec. B. A.

(1) Discuss the date of the Mudrârâkshasa. (2) Translate into English :—III. 3, 5. VII. 5. (3) Explain :—(*a*) V 10; (*b*) पाऊण निरवसेसं &c. II. 11. (*c*) अयमपरो गण्डस्योपरि स्फोटः । (*d*) अधिकारपदं नाम......शङ्कास्थानम् । (*e*) मयापि लेखस्याशून्यार्थं किमपि प्रेषितम् । (*f*) त्वमपि स्वाधिकारशून्यं कुरु । (*g*) वैरोचनपुरःसरेण पदातिलोकेन लोष्ठघातं हतः । (*h*) दुराराध्या......आत्मवद्भिरपि राजभिः । (4) Write gramatical notes on लोष्ठघातं and औशनिरीयं. 5. Contrast the character of Chân. with that of Râkshasa.

1896. Inter. Ex.

1. Translate :—(*a*) चन्द्रोपरागं......बुधयोगः । (*b*) p. 162. sl. 14. (*c*) p. 81. sl. 15. 2. (*a*) Define प्रस्तावना and mention which kind of प्रस्तावना is indicated by आः क एष &c. above. (*b*) Sketch briefly the character of the two kings alluded to by द्रव्यं and अद्रव्यं in verse 1. (*b*) 3. State in what connection the following sentences occur-(*a*) दैवेनोपहयसे......विपर्यस्यति. (*b*) दैवमविद्वांसः प्रमाणयन्ति. (*c*) मम तावद्यद्भवति तद्भवतु. (*d*) अयमपरो गण्डस्योपरि स्फोटः । 4. (*a*) Give the meaning of अस्मत्तो न किंचित्परिहास्यते; संभावितमेवेदमस्मद्विधैर्भवतः; उपश्लोकयितव्यः; आत्यन्तिको विश्लेषः । (*b*) Derive जितकाशी, सांवत्सरिक, निष्कासिष्ये, परायत्तः.

1900 Inter. Ex.

(1) Translate into English :—(*a*) आस्वाद्यारूढकोपस्फुरण...नन्दाः पर्यायo इताः पश्यतो राक्षसस्य ॥ (*b*) पितृन्भ्रातृन...वणिक्त्वेपि वणिजः ॥ (2) Explain with reference to the context:—(*a*) फलयोगमवाप्य...न शुचेव...व्रतं प्रतुष्टचं ॥ (*b*) न खल्वनिश्चितार्थं &c. p. 132. (*c*) पूर्वमनृतमिदानीमासीदिति परस्परविरोधिनी

वचने । (*d*) दिष्ट्या न सचिवायत्ततन्त्रोस्मि । (3)' Quote or refer to passages where the poet makes his characters attribute human feelings to objects not human. (4) Compare the characters of Râk. and Châṇakya. Give references in support of your answer.

1902.

I. Translate into Eng.—(*a*) प्रत्यग्रोन्मेष &c. III. 21. (*b*) स्वस्ति यथास्थानं कुतोपि...वाचिकं चासतमादस्माच्छ्रोतव्यं. pp. 124–5. Fxplain the several references contained in (*b*) 2 Explain with reference to the context:—(*a*) कायस्थ इति लघ्वी मात्रा. (*b*) अयं कुसुमपुरवृत्तान्तज्ञो भवत्प्रणिधिरिति गाथार्थः । (*c*) नमः सर्वकार्यप्रतिपत्तिहेतवे सुहृत्स्नेहाय. 3. (*a*) Give a description of the जीर्णोद्यान in English. (*b*) State what you know of Chandragupta and the dynasty to which he belonged (*c*) Discuss the character of Châṇakya. (*d*) Write notes on—औशानरीयं यशः, अर्हतः प्रणमामः, बुद्धानामपि चेष्टितं...क्लिष्टम्, and श्रावक. 4. Explain all the mythological allusions in the following stanza—कर्णनेव. &c. II. 15.
